COMPETING WITH IT

COMPETING WITH IT

Leading a Digital Business

Colin Ashurst

 macmillan education palgrave

First published 2015 by
PALGRAVE

Palgrave in the UK is an imprint of Macmillan Publishers Limited, registered in England, company number 785998, of 4 Crinan Street, London N1 9XW.

Palgrave Macmillan in the US is a division of St Martin's Press LLC, 175 Fifth Avenue, New York, NY 10010.

Palgrave is a global imprint of the above companies and is represented throughout the world.

Palgrave® and Macmillan® are registered trademarks in the United States, the United Kingdom, Europe and other countries.

ISBN 978–1–137–26997–3

This book is printed on paper suitable for recycling and made from fully managed and sustained forest sources. Logging, pulping and manufacturing processes are expected to conform to the environmental regulations of the country of origin.

A catalogue record for this book is available from the British Library.

A catalog record for this book is available from the Library of Congress.

Printed in China

CONTENTS

FIGURES, TABLES AND BOXES

Figures

Tables

Boxes

INTRODUCTION

In *Competing with IT*, I draw on my own research and practical experience as well as strong foundations in management research and practice. My aim is to provide a new perspective on how to realize the strategic potential of information technology (IT) and create value for customers, employees and other stakeholders and as a result create value for the organization and deliver competitive advantage.

Competing with IT is aimed at a very broad management audience. Virtually every organization is a digital business, and IT is a critical element of strategy formulation and execution, as well as business operations and service delivery, with the inevitable need for continuous improvement. Competitive advantage depends on a complex mix of capabilities embedded in the organization as a whole, and goes far beyond management of the technology itself and the IT function.

Key conceptual foundations for the book are as follows:

- the emphasis of strategy on benefits to customers and other stakeholders, and the role of innovation enabled by creating a climate where innovation can occur;
- the focus on realization of value from IT through business change and enabling *people* to do things differently;
- the emphasis on an 'agile' approach to projects that works well in scenarios of significant innovation and also enables individuals to work together successfully in teams and to maximize their contribution;
- recognition that IT is an 'intellectual technology' and value requires a process of learning and innovation as individuals, teams and organization explore the potential of the technology and learn how to realize benefits in a complex and rapidly changing environment;
- the emphasis on the need to develop an organization-wide capability to compete with IT through a process of strategic change.

My emphasis is on putting ideas into practice to make a difference. I hope the book balances providing insights into the latest thinking with helping you make a difference, whatever your role and area of influence.

Often during the book I refer to 'we', reflecting the fact that the ideas presented are in reality the result of learning together from and with many others over many years.

LEADERS OF DIGITAL BUSINESS

The core issues of competing with IT are the same, regardless of the size or sector of the organization. These are business issues, which must be owned by leaders across an organization. Unfortunately there is an 'IT attention deficit' (Huff et al., 2006), and many business leaders do not have the motivation or expertise to fulfil their role as leaders of IT-enabled transformation.

This book contributes to tackling the IT attention deficit and aims to help current and future business leaders develop as leaders of a digital business. You may be in one of a wide variety of roles:

- senior managers involved in establishing business and information systems strategy, including the CEO and top management team;
- sponsors and executive stakeholders responsible for major change programmes;
- operational and line managers who want to influence and establish control over changes affecting your business units;
- chief information officers and senior IT managers – particularly those involved in working closely with business colleagues;
- senior managers in the human resources (HR) function, particularly where there is a clear consulting role and a focus on organizational change and improvement;
- management consultants, consultants and managers at IT solution and service providers;
- those involved in transformation programmes in specific scenarios, such as e-commerce, knowledge management, knowledge work and virtual work, and customer relationship management;
- those engaged in innovation within organizations;
- those wanting to establish/improve the organizational capability to succeed with change and transformation programmes;
- individuals involved in IT and business transformation projects;
- students of MBA and other educational programmes and those working to develop into any of these roles.

Business managers do not need to develop the same specialist experience as their IT colleagues, but they do need the knowledge, skills and confidence to play significant roles in realizing benefits from IT investments effectively: they need to be 'IT-savvy' leaders of digital businesses. IT professionals need to be more 'business-savvy' and to learn to speak the same language as their business colleagues.

BIG PICTURE

The goal of *Competing with IT* is to provide insights into the issues and opportunities of realizing value from IT, as well as to help develop expertise with a range of practical tools to enable individuals to make a difference in their teams and wider organizations. My goal is to draw on my experience and the work of many others to provide a fresh perspective on succeeding with digital business and gaining competitive advantage from IT.

Digital business is a reality for all of us. It's possible to experiment more easily, reach further and scale faster. All aspects of an organization are involved, and whole industries are being reshaped. The opportunities for leaders to outpace and outperform the competition are huge. However, the core leadership principles and practices of competing with IT have not changed; we just need to adopt them more broadly across organizations and apply them more consistently and effectively.

This book is aimed at anyone who wants to help their team, department or organization realize the strategic potential of IT. It tackles the real-world challenges of succeeding with business innovation and change in a digital business.

THE STRUCTURE OF THE BOOK

In outline, *Competing with IT* is structured as follows:

- The starting-point is benefits realization from projects of IT-enabled change and transformation (Chapters 1–7). This establishes critical foundations for later sections.
- The focus then shifts to strategy and management of the overall portfolio of investments in IT. Many of the concepts and tools related to specific projects remain important (Chapters 8–10).
- The final section addresses wider organizational issues, including building the organizational capability to gain competitive advantage from IT through innovation and transformation (Chapters 12–14).

I have tackled projects first, and then strategy (i.e., which projects to invest in), because projects are part of day-to-day reality for more people. From experience in the classroom, covering projects first helps to establish a shared understanding of principles and practices for a benefits-driven approach before moving on to strategy and wider considerations of organizational capability.

Students regularly argue that this book is really about leading change and innovation and that the IT element is incidental. I wouldn't disagree, and my experience is that the concepts adapt very easily to a wide range of scenarios.

REFERENCE

Huff, S., Maher, M. and Munro, M. (2006) Information Technology and the Board of Directors: Is There an IT Attention Deficit? *MIS Quarterly Executive*, Vol. 5 (1): 55–68.

CHAPTER 1
FOUNDATIONS FOR A NEW PERSPECTIVE

IN THIS CHAPTER WE STUDY:

- the paradox of information technology (IT) – the tension between rapid innovations in technology creating strategic opportunities, with the high risk of IT investment failure;
- key foundations for the approach to competing with IT in a digital business;
- the importance of changing what people do and the concept of a 'toolkit' as a way of capturing and sharing effective practice.

THE PARADOX OF IT: OPPORTUNITIES AND FAILURES

HISTORICAL PERSPECTIVE

IT has had a dramatic impact on the world over the last 40 years. In my working life the changes have been dramatic. In my first year at university, about 40 years ago, I completed a computing module, which was essentially writing a fairly simple programme in Fortran. I think the biggest challenge was catching all the typing errors on the punched cards, as there was no spellchecker. I was at Durham, a reasonably-sized research-oriented university, yet the computer that the programme finally ran on, overnight in batch mode, was 15 miles up the road at our neighbour Newcastle upon Tyne. Presumably we didn't have a computer that was available for student work.

Twenty years ago I was working for Asda, a UK food retailer with more than 200 superstores. I remember the Computer Services Director explaining how we now had 1 Terabyte (Tb) of disk storage in our large, secure, air-conditioned data centre. That 1Tb supported all the mainframe systems that were used in the stores and head office and probably cost several millions of pounds. As I write this paragraph, I have a 1Tb back-up disk on my desk which cost £65 a year or so ago. That's Moore's Law in action (Box 1.1). I wonder what the equivalent is today as you read the book.

Box 1.1 Moore's Law

Named after Gordon Moore, the co-founder of Intel, this rule of thumb suggests that the number of components in integrated circuits will double approximately every two years. The 'law' has been remarkably accurate and has applied to many aspects of computer and network performance.

As a result, technology has developed at an astounding speed. Around 15 years ago a Terabyte of disk storage would have filled a large data centre and cost millions of pounds. Now you can have a 1Tb external drive plugged into your laptop for around £65, and the 2Tb memory stick is on its way. Similar developments have affected processor power and communication networks. As Bill Gates is reputed to have said: 'If GM had kept up with technology like the computer industry has, we would all be driving $25 cars that got 1,000 mpg.'

The impact of IT on our lives and on organizations has been dramatic. Vast organizations have evolved rapidly: Amazon, Google, Facebook and more.

Others have grown through all of those 40 years but have been on something of a roller coaster: for example, Microsoft and Apple. Many existing organizations have struggled to adapt, and some organizations and even industries are still struggling. Other traditional organizations – John Lewis as a UK retailer, for example – have handled the transition to 'bricks and clicks' very well.

Looking around the world, IT is having a massive impact as economies develop. Outsourcing and offshoring of IT to India have resulted in the rapid growth of IT services organizations competing around the world. In Africa the rapid adoption of mobile phones and their use for payments has compensated for the limited reach of traditional banking infrastructure. It will be important to consider the global picture as we explore opportunities and how to realize them.

We see the impact across sectors, with IT having a major impact in healthcare and the broader public sector. There have been many technology start-ups, and many start-ups and small businesses have used technology very effectively to compete with large organizations and around the world.

In a very real sense every business (and organization) is now a digital business. Even if the products and services are still physical, how they are marketed, sold and supported will almost certainly depend on technology. IT has always been an issue for the CEO, the Board and the management team as a whole. In the digital business world today and in the future it is vital that business managers have the knowledge and expertise to enable their organization to realize the strategic potential of IT and to compete with IT.

CONTINUED IT INNOVATION

Innovation in IT is continuing at a very rapid pace and will continue to provide new opportunities for organizations. IT has a critical role to play in the success of all sizes of organization, from the one-person start-up to the very largest. Erik Brynjolfsson has researched the contribution of IT to productivity and economic performance for many years. He now concludes that for some it is making a real difference to their competitive position:

> I really think that the way companies implement business processes, organizational change, and IT-driven innovation is what differentiates the leaders from the lagers. Rather than leveling the playing field, IT is actually leading to greater discrepancies. In most industries the top companies are *pulling further away* from the companies in the middle and the bottom of the competitive spectrum.
>
> Erik Brynjolfsson. *MIT Sloan Management Review*,
> Spring 2010; emphasis added

One of the factors that sets the leading organizations apart is their ability to realize benefits from IT-enabled change. Note that it is not about the technology itself.

Technology by itself is not the source of benefits. Benefits come when the technology is used to enable *people* to do things differently. Advantage comes from a complex mix of capabilities, including business process management, organizational change and IT-driven innovation. Technology developments have enabled rapid innovation across all sectors of the economy, enabling new products, services and ways of working. The challenge for individuals and organizations is to determine how to exploit existing and new technologies to gain advantage.

PERVASIVE IMPACT OF IT

The improved price-performance of IT and the increasing power of software, often available on a pay-per-use basis over the Internet (software as a service/cloud computing), have made IT pervasive. There will continue to be opportunities for cost savings from improved efficiency, and for improved effectiveness through integration within and between organizations. Newer trends, including mobile and collaborative technologies (e.g., Web 2.0), are changing customer expectations and bringing new opportunities for innovation.

A key challenge for organizations is to maintain a competitive advantage in this uncertain and rapidly changing environment. Which technologies do you invest in? When do you invest? When is it important to be an early adopter? Which specific vendors and variants of a technology should you select? How do you make use of these technologies to gain competitive advantage, given the needs of key stakeholders and the capabilities of your organization?

In the book *The World Is Flat* Thomas Friedman (2007) discusses '10 Flatteners' that together have resulted in transformational change over the last five to ten years. The world is clearly not (yet) flat, with billions still excluded by poverty from the benefits of IT. However, the core argument that the convergence of broadband, the PC, open standards and powerful software have created huge challenges and opportunities is right. Friedman potentially underestimates the importance of social relationships and the power of inertia, but it would be a risk to rely on these factors as insulation from the forces of change.

Friedman argues that the flat world crept up on us while we were asleep, distracted and depressed in the aftermath of the dot-com bubble and bust in the first years of the 21st century. In our consideration of competing with IT, it is important to consider our response to these flatteners and other IT-based business and social trends. We can also consider what might be coming next, so we are not caught sleeping again.

Box 1.2 provides a perspective on current technology trends, and throughout the book we introduce principles and tools for taking advantage of the opportunities resulting from these and other technology developments. What are the opportunities for your organization?

Box 1.2   Major technology trends

Mobile computing. This is the tenth flattener. Increasing bandwidth, more reliable connectivity and the power of new devices mean that new opportunities are emerging rapidly. We are moving to a situation where we have constant access to a full range of IT services and our own data across a wide range of devices.

Enabling knowledge work. There is a switch in focus from using IT to *automate* transactions to using it to *informate* and contribute to the creativity and productivity of individuals and teams. Many technologies are available, but we have hardly begun to learn to exploit their potential.

Information management (big data). New technology is providing organizations with vast stores of data: for example, the 'click stream' data of website usage or 'basket data' from retailer loyalty systems. The challenge is making use of this data to gain insight into how to create value for customers and to improve decision-making. Many tools – for example, for visualization – are becoming more widely available to help analysis and decision-making.

Cloud computing. I am using this as a broad term encompassing web services, software as a service and utility computing. These developments are making powerful, enterprise-level software and scalable IT infrastructures available on a pay-as-you-go basis. The open, Internet standards also mean that there are many opportunities for integration between systems and organizations. As a result, small organizations are much better placed to compete with large organizations, and large organizations have a range of new options to consider when planning how to supply their IT needs. It is possible to get new products and services to market much faster, and with fewer resources, than before.

CHANGING ORGANIZATIONAL CONTEXT: IMPACT ON INDIVIDUALS AND SOCIETY

The context in which organizations are operating has also changed. Laptops, smartphones and tablets mean that millions of consumers and employees are used to using powerful technology 24 hours a day, seven days a week. This is increasing demands on organizations that want to attract and retain customers and staff.

Friedman refers to 'uploading' as the fourth flattener: people making a contribution via the Internet. There are many examples of 'crowd-sourcing' (Wikipedia, for example) and open innovation (Chesbrough, 2003), which illustrate the willingness of vast numbers of individuals to contribute (time, intellect, knowledge) and show what can be achieved through collective knowledge and action. There is a real sense that every business is now a digital business (Bharadwaj et al., 2013).

Organizations are starting to realize significant benefits from these trends. But these trends also bring major threats to many existing business models.

SIGNIFICANT RISK OF IT PROJECT FAILURE

Alongside the opportunities provided by continuing innovation in IT, a primary driver for the book is the continuing failure of organizations to realize the full potential of investments in IT. This is seen in the continuing high failure rates of investments in IT in terms of benefits delivered, which have stayed at around 70–80% over the last 30 years (Clegg et al., 1997; Eason, 1988; B.C.S., 2004). Socio-technical approaches and benefits-driven approaches for IT have been available for 20 years (Mumford, 1995; Ward et al., 1996; Avison et al., 1998), but the lack of improvement in project success rates suggests that they have had a limited impact on how organizations approach IT investments in practice.

There is room to question these figures. Are they measuring the right things at the right time? Did the organizations make sensible choices about which projects to invest in? The issue is not the precise failure rate. What we do know is that too many projects fail to deliver the intended and potential benefits.

The series of Chaos Reports from the Standish Group (www.standishgroup.com) are widely quoted. The 2012 Chaos results 'show another increase in project success rates, with 39% of all projects succeeding (delivered on time, on budget, with required features and functions); 43% were challenged (late, over budget, and/or with less than the required features and functions); and 18% failed (cancelled prior to completion or delivered and never used)'. It's important to note that the measure of success they use is 'on time and on budget', and relates to feature delivery, not benefits realization. It's more than likely that the good news from 2012 is not as good as it sounds.

This situation has not changed much over the last 30–40 years; in many senses, the challenge is getting greater as the focus shifts from automation to innovation and achieving more with fewer resources. If there were an easy answer to this high project failure rate, surely we would have found it by now. Box 1.3 provides a view on project success factors.

Box 1.3   Project success factors

The study by Clegg et al. (1997: p. 863), which addresses over 14,000 projects, takes a broad view of project success and focuses on benefits from organizational change. It identifies a wide range of success factors, for example:

- Successful organizations adopt an integrated approach to organizational and technical change. The technical, organizational and people issues are seen to be inextricably linked, and successful change requires their joint management.

- Active consideration is given to the way in which work is organized and jobs are designed: these will almost certainly need to be changed to improve effectiveness.

- Methods are used to help organizations explicitly incorporate these human and organizational factors.

- Substantial resources are invested in these human and organizational factors. These may amount to 50% of the total cost of change.

As these examples indicate, the causes of failure and related success factors identified by Clegg et al. (1997) emphasize success through a focus on human factors and organizational change. This provides a good starting-point for consideration of a benefits perspective on a project.

The teaching and research that underpin this book are seeking to gain insights into how organizations can develop the capability required to succeed in realizing the potential of investments in IT to deliver benefits to stakeholders and improve organizational performance by competing with IT.

Note: There is an important distinction between Information Systems (IS) and Information Technology (IT). One way to approach it is that IS is the information and IT being *used* by people. IT is the technology itself: the hardware and software and networks. In the book we use IT as shorthand and will normally be referring to IS and IT. Benefits and competitive advantage don't come from the technology itself – value comes from people using the technology and the information it provides.

KEY THEMES IN OUTLINE

A 'fourth era' of IT is proposed (Peppard and Ward, 2004), based on the concept of an IS *capability* being the enabler of competitive advantage from IT: that is, sustained competitive advantage comes not from any one project or solution but from the ability continually to provide a stream of temporary sources of advantage. Empirical studies (e.g., Santhanam and Hartono, 2003) have indicated a strong link between IT capability and firm performance, and suggest that there is an opportunity to get a sustained advantage.

The idea of an IS capability or 'benefits realization capability' (Ashurst et al., 2008) is particularly relevant to the challenge of benefits realization from investments in IT, as it facilitates exploration of the organization as a whole and not just the IT function. As Peppard (2007) notes, the challenge for management is not to 'manage IT' but to 'manage to generate value through IT', with the understanding that the required knowledge and expertise are distributed across the organization and are not just in the IT function. In the book we provide a framework for this benefits realization capability and use the idea of a benefits realization *toolkit* to share specific *practices* that contribute to the development of the capability in organizations.

A number of key themes are developed though the book as follows:

1. Benefits from IT come from 'people doing things differently', not from the technology itself (Ward and Daniel, 2012): that is, benefits arise from how people *use* the technology and information. This means that realizing benefits from IT is an organization-wide issue, which requires leadership from all areas and levels of the organization. It also implies that benefits come from a broad approach to change: to behaviour and to attitudes, not just from implementing new technology and changing the formal organization, for example of policies and structures.

2. Every business is a Digital Business, and a focus on value from IT should be embedded in management practices across the organization, from strategy and setting priorities to delivering change, to exploiting information and systems in service delivery and through continuous improvement.

3. IT investments are increasingly contributing to business innovation, resulting in new products, services and ways of working. In many cases projects require creative, multi-disciplinary teamwork. Benefits-led approaches must support these teams, enabling them to work together effectively in a wide range of situations. In many cases there will be a drive to innovate to create new sources of value rather than simply solving clear-cut problems to improve efficiency or effectiveness.

4. Successful completion of a benefits-led investment in IT is only the start of benefits realization. There must be a focus on Benefits Exploitation through the life of an IT system. IT departments and organizations have neglected this area. There are important opportunities to realize value and major implications for the management *competences* required across the organization.

5. Benefits realization requires a focus on portfolio management and broad organizational factors as well as the management of individual projects. For example, 'Which projects should we invest in?' is a key question, which has to be considered at a portfolio level.

6. There is a considerable gap between what we know about the value of a 'benefits-led' approach and the extent of effective adoption of these approaches in organizations. A key challenge is overcoming this 'knowing–doing' gap (Pfeffer and Sutton, 1999). We tackle this from the perspective of developing the organizational capability for benefits realization. Developing this benefits realization capability is itself a strategic change programme, which involves changing attitudes and behaviour – not just the adoption of a new approach to projects. The concept of the benefits toolkit is a contribution to the development of this capability, and the gradual adoption of a selection of 'tools' can help make an important difference.

The starting-point is a focus on specific projects (chapters 1–7), as this provides a foundation for the exploration of the wider issues of strategy (chapters 8–11) and then capability development (chapters 12–14). It also reflects the reality that you can very rarely put everything on hold while you figure out the strategy. There is always a requirement for change through projects. There is also a strong argument that projects are the best place to start in practice, as the insights gained will be crucial in determining strategy. For example, has the organization got the capability to deliver the projects required to realize the strategy?

A NEW PERSPECTIVE: LEADING A DIGITAL BUSINESS

Being able to realize the strategic potential of information technology to deliver value to customers and other stakeholders and to improve organizational performance is a crucial issue for every organization. The challenge is simply to achieve the benefits, get value for money and avoid the risk of failure – in an environment where the technology, customer expectations and business environment are changing rapidly! This is what is required of leaders of a digital business.

Given the continued failure rate of investments in change over an extended period, there is a need for a different approach. There seems little point in repeating what has been said before, even if it is presented with more recent examples. In this book we seek to provide a new perspective and hope to make a significant contribution to equipping individuals as leaders of digital businesses who enable their organizations to succeed in competing with IT.

Key aspects of this new perspective are developed through the book and summarized in this section.

CLOSING THE LOOP: STRATEGY, IMPLEMENTATION AND CONTINUOUS IMPROVEMENT

There is a tendency to focus on either strategy or change projects and, in doing that, to fragment key elements of what is really one topic. We take a holistic approach and tackle the key elements that together enable an organization to realize value. In particular, we tackle both strategy and the implementation of strategy – making strategy happen through programmes and projects of change. While the 'biggest gains come from doing the right things' (Earl and Feeny, 1994) – that is, from setting the direction through the strategy and priority-setting – effective change to implement the strategy is also vital as, in our view, in a fast-changing world, there must be a very close relationship between the direction and the delivery of change.

We also focus on sustaining the changes and exploiting the new information and business capabilities delivered. Part of the reason for the high failure rate of projects is that measurements are taken too soon after the software solution goes live. Realization of benefits takes time, and it is vital to consider the activities after the delivery of the software solution and also after the handover to operational management that will lead to success. We need to focus more on exploiting information and the capabilities of the systems we have through their operational lives. This includes handling the extensive demands for ongoing incremental change and continuous improvement.

Figure 1.1 provides one way of looking at the different areas we are addressing.

ORGANIZATIONAL COMPLEXITY: DIFFERENT STAKEHOLDER PERSPECTIVES

Knowing *what* to do can be the biggest challenge. Different stakeholders have different perspectives and will see different changes as benefits. Traditional project and systems development approaches often skip quickly over defining

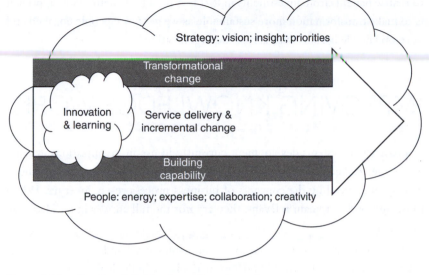

Figure 1.1 Leading the digital business: Key elements

what the problem is and jump into establishing objectives, requirements and the target solution. The situations we are tackling are complex, and time is required to understand the real problem and explore possible solutions. We need to recognize the challenges that come from the different perspectives of different stakeholders in both deciding what to do and then in succeeding with change to achieve the objectives.

We tackle the challenge of identifying different perspectives as part of identifying opportunities for transformation and benefits planning. We also consider building support, negotiating with stakeholders and gaining their involvement as part of successful delivery of the benefits.

LEADING CHANGE: EMPHASIZE PEOPLE AND PROCESS

Approaches to projects often focus on the project *process*, resulting in a lot of effort devoted to complying with a set of rules: for example, on progress reporting. PRINCE2, which is widely used in the UK, is just one example of this approach. It strongly emphasizes the value of an 'organized and controlled' start, middle and end to a project as key elements of the approach.

Good project managers have always focused on teamwork and communication, and seen leadership as an important part of their role. More recently, 'agile' approaches to projects and systems development have emphasized the importance of people and teamwork and recognized that process is simply a means to an end and that it must be adding value. We adopt this focus and extend it to the wider issues of stakeholder engagement and the management of change

15

to realize benefits from investments in IS/IT. A broader benefit of our approach is to make transformation more sustainable as we get more people engaged and develop knowledge and skills across the organization.

IMPROVING KNOWLEDGE WORK

Approaches to systems development currently in use in organizations evolved when the challenge was automating transactional processes, and have been heavily influenced by the concepts of business process re-engineering. While these approaches remain relevant, they are not the full answer in a wide range of scenarios.

IT is increasingly being used to enable professional and knowledge workers to work more effectively and productively as individuals and teams and as part of broader communities. In these scenarios the value of IT is often about enabling communication and enhancing the information-processing and decision-making capabilities of people.

In knowledge work and other scenarios, IT is an 'intellectual technology', not an industrial technology, in that it has properties that are not fixed on implementation but can be 'innovated endlessly, depending on its interaction with the intellect of the human beings who implement and use it' (Lee 1999: p. 8). This can lead to an ongoing cycle of innovation and change as the technology extends the intellects of its users leading to further innovation. This suggests a much more complex process than 'adoption' or diffusion of an innovation. We need to adapt the approach we take to IT investments to realize the potential benefits in these scenarios.

DEVELOPING BUSINESS COMPETENCES

The focus of business strategy is increasingly on developing organizational competences or capabilities that contribute to competitive advantage. From an IT perspective, this is helpful as this approach encourages addressing many different aspects of the organization and not just the business process perspective that has been the typical focus of IT projects. For example, a focus on developing competences might involve consideration of roles, performance measures, knowledge and information, working practices, culture and structures.

A logical next step is to make the focus of an IT project the development and enhancement of these organizational competences. This requires explicit consideration of a much richer view of the organization as part of the design and change process.

LEARNING AND INNOVATION

Existing project methods and project practices focus on delivery of a solution to meet clearly defined objectives. However, in many situations, a project exploiting IT is likely to involve significant innovation and result in new products and services and new ways of working. In these situations methods have to address the challenges of doing something new – the solution is not clear at the start, the customer and end-users cannot clearly state their requirements. We need to extend the range of approaches to projects and provide new tools and ways of working that fit these situations. We view a project as a creative process for a multi-disciplinary team and draw on the principles and practices of design thinking.

We also need to extend the focus on innovation to our approach to strategy. Very often, the challenge is to create a new market or to find an opportunity for a new product or service. This requires us to look beyond the techniques that have worked well in the past where the focus has often been competing better with existing products or in existing markets.

ESTABLISHING A LEADERSHIP TOOLKIT FOR BENEFITS REALIZATION

There is no single right way to approach benefits realization from IT. The approach needs to be adapted to reflect the specific situation and the people involved. Yet to avoid constant reinventing of wheels, to enable the movement of people between projects and to enable the sharing of ideas and learning there needs to be some level of consistency in how projects are approached. We find a balance between these opposing forces by advocating an approach that reflects how experienced and successful organizations and project teams work in practice.

We set out a number of key principles that guide the approach and then set out an overall framework for the lifecycle of a benefits realization project. This provides consistency and shared language within and across projects. We build on this by providing a 'toolkit' of practices that can be adapted according to the needs of the specific situation. Some of these will be used in virtually every case; others will be used only in specific cases. The toolkit enables sharing and learning, but it balances this with flexibility and the opportunity for continuous improvement. Both the concept of the toolkit and the tools within it will be of value for leaders across an organization.

The tools of leadership are many and varied: stakeholder mapping, benefits mapping, risk management, designing a workshop, giving feedback and pitching an idea are just a few examples. The key to the toolkit is its breadth and flexibility – the tools are at the service of the leader and team, they are no longer constrained by the requirements of the methodology. This 'flip' in perspective is important and also shifts ownership for effectiveness to 'us' rather than the 'them' who established the methodology.

The toolkit also enables individuals to share these ideas within their organizations. Often improvements to ways of working can be made incrementally and there is the opportunity to use individual tools to start to make a difference. In practice, individuals, teams and organizations will build expertise in using the tools and learn to adapt them as they apply them in a range of situations.

BUILDING AN ORGANIZATION-WIDE CAPABILITY FOR COMPETING WITH IT

Many attempts to tackle the failure rate of IT projects have themselves failed. This reflects a poor analysis of the problem and attempts to implement the wrong solutions. Many attempts have focused on new technology (new software development tools), new processes/methods (PRINCE2/Capability Maturity Model/COBIT) or new people and structures through outsourcing arrangements. Virtually all these attempts have approached this as a problem for the IT function. But realizing value from IT depends on the organization as a whole. Our focus is on developing an organization-wide capability to compete through IT. This has significant implications, for example for the education and roles of people at all levels across the organization.

It is essential to ask the right questions – not 'how can we reshape the IT function?' or 'how can we improve the delivery of IT projects?' but 'how can this organization develop its capability to realize the potential of IT to deliver value to stakeholders and improve performance?'

The organizational capability for benefits realization is considered at three levels: firstly, the practices adopted on specific projects and the success of the projects in benefits realization; secondly, the management of the entire portfolio of IT and change projects, including deciding which projects to invest in, sharing learning from project to project and resource planning and development; and finally, both projects and the overall portfolio are considered in the overall organizational context – for example, the impact of organizational structures, performance measures, management education and career development.

DEVELOPING LEADERS OF DIGITAL BUSINESS

A key implication of the focus we are taking in *Competing with IT* is that to succeed an organization needs to develop individuals who are capable of being effective *leaders of digital business*.

We have provided practical foundations through the toolkit – of *what* to do. With the wider discussion of key principles and examples of specific cases, we have also addressed *why* benefits realization should be approached in this way. By bringing together the 'what' and the 'why' we provide a better basis for people adopting this new approach.

Business leadership of transformational and major changes as well as ongoing service delivery and incremental improvement mean that a broad portfolio of leadership competences is required across the organization, including: process design and management; information management; benefits-driven project management; change management and multi-disciplinary team working. Leaders at every level can be ambidextrous, drawing on core principles and practices to run and improve their organization today, as well as creating the organization for tomorrow.

MAKING COMMON SENSE COMMON PRACTICE

Many of the ideas in the book are often described as common sense. They are not yet common practice. We've referred to the 'knowing–doing gap', which is certainly part of the challenge.

There is also a sense that we are talking about 'craft' skills (Sennett, 2009) and that these can only develop over time, with experience and appropriate support as teams and organizations establish a common language and shared mindset. This craft perspective influences how we approach leadership and organizational capability development to make common sense common practice.

LEADING AS A CRAFTSMAN

A key lesson is that benefits realization from IT depends on the *quality* of enactment of the practices and not simply which practices are adopted. This in turn depends on the knowledge, skills (know-what/know-how) and the 'know-why' (Pfeffer and Sutton, 1999) of a focus on benefits realization.

The skilled professionals engaged in projects are not followers of rigid methods but highly motivated 'craftsmen' (Sennett, 2009). They are passionate about the job, and skilled in using a range of tools, which they can adapt, based on experience, to the specific situation they are facing. Sharing and adopting practices provides a way to improve performance.

There are also strong links with reflective practice (Schon, 1984) and the education of professionals. Key points are the need for 'learning by doing' (the apprenticeship of the craftsman) and that craftsmen are dedicated to *good work for its own sake* ... their labour is not simply a means to another end (Sennett, 2009: p. 20). The goal here is benefits realization for stakeholders.

The tools of the craftsman are often deceptively simple, and can be used at a basic or an advanced level. They are a way for professionals to capture and share knowledge. Building leadership and organizational competences is not just about introducing the tools; it is also about helping individuals, teams and the wider organization learn how and when to use them and developing high levels of expertise in their use (Box 1.4). The expert probably has more tools available to them than the novice, but they certainly know how to use them very effectively in a wide range of situations. This approach depends on the (self-)*discipline* of the team, as opposed to the (imposed) *control* of management.

A common reaction to the benefits approach is that it is (just) 'common sense'. However, common sense is clearly not common practice. I hope that the perspective of the development of craft skills will contribute to the shift from common sense to common (skilled) practice. It is not knowing about the tools that counts; it's *using* them effectively at the right times. This craft perspective provides a fresh approach to the development of individual and organizational competences. Box 1.4 illustrates two perspectives on managing risk. The second gives more sense of craftsmanship.

Box 1.4   Risk management as a craftsman

The project manager reported on risk to the project board every two weeks using the red/amber/green system in relation to a number of key headings (budget, timescale, resourcing). He also updated the 'top ten risks log'.

Members of the project team didn't participate in the reporting or updating the risk log. In fact, they didn't get to see them. They were quite worried that things were going wrong, but no one seemed to want to listen to their concerns.

*   *   *

The project manager had a risk review meeting with the team every two weeks prior to preparing her report for the project board. She kept it separate from the progress and planning meetings to ensure there was time and energy to focus. The team worked together to identify, prioritize and respond to risks. Everyone had a chance to participate. She was very clear that the team owned the risk register and plan – the fact that you had raised a risk didn't mean you got stuck with taking action.

At key milestones the project manager and sponsor ran a risk review with the project board and other key stakeholders. It was important to engage them, get their perspectives and get them to take ownership as business leaders.

*   *   *

Together these elements contribute to a radically different approach to leading a digital business. Virtually every organization is a digital business, and IT is a critical element of strategy formulation and execution, as well as business operations and service delivery, with the inevitable need for continuous improvement. Competitive advantage depends on a complex mix of capabilities embedded in the organization as a whole and goes far beyond management of the technology itself and the IT function.

Leading a digital business is the job of the many, not just the few in very senior positions. The concepts and practices are highly scalable. From my perspective they apply in virtually every situation, whether I'm working on my own, working with a small team or involved in a much larger role. It's about agile, benefits-driven projects and managing strategically as a way of life. In a sense this is about managing and leading effectively in the 21st century.

A lot of what is done today to manage IT in organizations is still relevant. There is no need to throw away all the accumulated knowledge. However, by taking a fresh perspective we develop a different view of the world and put this knowledge and experience to use with a different emphasis.

In this book I have *not* attempted to cover the standard topics of leadership. What I hope I have done is address some aspects of the practicalities of what effective leaders do.

DEVELOPING EFFECTIVE PRACTICE: THE LEADERSHIP TOOLKIT FOR BENEFITS REALIZATION

We introduced the idea of the leadership toolkit for benefits realization earlier. In this section we take the discussion further...

What did you do at work today? Perhaps there was a meeting, perhaps quite a number of them. Some emails, phone calls and interruptions from people passing by. Did you write a report, a presentation or a progress report? Did you spend time helping, advising or reviewing the progress of others?

How effective were you? What did you achieve? What obstacles got in your way?

Were you more effective than last week or last year? Did you put into practice what you had learned from your colleagues, from the last course or educational programme, to work more effectively?

IMPROVING EFFECTIVENESS?

For most of us, one day is not too different from the next, even if you are in a varied and challenging role. We do similar things and we use a core set of routines – a personal 'toolkit' to tackle what we do day to day. For example, we approach planning a meeting or preparing a presentation in much the same way. Many successful managers work this way and can quickly explain the structure they use for a presentation or a proposal or how they approach other activities.

This toolkit only changes slowly. Even when we change roles and employers, many of these activities and the tools we use to tackle them stay the same. Often the formal processes and procedures of the organization have only a limited impact on what we do – we operate based on our experience and perhaps our professional education within our specific discipline.

DOES EFFECTIVENESS MATTER?

In many of the scenarios that we face day to day and that are at the core of our roles as professionals and knowledge workers there are huge variations in the effectiveness of individuals. You will know who runs meetings effectively in your organization, for example.

Research into the productivity of software developers highlighted a 10:1 difference in productivity between the best and the worst individuals and teams (DeMarco and Lister, 1999). That is a *big* difference – and it wasn't due to seniority, years of experience or technology. There are probably similar, very large differences in other knowledge work scenarios. What a difference if you and your team are among the most productive.

So, what do you do if you are a manager and you want to improve the performance of your team, department or organization? What do you do if you want to improve your own effectiveness?

HOW CAN WE IMPROVE THE EFFECTIVENESS OF INDIVIDUALS AND TEAMS?

There is a view that being effective – or a good leader, for example – depends on intangible, tacit skills, and it is not possible to make them explicit. There might be some element of truth in that. But does that mean we can do nothing to improve performance? No. Tacit skills could be articulated readily if organizational members were simply asked the question 'How do you do that?' Very often, we can capture, or codify, important elements that lead to effectiveness and share them. The tension between codifying nothing, thereby risking the loss of important information, and trying to codify everything, risking banality, is at the very core of attempts at knowledge management. There is an 'optimal amount of structure', and if knowledge is to remain useful once made explicit, a link with the context in which the knowledge was used, and thus in which it might be reused, must be retained.

The challenge is to tackle problems by cutting them up into chunks that can be analysed, understood and handled. This is a key strategy of successful managers – they are able to tackle a wide variety of problems by improvising and making use of relevant techniques from their 'toolkit'. So, improving performance requires extending the toolkit, getting better at using the tools in it effectively and learning how to break problems down so that they can be tackled with the tools available.

There are a number of different levels at which to approach this broad issue of capturing and sharing knowledge in a way that makes an impact. In *The Checklist Manifesto* (2011) Atul argues strongly for the use of checklists to improve the outcomes of professional work, using examples that include surgeons and airline pilots. A checklist can certainly be valuable to help ensure we consistently do the right things in the right order. It can complement the broader approach of developing a toolkit and indeed can be part of specific tools.

A NEW APPROACH TO IMPROVING EFFECTIVENESS

Some of us formalize our 'toolkit' with a collection of templates and a record of ideas of how to tackle common activities, so that we avoid reinventing the wheel, for example, each time we want to plan a meeting, facilitate a workshop or conduct an interview. This approach can help us maintain and extend our knowledge over time. It turns out to be an effective approach to learning and knowledge management and is a good way to improve our own efficiency and effectiveness and to share ideas or provide advice to others.

To improve effectiveness it makes sense to go 'with the grain' of how people think and work. What if we try and build on this idea of a personal toolkit? What if we find a consistent structure and make it a collaborative activity so that we have a shared toolkit connecting people so that they can think together, enabling individual and group learning and bringing together different people with different experiences, allowing them to contribute their knowledge in a team?

The benefits realization toolkit builds on these ideas. The toolkit is a collection of techniques that can be used during a project and when tackling the wider challenges of benefits realization from IT. We have introduced a number of the tools in this book: for example, 'stakeholder analysis'.

The toolkit is different from a 'methodology'. It addresses people and team-work as well as the more process-oriented aspects of a project (for example, risk management). By using the term 'toolkit' we aim to highlight that *when* and *how* to use the tools is up to the project team. The tools are there to help them achieve their goals. Many of the tools are very simple. Success depends on using them effectively, which requires experience.

The toolkit provides a basis for a shared language and a way of working that enables business and IT leaders, and multi-disciplinary teams engaged in realizing benefits from IT-enabled change, to work together effectively. In practice, individuals, teams and organizations will build expertise in using the tools and learn to adapt them as they apply them in a range of situations.

THE TOOLKIT . . .

The example 'round tables' (Box 1.5) shows how the 'tools' can be documented. It comes from guidelines we developed with participants at a series of workshops.

The simple example was one of a number used to document agreed ways of working for a networking group bringing together business and academic participants.

Box 1.5   Round tables: A simple example of the patterns format for capturing and sharing knowledge

Forum meetings are held at round tables to encourage discussion.

At forum meetings we want to develop an atmosphere of learning from each other. This means that the speakers must not dominate the sessions and that there must be opportunities for interaction in small groups and across all the attendees.

* * *

Traditional programmes tend to line up their students in large tiered lecture theatres so that they can focus on the speakers. By contrast, in the forum we will restrict numbers in order to maximize debate.

> *We will be seated café-style, at round tables,* in order to enable engagement in immediate and deep discussion whenever an opportunity presents itself. This layout encourages fast and efficient interaction to take place within and across table groups.
>
> *   *   *
>
> The round tables, by themselves are not sufficient to ensure that we have participative sessions. We will also rely on the '50:50 rule', 'learning by doing' and the 'variety of meetings' to encourage discussion, debate and learning from each other.

The toolkit is built on the ideas of practices and *patterns* (Box 1.6). The structure provides a link with the specific context(s) in which the knowledge is useful. In addition to the 'solution' (recommendation for action to improve the problematic situation), a rationale is provided to give insight into the complexities of the situation and the reasons the solution works. Rationale and context are vital so that users have the understanding to adapt and improvise as they apply the knowledge in their situation.

In the 'round tables' example we adopted the following structure:

- **Name**: the name seeks to capture the essence of the pattern.
- **Summary** (often with picture): the summary supports the name and tries to reinforce the understanding of the pattern.
- **Context**: this is a brief statement that indicates the context and relevance of the pattern.

*   *   *

- **Rationale** – The rationale explains the different forces involved in the problematic situation and how the solution responds to these forces. In these examples this section is kept brief. The proposed *solution* is in italics.

*   *   *

- **Links** are given to related tools.

Box 1.6   The toolkit: A pragmatic approach to sharing and applying knowledge

The concept of the toolkit reflects the way people work in organizations as individuals and teams. What they actually do is heavily influenced by experience and locally defined working practices or routines, rather than more formally defined business processes.

The toolkit draws on the idea of patterns (Jessop, 2004) as a way of capturing and sharing knowledge to tackle complex situations. The pattern format is intended to help build understanding, make clear in what context(s) the knowledge is relevant and provide scope for improvisation in tackling a specific situation.

The toolkit contributes to the craft skills, the craftsmanship, of the manager in a digital business.

THE TOOLKIT – IN THIS BOOK

The toolkit/patterns approach can be used to capture and share knowledge in many situations.

In this book we describe core elements of the benefits toolkit in some detail and outline a number of additional tools. Core tools are highlighted by a ^{T} in the relevant section heading.

IN SUMMARY

Benefits realization from IT is not primarily a technology issue: it's about people, leadership, strategy, management of change and many other factors. Success depends on the capability of the organization as a whole, not just the IT function.

Being able to realize the strategic potential of IT to deliver value to customers and other stakeholders, and to improve organizational performance, is a crucial issue for every organization. The challenge is simply to achieve the benefits, get value for money and avoid the risk of failure – in an environment where the technology, customer expectations and business environment are changing rapidly!

There is a need for vision and leadership. The need for effective leadership of business transformation in the digital business is greater than ever before. While we have much less money to spend, we must spend it much more effectively. We must also put much more effort into exploiting the potential of all the investments in IT we have made in the past. In many organizations the potential of the IT systems and the information they provide is seriously under-exploited – we need to focus on nurturing and realizing the potential of these significant organizational assets.

The core issues of benefits realization are the same regardless of the size or sector of the organization. These are business issues, and this book is aimed at building a common language between professionals from business and IT. We want to see business-savvy IT professionals and IT-savvy business leaders.

The book builds on a strong foundation of well-researched and well-tested ideas. It also provides a fresh perspective intended to help overcome the 'IT attention deficit' and enable individuals and organizations to be more successful in competing with IT.

TAKING IT FURTHER

FURTHER READING AND RESOURCES

Throughout the book I'll use this 'Further Reading and Resources' section to make suggestions about other sources of information. Often I'll highlight 'classic' articles that have made a lasting contribution to current thinking. Also I'll try and point to a small number of articles and books to help you deepen and expand your knowledge.

What you can access will depend on time and also on whether you have access to the libraries of e-journals, which unfortunately can be hidden behind university firewalls.

This article by Chris Clegg and others provides a great introduction:

Clegg, C., Axtell, C., Damodaran, L., Farbey, B., Hull, R., Lloyd-Jones, R., Nicholls, J., Sell, R. and Tomlinson, C. (1997) Information Technology: A Study of Performance and the Role of Human and Organizational Factors. *Ergonomics*, Vol. 40 (9): 851–871.

Many of the other articles and books referenced here we'll revisit, and I'll highlight more of them in the context of later chapters.

TALKING POINTS

Use these questions to help reflect on this chapter and explore the challenges of putting the ideas into practice:

1. What are the key issues you face when trying to use IT systems to get work done?

2. What experience do you have of failed IT projects? What has gone wrong and why?

3. What experience do you have of successful IT projects? What has worked and why?

4. To what extent are the latest technologies in use in your organization – why/why not?

5. What are the next big innovations likely to affect your organization/market?

6. What are you doing or can you do to take advantage of the new opportunities created by IT?

7. What are the key elements of your toolkit for management and leadership? (Think about how you respond when asked for advice.)

KEY DEBATES

In this short book I've given priority to setting out the *how* and *why* of leading in a digital business. I have passed over a number of contentious issues where there are competing perspectives and points of view. The 'Key Debates' section at the end of each chapter raises some of these issues.

IT IS A COMMODITY

As IT is commercially available to all, it is just a commodity and not a source of competitive advantage. The strategic challenge is simply to manage costs through effective procurement and outsourcing. The IT function and IT director will be relatively low-profile operational roles.

How does this IT as a commodity perspective relate to the view put forward in *Competing with IT*? What is your view, and why?

CASE STUDY 1.1

The book focuses principally on enduring principles and practices rather than examples of fast-changing technology. The *Journal of Information Technology Teaching Cases* (Palgrave Macmillan) is used to provide resources for exploring specific situations and relating 'theory' to practice. A brief outline of a relevant case is given at the end of each chapter.

The case study provides an opportunity to explore the challenges encountered when managing an IT project.

Journal of Information Technology Teaching Cases, Vol. 4 (2014): 34–40.

Keep IT simple – the challenge of interlaced IT architecture at Gothaer Systems

Dirk Basten, Dominik Joosten, Werner Mellis and Cornelia Wallmueller

The German direct insurer Gothaer Insurance Group is among the largest insurance companies in Germany. In recent years Gothaer was facing the challenge of replacing its existing collection systems. The replacement system was one of SAP's key modules for Insurance Solution, a standard software product called FS-CD (Financial Services-Collections and Disbursements). The first stage of the project significantly exceeded time and budget objectives. The second stage was expected to encounter serious technical problems. Consequently, the entire project was called into question. A meeting of the IT steering committee was scheduled at short notice to decide on the project's continuance. This case chronicles the series of events leading to that upcoming steering committee meeting.

REFERENCES

Ashurst, C., Doherty, N.F., and Peppard, J. (2008) Improving the Impact of IT Development Projects: The Benefits Realization Capability Model. *European Journal of Information Systems*, Vol. 17 (4): 352–370.

Atul, G. (2011) *The Checklist Manifesto*, London: Profile Books.

Avison, D.E., Wood-Harper, A.T., Vidgen, R.T. and Wood, J.R.G. (1998) A Further Exploration of Information Systems Development: The Evolution of Multiview 2. *Information Technology and People*, Vol. 11 (2): 124–139.

B.C.S. (2004) *The Challenges of Complex IT Projects*, British Computer Society.

Bharadwaj, A., El Sawy, O., Pavlou, P. and Venkatraman, N. (2013) Digital Business Strategy: Toward a Next Generation of Insights. *MIS Quarterly*, Vol. 37 (2): 471–482.

Brynjolfsson, E. (2010) The 4 Ways IT Is Revolutionizing Innovation – An Interview with Eric Brynjolfsson. *MIT Sloan Management Review*, Vol. 51 (3): 51–56.

Chesbrough, H.W. (2003) The Era of Open Innovation. *MIT Sloan Management Review*, Vol. 44 (3): 35–41.

Clegg, C., Axtell, C., Damodaran, L., Farbey, B., Hull, R., Lloyd-Jones, R., Nicholls, J., Sell, R. and Tomlinson, C. (1997) Information Technology: A Study of Performance and the Role of Human and Organizational Factors. *Ergonomics*, Vol. 40 (9).

DeMarco, T. and Lister, T. (1999) *Peopleware: Productive Projects & Teams*, 2nd edition, Dorset House Publishing.

Earl, M. and Feeny, D. (1994) Is Your CIO Adding Value? *Sloan Management Review*, Vol. 35 (3): 11–20.

Eason, K. (1988) *Information Technology and Organizational Change*, London: Taylor & Francis.

Freidman, T. (2007) *The World Is Flat: The Globalized World in the Twenty-First Century*. Penguin.

Jessop, A. (2004) Pattern Language: A Framework for Learning. *European Journal of Operational Research*, Vol. 153 (2): 457–465.

Lee, A.S. (1999) Researching MIS, in Currie, W. and Galliers, B. (eds.) *Rethinking Management Information Systems*. Oxford: Oxford University Press, 7–27.

Mumford, E. (1995) *Effective Systems Design and Requirements Analysis: The ETHICS Approach to Computer System Design*. Basingstoke: Palgrave Macmillan.

Peppard, J. and Ward, J. (2004) Beyond Strategic Information Systems: Towards an IS Capability. *Journal of Strategic Information Systems*, Vol. 13 (2): 167–194.

Peppard, J. (2007) The Conundrum of IT Management. *European Journal of Information Systems*, Vol. 16: 336–345.

Pfeffer, J. and Sutton, R. (1999) Knowing 'What' to Do Is Not Enough. *California Management Review*, Vol. 42 (1): 83–108.

Santhanam, R. and Hartono, E. (2003) Issues in Linking Information Technology Capability to Firm Performance. *MIS Quarterly*, Vol. 27 (1): 125–165.

Schon, D. (1984) *The Reflective Practitioner: How Professionals Think in Action*, Basic Books.

Sennett, R. (2009) *The Craftsman*, London: Penguin Books.

Ward, J., Taylor, P. and Bond, P. (1996) Evaluation and Realization of IS/IT Benefits: An Empirical Study of Current Practice. *European Journal of Information Systems* 4: pp. 214–255.

Ward, J. and Daniel, E. (2012) *Benefits Management*, John Wiley & Sons Inc.

CHAPTER 2
A BENEFITS FRAMEWORK FOR PLANNING PROJECTS: EXPLORING OPPORTUNITIES

IN THIS CHAPTER WE STUDY:

- principles for a benefit-led approach to investments in IT;
- the value of a framework for projects;
- foundation practices for a benefits approach to projects;
- the first stage of a project lifecycle – exploring and clarifying opportunities for improvement.

A BENEFITS-LED APPROACH TO PROJECTS

FROM TECHNOLOGY IMPLEMENTATION TO BENEFITS REALIZATION

The fundamental key to project success, and reducing the reported >70% failure rate of IT projects, is recognizing that the technology by itself is simply a cost. Indeed, the application of identical technologies, in very similar organizational contexts, can often result in radically different organizational outcomes (Orlikowski, 1992).

The benefits come from *using* the technology to enable *people* to do things differently. Our benefits-driven approach focuses on these people – customers, employees and other stakeholders of the organization. We seek to identify very clearly what the potential benefits are for these stakeholders and to focus the project on delivering them. Benefits realization should be the goal of activity from planning through delivery to exploitation. The focus is on benefits from start to finish: 'What are the potential benefits and how do we bring them about?'

To explore the extent of adoption of benefits-driven approaches I carried out over 50 case studies in a wide range of sectors and locations (Ashurst, 2007). This research revealed a very substantial gap between what we *know* about the value of adopting a strong benefits focus when managing projects, and what happens in *practice*, where the focus is overwhelmingly on delivery of a technical solution. The vast majority of the projects investigated focused on the design and delivery of an IT solution, with only limited consideration of wider issues. There was no example of explicit adoption of a well-integrated portfolio of practices for benefits realization which we could truthfully label a *benefits-driven* approach.

Most organizations produce a business case before starting an investment in IT. Many think this means they are focusing on benefits. However, in most cases the business case is simply there to release the money and other resources, and is only very loosely linked to the *activity* of the project, which often becomes delivery of a technology solution. This is the IT 'mindset' – that delivery of the technology means that the job is done.

The discussion in chapters 2 and 3 reflects Benefits Management (Ward and Daniel, 2012) and agile approaches to projects (Highsmith, 2004). Work by Eason (1988), who sets out a project process that addresses the non-technical aspects of an IT project and makes provision for organizational learning as part of the process, is an important reference point. Wider work on socio-technical approaches to IT also provides an important foundation.

OVERVIEW OF THE APPROACH: BRINGING TOGETHER BENEFITS AND AGILE THINKING

Benefits-led and agile approaches to IT are well established. Although adoption is increasing, they are still not 'mainstream'.

From this perspective key elements of the approach to IT investments include:

- *Understanding the opportunities* provided by IS/IT in different business scenarios, and how to explore the opportunities in a specific situation.
- A *benefits-driven approach* to the project lifecycle that focuses on realizing benefits for stakeholders. A key factor is to ensure alignment with the organizational strategy. Further factors are clear ownership and measurement of the benefits, and management of relevant organizational changes (for example, to process, roles, structures, performance measures, etc.) that will bring about the benefits.
- Effective use of a basic *framework for project management* that provides a foundation of key practices such as risk management and milestone-based control.
- A focus on people – this is reflected in an *agile approach to projects* which recognizes the crucial role of building and leading effective teams, and engaging with customers and other stakeholders.
- The agile perspective also emphasizes the importance of *innovation* to explore about and deliver new sources of value. This brings a focus on the user-centric *design* of new IT solutions and ways of working.
- *Adapting the approach to projects* to reflect the context of the specific project, and also the people involved in the project as project team members and as stakeholders.

All these elements, taken together, represent a substantial shift from more traditional technology- and requirements-driven approaches to projects.

THE BENEFITS-DRIVEN APPROACH PROVIDES A COMMON LANGUAGE

The benefits-driven approach provides the basis for a *common language*, enabling the different players involved in these complex, challenging ventures to work together effectively in high-performing, multi-disciplinary teams.

There are a number of reasons for starting here. Firstly, there is the perspective of individuals: projects are the right place to start to learn the ideas and practices of a benefits-driven approach. This is a concrete starting-point, which is within the experience of many readers. Starting here provides a foundation for moving on to consider a benefits-driven approach to business/IT strategy and management of the IT portfolio.

Secondly, from an organizational perspective it is important to develop an enhanced ability to realize benefits from projects and programmes. Strategy discussions will progress more smoothly once the potential strategic contribution of IS/IT has been demonstrated and the credibility of the IT function is enhanced.

PROJECTS IN ORGANIZATIONS

Where do you find projects in organizations? Everywhere. Some organizations are built around a collection of projects – consulting, advertising and engineering, for example. In a typical organization they are found in virtually every area. Take a retailer, for example: projects in IT, of course, and also new store development, store refurbishment, marketing campaigns, implementing regulation changes affecting the stores, introduction of a new line of business on the web.

Even more than this, projects can be a *way of life*, a way to manage effectively a variety of activities within an organization. In a business school, for example, this includes introducing a new degree programme, revision to an existing programme to strengthen its competitive position, centrally driven changes to assessment practice or other policies related to learning and teaching, and a campaign built around a well-known visiting speaker. For the manager driving change and improvement in an organization this view of projects as a *way of life* for the work of individuals and teams is extremely valuable.

PRINCIPLES FOR BENEFITS REALIZATION

Shifting focus from technology implementation to benefits realization is the development of a 'benefits mindset'. This benefits mindset is the foundation for the approach to benefits realization from IT-enabled change. The starting-point is to consider 'What benefits can we deliver for stakeholders?', and *not* 'What software and technology features are required?'

An important test of the presence of the benefits mindset is to consider whether people think and talk about benefits for stakeholders as opposed to technology features. We certainly want to consider the technology, and to do that from the early stages of the project, as we consider what is possible. However, we shift our focus to benefits and new ways of working that are *enabled* by the technology and wider organizational changes.

Classic objections to a benefits-driven approach are 'We have a robust business case' and perhaps 'We've already taken the savings out of the departmental budgets.' A benefits-driven approach is much more than a robust business case: it's about a focus on delivering value for stakeholders (not just cutting budgets), on the changes that will result in the benefits and on the ownership of both the benefits and the related changes.

The principles for benefits realization (Box 2.1) draw on a number of sources and make aspects of the 'benefits mindset' more explicit. The principles provide important context for the details of the benefits-driven approach we set out. If there are doubts about how to approach a specific situation, the principles provide a valuable reference point.

Box 2.1   Principles for a benefits-driven approach

1. Performance only improves when people do things differently.

2. Motivated individuals and teams, with the environment and leadership they need, will deliver innovation and value.

3. Focus on the delivery of value to customers and other stakeholders throughout the lifecycle.

4. Realization of benefits will depend on the participation of all relevant stakeholders.

5. Benefits arise when new capabilities are exploited and managed to the advantage of stakeholders.

6. Exploitation of the potential of IT requires a major form of organizational and individual learning.

The principles draw on work by:

The Agile Alliance: www.agilealliance.org;

Chris Clegg (Clegg, 2000);

Ken Eason (Eason, 1988);

David Preedy and the Microsoft Solutions Framework team (MSF v3): MSF was an early agile approach to projects widely used by Microsoft Consulting;

John Ward: for example, Ward et al., (1996), Ward and Daniel (2012).

PERFORMANCE ONLY IMPROVES WHEN *PEOPLE* DO THINGS DIFFERENTLY

The first principle makes the point that the technology itself is not the source of benefits. Benefits arise when *people* do things differently. It follows directly that the project needs to focus on the benefits for people (stakeholders), the new ways of working (what are they doing differently) and the enabling changes required to bring about these new ways of working. We might continue to use 'IT project' as a shorthand, but really we are talking about projects and programmes of IT-enabled *business change*.

This principle comes directly from the work of John Ward and the IS team at Cranfield on Benefits Management – see Further Reading.

MOTIVATED INDIVIDUALS AND TEAMS, WITH THE ENVIRONMENT AND LEADERSHIP THEY NEED, WILL DELIVER INNOVATION AND VALUE

At the heart of the approach is a focus on people. The emphasis is on people rather than process. In part, this is an attempt to counteract the traditional focus on process over people, which underplays the role of committed individuals and effective teams in successful benefits realization.

The focus on people affects all aspects of the project:

- the leadership of the sponsor and project management;
- effective engagement of customers and other stakeholders;
- effective teamwork and creating an environment where the team can work effectively.

The foundation for this emphasis is not a desire to create a 'nice' working environment or to keep people happy. It is recognition that empowered individuals and effective teamwork are key contributors to a successful project. Research published in *Peopleware* (DeMarco and Lister, 1999) indicates that there is a staggering 10:1 productivity difference between developers and development teams. This difference is largely due to a combination of factors:

- the creation of an effective working environment – where the team can work together in one place;
- providing the freedom for individuals to take responsibility for their work;
- developing an effective team.

We draw on the *agile* principles (see www.agilealliance.org) to emphasize the importance of motivated, empowered teams. The people involved are skilled, professional, knowledge workers. The challenges involved in benefits realization are complex. In all projects, and specifically when innovation is a goal, it is vital to focus on skills and enabling people to work together effectively in multi-disciplinary teams.

We emphasize key principles and a simple set of practices to help to build a common language and approach for multi-disciplinary teams. The aim is to create an environment where skilled, professional workers can succeed, rather than to attempt to improve performance by imposing a detailed process and tight controls. We often characterize this as a shift from (top-down) management control to (self-)discipline.

FOCUS ON THE DELIVERY OF VALUE TO CUSTOMERS AND OTHER STAKEHOLDERS THROUGHOUT THE LIFECYCLE

Principle 3 builds on Principle 1 to emphasize that the benefits focus relates to customers and other stakeholders. The emphasis must continue throughout the lifecycle of the investment.

The initial emphasis when exploring an opportunity is on benefits rather than technology implementation. The project itself becomes IT-enabled business change that tackles people, process and technology.

The focus on benefits continues throughout the project lifecycle and the subsequent lifetime of the 'assets', the new technology and business processes (or new business service) that have resulted from the investment.

REALIZATION OF BENEFITS WILL DEPEND ON THE PARTICIPATION OF ALL RELEVANT STAKEHOLDERS

This principle builds on Principle 2. Benefits realization depends on engagement with the stakeholders and their active participation through the project. The practices required to engage key groups will vary, but the principle makes clear that the project scope is not delivering technology, but active participation of stakeholders to provide their insights and to bring about change.

BENEFITS ARISE WHEN NEW CAPABILITIES ARE EXPLOITED AND MANAGED TO THE ADVANTAGE OF STAKEHOLDERS

The investment in IT-enabled change results in a new organizational capability: technology, processes, information and people educated in using the information and systems. For example, this might be a new e-commerce capability or a capability for customer relationship management. Benefits arise over an extended period, based on how these capabilities are exploited and managed.

Typically, there is an extended process of learning as the new capabilities are explored, skills are developed and the opportunities for the customer are discovered. This process needs to be actively managed or the capability will stagnate, remaining as it was when the systems went live and the changes first introduced.

EXPLOITATION OF THE POTENTIAL OF IT REQUIRES A MAJOR FORM OF ORGANIZATIONAL AND INDIVIDUAL LEARNING

This principle is closely related to Principle 5. It has particular relevance to our focus on benefits from innovation and the perspective of IT as an 'intellectual' technology (Lee, 1999). It makes the crucial point that this is not a simple linear process: (1) define requirements; (2) design and implement a system; (3) realize benefits. The traditional 'waterfall' model of the project lifecycle was based on the importance of getting the planning and design 'right' at the start of the project and then strictly controlling (preventing) change. This thinking is flawed, particularly if the scenario involves innovation. The strategic potential of IT is realized through a much more complex process of organizational learning and change, during and after the project.

While it is important to have a clear understanding of the problematic situation to be tackled or the vision for the project, the focus on the precise definition of outcomes in a business case before the project starts is an illustration of flawed thinking that stifles innovation. We need a more truly commercial approach, which reflects the vision of the entrepreneur. The project should reflect the principles of an agile approach 'responding to change over following a plan'. The requirements and design emerge from the project process because of learning and the innovative ways of working of the team.

We can still set some requirements, but we focus on the vision and the benefits for stakeholders and take a phased, incremental approach because we know that during a project we are likely to discover new possibilities, which we can capture through further phases of change, which in turn will lead to new learning.

Over all, the principles encapsulate a benefits 'mindset' which provides a crucial foundation for a benefits-driven approach to be successfully adopted (Box 2.2).

Box 2.2 Mindset and paradigm

One factor underlying the problems with adoption of benefits-related methods is potentially a 'paradigm filter' (Johnson, 1992). Steel (2000) says: 'a paradigm is a self-consistent set of ideas and beliefs which acts as a filter, influencing how we perceive and how we make sense.'

> The predominant paradigm is still one where the implementation of technology on time and on budget is taken as success.
>
> We have to stress the underlying principles of benefits realization, the 'know-why' to help enable a shift to a new paradigm or new mindset.

A FRAMEWORK FOR PROJECTS

THE VALUE OF A PROJECT FRAMEWORK

In our view, a project framework is different from a project method or methodology in important ways. It has a number of important elements: guiding *principles* that make clear important views about what leads to success; a clear *framework* for the project lifecycle, breaking it down into specific stages with defined deliverables; and specific *practices* or tools that can be adopted at different stages. It is not prescriptive. The framework provides guidance for teams to help them work effectively. A project framework has considerable value for an individual project and for the organization managing a diverse portfolio of projects.

For a specific project, the framework breaks the project down into a number of clear stages, each with specific deliverables. This should help the project team be clear about its role and the focus of its activities at any particular stage. It also helps the team communicate with management and other stakeholders. The splitting of the project into a number of clear stages, none of which is more than a few weeks in duration, also provides focus and motivation for the team. Innovation often brings many options and much uncertainty; the focus on short-term goals balances space to innovate with a drive for closure and progress.

At the organizational level there are many additional benefits of adopting a consistent framework for projects. A consistent approach helps management control the entire portfolio of investments and enables groups that have to be involved in many projects (for example, IT infrastructure and security) to engage effectively at the right time.

A consistent framework also provides a basis for sharing learning between projects and avoids 'reinventing the wheel' in areas that do not add a great deal of value ('How should we format the progress report on this project?'). Practices can be reused at many levels: for example, a communications strategy addressing how to engage with the diverse groups in a professional organization, or a document setting out team structure and roles, or perhaps a web-based environment and set of templates for project team collaboration and stakeholder engagement. This shared learning increases effectiveness by communicating good ideas and increases efficiency by avoiding time-consuming duplication of effort. Perhaps most importantly, the shared framework and practices help the rapid formation of effective teams as projects are established and as people move from project to project.

ESTABLISH A BENEFITS-DRIVEN PROJECT FRAMEWORK[T]: INTRODUCING e^{4+1}

In this chapter we introduce the e^{4+1} project framework (Figure 2.1). It draws on experience of both traditional approaches to projects, such as PRINCE2, and 'agile' approaches that have their roots in software development and design. e^{4+1} has a number of specific features.

Firstly, it focuses on people throughout the lifecycle, recognizing that success comes from motivated, effective multi-disciplinary teams and that project processes should be designed primarily to help the team and their stakeholders work effectively to deliver benefits.

Secondly, e^{4+1} takes the view that a project starts from the initial idea. The goal is to bring focus and momentum from this early stage, rather than the traditional starting-point, often months or years later, when the idea has been developed into a business case and project plan. This early focus and momentum are crucial in a fast-moving business environment and for managing the allocation of scarce organizational resources to the highest-value ideas.

e^{4+1} also continues beyond the traditional end-point of projects. Most projects end soon after the cutover to the new systems and processes. In e^{4+1} we take the view that benefits are only realized from the new ways of working that result from the cutover and that these take time to bed in and develop. In many

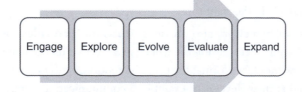

Figure 2.1 Outline of the e^{4+1} project framework

situations, crucial learning about the benefits and how to realize them takes place at this stage and the project team needs to continue its focus on benefits at this stage so we go beyond e^4 to e^{4+1} with the final 'Expand' stage.

e^{4+1} has an explicit focus on benefits for stakeholders rather than the delivery or procurement of software.

Finally, e^{4+1} reflects our view that there are serious flaws in the assumptions underlying traditional approaches to projects. Especially in scenarios where innovation is the goal, the approach to a project has to enable significant learning about what is possible and what is beneficial for the stakeholders during the life of the project. Innovative projects have to enable adaptation and change and they have to establish a simple, effective framework of management and control that does not stifle innovation and progress with bureaucracy. To put it bluntly, the traditional model, in which you define in detail *exactly* what the outcomes will be before you start a project, is nonsense if the goal is business innovation. The early stages of e^{4+1} emphasize creating space for innovation before the focus shifts to delivery.

In this section we provide an initial outline of key elements of the e^{4+1} framework. Later, we work through each stage in more detail, exploring specific benefits-driven practices.

LINKING e^{4+1} TO YOUR ORGANIZATION

We have used e^{4+1} to illustrate good practice and provide a basis for making a difference in organizations. Where you already have a project framework, you will probably need to work out how you can use key principles and practices from e^{4+1} to make improvements. The specific principles and practices as represented in the benefits toolkit can be adopted incrementally regardless of the specific project framework in your organization.

In any case, there is a lot of value in having a consistent project framework, and e^{4+1} embodies a number of important features.

e^{4+1} IN OUTLINE
Engage
There are always so many ideas, too many opportunities to invest time and resources in every one. How do you decide where to focus? How can you know at the start what the possibilities are?

In scenarios involving innovation, perhaps exploiting new technology, or just trying an idea learned from elsewhere that is new to the organization, you just cannot be sure of the potential benefits. What will the customers really think? Can we adopt an idea that has worked well in another organization? The traditional approach based on the business plan, detailed planning and requirements documented and signed off up front, brings a perception of certainty and control, but the high failure rate of projects confirms that the reality is different.

Engage is the start of a process of exploration and learning. It is the start of a series of small steps to discover and create possibilities, and gradually to focus on good ideas that have real potential for stakeholders and the organization.

Engage should be a rapid stage. The goal is to outline the opportunity by identifying and bringing together a group of key stakeholders who would need to be involved in further steps. The output is a brief outline of the opportunity (a single-page 'concept' document, perhaps) and agreement on whether to proceed further.

Explore

Explore builds on the rapid initial work done during Engage to establish a clear and agreed vision for the project and a benefits realization plan. The emphasis on learning and stakeholder engagement continues to be vital at this stage. The vision helps establish the broad goals for the project based on the contribution to the strategic objectives of the organization and the potential benefits to stakeholders.

The *benefits realization plan* is the critical deliverable from this stage. It brings together an agreed statement of:

- what the benefits are;
- how they will be measured;
- who is responsible for delivering them (and when);
- what changes are required to realize them.

The *solution concept* is also vital. It provides an initial view of the solution in both business and technical terms. In many cases, early prototyping will have been important in exploring what works to provide benefits for the different stakeholders.

The completion of the Explore stage is a second major project milestone and 'go/no-go' decision point. If innovation is an important driver, it is important to take some risks and explore different opportunities. As a result, not every project is successful, and it is good practice to stop some projects at this point.

Evolve

The project team will be mobilized at this point if this has not started earlier. Alongside starting to build an effective team, a key challenge is to ensure the team has a clear understanding of the vision for the project that has been established in previous phases, and that there is commitment to delivering the intended benefits.

Evolve will usually be a major stage and will often be subdivided into a number of smaller stages. Following an agile software development approach, Evolve will be split based on incremental delivery of elements of the underlying technical solution. In any case, it will often be useful to have a number of sub-stages to provide short-term goals and to enable regular reflection and learning. In many cases, the solution and related benefit realization plan will continue to evolve as the project continues. Typically, there will be a 'phased freeze' as elements of the solution and plan are brought under change control (Box 2.3).

Box 2.3   Phased freeze

The architect develops a conceptual design for the building, which gains enthusiastic approval. This provides a basis for starting work – by digging the foundations. Later on, the steelwork is put in place, providing a skeleton to build on. Only much later on will the details emerge – of the layout of each floor, of lighting, colours and furnishings.

With the right skills in the team, an IT system design emerges in a similar way. Technology infrastructure and core database design are 'baselined' early. Details of user interface can follow much later: the 'phased freeze' balances maintaining flexibility and achieving progress.

Evaluate

Major and interim project milestones provide important opportunities for review and reflection. Evaluate is the key opportunity for a benefits review to consider:

- What benefits have been realized?

- What action is required to sustain and develop these benefits?

- Is there a way to deliver any planned benefits that have not yet been realized?

- Have there been any unexpected benefits, and how can these be developed further?

- What learning is there for future projects and the wider organization?

Although conceptually simple, the challenge is to ensure that evaluation happens and that an environment is created where genuine learning can occur. The review needs to take place soon after implementation, but not too soon: there needs to be time for a benefits perspective to be possible, avoiding a focus on technical issues relating to 'going live'.

Expand

The framework is e^{4+1} not e^5 to emphasize Expand and to show that it is different from the other stages. Expand is the stage after a traditional perspective would say the project is complete. This 'post-live' period is crucial to the project, and it is vital to continue the focus on benefits realization. Expand could be considered as ongoing management of the production service, but value of Expand for benefits realization means that it is important to include it as part of the project framework.

Preparations for Expand will have taken place throughout the project, specifically the activities relating to stakeholder engagement. During this stage responsibilities will usually be handed over from the project team to operational management.

THE FRAMEWORK IN CONTEXT

There are many other approaches to projects, many with substantial backing from professional bodies and other groups. e^{4+1} provides a fresh perspective on projects that is valuable for both newcomers to the world of project management and experienced project managers. We hope it will help organizations succeed with innovation and make engagement in projects more rewarding and fun for individuals.

Many organizations have no overall project framework, and in many cases each project manager has to start from scratch in determining how to plan and manage a project. e^{4+1} can provide considerable value for an individual project or across an entire portfolio of projects. It brings the flexibility for learning and adaptation that is absent from traditional approaches. It has a focus on specific milestones and deliverables.

e^{4+1} provides a response to the suggestion by De Meyer et al. (2002) that there is a need to find the balance between planning and learning and to set out different roles for the project manager and different approaches to managing tasks and relationships depending on the type/extent of uncertainty:

> Openness to learning is new to many companies but it's obvious from the many spectacular project failures that the time has come to rethink some of the traditions of project management. In an era of rapid change, uncertainty is the rule not an exception. Companies that understand that have the greatest chance to produce spectacular project successes.
>
> (De Meyer et al., 2002, p. 67)

e^{4+1} can be used as a framework for projects small or large wherever they are found in organizations. Secondly, and perhaps most importantly, it is designed to reflect a new way of thinking about projects and how to succeed with benefits realization from projects and specifically investments in IT-enabled change. In this sense, it highlights key principles and practices, which will be valuable irrespective of the explicit adoption of the e^{4+1} framework. Finally, it can be used as a basis for adapting and enhancing whatever approach to projects is currently in place within an organization.

FOUNDATION PRACTICES FOR A BENEFITS-LED APPROACH

In this section we introduce three specific practices, which provide a foundation for a benefits-led approach to IT-enabled change. They are relevant throughout the project lifecycle.

PHASE BENEFITS DELIVERY[T]

In practice, a traditional 'waterfall' approach to projects often results in large, long projects as the team attempts to deliver all possible user requirements. For very good reasons the agile approach breaks away from this 'one shot' approach to change.

Agile projects keep teams small, have short durations (no longer than six to nine months, and much shorter where possible) and deliver the business solution (benefits) in phases over a series of these short projects or 'versioned releases' (Figure 2.2).

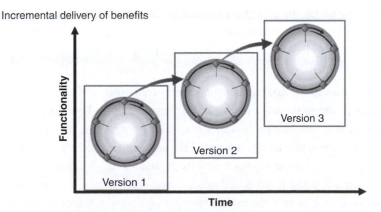

Minimize risks by breaking large projects into multiple versions. Reduce time to realization of benefits.

Figure 2.2 Phase benefits delivery

The first benefit of this incremental approach is that smaller, shorter projects are much easier to manage and control. The risks are substantially lower than with larger projects as complexity increases exponentially with the scale of the project. The shorter project also means that benefits are realized earlier.

In addition, small teams tend to be more innovative, and the short timescales are likely to result in greater motivation and stronger ownership.

A further benefit, which is crucial, is that delivery over a series of releases provides an opportunity for organizational learning. In scenarios of significant change and innovation it allows the organization and customers to learn more about the potential benefits and how to realize them.

MILESTONE-BASED CONTROL[T]

The focus of project management should be on the major milestones (stage ends) determined by the project lifecycle. If the project is kept short (as it should be), this will typically provide a major review point every four to six weeks, which provides a motivating target for the project team and reduces the risk of slippage between milestones for the sponsor and project board.

The deliverables at each milestone should be clearly defined. In some organizations a standard lifecycle is defined, with the same stages and major deliverables for each project.

BENEFITS-DRIVEN TRADE-OFFS[T]

The business case and project plans essentially balance three things: resources (including costs), the project timescale and the 'features' being delivered. Plans are without exception based on incomplete information. As the project progresses, the project team, project manager, project sponsor and project board will have to make decisions in response to new information.

The concept of making 'benefits-driven trade-offs' is that as part of initial project planning there should be a clear agreement on how decisions will be made as new information becomes available: for example, new requirements, more accurate estimates or evidence of the productivity of the project team. For most projects the right approach is to fix the team size, set a target delivery date and then adjust the features delivered, if necessary, as new information arises. This avoids the twin problems of throwing additional resources at a struggling project with little impact, and continually putting back the deadline to try to deliver everything that is wanted in one go.

The delivery of benefits provides an overall context for the trade-off decisions and fits closely with the phasing of benefits delivery.

ENGAGE: EXPLORING AN OPPORTUNITY

FOCUS ON BENEFITS FROM DAY 1

Engage is a rapid first stage of the project to turn an idea into the initial outline of an opportunity, which has the support of a key group of stakeholders. It also provides a way to filter out ideas that are not worth investigating further, or at least not at the moment.

Ideas can come from many sources; it is important to create an environment where ideas are encouraged and treated seriously and where decision-makers are open to new opportunities. We consider the importance of generating ideas and explore ways of thinking about business value from IT that help assess an idea. We then explore two important practices that underpin activity at this stage:

- stakeholder mapping: a valuable way to start with a focus on the customer and other stakeholders;

- the IT and Change Portfolio, which helps determine priorities based on alignment with the strategic objectives of the organization.

SOURCES OF VALUE FROM IT

IT makes different contributions to organizational performance in different scenarios. The opportunities for realizing value depend on the strategy, structure and culture of the organization. Many different frameworks can be used to classify the different sources of value from IT.

We have taken a straightforward model to help consider the different sources of value from IT, as it provides helpful insights when considering real-world situations (Box 2.4).

Many early IT investments were made to automate activities (payroll calculation, accounts payable etc.). Increasingly IT is being used in scenarios where the value comes from informating, embedding or communicating. In any scenario it is important to consider which of these sources of value are relevant and to explore if there are benefits in other areas.

Box 2.4   Sources of value from IT

Automate: substituting technology for labour
Informate: complementing human information-processing capabilities
Embed: replacing and enhancing mechanical and electro-mechanical controls

---

Communicate/collaborate: enhancing information-sharing capabilities
Source: Cash et al. (1994) *Building the Information Age Organization* –
building on Zuboff (1988) *In the Age of the Smart Machine*

Examples of sources of value from IT

Automate: matching of invoices, orders and goods received notes by an
accounts payable system; payroll processing; an e-commerce initiative;
online check-in for a flight.

Informate: a business scorecard-reporting system that provides managers with access to top-level performance indicators and the ability to
'drill down' to see more information about any trends/changes.

Embed: the car that alerts the driver that it needs a service; the automated
risk assessment of a mortgage application.

Communicate/collaborate: a worldwide virtual team in a consulting
organization – asking for and sharing advice by using an email discussion group and an intranet site for sharing valuable documents and other
resources.

INSIGHT AND INNOVATION

Ideas, insights and awareness of the problems that provide opportunities for
innovation are all around us. Most people are full of ideas and are keen to act
on them if they are given half a chance. It is only in unhealthy organizations that
people just accept the current situation, however ineffective and inefficient it is.

Some ideas will come top-down from senior management as part of a strategic planning process. Many others will come from staff, customers, partners
and competitors, if we keep our eyes and ears open and we encourage people to
share the ideas and insights they have (Figure 2.3).

There may also be opportunities to go out and search for ideas – perhaps at
relevant conferences, online or by specifically working to build up a network of
relationships with individuals who may provide valuable ideas.

Taking time to develop an understanding of the business potential of new
technologies is also important. This might involve investing time in researching
online and developing relationships with technical specialists internally as well
as key vendors.

Many individuals and organizations have become risk-averse because of
previous bad experiences: for example, being taken in by vendor hype about a
new technology or by the failure of a major project. Given the pace of technology and business innovation, most organizations can no longer take this
approach and simply follow and wait. A much better approach is to take some
risks and learn from experience. The key is to ensure that the risks are limited
and that a new project does not put the future of the business at risk.

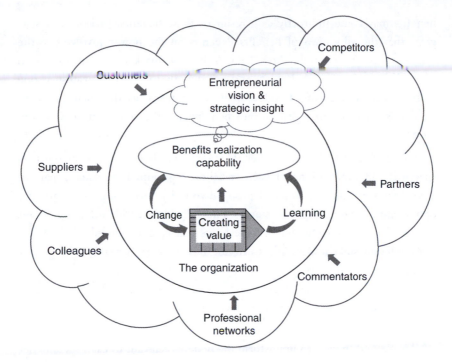

Figure 2.3 Ideas enabling innovation

STAKEHOLDER MAPPING[T]: START WITH A FOCUS ON BENEFITS FOR STAKEHOLDERS

It is important to start a project with a clear perspective on how to create value for customers and other stakeholders (see definition in Box 2.5). This counters the organizational perspective, which can often be reduced to 'make money'. While this is valid, perhaps translated outside the private sector into being 'cost-effective', it does not tell us 'how'. The key to understanding 'how' is to start with a focus on benefits for stakeholders.

Box 2.5   Stakeholder(s)

An individual or group of people who will benefit from the investment or are either directly or indirectly involved in making or are affected by the changes needed to realize the benefits.

See: Ward and Daniel (2012) *Benefits Management*

Jurison (1996) identifies that the benefits of IS/IT will often be benefits for specific stakeholders, including customers and employees, and that organizational benefits may come indirectly as a result of these benefits. Jurison also suggests that the allocation of benefits depends on the power involved in the relationships: for example, how competitive the market is. The extent to which benefits go to stakeholders and not directly to the organization is one reason many studies of IT value show low returns, as the focus of these studies is typically on (bottom-line) benefits for the organization (Jurison, 1996).

One powerful technique, stakeholder mapping, is to brainstorm the perspectives and expectations of each stakeholder group. It is usually part of a workshop session with a small group involved in exploring or identifying opportunities. There are two stages. The first involves identifying relevant stakeholders and stakeholder groups. Some judgement is involved to determine relevant stakeholders and to decide how to segment stakeholders. For example, in the university we would virtually always consider students as a number of groups – undergraduate, postgraduate taught, MBA, postgraduate research, executive – as there are different expectations to take into account.

The second stage is to brainstorm the benefits relevant to each stakeholder group. That is, to consider what benefits they might gain or, from a slightly different angle, how the project that is envisaged might affect them in terms of both benefits and 'dis-benefits'.

We can use the stakeholder mapping model with a small group of people. At this early stage it may reveal some gaps in our knowledge, which is fine as we can deal with that later if we proceed with work to turn the idea into a project. We can also decide later how to validate our understanding of the benefits for different stakeholders.

You can add to the process by thinking about your expectations of the stakeholder; it is particularly relevant for partners and suppliers, but is useful for other groups as well.

We can use the approach in at least two ways. One starting-point would be to use it to develop ideas – by just taking a very open view of the situation and exploring expectations, or potential benefits that are not being met. This could result in various opportunities for making improvements, or doing new things, being identified. The second scenario is to use the approach to explore a specific idea. The approach is much the same, but the aim is to ensure we start with a stakeholder perspective and use this to develop a better understanding of the opportunity and its implications.

Getting the right people involved in the initial analysis will mean that a lot of knowledge about the different stakeholders is already available. At later stages of the project it will be important to explore further and to test out the initial understanding.

THE IT AND CHANGE PORTFOLIO[T]: CLARIFYING STRATEGIC ALIGNMENT

An important starting-point for realizing value from investments in IT is the IT and Change Portfolio. This describes the investments in applications and services (those already in place, those planned and future possible applications), not in terms of technology but in terms of their role and contribution to business performance (Figure 2.4 and Box 2.6).

	Competitive	Exploratory
Transformational change/doing new things	*Critical to* achieving strategic objectives	*May be important* in achieving future success
Improving the current business	Critical to existing business operations	*Valuable but not critical* to success
	Qualifying	Support

Figure 2.4 The IT and Change Portfolio

Based on Ward and Peppard (2002) and McFarlan (1981).

The portfolio enables senior business and IT managers to work together to get a clearer focus on doing the right things: setting priorities and ensuring strategic alignment of investments in IT-enabled change. The portfolio is based on a paper by McFarlan (*Harvard Business Review*, 1981) and work by Ward and Peppard (see their book *Strategic Planning for Information Systems*, 2002).

There are four classes of contribution to business performance. *Qualifying* systems are those where the IT is so embedded and necessary that, if the system failed, the organization would suffer extensively: for example, an airline booking system. In any given industry or sector, organizations will have more or less the same qualifying portfolio.

Support systems are about improving efficiency. Their failure does not have far-reaching consequences: for example, training records unavailable for a week. Eventually, of course, if the records remained unavailable for a significant period there would be some impact on performance.

Competitive and Exploratory are quite different, although they both concern themselves with the future. Competitive systems are not just very big systems – they are those that genuinely contribute to the business's plans and strategies. When these are implemented, people will work in very different ways – ways that will confer a competitive advantage, for instance. The system does not deliver the strategic benefit – that comes from the change in the way business will be done – but the system is nevertheless crucial to the business change: for example, an integrated international supply chain system needed for truly global operation.

Exploratory investments are the Research & Development of IT activity – prototypes and pilots of ideas that may confer large benefits. These projects are the basis for innovation. The uncertainty means that large sums of money should *not* be laid out until some preliminary business experimentation has taken place to explore if the benefits really exist and how they can be realized.

Box 2.6   Examples of investments related to the IT and Change Portfolio

It is dangerous to give examples, as they might be turned into rules: for example, customer relationship management is Competitive. There are no rules. It all depends on the strategy and strategic context of the organization.

The first ATM (cash machine) was Competitive for a while. Then it was copied by the rest of the retail banking industry and became Qualifying. Now many banks do not own any ATMs and are just part of a consortium. Therefore, for these banks they are Support.

When we explored the systems used by my consulting group, we felt that a spreadsheet was the only Competitive application – it was used to allocate people (always a scarce resource) to projects.

The difference between Competitive and Exploratory is often about scale and confidence (certainty). The real value of an Exploratory project may be to reduce the risk of a multi-million dollar Competitive project.

In a business value sense, the portfolio charts the benefit lifecycle of an IT investment. A promising idea is tested for proof of benefits as an Exploratory activity; if it is worthwhile, it is implemented and confers Competitive advantage. Because it is good, it is copied by the industry and thus is classed as Qualifying. In time, as better IT offerings emerge, the application may migrate to Support.

USING THE PORTFOLIO

The portfolio can be used to help review current IT systems and services, to manage current projects and to explore priorities for future investments in IT. It provides a very powerful basis for bringing together senior business and IT stakeholders to make informed decisions based on a common, business-oriented language.

Our challenge is to decide whether to proceed with more detailed investigation of an idea so we can move forward with a successful investment. The IT and Change Portfolio allows key stakeholders to discuss and agree on the potential strategic contribution of a specific idea. This might cause some debate, particularly at this early stage, but it is helpful to take an initial view on where an investment sits in the portfolio.

It might make sense to investigate further an idea in any area of the portfolio, but the reasons would be different. For example, in Support – as the definition is 'valuable but not critical' – we should avoid making changes unless there is a clear financial payback. In Competitive and Exploratory, innovation will be a key driver, and alignment with strategic objectives and creation of new sources of value are likely to be important.

OPPORTUNITY EVALUATION[T]: READY TO MOVE FORWARD?

Using stakeholder mapping and the IT and Change Portfolio will provide new insights into an idea and whether to proceed with further investigation. We have not focused on cost or a return on investment analysis in any detail at this stage – that comes later.

The key at this stage is that the tools are simple to use. They provide a way for a small group of people to explore an idea and learn about the possibilities by working together. Although there will be an output on paper from the process, the key result is a shared understanding of the opportunity and hopefully a growing basis for working together on this or future opportunities.

The output from the work should include a 'one-pager' summarizing the opportunity and making a recommendation (Box 2.7). It usually makes sense to write up the stakeholder analysis, particularly if this is done in 'real time' as part of the workshop. Recommendations can include: proceed with more detailed investigation straight away; proceed but at some agreed future date (for example, after the year end); worth investigating at some point; or no further action (Figure 2.5).

Box 2.7 Opportunity evaluation: Outline of the benefits assessment as a concept paper

A very short (one-page) summary of the opportunity

- Why is it worth doing (strategic contribution and portfolio contribution)?
- What are the benefits (for customers, other stakeholders and the organization as a whole)?
- Who are the key players (to move forward from here)?
- How does it leverage existing resources and capabilities?
- What are the main areas of uncertainty and risk?

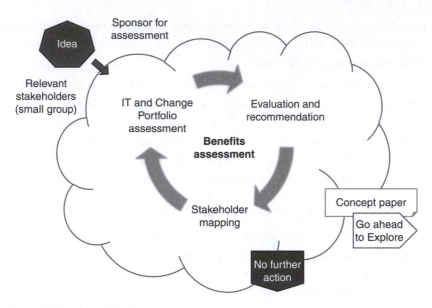

Figure 2.5 Outline of the Engage stage

Figure 2.5 provides an overview of the Engage stage.

Work on the idea may continue, or it may now be clear that it is part of a bigger strategic initiative. Moving ahead requires commitment of valuable resources, so a key element of the decision to proceed has to be to think about who are the right people to involve in the next stage, what level of effort is required and if they have the time available. Engage focuses effort in order to build momentum for delivering results.

MAKING IT HAPPEN

Two big questions remain: who should be involved at this stage, and who makes the decision about going ahead? To a certain extent, these are unanswerable in the abstract– it depends on the organization and the idea. For example, at this stage it might seem that the impact is within a particular department, but this might change as a greater understanding develops. In practical terms the investigation should involve representatives of those who might be planning and delivering the investment (IT function?) as well as potential sponsors and business areas affected. At this stage there is no need to be comprehensive; work with customers and other directly affected stakeholders might come later.

The need for broader engagement in the decision will depend on the seniority of the sponsor engaged to date and the scale of the opportunity. It usually makes sense to share the decision-making process with one or more groups that can provide a broader perspective – for example, of a product roadmap or IT strategy and architecture. There is an important balance to strike here – particularly as we are focusing on enabling innovation. Shared decision-making can be a good thing, and, approached in the right way, valuable insight and additional resources can be gathered in the process. There is also a major risk that all innovation is killed by over-cautious, committee-based decision-making. Engage is about focusing the entrepreneurial effort of individuals within the organization and must not inadvertently kill it. It needs to be a short, value-adding process.

IN SUMMARY

A benefits-led approach to investments in IT and organizational change is represented by a number of underlying principles. Together these reflect a benefits 'mindset' in contrast to the technology mindset that drives much of IT investment.

A clear project framework is important, and we have used e^{4+1} to highlight a number of key factors, including applying project disciplines from an early stage and following through beyond initial implementation and 'go live' to ensure benefits realization.

Engage provides the first phase of the project lifecycle, exploring an opportunity from strategic and stakeholder perspectives prior to investment of energy in developing a benefits realization plan and mobilizing a project team.

TAKING IT FURTHER

FURTHER READING AND RESOURCES
Key books for further reading include:

Ward, J. and Daniel, E. (2012) *Benefits Management*, John Wiley & Sons Inc.

John Ward's work provides a crucial insight into how to approach IS in organizations.

Highsmith, Jim (2004) *Agile Project Management*, Addison-Wesley.

A valuable book addressing the principles and practices of an agile approach to project management. The approach is intended to apply to IS projects and other product development scenarios. Lots of practical guidance.

Peter Checkland's work is an opportunity to dive deeper into some challenging issues:

Checkland, P. and Poulter, J. (2006) *Learning for Action*, Wiley.

Checkland, Peter and Holwell, Sue (1999) *Information, Systems, and Information Systems: Making Sense of the Field*, Wiley.

Checkland, P. and Scholes, J. (1999) *Soft Systems Methodology: A 30-year Retrospective*, Wiley.

Articles to start with include:

Markus, M. L. (2004) Technochange Management: Using IT to Drive Organizational Change. *Journal of Information Technology*, Vol. 19 (1): 4–20.

Markus provides another perspective on the same issues.

Peppard, J. and Ward, J. (2005) Unlocking Sustained Business Value from IT Investments. *California Management Review*, Fall, 2005: 52–69.

Good overviews of the Cranfield work on benefits management.

TALKING POINTS

Use these questions to help reflect on this chapter and explore the challenges of putting the ideas into practice:

1. What is your experience of IT projects? Has the focus been on technology implementation or the wider issues of business change to realize benefits?

2. How consistent is the approach to projects in your organization?

3. Why is a clear and consistent project framework valuable to an individual project team and the organization as a whole?

4. Is an emphasis on (self-)discipline of the project team rather than top-down management control realistic? What are the risks and potential benefits? What are the limits?

5. What are the implications of the principles for benefits realization for the governance and leadership of investments in IT?

6. What are the key features of e^{4+1}? How does it relate to your experience of projects?

7. How well established and consistently applied is the project framework in your organization? How does it differ from e^{4+1}?

8. How might you take advantage of the principles and practices outlined in this chapter (including e^{4+1}) to add value to the project framework in place in your organization?

9. In this chapter reference has been made to 'waterfall' approaches to projects and their limitations. What are their strengths and limitations? How might you adopt an agile approach without losing out on the strengths of these approaches?

10. How might we enable organizational learning to exploit the potential of IT (Principle 6)?

11. Pick a scenario in your organization: what are the opportunities for benefits in the context of the sources of value from IT (Box 2.7)?

12. What challenges might you face in developing a stakeholder map?

13. How might the portfolio influence your decision on proceeding with work on a potential investment?

14. What are the implications if a proposed investment seems to relate to more than one category in the portfolio?

15. How could you take into account what's possible when carrying out Engage (and Explore)?

16. What guidelines could you propose for when to apply Engage?

KEY DEBATES

The business case and clear metrics drive benefits realization

In practice, an alternative approach is to focus directly on metrics and specifically on financial return from the planned investment. The departmental budget is changed to reflect the savings (etc.) in the business case. IT are responsible for delivering the system. The department/business unit are responsible for operating with the new system and meeting their targets. From this perspective planning is about the financial business case.

Can this approach work? In what situations?

CASE STUDY 2.1

The case is an interesting example of benefits focus – exploring a long-term perspective and the role of partnerships.

Journal of Information Technology Teaching Cases, Vol. 3 (2013): 16–28.

Innovation through collaborative partnerships: creating the MSN News for iPad app at VanceInfo Technologies

Pamela Abbott, Yingqin Zheng and Rong Du

This teaching case focuses on a collaborative project between a major software and services outsourcing company in China (VanceInfo Technologies) and one of its major Western clients (Microsoft Inc.). VanceInfo and Microsoft had been engaged in a long-term client/vendor relationship since 1997, and the project had been the result of this long-term partnership arrangement. The project was deemed quite successful and innovative; hence it provided an opportunity to determine how collaborative innovation could work between two remote and culturally different supply chain partners and how the lessons from this project could be used to inform single sign on (SSO) providers of ways in which they could move up the value chain to more client-focused value added services. The case looks in depth at the actual working practices that enabled the distributed Microsoft/VanceInfo team to produce a market-led innovative product. Agile methods were highly integral to the functioning of those work practices and are quite carefully scrutinized from the point of view of how they were adapted for use in a distributed, cross-cultural environment. Users of the case study will be asked to formulate answers to several questions geared towards providing general guidelines that SSO providers can follow to achieve similar successful outcomes.

REFERENCES

Ashurst, C. (2007) Realizing Benefits from IS/IT: Exploring the Practices and Competences Required to Succeed, PhD thesis, University of Loughborough, UK.

Cash, J., Eccles. R., Nohira. N. and Nolan, R. (1994) *Building the Information Age Organization: Structure, Control and Information Technologies*, Richard Irwin, Inc.

Clegg, C. W. (2000) Socio-Technical Principles for System Design. *Applied Ergonomics*, Vol. 31: 463–477.

DeMarco, T. and Lister, T. (1999), *Peopleware: Productive Projects and Teams* (Second Edition), Dorset House.

De Meyer, A., Loch, C.H. and Pich, M.T. (2002) Managing Project Uncertainty: From Variation to Chaos. *MIT Sloan Management Review*, Winter 2002.

Eason, K. (1988) *Information Technology and Organizational Change*, Taylor & Francis.

Highsmith, J. (2004) *Agile Project Management*, Addison-Wesley.

Johnson, G. (1992) Managing Strategic Change – Strategy, Culture and Action. *Long Range Planning*, Vol. 25 (1): 28–36.

Jurison, J. (1996) Towards More Effective Management of Information Technology Benefits. *Journal of Strategic Information Systems*, Vol. 5: 263–274.

Lee, A.S. (1999) Researching MIS, in Currie, W. and Galliers, B. (eds.) *Rethinking Management Information Systems*, Oxford University Press.

McFarlan, F. (1981) Portfolio Approach to Information Systems. *Harvard Business Review*, Vol. 59 (5): 142–150.

Orlikowski, W.J. (1992) The Duality of Technology: Rethinking the Concept of Technology in Organizations. *Organization Science*, Vol. 3 (2): 398–427.

Steel, R. (2000) New Insights on Organizational Change. *Organizations & People*, Vol. 7 (2): 2–9.

Ward, J. and Daniel, E. (2012) *Benefits Management*. John Wiley & Sons Inc.

Ward, J. and Peppard, J. (2002) *Strategic Planning for Information Systems* (Third edition). John Wiley and Sons.

Ward, J., Taylor, P. and Bond, P. (1996) Evaluation and Realization of IS/IT Benefits: An Empirical Study of Current Practice. *European Journal of Information Systems*, Vol. 4: 214–255.

Zuboff, S. (1988) *In the Age of the Smart Machine*, Basic Books.

CHAPTER 3
ESTABLISHING THE VISION: DEVELOPING THE BENEFITS REALIZATION PLAN

IN THIS CHAPTER WE STUDY:

- a strategic perspective on an investment in IT and business change;
- aligning an investment with benefits for stakeholders;
- the second stage of a project lifecycle – developing the benefits realization plan to address what the benefits will be and how they will be realized.

EXPLORE: DEVELOPING THE BENEFITS REALIZATION PLAN

OVERVIEW OF THE PHASE

As we enter the Explore stage, we are going to be working on an opportunity which has been the subject of preliminary work during Engage. The goal is to develop a benefits realization plan and an initial solution concept prior to a critical decision point on further investment.

There are a number of activities at this stage, each supported by key elements of the toolkit. Initially we will take a step-by-step approach to explain how the tools can be used in the development of the benefits realization plan. One key issue to consider is whether there is a decision, in principle, that a project will go ahead and that the work during Explore is about shaping the project and starting to build a team so that momentum is gained to deliver the benefits. Alternatively, a more tentative approach can be adopted with the benefits realization plan as the basis for a stronger go/no-go decision; building the team and the momentum of the project can be deferred until the next stage (Evolve).

Benefits Management is 'the process of organizing and managing such that the potential benefits arising from the use of IT are actually realized' (Ward and Elvin, 1999, p. 197; also Ward and Murray, 2000). Its contribution is that it provides concepts and techniques to enable the project team to focus on managing the project to ensure the benefits are realized. Benefits management is designed to identify and then deliver the benefits. In this chapter, as elsewhere, we are drawing on these ideas.

Activities in the Explore stage build directly on the work done during Engage. These include: driver analysis; the benefits and change assessment; stakeholder analysis; exploring perspectives on design; and, finally, developing a benefits realization plan (Figure 3.1).

START WITH THE END IN MIND – THE BENEFITS REALIZATION PLAN[T]

The benefits realization plan identifies:

- why the project is required and what the high level goals are;
- what the benefits are; and for all of the benefits ...
- how they will be measured and what the targets are;
- when they are due to arise;
- which stakeholders they relate to;

- who is responsible for delivery;
- what business changes are required to realize them (and who is responsible for these changes);
- what enablers are required in support of the business changes, including IT functionality.

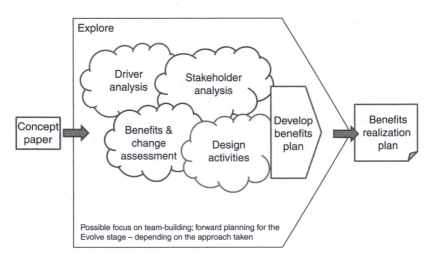

Figure 3.1 Key activities during the Explore stage

The questions themselves (Figure 3.2) can be used as a checklist when preparing and reviewing a business case. This works for new practitioners of a benefits-driven approach who are not yet familiar with the specific techniques, and for experts it is a way to summarize the key issues.

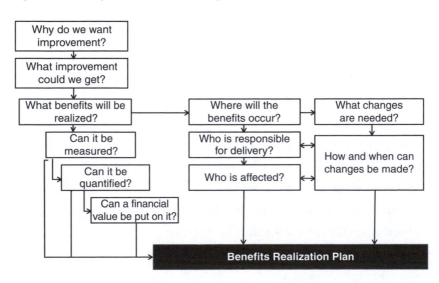

Figure 3.2 Outline of benefits planning – key questions
Source: Based on Benefits Management (2006) Ward and Daniel.

The outcome of benefits planning will be a benefits delivery or *benefits realization plan* setting out *what* the benefits are and *how* they are going to be realized. Although in theory all these topics should be covered by a business case, it is likely that in practice the focus is on *what* the benefits will be, rather than on *how* they are realized. In addition, in many cases the approval of the business case is just another hurdle to be tackled, and for many reasons the project then becomes an IT-driven technology implementation. The aim of the benefits realization plan is that it should continue to have a central role in the management of the project.

It is worth exploring in more detail what we mean by these questions.

Why do we want improvement?

The crucial first step is to get a clear understanding of why there is a need to do anything. What are the internal or external *drivers* for change? Change is risky, so we need to have a good reason for starting. This requires a good understanding of the problem or opportunity and a decision by (senior) management that action is required. We refer to the reasons why change is required as the 'business drivers' or drivers.

Initial work on the project as part of Engage will have started to clarify this.

What improvement do we want/could we get?

Once the need for action has been identified, the next step is to agree on the overall objectives for the investment in change. This is about developing an understanding of the desired end-state: what does it look like when we have succeeded? This provides the *vision* for the project.

The *investment objectives* are a choice made by management. The drivers require action, but in most circumstances what action to take requires consideration of a range of options and a decision by management. For example, if the goal is to improve customer satisfaction, one starting point might be to invest in a customer relationship management (CRM) system. Another option would be to change employee recruitment practices to focus on employees more likely to provide a friendly and helpful service. Yet another response would be to reassess product and service design.

Many projects fail at this point because the *why* (the drivers) and the *what* (the investment objectives/vision) are not clear, or at least they have been defined in technical terms.

If the problem is particularly complex and messy, as they often are, it can be helpful to use Soft Systems techniques as a way of getting a better understanding of what the problem is and what would be an improvement (see Further Reading in Chapter 2: for example, *Learning for Action* by Peter Checkland and

John Poulter (2006)). More recent work on 'design thinking' (Brown, 2008) provides an alternative way to approach complex situations.

What benefits will be realized?

Having established the objectives, the next step is to clarify the benefits for relevant groups of stakeholders. Essentially, the question to consider is: 'what benefits would need to be realized to enable us to say that the objectives have been achieved?' This provides more detail to build on the initial statement of the objectives.

At this stage it is also important to consider the benefits and the extent to which they can be measured or quantified, and whether a financial benefit can be agreed.

Where will the benefits occur?

Where will the benefits occur? Often a change will have impacts in many areas of the organization. Which departments/business units/business processes are affected, and where will any benefits show up in departmental performance metrics or in business process performance measures?

What changes are needed?

What changes are needed to bring about the benefits (i.e., who is doing what differently)? This question requires a response in some detail to make clear what areas of the business need to change and how. For example, changes may include: training and education; structures; roles; locations; performance measures; reward and recognition; processes; working practices; behaviour; leadership. The approach to change will vary to reflect the context and which aspects of the business are being changed.

Who is responsible for delivery?

Who is responsible for delivery of the benefits (and the changes required to bring them about)? Depending on the responses to the previous question, this is likely to be senior managers across the business who are responsible for the departments and processes affected. This provides fresh insight into the changes required and the potential difficulty of the project.

Who will be affected?

As a result of the previous analysis, it now starts to become clear which stakeholders are affected and in what way. Who will benefit? Where will dis-benefits occur? What are the implications for the change programme and benefits realization?

How and when can changes be made?

It should now be possible to consider how/if the necessary changes can be made and develop the benefits realization plan.

These questions provide a starting-point for putting benefits planning into action. They provide the basis for a quick review of an investment proposal or an initial, rapid planning exercise. The leadership toolkit for benefits realization provides help to carry out a more in-depth investigation.

Focus on people: Enabling innovation

The detailed tools and techniques of a benefits-led approach are simply a means to an end – which is to enable a group of people to work together effectively to explore a valuable opportunity, develop a vision and concept for the solution, develop a benefits realization plan and then work together to realize the potential benefits.

The key success factor is getting the right people working together as effectively as possible. This is far from trivial, and it will often be particularly challenging to bring together a group representing different areas of the organization, with different backgrounds and skills, with different objectives and perspectives on priorities, to work together to innovate in products, services and ways of working. The tools presented here can and do contribute to this process, but using the tools must not become an end in itself. The skills of the facilitators and the team as a whole are critical.

It is particularly important to approach this stage of the project as a creative activity. The traditional model is often to carry out a series of interviews capturing details of possible benefits and requirements and then to compile a consolidated list. Our focus is on a series of *workshop* activities which allow people to work and think together, and which provide an opportunity for a more in-depth exploration of possible improvements. The benefits realization plan is only one outcome; more important is to start to build a team of people with a shared vision of the potential benefits and a commitment to bringing them about. Techniques such as brainstorming and the ability to design and facilitate effective workshops, which stimulate ideas and energy, are essential.

DRIVER ANALYSIS[T]

Driver analysis is a way to investigate 'why do we want the improvement?' and 'what are the overall objectives of the investment?' These are the key questions used to start work on the benefits realization plan. Driver analysis clarifies the potential contribution of the project to the organizational strategy (strategic alignment) and, as a result, helps set the priority for the project. Driver analysis builds on the work already done on stakeholder mapping, typically bringing in a strategic, top-down perspective to complement the 'bottom-up' stakeholder focus.

Understanding the drivers reveals the strength of ownership for the project at senior levels in the business. It clarifies how the investment should link into business plans and allows IT expenditure proposals to be seen as an investment in developing the organization's capability. The rationale for analysing the drivers is that:

- The beginning is the best place to stop bad projects (weak or insufficient rationale).
- It sets out how the investment should link into strategic objectives both in terms of project objectives and scope.
- It reveals the strength of ownership at senior levels in the business and identifies the sponsor(s) and their interests.
- At a high level, it determines how success will be recognized.
- It locates IT expenditure proposals as an investment in the future of the organization's capability – not merely parting with money to acquire modern technology.

A 'driver' is something that is putting pressure on the organization to change in some way. Driver analysis aims to understand the drivers, and then decide on investment objectives for the project. The investment objective is a high-level statement of the desired end-state: that is, just where the finishing-line is in the race. It doesn't cover *what* has to be done to get there, or *how* – those choices are made later.

It is worth noting that, by their nature, drivers cannot be changed or made to go away – they exist independently of any kind of programme or project. The investment objectives represent what an organization *chooses* to do about the drivers.

TECHNIQUES FOR DRIVER ANALYSIS

There are many techniques that can be used for driver analysis. They come from strategic management, and we just apply them with a focus on IT. The choice of tools depends on a range of factors, including the time available and what participants are already familiar with.

The analysis of competitive position is a key technique for driver analysis (Table 3.1 and Figure 3.3). The technique works at two levels. Firstly, it can be used to consider the overall competitive positioning of the organization. Which of three dimensions is the primary focus of the organizational strategy: customer intimacy, operational excellence or product leadership?

The logic is that successful organizations will *focus* – not try to be best at everything. If this can be agreed, it provides valuable context and focus for the more detailed analysis and planning activities.

Organization	Strategic focus
Apple	Product innovation: leading-edge products or services
Amazon	Customer intimacy: unique value-adding solutions
Ryanair	Operational excellence: focus on best value

Table 3.1 Strategic focus of well-known organizations
Source: Adapted from Treacy and Wiersema, 1993.

Then, at a second level, managers are asked to assess where they are in relation to the competition for each of the three dimensions. The assessment is carried out for each customer segment or business unit, as appropriate to the investment scenario. Is your organization better or worse than the competition and by how much (from −5 (much worse) to +5 (much better))? A score of '0' means you are equivalent to the competition. The positioning is *relative* and will change over time as, by doing nothing; the relative position will erode because of competitive activity.

Projects addressing 'Survival' are usually copying the rest of the sector or industry in order to catch up. Those on the same level of competitors are typically either 'business as usual' or incremental improvement. Those designed to take the business 'ahead' (to 'Prosperity') may have an innovation and radical-change aspect to them, since by definition no one else in the industry is doing things this way.

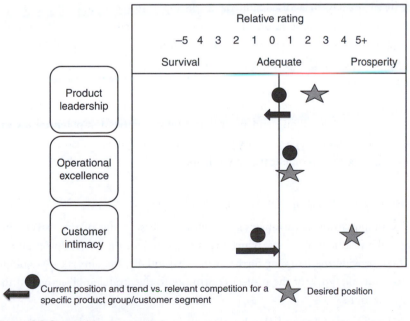

Figure 3.3 Competitive assessment
Source: Adapted from Treacy and Wiersema, 1993.

It is worth paying attention to the combinations of dimensions, since ultimately they interact: for example, good customer intimacy cannot be sustained for long if operations are below average and there is no clear product leadership.

SUCCEEDING WITH DRIVER ANALYSIS

There is a need to be reasonably persistent at the driver analysis stage since this is the point where it is best to re-scope projects or kill ones that should never have been started in the first place. The competitive assessment technique has proved very successful in helping to structure the discussions around drivers and what needs to be done about them. It attempts to set the drivers into the context of the organization's environment, especially its market-place. The technique also has the virtue that it is easily understood and quickly applied.

Many other tools and techniques can help identify drivers and objectives. They include PEST, SWOT and their variants, and also:

- 5-forces (Porter, 2008);
- value chain analysis (see Ward and Peppard, 2002)
- balanced scorecard (Kaplan and Norton, 1992, 1993, 1996a, 1996b);
- strategy mapping (Kaplan and Norton, 2004);
- value innovation (Kim and Mauborgne, 1997, 2005).

The different techniques can all be valuable. Some, such as the balanced scorecard, are particularly helpful if the organization already uses it. Some can be used quickly in a discussion or workshop (5-forces), and others need a more in-depth exercise to get the real value from them (value chain, strategy mapping). When used as part of driver analysis, these techniques help clarify how a potential investment contributes to the strategic objectives of the organization.

They can also be used in the context of developing IT strategy; the focus then becomes identifying and prioritizing opportunities for potential investments. Techniques, such as strategy mapping, that help to establish a view across the organization become extremely valuable.

THE CONTRIBUTION OF DRIVER ANALYSIS

The output from driver analysis is a clear understanding of the drivers and agreed investment objectives which provide a vision for the project/programme. These provide the basis for further work. Essentially, the aim is to be able to show how the goals of the project contribute to the strategic objectives of the organization.

The IT and Change Portfolio plays an important role in driver analysis as well as in the rest of the project. The portfolio provides a powerful shorthand for exploring and describing the contribution of the proposed investment to the strategy of the organization. The fit of the investment(s) with the portfolio was first considered during Engage. At this stage it is important to revisit the portfolio and reassess where the planned investment is.

If a project appears to be spread across several elements of the portfolio, it is possible it should be treated as a *programme* and split into components that each relate to one area of the portfolio. As the portfolio implies different projects need to be managed in different ways, it can be difficult to manage a project in the appropriate way if it does not fit into any one category.

It is important to develop shared use of key terms to avoid misunderstandings and to enable a clear focus on a number of important issues such as ownership for project goals vs. ongoing performance of an operational service (Box 3.1).

Box 3.1   Key terminology

Project: an initiative with specific goals, resources and timescales.
Programme: a broader strategic initiative, typically including a number of projects.
Service (or business process): the operational, business-as-usual activity, which is the target of the changes introduced by the project or programme.

*   *   *

All too often we see great confusion because these concepts are not used. A project merges into an ongoing programme of change, neither of which has accountabilities that are clearly distinguished from those for management of the ongoing service.

BENEFITS AND CHANGE ANALYSIS[T]

Having identified the drivers and investment objectives, the next stage is to identify the *benefits* that need to be delivered. A workshop approach is used to create a 'benefits dependency network' (or BDN: see Figure 3.4) that relates the business drivers with the project deliverables, including the IT solution. This network establishes a clear understanding of the overall business change plan and the contribution of technology.

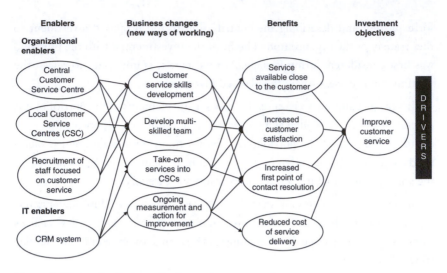

Figure 3.4 Example of a benefits dependency network
Source: Based on Benefits Management (2006) by Ward and Daniel.

The starting-point for the BDN is the set of drivers and investment objectives already defined. The next stage is to consider what benefits would be realized if the high-level investment objectives were achieved. The aim is to identify benefits relevant to specific stakeholders.

One way to do this is to have a large wall, a very large whiteboard or a number of sheets of flipchart paper available to capture the BDN. Each benefit is then written on a 'post-it' note that can be stuck onto the network.

Once the benefits have been identified, the business changes and then enabling changes are identified in a similar interactive process and positioned on the network using 'post-its'. The 'enabling changes' and 'business changes' respectively (see Box 3.2) define the one-off and ongoing changes in the business that are necessary to realize the benefits. The logic is to consider each benefit in turn and ask what needs to be done differently for this benefit to be achieved. It can be a messy process, but the use of 'post-its' enables changes to be made.

Box 3.2   Enabling changes vs. business changes

Enabling changes

- designing a new process;
- training;
- establishing new performance measures;
- defining new roles and responsibilities;

business changes (i.e., the new ways of working)

- working to a new process;
- key activities and controls.

The 'business changes' are the new ways of working that are essential for benefits realization. This is effectively the 'to be' state of the organization following delivery of the IT solution and enabling changes. It is important to take a broad perspective here; the enabling and business changes will relate to people, process and wider aspects of the organization.

A key contribution of the technique is the discussion that it generates in the workshop. This plays a key role in building a shared vision for the project. The workshop is often most effective if the business sponsor for the project is fully involved. The physical environment is also crucial – it is important that there is room for people move around, and to stand by the evolving network.

Although the network is built from right to left, once it has been developed, it can be read from left to right. It represents the cause-and-effect logic that underpins the project. If we implement the specified IT and make one-off enabling changes to the business and start to work in new ways (the business changes), then the required benefits will be achieved. As a result, we will have achieved the desired investment objectives, which have been defined in response to the drivers for change (Figure 3.5).

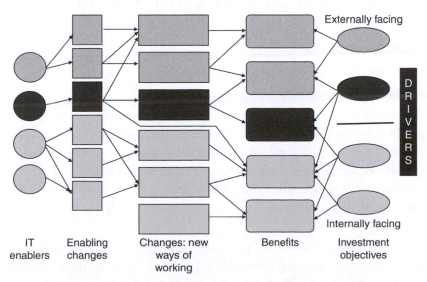

Different enablers/changes are aligned to deliver clusters of benefits

Figure 3.5 The benefits dependency network

Note: A simplified example based on a customer service/CRM programme.
Source: Based on Benefits Management (2006) by Ward and Daniel.

The BDN comes directly from the work of John Ward on Benefits Management – see Further Reading.

The network forms the basis for the two elements of the benefits delivery plan: 'What are the benefits?' and 'How are they going to be delivered?' Subsequent practices validate and refine the results from the development of the network.

This is a critical stage. Key elements are: the workshop approaches that allow creativity and build engagement; the inclusion of non-financial benefits that arises from the emphasis on benefits for stakeholders; and the identification of the changes required to deliver the benefits (i.e., *who* is going to do *what* differently). The 'benefits roadmap' (Box 3.3) provides a second workshop-based approach to tackling the same issues. The roadmap has a simpler structure and potentially provides a simpler starting-point.

Box 3.3   The benefits roadmap: An alternative technique for benefits and change assessment

The benefits roadmap (see *Information Paradox*, by John Thorp) is a technique that can be used at this stage instead of the benefits dependency network.

STAKEHOLDER ANALYSIS[T] AND RELATIONSHIP DEVELOPMENT

BUILDING DEEPER INSIGHT INTO THE CHALLENGES OF CHANGE

As Martinson and Chong (1999) note, IT-induced organizational change often results in user resistance and, in extreme cases, possibly even system rejection. Indeed, there is a growing consensus that the difficulties associated with predicting and managing the organizational change associated with information systems investments are the primary contributor to the high levels of failure associated with information systems implementation (Doherty et al., 2003; Peppard and Ward, 2005).

There are many aspects to stakeholder analysis and relationship development. The focus on engagement with stakeholders continues throughout the project, and the team will use a range of different perspectives to explore and manage stakeholder engagement and relationships. The stakeholder analysis approach outlined here is a structured tool building on the BDN; we typically use this alongside other tools that focus more specifically on how to approach *engagement* with the stakeholders. It builds on the early work done during Engage on stakeholder mapping.

Stakeholder analysis addresses the questions: 'who is responsible for delivery of the benefits?' and 'who is affected by the changes required?' A 'stakeholder analysis' is carried out to think through the benefits and 'dis-benefits' related to each stakeholder group and to assess the existing level of commitment to the change, the level of commitment required and the action that is needed to get to the required level of commitment.

A typical situation is that one group receives the benefits and another group is supposed to work differently so that the benefits are delivered. Often the benefits are not realized because of this mismatch and the lack of appropriate actions to manage the changes required. McKersie and Walton (1991) consider the relationship of organizational change with the successful introduction of IT: 'effective implementation of IT is at its core, a task of managing change.' They state: 'where ITs potential has not been exploited or its implementation delayed, we invariably find insufficient positive motivation on the part of some stakeholder group, competence gaps, or co-ordination failure.'

Identification of all the stakeholders, and analysis of their perspectives and attitudes to the changes implied by the project, is essential since no benefits will emerge if their involvement is not correctly managed. The following needs to be done:

- All stakeholders have to be identified.
- Their perceptions of benefits, dis-benefits and resistance, if any, need to be understood.
- Any changes that are needed by them must be made explicit.
- Their commitment to the project should be established, together with an appreciation of whether it needs to be changed or embraced in some other way.

AN APPROACH TO STAKEHOLDER ANALYSIS

One approach, developed by Benjamin and Levinson (1993) and used by Ward and Daniel (2012), is the use of the form in Figures 3.6 and 3.7.

Linking the benefits and the changes

Stakeholder	Changes needed	Perceived benefits (& dis-benefits)	Perceived Resistance

Figure 3.6 Stakeholder analysis
Source: Based on Benjamin and Levinson, 1993.

Each group of stakeholders is identified and their *perceived* benefits (or dis-benefits) are established. Any changes that the group itself must undertake for the benefits to appear are documented, as is their perceived resistance to those changes. This information is largely available from the BDN. As before, this can be done in various stages. A first step is just to involve relevant people in a workshop session, where relevant further work can then be done to validate and refine the analysis with more extensive engagement with the stakeholder group.

An assessment of the current capability of the stakeholders to adapt to the change is made (Figure 3.7). The next five columns are an aid to assessing the stakeholders' commitment and, hence, the amount of managing that has to be done to get the right degree of involvement. For each group, a 'C' (= current commitment) is marked in the appropriate column (e.g., 'anti') then an 'R' (= required commitment) is marked in the column where the stakeholder 'needs to be'. Clearly, the further apart the C and R are, the greater the amount of change intervention is needed. The final column is then used to record any actions required. These actions are new Changes and Enabling Changes in the benefits network (Figure 3.7).

Linking the benefits and the changes

Stakeholder	Commitment				Recommended Actions
	Anti	Let it happen	Help it happen	Make it happen	

Figure 3.7 Stakeholder analysis (II)
Source: Based on Benjamin and Levinson (1993) and Ward and Daniel (2012).

Experience shows that any stakeholder who is one column to the left of where they 'should be' can usually be influenced by their manager to make the transition (e.g., from 'anti' to 'none' or 'allow to help'). Where the change in commitment is two or more columns, there is an explicit change management task to be addressed. It must be addressed; otherwise the new way of working, and hence the benefits, will not happen. Where the transition needed is three or more columns, the stakeholder's position is likely to be a 'hearts and minds' issue. Very firm instruction will not work since the recipient is responding less from the head than from how he/she feels about the changes; they may feel very threatened and confused, so rational debate cannot be the first step.

Figures 3.6 and 3.7 are normally combined into one form, as in Figure 3.8.

It also follows that any 'two or more column shifts' should be entered in the BDN as enabling changes. Most workshops in creating BDN find it rel-atively easy to identify 'hard' enabling changes, such as 'Rewrite Standards

Linking the benefits and the changes

Stakeholder	Change needed	Perceived benefits (& dis-benefits)	Perceived Resistance	Capability	Commitment				Recommended actions
					Anti	Let it happen	Help it happen	Make it happen	

Figure 3.8 Example of stakeholder analysis

Manual to meet ISO9000' or 'Design New Procedure'. However, the 'softer', people-oriented issues either get missed or dismissed, sometimes under the easy catch-all of 'Culture and Politics', which technical personnel can regard as outside their domain of interest.

STAKEHOLDER INTERACTION

It is helpful to look at the overall set of stakeholders and to consider the various inter-relationships and priorities (Figure 3.9). It is usually wise to focus on those stakeholders who will experience the most changes. However, those who will get a lot of benefit but experience little change need managing as well, since they can become impatient with other stakeholders and try to force unreasonable rates of change progress, causing adverse reaction and sometimes disruption.

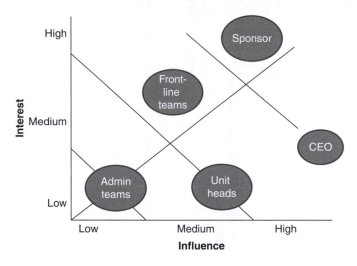

Figure 3.9 Stakeholder analysis – the bigger picture

SUCCEEDING WITH STAKEHOLDER ANALYSIS

New benefits should not appear at this point. If discussion shows there may be more, then the BDN activity needs revisiting. Appearance of more benefits could indicate that the attendees at the initial workshops were not representative enough.

Remember it is perceived benefits and perceived dis-benefits that matter here, since ultimately stakeholder reaction always boils down to one question – 'What's in it for me?' – a question that should always be answered, even if the answer is unpopular.

Success in stakeholder analysis can be judged by the following:

- All stakeholders are identified, informed and involved to an appropriate degree.

- All perceptions and commitments are documented and agreed as representing the current situation.

- Managers agree how the improvements will be tackled.

- Dis-benefits are properly discussed, documented and a management response given, or a date when the response will be forthcoming.

- There is sufficient clarity and agreement of the changes needed to form the entries in the benefits plan for explanation and discussion with the sponsor.

- Change responsibilities are documented as part of the project documentation.

CHECKPOINT: PROGRESS TOWARDS THE BENEFITS REALIZATION PLAN

Work on *drivers* has now clarified the strategic alignment of the proposed investment. The *benefits and change assessment* has provided a clearer understanding of the potential benefits and how they can be achieved. The stakeholder analysis builds on the benefits work and explores likely issues in making the changes happen. The large body of knowledge on change management is extremely relevant to stakeholder analysis and management, and further aspects are considered in Chapter 7.

DESIGN: EXPLORING THE POTENTIAL BENEFITS

The project is not a linear process, working from strategic vision to technology implementation. The stakeholder analysis has provided insight into the feasibility of changes within the organization. Work on design looks at further aspects of solution delivery to start to consider what options there are and their feasibility, cost-effectiveness and impact on timescales. Figure 3.10 provides a framework.

In Chapter 7 we build on this introduction to consider broader issues for 'design thinking' and enabling innovation (Kelley, 2001). In this section we consider a number of important topics, which provide foundations for the later discussion:

- shifting from requirements-gathering to user-centred design;

- adopting a business process perspective;

- technology opportunities as a basis for the design;

- establishing a shared business vision.

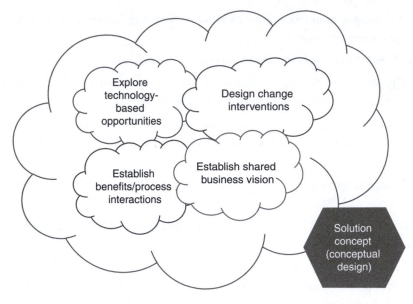

Figure 3.10 Design activities

In a traditional approach, this work on design would often follow later or be approached as procurement of a technology solution. We view this as an important element of the benefits realization process, which will add considerable value to the project. It is important that initial work takes place at this stage. Highsmith (2004) exemplifies this with an early focus on product architecture (p. 98). There will be implications for the skills required within the project team.

FROM REQUIREMENTS-GATHERING TO USER-CENTRED DESIGN

A classic starting-point for an IT project is to ask the users what their requirements are for a new system. Of course, some organizations bypass this step by letting senior management decide. In any case, there are a number of serious flaws.

What if the senior management view of the drivers for change and the high-level objectives have not (yet) been communicated effectively to other stakeholders? If communication has taken place, what if the users and other stakeholders have different ideas and priorities? Perhaps senior management have a vision based on dramatically improving customer service, but the front-line staff are under so much pressure that they can only envisage incremental changes to do away with some of the most pressing problems and causes of inefficiency? The requirements provided by the end-users are likely to be only loosely related to the vision defined by management.

In a scenario involving innovation, whether involving new technology or not, all stakeholders are likely to have trouble envisaging what is possible. Sessions to 'gather requirements' or document the 'as is' situation of the business process are likely to be of only limited value. A mindset shift is required: from requirements-gathering to innovation through user-centred design. The approach required is to engage a multi-disciplinary team in a process of exploration and innovation, which builds from the initial understanding of the opportunity to a vision and initial (conceptual) design.

At this early stage it is important to ensure that 'non-functional requirements' are considered, as these may have a crucial impact on the business case, design and feasibility of any project. These include requirements related to: security, privacy and confidentiality of information, availability, response times, scalability and resilience.

OPPORTUNITY-BASED DESIGN: EXPLORING THE POSSIBILITIES ENABLED BY THE TECHNOLOGY

The design process should involve consideration of the problems/opportunities from a user perspective and the opportunities provided by the technology. An understanding of the technology provides insight into what is possible and which options are easy to accomplish. The focus on the opportunities enabled by the technology helps to break out of making incremental improvements to the current situation and can provide an opportunity for business innovation.

Important implications of this practice are:

- the need for good knowledge of the technology within the team;
- an approach to the project lifecycle that allows learning;
- building opportunities for prototyping into the lifecycle as a way of exploring and getting feedback.

In early IT developments a waterfall (sequential) development process worked well. The project effectively started with a clean sheet of paper', and the initial focus of activity was getting a detailed understanding of user requirements. All functionality required to deliver the solution was then part of the design and development. Some companies even developed operating-system software and hardware following this logic.

Following this approach today is a serious mistake. There is no 'clean sheet of paper'. The design process needs to take account of the services available from the operating system, other purchased software (database, email, messaging, etc.) or available from the cloud from a rapidly increasing range of pay-as-you-go service providers. There will be very extensive services, such as security, back-up, transactional integrity, audit trails and error-handling, that can be simply incorporated into a solution. In addition, in many cases there may be significant application functionality that can be used. For example, when developing an e-commerce site, most organizations will incorporate purchased software providing much of the core functionality (catalogue, sales basket and pipeline, sales analysis). There will also be services to draw on from previous development projects within the organization. As a result, a successful project needs people with good knowledge of the technologies being used and the existing systems of the organization.

There are important implications for the people and skills involved in the project team, and the involvement from others across the organization, perhaps in strategy and architecture roles. The project team will probably need to prototype in a variety of ways to bring to life what's possible and contribute to the development of both the benefits plan and the solution concept (Box 3.4).

Box 3.4   Prototyping as a key enabler of learning and innovation

Prototyping plays a vital role from the earliest stages of work on a project. At the early stages it helps explore possibilities and develop a clearer sense of the underlying problem and the potential benefits.

Prototyping can take many forms. It should address the overall service and customer experience and not just the product or IT solution.

Prototyping may be very simple, with little technology involved: diagrams and pictures; simply acting out the relevant scenarios from the perspective of different stakeholders; writing 'day in the life of' stories, imagining different stakeholders talking about the envisaged future in the present tense.

Prototypes can also include simple system mock-ups, and in some case can extend to pilot systems making use of existing (perhaps packaged or bought-in) functionality.

From a traditional IT perspective this might be seen as redundant and a waste of time and effort, particularly at this early stage. The aim, however, is to get a much deeper understanding of the problematic situation, get a broad range of insights into opportunities and the potential benefits and get a much earlier view of what will really work in this situation. It is all too easy to fail to identify the real problems and to design solutions that are not workable in practice.

Sources: Kelly, 2001; Brown, 2008.

The need for projects to enable organizational learning Eason (1988) is highlighted by Garud (1997) from a different perspective: 'customers invariably use technological systems in ways different from how they were designed or produced'. With new products/technologies the full potential may not be clear even to the creators and suppliers. It is normal to find that new uses and the best ways to use the technology gradually emerge through experience and learning in the real world. The incremental approach to phased delivery of benefits is an important enabler of learning so that the real benefits of IT as an 'intellectual technology' can be realized. Orlikowski and Hofman (1997) make a similar point as they identify a series of anticipated, emergent and opportunity-based changes that together resulted in the realization of benefits from new technology.

Opportunity-based design applies to all projects. The need for this focus on opportunities is particularly strong when the project is implementation of a software package (enterprise resource planning (ERP), CRM, etc.). In this case it is essential to start from gaining an understanding of what the software can do and exploring which of the available options provides the best solution.

One recent case study we carried out revealed serious issues in this area. A package solution had been selected at a higher level in the organization and had been effectively imposed at a local level. The local implementation project did not compensate for the lack of requirements and selection process, and as a result the team did not gain an understanding of the solution and how it could improve local working practices. The project became focused on technology implementation because there had not been a need to focus on the business problem and user needs locally.

In summary, following a 'clean sheet of paper' approach and driving the design just from user requirements can result in missed opportunities for new ways of working, and in solutions that are not a good fit with the technology, are higher risk and take longer to deliver.

ESTABLISH BENEFITS AND BUSINESS PROCESS INTERACTION[T]

A further practice to consider as part of the design perspective is to consider benefits and process interactions. Virtually any aspect of an organization can be considered using this perspective (Garvin, 1998).

The business activity involved is considered as a process. A process has inputs, activities and outputs. Improvements can be made in terms of cost, speed and quality. Taking these aspects of a process produces a 3×3 matrix as shown in Figure 3.11.

The practice can be used as a starting-point to get an understanding of a scenario. In addition, if a BDN has already been developed, the 3×3 process perspective can be used to explore the completeness of the benefits identified. The benefits identified are mapped onto the 3×3 matrix. This typically identifies gaps in the analysis carried out when the BDN is prepared and is a starting-point for the identification of further possible benefits that fill in the gaps.

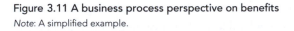

	Input	Activity	Output
Cost	?	Reduced cost of service delivery	Ongoing measurement to drive further improvements
Speed	Customer able to gain access to service close to home	First point of contact resolution	?
Quality	?	First point of contact resolution	Increased customer satisfaction

Figure 3.11 A business process perspective on benefits

Note: A simplified example.

It is also possible to carry out more extensive work from a business process perspective: for example, looking at the design of target business processes. The business process perspective also has limitations. Be particularly careful in professional and knowledge work situations not to try and define a process in too much detail.

ESTABLISH A SHARED BUSINESS VISION

One of the causes of project failure is getting lost in the detail of requirements capture and solution design. Different groups have different requirements and there can be a rapid growth of complexity as the team tries to accommodate the demands of each group. This can also result in conflict as each group fights for as much of the project resource as possible to be devoted to meeting their needs.

A second cause of failure is that understanding of the drivers for the project and the overall goals can be lost as the project progresses and different groups become involved. There may be clear business objectives in the minds of senior management, but often they are not understood or fully shared by users involved in the project or the project team.

A vision statement starts to address these issues. It provides a high-level view of the investment objectives and direction of the project. It enables flexibility at a more detailed level as the project progresses. It should also provide a motivational goal as the project team and other stakeholders make a commitment to realizing the vision.

The overall direction and goals for the project (objectives) are captured in a vision statement. The statement is short: a sentence or, at most, a short paragraph. The vision statement provides clarity of purpose and a motivational target for the project team and project stakeholders. As details of requirements, solution design and project plan change, the vision statement should provide a solid foundation to which the team can return. The vision statement should have a business focus, and everyone involved in the project should share an understanding of the vision.

Developing a short vision statement is difficult. It takes time to get the words just right. For the vision to be 'shared' there needs to be broad involvement in its development – it would typically form part of initial work on the project.

DESIGN – SUMMARY

The result of this early design activity is a much clearer understanding of the likely business and IT solution. For example, an initial solution overview for a project we are working on has a one-page diagram sketching information flows between a new website, Salesforce, which will provide a CRM solution, and an existing SAP system.

We have explored a design perspective and considered aspects of the business and IT solution that will contribute to benefits realization. There is much more work to do and much that is beyond the scope of this book; for example, user-centred practices for design of the system. Our aim is to promote innovation by using the design perspective alongside the other benefits-driven practices.

It is important to recognize that this will be a messy, creative process, but that in many situations it provides a much greater chance of success than the more ordered linear requirements-gathering process traditionally adopted, which provide only a *perception* of effectiveness and control.

THE BENEFITS REALIZATION PLAN[T]

At this stage it is possible to develop the benefits realization plan, which pulls together the results of the work on benefits planning. The benefits realization plan becomes a central part of the ongoing management of the project, with project reviews and milestone reviews driven by an emphasis on 'Are we on track to deliver the benefits?' rather than just progress against budgets and timetables. The benefit plan is kept up to date, reflecting learning and changes during the life of the project.

The emphasis at this stage is on developing a benefits realization plan that identifies:

- benefits and how they relate to different stakeholders/stakeholder groups (a benefit is an advantage for a stakeholder);
- owners for each benefit/benefit stream – there must be an owner to be included;
- measures related to each benefit – if the benefit isn't measurable (in some way) it isn't a benefit;
- who is going to do what differently (i.e., what business changes are required to deliver the benefits);
- how the changes will be brought about and who is responsible for them;
- how delivery is going to be phased – it is not helpful to try and focus on every possible benefit and measure.

Processes for project evaluation (investment appraisal) are often weak. There is an over-reliance on purely financial justification measures: the approval process is treated as a bureaucratic hurdle or hoop to be jumped through (Alshawi et al., 2003), and effective post-project appraisal is rare (Ballantine and Stray, 1999). As Irani et al. (2005) highlight, there is often 'no robust framework to evaluate costs and benefits' (p. 64) and no 'management process to govern and measure achievement of desired outcomes [. . . or] evaluate what benefits were actually achieved' (p. 65). Work by Irani et al. (2005) identifies that IS/IT investments affect multiple stakeholders and that this must be addressed in the evaluation process.

The development of the benefits realization plan seeks to address some of these issues.

IDENTIFY BENEFITS OWNERS

Based on the stakeholder analysis and the other work on benefits planning, owners for each benefit are agreed. This is an important business role on the project. Benefits owners are an important part of the project governance framework. At this stage the real level of commitment to the project will be put to the test.

STRUCTURE BENEFITS AND ESTABLISH TARGETS AND MEASURES[T]

The benefits are classified (see Figure 3.12) as to how explicit they are by ranking them as measurable, quantifiable and financial and according to whether the benefit allows:

	Stop doing things	Do things Better	Do New things
Financial	Reduced costs in back office functions	Reduced cost of service delivery	
Quantifiable		Increased first point of contact resolution	Service available close to the customer
Measurable		Improved customer satisfaction	

Figure 3.12 Structuring benefits

Note: A simplified example. See Ward and Daniel, 2012.

- the business to do something *new*;
- current activities to be improved (*better*);
- the elimination of certain activities (*stop*).

A quantifiable benefit is a measurable benefit where a specific target can be defined and agreed. For example, if the project involved increasing response rates from mail shots to customers as a result of better targeting, this is clearly *measurable*. It may be possible to do some work, perhaps a pilot, to get further evidence so that a realistic target can be set and the benefit can be made *quantifiable*.

The core difference is that, for the benefit to be *quantifiable*, we need to have a benefit *owner* who will sign up to take *responsibility* for the specific *target*. It is really about our level of knowledge and confidence in the forecast. Ideally, benefits will be *financial* and quantifiable, but the approach recognizes that this is not always possible. The financial element of the plan can be presented using whatever techniques are in use within the organization (Internal Rate of Return (IRR), Net Present Value (NPV), Payback Period, etc.).

It is essential not just to dismiss non-financial benefits as 'intangible'. The quantifiable and measurable categories should be used to highlight the many benefits – for example, related to customer satisfaction – that will not be *directly* financial, but that will have a major impact on organizational success in the longer term.

There should be a clear link with the IT and Change Portfolio. The extent to which the project is financially justified will depend on what type of project it is.

Effective measurement

Benefits management emphasizes the importance of *ownership* of benefits and of appropriate *measurement* of benefits. Measures are important for two reasons:

- Effective measurement provides information on the outcome of the investment providing accountability and enabling learning.

- Measurement causes changes in behaviour ('what gets measured gets done'), and as a result measures are a major driver of change and can determine whether the benefits arise (i.e., they don't just provide information on the benefits – the measures help bring them about).

Setting the right measures that are cost-effective and encourage behaviour that results in the desired benefits is difficult. Unexpected effects can easily arise.

It is also important to avoid turning measurement into a new area of bureaucracy. There should be a balance between using the tools to think through the potential benefits and the changes required to realize them, with the pragmatic case for a few, carefully chosen measures that will put the focus on key areas and will contribute to the required changes.

Getting measurement right is important, not just for approval of the project but also for actual delivery of the benefits. Performance measures can have significant impacts on behaviour (Simons, 1995), and there can be significant unintended impacts if the measures are not carefully designed. As Hemingway (Murray et al., 2001) points out, the impacts can also be very different if the measures are focused on teams or individuals. Approaches to performance measurement such as the balanced scorecard (Kaplan and Norton, 1993, 1996) and Performance Prism (Neely et al., 2000, 2002) are relevant.

INFORMATION FOR BENEFITS TRACKING

An additional consideration is the need for information to track the realization of benefits. The collection, analysis and presentation of the required information need to be considered as part of the solution design. Ideally this should link with planning for ongoing management of the performance of the new service/way of working/business process.

In many cases it becomes clear at this stage that weaknesses in the information currently available make it difficult or impossible to measure the current situation. So it will be impossible to compare 'before' and 'after' accurately. This is usually an inconvenience, rather than a reason for not doing anything. It is usually more important to press on and deliver improvements to customers rather than spending time and money putting in place better measurement of the current situation. Better ability to track further improvements will itself be a valuable outcome from the investment.

IDENTIFY AND DEFINE COSTS

In theory, costs are the straightforward part of the business case/benefits realization plan and are likely to be handled more easily than benefits. However, this is not an entirely straightforward area, and some aspects of costs are difficult to identify and relate to a project. This produces issues of accountability and adversely affects decision-making: for example, when comparing business cases which only contain some elements of the overall project costs – that is, those most easily and directly attributable to the project (Ward et al., 2007). It is all too easy to make a decision based on incomplete and misleading information.

The business case should address: one-off business and IT costs related to the project, including any new hardware and software; costs related to making the business changes; and ongoing impacts on business and IT costs. For example, the business changes may require training not related to a new system (perhaps a direct cost for external resources plus the indirect costs of people taken away from day-to-day activity to be trained). Alongside the benefits, the business costs may be increased by the cost of time spent analysing and using new information (as just one of many possible impacts).

The IT costs may include allocation of expenditure related to IT infrastructure that makes a critical contribution to the project: for example, a network or servers. Significant elements of these costs are often not included in business cases, which tend to focus on external and direct IT costs. In particular, the indirect costs of the business changes are often ignored.

Establishing fully accurate costing may not be possible or cost-effective, for example, as many individuals in IT and business areas will spend only a part of their time on a project and are unlikely to complete timesheets that enable this information to be captured and recorded.

There are also wider factors: for example, a fear that if end-user costs are identified they will become additional, real incremental costs for the business. In this case it may be better if the time spent on the required activities (training, process change, etc.) is simply absorbed in departmental budgets. This is a strong argument, but there are other very important factors that must be addressed. In the absence of a budget that fairly represents all project costs there may be a number of unintended, adverse consequences:

- The organization may undertake non-beneficial projects (i.e., the hidden, indirect costs exceed the benefits).
- The organization may undertake the 'wrong' projects: for example, a project with low direct costs and high indirect costs is likely to be approved over a project with higher direct costs, regardless of the respective benefits.

DESIGN A FRAMEWORK FOR BUSINESS CHANGE GOVERNANCE[T]

The overall aim of work at this stage is to be ready to proceed with the realization of benefits from the proposed investment in IT. A governance framework is likely to evolve from the stakeholder involvement and should be in place to approve the benefits realization plan and to lead the start of the next stage of the work.

The governance framework will ensure the right involvement and ownership for business change and benefits realization. The governance framework and related performance measures will have a significant impact on the focus of the project and the behaviour of individuals. The role and contribution of the project sponsor are key elements of the governance framework.

Basic control processes can be largely the same across a wide range of projects (the existence of a project board, a business sponsor, risk management, lessons learned, etc.). However, there is no single best design for a governance framework. The framework adopted should be adapted to meet the challenges of an individual project and to take into account the experience of those involved.

RISK ASSESSMENT[T]

The causes of project failure are well known. Many of the factors that are going to cause a project to get into trouble can be seen at the start of the project and certainly well before they have an impact. We have two main responses:

- Firstly, we design our approach to the project to take into account both the major sources of risks and the associated critical success factors. The practices outlined in this book address many of these areas.

- Secondly, we establish an effective risk management process that maintains a focus on risk throughout the life of the project.

The risk management process is straightforward in theory. The key to success is to put the process into practice and *use it* throughout the life of the project. Virtually all projects make some attempt at risk management. However, in many cases it is not used effectively.

A crucial success factor is to take a benefits perspective to risk management:

- *Scope*: the context for the risk management process is the delivery of measurable benefits on behalf of stakeholders. Many risks and issues will not relate specifically to the delivery of a software solution.

- *Involvement*: the benefits focus implies that the risk management process must involve stakeholders in the business change, not simply the IT solution. For example, user representatives on the project should be involved in risk meetings, and the overall project governance framework should include owners of the business changes and benefits.

- *Prioritization*: the primary basis for assessing the potential impact of a risk should be in relation to the realization of benefits.

It is important to carry out an initial risk assessment as part of the development of the benefits realization plan. This activity will allow the team to stand back from the detail and reflect on their work to date. Then the risk management process is kept alive through the life of the project.

PHASE BENEFITS DELIVERY$^\mathrm{T}$

Phasing benefits delivery is a fundamental principle underpinning the $\mathbf{e^{4+1}}$ approach.

Many projects grow to have very long timescales and very large project teams. Both these factors increase the complexity of project management – exponentially. Keeping the duration of projects short (say, four to six months) and using small teams significantly reduces their complexity and dramatically increases their chance of success. This approach also has the benefit of reducing the exposure of the project to changes in the organization or the market during the life of the project. Additional, major benefits are that the short project timescale means that 'time to benefit' is reduced and that there is an early opportunity to learn from the live operation of the service.

The implication is that large projects must be broken up into 'chunks' that can be delivered in four to six months. This is usually possible. Each small project is then seen as a 'versioned release' contributing to the overall project or programme goals. The split of a project into a number of versions can also enable different approaches to be taken to different versions: for example, based on the IT and Change Portfolio. In many scenarios where there is significant innovation and change the only real way to learn about what the end-user or customer actually wants is to get an initial version of the service in live operation.

This approach is also called 'iterative and incremental development'. Each version or iteration must contain functionality that enables the delivery of a new or improved service and specific benefits to stakeholders. Typically, functionality in a specific area will be delivered in stages: that is, incrementally over a number of releases. The approach applies both to bespoke developments and to software package implementations. When using a package, the emphasis is on phasing the business change and the adoption of software features rather than the software development.

The versioned release approach blurs the boundary between a project and a programme. The need to use a programme management approach will largely depend on the scale of activity and, in particular, on whether there are a number of projects/versions being delivered in parallel. (A programme addresses a broader business goal than an individual project and is made up of a number of projects. Programme-level roles, governance structures and processes are important, in addition to project-level arrangements.)

The BDN provides a basis for breaking the objectives down into a number of projects or 'versioned releases' based on groupings of changes and benefits. It is also important that the links between the IT solution and the benefits remain clear. This traceability is important to enable effective decision-making on trade-offs and changes through the life of the project.

The benefits realization plan is a vital foundation for the project. It should provide a focus for the activity of the team in later stages. It should also be treated as a *living document* and updated to reflect learning during the project.

At this stage, as in all areas of the project, considerable judgement is required. It is vital to balance two views. Firstly, every benefit has to have a measure and an owner to be included in the benefits realization plan. Secondly, benefits and related measures are vital aspects of communicating the project, and there should be a focus on a small number of benefits and very well-designed measures that help stakeholders understand what the project is about and help drive the desired changes. Both views are true, and they need to be reconciled in some way that is appropriate for the project. For example, the benefits plan might provide a comprehensive treatment of benefits, but stakeholder communication will be driven by a core set of benefits and measures and these can subsequently be updated; for example, during Expand as the focus shifts to capturing a second tier of benefits.

Benefits thinking must not be allowed to grow into an innovation-killing bureaucracy – it is designed to enable innovation and *contribute* to project success. The essence of the approach is to build real engagement with the goals and commitment to the delivery of benefits.

IN SUMMARY

The foundation for competing with IT is the ability of the organization to achieve benefits from specific investments. The development of the benefits realization plan, which is the focus of the Explore stage, is a crucial element of a benefits-driven approach to planning and building momentum with an investment in IT-enabled business change.

The benefits approach to projects also provides a foundation for later discussion of IT strategy. Projects are a key vehicle for the implementation of strategy, and the alignment of projects with strategic goals is vital. It is no coincidence that there are clear links between the principles and practices discussed here in relation to projects and the approach to strategy developed later in the book.

There are many considerations of ethics to address at this stage, including considerations of privacy and use of personal data. The focus on stakeholders and value to stakeholders provides a vital foundation for an ethical approach.

TAKING IT FURTHER

FURTHER READING AND RESOURCES

Key books for further reading include:

Ward, J. and Daniel, E. (2012) *Benefits Management*, John Wiley & Sons Inc.

John's work provides a crucial insight into how to approach IS in organizations.

Highsmith, Jim (2004) *Agile Project Management*, Boston, MA: Addison-Wesley.

Checkland, P. and Poulter, J. (2006) *Learning for Action*, Chichester: Wiley.

Checkland, Peter and Holwell, Sue (1999) *Information, Systems, and Information Systems: Making Sense of the Field*, Chichester: Wiley.

Checkland, P. and Scholes, J. (1999) *Soft Systems Methodology: A 30-Year Retrospective*, Chichester: Wiley.

Articles to start with:

Markus, M.L. (2004) Technochange Management: Using IT to Drive Organizational Change. *Journal of Information Technology*, Vol. 19 (1): 4–20.

Markus provides another perspective on the same issues.

Peppard, J., Ward, J. and Daniel, E. (2007) Managing the Realization of Business Benefits from IT Investments. *MIS Quarterly Executive*, Vol. 6 (1): 1–11.

Peppard, J. and Ward, J. (2005) Unlocking Sustained Business Value from IT Investments. *California Management Review*, Fall (2005): 52–69.

Good overviews of the Cranfield work on benefits management.

TALKING POINTS

Use these questions to help reflect on this chapter and explore the challenges of putting the ideas into practice:

1. Which driver analysis techniques would you adopt, and why?

2. What would be the challenges you would face in driver analysis, and how would you overcome them?

3. Does the portfolio suggest a natural sequence of investments?

4. It is suggested that developing the BDN is a workshop activity. What might be the challenges and how would you tackle them?

5. How might you build on the stakeholder analysis to get greater insight into how to approach the changes required?

6. How do you balance the two views of measurement: you measure what you get vs. you get what you measure?

7. How do you judge the effectiveness of a measure/set of measures?

8. What should you know about each benefit?

9. How would you judge the overall quality of a business case/benefits realization plan?

10. What are the barriers to adoption/effective application of a benefits-driven approach?

11. What are the implications for the role of the project sponsor of the benefits-driven approach?

12. How can 'politics' derail the development of an effective benefits realization plan?

13. Where is your organization in the journey from financial business case to benefits realization planning?

14. What are the implications for the skills/competences of the project team of taking a benefits-driven approach?

15. How does the competence for benefits planning differ from, or perhaps build on, the Engage and Evolve stages of the project lifecycle?

KEY DEBATES

Effective measurement – competing views

Metrics and measurement are crucial elements of both a business case and a benefits realization plan.

There are competing views about good practice. One approach is that every benefit must have a measure, target, timescale for realization and an owner. Realization of benefits is measured against this detailed plan. A second approach emphasizes that measures drive behaviour and that a small set of benefits should provide the focus for a change programme. This small set can evolve over time as targets are met and new opportunities emerge.

What is your view? How would you approach this in practice? Does the type of project affect your views?

CASE STUDY 3.1

The case explores the challenges of managing projects and developing an improved project capability.

Journal of Information Technology Teaching Cases, Vol. 4 (2014): 1–10.

IT project governance at Worthington Health-Care System

Ulrike Schultze

In 2012 the Chief Information Officer (CIO) of Worthington Health-Care System (WHCS), a St Louis company with 27 health-care facilities, was considering how to improve IT project governance.

Over the previous seven years three approaches to developing project oversight had been attempted, including a Project Management Office, a project Portfolio Management application (PlanView) and, more recently, an incremental approach to process improvement, which was meeting with increasing resistance. The CIO's challenge was to find an effective solution to IT project work and oversight at WHCS.

REFERENCES

Alshawi, S., Irani, Z. and Baldwin, L. (2003) Benchmarking Information Technology Investment and Benefits Extraction. *Benchmarking: An International Journal*, Special Issue, 'Benchmarking: Information and Communication Technologies', Vol. 10 (4): 414–423.

Ballantine, J.A. and Stray, S. (1999) Information Systems and Other Capital Investments. *Logistics Information Management*, Vol. 12: 78–93.

Benjamin, R.I. and Levinson, E. (1993) A Framework for Managing IT-Enabled Change. *Sloan Management Review*, Summer 1993: 23–33.

Brown, Tim. (2008) Design Thinking. *Harvard Business Review*, June 2008, Vol. 86 (6): 84–92, p. 9.

Doherty, N., King, M. and Al-Mushayt, O. (2003) The Impact of the Inadequacies in the Treatment of Organizational Issues on Information Systems Projects. *Information & Management*, Vol. 41: 49–62.

Eason, K. (1988) *Information Technology and Organizational Change*, London: Taylor & Francis.

Garud, R. (1997) On the Distinction between Know-How, Know-What and Know-Why in Technological Systems, in Anne Huff and Jim Walsh (eds.) *Advances in Strategic Management*, JAI Press, pp. 81–101.

Garvin, D.A. (1998) The Processes of Organization Management. *Sloan Management Review*, Summer 1998, Vol. 39 (4): 33–50.

Highsmith, J. (2004) *Agile Project Management*, Addison-Wesley.

Irani, Z., Love, P.E.D., Elliman, T., Jones, S. and Themistocleous, M. (2005) Evaluating e-Government: Learning from the Experiences of Two UK Local Authorities. *Information Systems Journal*, special issue on e-Government, Vol. 15 (1): 61–82.

Kaplan, R.S. and Norton, D.P. (1992) The Balanced Scorecard: Measures that Drive Performance. *Harvard Business Review*, Vol. 70 (1): 71–79.

Kaplan, R.S. and Norton, D.P. (1993) Putting the Balanced Scorecard to Work. *Harvard Business Review*, Vol. 71 (5): 134–147.

Kaplan, R.S. and Norton, D.P. (1996a) Using the Balanced Scorecard as a Strategic Management System. *Harvard Business Review*, Vol. 74 (1): 75–85.

Kaplan, R.S. and Norton, D.P. (1996b) *Balanced Scorecard: Translating Strategy into Action*. Boston: Harvard Business School Press.

Kaplan, R.S. and Norton, D.P. (2004) *Strategy Maps: Converting Intangible Assets into Tangible Outcomes*, Boston: Harvard Business School Press.

Kelley, Thomas. (2001) *The Art of Innovation: Lessons in Creativity from IDEO, America's Leading Design Firm*. London: Harper Collins Business.

Kim, W. Chan and Mauborgne, Renee (1997) Value Innovation: The Strategic Logic of High Growth. *Harvard Business Review*, Vol. 75 (3): 103–112.

Kim, W. Chan and Mauborgne, Renée (2005) *Blue Ocean Strategy: How to Create Uncontested Market Space and Make Competition Irrelevant*. Boston: Harvard Business Press.

Martinson, M.G. and Chong, P.K. (1999) The Influence of Human Factors and Specialist Involvement on Information Systems Success. *Human Relations*, Vol. 52 (1): 123–152.

McKersie, R.B. and Walton, R.E. (1991) Organizational Change, in Scott Morton and Michael S. (eds.) *The Corporation of the 1990s: Information Technology and Organizational Transformation*. Oxford University Press, p. 244.

Murray, P., with Ward, J., Elvin, R. and Hemingway, C. (2001) *Advanced Benefits Management*. Cranfield School of Management, Information Systems Research Centre, Document Number – ISRC-200107.

Neely, A., Adams, C. and Kennerley, M. (2002) *The Performance Prism: The Scorecard for Measuring and Managing Business Success*. London: FT Prentice Hall.

Neely, A., Mills, J., Platts, K., Richards, H., Gregory, M., Bourne, M. and Kennerley, M. (2000) Performance Measurement System Design: Developing and Testing a Process Based Approach. *International Journal of Production & Operations Management*, Vol. 20 (10): 1119–1146.

Orlikowski, W.J. and Hofman, J.D. (1997) An Improvisational Model for Change Management: The Case of Groupware Technologies. *Sloan Management Review*, Vol. 48 (1): 52–75.

Peppard, J. and Ward, J. (2005) Unlocking Sustained Business Value from IT Investments. *California Management Review*, Vol. 86 (1): 78–93.

Porter, M.E. (2008) The Five Competitive Forces That Shape Strategy. *Harvard Business Review*, January 2008, 78–93.

Simons (1995) *Levers of Control*. Boston: Harvard Business School Press.

Treacy, M. and Wiersema, F. (1993) Customer Intimacy and Other Value Disciplines. *Harvard Business Review*, Vol. 71 (1): 84–93.

Ward, J. and Elvin, R. (1999) A New Framework for Managing IT-Enabled Business Change. *Information Systems Journal*, Vol. 9 (3): 197–222.

Ward, J. and Murray, P. (2000) *Benefits Management Best Practice Guidelines*. Cranfield.

Ward, J. and Peppard, J. (2002) *Strategic Planning for Information Systems* (Third edition) John Wiley and Sons.

Ward, J., De Hertogh, S. and Viaene, S. (2007) Managing Benefits from IS/IT Investments: An Empirical Investigation into Current Practice. *40th Annual Hawaii International Conference on System Sciences*.

Ward, J. and Daniel, E. (2012) *Benefits Management*, Chichester: John Wiley & Sons Inc.

CHAPTER 4

BUILDING MOMENTUM – DELIVERING THE BENEFITS

IN THIS CHAPTER WE STUDY:

- building the team and delivering a project – the core of traditional approaches to projects;
- maintaining a focus on benefits realization.

BUILDING MOMENTUM

The foundations of a successful project are laid at the very early stages (Kappelman et al., 2006). It is also true that the seeds of failure are often sown at the beginning of a project. Many projects proceed when the problems that will emerge later and cause major problems or failure are clear to see (Myers, 1994). One major success factor for organizations trying to compete with IT is to stop failing projects, and the best time to do this is right at the beginning, preferably before they start.

The emphasis during Engage and Explore has been on ensuring that there are clear goals for the project (defined in terms of benefits) and that these align with the needs of stakeholders and the strategy of the organization. This alignment is not so much about approval of a piece of paper (the benefits realization plan in this case) as about a core group of people with a shared vision committed to making it happen.

So far, we have established a clear benefits realization plan setting out the intended benefits for stakeholders and how we are going to realize them. We have also established at least a conceptual design as a basis for further work on the business and IT solution.

Moving on to Evolve, the focus is now on building an effective, multi-disciplinary project team and gaining momentum to deliver the intended benefits. In many organizations the 'project' starts at this stage, after approval of a business case. Key areas to focus on at this stage include:

- designing the business and IT solution that will enable benefits to be realized;
- managing change, including continued effective engagement with stakeholders;
- maintaining control of the project;
- enabling learning and flexibility.

EVOLVE

ESTABLISHING THE CONTEXT: AGILE APPROACHES TO PROJECTS

At the Evolve stage the project is moving beyond planning to delivery. As the name of the phase suggests, there is further opportunity for learning and change, but if earlier stages have been successful this will normally be within well-established boundaries.

In this section we drill further into the core of project management and agile approaches to projects. This provides important context for discussion of key practices for the Evolve stage.

Formal definitions provide a starting-point for understanding 'What is a project?'

A unique set of activities, with definite starting and finishing points, undertaken by an individual or organization to meet specific objectives within defined schedule, cost and performance parameters

(BS6079, *Association for Project Management (APM)
Body of Knowledge*)

It is helpful to expand on the formal definitions of a project by considering a number of general characteristics of projects.

Projects

- are carried out to create specific results or products and to achieve specific aims and benefits. The project itself is simply a means to an end.

- have an element of uniqueness. This emphasis distinguishes a project from a business process – where there is an emphasis on consistency. It is important not to push this factor too far, as the trend to mass customization (and, for example, 1:1 marketing) emphasizes variety from business processes, and project-based organizations (consulting, engineering and others) emphasize consistency in projects.

- have resources – for example, of people, money, equipment – and constraints – including targets related to time, cost and performance.

- follow a lifecycle and contain stages. Each stage includes a number of activities and deliverables, and is typically completed by a phase-end milestone.

- have a definite start and finish.

- are complex.

- involve uncertainty.

The nature and role of project management follow from the definition of a project. Project management is: 'planning, monitoring and controlling all aspects of a project and motivation of all those involved to achieve the project objectives on time and to the specified cost, quality and performance' (*APM Body of Knowledge*).

It is also helpful to see that there are many aspects to successful project management: 'projects do not succeed just by assiduous adherence to a mechanical process [...] successful projects are managed with enthusiasm, vision, single-mindedness and integrity' (BS6079).

'Agile' approaches to projects have evolved in cultures where 'technical' skills are valued. These technical skills come in many forms and include the professional skills of end-user groups. In agile approaches the emphasis is on success through people, creating an environment where multi-disciplinary teams can work together effectively delivering benefits through innovation and business change. The role of the project manager becomes leadership of a multi-disciplinary team of people with professional skills. The project manager, as 'first among equals', often plays a facilitating role. In a sense, agile approaches are a reaction against traditional approaches, which can represent a hierarchical model with the project manager 'in charge' and an over-emphasis on the project process rather than the various professional and technical skills of the team members.

The 'Agile Manifesto' (Box 4.1), written by a group of thought leaders in this area, captures the key principles of an agile approach.

Box 4.1   Agile Manifesto – Principles

We are uncovering better ways of developing software by doing it and helping others do it. Through this work we have come to value:

- Individuals and interactions over processes and tools.
- Working software over comprehensive documentation.
- Customer collaboration over contract negotiation.
- Responding to change over following a plan.

That is, while there is value in the items on the right, we value the items on the left more.

www.agilemanifesto.org

For many organizations these principles represent a fundamental, radical shift from how they currently approach projects. We explore each principle in turn.

Individuals and interactions over processes and tools

Projects can develop an emphasis on specific techniques, tools and deliverables. Huge effort is expended on interim deliverables, such as requirements and design *documents*, which are simply a *means to an end*. Agile approaches emphasize people and their interactions. This is very clear in the practice of having a 'co-located' team – a team with a 'team room' to work in where they can communicate easily.

Working software over comprehensive documentation

Agile approaches, with their history in IT development, focus on working software. They tackle technical issues and start software development early in the lifecycle. This reflects the importance of working software as an output (rather than the design document). It also reflects that, as people see early versions of working software, they will have a better understanding of what they need and what is possible. This reflects the value of prototypes and pilots of many kinds.

It is important not to see this as implying *no* documentation. The development is just not driven by documentation, and documents are produced where they genuinely add value.

Customer collaboration over contract negotiation

Even within an organization, the relationship between business and IT functions can work in a formal, contractual style. This often reflects lack of trust. The extent of IT outsourcing also means that there are actual contractual relationships involved in many projects.

Given the inevitable uncertainty over requirements and the need for learning, this contractual emphasis is problematic. However, there are ways of setting contracts that at least begin to reflect the need for flexibility and close collaboration.

Agile approaches emphasize project teams working directly with the customer. This also removes much bureaucracy and accelerates the project process.

Responding to change over following a plan

Agile approaches recognize that change is inevitable and seek to make it possible and cost-effective. This is possible if project processes are kept simple and the strong technical skills in the team are used to establish a solution design that enables change.

Box 4.2 provides more of the 'Agile Manifesto'. Each point is a valuable foundation for the overall approach we are adopting.

Box 4.2   Agile Manifesto – Principles for agile development teams

Business people and developers must work together daily throughout the project.

Build projects around motivated individuals. Give them the environment and support they need, and trust them to get the job done.

The most efficient and effective method of conveying information to and within a development team is face-to-face conversation.

> The best architectures, requirements, and designs emerge from self-organizing teams.
>
> At regular intervals, the team reflects on how to become more effective, then tunes and adjusts its behavior accordingly.
>
> Agile processes promote sustainable development. The sponsors, developers, and users should be able to maintain a constant pace indefinitely.
>
> www.agilealliance.org

An agile approach applies a shift in emphasis from *process* to *people* as the most important factor in succeeding with a project. The aim is to have *just enough* process. A well-managed agile project balances this focus on people and flexibility with maintaining discipline and control. Control is achieved with the minimum of additional work in a way that seeks to *add value* to the project, rather than adding effort and cost in seeking to comply with an externally imposed framework of controls. The key question to consider at every stage is: 'How does this activity help the team realize benefits?'

Research into project management identifies a number of broad success factors. Sauer and Cuthbertson (2003, p. 61) identify the need for greater top management support, more commitment from users and more power and decision-making authority for project managers as key success factors. The B.C.S. report (2004) highlights a slightly different range of factors including client–supplier relationships, contractual arrangements, evolutionary project management and requirements management. This is one of the few reports to highlight software engineering as an issue and in the summary highlights the need for greater professionalism in software engineering, improved management education in relation to IT and project management, and more effective risk management.

Key factors noted by Yetton et al. (2000) are:

- Project team dynamics have a positive impact on budget variance. Good dynamics are encouraged by good planning – encouraging a stable team that performs effectively. Effective management of both social and technical processes is required.
- Risk management resulted in reduced budget variances.
- Senior management support, which depends on the strategic nature of the project, has a powerful effect on successful completion.
- User participation assists the successful completion of projects.

It is suggested by Yetton et al. (2000) that senior management and user management participation provide continuity across development and deployment stages and help build an implementation capability during development.

Although we have adopted a project mindset from the beginning of Engage, it is as we move into Evolve that the full project management toolkit becomes indispensable and these success factors need to be addressed in the approach adopted.

TEAM DESIGN FOR BENEFITS REALIZATION[T]

The project team that is put in place must be structured around the goal of realizing benefits from business change and must provide a foundation for effective teamwork and communication. A key success factor noted in the study by Yetton et al. (2000) is project team dynamics.

The project team members work together to deliver the objectives of the project. There will typically be a core team who work full-time on the project and others who play key roles, but who are only part-time members of the team. As an example, specialist technical IT staff in the areas of networking or security may have to provide input to all projects.

The team model (Figures 4.1 and Box 4.3) provides a starting-point for establishing a team design for a specific project. The example outlined is based on Version 3 (June 2003) of the Microsoft Solutions Framework, as used by Microsoft Consulting teams. The team can be as small as three people (i.e., by a sensible combination of roles), and there is no limit to the upper size, although keeping the team small is a key success factor. In practice, a team of more than 40–50 would be a *very* large agile project team.

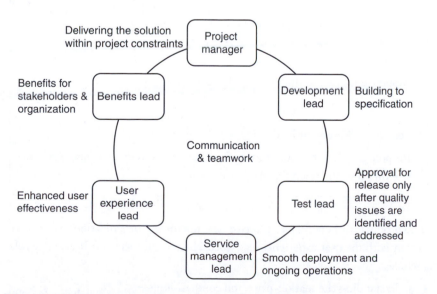

Figure 4.1 Project team model focused on benefits realization
Source: Based on Microsoft Solutions Framework V3.

The bulk of project resources are in the software development and test areas. However, in retail and banking scenarios, where there are many stores or branches, the end-user deployment and training activities may require the majority of the resource allocated to the project.

Box 4.3   Team roles

Product or benefits lead

Works on behalf of the sponsor to ensure the realization of benefits for the organization. The role leads the benefits focus and will lead on business process and change issues.

Project manager

The role of the project manager is to work with the team, and on behalf of the project sponsor, to ensure the project is successful. This includes working with the team leads to deliver the project – to time, cost and performance priorities.

User experience lead

Focuses on benefits for the end-user. The role includes usability and user education. Works very closely with the benefits lead on work design/business processes. This role often has the overall responsibility for communications strategy.

Development lead

Responsible for development of the IT solution.

Test lead

Responsible for testing of the IT solution and the wider business process/changes.

Service management lead

Responsible for the smooth transition of the system and new ways of working into the operational environment.

The product (or benefits) lead (focus: benefits for the organization) works very closely with the user experience lead (focus: benefits for the end-user). The role includes:

- understanding the market-place and competition;
- understanding the customer and what would add value to them;

- responsibility for realizing benefits from the product/service over its lifetime;
- phased delivery of the product/service to enable early benefits and understanding of the customer opportunity;
- continued innovation and improvements to deliver value;
- establishing performance measures to assess benefits and to drive learning and improvement;
- working with a range of other disciplines to realize the potential benefits.

It is essential that the six key roles are represented in the team from the start of the project, as the different perspectives and skills they bring all have a vital contribution. One way to approach this is with an initial team of three: a technical lead (perhaps a solution architect, covering all the technical roles), a benefits lead (covering benefits and user experience) and a project or programme manager.

In many traditional projects the project team structure and management style are very hierarchical. Communication channels are formal, and the project manager may be the only one to speak to the sponsor. The implicit model behind this approach is that 'the project manager knows best'.

An agile project requires a very different approach. There is a strong emphasis on teamwork, along with individual responsibility and empowerment, and open communication. Agile approaches are based on the belief that motivated individuals are key to successful projects and also that open communication between the different disciplines is essential for the identification and delivery of a successful business solution, particularly where there is a need for innovation.

Traditional approaches often focus on 'control', imposed 'top down' on the team. Agile approaches emphasize 'discipline': the good practices established and owned by a motivated and skilled team (Boehm and Turner, 2004).

In practice, it can be helpful to design the roles around the people – as well as find the people to fill the required roles. The challenge is to ensure that the overall team is effective. Team roles are likely to change and evolve during the project as the balance of different types of work changes and different strengths emerge and are required. Note that the split between the project roles and the ongoing responsibility for the service will vary from project to project.

The project manager

The role of the project manager is to work with the team, and on behalf of the project sponsor, to ensure the project is successful. This includes working with the team leads to:

- deliver the project – to time, cost and performance priorities;
- build, lead and motivate the project team throughout the project;

- ensure work is allocated and responsibilities identified;
- keep the sponsor and senior management informed of progress/problems;
- recommend termination of the project, if justified;
- ensure there is a focus on communication between the team, organization, suppliers, etc.

Effective teamwork and communication

Success of a project depends on the people involved. The effective teamwork of the project team and the engagement with wider stakeholders make the difference between success and failure.

The project team design must ensure ownership of:

- effective teamwork– this should be the project manager or one of the team leads who has real commitment to this area and relevant experience;
- communication with and involvement of stakeholders – the different project leads (and potentially other team members) should have responsibility for working with agreed stakeholders;
- use of IT to enable communication and effective teamworking.

There are many other practices to consider: selection of team members, location of the team, team meetings etc. The work of Ancona et al. (2002, 2008) on X-Teams provides interesting insights into what makes a team successful. They particularly emphasize flexible membership and extensive ties outside the team with relevant stakeholders inside and outside the organisation. The model fits well with the challenges facing our project teams.

Use of technology to enable effective teamwork and communication

Getting people communicating directly with others is a key part of an agile approach. If the team is working in the same workspace ('co-located'), they can talk face to face or gather around a whiteboard to work on a problem. Diagrams on whiteboards and flipchart paper will be on the walls – providing a record of discussions and decisions and being there to refer to later. If the detail isn't clear, you can always ask the colleague who drew the diagram in the first place.

This approach eliminates huge efforts producing reports and documents that are largely there for compliance reasons – so that risk-averse managers can refer to a paper trail when things go wrong. For the people doing the work their elimination is no loss – they probably didn't use them anyway.

Even in this environment of face-to-face discussion and simple diagrams on flipcharts and whiteboards, technology is important. Some documents are required. Some contributors to the project cannot work full-time with the team.

Core team members may have to travel as part of the project. A wide range of stakeholders need to be kept in touch and involved. Management need to be kept informed.

For all these reasons the team needs to be able to make effective use of IT to enhance their effectiveness as individuals and as a team, as well as their ability to communicate with broader stakeholders in the project.

There are a number of implications. The team needs someone who can provide a lead to ensure that individuals and the team as whole are making effective use of IT. This can involve establishing agreed protocols for the use of email, phone and instant messaging, as well as talking to each other. It also involves the use of project management, intranet and portal solutions for teamworking and wider communication.

There are practices for the toolkit here as well. These can form the basis for capturing and sharing learning and for enabling teams to get these aspects of the project working well as quickly as possible. The team design and working practices will depend on the specific project, and the IT and Change Portfolio will be an important influence (Box 4.4).

Box 4.4   Approach to a competitive project – An example

The project was a competitive project, and the project team was expected to grow to 12–15 people. There was a good work area where all the team members could be located, but some element of mobile working was going to be involved (visiting customers and other stakeholders, working from home, etc.). There were a number of project stakeholders within and outside the organization.

The project manager decided to retain primary responsibility for effective teamwork, partly to demonstrate its importance. She also arranged to bring in a specialist from the HR team to help with the project kick-off workshop and various other team-building activities.

The sponsor took responsibility for communication with a number of the key business stakeholders. The product manager also had a specific role.

One of the two user-experience members of the team had specific experience of using a range of communication technologies and worked with the project manager to:

- establish a team workspace and set up information management for the team (including handling of core documents, risk and issues logs, etc.);
- establish a project intranet site that provided information and a communication channel to stakeholders outside the core team;

- establish an agreed communication etiquette for the team (e.g., how and when to use email, phone, face-to-face communication, etc.);
- provide guidance on the communication etiquette and use of the various technologies to team members;
- ensure there was time to reflect, learn and improve.

Sharing the vision as the team grows

There will almost certainly be new people joining the team at this stage. If it did not happen during the previous Explore stage, work on building the team will have to start.

It is vital to pay attention to ensuring the team has a clear understanding and commitment to the drivers and vision for the project. Do not leave this to chance or rely on them simply reading the benefits realization plan. This is a crucial 'hearts and minds' issue, which the sponsor should own. If the team members do not understand the reasons for the investment (drivers) and the high-level goals (vision and investment objectives), they will be unable to use their judgement effectively to drive innovation during the project, and the chances are that the project will rapidly shift focus to technology delivery.

Building the team

Getting the right people engaged in all the different team and stakeholder roles is vital. There may be some tough decisions to take during the project to make changes if this is not right first time. In any case, structures and roles are likely to need to evolve during the project.

The priority is to get the right people engaged in the core team and other roles. Then the goal is to create the right environment so they can work together effectively. You can't assume that this will just happen. Selecting the people and building a high-performing team require considerable effort and attention. Again, the agile principles provide valuable guidance. It is also important to note that there is no single right way to structure the project team and governance framework.

Getting the right people is more than just getting the right job titles. It is getting the best mix of enthusiasts, critical friends, experts and idea generators (Kelley, 2008).

BUSINESS CHANGE GOVERNANCE FRAMEWORK[T]

The governance framework brings together key stakeholders in the project to contribute to benefits realization. Key areas to consider include: the project sponsor, the project board and end-user involvement.

Ward and Elvin (1999) summarize the results of an 'IT and Change' research project. The aim of the project was to establish a project framework to manage IT-enabled change. The importance of the organizational context for the change project is highlighted (both internal and external), as is the fact that the context will evolve during the project and will be affected by the project (as there is some degree of mutual interdependence). Problems in the projects studied arose from an unsuitable change process, and particularly from inadequate or inappropriate stakeholder involvement, and from underestimating the scale and complexity of the business changes. The business change governance framework needs to anticipate challenges in these areas and can draw on the benefits dependency network (Ward and Daniel, 2012) as the starting-point for the high-level work breakdown structure and as a basis for focusing project activity on benefits delivery.

The project sponsor

The project sponsor has overall responsibility for the project on behalf of the organization. The primary objective of the role is to ensure the investment is successful and that the intended benefits are realized. The nature of the role will vary considerably, depending on the nature and size of the project. It can be a significant, challenging role and may in some cases be full-time.

The authority and credibility of the sponsor will often be critical in gaining support for the project and for making the required changes to the organization happen. The sponsor will often have to work with and influence senior business colleagues who are responsible for benefits and related changes.

Box 4.5 provides an example of a role description for a project sponsor.

Box 4.5 The role of a project sponsor

The role of a project sponsor in his own words … 'My role as project exec. was:

- challenging of detailed reports;
- co-ordination – handling tensions between different stakeholders, making it happen at board meetings and in between;
- 'coaching' outside the meeting (e.g., other senior stakeholders);
- clarifying roles and making sure people worked as a team;
- anticipating weak areas (e.g., post-implementation capacity to operate the system; I commissioned a report on knowledge transfer and post-live admin);
- being sensitive to communications;
- managing expectations.

This 'took up a lot of time – a substantial number of hours each week for a year'. 'I gave him [the project manager] the support he needed', he had 'daily contact with the project exec'.

The extent and type of involvement required from the sponsor will vary according to the type of project (Box 4.6). Too much executive involvement can be a bad thing (Support projects).

Box 4.6   Leadership roles for different types of project

Competitive

A senior manager with credibility with the top management team must be actively involved with the project for all or a significant part of their time. The focus of the role is on alignment with strategy and maximizing the business opportunity from this innovative project.

Exploratory

The senior management role is primarily about creating a climate where Exploratory projects can happen.

There will be significant/credible business involvement in the project team (product/project manager).

Qualifying

There is a significant requirement for senior operational management leadership. Focus areas will include ensuring involvement and support from the range of business areas affected, managing the business risks, ensuring a continued focus on benefits through the steering committee and milestone reviews.

Support

The senior management role focuses on ensuring that there is a clear business case for the project and the focus is on a 'good enough' (80–20) solution.

There may not be a need for significant ongoing involvement.

The project board

The project board is an important part of the overall management framework or 'governance' framework for projects. It provides a forum for the project sponsor and project manager to work with other key stakeholders in the project.

The project board meets at the end of project stages and/or on a regular basis (two-weekly/monthly) and takes major decisions on the project.

The composition of the project board will depend on many factors. On large projects the project sponsor will need to include senior managers from other business areas to enable them to be involved in key project decisions. It also includes user representatives, a senior manager from the area(s) affected and a senior IT manager (a representative of the Chief Information Officer/IT Director and potentially the external supplier of software/services).

Some project managers find it helpful to establish other groups (vision or strategy group, user representatives) that allow the project board to focus on progress towards benefits against timescale and cost. The other groups provide a forum for exploration and communication of wider project issues.

End-user involvement

Getting the right level of user involvement is hard. In many organizations it is very difficult to release good people to be part of project teams – they are too valuable where they are.

Having made people available, getting them involved effectively is difficult. There is a tendency for projects to focus on technology issues and to use techniques and a 'language' that makes it hard for users to contribute. One of the advantages of a benefits-driven approach is that it makes a shift in language away from technology towards business issues.

It is important to think through what is required to enable people to work effectively as they become part of a project team. For example, what induction is required, or is any specific training relevant? In many cases it would be valuable to include education to introduce and reinforce relevant aspects of the 'toolkit'.

There is also a balance to make between full-time involvement in the team of a small number of users and wider involvement of all, or part, of the wider user community. Users who become part of the project team, perhaps on secondment, may, paradoxically, be treated as outsiders by their old team and not seen as *representatives* of end-user views or able to take decisions on behalf of end-users.

It is helpful to recognize that in many cases there will be a significant learning process for individuals and teams during and following implementation. There is no way to eliminate this. Even with good and effective user involvement throughout the project, new users have to go through a learning process as part of training and deployment. The project needs the resources, time and focus to enable and support this learning process. In many cases this means significantly more than a one-off, 'press this button', training course.

It is important to recognize that there will be many different end-user viewpoints and different perspectives on the opportunities and requirements.

Within a stakeholder group (defined by the benefits and changes involved) further segmentation may be valuable – for example, some users may be natural 'early adopters' and can be valuable in providing feedback and promoting adoption. The level of segmentation will often be increased as the project progresses. It is helpful to tailor the communication and engagement approach to the different segments.

Designing the governance framework

We have already discussed a number of important elements of the governance framework: the role of the sponsor, project team and project board. The governance framework is designed to meet the needs of the specific situation, take account of key individuals and what they can contribute, and specifically to address IT-enabled business change rather than technology delivery. The business focus means that benefits owners should be included in the framework as members of the project board, for example.

Effective governance is really about behaviour, not structure. Do the senior managers actually turn up, or do they send deputies? Does action take place outside project board meetings so that the meetings themselves can be effective? Is there shared ownership for solving problems, or is it a game of politics? Is there willingness to learn and adapt as the project progresses?

When we work with projects, these issues of leadership and behaviour really make the difference. Even where there is a good governance framework on paper, there are often problems in practice. The project sponsor and manager have important roles in ensuring the governance framework works effectively.

A colleague referred to the governance framework as providing the heartbeat of the project. For example, if the main project meeting is monthly and nobody has done much follow-through between meetings, the heartbeat is very slow. If the agile practice of daily meetings is adopted, maybe the heartbeat is racing – but that is OK – for limited periods. A combination of a focused daily or weekly meeting with project board meetings at regular milestones (roughly every four weeks) is often a good way to drive progress. Box 4.7 provides an example.

Box 4.7   Example of a governance framework for a competitive project

The key elements of the governance framework for a competitive project included:

- weekly progress reports (brief) from each sub-team;
- weekly team leads meeting with the project manager and sponsor;
- fortnightly risk meeting (team leads and others);

- milestone-based steering committee meetings involving all benefits owners at the end of each project phase (no phase lasting longer than four to six weeks);
- regular meetings with key stakeholders.

In addition, milestone reviews were carried out, and there was a range of activities to communicate with/involve wider stakeholder groups (end-users, help desk, etc.).

PLANNING AND CONTROL

This section addresses a number of aspects of project planning that build on the benefits foundations already established. Useful context comes from a study of product portfolio management (Cooper et al., 1999) which identified three success factors: an explicit, consistently used approach – which is strongly supported by management and applied to all projects (the actual approach used is less important); multiple evaluation methods – such as financial, strategic, etc.; and a fit with the overall management style of the organization.

Topics covered are:
- the project framework – the detailed aspects of the Evolve stage;
- work breakdown structure;
- estimating;
- living documents;
- benefits-driven change control;
- risk management;
- milestone review;
- aspects of the project plan and project planning;
- trade-off strategy.

The 'Agile Manifesto' again provides important context – with benefits as the focus rather than software (Box 4.8).

Box 4.8 Further aspects of the 'Agile Manifesto'

Our highest priority is to satisfy the customer through early and continuous delivery of valuable software.

Welcome changing requirements, even late in development. Agile processes harness change for the customer's competitive advantage.

Deliver working software frequently, from a couple of weeks to a couple of months, with a preference to the shorter timescale.

Working software is the primary measure of progress.

Continuous attention to technical excellence and good design enhances agility.

Simplicity – the art of maximizing the amount of work not done – is essential.

www.agilealliance.org

Project framework – milestones and deliverables

The e^{4+1} project framework provides a broad framework that is suitable for many types of project. It has been designed specifically to start before traditional projects and to capture ideas and manage them as projects from the beginning. It also goes beyond the completion of traditional projects with Evaluate and Expand, to take a benefits perspective on post-project review and focus on developing the benefits being realized. As a result, much of traditional project activity is within one phase of e^{4+1} – **Evolve**. Therefore it is helpful to consider how Evolve can itself be broken down into a series of stages with clear deliverables and milestones. This is particularly important for larger projects.

Box 4.9 sets out an example of detail within the Evolve phase. It is based on the Microsoft Solutions Framework (MSF). MSF is a very effective framework and was an important source of inspiration and ideas for aspects of the book. Although developed before 'agile' became fashionable, it embodies many of the same principles.

Box 4.9   Example of project lifecycle for the Evolve stage

Planning: Project plan approved

- project plan and project schedule;
- project structure;
- risk assessment;
- technology validation (often completed earlier);
- communications strategy;
- functional specification;
- solution design.

Developing: Scope complete

- solution code;
- draft training materials;

- draft documentation: deployment processes, operational procedures, support and troubleshooting;
- marketing materials.

Stabilizing: Release readiness

Release-ready versions of:

- source code and executables,
- end-user help and training materials,
- operations documentation.

Deploying: Deployment complete

- new systems and ways of working operational.

The example draws on the Microsoft Solution Framework V3.

Work breakdown structure

Establishing a work breakdown structure (WBS) is an important early step in project planning. The project manager and team start with the high-level goals of the project and identify the 'products' or deliverables and the major activities required as part of the project in order to achieve the goals. At its lowest level, the WBS should show tasks that can be allocated to an individual and completed in one progress-reporting period (typically a week – though potentially a day at key stages and in some agile methods). This lowest level of detail is established on a rolling basis as the project progresses.

The WBS provides a basis for controlling the project – for resource planning and for estimating effort, elapsed time and cost – and provides a valuable input to risk identification.

Some agile approaches argue that the WBS should be discarded, arguing instead for a list of features and an evolving, bottom-up estimate of effort required from the developers. SCRUM (Box 4.10) provides an important example.

Box 4.10   Scrum: An alternative approach to project scheduling

Scrum is an example of a popular, iterative and incremental agile development method that can be applied to a wide variety of projects.

Elements of the approach include having a 'product backlog', essentially a stack of requirements to be tackled at some point, and a series of 'sprints', typically two-week development periods where a number of requirements are tackled. It's a time-boxed approach in that a number of two-week sprints would be included in the project plan and the features delivered would depend on the progress of the team over each period.

The approach shifts the emphasis of estimating to the specific requirements to be tackled in each sprint and provides an opportunity for the team to learn and improve as it goes in terms of both estimating and solution delivery.

This model fits well within the overall approach described in the book and the Evolve phase of a project would be time-boxed with a number of interim milestones (effectively sprints).

Estimating

Establishing estimates of effort, duration and cost are a key part of project planning. There are two basic approaches – 'top-down' and 'bottom-up'. Both approaches are normally required. A 'top-down' estimate is based on a broad understanding of the scope and complexity of the project. The estimate comes from comparing the project to other similar projects. The 'bottom-up' estimate is developed by establishing a WBS and then estimating effort/duration/costs for activities at the lowest level on the WBS. An overall project estimate is then established simply by adding up the individual estimates. The top-down and bottom-up estimates are compared and an overall estimate for the project negotiated and agreed.

In many projects a key element of the total estimate will depend on costs proposed by potential suppliers as a result of a procurement process.

Estimating is an art not a science, and a number of elements of the approach to projects address the inevitable uncertainty in the initial estimates and budgets. The practice of making benefits-driven trade-offs is important, as the one thing we do know about the estimate is that it will not be 100% accurate.

Living documents

The production of documents on a project (requirements, plans, designs, etc.) can become an end in itself. It is easy to lose sight of the fact that these documents are only a means to an end, which is the goal of providing benefits to stakeholders. In particular, there can be huge effort involved in getting a document 'just right' because this is (often correctly) seen as the last chance to make changes: for example, to requirements. This causes extra effort and delay. It can also prevent learning and change.

An agile approach seeks to 'maximize the amount of work *not* done' – in part by eliminating and streamlining documentation deliverables. There is still considerable documentation required, and the Living Documents practice addresses how this is produced.

The approach of 'baseline early – freeze late' is used. Many aspects of a deliverable can be captured quickly (following the 80:20 rule: i.e., 80% of the output is delivered in 20% of the time). The deliverable can then be 'baselined' and brought under change control. This allows other parts of the project to proceed based on this '80% complete' version. For example, it avoids excessive delays, which can result if the project attempts to ensure requirements and specifications are 100% complete and locked down before development start. The deliverable is kept under change control and is 'frozen' as late as possible.

Having a standard project framework also means that effort is saved and quality is improved by using templates for key deliverables and by reusing sections that address aspects of the project approach that do not need to vary (much) from project to project.

Benefits-driven change control[T]

Change is inevitable. In fact, change can often be a positive response to learning about new opportunities for benefits during a project. Engage and Explore are designed to encourage innovation and learning about the problem and potential solutions.

Control of change is an important discipline and has formed part of traditional project and systems development methods. Too much change can mean that a project never delivers. Completely preventing change is unrealistic, as there will always be learning during the course of a project and this may be significant. Particularly in scenarios where the benefits arise from innovation rather than incremental change, there will be a creative process of learning and discovery as possibilities are explored.

The change control process needs to evaluate change requests and decide if action is required in the current or a future release. The time-boxed approach means that delivery dates are only changed as a last resort, but within and between releases there is flexibility in the specific features that are prioritized for delivery.

Benefits-driven change control builds on a traditional approach to change control and ensures that changes are evaluated primarily on the basis of their impact on benefits rather than software features (Box 4.11).

Box 4.11   Change control: Example from recent research

The project sponsor worked with the project manager to establish a benefits-driven framework for change control. A contingency of 15% of the project budget was set aside as a provision for changes and other contingencies. This contingency was to be managed by the project board. If additional funds were required, approval would depend on normal financial approval processes.

There is a tendency to subject requests for changes to very high levels of scrutiny, often beyond that applied to the original business case. The change control framework must not be too onerous or it will result in important changes not being progressed or the change control system being bypassed.

Risk management[T]

Risk management is a critical project activity and should be an ongoing process throughout the project. It is important to balance the effort given to this area – work is required to identify possible risks and also to take *action* to reduce their likelihood and/or impact. Often organizational politics or some form of organizational blindness can mean it is very difficult to get agreement to action.

We advocate a simple approach to risk management, on the basis that actively managing risks is the goal and that there is little value added by attempting to get too precise in the quantification of probability or financial impact (Box 4.12).

Where an organization has an established approach to risk management, it is probably most effective to keep using it. Just check how effectively it is being used and if the risks are being considered in relation to benefits realization rather than technology delivery.

Box 4.12 Risk management process

The risk management process has six stages:

1. Identify: a range of techniques can be used to identify risks (brainstorming, interviews and checklists). The identification process should be started as early as possible and continue throughout the project. It should draw on the experience of project team members.

2. Analyse and prioritize: a project-specific scale is used to assess the probability and potential impact of each risk: normally either High, Medium and Low or Very High, High, Medium, Low, Very Low. Risks are plotted on a probability/impact grid, and the top ten risks are identified.

3. Plan and schedule: with a focus on the top risks, strategies, plans and actions are agreed and incorporated in wider project plans. For each of the top risks a suitable response strategy and, where appropriate, a contingency plan are agreed.

For each risk consider:

- mitigating actions (to reduce the probability or impact);
- contingency actions: what to do if it the risk happens;
- ownership for the actions;
- when to review.

4. Track and report: the probability and impact of the risks are kept under review, and the progress of any agreed actions is monitored.

5. Control: the risk management process is kept under review through project team and steering group meetings.

6. Learn: lessons learned about the risk management process are captured for the benefit of future phases and projects. Checklists and other resources are updated.

Risk management is an ongoing process throughout the life of the project.

Milestone-based control[T]

Management focus should be on the major milestones (stage ends) determined by the project lifecycle. If the project is kept short (as it should be), this will typically provide a major review point every four to six weeks, which becomes a motivating target for the project team and for the sponsor and project board, reducing the risk of slippage between milestones.

The deliverables at each milestone should be clearly defined. In some organizations a standard lifecycle is defined with the same stages and major deliverables for each project. We strongly recommend this approach, and the book provides an example of a lifecycle framework.

Each milestone is also an opportunity to reflect on progress and to *learn* from the project to date (Box 4.13). We address this benefits review activity in our discussion of the Evaluate stage of the lifecycle.

Box 4.13   Milestone review: Key questions

Have we achieved our goals for this stage? (Are specific deliverables complete?)

Are we ready to proceed to the next stage, with resources and plans in place?

Are we still on track to deliver benefits that justify the project?

Is the risk assessment up to date, and have appropriate actions been planned or taken?

What have we learned that will enable us to work more effectively in future stages, and how are we going to make it happen?

The project plan

Project planning is an ongoing process throughout the project. Plans are updated and changed as the project progresses. Typically, there will be a high-level plan for the overall project and a detailed plan for the current and next stage.

The project plan is far more than a timetable. It needs to address a range of questions:

- Why – is the project being undertaken?
- What – are the aims and target benefits?
- Who – is involved in delivering the benefits?
- What – is the business solution required?
- When – will the project be completed?
- How – will the project be carried out?

At the early stages of the project, the plan may be a one- or two-page document. As the project progresses, it may become a much more substantial document. According to the preferences of the organization, a range of specific areas will have to be addressed either in sub-plans or as part of the overall document (Box 4.14).

Box 4.14 · Aspects of the project plan

- benefits plan: benefits, measures, targets, timescales, owners, plans for tracking;
- change plan – related to the benefits plan;
- governance framework, including benefits ownership;
- team structure;
- communications and user engagement strategy;
- security strategy;
- test strategy;
- deployment strategy;
- training plan;
- cutover plan;
- trade-off strategy;
- milestones and deliverables;
- assumptions and constraints;
- risk management strategy, current assessment and action plan.

Benefits-driven trade-offs[T]

The trade-off strategy should be made explicit as part of the project plan. In most cases the timescale is key and a small team works to deliver a release to the timetable. Resourcing might evolve during the project, but the primary decision is to take a time-boxed approach and treat features as the key variable. The technical design needs to enable features to be moved from release to release, if required, to enable the implementation timescales to be met.

Figure 4.2 shows a typical agile approach to trade-offs. Resources are fixed (small teams are effective, and adding people in response to problems is often not effective), a schedule (timescale) is chosen and then features are adjusted to enable the team to deliver to the timescale.

Design

The design of the business solution required to enable benefits realization was considered at the Explore stage. Work now progresses to design and build a solution, including an IT solution. This could include design and build of a bespoke system, configuring package software or making use of cloud services. Specific practices related to software development, testing and implementation, including user-centred software design, are beyond the scope of this book.

In Chapter 7 there will be further coverage of this area as we consider 'design thinking' as a way to tackle change and benefits realization in complex and problematic situations.

	Fixed	Chosen	Adjustable
Resources	✔		
Schedule		✔	
Features			✔

Given fixed Resources, we will choose a Schedule, and adjust Features as necessary.

Figure 4.2 Trade-off strategy for a typical agile (time-boxed) project

Delivering the change programme

The benefits realization plan helps to define what changes are required to realize the benefits. During Evolve the focus shifts to actually delivering the change programme. The changes and the types of interventions required to realize them will be of many kinds. In this section we explore a number of important aspects of successfully delivering the change programme.

Stakeholder communications and engagement[T]

Our focus on stakeholder engagement highlights the importance of the communications strategy and role. This is a vital part of benefits realization.

Who is being communicated with about what? When is communication required? What method should be used for each communication? These are all vital decisions. How to enable feedback and effective two-way communication is also an important element of the overall strategy.

In many cases one of the team leaders will take on the role of 'communications lead'. This will often be the user experience lead or benefits lead. The aim is to bring specific expertise in communication with stakeholders, and to support other team members as they engage with different stakeholders.

Marketing perspectives and practices have an important contribution to make. Thinking about 'brand' and communicating the benefits to customers and other end-users may be critical in establishing adoption and usage.

Phased deployment[T] and benefits ramp-up

Well-executed waterfall and agile projects ensure that new business processes are defined alongside the system and are tested, along with training materials, as part of final user testing of the system. However, in many cases these effectively become frozen at this stage and, even if there is a pilot deployment of the solution, the pressure to complete deployment tends to prevent any significant changes:

> One engagement was deploying a solution to a number of countries in a phased roll-out. However, the target dates meant that there was no time in the schedule to allow for any learning from the initial deployment to be incorporated in the planning.
>
> (quote from a recent research project)

There is a major risk that business processes and training are frozen just as some of the most significant learning is taking place as the solution is deployed in the real world. It is important to build in genuine opportunities for learning about the potential benefits and how best to realize them as part of the deployment process.

Cutover: Implementation, training and education

At each stage of the deployment detailed planning for implementation will be required as well as training and education aimed at different stakeholder groups. Even with the best-designed systems and built-in help, etc., this is often a major activity for the project team.

Training and education contribute to the implementation of organizational changes and are a major part of a project. Very often there is underinvestment in this area. It is important to design the training with a benefits focus as part of the wider activity to realize benefits.

Summary: Delivering the changes

Delivering the business changes required to realize the benefits is a vital element of the project. One guideline suggests that at least 50% of project budget should be allocated to these people-related activities (Clegg et al., 1997).

The changes are complex, and the results of actions can be unpredictable. It is vital that the sponsor, project team and other key stakeholders continue to focus on this area.

ENABLING LEARNING AND FLEXIBILITY

A traditional approach to projects emphasizes the cost of making changes to the desired results or products that are the outcome of the project. The cost of making changes increases as the project continues. For example, at the start of a project changing requirements is only a matter of changing a list of bullet points in a Word document. Towards the end of the project it could require changes to software, training materials and user procedures, as well as significant re-testing of the solution. The fact that the cost of change rises rapidly (exponentially) means that:

- Approaches to projects place a huge emphasis on planning, and trying to avoid the need for change. This may extend to preventing changes even if they are important.

- Managing and controlling change are a critical element of project management.

- Reducing the cost of change is in a sense the 'holy grail' of project management.

Traditional approaches to project management respond to this with a huge focus on planning – trying to get it right first time and on controlling (preventing) change. The agile response is to *enable* learning and change and to manage the project to reduce the cost of change.

IN SUMMARY

Evolve is the core of the project where the ideas and plans are brought to life.

The shape of the Evolve stage will vary significantly from project to project: for example, is it a bespoke development, a package implementation or exploitation of elements of the existing IT infrastructure? The guiding principles and key practices remain the same. Inevitably experience and judgement will determine how they are applied in the specific situation.

We have seen how many organizations approach projects and observed a wide range of strengths and weaknesses. Many are competent at traditional projects but struggle when innovation is required. Others are effective at technology delivery but cannot effectively tackle IT-enabled organizational change. Many waste months drifting from idea, through business case into project kick-off. Most switch attention to the *next* project far too quickly rather than continuing to focus on realizing the benefits from the investment they have already made.

In virtually every case a critical area for improvement is to develop the skills of the people involved to work together effectively. The issue is rarely technical skills. Projects are challenging; they require complex multi-disciplinary teamwork, which requires high-level skills in many areas. These need to be developed over time and require education, and ongoing support in an enabling environment.

The agile principle is critical: 'Simplicity – the art of maximizing the amount of work **not** done'. Remember that a lot of project processes are about the perception of control and are designed to keep nervous management, who do not trust their teams, happy.

TAKING IT FURTHER

FURTHER READING AND RESOURCES

There are many avenues for further reading using the references as a starting point. Suggestions include:

Teamwork

Ancona, Deborah, Bresman, Henrik and Kaeufer, Katrin (2002) The Comparative Advantage of X-Teams. *MIT Sloan Management Review*, Spring 2002, Vol. 43 (3): 33–39.

Agile approaches to projects

Boehm, B. and Turner, R. (2004) *Balancing Agility and Discipline: A Guide for the Perplexed*, Boston, MA: Addison-Wesley.

Learning and sharing knowledge

Garvin, D.A. (1993) Building a Learning Organization. *Harvard Business Review*, July–August, Vol. 71 (4): 78–91.

Wenger, W., McDermott, R. and Snyder, W.M. (2002) *Cultivating Communities of Practice*, Boston: Harvard Business School Press.

Leading change

Todnam, R. (2005) Organizational Change Management: A Critical Review. *Journal of Change Management*, Vol. 5 (4): 369–380.

Kotter, John P. and Schlesinger, Leonard A. (2008) Choosing Strategies for Change. *Harvard Business Review*, July–August 2008, Vol. 86/7–8.

Kotter, John P. (2008) Leading Change. *Harvard Business Review*, January 2007, Vol. 85 (1): 96–103.

TALKING POINTS

Use these questions to help reflect on this chapter and explore the challenges of putting the ideas into practice:

1. How would you apply the team model to a small project/team?

2. How would you apply the team model to a large project?

3. What are the implications of using package software or web services for the approach to the project?

4. What would be the role of a software supplier in a benefits-led project? What might be the challenges of incorporating them into a project team?

5. What purchasing/procurement issues do you envisage if you are taking a benefits-led approach and seeking to enable innovation?

6. What problems do you envisage if you try adopting a benefits-led approach? How might you overcome them?

7. How might you approach adopting a benefits-led approach on a particular project?

8. How might you approach getting adoption of benefits-led approaches across all projects in an organization?

9. How might we need to adapt the approach to a project to reflect the IT and Change Portfolio?

10. How does a benefits-led approach contribute to handling typical problems with projects including power and politics?

KEY DEBATES

Making procurement work for benefits realization

There can be a tension between a focus on procurement, often to minimize costs, and a benefits-driven approach, which typically focuses on maximizing benefits.

Procurement is a major driver for a traditional, waterfall approach to projects. Requirements are defined in detail and then provide a basis for a formal statement of requirements and services required. Potential suppliers then submit bids for the work, and there is a formal selection process.

It is undoubtedly the case that with many suppliers there is a lot of room for negotiation and the customers with good procurement expertise can negotiate a much better overall deal.

How might you approach procurement when adopting a more agile, benefits-driven approach? What are the implications for the contribution of the supplier and governance of the relationship? How might the approach differ for different types of projects?

CASE STUDY 4.1

The case study provides an opportunity to explore challenges of benefits realization.

Journal of Information Technology Teaching Cases, Vol. 3 (2013): 96–105.

Saving costs using smart call routing: aligning business and IT through finance

This case describes the effective information technology (IT) business alignment considerations that led to the successful implementation of a telecommunication platform designed to efficiently route cell phone calls in a financial institution in Chile. The company had several branches throughout the country, including its headquarters in Santiago. This initiative was part of a Technology Cost Savings strategy generated in response to the 2008 crisis. The idea behind it was to align internal business leaders with the IT team in order to optimize these costs, realizing a more efficient telecommunication platform, and to work together, as several cost-reducing initiatives were being executed at the same time. Achievements were thoroughly reviewed by the board of directors, and thus pressure to clean up the house was high. At that time, when users called a cellular phone from a landline, the call was charged using a fee much higher than a mobile company rate. The goal of the project was naturally to optimize these charges. An automatic call routing was designed, discussed and executed with the participation of the business leaders, based on each branch's demand and projected growth. The case relates the project lifecycle: the mistakes made at the beginning, the initial platform tests and bottlenecks, the rejection and frustration of the business, and a posterior crisis control and recovery phase. IT alignment and sponsorship from the directors were crucial, as there was no way back. All these factors, plus the additional IT activities competing for business attention, made this project both a challenging and learning experience.

REFERENCES

Ancona, Deborah, Bresman, Henrik and Kaeufer, Katrin (2002) The Comparative Advantage of X-Teams. *MIT Sloan Management Review*, Spring 2002, Vol. 43 (3): 33–39.

Ancona, Deborah, Backman, Elaine and Bresman, Henrik (2008) X-Teams: New Ways of Leading in a New World. *Ivey Business Journal*, May/June 2008, Vol. 72 (3): 1–8.

Association for Project Management (2006) *APM Body of Knowledge* (5th edition). Princes Risborough: Association for Project Management.

B.C.S. (2004) *The Challenges of Complex IT Projects*, London: British Computer Society.

Boehm, B. and Turner, R. (2004) *Balancing Agility and Discipline: A Guide for the Perplexed*, Boston, MA: Addison-Wesley.

Clegg, C., Axtell, C., Damodaran, L., Farbey, B., Hull, R., Lloyd-Jones, R., Nicholls, J., Sell, R. and Tomlinson, C. (1997) Information Technology: A Study of Performance and the Role of Human and Organizational Factors. *Ergonomics*, Vol. 40 (9): 851–871.

Cooper, R.G., Edgett, S.J. and Kleinschmidt, E.J. (1999) New Product Portfolio Management: Practices and Performance. *Journal of Product Innovation Management*, Vol. 16 (4): 333–350.

Kappelman, L.A., McKeeman, R. and Zhang, L. (2006) Early Warning Signs of IT Project Failure: The Dominant Dozen. *Information Systems Management*, Fall 2006, Vol. 2 (4): 31–36.

Kelley, T. (2008) *The Ten Faces of Innovation: Strategies for Heightening Creativity*, London: Profile Business.

Myers, M.D. (1994) A Disaster for Everyone To See: An Interpretive Analysis of a Failed IS Project. *Accounting, Management and Information Technologies*, Vol. 4 (4): 185–201.

Sauer, C. and Cuthbertson, C. (2003) *The State of IT Project Management in the UK 2002–2003*, Oxford: Templeton College.

Ward, J. and Daniel, E. (2012) *Benefits Management*, Chichester: John Wiley & Sons Inc.

Ward, J. and Elvin, R. (1999) A New Framework for Managing IT-Enabled Business Change. *Information Systems Journal*, Vol. 9 (3): 197–222.

Yetton, P., Martin, A., Sharma, R. and Johnston, K. (2000) A Model of Information Systems Development Project Performance. *Information Systems Journal*, Vol. 10: 263–289.

CHAPTER 5
ASSESSING THE BENEFITS – EVALUATION

IN THIS CHAPTER WE STUDY:

- evaluating the results of a project and enabling learning through the project lifecycle;

- sharing learning in the form of specific practices in order to improve performance;

- a framework of business competences for benefits realization as the source of competitive advantage from IT.

EVALUATE

WHY BOTHER?

Is there any point carrying out a *benefits review*? Why not just call the project a success and move on to the next project or job? Is that not what usually happens?

Post-implementation reviews are not consistently carried out in most organizations. As a result, a major opportunity for learning is lost. In the minority of cases where a post-implementation review is carried out, it is often soon after the IT solution goes live and focuses principally on the success of the IT solution delivery.

The benefits review builds on this and has an explicit focus on benefits. As a result, the gap between 'going live' and the review has to be extended to provide time for benefits to be established. In some cases follow-up reviews are required to assess the benefits: for example, at the year-end or 12 months after the project.

The 'Agile Manifesto' brings a still broader focus – which we adopt here:

> At regular intervals, the team reflects on how to become more effective, then tunes and adjusts its behavior accordingly.
>
> www.agilemanifesto.org

Benefits review becomes an ongoing process throughout a project, with the Evaluate stage providing a major focus.

A strand of research into IT evaluation has explored this area. As work by Farbey et al. (1999) indicates, there is a considerable opportunity to improve evaluation practice. Serafeimidis and Smithson (1999, 2000) have also highlighted the difficulty in improving evaluation practice and suggested that this is itself an organizational change, and that a paradigm shift is required to see evaluation as an ongoing process and to adopt a wider, contingent framework.

Farbey et al. (1995) also point out that benefits often come from a major programme of business change and that the value is from the whole programme. There is a danger of sub-optimization if the focus is on each project in isolation. The benefits from an IT project will not all arise immediately on implementation of the technology. A successful infrastructure project, in particular, can be seen as providing a competence that can then be exploited by the organization, potentially in a series of further projects.

Ward sets out benefits management as a part of the overall project process (Ward et al., 1996). This is consistent with Farbey et al. (1999) and Walsham (1999), who see the importance of evaluation being ongoing, and part of the natural work of the project. Ward and Elvin (1999) propose a project framework that starts to try and address this. The approach taken here follows this logic.

A broad guideline is that those who participate in a benefits review are most likely to learn lessons from the project. The best way of sharing the lessons with other projects is often moving team members on to be part of new project teams when the time is right.

The organizational culture can have a major effect on the ability to carry out reviews and on their success. In many organizations admitting there is anything to learn is still hard, and also personnel move so quickly from role to role there can be a lack of continuity between planning the project and reviewing the benefits.

The benefits review is intended to enable learning from success and failure (and avoid repeating mistakes), and to increase the benefits realized from IT investments. Specific objectives are:

- to understand any changes in the business context or learning during the project that have an impact on the intended benefits;

- to identify the intended benefits that have been achieved;

- to identify the intended benefits that have not been achieved, the reasons why, and to decide whether any action to enable their realization is appropriate;

- to identify the benefits that have been achieved that were not expected;

- to identify any dis-benefits that have arisen and decide on any action to deal with them;

- to identify any further benefits, which can now be obtained and agree whether action should be taken to realize them (at some point projects reach the 80:20 point and resources should be reallocated to achieve bigger returns elsewhere);

- to understand what types of benefits can be achieved and to determine the causes of success and failure, in order to provide better insight for other projects at the benefits planning stage;

- to understand better how the benefits management process works, and hence to be able to improve the process.

(based on Ward, J. and Murray, P. (2000) *Benefits Management Best Practice Guidelines*, Information Systems Research Centre – Cranfield School of Management)

The review should involve key project stakeholders and should be based on relevant evidence. It is important to design and facilitate a workshop session that enables different stakeholders to contribute (Box 5.1). In some cases it will be valuable to run a number of different sessions with individual stakeholder groups. The example describes one effective approach we have taken to running a benefits review session.

Box 5.1 Example of an approach to a benefits review

The sponsor called key team members representing different stakeholders together for a two-hour workshop. A facilitator, not connected with the project, was lined up, and a member of the team was asked to work as 'documenter' – typing the discussion and findings during the workshop.

The workshop started with a brief introduction to the purpose and objectives. The participants were asked to discuss 'Why did the project need to be undertaken?' and 'What were the overall objectives?'

Participants were then asked: 'What were the outcomes (benefits/dis-benefits)?' These were quickly explored by considering if the benefits were as planned and what unexpected benefits there had been.

Then the participants were asked to take some time thinking individually and writing on large post-its: what practices had worked well – and where there are opportunities for improvement. They were asked to consider before, during and, finally, after the project.

After about ten minutes, each participant put his or her post-its on the wall one by one, briefly explaining the point and gradually filling a rough 2 × 3 matrix. This allowed everybody to speak and make his or her contribution.

The facilitator followed up with questions to explore the major points made and to try and explore the underlying causes and opportunities for action.

Getting a shared focus on five priority areas for action and exploring what to do in each area wrapped up the session.

As the discussion was documented during the meeting, a draft report was issued for feedback the same day.

* * *

Note: as part of exploring each key issue, it is important to consider if any problems are to do with lack of compliance with existing policy and frameworks, or if there is a need for new or changed policy and practice. It is also important to think hard about the underlying causes – keep asking 'why?'

It is important to note that, as with risk management, reflection and learning should be an ongoing activity. The core benefits review carried out at the Evaluate stage of the lifecycle can be adapted for use during other stages of the project. The core of the practice is the same – the specific questions just need to be adapted slightly to the relevant stage of the project (Box 5.2).

Box 5.2   Approach to benefits review at different stages of the lifecycle

Engage

Is the opportunity worth investigating further?
Are we ready to develop the benefits realization plan?

Explore

Is there a clear benefits realization plan?
Is everything in place to proceed with the project?

Evolve

Milestone reviews at each stage: are we on track to realize benefits? (Note that we expect the target benefits may change due to learning during the project.)
The milestone review also considers:

- Have planned deliverables been completed?
- Is everything in place for the next stage of the project?
- Has the risk assessment been updated?
- What are the lessons learned that could help increase the effectiveness of project activity?

Evaluate

Benefits review: what benefits were realized (planned and unplanned)? What further benefits can be realized? What lessons can be learned for future projects?

Expand

Benefits review – periodic review of the production service: how can we sustain and improve benefits?

EFFECTIVE MEASUREMENT OF BENEFITS

'You get what you measure' – performance measurement is a strong driver of behaviour. As a result, the measures that are put in place and the targets that are set will have a significant impact on the benefits that are actually realized. Measurement is not just about assessing the results – measurement makes things happen.

Unfortunately, it is hard to predict the precise impact of specific measurements, and there are often unexpected effects.

Measuring what is easy to measure may not be the right thing to do. Getting the data to measure what really matters can be difficult (Box 5.3).

Box 5.3   Effective measurement?

The supermarket was getting long queues of customers at the checkouts on a regular basis. One step they took to address this was to focus on the performance of checkout staff. From the new electronic point of sale (EPOS) system they were able to measure 'items scanned per minute', so they introduced a daily report in each store showing the performance of each operator on each shift.

Performance of checkout operators increased.

However, the store manager saw that there was still a problem. The system was only measuring one part of the whole checkout process: the time between the scanning of the first and last item for each customer. Checkout operators were scanning the goods so rapidly that the shoppers couldn't keep up with the packing. There was a big pile of shopping at the end of the belt – with the customer frantically trying to pack it into bags – and the checkout operators were sitting waiting for the next customer – doing nothing.

So they decided to experiment with a different set of measures . . .

Having identified benefits and associated measures, it is important to consider the likely impact of the individual measures, and the overall set of measures on behaviour.

The Balanced Scorecard concept (Kaplan and Norton, 1993) indicates that we need a 'basket' of measures, which together bring the right emphasis on behaviour. Neely et al. (2002) also provide useful guidelines on what makes an effective set of measures. Consider a sales role: A measure based on orders taken would be a starting-point. But, by itself, what behaviour might it drive? Other measures required might include:

- credit notes and bad debts (to assess what income was actually received);
- repeat business (as an indicator of customer satisfaction);
- order accuracy (problems highlighted by manufacturing).

Effective measurement is difficult. It comes into focus during the development of the benefits realization plan and should remain a focus during the project. Very often measures will need to evolve over time to shift the emphasis as different opportunities come into focus. A particular problem, and opportunity, is that often there is no effective measurement of the situation *before* the project: the project itself produced the capability to start to measure. Do not use this as an excuse to do nothing, or to spend a lot of time or money creating a baseline simply so you can measure the benefits more accurately. Keep the focus of activity on creating value.

PAYBACK FROM EVALUATE

The practices of Evaluate can make an important difference through the life of the project and in realizing benefits from an investment through its operational life.

Wider benefits will also come from sharing the learning more broadly to current and future projects and the wider organization.

SHARING THE LEARNING

Succeeding in implementing actions based on the learning from a benefits review is another major challenge. Research suggests that the rate of conversion from opportunities identified to *action taken* and improvements made is low. One of the best ways to learn is for an individual to be part of a benefits review session. In addition, as individuals move onto other projects, they are likely to take their learning with them.

We want to explore two different perspectives which help us understand how to share learning and put it into practice. In an article and book about the 'Learning Organization', David Garvin (1993, 2000) refers to three overlapping stages of organizational learning:

- cognitive: members of the organization are exposed to new ideas, expand their knowledge and begin to *think* differently;
- behavioural: employees begin to internalize new insights and alter *behaviour*;
- performance improvement: changes in behaviour lead to measurable *performance improvement*.

We need learning at all three stages. Garvin defines a 'Learning Organization' as an organization skilled at *creating, acquiring, interpreting, transferring* and *retaining knowledge* and at *purposefully modifying* its *behaviour* to reflect new knowledge and insights (Garvin, 2000). This is an important element of our overall benefits realization capability – deliberately to modify behaviour. He goes on to identify a number of enablers of learning:

- create the opportunity to learn from all experiences – both good and bad – and admit to failures;
- foster an environment that is conducive to learning – make time to really understand customer needs, to think and to reflect;

- open up boundaries and stimulate the exchange of ideas;
- create learning forums – reviews of strategy or cross-functional processes, including internal benchmarking.

A second perspective on learning is provided by Pfeffer and Sutton (1999, 2004), who refer to the gap between what we know and what we do. This 'knowing–doing' gap is a serious issue in the arena of IT-enabled change, as many valuable and widely known practices are not effectively adopted. The lack of adoption of the practice of carrying out a post-implementation review (benefits review) is just one of many examples.

Pfeffer and Sutton suggest that a major reason for the gap is that education and development focus on 'know-what' (to do) rather than 'know-why' (the underlying principles) and 'know-how' (the skills built up from experience of putting the knowledge into practice).

It is clear that, although we can have valuable benefits review sessions, the results will be limited if we do not take purposeful action to follow them up. Learning can be shared in a number of ways, and this has to be planned and managed (Box 5.4).

Box 5.4 Approaches to sharing learning

Updating policy and evolving the project framework (i.e., making change in the formal organization)
Introduce a specific project lifecycle framework (such as e^{4+1}).
Introduce a 'product manager' role into project teams.
Focus project board activity on milestone reviews.

Capturing and sharing reusable resources

A communications strategy (or other deliverables relating to the approach to the project) may be highly reusable.

Capturing aspects of tacit knowledge

A project team has a 'brown bag' session (open workshop over lunch) to share their experience in a specific area.
The team writes a short case study or prepares a podcast.
Learning is captured as a new 'practice' to add to the toolkit.

Sharing knowledge through people

Key players from a successful project are moved into other teams specifically with the goal of sharing their experience of new ways of working.

Training and education

Standard courses are updated to reflect learning.

A course is provided to introduce an agile, benefits-driven approach to projects.

Education is provided in specific areas identified as priorities.

Experiments

An agile approach is piloted on an exploratory project using an external coach to support the new way of working.

Reward and recognition

The CIO uses regular departmental briefings to recognize innovators.

Using networks

Staff are encouraged to participate in external professional networks and attend conferences – with an emphasis on bringing back ideas to share with colleagues.

THE ROLE OF THE TOOLKIT[T]

Background

Earlier in the book we provided a brief introduction to patterns. We now make some links to thinking about knowledge management and organizational learning.

Thinking on *patterns* has developed from a number of sources, including the work of Alexander et al. (1977) in architecture. In essence, a pattern is an outline of 'what works' based on observation of practice. Software developers have adopted the concept of 'patterns', and more recently patterns have been used by those interested in software development processes and IT education (Coplein and Harrison, 2005).

From an IT development perspective Nandhakumar and Avison (1999) highlight the limitations of formal methodologies, which often represent only a 'convenient fiction', to provide an appearance of control, but bear little relationship to how work actually gets done: the methodology represents a focus on the formal process rather than the actual *practices* that relate to how people do their work. Brown and Duguid (2000; see Chapter 4) provide a similar critique of business process re-engineering.

Practices and patterns

'Practice' is an increasingly widely used term, and a range of descriptions and definitions have emerged. Wenger et al. (2002) suggest the following definition: 'a set of socially defined ways of doing things in a specific domain: a set of common approaches and shared standards that create a basis for action, problem solving, performance and accountability'.

Not only does the concept of a practice appear to be very closely aligned with how people actually work, but it is also particularly relevant in knowledge-intensive activities, such as IT projects, where much of the effort is based on the experiences of individual and teams. Moreover, the concept of practice relates to the informal organization and how work is actually done by individuals and groups.

For our purposes we have made the following distinction:

- A *practice* relates to an approach to getting work done in a specific context. Some authors refer to practices as 'routines'. Practices are what people do within your organization.

- A *pattern* is an abstraction, a description of a practice. It must lose some of the richness and uniqueness of the related practice, but it provides a way to identify and communicate what works. We have used the concept of patterns as a basis for the benefits-driven toolkit for IT-enabled change.

In this book we have provided brief outlines of some of the tools to contribute to the adoption of the specific ideas. The idea of 'tools' and the format of a 'pattern' provides a valuable way for an organization to approach capturing and sharing good practices identified locally.

Practices, knowledge management and organizational learning

An important strand of thinking about knowledge management is the distinction between explicit and tacit knowledge. This categorization of knowledge as either explicit or tacit is likely to be misleading: there are different levels of tacit knowledge and of skills. In some cases, important aspects of tacit knowledge can be made explicit while retaining much of its value. For example, some 'tacit skills could be articulated readily if organizational members were simply asked the question "how do you do that?"' (Ambrosini and Bowman, 2001).

Thompson and Walsham (2004) showed that, if knowledge is to remain useful once made explicit, a link with the *context* in which the knowledge was used and so in which it might be reused must be retained. They also noted that, while the ideal of 'strictly explicit knowledge is self-contradictory', there are still opportunities to codify some aspects of knowledge that will be useful, particularly with a specific context as provided by, for example, a community of practice. Kamoche et al. (2003) use the jazz metaphor of improvisation in suggesting that there is an 'optimal amount of structure'.

The jazz analogy is that skilled professionals, whether jazz musicians or people engaged in a multi-disciplinary team to deliver IT-enabled change, need some common understanding to work together. This is not a score to follow note by note but a common language: common ways of working provided, for example, by the benefits principles and toolkit.

The tension between codifying nothing, thereby risking the loss of important information, and trying to codify everything, risking banality, is at the very core of attempts at knowledge management.

The codification of practice into knowledge is of its essence an active and social task 'connecting people so that they can think together' (Alvesson and Karreman, 2001), bringing together different people with different experience and enabling them to contribute their knowledge in a team (Becker, 2001). The goal is to enable group learning by the 'sharing of individual interpretations to develop a common understanding' (Bontis et al., 2002).

In summary: the format provided by a pattern provides a powerful way to capture and share knowledge in complex, knowledge-intensive environments where it is impossible to make key aspects of knowledge fully explicit. This is the foundation for the concept and structure of the benefits toolkit.

The skilled professionals engaged in projects are not followers of rigid methods but highly motivated 'craftsmen', passionate about the job and skilled in using a range of tools, which they can adapt, based on experience to the specific situation they are facing. Building the capability for benefits realization into an organization is at its core an issue of broad and skilled adoption of key practices.

FIRST STEPS TO A BENEFITS-DRIVEN APPROACH

Benefits review (Evaluate) is a classic area where common sense is far from common practice. It is also one of the best places to start with a benefits-driven approach. Carry out benefits reviews of recently completed and a few in-progress projects and see what you learn. Then make some targeted improvements, and use the learning to plan broader adoption of benefits-driven ways of working.

BUILDING COMPETENCES FOR BENEFITS REALIZATION

FROM PROJECT FRAMEWORK TO ORGANIZATIONAL COMPETENCES

The idea of a 'benefits realization capability' is particularly relevant to the challenge of benefits realization from investments in IT, as it encourages exploration of the organization as a whole, going beyond individual projects and the role of the IT function. In this book we are making use of a model of the organizational competences that contribute to this benefits realization capability.

We use the following definitions:

Benefits realization . . .

- delivering value to customers and other stakeholders, and improving organizational performance through benefits-driven programmes and projects of IT-enabled change.

Benefits realization capability . . .

- the organization-wide capability to consistently realize value from investments in IT-enabled change and transformation.

FRAMEWORK OF COMPETENCES

The benefits realization capability of an organization comprises four distinct yet highly interrelated competences (Ashurst et al., 2008, Figure 5.1).

- **benefits planning**: benefits do not simply emerge, as if by magic, from the introduction of a new technology – their realization needs to be carefully planned and managed from the very beginning of thinking about any investment in change. Benefits planning includes a strategic perspective, enabling innovation and deciding which projects to undertake, as well as benefits-focused planning of individual projects.

- **benefits delivery**: benefits primarily arise from the organizational change that accompanies an IT implementation, rather than directly from the technology itself. The benefits and related changes need to be the focus of activity.

- **benefits review**: organizations must monitor and evaluate results on an ongoing basis. This will improve the results of individual projects and ensure that the organization's ability to deliver business value improves over time.

- **benefits exploitation**: the quest to leverage benefits from business software should not cease as soon as it has been implemented. Continued focus is required over the life of the investment.

These competences have both explicit and tacit elements and can be hard for managers to deal with. One way of bringing a competence to life is through adoption of a *toolkit* of *practices*, each of which can be tailored to the needs and circumstances of a specific organization. The concept of a 'practice' is a way to capture and communicate 'what works', how to get things done.

A competence is essentially 'the ability to . . .' – in this case, 'realize benefits from IT-enabled organizational change'. It is important to emphasize this

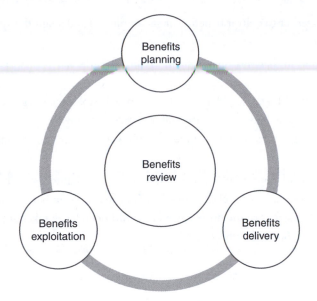

Figure 5.1 Organizational competences for benefits realization

view of competences and capabilities, as the real management challenge is building these competences, rather than success with any particular project. Later chapters explore wider perspectives on these competences for benefits realization: for example, strategy and portfolio management. Capability development is the focus of Chapter 14.

IN SUMMARY

In this chapter we have explored the Evaluate stage of the project lifecycle. Evaluate builds on the post-implementation review of benefits and lessons learned that is part of most project lifecycles. We adopt a clear benefits focus and emphasize the important of ensuring the review takes place as a key driver of learning and benefits realization for the individual project and the wider organization.

In chapters 2–5 we have explored the principles and practices of a benefits-driven approach to IT projects and delivering change. In the context of competing with IT this is a major subject area. Strategy without implementation and hence results is a waste of time. These results come from implementing the strategy through benefits-driven projects and programmes.

The e^{4+1} framework and toolkit can be applied to a very wide variety of projects. In every case it's important to focus on the goal (i.e., enabling a team to work together to deliver benefits for stakeholders) and adapt the approach as necessary.

Research in benefits management (Lin and Pervan, 2003; Lin et al., 2005) suggests there may be some progress in the adoption of benefits-led approaches to IT-enabled change. More general experience suggests there is still a major gap between theory and practice. In most cases a number of relatively small steps to adopt initial benefits 'tools' can start to make a big difference.

The Expand stage of e^{++1}, discussed in the next chapter, goes beyond the scope of traditional approaches to projects. There are a number of implications for the earlier stages of the project, which would need to be taken into account alongside the topics already covered.

TAKING IT FURTHER

FURTHER READING AND RESOURCES

There are many avenues for further reading, using the references as a starting-point. Suggestions include:

TEAMWORK

Ancona, Deborah, Bresman, Henrik, Kaeufer, Katrin (2002) The Comparative Advantage of X-Teams. *MIT Sloan Management Review*, Spring 2002, Vol. 43 (3): 33–39.

Agile Approaches to Projects
Boehm, B. and Turner, R. (2004) *Balancing Agility and Discipline: A Guide for the Perplexed*, Addison-Wesley, Boston, MA.

Learning and Sharing Knowledge
Garvin, D.A. (1993) Building a Learning Organization. *Harvard Business Review*, July–August, Vol. 71 (4): 78–91.

Wenger, W., McDermott, R. and Snyder, W.M. (2002) *Cultivating Communities of Practice*, Boston: Harvard Business School Press.

IT Project Evaluation
Farbey, B., Land, F. and Targett, D. (1993) *How to Assess Your IT Investment*, Butterworth-Heinemann, Oxford.

Farbey, B., Land, F. and Targett, D. (1999) Moving IS Evaluation Forward: Learning Themes and Research Issues. *Journal of Strategic Information Systems*, Vol. 8: 189–207.

Walsham, G. (1999) Interpretive Evaluation Systems Design for Information Systems, in Willcocks, L. and Lester, S. (eds.) *Beyond the IT Productivity Paradox*, Wiley, Chichester.

TALKING POINTS

Use these questions to help reflect on this chapter and explore the challenges of putting the ideas into practice:

1. Consider practice in your organization: how consistently/effectively is the benefits review carried out?

2. How might power and politics interfere with evaluation of the results of a project?

3. How would you judge whether you had a good measure and set of measures for a particular project?

4. What might a scorecard (set of metrics) evaluating all projects in an organization contain?

5. How do professionals learn? What are the implications for improving project practice and sharing learning?

6. How is learning captured and shared across projects in your organization?

7. What additional practices could we add to the toolkit for benefits realization?

8. How does a focus on developing organizational competences for benefits realization differ from implementing a new project methodology?

9. How does the competence for benefits review differ from, or perhaps build on, the Evaluate stage of the project lifecycle?

KEY DEBATES

Power and politics

It is true that benefits-driven projects are really about people – the sponsor, the projects manager and team, benefits owners, the project board, many other stakeholders. Even which projects are selected for investment can be seen as largely a political decision, influenced by the power of the actors involved.

One response to this is to focus directly on power and politics as the way to achieve success. The project process and toolkit are seen as having limited impact.

What is your view and experience? Acknowledging the importance of communication, power and politics, what is the role of the framework and toolkit for benefits realization? How might we extend the toolkit to address power and politics more directly?

CASE STUDY 5.1

The case explores evaluation of impact and knowledge-sharing.

Journal of Information Technology Teaching Cases, Vol. 3 (2013): 43–50.

SYSCO's best business practices (BBPs)

Daniel E. O'Leary

The purpose of this paper is to present a case about SYSCO's 'Best Business Practices' (BBPs). The analysis focuses on both the system and the impact of the system, particularly the measurable effects and the overall organizational impact. Perhaps the most interesting issue is how a system for BBPs is used to manage a highly decentralized firm and push the individual corporate entities to better performance, without requiring specific processes or best practices. Use of the system is illustrated through an example.

REFERENCES

Alexander, C., Ishikawa, S. and Silverstein, M. (1977) *A Pattern Language*, New York: Oxford University Press.

Alvesson, M. and Karreman, D. (2001) Odd Couple: Making Sense of the Curious Concept of Knowledge Management. *Journal of Management Studies*, Vol. 38 (7): 995–1018.

Ambrosini, V. and Bowman, C. (2001) Tacit Knowledge: Some Suggestions for Operationalization. *Journal of Management Studies*, Vol. 38 (6): 811–829.

Ashurst, C., Doherty, N.F. and Peppard, J. (2008) Improving the Impact of IT Development Projects: The Benefits Realization Capability Model. *European Journal of Information Systems*, Vol. 17 (4): 352–370.

Becker, M. (2001) Managing Dispersed Knowledge: Organizational Problems, Managerial Strategies, and Their Effectiveness. *Journal of Management Studies*, Vol. 38 (7): 1037–1051.

Bontis, N., Crossman, M. and Hulland, J. (2002) Managing and Organizational Learning System by Aligning Stocks and Flows. *Journal of Management Studies*, Vol. 39 (4): 437–469.

Brown, J.S. and Duguid, P. (2000) *The Social Life of Information*, Boston: Harvard Business School Press.

Coplein, J. and Harrison, N. (2005) *Organizational Patterns for Agile Software Development*, Pearson Prentice Hall.

Farbey, B., Land, F.F. and Targett, D. (1995) A Taxonomy of Information Systems Applications – The Benefits Evaluation Ladder. *European Journal of Information Systems*, Vol. 4 (1): 41–50.

Farbey, B., Land, F. and Targett, D. (1999) Moving IS Evaluation Forward: Learning Themes and Research Issues. *Journal of Strategic Information Systems*, Vol. 8: 189–207.

Garvin, D.A. (1993) Building a Learning Organization. *Harvard Business Review*, July–August, Vol. 71 (4): 78–91.

Garvin, D.A. (2000) *Learning in Action: Putting the Learning Organization to Work*, Harvard Business School Press.

Kamoche, K., Pina e Cunha, M. and Vieira da Cunha, J. (2003) Towards a Theory of Organizational Improvisation: Looking Beyond the Jazz Metaphor. *Journal of Management Studies*, Vol. 40 (8): 2023–2051.

Kaplan, R.S. and Norton, D.P. (1993) Putting the Balanced Scorecard to Work. *Harvard Business Review*, September–October, 71 (5): 134–147, 2–16.

Lin, C. and Pervan, G. (2003) The Practice of IS/IT Benefits Management in Large Australian Organizations. *Information & Management*, Vol. 41 (1): 13–24.

Lin, C., Pervan, G. and McDermid, D. (2005) IS/IT Investment Evaluation and Benefits Realization Issues in Australia. *Journal of Research and Practice in Information Technology*, Vol. 37 (3): 235–251.

Nandhakumar, J. and Avison, D. (1999) The Fiction of Methodological Development: A Field Study of Information Systems. *Information Technology and People*, Vol. 12 (2): 176–191.

Neely, A., Adams, C. and Kennerley, M. (2002) *The Performance Prism: The Scorecard for Measuring and Managing Business Success*, London: FT Prentice Hall.

Pfeffer, J. and Sutton, R. (1999) Knowing 'What' to Do Is Not Enough. *California Management Review*, Vol. 42 (1): 83–108.

Pfeffer, J. and Sutton, R. (2004) *The Knowing-Doing Gap: How Smart Companies Turn Knowledge into Action*, Boston, MA: Harvard Business School Press.

Serafeimidis, V. and Smithson, S. (1999) Rethinking Approaches to Information Systems Investment Evaluation, *Logistics Information Management*, Vol. 12 (1/2): 94–107.

Serafeimidis, V. and Smithson, S. (2000) Information Systems Evaluation in Practice: A Case Study of Organizational Change. *Journal of Information Technology*, Vol. 15 (2): 93–105.

Thompson, M. and Walsham, G. (2004) Placing Knowledge Management in Context. *Journal of Management Studies*, Vol. 41 (5): 725–747.

Walsham, G. (1999) Interpretive Evaluation Systems Design for Information Systems, in Willcocks and Lester (eds.) *Beyond the IT Productivity Paradox*, Chichester: Wiley.

Ward, J. and Murray, P. (2000) *Benefits Management Best Practice Guidelines*, Cranfield.

Ward, J., Taylor, P. and Bond, P. (1996) Evaluation and Realization of IS/IT Benefits: An Empirical Study of Current Practice. *European Journal of Information Systems*, Vol. 4: 214–225.

Wenger, W., McDermott, R. and Snyder, W.M. (2002) *Cultivating Communities of Practice*, Harvard Business School Press.

CHAPTER 6
MAKING THE MOST OF INVESTMENTS IN IT

IN THIS CHAPTER WE STUDY:

- activities following a project to harvest the benefits;
- using IT to contribute to knowledge worker productivity;
- business capabilities required to take advantage of the potential of IT, including business process, information and knowledge management;
- the implications of working harder to realize benefits from existing information and IT.

GOING BEYOND PROJECT DELIVERY

The implicit assumption in the approach to many IT projects is that, when the technology goes live, the benefit will be realized. On this basis the project team is often disbanded seven or 14 days after 'go live', with a tiny core of people with technical skills kept available for bug-fixing. The rest move rapidly onto other projects.

The reality is that the technology going live is just an important milestone on the journey to benefits realization. When the technology is implemented, benefits realization has only just started. This chapter explores post-project benefits realization during the lifetime of the new systems and business processes. This is the Expand phase of the e^{4+1} lifecycle introduced in chapters 2 to 5.

We also explore the neglected area of exploiting IT to enable knowledge worker productivity, as this illustrates many of the general issues of post-project benefits realization. There are significant implication for systems design, project delivery and the scope of IT services.

Drawing on the discussion of Expand and knowledge worker productivity, we then look at some of the broader issues of developing the organizational capability to realize benefits from IT – with an emphasis on the 'benefits exploitation' competence (Ashurst et al., 2008). This means we need to consider important perspectives on the use of IT, including business process management, information management/business intelligence and knowledge management.

In this area, as in many others addressed in the book, there are many opportunities for action at a local level, whatever your role in the organization.

FROM INDUSTRIAL TECHNOLOGY TO INTELLECTUAL TECHNOLOGY

Many IT projects are not straightforward cases of 'adoption' of new technology. A new technology can be put to a very wide variety of uses within an organization, and benefits realization depends not just on the technology but also on complementary organizational resources and competences (Melville et al., 2004). Lee (1999, p. 7) makes a similar point and suggests: 'There are rich organizational and political processes whereby a set of information technology is instantiated and there are also rich organizational and political processes pertaining to the continual managing, maintaining and changing of the information technology instantiation'.

These perspectives support the view that value is not about the technology. It is about how it is *used* by people within the context of on organization comprising processes, information flows, structures and performance measures (and many other dimensions).

Lee (1999) also suggests 'MIS involves information technology as a form of *intellectual* technology'. Information technology is an intellectual technology, not an industrial technology, in that it has properties that are not fixed on implementation but which can be 'innovated endlessly, depending on its interaction with the intellect of the human beings who implement and use it' (Lee, 1999, p. 8). This can lead to an ongoing cycle of innovation and change as the technology extends the intellects of its users, leading to further innovation.

Ongoing innovation works at many levels. In some cases – for example, high-volume transaction processing systems in the supply chain at a retailer – the scope for innovation in the short term is limited. But even in these cases, performance – for example, in terms of stock outs and waste – may differ considerably from one store to the next, showing the importance of the people involved. In other situations, as we'll explore when we consider knowledge worker productivity, there are high levels of innovation as individuals and teams make use of widely available technologies to enable innovation in working practices.

Another perspective is that IT products can be used in scenarios not envisaged by the supplier. I remember clearly working with friends and colleagues at Microsoft when BizTalk was introduced as a systems integration and business process management middleware product. Consultants using it with early-adopter customers found that the processing times were so good that it could be used for handling some of the complex integration required at the front end of a website, not just background transactions handling fulfilment of orders. A whole new range of opportunities for using the technology emerged from use. As we noted earlier: 'customers invariably use technological systems in ways different from how they were designed or produced' (Garud, 1997).

This suggests a much more complex process than 'adoption' or diffusion of an innovation. Thomke and von Hippel (2002) make a related point in their proposal for the provision of 'toolkits' to enable customers to be a key part of innovation activity. Many IT products effectively provide the organization or the individual with a toolkit that enables ongoing innovation.

There are almost certainly macro and micro level processes to manage here. At a macro level, the use of programmes containing multiple projects and the core idea of 'versioned release' is a key way to build in opportunities for learning and evolution. At a micro level, benefits exploitation (Ashurst et al., 2008) provides a focus on developing a key capability across an organization, which in many cases involves further local innovation as the IT is used.

TACKLING KEY RISKS TO BENEFITS REALIZATION

The goal of an organization making an investment in IT is benefits realization over the lifetime of the investment. Post-project focus on benefits realization and benefits exploitation is an important area often neglected by organizations.

In our recent project Exploring Business Transformation (Ashurst and Hodges, 2010), which involved 65 interviews with business and IT managers from a very wide range of organizations, we covered the area of benefits exploitation. Very often, it is left to chance: 'end users of systems lack knowledge – it's a case of loss of knowledge through staff turnover and passing on knowledge informally from one to the other' (business manager, financial services). The knowledge of what is possible and how to realize the full potential of the new technology is quickly fragmented and lost. When many organizations are still using systems 20 or more years old, this is an important area. This view was reinforced in our recent survey of senior business managers, where exploitation of existing systems and information was the area of lowest satisfaction when we explored how effectively benefits are being realized from IT.

Risk management can play a constructive role in benefits realization, not least because many of the things that go wrong are very predictable. Key risks that we address in this chapter include:

- keeping a focus on information use;
- providing an opportunity for continued learning after delivery of the technology solution;
- hitting a moving target – managing investments in IT-enabled change where the business is already changing rapidly;
- preparing the organization for further change. The outcome of the change programme will be a 'change-ready' organization equipped for further change, rather than an organization which has simply changed from one state to another.

Keeping a focus on information use

Although we talk about *information* systems and *information* technology, we often focus on the system/technology rather than the information itself. We can do more to focus on the information and how it is used by different stakeholders in decision-making, providing a service for customers and in monitoring and controlling the overall system. One of the classic challenges for a benefits-led approach is that we don't have the information to assess the current situation or to track the intended benefits from the investment.

Approach to projects – Providing an opportunity for learning

Many organizations have traditionally adopted a very technical mindset when approaching major IT projects. Introducing a major system across multiple sites in a large organization, perhaps retail or banking, is treated as a manufacturing situation: get the design right, test it, then deploy the technology solution in lots of places.

While this model is certainly helpful and it is important to capture economies of scale, there are major areas of risk. The time for an effective pilot, perhaps in one or more initial branches, stores or business units, is often squeezed because of the rush to finish the project or delays at earlier stages in the process.

As a result, although a pilot does take place, there is no time to listen to feedback or respond with changes beyond dealing with major technical flaws (poor response times, clear faults in functionality highlighted by testing). In many cases what this means in practice is that the system is effectively fixed and that all that is being piloted is the deployment and training as implementation teams gear up for wider roll-out. Any real space for learning is squeezed out because of the tight timescales and the major investments made in training materials and training trainers and implementation teams.

Wider learning opportunities of how best to work with the technology to realize benefits often get forced out. A major contributing factor is a lack of investment in the non-technical aspects of a project. Clegg et al. (1997) highlighted major sources of project failure and suggested that around 50% of project effort and budgets should relate to people rather than technology. This is often neglected. These problems reflect the difficulty faced by the project team and the end-users and other stakeholders in working together and understanding what is possible.

Often it makes sense to take more time at the early stages in order to go faster to overall benefits realization. This would mean an earlier, more informal, pilot where there is genuine opportunity for learning. Training and implementation approaches might then emerge based on the learning.

A second major challenge is to provide for learning at each local level (store, branch, department, team). Even in a very standardized operation (McDonald's, perhaps) there will be some need for limited and informal localization. In many cases the challenges will be significant: for example, a foreign subsidiary with 200 staff where the parent has 10,000. On paper processes may seem very similar, but in practice the differences are significant. For example, in the US the scale might mean staff specialize and can take the time to learn complex systems; in the subsidiary they will have to cover a wider range of roles and will only be occasional users of specific IT functionality. Even where organizations are fairly similar – perhaps rolling out self-service functionality from the human resources and payroll system to the many academic schools and departments across a university – there is a need for learning at a local level, because the benefits arise from people doing things differently and there is inevitably a change process for individuals and local organizations.

From a change management perspective a key response to this risk has been to address how to embed and sustain change. The aim is to ensure that new ways of working are adopted and that the organization does not revert to working how it has always worked, but with a new system in place.

Hitting a moving target

The challenge is not simply understanding a relatively stable situation and introducing IT and wider business changes to move to a new, but relatively stable situation. The business areas targeted by the investment are in a constant state of flux, driven by both external and internal factors. The changes required to achieve any particular desired outcomes are at best only partially understood. Also, from an intellectual technology perspective we know that the introduction of new technology is itself going to drive further change and innovation.

The innovation and change will almost certainly need to continue beyond the end of any project or programme and will need to be considered as part of the continuing management of business activities. This is where the organizational competence of benefits exploitation fits. It is much wider than an aspect of the project lifecycle.

Preparing the organization for further change

The fact that we are trying to hit a moving target is much more than a problem that makes change difficult. In a sense it is part of what success looks like. We want the organization to be a moving target: ongoing improvement, change and innovation at many levels are what we are enabling as we establish the benefits realization capability of the organization. The capability is required for the small number of strategic transformation projects, and needs to be embedded across the organization for continuous, local and incremental change.

In this section we address these risks in a number of ways. This is an area typically neglected by organizations, which is a crucial part of the benefits realization capability and where there are opportunities for action at a local and organizational level. In Chapter 14 we return to these themes in the context of developing the overall IT capability of the organization.

EXPAND

FOCUS ON EXPAND AND BENEFITS EXPLOITATION TO ENABLE BENEFITS REALIZATION

From a project perspective the e^{4+1} framework for a project includes the Expand stage to highlight the importance of this area and establish key practices.

In this chapter we address both the Expand stage of the project lifecycle and wider aspects of benefits exploitation. We take the view that these are crucial factors in benefits realization.

EXPAND IN THE CONTEXT OF THE EARLIER STAGES OF THE PROJECT

During earlier stages of the project work will have taken place on designing new working practices and business processes to contribute to benefits realization. These will have been documented in some form and will have become a basis for final stages of testing and for pilot training and implementation as part of the overall change plan enabling 'people to do things differently'.

Expand is a key enabler of benefits realization and needs to be considered from the beginning of the project, not least in terms of the structure and staffing of the team. Key considerations at the Expand stage include:

- going beyond delivering training for users during initial implementation to provision for ongoing user support and training as staff move on and new users arrive;

- going beyond fixing bugs to proactive support to enable end-users and the organization to get the most from the solution in the context of ongoing changes to the business;

- going beyond implementation to developing the ability to evolve and adapt in response to business changes and as new opportunities to improve efficiency and effectiveness are discovered. This might be reflected in the original software selection, in the overall solution design, and how processes and guidance for users are documented so that they can be updated and changes communicated and implemented.

- going beyond handover from a project team to line or operational management to developing the knowledge and competences for benefits realization during the life of the system. There is a risk of losing vital knowledge of the business system at this stage. In most cases it is important to keep relevant members of the project team available during a transition period as benefits are established. A key outcome of the project is the capability for continued change and improvement. This is likely to require a major emphasis on building the capability to lead benefits-driven change in business areas;

- going beyond getting benefits from a specific system to tackling wider issues of digital literacy and knowledge worker productivity to enable the organization to build the overall capability to realize benefits from IT.

It is vital to consider Expand as an integral part of the project and to address relevant issues from the beginning. The potential contribution to controlling project and lifecycle costs and ensuring effective benefits realization is critical. For example, decisions about the project and solution, perhaps reducing the need for training, may need to be made at an early stage.

One approach is to consider Expand from the perspective of service management and to see this stage as the handover from project to operational management (see Box 6.1).

Box 6.1   Service management

Business and IT service management is well defined in standards such as ITIL®and ISO/IEC 20000 and forms part of the IT-CMF capability framework.

From an IT perspective, service management is commonly seen as the day-to-day management of the IT infrastructure and operation of systems in terms of security, back-up, help desk and user support. It has evolved from the days when IT operators placed tapes in the machines and ran jobs manually. Service management typically involves a significant proportion of people and budgets, with >70% of the IT budget devoted to current systems.

From the business perspective service management provides a focus on customer service and value, going beyond the potentially internal orientation of business process management.

From a business perspective it is important to consider the overall customer experience and service from the beginning of the project. And from both a business and an IT perspective service management considerations will be key drivers of the project, for example:

- ensuring that alerts are built in, highlighting potential delays to customer orders and prompting action;

- enabling system changes responding to faults to be implemented with no impact on customers.

Practices in the area of Expand are not yet well defined, so as a starting-point we will share some ideas through a case study. I've used an example of a major system from the university context – this draws on a case study carried out as part of a research project (Ashurst, 2012). See example practices in Box 6.2.

Box 6.2 Examples of practices for Expand

A regular review of e-Learning environment (eL) usage, including an annual end-user survey, is carried out to understand satisfaction, identify problems and opportunities, and to provide input into future developments.

An annual user conference, which provides an opportunity for end-users to share how they are using the system and for good ideas to be communicated. The team provides additional input to the conference based on their work with the solution providers, and other organizations using the software.

Regular updates to help guides and training courses that address how to get the most value from the system. Help information is now provided in the form of a wiki, enabling broad participation in sharing ideas and advice.

Consultancy services to end-users, and user departments, with the aim of tackling specific projects to help them realize additional value from using the system: 'we'll put in time to run a series of short seminars to provide updates on the new features and then we can work one-to-one with people who want specific advice.'

How can these practices be adapted for your context?

At a university, one of the major systems is the eL, which is used by all members of teaching staff and all students. eL has a great many capabilities and can be used in many different ways to contribute to learning and the student experience. At a basic level, it is a way of making lecture notes available to students. At another level, it allows discussion groups, podcasts, wikis and interactive exercises. Which of these capabilities are used depends on the knowledge and interests of each member of staff and how they see eL helping their students.

eL is a good example of an IT system as a form of *intellectual* technology. Individual teaching staff will use different elements of the system and use them in a wide variety of ways, often coming up with novel and valuable approaches, which would be of interest to other colleagues. This is a real challenge for many IT functions where the approach to projects is designed for an industrial technology – the way the system will be used is defined as part of the design and implementation. This approach might have worked for automating transactions, but it is much less helpful when we use IT to help professional and knowledge workers.

The case study university has some good practices in place, which address the need for benefits exploitation – for continued learning and innovation. There is leadership for the usage and exploitation of eL across the organization with support from a small, central team: 'our aim is to work with academic staff to help them enhance learning for students.' Responsibilities of the team include testing and releasing regular upgrades from the software suppliers, support and training for users, sharing good ideas and good practice. The team has a strong mixture of technical and business skills, in this case expertise in the design of eL.

The impact of these practices is to encourage gradual benefits exploitation as individuals and departments experiment and innovate, building on existing usage. This scale of investment is certainly not appropriate in every case, but it is here, as teaching and learning are the core business of the university. The example does demonstrate some good practices that can be adapted for different scenarios in many types of organizations.

KEY PRACTICES FOR EXPAND

Key practices to consider include:

- benefits-led training (and education);
- evaluation – ongoing benefits review;
- team design;
- super users;
- governance framework;
- portfolio perspective.

The discussion about knowledge worker productivity, business intelligence and knowledge management in the later part of the chapter is also directly relevant.

Benefits-led training and education

Training and education are important factors in realizing benefits. Training/educational activities should address the contribution of the project to organizational performance and focus on how benefits are realized, rather than just on how to use the IS/IT system. Very often there is underinvestment in this area. It is important to design the training with a benefits focus as part of the wider activity to realize benefits. It is also important to design the training in such a way that changes during the life of the project can be accommodated effectively. Also there will be a need for continued provision of training to meet the needs of new staff as well as to enable continued learning and fuller exploitation of the system.

The product manager and user experience lead (see the team model in Chapter 3) often work together to develop an educational programme before, during and after the cutover to the new system and the implementation of organizational changes. The education starts with why the changes were required (business drivers) and highlights the intended benefits for different stakeholders.

The aim of the educational programme is to equip participants to realize the intended benefits. By taking a broader perspective, participants are better able to contribute to successful benefits realization than if they had simply been shown what 'buttons to press'. In one case study (Ashurst, 2012, Chapter 5) the project was part of a programme of activity to improve customer service. The team took the decision to start with education to develop the customer service focus of the department; systems changes and related education followed some time later.

Evaluate – ongoing benefits review

Evaluate provides an important starting-point for consideration of Expand. The focus on benefits realized, and specifically on opportunities for realizing further benefits naturally provides a link into Expand.

The benefits review[T] applies through the life of the systems as at earlier stages of the project lifecycle. The review provides the basis for an annual review of benefits realization and consideration of further opportunities for improvement as part of a phased delivery strategy and also in response to changing customer needs and evolving business capabilities.

An important opportunity is to carry out a benefits review periodically during the operational life of a system (perhaps better to focus on the operational service or the wider business process). This is a natural fit where there is the concept of business ownership of systems and a relationship management role in IT. However, the tools can be applied regardless of formal structures.

Team design

There are two main drivers for ongoing change following the introduction of a new investment: firstly, changes to customer expectations and market conditions; and secondly, gradual learning about what the system can do and how to work most effectively to realize benefits. Depending on the priority of the business area, it is important to provide support to enable practices to evolve to respond to these drivers and to share new learning and innovations.

Where there is a particularly important and widely used service – for example, as in the eLearning example in the university case – it may be appropriate to have a team in place dedicated to continued benefits realization. The team will need a range of skills, including knowledge of the technology and the business domain. Their role could include providing formal courses, providing help materials supported by email and telephone, organizing good practice sharing sessions, providing workshops on new features, providing advice and consultancy on how to make use of the features available to support learning objectives. One strategy is to incorporate these roles as part of a wide service improvement capability within a business area.

Super users

In a large organization major systems will be used in many different departments. Benefits exploitation will require system and business process expertise distributed across the organization. Provision of training – for example, for new staff – is helpful but by itself may not be enough.

For many important systems and processes it can be helpful to encourage the development of 'super users': individuals with an interest and aptitude who can develop higher levels of knowledge and can provide support and advice to colleagues. These individuals can also provide the core of a user community for a central team to work with.

The development of super users can be encouraged through the normal staff development process. It can be applied in many situations. It is likely that different individuals will develop operational/process expertise and others management information and control/analytical expertise. The idea can work with major 'line of business systems' (ERP, CRM, etc.) and also with the much-neglected office systems (Word, Excel, etc.) that are used by many people for many hours each week.

Governance framework

Just as there is no single best design for a project governance framework, so there is no single right answer for the framework required to support and encourage ongoing benefits realization. An important starting-point is to make a distinction between the programme or project that is bringing about change and the ongoing operational management of the business activities.

For example, in one recent case study the 'project' that participants referred to was actually a strategic programme, made up of a number of individual projects, and also the ongoing management of a business service that had resulted from initial projects within the programme. The service now had several thousand users across significant areas of the organization. The important point is not what the elements were called; this is not a pedantic point. The key thing is that the different elements had not been differentiated, and as a result they were not being managed in the most effective ways. There was one governance structure working across the 'project', which in fact was a programme, collection of projects and business service. To illustrate some of the different considerations:

Project: are we on track to deliver a solution that will provide the intended benefits within planned constrained of time and cost?

Programme: what can we learn from work to date that will help shape the next projects to achieve the strategic objectives?

Service: what are we learning from working with end-users that we can use to inform training for future users, enhance help desk and support processes, and influence the detail of further projects?

At this stage the two elements of the ambidextrous organization are coming together in the transition from Explore to Exploit: exploring and innovating to create the 'business for tomorrow' and at the same time making sure that the 'business of today' operates effectively and continues to develop. It is not surprising that there are often problems, as there are differences in culture and the competences required. It can be helpful to try and establish a common language that helps the individuals involved talk about the different concepts – project, programme and service management. Box 6.3 provides further examples of approaches to continued benefits realization.

Box 6.3   Maintaining a focus on benefits: Examples of approaches adopted

Systems administration team

The organization implemented a major ERP system, with the finance function taking a lead role. A new team was established to take responsibility for the use of the system, including: continuing to develop reports, maintaining master data including coding structures, user training and support in terms of how best to use the systems.

Value assurance team

The value assurance team was established as part of a major ERP project. Their focus was to work with end-user teams to help ensure target benefits were being realized and to be a catalyst for identifying and acting on new opportunities.

Productivity coach

The organization had implemented SharePoint to support internal collaboration and effective working for teams and departments. The productivity coach, who also had in-depth knowledge of the related Office products, worked with small groups of end-users to identify opportunities and support implementation. The aims were to tackle local issues, build expertise and share good practices and solutions (e.g., templates for sites).

PORTFOLIO PERSPECTIVE

It is important here, as elsewhere, to take a portfolio approach. Flexibility and continued benefits realization come at a cost. It is important to match the level of investment in terms of management attention and resources to the situation. The IT and Change Portfolio provides insight into the strategic contribution of the system and business process. Factors to consider also include: number of users; number of customers and other stakeholders affected; staff turnover in user and operational management roles; day-to-day flexibility required and extent of change; nature of business activity and approach taken to management (e.g., from top-down control of a transactional process to individuals and teams of professionals and knowledge workers with significant autonomy).

At the portfolio level consideration of benefits exploitation shifts the focus from management of investment in change to management of systems/services/processes over their full lifecycle. There are significant technical considerations, including fit with the evolving technical infrastructure, continued vendor support and availability of technical skills for support and maintenance. There are also significant business issues, as we have noted. The portfolio perspective provides an overview across the organization to ensure clear accountabilities for continued benefits realization and to manage a periodic review process.

There will inevitably be a need for business and IT involvement in benefits exploitation. The perspective provides a basis for a valuable discussion about how different areas of the organization can work together to sustain and develop benefits. The portfolio perspective provides a good starting-point for building a focus on benefits exploitation at a local level in a business unit or department. It provides a valuable element of a wider business planning process (Box 6.4).

Box 6.4   Benefits exploitation: Using the portfolio within a business unit/department/team

The portfolio provides an important contribution to strategic management at any level of the organization. Depending on the context, the constraints vary. For example, at a team level many of the systems are given and the question becomes how can we best use the existing systems and information. Even at a very local level there will be many options to realize value from Office and Cloud solutions.

As part of a strategic review (annual planning) a team can consider the following questions using the IT and Change Portfolio to help structure and prioritize.

Bottom-up

- What systems do we currently use?

- How important are they to our day-to-day operations?

- What more can we do to take advantage of the information and services provided by these systems to create value for stakeholders and to work more effectively?

Top-down

- What are the key strategic goals and objectives for the organization and team?

- What business processes are required to deliver value to stakeholders? What knowledge and information is are required? How effectively are these needs met by current systems?

- What are the key decisions being made, and what information is required? Is this information available?

- What are the key performance measures, and how effectively are we able to measure them?

- What expertise is there in the team of for using the capabilities of key systems? How are we making use of and continuing to develop that expertise?

- What are the priorities for action?

DESIGNING THE APPROACH TO EXPAND

Here, as elsewhere, the practices for benefits realization are very scalable and can be applied in the smallest team or organization. There is no need for a top-down approach or senior management support in order to start to make a difference. Then, depending on the level of the organization at which the practices are applied, the scope, effort and degrees of freedom for action will change.

Expand is also a lot more than ongoing benefits review and evaluation of the benefits. Planning for this stage of the project should start at the earliest stage, with consideration of the nature of the problem and the overall approach being taken to benefits realization. There will be implications for team design and the overall structure and phasing of the project.

For example, is this a traditional IT scenario which requires automation and high-volume transaction processing, perhaps an Internet e-commerce solution? Or is this a scenario where the project will effectively deliver the end-users new information and tools and there will be considerable evolution in how they are used? In the area of knowledge worker productivity, explored later in the chapter, the initial introduction of technology is relatively straightforward, but much of the value comes from thinking through how the technology can be used most effectively at a local level, and this is often left to chance.

BUILDING THE BENEFITS EXPLOITATION CAPABILITY

Bringing Expand into the scope of the project means that thinking about team design needs to shift. At the early stages of the project there will clearly need to be roles focusing on business changes and benefits realization, not just technology delivery. As the system nears implementation, and then through initial pilots, there will be an increasing focus on ongoing benefits realization. It is likely that individuals will emerge with an aptitude for end-user support and training and for working as 'super users', who for at least part of their role can be experts and advisers in how to get the most out of the systems.

Where we are working with versioned release and complex programmes, not just individual one-off projects, the issues are complex. Work on a new project/release will be taking place alongside operation and evolution of the existing system(s). Decisions will depend on the specific context, but it is likely that a programme management structure will provide an emphasis on overall architecture, learning across projects and ongoing benefits realization.

From a traditional change management perspective the focus at this stage has often been on 'sustaining change': that is, on preventing old ways of working taking their place alongside the new system. While this is important, we have looked at a bigger picture of enabling flexibility and further change to contribute to benefits realization. The goal is not to sustain but to accelerate continuous improvement.

From an IT function perspective Expand/benefits exploitation is often neglected, as the core 'IT system' may need little change, with evolution enabled through capabilities to tailor screens, workflow and reporting which are part of the system. However, from an end-user perspective, often the skills have not been established to make use of these capabilities and there is effectively no ownership of or capability for ongoing benefits exploitation.

An important element in developing the capability for benefits exploitation is a shift in *mindset*. The shift from technology implementation to benefits realization implies a shift from a fairly simple deterministic world where a project moves through requirements – to design, build, test and implementation – to a much more complex world where there is flexibility and co-evolution of technology, people and processes as intellectual technologies contribute to organizational flexibility and ongoing benefits realization.

Investing in Expand and benefits exploitation is 'sharpening the saw' (Covey, 2004) for the organization. You may get away without, it but you will quickly become inefficient and ineffective.

LEADING THE DIGITAL BUSINESS

A major implication of the importance of benefits exploitation is that leaders in the digital business need to have a broad range of abilities related to the management and use of IT. These abilities are required across the organization as part of all management and other leadership roles. This book focuses directly on core aspects of these abilities – specifically, delivering change through agile, benefits-driven projects – and then the broader issues of strategy and the management of the IT and Change Portfolio. Further aspects of these core leadership abilities are explored more briefly in this chapter: improving knowledge worker productivity; business process management; information management and knowledge management. These are all vital elements of the organization-wide IT capability.

KNOWLEDGE WORKER PRODUCTIVITY

THE CHALLENGE

'Knowledge worker productivity' should be a major topic for organizations seeking to realize benefits from investments in IT. Surprisingly, it isn't. We explore the issues and opportunities in this section.

Peter Drucker popularized the term 'knowledge worker' and has come back to it many times in his writing. In a 1999 article he states that the unique contribution of management in the 20th century was the 50-fold increase in the productivity of manual workers and proposes that 'the most important contribution management needs to make in the 21st century is to similarly increase the productivity of knowledge work and knowledge workers. The most valuable asset of the 21st century institution will be its knowledge workers.'

Drucker goes on to outline six factors that determine knowledge worker productivity:

1. Determining the task – how the knowledge worker contributes. Understanding what hampers the knowledge worker from concentrating on the task and eliminating it.

2. Imposing responsibility on the knowledge workers themselves for their productivity. They have to manage themselves. They have to have autonomy.

3. Continuous innovation has to be part of the work and the responsibility of knowledge workers.

4. Knowledge work requires continuous learning and continuous teaching by the knowledge worker.

5. Productivity of knowledge work is not – at least, not primarily – a matter of quantity. Quality is at least as important.

6. Knowledge workers should be treated as an asset rather than a cost. Knowledge workers need to want to work for the organization, and attracting and retaining the best knowledge workers are a key role for management.

In a compilation of his writing Drucker (2003) emphasizes effectiveness as the most important area for knowledge workers: 'Increasing effectiveness may well be the only area where we can hope significantly to raise the level of the knowledge workers' performance, achievement and satisfaction. Can effectiveness be learned? Yes. Effectiveness is a habit – that is a complex of practices. And practices can always be learned.'

A second key starting-point for exploring knowledge worker productivity is research into workforce agility (Breu et al., 2002). The aim was to develop a deeper understanding of what attributes contribute to workforce agility and the relevance of information systems and information technology to workforce agility. Workforce agility was defined as one element of enterprise agility, and is very closely aligned to the concept of effective knowledge workers.

Agile enterprise

- 'The successful exploitation of competitive bases (speed, flexibility, innovation, quality) through the integration of reconfigurable resources and best practices in a knowledge-rich environment to provide customer-driven products and services in a fast changing market environment.'

Agile workforce

'Knowledge workers with the knowledge and skills needed to deliver enterprise agility. Key components include:

– speed of action

– flexibility to change.'

The study identified key attributes of workforce agility and also identified an important role for information systems. One major finding was the relative importance of new working models encouraging collaboration: particularly virtual teams within an organization and across organizations, and communities of practice. Other sources of benefits were mobile technologies, e-training and better access to information.

Consider your organization:

- Who determines the level of investment to improve knowledge work productivity?
- Who has responsibility for realizing the potential of a major investment in desktop infrastructure to improve organizational performance?
- Who is responsible for knowledge work productivity?

Typical answers, which include 'The IT function', 'The management team', 'HR provide some training in Word and Outlook' and 'What do you mean?', are all inadequate. A particular challenge is that all the support functions in the organization (HR, IT, facilities/property) have a crucial role to play.

THE ROLE OF IT IN KNOWLEDGE WORKER PRODUCTIVITY

We explored the role of IT in knowledge worker productivity in a recent survey of a wide variety of managers and knowledge workers (part-time MBA students across all our executive MBA programmes and participants of executive workshops). We found that knowledge workers spend around 20 hours a week using elements of Microsoft Office (Word, PowerPoint, Excel) and another 10–20 hours a week using email. While this is self-reported and possibly not totally accurate, it is line with our experience. Evidence from much more in-depth studies, for example by Microsoft, supports our indicative results. The majority of the working week for most professional and knowledge workers is spent using a few basic applications.

I've asked as many managers as I can how their organizations help knowledge workers understand how to exploit Microsoft Office and other tools to improve their productivity. My 'sample' has included all sorts of organizations, including some large global businesses. There are typically three parts to the answer:

- 'We have a help desk that you can contact if there is a problem. The help desk also uses the intranet to provide some self-help and learning material.'
- 'We also provide a range of classroom-based courses on key applications.'
- 'In practice you just pick stuff up as you go.'

Evidence of the lack of exploitation of key applications indicates that this does not go nearly far enough to really enable productivity. The evidence from Microsoft that 80% of new features requested for Office are already in the product supports this.

Day-to-day examples

In relation to knowledge worker productivity, word processing is a valuable place to start: many knowledge workers spend a large part of their week working with Word, Excel, PowerPoint and email. To illustrate the issues I often use a number of very quick demonstrations in MBA and other classes. MBA students, along with academics and many others produce a lot of long documents, for example in the case of an MBA student a 12–15,000-word dissertation.

Paragraph **Styles** have been available as part of word processor functionality for many years. Yet from my informal research less than 50% of people know of them or use them, preferring to format each heading, etc. by selecting the text and then choosing Bold, Font Size, etc. as required. That might be no real problem for a one- or two-page document, but for long documents there is a real hit on productivity. Using Styles by itself is valuable, as it means you can very quickly alter the styles to reformat the whole document at once. More than that, it provides a foundation for using other features such as Table of Contents and Navigation (by Styles), which are also major time-savers.

At quite a different level, I've noticed the impact of PowerPoint 2007 (and more recent versions) on my presentations. I need to use slides a lot in presentations and teaching – I like to try and use diagrams, not just endless bullet points. The 'new' Smart Art feature can probably save me 15 minutes or more a slide in preparation time, and I was very competent with PowerPoint anyway. And it also has an impact on quality – it's challenging me to think in a different way about communication. Yet again a lot of people don't know it's there. It's great to be able to demonstrate it and from some get the reaction that you've just done a magic trick when you transform a few bullet points into a colourful diagram in seconds.

These are just small examples. How many people in your organization are wasting hours each week because they only have a basic level of knowledge of key tools? What if we could free up some of this time related to the work of individuals, teams and business processes? What if better knowledge resulted in improved quality (of customer service perhaps) and greater innovation, not just improved efficiency? The evidence from DeMarco and Lister (1999) that there is a 10:1 difference in the productivity of IT developers and development teams suggests there are big opportunities for improvement if anything like this difference applies in other scenarios.

Role of the IT function

The IT function of an organization is usually happy as long as the technology works; the human resources function may pay for some formal training. But no one really tackles how individuals, teams and departments can exploit the full potential of these tools to improve the effectiveness of information and knowledge workers. So what are we going to do about knowledge worker productivity?

BUILDING PRODUCTIVITY

There are three broad areas where IT can be used to help improve the productivity of knowledge workers. Realizing value in each of these areas brings different challenges for the organization.

Eliminate 'non-value-adding' tasks

'Non-value-adding' tasks are any activities outside the core 'task' of the knowledge worker. IT is used to eliminate or automate these activities. Many organizations have put a lot of effort into this area: for example, with online expense claims, purchasing, travel booking and HR administration. Microsoft, for example, eliminated all paper forms over a decade ago. What would be the value of switching from spending 30% of time on the 'core task' and 70% of time on other things to 70% of time on the core task?

Many organizations have a made a lot of progress in this area. There are many opportunities for a wide range of solutions, both standalone and integrated with core systems. Examples include finance, payroll and human resources. The concept of an 'employee portal' provides a way of bringing many of these solutions into an easy-to-use intranet format.

Although many organizations have made good progress, many still have a long way to go.

Specialist support for the core task

There is often an opportunity to develop and use specialist IT solutions that automate or in other ways improve the productivity of the knowledge worker in relation to the 'core task'. For example, engineers might use computer-aided design (CAD) tools. These solutions will often relate to a specific area of expertise.

This is another area where there has been a lot of progress and is well supported in many organizations. The falling costs of IT, particularly hardware, are making it possible to make these solutions available to wider groups of users.

A particular challenge for organizations is to learn to deliver solutions to meet the needs of knowledge workers. This can often helpfully be seen as improving working practices rather than re-engineering processes. IT can provide new tools, and the knowledge worker retains discretion over how to use them.

General support for the core task

There is an opportunity to make better use of general IT solutions to help improve productivity. As we have seen, many knowledge workers spend large amounts of the working week using software such as Outlook, Excel and Word and search tools such as Google. The challenge is often to help them to get the most out of investments that have already been made. As the work by Breu et al. (2002) showed, some of the greatest benefits come from enabling people to communicate and collaborate.

MAKING A START

Where do you want to start: with your own productivity, with your team or with the organization as a whole? There are opportunities at every level. To get started there are many opportunities for quick wins that start to free up a little time and also create a sense of what's possible (Box 6.5).

Box 6.5   Making a start with knowledge worker productivity

Overcoming the challenge of 'you don't know what you don't know'

A key challenge in improving knowledge worker productivity is that 'you don't know what you don't know' – 'unknown unknowns', if you like. Based on input from Peter Murray, who played an important role in the team working on benefits management with John Ward at Cranfield, and particularly his work on knowledge management, we've applied the well-known 'Johari window' to knowledge worker productivity.

There are both known and unknown unknowns:

- known unknowns: features that we know about that would be helpful if you used them, but perhaps because of the learning curve;

- unknown unknowns: the many features we don't know about and can't even have tried using.

In each case there are simple steps that can be taken to at least start to make a difference. What would you do?

BUILDING CAPABILITIES FOR DIGITAL BUSINESS

VALUE CHAIN PERSPECTIVE AND STRATEGIC CONTRIBUTION OF IT

The value chain (Porter, 1985) was originally used in a manufacturing context. It is also valuable in wider scenarios and has evolved to include value shop and value network perspectives (Stabell and Fjeldstad, 1998). The concept provides a familiar starting-point for considering how information and IT are used to contribute to value creation across the organization as a whole.

Early uses of IT involved financial transactions and accounting and also payroll processing. This rapidly expanded to transaction processing across the organization and then supply chain with integrated finance systems, then enterprise resource planning and most recently enterprise systems. There has been an increasing reliance on package solutions as the economies of scale for the development of these highly complex systems have given the advantage to large software vendors such as SAP, Oracle and Salesforce. These systems have become highly efficient and process transactions on a huge scale.

Much value is also created in other areas of the value chain where the emphasis is less on the speedy and efficient handling of transactions. Examples might include: attracting, developing and retaining great people; product and service innovation to create new value for customers; and, hopefully, the management of IT-enabled change.

The use of IT in these areas brings new challenges, as we have considered in the exploration of knowledge worker productivity. In later sections of this chapter we explore three of these areas: business process management, information management and knowledge management.

Each of these areas is a major topic and an area where some organizations have made huge investments and considerable progress. Our aim here is to explore the broad capability of benefits exploitation, which is particularly relevant in relation to the use of intellectual technologies in these areas.

BUSINESS PROCESS MANAGEMENT

The business process perspective is widely used in IT projects as a basis for understanding the context of the project and developing the requirements for solution design. It is also well accepted in practice that the project should address the IT system in the context of the relevant business process – for example, during testing and in user training. The approach is most frequently used in process automation projects and in scenarios such as enterprise resource planning, customer relationship management or supply chain management.

Garvin (1998) provides an in-depth study of processes of organization and management that applies the process perspective very broadly. In particular, Garvin considers management activities as processes (Box 6.6). He argues that successful improvement programmes require explicit attention to the organization's characteristic patterns of decision-making, communication and learning.

Box 6.6   Categories of organizational processes

Work processes

- Operational processes – processes that create, produce and deliver products and services that customers want.

- Administrative processes – other processes that are still necessary for running the business.

Behavioural processes

Three main categories of behavioural process are proposed:

- Decision-making processes. The activities are typically complex and cannot be reduced to a sequential series of steps.

- Communication processes. Processes are complex and can be characterized using a number of dimensions.

- Organizational learning processes – knowledge acquisition, interpretation, dissemination and retention.

Change processes

Change processes fall into two main categories:

- Autonomous – these have a life of their own and proceed because of an internal dynamic. Examples include the evolution of an organization from entrepreneurial start-up to a more structured, professionally managed firm or industry shifts from revolutionary changes in technology.

- Induced – all planned change efforts fall into this category.

Managerial processes

The bulk of management activity to 'get things done' involves working with people to harmonize interests, gain support and get the organization moving in the right direction. The process – how things are done – is typically more important than the content. There are three main categories of managerial process:

- direction-setting processes;
- negotiation and selling processes;
- monitoring and control processes.

See Garvin (1998).

Work by Edwards and Peppard (1997) and Braganza (2001) provides an approach to establishing processes to meet the expectations of organizational stakeholders and to classify and manage processes according to their contribution to the business. The work by Garvin, Edwards, Braganza, etc. indicates the opportunity of taking a broader perspective on processes than typically happens in practice and brings in areas of the organization that are not traditionally seen or managed as processes. Key implications for benefits realization are that all processes are not the same and different processes need to be managed, and changed in different ways. Peppard (2003) made a similar point when viewing the organization as a bundle of services.

Brown and Duguid (2000, Chapter 4) examine the limitations and failure of business process re-engineering and develop a distinction between *practice* and *process*. Practice is about 'how' a job gets done and is often managed bottom-up, as opposed to the top-down approach to processes. The description of practice is very similar to that used by Garvin (1998) for behavioural processes. As a result, although different terminology is used, the two accounts agree on the importance of 'practice' when attempting to make changes and improvements.

Bohn (1994) provides a model of the different stages or levels of knowledge for a technological process – essentially covering a spectrum from tacit knowledge to explicit, scientific knowledge and building on the tacit vs. explicit model used by Nonaka (1991). In addition, Bohn highlights with the idea of the 'knowledge tree' that the different aspects of the process will not be understood to the same level of knowledge. A key insight from the model is that the best way of managing a process varies according to the stage of knowledge; 'the higher the stage of knowledge, the closer the process is to "science", and the more formally it can be managed' (Bohn, 1994, p. 66). If there is a high level of knowledge about a process, we can either automate it effectively or use unskilled workers adhering to strict procedures. If there is a low level of knowledge, 'this requires experienced and skilled people who use their own judgment each moment' (Bohn, 1994, p. 67).

The business process management perspective remains important, and new technologies are enabling more flexible, agile management of processes within and between organizations (Smith and Fingar, 2006; Sinur et al., 2013).

Process design and management capabilities are important at many levels of the organization. Many organizations have adopted 'lean' approaches (Bicheno and Holweg, 2008), which have been pioneered at the Japanese car manufacturers, including Toyota (Liker, 2003). Lean 'tools' can be used in a very similar way to many of the benefits tools, equipping individuals and teams to make improvements at a local level (Box 6.7).

Box 6.7   Business process management: Making local improvements

The following quotes from recent interviews illustrate an organization that has successfully built a strong change capability in the teams running major transactional processes.

We had some key officers (40 people) that were trained in Lean principles and they led workshops.

We look at every single service area, see where the waste is and try and streamline the process. And we do that from the customer's point of view, but also from the officer's point of view delivering it.

You have your toolkit and you just have a lot of things that you can draw on, and you use the appropriate tool for the appropriate task.

Those guys are probably into year five or more of doing it now so it's just much more natural to them. In that sense for me it's akin to things like equality, health and safety, these should not be add-ons they should be intrinsic around how you are and what you do.

It was about establishing that an intervention can make things better, and it's understanding how to select those things and how to focus them' The action 'not only fixes the problems, it builds confidence, it builds ability, it gives people that sense that we can actually fix this.

People make suggestions all the time, because they're acted on.

We want and have leaders who innovate and change and excite people to get involved. We want a new leadership style and way of working. We redesign around the customer.

INFORMATION MANAGEMENT AND BUSINESS INTELLIGENCE

A major theme in the continued rapid evolution of information and communication technologies is 'ubiquitous computing' (Weiser, 1991). In 'The Computer for the 21st Century' Weiser suggests that the 'most profound technologies are those that disappear'. He contrasts ubiquitous computing with virtual reality. Ubiquitous computing seeks to enhance the world that already exists, and virtual reality seeks to simulate the real world. A key goal is to make technology a seamless part of life: 'ubiquitous computers reside in the human world and pose no barrier to personal communications.'

Making computers 'disappear' in this way is a major challenge and a significant change from how they are often used. There are major implications for how we design and use the technology – making technology disappear is 'a fundamental consequence not of technology but of human psychology. Whenever people learn something sufficiently well, they cease to be aware of it' (Weiser, 1991).

Weiser (1991) also relates ubiquitous computing directly to the problem of 'information overload':

> Most importantly ubiquitous computers will help overcome the problem of information overload. There is more information available at our fingertips during a walk in the woods than in any computer system – yet people find a walk in the woods relaxing and computers frustrating. Machines that fit the human environment, instead of forcing humans to enter theirs will make using a computer as refreshing as taking a walk in the woods.

Weiser (1991) suggested: 'like the pc, ubiquitous computing will enable nothing fundamentally new'; however, 'by making everything easier and faster to do it will transform what is apparently possible.' With the potential for making transformational changes possible it will be important for organizations to undertake Exploratory projects.

As benefits are expected to come not only from the technology but also from the information it provides, with people learning how to use it so well that they cease to be aware of it (Weiser, 1991), it is important to consider a framework of *information competences* that address the organization as a whole (Ward and Peppard, 2002) and not just the IT requirements.

Much of the academic and practitioner IT literature still does not make a clear distinction between the management of information and the management of information systems and technology (Checkland and Holwell, 1998). Most publications are primarily focused on IT management and have very little to say about managing information. In our thinking we have focused on information and how it can be effectively managed and exploited.

Competences for information management were identified by Marchand et al. (2001) in their discussion of the competences that an organization must develop to manage and use information effectively. By developing these competences the organization positions itself to utilize its information assets

Competence	Description	Source
Information Strategy	The ability to identify and evaluate the implications and opportunities related to the management and exploitation of information as part of business strategy formulation	Based on Ward and Peppard (2002)
Information Management	The ability of a company to manage information effectively over its lifecycle	Marchand et al. (2000)
Information Exploitation	The ability to maximize the benefits realized from information and related ICT investments through effective use of information	Ward and Peppard (2002) (adapted)
Information Behaviours and Values	The ability of a company to instil and promote behaviours and values in its people for the effective use of information	Marchand et al. (2000)
Information Systems/ Technology	The ability of a company to manage appropriate IT applications and infrastructure effectively in support of information management and exploitation	Marchand et al. (2000) (adapted)

Table 6.1 Information competences

effectively. Competences related to collecting, organizing and processing information must be developed to achieve this (Marchand et al., 2000). Marchand et al. (2000) identify three broad areas of capability (competence): information management practices; information value and behaviour; and information technology practices.

Marchand (1997) argued that 'excellence in information management will be the difference that makes the difference'. Achieving this will not only assist organizations to realize the value of their information assets; it will also enable them to exploit these assets much more effectively. This is a critical business issue: 'I have a simple and strong belief, how you gather, manage and use information will determine whether you win or lose' (Gates, 2001).

We have presented in Table 6.1 a framework that encapsulates and builds on current thinking on information competences (Ashurst and Doig, 2005).

The framework builds on the three competences identified by Marchand et al. (2001) and suggests that:

- Information exploitation needs to be a competence and is distinct from information management – this reflects the exploitation capability proposed by Ward and Peppard (2002). However, the competence as we have envisaged it is different from that envisaged by Ward and Peppard, as their focus is on exploitation of the benefits from IS-enabled organizational change rather than from information.

- Information strategy needs to be an explicit capability – this is addressed by Ward and Peppard but not by Marchand et al.

Information management competences

Information management competences are addressed in the existing work by Marchand et al. (2002) and Collins (1996). Table 6.2 provides an initial view of the micro-competences required for effective information management.

Competence	Definition
Sensing	The ability to detect and identify information that might be of value to the organization.
Collecting	The ability to establish systematic processes for gathering relevant information.
Organizing	The ability to assemble information from a range of sources and index and classify as required.
Provision	The ability to provide information in an appropriate form, so that it can be used effectively.
Maintenance	The ability to keep information so that it is current and available as required.
Renewal	The ability to keep the focus of information management on information that is of high value to the organization.
Custodianship	The ability to define how information will be managed and to identify by whom it will be managed.

Table 6.2 Information management competences

Information exploitation competences

Information exploitation is not prominent in the model put forward by Marchand et al. (2000). Collins (1996) refers to the *use* of information as part of the overall information management lifecycle, but we do not consider that this reflects the importance of this area or provides a strong enough starting-point for this research. Table 6.3 provides an initial view of the micro competences required for effective information exploitation.

Competence	Definition
Access	The ability to ensure that all required elements of information exist within the organization and can be readily retrieved by information consumers
Analyse	The ability to analyse information using a range of techniques appropriate for the objectives, context and information
Interpret	The ability to understand and interpret the information, making judgements on its accuracy and relevance
Communicate	The ability to communicate and share the information in formats that will enable others to understand it and use it as a basis for decision-making and action
Decision-making and action	The ability to take decisions and action based on relevant information
Renewal	The ability to keep the focus of information exploitation on information that is of high value to the organization

Table 6.3 Competences for information exploitation

Information management competences in practice

Effective use of information is an important source of benefits. As in other areas, results depend on a blend of competences underpinned by technology and people with knowledge and expertise. The expertise required can be varied: from understanding of performance measurement and what makes a helpful set of measures to more mathematical understanding to identify relevant fluctuations in performance or discover new insights from data, to the ability to present information visually in ways that encourage insight and understanding. In addition, a good understanding of the sources of data is vital: where they are, what they represent in the operational systems and what the subtle differences in definition are that make 'one version of the truth' so hard to achieve.

At an operational level information management tackles the delivery of information to monitor and control processes and to assess performance against operational targets. Key requirements will include being able to follow through from any variances to 'drill down' and explore the underlying issue and having 'alerts' in place so that there is early warning of a problem. A key challenge is often to bring together information from a range of sources in order to gain a balanced view of the process and customer service.

At a higher level, management information systems should be providing a broader view across the organization, and decision support systems will enable more exploratory use of information for specific investigations. The Internet has made available vast new sources of information related to many aspects of an organization: for example, details of customer usage of the website; shopping history of individual customers; employee movements and performance; alerts and performance information from individual machines and equipment as part of the 'internet of things'. The 'big data' challenge is to make use of all this information, where the key is to develop a range of competences as outlined in Tables 6.1 to 6.3. In many organizations there are major opportunities for making better use of existing information (Box 6.8).

As a cautionary note it is interesting that, in a recent update to his classic work on the role of management, Mintzberg (2013) makes clear that managers still rely to a great extent on informal communication and personal networks to get information and to understand what information means.

Box 6.8   An information management case study

A new IT Director made it a priority to visit senior managers to understand their perceptions of IT systems and services. In one case he was surprised to hear that 'SAP is a major problem: it just doesn't provide the information I need to run my business'. The IT Director knew SAP well and asked for more information. After the meeting he went straight to the SAP support team, and within 24 hours the manager had a report showing the information he wanted. In many cases lack of knowledge, bureaucratic barriers and lack of motivation to tackle problems lead to missed opportunities for benefits realization.

KNOWLEDGE MANAGEMENT

Knowledge management is a further area where there has been much activity and investment and where there remain many opportunities to create value. It is a complex area where many different approaches are used to tackle a variety of issues.

Many knowledge management initiatives effectively redefine knowledge as information and then take a technology-based approach (Brown and Duguid, 2000). This is one of the key causes of failure. Knowledge implies a 'knower' and is quite different from information – which can be held in a database.

The categorization of knowledge as either explicit or tacit is likely to be misleading: there are different levels of tacit knowledge and of skills (Ambrosini and Bowman, 2001). In some cases important aspects of tacit knowledge can be made explicit while retaining much of its value. For example, some tacit skills could be articulated readily if organizational members were simply asked the question 'How do you do that?' (Ambrosini and Bowman, 2001).

A closely related issue is the consideration of the form in which knowledge can be captured and shared. Although 'tacit knowledge has resisted operationalization' (Ambrosini and Bowman, 2001), there have nonetheless been many attempts within organizations to manage knowledge using a variety of 'organizational memory systems' to make 'experiential knowledge accessible' (Fernando, 2000). These organizational memory systems include documents and repositories and 'also organizational routines, processes, practices and norms' (Alvesson and Karreman, 2001). The tension between codifying nothing, thereby risking the loss of important information, and trying to codify everything, risking banality, is at the very core of attempts at knowledge management and its precursor, expert systems.

There are two broad approaches to knowledge management – codification and personalization (Hansen et al., 1999). They are both valuable – when used in the right context. They relate directly to the approaches found in practice, which can be summarized as collecting documents in databases and connecting people (Box 6.9).

Box 6.9   Two strategies for managing knowledge

Codification

Provide high-quality, reliable and fast information systems implementation by reusing codified knowledge.

Personalization

Provide creative, rigorous advice on high-level strategic problems by channelling individual expertise.

*   *   *

A successful knowledge management strategy requires elements of both approaches, with a roughly 80:20 emphasis on one of the approaches, depending on the needs of the business.

Key questions help determine the right strategy:

- Do you offer a standardized or customized product?
- Do you have a mature or innovative product?
- Do your people rely on explicit or tacit knowledge to solve problems?

See: What's your strategy for managing knowledge, Harvard Business Review, March-April 1999.

The codification strategy will work at various levels: for example, resulting in a skeleton project plan that captures and reproduces core information about 'how we do projects around here' and can provide a lot of value locally or across an organization. The skeleton is then tailored for a specific project. Other examples of codification include sharing anonymized versions of client reports in a consulting organization, or the use of Frequently Asked Questions to communicate within a help desk team or to provide guidance to customers.

The personalization strategy is about who you know, about finding the expert and getting a response. The technology involved can vary from none, as face-to-face conversations are still valuable, through email circulation lists for specific interest groups, through to use of a variety of social technologies.

Communities of practice

An empirical study by Thompson and Walsham (2004) showed that, if knowledge is to remain useful once made explicit, a link with the context in which the knowledge was used and so in which it might be reused must be retained. They also noted that, while the ideal of 'strictly explicit knowledge is self-contradictory', there are still opportunities to codify some aspects of knowledge that will be useful, particularly with a specific context as provided by, for example, a community of practice.

Communities of practice as described by Wenger et al. (2002) have grown up informally in organizations and have been recognized as sources of significant value (Box 6.10). A key challenge faced by management is how to exploit this value and develop a capability to nurture and sustain communities of practice. Wenger et al. (2002) provide guidelines for how to develop and sustain a community.

Box 6.10   What is a community of practice?

Communities of practice are groups of people who share a concern, a set of problems or a passion about a topic, and who deepen their knowledge and expertise in this area by interacting on an ongoing basis.

A framework for realizing value from communities is put forward by Wenger et al., in *Cultivating Communities of Practice* (2002): the 'double-knit' organization involves the combined contribution to learning of teams aligned to business processes and communities of practice. For example, the process and team structure in an organization will bring together a range of disciplines to deliver services for a specific customer, while individuals in these teams will draw on support from their discipline-based communities with links around the organization and in many cases outside the organization. In an IT team, for example, specialists in testing will have strong links with other testing specialists across organizational boundaries. These links will be a valuable source of learning and problem-solving.

Benefits from knowledge management

Many knowledge management initiatives have been IT-/technology-led projects that involve collecting lots of information (explicit knowledge) in the form of documents in databases and then hoping this will provide business value. Murray (2002) has built on the benefits management approach and proposed an approach to knowledge management to make it a demand-led business activity rather than technology-driven supply-side activity. The approach proposed is to use the benefit approach to start with a major business issue, understand what business results are wanted, what actions are needed to realise them and as a result what knowledge and information are required.

Knowledge management provides another approach to benefits realization. There will be opportunities at many levels with an organization. The foundation for success is to take a benefits-driven approach.

MANAGEMENT FRAMEWORK: LEADING THE DIGITAL BUSINESS

There have been predictions of technology having a significant impact on the role of management for some time. Rockart and Short (writing in Scott Morton, 1991) explored the implications for the role of management in a move to a networked firm – a new style of organization within and between businesses. Zuboff (1988) proposed that a paradigm shift is required to take advantage of the new 'informating' capability. There will be impacts on roles and relationships – information is made more widely available, and the role of middle management changes to include developing the skills of staff on the front line. There will also be a need for structures that foster a learning environment – for example, that allow admission of mistakes.

While in some respects management is little changed (Mintzberg, 2013), it is also true that we can see evidence of major change (Birkinshaw, 2010).

There are implications for operational management, who need a very broad range of competences to take part in major, transformational projects and also need to lead incremental and local change in their teams and business units. The benefits-led approach to projects and strategy set out in this book is an important element of the competences required. The areas discussed in this chapter – knowledge worker productivity, business process management and knowledge management – are also important alongside the ability to motivate and lead individuals and teams.

Senior managers need to overcome the 'IT attention deficit' (Huff et al., 2006) to become leaders of the digital organization. Again this can be underpinned by the principles and practices of a benefits-led approach, which contribute to managing strategically.

MOVING TOWARDS BENEFITS EXPLOITATION

In every organization we have worked with there are major opportunities for action to increase the benefits realized from *existing* systems. Who is responsible for exploitation of benefits from each system in your organization? What are the good practices? How proactive is the role of the IT function? What if the role of the help desk shifted away from responding to problems and towards helping end-users realize benefits from the systems?

As with many other aspects of a benefits-driven approach, the key is just to make a start and to learn by doing:

- Review projects completed 12–18 months ago: what is the current position in terms of benefits realization? What additional opportunities are there?

- Carry out a benefits review of major systems or services, including Microsoft Office and any major package applications (SAP, etc.). Think hard about how effectively the information and system capabilities are being used.

- Review current projects and consider the effectiveness of arrangements for Expand (see the next section).

IMPLICATIONS FOR CURRENT PROJECTS

We initially tackle Expand when setting up the project, as the governance framework will establish key foundations. Specific areas to consider include:

- inclusion of senior operational managers from the areas affected;

- bringing members of key user areas into the project team;

- ensuring the communications and stakeholder engagement strategy considers post-project roles and support for benefits exploitation;

- planning for the development of competences for information management, business process, management, knowledge management, knowledge worker productivity and, most importantly, continued benefits-driven change;

- using the training and deployment strategy to build expertise in key business areas and planning for key individuals to continue to play a role;

- designing the system for ease of use and ease of training;

- designing any help and training materials to make them easy to keep up to date.

One organization used the idea of a 'Benefits Assurance Team' to provide a post-live focus on building benefits realization (Box 6.11).

Box 6.11   An approach to benefits ramp-up

The project had adopted the practice of 'phase benefits delivery'. It was decided to establish a Benefits Assurance Team combining product management and user experience expertise. The Benefits Assurance Team had a range of roles:

- supporting new ways of working – helping the operational management team 'bed in' the new ways of working and start to make improvements based on early learning;
- monitoring the early results of benefits tracking and exploring options to realize and/or increase benefits;
- following up the original training and making sure that staff were confident in both the systems and the ways of working;
- working closely with operational management to ensure that they were able to manage the changed operations;
- planning for the benefits realization review;
- running workshops with small teams, using a combination of lean and benefits 'tools' to explore opportunities for improvement for individual teams and processes.

IMPLICATIONS FOR THE IT FUNCTION: SYSTEMS DEVELOPMENT

There are also significant implications for the IT function that will affect both systems development and the operational/support roles of the function. How can we establish a framework for knowledge worker effectiveness that includes support closely related to the work context where it is most effective?

The paper from Kidd (1994) continues to provide profound insights into the implications for the IT function and IT systems. The core of the argument is that the importance of knowledge is in the process of informing and changing the knowledge worker. We should explore the value of technology in enabling the *act of knowing* rather than seeing it as a repository of knowledge.

Often knowledge workers cannot classify information until they have been informed by it, and at that point it is not needed. This links with the piles of papers often found on the desk or in the room of a knowledge worker.

Knowledge workers are often interrupted, for example by phone calls. The pattern of marks on the paper (the piles on the desk, the notebook) is important; they provide the context to help the worker get back to where they were before the interruption. If the information is forced into a database, it becomes hard to find because it is not clear how to classify it.

The implication is that we need to rethink many attempts to capture knowledge in databases. We know that from the many project failures. But more importantly, along with Zuboff, Kidd suggests that the information and technology should be seen as supporting the worker. They provide tools and resources that the worker can use to get the job done. Too often we jump in and try and define a process with the worker effectively a part in the machine.

Peppard and Hemingway (2009) address the issues in a complementary way, as they discuss a 'design for use' (D4U) paradigm for systems development in contrast to our current 'design to build' (D2B) model (i.e., with a focus on the technology, not the information and user).

They draw on the work of Marchand et al. (2001) and others to suggest 'that a key part of any D4U project is helping decision makers to acquire and use information within the context of their relationships with colleagues and the organizational structures, rules and processes that influence how they make decisions'. The focus is on the information content in people's work and on the context in which the work is taking place. Table 6.4 contrasts D4U and D2B.

	D2B project paradigm	D4U project paradigm
Objective	Technology deployment	Information use
Focus of improvement	Data flows	Communication
Outcome	Optimized business processes	Improved decision-making
Implementation rationale	Process rationalization and systems analysis	Organization change and decision analysis
Design process	Create abstract data model to enable all uses of data	Represent cause–effect relationships relevant to specific decisions
Artefact	Technology	Human Cognitive (i.e., decisions, attention to information artefacts)
Conception of events	Data changing (i.e., database transactions)	Cognitive (e.g., decisions)

Table 6.4 Design for use paradigm

IMPLICATIONS FOR THE IT FUNCTION: THE KNOWLEDGE WORKER SUPPORT CENTRE

The role of support arrangements provided by the IT function is also critical. Organizations have taken many approaches to providing users of desktop technologies with support. Many went through a period of investment in an information centre in the 1980s as PC use exploded, which was heavily involved in support and in developing systems for end-users. More recently, cost-cutting within IT has found support teams an easy target, and organizations have restricted the scope of support to providing a technical service to ensure that 'PCs' continue to function and handling specific technical problems.

A service is required to provide support for knowledge workers that addresses the *use* of technology to increase the effectiveness of end-user performance. It should not be restricted to purely technical issues. This is applying the concepts of Expand and benefits exploitation to the systems that key value-adding workers use most of the time.

A key decision for an IT function is what balance should be struck between providing the service and facilitating the local services and arrangements within the business areas. The IT support arrangements need to work closely with the support arrangements in business areas already outlined and, in particular, need to facilitate more informal arrangements in place locally.

Over all, we envisage a three-tier support model:

Tier 1 support is provided by the local informal support arrangements. This may also include more extended support through local communities (see below).

Tier 2 support is provided by the central knowledge worker support team(s). This service, using email, telephone and web, aims to help the users exploit the available technology to improve their performance and productivity. It should start from the perspective of 'How do I do task x?' not just how a specific product works.

Tier 3 support addresses more advanced technical issues and also services to support end-user systems needs: for example, a requirement for a sophisticated spreadsheet.

The opportunities for shared learning, good practices and reusable resources are significant. This certainly seems a key opportunity for the IT function, through brown bag sessions, showcases, online forums, etc.

ENHANCING EXISTING, INFORMAL SUPPORT ARRANGEMENTS WITHIN BUSINESS UNITS

Education in the use of technology is most effective if closely related to the work context and the effective exploitation of technology is significantly influenced by support from the user's peer group. A key focus is to build on and enhance the effectiveness of the existing *ad hoc* and informal arrangements. Drucker supports this position: 'knowledge work requires continuous learning and continuous teaching by the knowledge worker.'

So, areas to consider include:

- *Formal activities*. Education for new workers or on the introduction of new technology should be related to the work context, as should help and guidance material. The evolution of portal and e-Learning technologies provide a number of opportunities: for example, training and other guidance and support resources can be linked to directly from guidance/documentation on business processes. There is also the opportunity to make this user-owned.

- *Peer group and community support*. It is important to recognize, encourage and facilitate peer group and community support. Specific steps could include reward and recognition for local experts and recognizing these existing informal roles in more formal team role descriptions and performance measures. Provide enhanced training and support for these local experts. Also, establish and facilitate a community (or communities) that can bring these people together and enable them to learn from each other.

- *Local/informal/community support arrangements*. These should be encouraged by the 'formal' IT support teams and arrangements. This is key area where end-user innovation and skills need to be encouraged.

Key context has to be that 'improving how the job is done' is part of the job at every level of the organization. There needs to be a drive for innovation, improvement and change at a local level by individuals throughout the organization. The overall management framework needs to encourage this initiative and enable it to make an impact. Do people see the opportunities for improvement, and, having spotted them, do they do something about it, and are they able to see the idea through to get results?

BIGGER PICTURE

In the digital business 'digital literacy' is vital. This goes beyond using a smartphone all day every day. There is a leap to make from the day-to-day personal use of technology to effective use in the workplace. Expertise in knowledge worker productivity and information management are core elements. Expertise in business process management, knowledge management and organizational learning is also crucial. Principles and practices of a benefits-led approach to setting and implementing strategy through a series of projects are also critical.

This chapter was positioned as about Expand as the final stage of a project and the wider competence of benefits exploitation. However, taking the organization as a 'fractal', as we look at each team or business unit as an organization in its own right, the entire framework of competences for benefits realization becomes relevant, enabling strategic thinking, change and review to drive continuous change and improvement at a local level. The difference in scale is simply one of context, requiring thinking about how best to apply the ideas, but from our perspective the core concepts are the same.

What this means is that, whatever your role, you can take these ideas and use them to make a difference to benefits realization in your organization, whatever that is.

TAKING IT FURTHER

FURTHER READING AND RESOURCES

The following readings provide a useful introduction to key topics covered in this chapter:

Process perspective

Bohn, R. (1994) Measuring and Managing Technological Knowledge. *MIT Sloan Management Review*, Fall 1994, Vol. 36 (1): 61–73.

Garvin, D.A. (1998) The Processes of Organization Management. *Sloan Management Review*, Summer 1998, Vol. 39 (4): 33–50.

Information management

Marchand, D.A., Kettinger, W.J. and Rollins, J.D. (2000) Information Orientation: People Technology and the Bottom Line. *MIT Sloan Management Review*, Summer 2000, Vol. 41 (4): 69–80.

Knowledge and knowledge management

Grant, R. (1996) Toward a Knowledge-Based Theory of the Firm. *Strategic Management Journal*. Winter 1996, Vol. 17 (Winter Special Issue): 109–122.

Hansen, M., Nohira, N. and Tierney, T. (1999) What's Your Strategy for Managing Knowledge? *Harvard Business Review*. March–April, Vol. 77 (2): 106–116.

Systems for the professional and knowledge worker

Kidd, A. (1994) *The Marks Are on the Knowledge Worker*. Human Factors in Computing – CHI 94 conference.

Service management

Peppard, J. (2003) Managing IT as a Portfolio of Services. *European Management Journal*. Vol. 21 (4): 467–483.

TALKING POINTS

Use these questions to help reflect on this chapter and explore the challenges of putting the ideas into practice:

1. What are the barriers to improving your productivity as a knowledge worker?

2. What could you do to improve the productivity of your team?

3. Consider specific scenarios for your own work or your team – what specific steps could you take to improve productivity? Consider perhaps: a meeting, a project review, a project, progress report, specific activities that are important for your work.

4. How competent is your business unit in the competences outlined in this chapter (knowledge worker productivity; information management; knowledge management; business process management)? What other competences are required to enable benefits exploitation?

5. What are the implications for the role of management?

6. How well does management development within your organization address these issues?

7. How could you make use of participation in benefits-led projects to build capabilities for benefits realization into the organization?

8. How might the IT function provide greater support for knowledge worker productivity?

KEY DEBATES

Embedding expertise across the organization vs. specialist teams

The view put forward in this chapter is that improving how the job is done is part of the job (see Drucker on knowledge workers). The implication is that business leaders need a broad range of competences for change and improvement.

An alternative view is that a more cost-effective approach is to focus managers and teams on running the business. Central, specialist teams are the place for project, change and business process management expertise.

What is your view? What are the benefits and risks of the two approaches? How would you find the right balance in a particular context?

CASE STUDY 6.1

The case illustrates an interesting challenge of knowledge worker productivity and the use of new technology – end-user innovation in the use of IT.

Journal of Information Technology Teaching Cases, Vol. 3 (2013): 1–8.

Tactical NAV: Innovation in the US Army

Dennis A. Adams, Blake Ives and Iris Junglas

Increasingly, employees are innovating with their own consumer technologies (such as smartphones and tablets), rather than looking to their companies' IT departments to lead technical innovation. This can give rise to tension between employees and IT departments, and this tension is particularly pronounced in the US military, where long systems development times run headlong into young, technology-savvy soldiers arriving in camp with smartphones, sophisticated applications and high expectations. In this case study, this phenomenon plays out in the person of a US Army captain who, using resources obtained via the Internet and while on a tour of duty in Afghanistan, develops and sells an inexpensive iPhone application – Tactical NAV – that provides soldiers with a sophisticated navigation tool.

REFERENCES

Alvesson, M. and Karreman, D. (2001) Odd Couple: Making Sense of the Curious Concept of Knowledge Management. *Journal of Management Studies*, Vol. 38 (7): 995–1018.

Ambrosini, V. and Bowman, C. (2001) Tacit Knowledge: Some Suggestions for Operationalization. *Journal of Management Studies*, Vol. 38 (6): 811–829.

Ashurst, C., Doherty, N.F., and Peppard, J. (2008) Improving the Impact of IT Development Projects: The Benefits Realization Capability Model. *European Journal of Information Systems*, Vol. 17 (4): 352–370.

Ashurst, C. and Doig, D. (2005) Information Competences: The Cornerstone of Effective Ambient Intelligence in a Business Context, Paper presented to the UK Academy of Information Systems Conference.

Ashurst, C. and Hodges, J. (2010) Exploring Business Transformation: The Challenges of Developing a Benefits Realization Capability. *Journal of Change Management*, Vol. 10 (2): 217–237.

Ashurst, C. (2012). *Benefits Realization from Information Technology*, Basingstoke: Palgrave Macmillan.

Bicheno, J. and Holweg, M. (2008) *The Lean Toolbox 4th Edition: The Essential Guide to Lean Transformation*, 4th edition, Picsie Books.

Birkinshaw, J. (2010) *Reinventing Management*, John Wiley & Sons.

Bohn, R. (1994) Measuring and Managing Technological Knowledge. *MIT Sloan Management Review*, Fall 1994, Vol. 36 (1): 61–73.

Braganza, A. (2001) *Radical Process Change: A Best Practice Blueprint*, CBI – John Wiley and Sons.

Breu, K., Hemingway, C.J. and Strathern, M. (2002) Workforce Agility: The New Employee Strategy for the Knowledge Economy. *Journal of Information Technology*, Vol. 17 (1): 21–31.

Brown, J.S. and Duguid, P. (2000) *The Social Life of Information*, Harvard Business School Press (Chapter 4).

Checkland, P. and Holwell, S. (1998) *Information, Systems and Information Systems*, John Wiley & Sons.

Clegg, C., Axtell, C., Damodaran, L., Farbey, B., Hull, R., LloydJones, R., Nicholls, J., Sell, R. and Tomlinson, C. (1997) Information Technology: A Study of Performance and the Role of Human and Organizational Factors. *Ergonomics*, Vol. 40 (9): 851–871.

Collins, B. (1996) Practicalities of Information Management, in Best, D. P. (ed.) *The Fourth Resource – Information and its Management*, Aldershot: Aslib/Gower. pp. 851–871.

Covey, S. (2004) *The 7 Habits of Highly Effective People*, Free Press.

DeMarco, T. and Lister, T. (1999), *Peopleware: Productive Projects and Teams*, 2nd edition, Dorset House.

Drucker, P. (2003) *The Essential Drucker: The Best of Sixty Years of Peter Drucker's Essential Writings on Management*, Collins Business.

Edwards, C. and Peppard, J. (1997) Operationalizing Strategy through Process. *Long Range Planning*, Vol. 30 (5): 753–767.

Fernando, O. (2000) Memory Systems in Organizations: An Empirical Investigation of Mechanisms for Knowledge Collection, Storage and Access. *Journal of Management Studies*, Vol. 37 (6): 811–832.

Garud, R. (1997) On the Distinction between Know-How, Know-What and Know-Why in Technological Systems. *Advances in Strategic Management*, 81–101.

Garvin, D.A. (1998) The Processes of Organization Management. *Sloan Management Review*, Summer 1998, Vol. 39 (4): 35–50.

Gates, W. (2001) *Business at the Speed of Thought*, E-Penguin Press.

Hansen, M., Nohira, N. and Tierney, T. (1999) What's Your Strategy for Managing Knowledge? *Harvard Business Review*, March–April, Vol. 77 (2): 106–116.

Huff, S., Maher, M. and Munro, M. (2006) Information Technology and the Board of Directors: Is There an IT Attention Deficit? *MIS Quarterly Executive*, Vol. 5 (1): 55–68.

Kidd, A. (1994) The Marks Are on the Knowledge Worker. Human Factors in Computing – CHI 94 Conference, New York.

Lee, A.S. (1999) Researching MIS, in Currie, W. and Galliers, B. (eds.) *Rethinking Management Information Systems*, Oxford University Press. pp. 7–27.

Liker, J. (2003) *The Toyota Way: 14 Management Principles from the World's Greatest Manufacturer*, McGraw-Hill.

Marchand, D.A., Kettinger ,W.J., and Rollins, J.D., (2000) Information Orientation: People Technology and the Bottom Line. *MIT Sloan Management Review*, Summer 2000, Vol. 41 (4): 69–80.

Marchand, D.A. (1997) Competing with Information: Know What You Want. *FT Mastering Management Reader,* July/August, Vol. 3: 7–12.

Marchand, D.A., Kettinger, W.J., and Rollins, J.D. (2001) *Making the Invisible Visible*, Chichester: John Wiley.

Marchand, D., Kettinger, W. and Rollins, J. (2002) Information Orientation: People, Technology and the Bottom Line. *Sloan Management Review*, Vol. 41 (4): 69–80.

Melville, N., Kraemer, K., and Gurbaxani, V. (2004) Information Technology and Organizational Performance: An Integrative Model of IT Business Value. *MIS Quarterly*, Vol. 28 (2): 283–322.

Mintzberg, H. (2013) *Managing*, Pearson Education Ltd.

Murray, P. (2002) Knowledge Management as a Sustained Competitive Advantage. *Ivey Business Journal*, Vol. 66 (4): 71–76.

Nonaka, I. (1991) The Knowledge-Creating Company. *Harvard Business Review*, November/December 91, Vol. 69 (6): 96–104.

Peppard, J. (2003) Managing IT as a Portfolio of Services. *European Management Journal*, Vol. 21 (4): 467–483.

Peppard, J. and Hemingway, C. (2009) 'Design-for-Use': A Paradigm for Successful Information Technology Projects. Draft of paper submitted to Business Horizons, accessed from Cranfield School of Management website.

Porter, M. (1985) *Competitive Advantage*, Free Press.

Scott Morton, M. (ed.) (1991) *Organizational Change. The Corporation of the 1990s: Information Technology and Organizational Transformation*, Oxford University Press.

Sinur, J., Odell, J. and Fingar, P. (2013) *Business Process Management: The Next Wave*, Meghan-Kiffer Press.

Smith, H. and Fingar, P. (2006); *Business Process Management: The Third Wave*, Meghan-Kiffer Press.

Stabell, C. and Fjeldstad, Ø. (1998) Configuring Value for Competitive Advantage: On Chains, Shops, and Networks. *Strategic Management Journal*, Vol. 19 (5): 413–437.

Thomke, S. and von Hippel, E. (2002) Customers as Innovators: A New Way to Create Value. *Harvard Business Review*, Vol. 80 (4): 74–81.

Thompson, M. and Walsham, G. (2004) Placing Knowledge Management in Context. *Journal of Management Studies*, Vol. 41 (5): 725–747.

Ward, J. and Peppard, J. (2002) *Strategic Planning for Information Systems*, 3rd edition, John Wiley and Sons.

Weiser, M. (1991) The Computer for the 21st Century. *Scientific American*, Vol. 265 (3), September 1991: 94–104.

Wenger, W., McDermott, R. and Snyder, W. (2002) *Cultivating Communities of Practice*, Harvard Business School Press.

Zuboff, S. (1988) *In the Age of the Smart Machine*, Basic Books.

CHAPTER 7
DIGGING DEEPER INTO THE ISSUES OF DESIGN AND CHANGE

IN THIS CHAPTER WE STUDY:

- benefits-driven projects as organizational change initiatives;
- design thinking as a set of principles and practices as a way to get insight into opportunities for change and to encourage creativity and innovation;
- different perspectives on the organization being changed as a result of the investment;
- the implications for projects of the emphasis on change.

ORGANIZATIONAL CAPABILITIES: A FOUNDATION FOR THE APPROACH TO DESIGN AND CHANGE

THE STORY SO FAR

In chapters 2–4 we established a framework and toolkit for an agile, benefits-driven project. Compared to a more traditional approach we emphasized:

- a shift of focus to people, the benefits for the customer and other stakeholders, and the recognition that benefits come from people doing things differently so that they arise from business change;

- the emphasis of building engagement and commitment to change with leadership from a business sponsor and a multi-disciplinary team, with the principle and practices of a benefits-led approach helping the team and wider stakeholders work effectively;

- starting the project from the first idea (Engage) to build momentum from idea to results;

- going beyond a traditional business case which focuses on what the benefits are to a benefits realization plan that tackles *how* the benefits relate to different stakeholders and *how* they will be realized (Explore);

- adopting an agile approach to balance disciplined and rapid delivery with the opportunity to learn and adapt through the project (Evolve);

- focusing on how benefits will be measured, and relevant targets from the earliest stages of the project; taking a benefits perspective to assess the results of the project and to guide further learning and action (Evaluate);

- continuing beyond software or solution delivery to build benefits realization (Expand);

- the benefits of a clear, consistent project framework across a wide variety of projects and contexts;

- the importance of a 'toolkit' that provides the basis for a common language and effective multi-disciplinary teamworking;

- the need to adapt how the framework and toolkit are applied in different contexts guided by factors including the IT and Change Portfolio;

- the foundation provided by a core set of principles that underpin the approach and provide a reference point for decision-making.

In this chapter I am going to introduce some ideas and tools that build on what has gone before. There is an argument that I could have brought this material into earlier chapters; however, experience in the classroom and with practitioners suggests that for most people it is better to build up the ideas in stages, even if this means going over the same broad area several times.

The logic here is similar to how we use the investment portfolio to help prioritize investments in IT. It makes sense to tackle core operational areas first, so there are sound foundations as a base for strategic investments. Similarly, if we lead straight into some of the issues of organizational change and design thinking in this chapter, we may be answering questions people are not (yet) asking when the issues they are facing are about getting very basic elements of benefits realization established.

I've already made a major leap by starting with agile, benefits-driven approaches to projects rather than a more traditional approach. The next step is to look in more detail at issues of organizational change and also to consider how 'design thinking' fits with a wide range of scenarios and contributes to benefits realization from innovation.

Firstly, benefits-driven approaches build on a long history of thinking about socio-technical systems (Box 7.1) and the need to consider many perspectives on an organization when seeking changes to enable benefits realization (process, practice, structure, etc.). Benefits ideas provide guidance on identifying in broad terms what changes are required and in identifying the stakeholders involved. However, we have not yet tackled these areas.

Box 7.1   Socio-technical perspectives in brief

In summary, important aspects of a socio-technical perspective on information systems include:

- Tackling a broad range of organizational issues throughout the project process is a key contributor to success (for example, organizational alignment, human-centred and transitional issues need to be addressed).

- The focus must be on work design and understanding wider cultural issues etc., not simply systems design.

- Close involvement of users and other stakeholders throughout the project is vital.

- Flexibility of the project process and organizational learning through the life of the project is important – reflecting both the changing organizational context and a deepening understanding of the opportunities.

Eason (1988); Clegg et al. (1997); Clegg (2000); Avison et al. (1998); Mumford (1995)

Secondly, although the benefits thinking and tools are helpful in trying to get an insight into the opportunities, in terms of standing back and getting deep insight into a complex situation and what problem is being solved they provide only limited help. Various other approaches can be applied. Soft systems (see Box 7.2) provides a valuable framework and set of tools, but it is hard to do it justice within the confines of this book. Instead, we have focused on design thinking: in essence this provides us with a way to explore a problematic situation and clarify the opportunities for delivering value to stakeholders. There is a good fit with everything we have covered so far.

Box 7.2   Soft systems thinking

Soft-systems thinking and methods come from the work of Peter Checkland (see Further Reading). It is one part of a much wider body of knowledge and practice called systems thinking. In essence the key is the much-used phrase 'the whole is greater than the sum of the parts'. The system is a number of interrelated and interacting elements, and systems thinking is about exploring the system, as opposed to a reductionist view that identifies individual elements and then focuses on them in isolation. Business process design and management, which we refer to elsewhere (Chapter 6), is another example of systems thinking.

Soft systems provides a variety of tools to help explore and model complex situations in order to gain new insights and deeper understanding. The models help *think about the real world* situation; they don't claim to represent the actual real world as perhaps a business process model might. There is a strong emphasis on the different views of stakeholders, and some of the tools – for example, *rich pictures* – can be valuable used independently. A variety of models might, for instance, be used to help explore a situation from the perspective of different stakeholders, seeking to bring new insights into view.

The approach is powerful and fits at the early stage of a project to explore a complex situation and get a clearer understanding of what problem is being tackled.

A 'rich picture' (see Figure 7.1) is a valuable element of the soft systems toolkit.

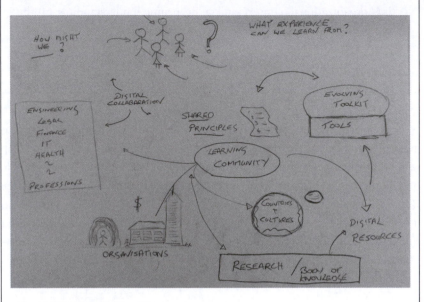

Figure 7.1 Example of a rich picture

Source: Hand-drawn for speed and simple capture of ideas.

Further reading on systems thinking includes:

- Senge, P. (2006) *The Fifth Discipline: The Art and Practice of the Learning Organization*. 2nd edition. London: Random House Business.
- Midgley, G. (ed.) (2003) *Systems Thinking*. London: Sage.

Organizational change

In terms of organizational change, to date we have used elements of the toolkit, including stakeholder analysis and management and the benefits dependency network, to identify the changes required and start to think about how to make them happen. The aim is to take this further and extend our toolkit for exploring the challenges of change in a specific situation and for designing and delivering the changes required. The work we have already done in taking an agile, benefits-driven approach provides a vital starting-point. The foundation of the benefits approach in a focus on benefits for specific stakeholders provides an insight into 'What's in it for me?' as seen by each stakeholder/stakeholder group. The phased delivery of the agile approach provides an opportunity (alongside many other benefits) to learn from real-world experience, building engagement through adapting to the real needs of users.

Design-led thinking

Design thinking is one way to tackle another set of limitations in what we have done so far. Benefits and agile approaches work very well in getting people engaged in project planning and delivery. The development of the benefits dependency network, for example, should be an interactive workshop involving the sponsor, core team members and other stakeholders. This allows high levels of communication and collaboration, allowing creative approaches to solving problems and identifying opportunities based on the workshop approach and the interaction of different people and different perspectives.

There is a risk, however, in complex situations or where there is significant change or a major opportunity for innovation, that the benefits network dives too quickly into solution development when more time is required to understand the problematic situation. Design thinking provides a way of building on the existing agile, benefits-driven approach. The underlying principles are a good fit, specifically with a focus on value for stakeholders. Design thinking emphasizes taking time to understand stakeholder needs and provides interesting tools to help. It also emphasizes prototyping and rapid cycles of feedback and learning. In this context the early prototyping is to help understand the problem and to get new insights into opportunities. The assumption is that, in complex situations and where there is innovation, traditional approaches of requirements-gathering are inadequate and often inappropriate.

Develop the skills of the craftsman

From the perspective of the craftsman I suspect we are now moving beyond competence to mastery. At this level, although you are still using the same tools, you are able to use them in a very different way – you have time to concentrate on the people and the nuances of the situation rather than the technicalities of the tools. You are very much in charge, rather than being a prisoner of the technicalities of the tools. If it helps, think of Tom Cruise in *The Last Samurai* – after much practice and a lot of hard knocks he achieves mastery over the sword and is suddenly able to be fully in the moment and work at a very different level.

It is important that the tools are simple – and are kept simple. What is important is our ability to use them in collaboration with other people. We need to keep the barriers to entry low so that we can include new members in the team and wider stakeholders quickly and effectively, even if it takes them a longer period to develop their mastery in the use of the tools. At this stage we are making advanced use of the existing toolkit for an agile and benefits-driven approach to a project; in the sense of adapting how we use them to reflect the specific context and the people involved, we are also adding in new tools to dig deeper into the challenges of change and to enable innovation.

The distinction between projects, programmes and the overall portfolio makes a valuable contribution to our ability to adapt our approach to a specific context. With a programme we can approach individual projects in different ways: for example, reflecting the uncertainty and scale of innovation required (see Box 7.3).

Box 7.3   Designing programmes and project to realize benefits

It is important to consider each project in the context of programme and portfolio perspectives.

For example, within a programme it may be possible to move quickly to tackle existing problems, alongside an exploratory pilot to get insight into further opportunities. So when some of the basic issues are resolved and there is more energy and opportunity to tackle new things, there is a much stronger basis for moving forward quickly into a further phase because of the exploratory work.

At a portfolio level it becomes possible to gain a perspective looking across the different projects and programmes. You can start to look beyond where projects fit on the IT and Change Portfolio to how this influences your approach to each project. The knowledge of individuals – for example, where is there real expertise in benefits approaches – and adoption of different aspects of the toolkit can be considered. There is an important role at portfolio level to help build the team on each project and to help adapt the approach to reflect the team and wider project context.

DESIGN THINKING

Design thinking as a concept, a discipline and set of practices, has emerged from work on product design and has been applied to product, service, experience and organizational design and to tackling complex societal issues. The starting-point is the view that in many cases we are tackling complex, problematic situations where it's hard to be clear what the real problem is, and at the start the specific improvements that are possible or desirable may not be clear.

Tim Brown, CEO of design firm IDEO, describes it as follows:

'design thinking' – a methodology that imbues the full spectrum of innovation activities with a human-centred design ethos. By this I mean that innovation is powered by a thorough understanding, through direct observation, of what people want and need in their lives and what they like or dislike about the way particular products are made, packaged, marketed, sold, and supported. [...] It is a discipline that uses the designer's sensibility and methods to match people's needs with what is technologically feasible and what a viable business strategy can convert into customer value and market opportunity.

(Brown, 2008, p. 86)

The approach brings together a multi-disciplinary team and provides a toolkit and set of principles to help them. IDEO is one organization that has contributed to the development of design thinking. In the book *The Art of Innovation* (2001) Tom Kelley tells their story and uses their demonstration project developing a new supermarket shopping trolley, which was the subject of a US, *Nightline* TV programme and can now be found on YouTube.

The story of IDEO developing the new shopping trolley provides a good illustration of design thinking in action. The brief was simply to develop 'a better shopping' trolley. The trolley was to be designed for customers of a chain of specialist food retailers with relatively small supermarket stores, rather than vast superstores such as Walmart.

The project takes place over a week. On Monday a multi-disciplinary team of around 10–12 people meets in the large room that is going to be the focus for project activity. The project leader is chosen because he is good at working with groups, rather than because of seniority or specific expertise. They brainstorm and share ideas before going out to gather information. We see them observing shoppers and taking pictures in the store, talking to staff in the store and the man responsible for the trolleys in the car park. The team members gain insights from their observations and the views of these experts. They come back together and share what they have learned. The walls start to fill with pictures and drawings. We see a few people starting to experiment with aspects of building trolleys. At no stage do we see them asking for 'requirements'. Instead they try to build a deep empathy with, and understanding of, the needs of different stakeholders and use their design expertise to start to explore opportunities.

On Tuesday there is a 'deep dive', a brainstorming session to get further insight into opportunities. Their rules for brainstorming are well established and are written around the room (Box 7.4). The team is used to working together; one of them reflects that he is a newcomer – with only six years' experience! They vote on features that are 'cool and buildable' to get views from across the team, rather than getting a decision from the project manager.

By lunchtime there are signs of drift as the brainstorm continues. A group of 'adults' intervene, based not on seniority but on status in the group. At this milestone they decide to split into sub-teams and spend the rest of the day building four different prototypes – each one optimized to an area of need or a different stakeholder group (safety, shopper, children and store manager). At the end of the afternoon each group shares its prototype with the wider group, not just by showing it but also by acting out a short demonstration of how it could be used. One group prototypes a feature for a shopper to contact a store assistant when they can't find a product. At this stage it's just brought to life with the plastic head from a shower representing a microphone, but we get the idea. When they look at the prototypes at the end of the day, they decide that none of them is quite right ('fail often in order to succeed sooner'), but they all contribute elements to a final design.

Wednesday is spent on the final design, which is then built on Thursday, with a team working through the night. The final shopping cart is revealed on Friday morning, and then the team goes back to the supermarket with the completed cart to try it out and get feedback.

Key practices demonstrated are observation, brainstorming and prototyping, each carried out by an experienced, multi-disciplinary team. Together they add up to a radically different approach to a project. The project did depend on having a team available to take the final design and build it in their machine shop. To a degree these technical and engineering skills were available throughout the project as we saw core team members getting involved with building prototypes from the morning of the first day. The many prototypes helped evolve key aspects of the final design. The technical skills within the team also helped ensure that the design was buildable and cost-effective. As Dave Kelley, the founder of IDEO, notes, the finished result is beautiful and also functional.

There will be much that is familiar to those with experience of agile projects, but clearly this has nothing to do with software development. As important as the specific practices are the overall mindset and the space where the work took place. Brown (2008) describes the lifecycle as 'Inspiration, Ideation and Implementation', while Kelly (2001) uses 'Observe, Brainstorm, Prototype and Learn'. In practice they are describing the same core approach, taking time to understand stakeholder needs and refine an understanding of the 'problem' and then to use brainstorming and prototyping in an iterative cycle of creativity and learning.

The business of IDEO has extended from product to service design to helping organizations become more innovative. Design thinking has made a major impact on innovation at other organizations and in a range of sectors, including health-care.

By its nature design thinking cannot be tied down to a specific set of rules. IDEO have shared a toolkit (a set of 'method cards', a toolkit for educators and a human-centred design toolkit). Stanford Design School also shares a range of resources for design thinking (see Box 7.5).

Box 7.5   Resources for design thinking (examples)

IDEO

Human-centred design toolkit
http://www.ideo.com/work/human-centered-design-toolkit/

Toolkit for educators

http://designthinkingforeducators.com

Method cards

http://www.ideo.com/work/method-cards/

d.school Stanford

https://dschool.stanford.edu/use-our-methods/
https://dschool.stanford.edu/groups/designresources/

CREATIVE SPACE

In the video we see the IDEO team working in a large team room with lots of wall space to use as they work and lots of space for sub-groups to break out, including when they want to work on prototypes. Dave Kelley also talks about the influence of space on creativity.

IDEO certainly provides a good illustration of the agile principle of maximizing the amount of work *not* done (http://agilemanifesto.org). The prototypes and the willingness to allow the time for the team to dedicate to work together in the same space enable communication and creative collaboration, minimizing the need for layers of requirements and design documentation. The approach also illustrates the importance of a multi-disciplinary team and having people working together through the project rather than in isolation.

ROLES IN THE TEAM

In *The Ten Faces of Innovation* Tom Kelley (2008) provides an outline of ten different roles that contribute to innovation based on IDEO experience at many organizations, including Kraft, Samsung and Procter & Gamble (see Box 7.6). The book provides an outline of the ten roles that foster innovation. Kelley also criticizes the 'devil's advocate' as a great killer of innovation who avoids taking responsibility.

Box 7.6 The ten faces of innovation

Learning Personas

The Anthropologist: ventures into the field to observe people interacting with products, services and experiences.

The Experimenter: celebrates the process of innovation, taking calculated risks, and tests and re-tests scenarios.

The Cross-Pollinator: develops connections between apparently unrelated ideas to get fresh insights.

Organizing Personas

The Hurdler: a tireless problem-solver with the optimism to tackle something that's never been done before.

The Collaborator: truly values the team over the individual and coaxes and coaches the team to build confidence and skills.

The Director: sees the bigger picture and targets opportunities.

Building Personas

The Experience Architect: focuses on creating remarkable experiences for individuals.

> **The Set Designer**: creates work environments that stimulate creativity.
>
> **The Storyteller**: captures the imagination and creates a vision with narrative in story, video or many other forms.
>
> **The Caregiver**: has empathy and guides the client through the process to provide them with a comfortable, human-centred experience.

MEASURE TO LEARN

Design principles and practices are to be found in many places. In *Lean Start-Up*, Ries (2011) emphasizes the importance of using measures to learn and not simply as 'vanity metrics'. The concept of 'cohort analysis' is used to get insight into different customer groups related, for example, to different versions of a product, or process, perhaps testing different assumptions and providing information to inform decision-making and action.

The idea of the 'minimum viable product' builds on prototyping, with the aim of getting early feedback from real customers to enable further product or business development. The measures are designed to help guide continued development. These ideas relate to organizations of all types, and not just start-ups.

Steve Blank (Blank, 2013) provides many resources for a lean approach to start-ups (see steveblank.com and the How to Build a Startup course on www.udacity.com).

ADOPTING DESIGN THINKING

Design thinking applies in a wide range of scenarios. In relation to benefits realization from IT-enabled change it complements agile and benefits approaches and provides a way to tackle both problematic situations and new opportunities provided by technology. The focus on design – that is, on user experience and value for the end-user – is well aligned with benefits thinking.

As with earlier work on agile and benefits approaches, there can be major barriers to adoption in an organization. Risk-averse and bottom-line-focused management fail to see that it is better to get a good understanding of what problem is being tackled or where there are really opportunities for value. They prefer diving into the project and the perception of progress, even if the wrong problem is being solved or the project grinds to a halt or fails completely at a later stage.

The design approach also brings a new meaning to a user-centric approach. It reflects that asking for 'user requirements' in many situations is naïve at best. What if the possibilities are radically different from the current situation? How well does end-user understanding of current problems align with a vision from management of new directions for the organization or with the real issues customers are facing?

At a project level there are many starting-points for adopting the principle and practices of design thinking. Consider going out and observing end-users as they engage in relevant activities or use current and competitor products. Create empathy for the end-users by developing a range of rich personas that bring to them to life as people. Use brainstorming effectively to identify multiple possible solutions as a starting-point for further thinking. Reflect on and revise the problem statement during the project as your understanding evolves. State the problem in the form of an open question: 'How might we...?' (e.g., 'How might we build a better shopping trolley?'), avoiding defining the solution from the beginning (Kelley and Kelley, 2013, p. 238). Build prototypes early and often. The rapid learning-by-doing approach through rapid cycles of prototyping has huge potential (Box 7.7).

Box 7.7   Simple prototypes

Brown (2008) emphasizes the importance of prototyping, whether the goal is a new product, a service or a new user experience. The aim is to get useful feedback and learn. The prototype does not need to be complex or expensive; in fact, if the prototype is too polished, it may stifle feedback.

Prototyping can take many forms:

- a 3-D model made in five to ten minutes from a collection of bits and pieces and then brought to life by the story told by the team who built it;

- acting out the scenario;

- a picture and user story;

- a short video.

Teams can develop multiple prototypes, perhaps starting from the perspective of different stakeholders. As teams present, tell stories or act their scenarios, it is helpful to take a video to help capture all the ideas and insights.

Design principles and practices influence the whole project lifecycle. During Engage and Explore design thinking can help develop an understanding of issues and needs, and to explore the problem resulting in a problem statement ('How might we...?'), then during Explore and Evolve design thinking can be used to explore potential 'solutions': that is, opportunities to create value.

I've argued (Ashurst, 2012) that many practices can be applied to a project focused on either IT solution delivery or benefits realization. The difference is not in the core of the practice itself but in the problem it's applied to and the mindset adopted.

I used the example of risk management, based on observations in a number of different cases. The core of the risk management activity was very similar. The difference was in how the goals of the project were defined: was the focus on solution delivery or benefits realization? Risk management as a practice is essentially the same – the difference is the *goal it is applied to*.

This strong similarity of the core practice for solutions delivery and benefits realization applies to a range of other practices. In the research project I reported, there were cases where an agile approach was adopted with a focus on involving people and effective teamwork. A number of practices related to solution delivery would, with a change of objective, become practices that contribute to benefits realization. This suggests that, for some situations, the critical factor for adoption of benefits-driven approaches is a change of *perspective* to focus explicitly on benefits as a goal, and that if this can happen, actual day-to-day *practice* does not need to change significantly. Existing skills are relevant with this change of perspective – which we might also call a change of *paradigm* or *mindset*.

In a more recent project (Ashurst et al., 2012) we noted a similar phenomenon. In this case we had studied ten cases of IT-enabled innovation in different organizations. We were exploring the practices adopted and the factors enabling the organizations to innovate. The detailed analysis outlined in the findings and discussion sections highlights many factors. However, following Lee (1999) and Checkland and Scholes (1999), it is important to consider the 'system' as whole. At this 'bigger picture' level a key finding is that many of the practices contributing to innovation are familiar from previous work: for example, on agile and benefits-led approaches. On the other hand, something is very different. Ashurst (2012) makes a similar point in relation to the difference between benefits-led and technology-focused approaches to IT investments, suggesting that the issue is not different methods but different 'paradigms'.

Steel (2000) says 'a paradigm is a self-consistent set of ideas and beliefs which acts as a filter, influencing how we perceive and how we make sense'. It seems that an innovation approach to IT represents a 'third paradigm', which is significantly different from previous paradigms (technology implementation and benefits-led). The difference is the attitude or mindset, more than the specific practices, and the challenge of making a paradigm shift will be the major barrier to developing the capability for IT-enabled business innovation in many organizations and IT functions. To reflect on what this paradigm is like, watch the IDEO Nightline Deep Dive, which is on YouTube as three short videos.

DESIGNING THE APPROACH TO CHANGE

TAKING A BROADER VIEW OF THE 'ORGANIZATION'

The benefits perspective implies that benefits are realized as a result of 'business changes' ('the new ways of working that are required to ensure the desired benefits are realized', Ward and Daniel, 2006, p. 109). By taking a stakeholder perspective we avoid the constraints imposed by departmental and organizational boundaries. Benefits realization will often involve changes across a range of organizations and involve stakeholders who are not part of any organization (e.g., customers) in the context of the project. When we refer to 'organization', we usually have in mind this complex scenario rather than the boundaries of a particular legal entity.

The scale and scope of changes will vary from project to project. In this section we start to develop a broader review of what is changing and establish a framework of the different types of organizational change to help ensure that benefits planning addresses all the issues that are relevant in a particular situation. If the context is a new organization, perhaps a new business unit or a start-up, the focus will shift to the capabilities required, rather than the changes.

The organization is extremely complex. It exists in a rapidly changing environment, and its strategy and performance depend on the interaction of a wide range of stakeholders with different objectives and contributions to make. No one perspective can adequately describe the organization, and in many cases it is likely that there will be unexpected results from change initiatives (both good and bad). It is important to consider the interaction of the investment with the organization as broadly as possible to consider both the potential risks and the range of interventions required to succeed in realizing the benefits.

PROCESSES

The process approach provides a way of breaking down the organization into smaller units that are more relevant for considering the impact of IT. The process model is scalable in that a process can be broken down into a small number of high-level components or into a larger number of more detailed activities. (See Chapter 6, 'Business Process Management'.)

Work by Edwards and Peppard (1997) and Braganza (2001) provides:

- an approach to process design based on meeting stakeholder expectations.

- a classification model for processes based on their impact on the business. The classification model includes 'competitive' and 'transformational' processes which are likely to include areas of the business not traditionally considered as processes.

- an approach to identifying information/knowledge requirements based on the initial process design. This provides a link to knowledge/community perspectives of the business.

The model also starts to address decision-making about when to focus on cross-functional business processes and when to use functional organization models.

The process perspective is widely used in IT projects as a basis for understanding the context of the project and developing the requirements for solution design. It is also well accepted that the project should address the IT system in the context of the relevant business process – for example, during testing and in user training. The approach is most frequently used in process automation projects and in scenarios such as ERP, CRM or Supply Chain Management (SCM).

The work by Garvin, Edwards, Braganza, etc. indicates the opportunity of taking a broader perspective on processes and brings in areas of the organization that are not traditionally seen or managed as processes. A key implication is that not all processes are the same and that different processes need to be managed in different ways.

WORKING PRACTICES

Brown and Duguid (2000, see Chapter 4) examine the limitations and failure of the business process re-engineering movement. A distinction between process and practice is developed.

Process is typically addressed top-down and focused on inputs and outputs: on *what* is required, not *how* the job is done. Business change from re-engineering is usually substantial and one-off. Business process re-engineering projects have typically succeeded in only a small number of scenarios: for example, procurement.

Practice is about *how* a job gets done. It is often 'managed' bottom-up and requires a focus on information and knowledge. It is about collaboration and improvisation and applies to a wide range of scenarios, particularly complex 'processes' requiring high levels of skill.

Communities of practice as described by Wenger et al. (2002) relate very closely to the concept of practice put forward by Seely and Brown. Wenger refers to the 'double-knit' organization and shows the combined contribution to learning of business processes/teams and communities of practice.

We are working on the assumption that in seeking to understand an organization and to plan and manage change, both process and practice perspectives are valuable. Even if the process perspective is a good representation of reality, there will still inevitably be local working practices: for example, within a 'black box' in the process description or in gaps around the formal process.

PROCESS VS. PRACTICE

Brown and Duguid (2000) explore how change is often handled from both process and practice perspectives.

They suggest that a process perspective has, at least historically, resulted in top-down changes often led from the 'outside' of the organizational unit affected. There is a focus on rules and procedures, and change tends to be one-off and discontinuous, with major change efforts and then periods of stability.

From a practice perspective there is much more likelihood of bottom-up change led from 'inside' and with a greater focus on *how* the job gets done rather than on *what* to do. Change often requires collaboration and improvisation and is likely to be continuous with a focus on continuous innovation and improvement. This perspective fits well with the knowledge-based view of the firm put forward by Grant (1996a).

RESOURCE-BASED VIEW OF THE ORGANIZATION: COMPETENCE-BASED DESIGN

A key starting-point for this book is the resource-based perspective, which considers an organization as interrelated resources, competences and capabilities (Figure 7.2). We view this as a very powerful perspective for both developing and implementing strategy. It seems a good fit with the real world. Unfortunately, one of the drawbacks of the approach to date is that it can be hard to operationalize, and there is no simple way of identifying, classifying or designing competences and capabilities.

Resources, capabilities, competences and practices are all important concepts that have already received much attention in the general and strategic management literatures (e.g., Barney, 1991; Grant, 1996b; Teece et al., 1997; Brown and Duguid, 2000; Helfat and Peteraf, 2003). In this section we illustrate how these theoretical constructs can be applied to the task of delivering specified benefits from IT investments.

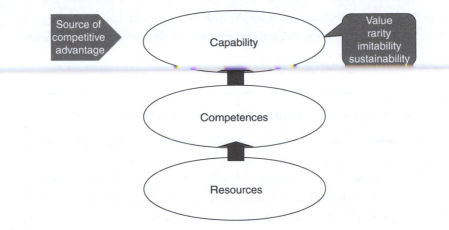

Figure 7.2 Resource-based perspective

Over the past 25 years there has been significant interest in the process by which organizations can assemble a unique portfolio of resources that will render them a competitive advantage. The resource-based view (RBV) of the firm (Wernerfelt, 1984; Barney, 1991) suggests that organizations should invest in those assets and resources that they believe will best assist them in successfully gaining a sustainable competitive advantage. In this context, resources have been defined as 'stocks of available factors that are owned or controlled by the firm' (Amit and Schoemaker, 1993). From a competitive perspective not all resources are equally valuable. An organization's primary source of competitive advantage will be through those resources that are simultaneously valuable, rare, imperfectly imitable and non-substitutable – the so-called 'VRIN' conditions (Barney, 1991). While resources are clearly a critical element of the RBV, there is a growing recognition that resources, *per se*, do not create value. Rather, value is created by an organization's ability to mobilize, marshal and utilize these resources, through the application of capabilities and competences (Grant, 1996b; Bowman and Ambrosini, 2000). It can be argued that organizations will only attain a sustainable competitive advantage if they can assemble a set of competences that can be consistently applied (Teece and Pisano, 1994) and that competitors find difficult to imitate (Barney, 1991; Prahalad and Hamel, 1990).

The literature is not consistent in the use of the terms involved. A composite model is as follows. The term 'resource' is used in a very inclusive way – it covers not just all the usual elements, such as money, people, skills, capital, etc., but also 'softer' resources such as credibility, brand, IP, procedures and so on. 'Competence' is used more specifically as an attribute at the organization level (skills are deemed to be held at the individual level). An organization is competent if it manages and deploys its resources effectively and efficiently. Finally a 'capability' is the combination of competences and resources deployed in the market-place such that customers see the organization as having some competitive advantage. Thus resources and competences are internal, while capabilities are recognized externally (Box 7.8).

Box 7.8   Resources, competences and capabilities: An example

Capability: the organization-wide capability to realize value consistently from investments in IT-enabled change and transformation.

Competences: the four competences of benefits planning, benefits delivery, benefits exploitation and benefits review which are brought to life through the e^{4+1} framework and the benefits toolkit.

Resources: the skills and energy of individuals; the 'toolkit' of effective working practices, enabling organizational structures, processes and environment.

An example of using the terms this way is branding. In this terminology a 'brand' is a resource; developing a brand is a competence (it requires managerial skill and action applied to the resource); creating new brands successfully is a capability (i.e., this is the element that the market recognizes).

If we view an organization as a collection of competences (Neely et al., 2002; Kaplan and Norton, 2004), it makes sense to take a competence-based approach when exploring the current situation and in setting out what success of a change programme looks like – that is, to develop a business competence-based design (i.e., 'as-is' and 'to be').

Business competence-based design works at two broad levels. Firstly, it helps consider the outcome of the investment as new and improved resources, competences and capabilities. Secondly, it helps define these elements in more detail and explore the implications for the changes that are required. We need to use a range of perspectives to address the real-world complexity of an organization in developing a design for a new business solution, including:

- process – normally the starting-point. The process can be defined as 'the activities involved in delivering value to a stakeholder'.

- practices – how people actually work. It is important to consider this perspective as well as the process perspective, particularly in the many situations where the people have considerable discretion in how they approach activities.

- roles and skills – the jobs and skill requirements for individuals;

- structures – the formal organizational structure (geographical, product-based, process-based, span of control, etc.);

- information (and knowledge) – required to do the job and to manage and improve the process;
- management framework – the role of management and how they influence and control;
- performance measures – to monitor the process and to motivate individuals and teams;
- culture – a very broad perspective on 'how we do things around here'.

All of these 'dimensions' of an organization can be affected, sometimes significantly, by changes to information systems.

Early IT implementations were often designed around the automation of specific business processes. It is now clear that, although the process perspective is valuable, by itself it is not enough even in tightly controlled, transactional scenarios. In many settings where IT is being used by professional and knowledge workers, with considerable autonomy, a wide range of perspectives are relevant, and process has a more limited role to play. The focus on business competences when designing the outcome and planning the change programme helps ensure consideration of relevant perspectives.

EXPLORING THE CURRENT SITUATION AND THE CHANGES REQUIRED

Three models compete to provide a general framework for exploring difference perspectives on the organization. The 'cultural web' (Johnson and Scholes, 2002; see Figure 7.3) provides good coverage of both 'hard' and 'soft' aspects of the organization.

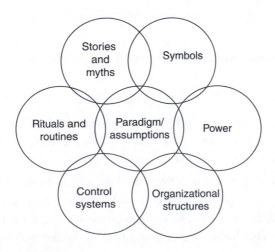

Figure 7.3 The cultural web
Source: Johnson and Scholes (2002).

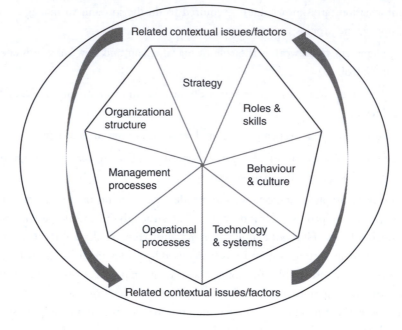

Figure 7.4 The change heptagon
Source: Based on Ward and Elvin (1999).

The '7-S' model also takes a broad view of the organization (Kaplan, 2005), as does the 'change heptagon' from Venkatraman and used by Ward and Elvin (1999). See Figure 7.4.

Any of these models can be used to help give shape to a workshop. They can also be used – for example, the change heptagon – to think about different aspects of the future vision priory to trying to establish a consolidated, multi-dimensional view of the desired outcome.

Just as there are established techniques for business process analysis and design, so methods for capability/competence mapping and design are evolving through experience in practice.

ESTABLISHING AN APPROACH TO CHANGE

There is a vast literature on planning, delivering and sustaining change. Our aim here is to introduce a few tools that can build on the foundations we have established and that can add value in a project context.

Balogun and Hope Hailey (2004) describe a model they call the 'change kaleidoscope', which provides criteria to help diagnose the context for change and to establish design choices for the approach to change. It can be used alongside existing models for benefits mapping and stakeholder analysis. Elements of the model are as follows:

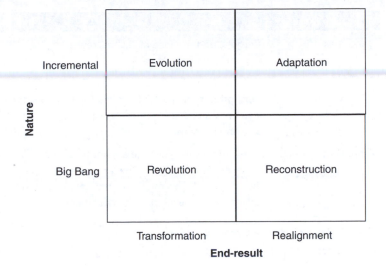

Figure 7.5 Types of change

Change Path. There are four types of change in terms of the end-result and the nature of the change (see Figure 7.5). This is about the change path, because over time more than one approach may be adopted: for example, a Revolution followed by Adaptation.

Change Start Point. There are two main approaches: 'top-down' and 'bottom-up'. They also refer to 'pockets of good practice' and 'pilot sites' as more minor categories.

Change Style. Change style parallels the top-down vs. bottom-up and focuses on management style. It ranges from Coercion through Direction, Participation, Collaboration and then finally Education and Delegation as the focus of ownership shifts from top management.

Change Target. The target refers to what is the initial focus of the change effort: Outputs, Behaviours, or Attitudes and Values.

Change Levers. The change levers relate directly to the target, and Balogun and Hope Hailey (2004) use the 'cultural web' as a way of exploring different levers to contribute to change. See Table 7.1. In our experience, change of behaviour (routine) through the adoption of new practices can result in changes to attitude and values, depending on how the practice is introduced.

Change Roles. The discussion of roles explores the 'pros' and 'cons' of different players taking the lead: senior leadership, external consultants, a change action team or functional delegation to operational managers.

Change target	Levers
Outcomes	Targets, performance measures, rewards, organizational structure.
Behaviours	Structures, performance measures controls supported by influencing stories and symbols: for example, stories of 'heroes' and routines, or actual working practices.
Attitudes and values	The aim here is to change assumptions and beliefs (or mindset/paradigm in the language we have used to date). This might be through education and personal development interventions.

Table 7.1 Matching change targets and levers

For each programme (and project) the aim is to use design choices on each of these dimensions to develop an overall approach to enable change. The analysis of contextual factors includes consideration of:

1. **Time**: how quickly is the change needed?

2. **Scope**: is the degree of change realignment or transformation, and how much of the organization is affected?

3. **Preservation**: what should be maintained and protected during the change (people, practices, other characteristics)?

4. **Diversity**: how diverse are the different groups within the organization?

5. **Capability**: what is the level of individual, managerial and organizational capability for change?

6. **Capacity**: what is the capacity of the organization in terms of money and people, and where does this initiative fit in terms of wider plans for change?

7. **Readiness**: how ready are relevant people in terms of awareness and motivation?

8. **Power**: does the change leader have the power necessary to influence the required scope and nature of changes?

Exploring the contextual factors and the dimensions for the design of change, as well as making use of work on benefits and stakeholders, the aim is to develop a change strategy and plan, and to get a team in place to lead the change. At the core of the exploration are people and their readiness in terms of motivation, energy and expertise to deliver the changes.

SUCCEEDING IN DELIVERING THE CHANGE

Kotter (1995, 2008) takes a different approach and focuses more on the leadership of change. The eight-step model is widely cited (see Box 7.9).

Bringing together ideas from Kotter with Hope Hailey and Balogun, and using competences as a way to understand the goal of a change programme, we have the basis for designing and delivering a change programme that will result in benefits realization. The principles already established of a phased, incremental approach with opportunities for learning remain critical.

IN SUMMARY

Previous chapters have established important foundations for an agile, benefits-driven approach to IT projects and for going beyond projects to a focus on benefits realization through the life of any investment in IT.

This chapter has taken a further step and introduced design thinking as a basis for approaching IT projects. Design thinking is a response to the complexity of the problems being tackled, which is not well addressed by traditional, requirements-driven approaches. We need to take more time exploring the problems and opportunities, to really understand the world of key stakeholders and create the space for innovation.

The second aim of the chapter was to explore some of the wider challenges of succeeding with business change. We have focused from the beginning on benefits arising when people do things differently, but to date we have only scratched the surface of planning and delivering change. This is another major topic, and in this chapter we tackled a number of factors that are important.

Design thinking and the approach to benefits from change explored here both focus directly on the stakeholder and as a result are complementary. The outcome of understanding these perspectives can be a further shift in mindset and also the development of expertise in additional 'tools' that will contribute to benefits realization.

TAKING IT FURTHER

FURTHER READING AND RESOURCES

The further reading provides an article supporting each of the two main themes in the chapter. Any one of the books would also provide a good introduction to design thinking.

Hope Hailey, V. and Balogun, J. (2002) Devising Context Sensitive Approaches to Change: The Example of Glaxo Wellcome. *Long Range Planning*, Vol. 35 (2): 153–178.

Brown, Tim (2008) Design Thinking. *Harvard Business Review*, Vol. 86 (6): 84–92, p. 9.

Kelley, Thomas (2001) *The Art of Innovation: Lessons in Creativity from IDEO, America's Leading Design Firm*, London: Harper Collins Business.

Kelley, T. (2008) *The Ten Faces of Innovation: Strategies for Heightening Creativity*, London: Profile Business.

Kelley, D. and Kelley, T. (2013) *Creative Confidence*, London: William Collins Books.

TALKING POINTS

Use these questions to help reflect on this chapter and explore the challenges of putting the ideas into practice:

1. Contrast the design-led approach with a more traditional approach to gathering requirements. What are the benefits and risks?

2. How would you adapt and apply the design-led approach to different types of projects?

3. Is the design-led approach just for some projects? Are at least elements of it relevant to all?

4. How would you manage the balance between (i) creating space to explore and learn and (ii) the need to make progress and deliver results, when adopting a design-led approach?

5. How does the discussion of change relate to your experience?

6. What are the implications of using a competence-based approach to design?

7. How might you handle different dimensions of change on a project or programme? Consider, perhaps: structure, process, roles, skills, behaviours, values. How might this relate to timescales and incremental change/phased delivery of benefits?

8. How is the approach to change designed/planned on projects in your experience?

9. What are the implications (risks) of using a bottom-up approach to change and education as a lever?

10. What other change-related tools and techniques would you want to draw on?

KEY DEBATES

Complexity of the benefits-driven approach

'This emphasis on a benefits-driven approach is just making a difficult job bigger and harder. We simply don't have the time.'

How would you respond? Are benefits driven approaches feasible in the 'real world'? What are the alternatives?

CASE STUDY 7.1

An exploration of the challenges of change in the important scenario of compliance driven projects.

Journal of Information Technology Teaching Cases, Vol. 1 (2011): 91–113.

The SOX compliance journey at Trinity Industries

Ulrike Schultze

Process and information technology changes in organizations are not always voluntary and motivated by strategic goals. Instead, they may be imposed on organizations by regulatory bodies and certifying agencies. This teaching case focuses on one company's multi-year journey of making process and information technology changes so as to comply with a new set of regulations known as the Sarbanes-Oxley Act (SOX). Even though SOX compliance work focuses on designing, implementing, and testing internal controls, these controls are nothing but activities designed to ensure that processes implicated in the production of financial information are completed correctly and that the financial representations they generate are reliable. Thus, despite its emphasis on internal controls, accounting and auditing, this teaching case provides students with insights into compliance-related process improvement and system integration in general.

REFERENCES

Amit, R. and Schoemaker, P.J.H. (1993) Strategic Assets and Organizational Rent. *Strategic Management Journal*, Vol. 14: 33–46.

Ashurst, C. (2012) *Benefits Realization from Information Technology*, Basingstoke: Palgrave Macmillan.

Ashurst, C., Freer, A., Ekdahl, J. and Gibbons, C. (2012) Exploring IT-Enabled Innovation: A New Paradigm? *International Journal of Information Management*, Vol. 32 (4): 326–336.

Avison, D.E., Wood-Harper, A.T., Vidgen, R.T. and Wood, J.R.G. (1998) A Further Exploration of Information Systems Development: The Evolution of Multiview 2. *Information Technology and People*, Vol. 11 (2).

Balogun, J. and Hope Hailey, V. (2004) *Exploring Strategic Change*, 2nd edition, Harlow: Pearson Education Ltd.

Barney, J.B. (1991) Firm Resources and Sustained Competitive Advantage. *Journal of Management*, Vol. 17: 99–120.

Blank, S. (2013) Why the Lean Start-Up Changes Everything. *Harvard Business Review*, Vol. 91 (5): 63–72.

Bowman, C. and Ambrosini, V. (2000) Value Creation versus Value Capture: Towards a Coherent Definition of Value in Strategy. *British Journal of Management*, Vol. 11: 1–15.

Braganza, A. (2001) *Radical Process Change: A Best Practice Blueprint*, Chichester: CBI – John Wiley and Sons.

Brown, J.S. and Duguid, P. (2000) *The Social Life of Information*, Harvard Business School Press (Chapter 4).

Brown, Tim (2008) Design Thinking. *Harvard Business Review*, Vol. 86 (6): 84–92.

Checkland, P. and Scholes, J. (1999) *Soft Systems Methodology: A 30-Year Retrospective*, Chichester: John Wiley and Sons.

Clegg, C.W. (2000) Socio-Technical Principles for System Design. *Applied Ergonomics*, Vol. 31: 463–477.

Clegg, C., Axtell, C., Damodaran, L., Farbey, B., Hull, R., Lloyd-Jones, R., Nicholls, J., Sell, R. and Tomlinson, C. (1997) Information Technology: A Study of Performance and the Role of Human and Organizational Factors. *Ergonomics*, Vol. 40 (9):851–871.

Eason, K. (1988) *Information Technology and Organizational Change*, London: Taylor & Francis.

Edwards, C. and Peppard, J. (1997) Operationalizing Strategy through Process. *Long Range Planning*, Vol. 30 (5): 753–767.

Grant, R. (1996a) Toward a Knowledge-Based Theory of the Firm. *Strategic Management Journal*, Vol. 17: 109–122.

Grant, R. (1996b) Prospering in Dynamically Competitive Environments: Organizational Capability as Knowledge Integration. *Organization Science*, Vol. 7: 375–387.

Helfat, C. and Peteraf, M. (2003) The Dynamic Resource-Based View: Capability Lifecycles. *Strategic Management Journal*, Vol. 24 (10): 997–1010.

Hope Hailey, V. and Balogun, J. (2002) Devising Context Sensitive Approaches to Change: The Example of Glaxo Wellcome. *Long Range Planning*, Vol. 35 (2): 153–178.

Johnson, G. and Scholes, K. (2002) *Exploring Corporate Strategy*, 6th edition, Harlow: FT Prentice Hall.

Kaplan, R. (2005) How the Balanced Scorecard Complements the McKinsey 7-S Model. *Strategy & Leadership*, Vol. 33 (3): 41–46.

Kaplan, R.S. and Norton, D.P. (2004) *Strategy Maps: Converting Intangible Assets into Tangible Outcomes*, Boston, MA: Harvard Business School Press.

Kelley, Thomas (2001) *The Art of Innovation: Lessons in Creativity from IDEO, America's Leading Design Firm*, London: Harper Collins Business.

Kelley, T. (2008) *The Ten Faces of Innovation: Strategies for Heightening Creativity*, London: Profile Business.

Kelley, D. and Kelley, T. (2013) *Creative Confidence*, London: William Collins Books.

Kotter, J. (1995) Leading Change: Why Transformation Efforts Fail. *Harvard Business Review*, March–April, Vol. 73 (2): 59–67.

Kotter, John P. (2008) Leading Change. *Harvard Business Review*, January 2007, Vol. 85 (1): 96–103.

Lee, A.S. (1999) Researching MIS, in Currie, W. and Galliers, B. (eds.) *Rethinking Management Information Systems*, London: Oxford University Press.

Mumford, E. (1995) *Effective Systems Design and Requirements Analysis: The Ethics Approach to Computer System Design*, Basingstoke: Palgrave Macmillan.

Neely, A., Adams, C. and Kennerley, M. (2002) *The Performance Prism: The Scorecard for Measuring and Managing Business Success*, London: FT Prentice Hall.

Prahalad, C.K. and Hamel, G. (1990) The Core Competencies of the Corporation. *Harvard Business Review*, Vol. 68 (3): 79–91.

Ries, E. (2011) *The Lean Startup*, London: Penguin Books.

Steel, R. (2000) New Insights on Organizational Change. *Organizations & People*, Vol. 7 (2): 2–9.

Teece, D. and Pisano, G. (1994) The Dynamic Capabilities of Firms: An Introduction. *Industrial and Corporate Change*, Vol. 3 (3): 537–556.

Teece, D., Pisano, G. and Shuen, A. (1997) Dynamic Capabilities and Strategic Management. *Strategic Management Journal*, Vol. 18 (7): 509–533.

Ward, J. and Daniel, E. (2006) *Benefits Management*, Chichester: John Wiley and Sons.

Ward, J. and Elvin, R. (1999) A New Framework for Managing IT-Enabled Business Change. *Information Systems Journal*, Vol. 9 (3): 197–222.

Wenger, W., McDermott, R. and Snyder, W.M. (2002) *Cultivating Communities of Practice*, Harvard Business School Press.

Wernerfelt, B. (1984) A Resourced-Based View of the Firm. *Strategic Management Journal*, Vol. 5: 171–180.

CHAPTER 8
STRATEGY – CREATING VALUE AND BUILDING COMPETITIVE ADVANTAGE

IN THIS CHAPTER WE STUDY:

- different perspectives on strategy;
- a framework for IT strategy;
- tools to help develop the strategy;
- approaching the strategy as a project.

THE VALUE OF STRATEGY IS IN IMPLEMENTATION

The value of work on strategy is delivered though implementation in a series of initiatives forming projects and programmes of change. The early part of the book has focused on a project level, providing the foundations for successful implementation of strategy. The focus now shifts to wider issues of IT strategy and IT portfolio management. This chapter builds on the benefits perspective and addresses how to take a strategic approach to set priorities for IT investments and establish an IT portfolio to deliver the business strategy and contribute to competitive advantage.

The pervasive and extensive impact of IT means that it is vital to move beyond views of the IT strategy as a functional strategy that follows on from the business strategy. The business strategy can only be established in the context of IT trends and opportunities, taking into account the potential of new waves of innovation. As every business is now a digital business (Accenture, 2014), the IT strategy and business strategy need to be considered together, and we refer to this as the 'digital business strategy'.

We draw on concepts and frameworks from wider work on business strategy and apply them to the challenges of developing and implementing the IT and digital business strategy. As in earlier chapters, the aim is to deliver results, and there are strong links between strategy and implementation via the portfolio, programmes and projects.

Later chapters will develop these ideas in a number of directions. The work on strategy develops the vision and provides an overall direction and purpose. Projects and programmes drive the implementation of the strategy and are managed as part of the overall management of the IT portfolio (Chapter 9). The architectural perspective provides a holistic view of the organization looking at key dimensions including information, process, technology and people, and ensures that developments contribute to a coherent, flexible set of systems in line with the strategy, avoiding fragmentation, duplication and excess costs (Chapter 10). New technologies, including those under the broad heading of 'social media', are having a major impact on individuals, organizations and society; they need to be taken into account as an important strand of gaining competitive advantage from IT as every business becomes a 'digital business' (Chapter 11). Governance, roles and structures are also important as part of the overall picture, and the role of CIO and IT function continue to be a focus of debate (Chapter 12). Innovation in technology continues to be a major driver of opportunities for competitive advantage. It is only a part of a wider picture of how the organization develops a capability for IT-enabled innovation

(Chapter 13). Finally, it is vital to consider the overall challenge of developing the IT capability of the organization. Peppard and Ward (2004) identified this as the basis for a fourth era of IT where the ability to realize value from IT is embedded within the organization. The capability relates to the realization of value from across the organization as a whole. Competitive advantage ultimately depends on developing this organization-wide capability and developing a generation of leaders equipped to lead the digital business (Chapter 14).

STRATEGIC CONTEXT

The strategic context is a perplexing mixture of uncertainty, rapid and sometimes disruptive change, and continuity.

In terms of continuity, the reasons for the failure of investments in IT have changed very little over the last 30 years. They have little or nothing to do with technology and a lot to do with people and organizational issues. Although how we work in organizations is changing – very quickly in some – there is also a lot that is little changed. Work on business process design and improvement today, for example, would be familiar to the Organization and Methods department of 30–50 years ago. Even at a technology level, some organizations are still using 20- to 30-year-old (or older) IT systems written in Cobol.

At a technology level the change has been remarkable. About 35 years ago I was doing a computing module at university, writing a Fortran programme using punched cards, with the deck submitted to operators for running and finally, when all the errors in typing had been eliminated, run overnight through the time-sharing arrangement to use a computer at another local university. About 20 years ago I was working at a major retailer, and we had our first PC connected to the Internet and the data centre as a whole held 1 Tb of disk storage. Enterprise applications – for example, financial systems – still ran on the mainframe, often with a 'green screen' interface, and had a multimillion pound price-tag. Now I have a 1 Tb back-up drive on my desk, Internet connections are ubiquitous and we are quickly moving to always having high bandwidth connections, regardless of location. Enterprise class applications can be run over the Internet and accessed on payment per user per month. Productivity and collaboration applications using the Internet and a wide range of devices, particularly phones and tablets, have enabled new ways of working within organizations and have enabled new arrangements for flexible working across individuals and organizations. In some case there has been a major impact on whole industries: retail, newspapers, music, film, etc.

Major directions for future development, at least in the medium term, seem fairly clear: proliferation of devices connecting people and 'things', pervasive availability of broadband, availability of powerful systems and services to organizations regardless of size, flexibility/agility of careers and organizational structures. The speed and timing of developments are less clear – when does reality catch up with the hype? In many cases the journey from initial proof of technology to broad adoption is still a long one.

There are many other drivers of change. In the last decade economies have been on a roller coaster, with major impacts across a range of countries. Rapid economic development is creating many new opportunities and also competitive challenges. Markets have very different characteristics: for example, due to demographic trends. Wider geopolitical trends are important, with conflicts as well as new economic groupings. Social trends also have a major impact, with social technologies playing a major role. Then, at a basic level, the weather seems to be having an increasing role to play, raising concerns about resilience and business continuity. Strategy development for organizations large and small takes place in a very complex environment.

We are taking the view that, regardless of uncertainty in the medium and longer term, it is vital to carry on developing the organization and creating value for stakeholders: 'doing nothing is not an option.' There are many opportunities for innovation and value creation based on existing technologies. Very often there is still value to be gained by doing the basics consistently well. Innovation will continue, and there is a good argument that we will face further major change over the next ten years, with more industries (retail, higher education?) affected by the disruptive impact of new technologies.

Very importantly, we also take the view that strategy is not simply an issue for senior managers of large corporations. Much of what we address is a matter of managing strategically, and is relevant at many levels of a large organization (regardless of sector) and also at smaller and medium-size organizations. The approach adopted is essentially about using the toolkit to get broad engagement in contributing to the strategy and managing strategically to get a better outcome and also to develop 'prepared minds' (Beinhocker and Kaplan, 2002), so that leaders at a local level are best able to take decisions and respond to insights and change with awareness of the overall direction and plans.

BUILDING ON STRONG FOUNDATIONS

From the perspective of this chapter, where the focus is on strategy, projects and programmes are about the *implementation* of strategy. They provide the means of bringing the vision to life, and, by ensuring the output of the strategy exercise includes outlines of key programmes and projects, the chances of the work on the strategy having an impact and delivering value are increased.

The book has been structured to address benefits realization from projects in the first chapters for two main reasons. Firstly, the initial focus on projects is closer to the experience and current role of many readers. Secondly, it provides an opportunity to introduce key ideas in a slightly simpler and more concrete context before moving on to the messier challenge of strategy development.

In any case, the result is that as we start to consider the development of IS/IT strategy we have strong foundations in place and can reuse and build on much of what we have already covered (Box 8.1).

Box 8.1   Foundations for the approach to strategy

Key foundations established in the earlier chapters include:

Benefits principles and tools: the focus on benefits for stakeholders and benefits as a result of people doing things differently is the basis for the work on strategy. Much of the benefits toolkit is also valuable. Work on advanced benefits management (Murray et al., 2001) showed how the BDN can be used at a strategic level, where each business change becomes a project or programme.

Stakeholder engagement and management: looking beyond the emphasis on value for stakeholders, engagement in developing and delivering the strategy is vital in terms of the quality of thinking and the successful delivery of change.

Programmes and projects to deliver change: much work on strategy stops short of implementation. The alignment between approaches to strategy and projects contributes to strong linkage between the vision and delivery of change to bring about results. The agile approach, with an emphasis on phased, incremental delivery, builds in flexibility to adapt.

Portfolio perspective: The IT and Change Portfolio was a critical part of the overall toolkit, helping reflect on the priority of a particular investment and adapt the approach taken to a specific project. At a strategy level we use the portfolio to look at the set of investments and the fit with organizational goals, as well as considering the impact of multiple projects: for example, when they affect the same business area and the overall capacity for change. The portfolio also provides the basis for ongoing management of existing assets (systems/processes/services) as well as investment in change. Effective use of the portfolio – for example, with Exploratory projects – is an important enabler of flexibility.

Driver analysis: at a project level, driver analysis helped set the goals of a potential project in the context of the strategy of the organization.

That is to say, it helped consider: 'How might this project contribute to strategic objectives?' In developing the strategy, we build on driver analysis and address a broader, more open question: 'Where might we invest in change in order to deliver benefits for stakeholders in line with the vision of the organization?'

TOWARDS COMPETITIVE ADVANTAGE

The framework for business value from IT in Figure 8.1 (Melville et al., 2004) provides a useful outline of perspectives to be considered. The linkage of IT through business processes to organizational performance can be explored via business process or value chain models or perhaps through capability maps. The organization is also considered in the context of its competitive environment, and work by Porter – for example, on 'five forces' and generic strategies – remains relevant. Then the bigger picture in terms of countries, markets and society can be considered through a 'PEST' analysis. (There are several variations on the PEST analysis. Essentially it involves exploring Political, Economic, Societal and Technological factors that impact on the strategy.) The framework also highlights the role of suppliers, partners and alliances, which are arguably increasingly important when competition is between different value chains and 'ecosystems'.

The Melville et al. (2004) framework makes clear how relevant context is at many different levels. It also reinforces that questions of the 'value of IT'

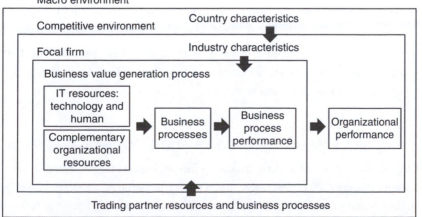

Figure 8.1 Framework for IT value (Melville et al.)

have to relate to a specific context and that value realization is not a matter of technology implementation, as it depends on complementary organizational resources (people and practices) and value is realized through business processes (people doing things).

PERSPECTIVES ON STRATEGY

Mintzberg (1994) differentiates between strategic thinking (vision) and strategic programming (i.e., detailed long-term plans) and highlights a strong emergent element of strategy as learning and change have an impact. The uncertainty in the world means that successful strategy is primarily about having a clear vision (Beinhocker and Kaplan, 2002) and the strategy process is about:

- 'prepared minds', so that the management team understand the vision and can take decisions in response to ongoing changes;
- encouraging and managing creativity and balancing top-down and bottom-up creativity.

Competitive advantage comes from a stream of continuous innovation and evolution that provides a stream of sources of temporary advantage (Beinhocker, 1997). Implementation of strategy is also impacted by the uncertainty of cause and effect, and the impact of change programmes is hard to predict. As a result, a portfolio approach, managing a range of investments of varying scale, has many advantages. It allows phased investments and enables competences to be developed over time (Bryan, 2002).

The implications for the benefits realization capability include:

- the expectation of change and the need for IT change programmes to be able to identify and respond to changes in the strategy and the wider organizational context;
- the need for a portfolio approach to IT investments to complement the business portfolio;
- the expectation that major change programmes will have to cope with both uncertainty of cause and effect in relation to actions to implement change and uncertainty about the target outcomes.

STRATEGIC PERSPECTIVE ON INNOVATION

Organizations have different attitudes to innovation and the adoption of technology. Rogers (1995) described five types of technology adopters based on timing of adoption: innovators, early adopters, early majority, late majority and laggards. The approach taken by an organization will depend on a range of factors, including perceptions of the effectiveness of the IT function and senior

Business strategy type	Characteristics – implication for innovation
Prospector	Willing to take a lead in innovation to develop market presence. Potentially early adopter and willing to take risks in order to learn.
Analyser	Monitors and analyses the external environment and may be quick to imitate others.
Defender	Will seek innovations in defence of market share, strengthening operational efficiency and customer relationships.
Reactor	Slow to change. Possibly pockets of innovation driven by specific champions.

Table 8.1 Business strategy types (Miles et al., 1978)

level business and IT relationships. At a business level, organizations generally take one of four approaches to strategy which will have a major impact on innovation and the role of IT (Miles et al., 1978) – see Table 8.1.

COMPETITIVE ADVANTAGE FROM CAPABILITIES

Barney (1995) sets his discussion of resources and capabilities in the context of the Strangths, Weaknesses, Opportunities and Threats (SWOT) framework. Michael Porter – for example, with his work on 'five forces' – considered the strategic opportunities from the industry structure and market within which the firm operates. This is the 'positioning' approach to strategy, focusing on the market and the opportunity and identifying how the firm positions itself, for example by cost leadership or differentiation, in order to compete.

The approach of resource-based theory is to look inside the firm at strengths and weaknesses that can be exploited to provide sources of competitive advantage. The view here is that in the short to medium term the firm cannot just change its capabilities to take on a new competitive position, so must focus on a strategy built around developing existing capabilities.

Resources and capabilities are terms that tend to be used interchangeably. The scope is broad, covering physical resources as well as factors such as history, trust, relationships and management control systems.

Barney proposes a number of criteria for evaluating resources and capabilities of a firm:

- *Value*: do a firm's resources and capabilities add value by enabling it to exploit opportunities and/or neutralize threats?
- *Rareness*: how many competing firms already possess these valuable resources and capabilities?

- *Imitability*: do firms without a resource or capability face a cost disadvantage in obtaining it compared with firms who already possess it?

Factors contributing to *imitability* include:

- the importance of history;
- the importance of numerous small decisions;
- the importance of socially complex resources;
- organization: is a firm organized to exploit the full competitive potential of its resources and capabilities?

Based on this analysis, sustained competitive advantage can only be achieved by managers exploiting the unique resources and capabilities of a firm. An additional key message is that firms cannot expect to 'purchase' competitive advantage in open markets (Barney, 1995).

Other writers in the area of resource-based theory use different terminology (e.g., 'core competences') to describe broadly similar concepts. Collis and Montgomery (1995) set out similar tests to identify a 'core competence'. They also stress that the capabilities/resource-based theory (RBT) perspective is complementary to the industry/market perspective and that both approaches are required.

Johnson and Scholes (*Exploring Corporate Strategy*, 6th edition, 2002) provide an outline of competences very similar to that of Barney. They identify (p. 175) rarity, causal ambiguity, complexity and culture as factors affecting the sustainability of the value of competences. They identify knowledge creation and integration as a critical factor. A subsequent discussion of strategic change (Chapter 11) is closely linked with their cultural web model (e.g., p. 230) and a discussion of the learning organization as an important 'lens' on the organization. In both cases there is an implication of a strong link between competences/capabilities and knowledge management/the learning organization.

The strategic implications of competing on resources are that management needs to continually invest to maintain and build valuable resources. In a situation where there are no competitive resources it may be possible to invest to build a competitive capability. One approach is to take on new challenges to build sequentially over a period of time as a capability is developed through learning and experience. From this perspective Collis and Montgomery (1995) liken the RBT approach to the development of a learning organization. A further implication is that management should leverage existing core capabilities more widely: for example, in entering new markets.

The fourth era of IT (Peppard and Ward, 2004) builds on this resource-based perspective and emphasizes IT as a crucial element of these organizational capabilities and the continual evolution of competitive advantage.

FRAMEWORK FOR IT STRATEGY

Our aim is to develop the IT strategy for the organization under consideration. We need an approach and set of tools that can be used in a variety of situations, from small to very large organizations and within a business unit of a larger organization. Key questions are: what are the priorities for action and investment to deliver benefits for stakeholders? And how can we build the capability of the organization to realize value from investments in IT?

The starting-point is to establish a framework for IT strategy. Then we revisit driver analysis and the IT and Change Portfolio and explore how to make use of these important elements of the overall toolkit in the context of strategy development. Then we consider setting priorities, and finally we reflect on wider factors that contribute to succeeding with the work on strategy.

OUTLINE OF A FRAMEWORK FOR IT STRATEGY

The emphasis on benefits realization follows through into the work on strategy. The working definition of strategy is 'an integrated set of actions *to provide benefits* over the long term to enterprise *stakeholders*' (based on work by John Ward: e.g., Ward and Peppard, 2002). A framework for IT strategy is set out in Figure 8.2. There are a number of important implications of the framework.

Firstly, the split of the strategy into three components is crucial. At the top level the business strategy provides a starting-point. It provides the overall direction and priorities for the organization. In some cases it may not be written down, at least in a form that is helpful for our purposes. However, it

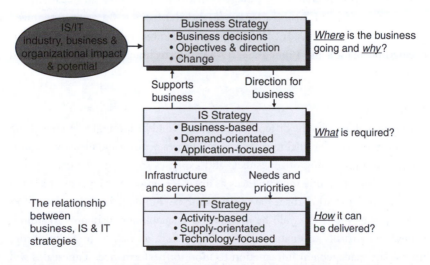

Figure 8.2 A framework for IT strategy (Earl (1989); Ward and Peppard (2002))

will always exist at some level, if only in the minds and actions of the executives. It is most helpful when, in addition to vision, mission, values and long-term key performance indicators, there are clear priorities and plans for investment and improvement.

IT strategy

The IS/IT strategy is deliberately split into two components. In some areas we have overlooked the important distinction between IS and IT. Here this is not possible, and we need to consider each aspect of the strategy. The IT strategy is about the technology – hardware, software, networks and issues of sourcing, supply, operation and maintenance of these IT assets. It also addresses the internal workings of the IT function. Over all the IT strategy tackles the *supply-side* perspective on the strategy and *how* the need set out by the business and IS strategy will be delivered.

Key considerations to address in the IT strategy might include: use of cloud-based applications; local vs. organization-wide applications; application integration; PC renewal; mobile security and support; data centre virtualization. There are many technical, contractual and management issues, and organizations have faced very rapid change over the last five to ten years. Key goals include availability, scalability, security, cost-effectiveness and flexibility. The technology infrastructure provides a very valuable capability for the organization and can be an important enabler of flexibility and responsiveness: for example, in rapidly launching a new application or location, or responding to acquisitions and de-mergers.

IS strategy

The information systems (IS) strategy is distinct from the IT strategy. The IS strategy is written in business language and the focus is on *what* is required to meet stakeholder needs. The language will often relate to services, processes, information and a functional (rather than technical) view of systems and applications.

IS vs. IT strategy

An example illustrates the difference between IS and IT strategies. A consulting organization may identify improving cash flow as a priority and identify the submission and processing of timesheets and expenses from consultants, and also the workflow around issuing invoices as areas for action, with a goal of issuing interim invoices within three days of the end of a billing period. In terms of IS strategy, the objectives could be established as enabling consultants to submit timesheets virtually to enable improved cash flow, as well as providing more up-to-date management information to monitor performance. Timescales will be considered and an initial benefits case set out.

Issues of how to deliver the business requirements are then matters for the IT strategy. For example, does this require an upgrade or replacement to the existing billing system? Is there a web page or perhaps and 'app' for consultants? Can Excel be used as the front end? It is also important to note that, even for a relatively simple example, there are many business change issues to consider. Are any current 'back office' functions eliminated? What will happen to the staff? What will be the problems in getting timely submission by all the consulting staff? Will there be contractual or practical issues with clients in trying to move to a faster billing and collection cycle?

In practice, within an organization the IS vs. IT distinction may not be made clear, or different terms might well be used. Ownership of the IS strategy is often problematic. Input is required from business and IT specialists, and there needs to be clear business engagement. Sometimes the IT function will take ownership, perhaps because of a perceived lack of interest from business executives. There is also a risk that business–IT dialogue is effectively about the IT strategy and is over-focused on technical issues. Both of these situations are likely to be a source of problems. The simple framework set out in Figure 8.2 provides a valuable basis for a common language, as it is very likely that different people will be involved in different aspects of strategy and effective communication across organizational and professional/disciplinary boundaries will be important.

The focus of this chapter (and book) is primarily on the IS strategy, as the target is a broad business management audience. We tackle some aspects of IT strategy, but there are many areas beyond our scope.

Developing the strategy: three perspectives

The strategy framework provides a number of starting-points and linkages (see Figure 8.3). Firstly (1), the classic starting-point is with the business strategy. Given the business strategy, what are the implications for the IS strategy? In some cases these will be very clear; in others the implications will be more hidden. Driver analysis provides an approach and set of tools for exploring the implications of the business strategy. Then, following this path, the implications for the IT strategy are considered: how will the business priorities articulated in the IS strategy be delivered?

The second perspective takes the IT strategy and existing infrastructure as a starting-point (2). Given the results of past decisions that have resulted in an operational IT infrastructure, applications and data, as well as an infrastructure in the sense of people, process and skills, what are the implications for how we assess priorities and deliver change? There is almost never a complete 'greenfield' situation, or, if there is, money is likely to be in short supply (a start-up). So there will always be many constraints and opportunities

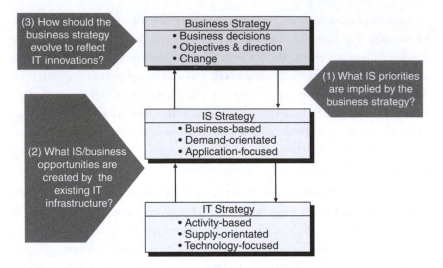

Figure 8.3 Three perspectives on developing the strategy

based on the results of past decisions and the evaluation of the current infrastructure.

In the real world, where there are always far more possibilities and potential projects than the capacity to deliver, this second perspective is important. Our choices of what to set as priorities (business and IS strategy) will be influenced by what we know of feasibility and risk (IT strategy). Some things will be straightforward; others will be very costly and difficult. For example, if a global organization has already invested in a high-bandwidth network to support centrally run systems, it may be straightforward to deploy instant messaging and desktop video conferencing to support improved communication and flexible working. Alternatively, the organization may have been an early adopter of enterprise systems (ERP) but now cannot afford to upgrade or replace to take advantage of new functionality and cloud-based services because the current solution is 'OK' and the cost and disruption of change are significant.

The third perspective (3) is effectively provided by the technology element of a PEST analysis. The aim is to consider how technology is changing over a timescale relevant to the strategy exercise. What business opportunities will these technology innovations bring? Will there be a need to change the business strategy? Is any action required now to explore and prepare for realizing benefits from these new developments?

Exploring opportunities across the organization

The opportunities and risks can be at many levels. New industries have evolved (search, apps); disruptive forces have undermined previous business models and market leaders (music). Existing businesses have taken advantage of new channels and business models (retail, airlines), and at a more local level technology has contributed to innovations with a major cumulative impact. For example, a bus operator is using information from the engine management system to provide a real-time feed to drivers showing how fuel-efficiently they are driving. Information is also tracked centrally, and there is a weekly competition for the best driver. Saving 4% of fuel costs is a useful contribution to profitability and the cumulative impact of this and other savings can be significant.

The 'top-down' analysis (1), 'bottom-up' analysis (2) and consideration of opportunities for innovation (3) are all important for a digital business. The scope of a particular strategy exercise can be agreed to address one or more of these perspectives. In each case a range of tools is available to contribute to getting people to work together to make informed decisions.

PORTFOLIO PERSPECTIVE

The IT and Change Portfolio is a core part of the strategy toolkit. Given that vision, mission, values are set as part of the business strategy, the emphasis for the IS strategy is on the set of investments to deliver benefits for stakeholders. We can analyse these investments in various ways, but the portfolio provides an important starting-point. The structure of the IS strategy also reflects the importance of the portfolio (Box 8.2).

Box 8.2   Basic structure and content of an IS strategy

Purpose of this version of the IS strategy.

Overview/summary of business strategy:

- to provide context; objectives and critical success factors; analysis of competitive forces and resulting issues affecting the IS strategy;

- context in terms of business priorities and implications for new and enhanced business capabilities.

Argument for:

- new IS opportunities (to gain advantage);

- critical improvement areas (to avoid disadvantage).

Summary of opportunities/problem issues:

- one page for each, explaining the application/opportunity/issue, rationale, potential benefits, any critical dependencies and initial actions to be taken;

- opportunities/issues should be separated into:
  - competitive, exploratory, qualifying and support
  - prioritization high/medium/low based on business timescales (e.g., H = within 6 months, M = 12 months, L = 2 years).

Review of current applications and current projects:

- overall resource implications of completing outstanding work and ongoing commitments (major components should be described in appendices);
- resources available to address new work;
- any critical issues requiring resolution within the existing strategy.

Future application portfolio;

Issues arising from the IS strategy;

Implications for development of the overall IS capability (see Chapter 14).

Source: The outline draws on Ward and Peppard (2002)

The portfolio provides a visual and analytical tool for a critical review of the whole set of investment proposals (Figure 8.4). Given the strategy of the organization, does the overall balance of proposals make sense? If the organization is innovative, are the exploratory projects exploring important new opportunities? What level of competitive projects is proposed, and is there the leadership and wider organizational capacity to handle them? What percentage of investment is into support projects, and is there a risk that this is getting too high? While support projects are important for addressing local and tactical requirements, they tend to be easy to justify, as they are or should be about saving money, so there is a tendency for too much investment in this area. Is there sufficient investment in qualifying systems? Although we might not want to fix what is not broken, there is also a case for 'investing while the sun is shining' and before the crisis hits.

There is no right answer to the question 'What percentage of budget should be spent in each area of the portfolio?' other than 'It depends'. The answer is what the management team agrees to, but the analysis will rapidly highlight 'wrong' answers.

It is important to note that in many organizations a large percentage of the IT budget is spent on current systems and priorities. Keeping this down to 75% of the total is typically good performance. As a result, reducing this cost and freeing up resources for investment in innovation and improvement are often a strategic priority. In addition, there are crucial strategic issues of change capability and capacity, which are addressed further in Chapter 14. At a basic level, if 75% or more of projects fail to deliver value, it is important to fix this problem rather than focus only on where to make the next set of investments, knowing that 75% of these are doomed to fail. The groundwork provided by chapters 1–7 tackles this area of succeeding with investments in change.

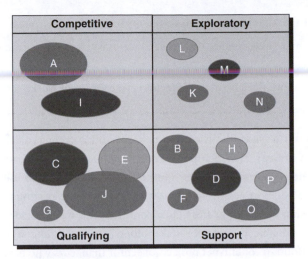

Figure 8.4 Using the IT and Change Portfolio to represent the IS strategy

The portfolio analysis should also be used to explore other dimensions. For example, how do the investments relate to different aspects of the organization in terms of processes and business units? What does the portfolio look like at a business unit level, where there will be the local impact of organizational projects as well as local projects? What is the ownership of projects in the portfolio? For example, there will be projects owned by the IT function, projects with IT components owned by business units and other functional areas as well as other investments in change with no direct IT components (e.g., education and culture initiative driven by HR).

There is also a time dimension to the portfolio that needs to be considered as part of the overall work on strategy. What are the current systems that are in place and supporting the operation and management of the organization? What are the current projects where investments are already being made to deliver new systems and services (see Box 8.3)? In a large organization it is not uncommon for there to be 100+ projects under way at any time.

Box 8.3 Different dimensions of the IT and Change Portfolio

The current business

- What processes/systems do have, and where do we need to improve?

Existing projects

- Are the projects we are working on still a priority?

> **The future** – benefits-driven investments in IS/IT and business change
>
> - What new investments do we need to make to support the current business?
> - How can we develop new products/services/ways of working?

It is important to assess both current systems and current projects as part of the work on strategy. How do these current systems align with existing business processes and organizational units? How effective are they from user/customer and technical/support perspectives? How well aligned are existing projects with current organizational priorities? How confident are we that current projects will deliver valuable benefits for stakeholders? It is not uncommon for the project portfolio to contain pet projects of senior managers who have long since moved on, to contain projects that no longer have real management support but carry on as a result of a dogged determination to 'finish what we started', and to contain projects that have become black holes sucking in resources and management attention in apparently doomed attempts to deliver something seen as very important. Depending on the maturity of strategic and portfolio management (see Chapter 9) in the organization, the review of current systems and the current project portfolio might be vital elements of the development of strategy to get a balanced sense of priorities, to see where resources can be freed up by completing or killing current projects and by getting a better insight into the capacity for change.

The extent of work required in relation to current systems will vary dramatically depending on the objectives of the work on IS/IT strategy and particularly the maturity of the organization in terms of benefits review and benefits exploitation (Ashurst et al., 2008).

DRIVER ANALYSIS

Driver analysis (see Box 8.4) provides a way to think about and explore the drivers for change (Why do we need to change? How pressing is the need for action, in the context of the risks associated with change?), and then set the investment objectives for the change programme (What is the vision? What does success look like?).

> **Box 8.4   Driver analysis: key definitions**
>
> **Drivers** (business drivers): views held by senior management as to what is important to the business – in a given timescale – such that they feel changes must occur. Drivers for change can be both internal and external, but are specific to the context in which the organization operates.

> **Investment objectives**: targets for achievement agreed for the invest-
> ment in relation to the drivers. As a set, they provide the vision for
> the investment and a description of what the situation should be on
> completion of the investment.
>
> **Business benefit**: an advantage on behalf of a particular stakeholder
> or group of stakeholders.
>
> **Stakeholder(s)**: an individual or group who will benefit from the
> investment or are either directly involved in making or are affected by
> the changes needed to realize the benefits.
>
> *Source*: Ward and Daniel (2006), p. 106–107

At the strategy level the key question is 'Where should we invest in order to deliver value for stakeholders?' It is about exploring opportunities and taking decisions to set priorities. So we are tackling a bigger question than when we used driver analysis at a project level, asking 'How does this proposed invest-ment contribute to the strategic objectives of the organization?' Resources and capacity for change are always limited compared with the many opportunities, so it is always essential to take decisions and set priorities.

It is vital to reflect that the drivers are the 'views held by senior manage-ment'. This is fundamental to the approach to strategy: from this perspective it is about people, their engagement and commitment to the direction and to taking action. Strategy is not primarily about analysis.

Driver analysis can draw on a very wide range of tools, particularly from the strategy domain. The tools used depend on the scope, resources and timescales of a particular strategy exercise. A key criterion for deciding which tools to use is how they enable people to get involved as really the tools are only a means to an end, enabling people to explore opportunities and set priorities. There is a risk that using the tool and completing the model becomes an end in itself. Which tools are already in use in the organization and familiar to participants is also an important consideration. It is important to avoid creating barriers to partic-ipation and engagement, and there is a risk that unfamiliar tools, particularly if introduced by the IT function, will lead to problems.

Tools for driver analysis

The competitive competences and five forces tools are useful starting-points (Chapter 3). SWOT and PEST can also be valuable. The stakeholder map and consideration of benefits to stakeholders using the Benefits Dependency Net-work is also a key foundation. Benefits visualization tools such as the BDN and benefits roadmap are a valuable part of the strategy toolkit. By being applied to a broader context they provide a way for a group to collaborate and work creatively to identify opportunities and dependencies. The structure they impose is a valuable aid to clear thinking. When used to help develop the strategy, the BDN focuses on enterprise stakeholders (in line with the definition of strategy) and the business changes are individual projects and programmes. In every case context and focus are vital, and the tools can be used very superficially or to produce deep insights.

Other tools are very valuable for getting a broad perspective of the organization and help address the risk of focusing only on the most visible needs and loudest voices. Value chain, business process and capability mapping all provide valuable ways of exploring this big picture and can have value in the longer term beyond the strategy exercise. These tools take longer to use, for example a few days or a few workshop sessions, and preferably need some experience, but they can still be used as part of a short strategy exercise. They reinforce the shift of focus from systems onto the business and make it easier to identify gaps: for example, 'How do we need to improve this business activity?', 'What systems support this business activity/capability, and how effective are they?' rather than 'How should we improve system X?' From experience the result is likely to be the identification of important business capabilities where there is currently little management attention and limited IT support.

The process of driver analysis

There is no getting away from the driver analysis as being a complex, messy process. Essentially the team uses a variety of tools to explore various perspectives on the organization and identify different opportunities for investment in the context of an understanding of different stakeholder groups and what they perceive as benefits. The value often comes from using a simple set of tools to work with a range of different organizational units and stakeholder groups to get different perspectives. The tools used can help cover a range of perspectives: an external view of markets and competitors to explore positioning; an internal view of capabilities and how they can be developed; and also a value innovation perspective (for example, Kim and Mauborgne, 2005), for example exploring how the major strands of IT innovation and wider socio-economic trends might create new opportunities (Box 8.5).

Box 8.5   Value innovation – A strategic perspective

In *Blue Ocean Strategy* (2005) contrast the tough competition in 'red oceans' where all the competitors are fighting on the basis of price or differentiation in terms of features, with the 'blue ocean' of calm beautiful waters where the competition is irrelevant. They provide a series of tools to help identify blue oceans – where you effectively create a new market by creating value for customers in a different way.

Examples include creating a very simple and easy-to-use mobile phone service when other players are competing on constant new features, and then a very clearly and simply labelled range of wine when others use very complex and pretentious language.

The 'blue ocean' approach parallels the discussion of design-led thinking in Chapter 5.

One tool we have found very useful is 'a day in the life of': this involves writing about the future in the present tense, as if it has already arrived, from the perspective of a specific stakeholder. It provides a way of releasing creativity and is a compelling way to communicate ideas. The scenario can also be brought to life in a short video acting out the future.

The prototyping of design thinking becomes experimentation through exploratory projects as new ideas are explored with employees and customers. Often it will be valuable to work with partners and to build alliances to increase the range of opportunities and the ability to deliver.

At this stage it is often helpful to develop an initial outline of each opportunity using an agreed format. These half- to one-page outlines force clarity of thinking, aid communication and can accelerate the next stage of more detailed work. These contribute to the strategy and also provide a first draft of concept papers for individual projects (Chapter 2).

It is also common and very helpful at this stage to identify and start tackling problems and opportunities for quick wins where action just needs to happen and there is no need for further consideration as part of the strategy.

SETTING PRIORITIES

Having identified a wide range of opportunities, the next stage is to start to focus the list and develop an agreed set of investment priorities. As a strategy exercise we are probably still working at a high level, so we are not yet at the stage of developing a full benefits realization plan. Relating this to the project lifecycle, we are effectively working on a preliminary view of the Engage phase for these possible projects.

So the key challenge is how to filter the *opportunities* identified into an agreed set of *priorities*. Key factors are who is involved in this decision and what criteria do they use. We return to the question of *who* from a governance perspective in Chapter 9. Here we just note that the outcome will depend on the people involved. This is not pure science, so getting the right people involved is vital.

In terms of the criteria used to make a decision, the key point is that it is vital to develop and use a set of criteria to help inform the decision so it does not depend entirely on politics. However, the criteria can only ever contribute to the decision-making as, again, we are not plugging numbers into mathematical algorithm.

From the driver analysis we know something about the reasons for each proposed investment and what it might involve. We have taken a view on how it contributes to the organization and strategic objectives, by using the IT and Change Portfolio. We know something about the degree of change involved (see Box 8.6). We also know something about the level of management commitment, if we have involved relevant people in the work to date.

Box 8.6   Degrees of change

The driver analysis will identify a range of project and programmes involving different degrees of change. One way of classifying them is:

- stop something – remove a problem;
- business as usual – sustain performance;
- incremental change – targeted improvement;
- innovation – radical change.

Source: Ward and Daniel (2006)

Each opportunity will have a range of characteristics, and it is helpful to get a broad view at an early stage (see Box 8.7). In addition, it is important to consider limitations on change capacity: for example, IT technical staff will be much more effective with technologies/systems they already know in the short/medium term, and each business area can only cope with a certain amount of change in any period of time. As a result there are restrictions, possibly significant ones, in how the overall change capability of the organization can be deployed across different projects. In many cases portfolio and agile perspectives will mean that short initial projects can be proposed as ways of starting to make progress at reduced risk and at the same time starting to enhance the change capability.

Box 8.7   Factors to consider in screening opportunities

- portfolio category;
- business process and departments effect;

- number of potential users;
- degree/type of business change;
- costs;
- benefits – types/magnitude;
- alignment and contribution to strategic goals;
- resources required to deliver and existing capability;
- business risk (e.g., uncertainty of market);
- technical risk;
- degree of sponsorship;
- confidence in understanding of customer value and market opportunity.

SUCCEEDING WITH THE IT STRATEGY

What does success look like in relation to the work on developing the strategy? The approach set out above draws on extensive experience and addresses the major problems with strategy exercises. At this point it is useful to provide a summary and to emphasize key points.

Firstly, you might say that acceptance of recommendations included in a strategy report or presentation is success. Going further, a stronger measure would be that action happens, that funds and people are committed to follow through the recommendations and that as a result of the strategy exercise there is commitment to and engagement in action. Over a longer time-frame the success of the strategy can be judged by results. Are the recommendations implemented? Are the intended benefits realized? Is further work done in the future to evolve the strategy?

The quality of the strategy is hard to judge. Factors might include the extent of engagement in identification of opportunities, decision-making and the buy-in to following through to implementation. The strategic alignment of the recommendations is important, as well as handling new insights and opportunities that have an impact on the existing business strategy.

A broader factor is the extent to which engagement in the strategy activity has given people new insights into the organization and its strategy so that they are better equipped to take local decisions and react to events: 'prepared minds' (Beinhocker and Kaplan, 2002) is a key outcome. In addition, engagement with development of the strategy will have helped participants learn to use elements of the strategy toolkit, which, because of its scalability and fairly small learning curve, will equip them to be able to use many of the tools in their local context. This will probably involve 'managing strategically' rather than formally developing strategy, but the tools will be valuable in many different contexts.

Work by Earl (1993) and also Doherty et al. (1999) into the success of different approaches to strategy (see Box 8.8) provides support for the approach set out in this chapter: the use of tools and methods as a means to an end and the focus on people.

Box 8.8   Approaches to IT strategy

Earl (1993) explored approaches to strategic information system planning in practice. There were two primary goals: aligning investment in IT with business goals, and exploiting IT for competitive advantage.

He identified five different approaches characterized by a mix of method, process and extent of focus on implementation:

- *organizational* – development of key themes for IS investment from a consensus view of priorities;
- *business-led* – business plans analysed to identify where IS is most critical;
- *administrative* – focus on budgets;
- *method-driven* – use of techniques, often from a consultancy;
- *technological* – focus on IT architecture.

In a broad quantitative study Doherty et al. identified three of the approaches set out by Earl and a fourth, which was an amalgam of method- and technology-driven. They also confirmed Earl's finding that an organizational approach is the most successful and administrative is the least successful.

Based on work by Earl and Doherty et al., we can summarize the organizational approach as follows:

- Use methods as required – fit for purpose.
- Emphasize senior management understanding and involvement.
- Build a multi-disciplinary team for the project.
- Encourage high levels of creativity.
- Focus on specific themes (a small number).
- Ensure a strong implementation focus.
- Ensure wide participation.
- Create a capacity to learn.
- Make strategy an ongoing activity rather than one-off.

STRATEGY AS A PROJECT AND PROCESS

It is helpful to explore both process and project perspectives on IT strategy development. A process is designed to deliver value to stakeholders and implies some level of consistency and repeatability. This will be valuable across a large organization and from year to year in any organization.

Strategy development should be ongoing. In many cases it is effective to have a first, fairly rapid attempt at strategy development to build engagement and get early results, including a clearer sense of priorities for future investments. Revisiting the strategy after six or 12 months will then allow effort to be made to take the work further in particular areas, looking at more business units, in more detail at a particular theme or process, or considering a longer time horizon, for example.

The work on each stage of strategy development is a project. As such, the key practices of a project should be applied. There needs to be a sponsor and multi-disciplinary team. Early work should include a stakeholder map and consideration of benefits to stakeholders.

It is important to adopt a versioned release strategy, as the work on strategy is an excellent fit with a time-boxed approach. A series of milestones with clear deliverables helps impose a shape and build momentum on a project that could easily drift. This focus on delivery avoids 'analysis paralysis' with the aim of getting early feedback and rapid results. There should be a sense of 'planning while building' as work on strategy proceeds in parallel with work on implementation and feedback and learning enhances both strands of work.

KEY PRINCIPLES: ESTABLISHING AN EFFECTIVE APPROACH

A traditional view of IS strategy has been that it is a response to 'demand-pull' from the business strategy (Earl, 1993). A 'technology-push' perspective is also well established (Herstatt and Lettl, 2004). These perspectives reflect the (planned) alignment of business and IS/IT strategies. The concept of co-evolution reflects a third perspective, often reflecting the messy reality of interaction of business, IS and IT (Peppard and Breu, 2003).

Mintzberg draws the distinction between strategic planning and strategic thinking. The concept of a long-term (e.g., five-year), detailed strategic plan

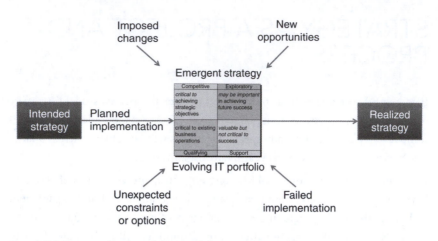

Figure 8.5 The contribution of the portfolio to strategic agility

with specific projects, deliverables and dates has been widely discredited. The approach put forward here is using a series of tools to help guide strategic thinking. Hopefully the direction and priorities are clear, but the investment programmes evolve over time and the strategy itself is kept under review.

There is a direct fit with the concepts of planned and emergent strategy (Figure 8.5). The portfolio and implementation through a series of short projects are important enablers of flexibility and responsiveness to a changing context. This 'strategic agility' can be an important source of advantage.

The approach encourages broad engagement and attempts to reflect both bottom-up and top-down input. Finally, while the approach encourages alignment of the IS/IT strategies with the business strategy, there is also room for co-evolution, for example as the consideration of new technologies drives change in the existing business strategy. A key aim is to enable making a more strategic way of working business as usual and to embed use of the relevant tools across the organization. In a digital business, handling uncertainty and a rapid pace of change, this is an important element of the overall 'IT capability'.

TAKING IT FURTHER

FURTHER READING AND RESOURCES

Carr, N.G. (2003) IT Doesn't Matter. *Harvard Business Review*, May, Vol. 81 (5): 41–49.

Carr created a fierce debate with his article 'IT Doesn't Matter'. Carr suggests that IT is a commodity and as a result cannot contribute to competitive advantage. This article addresses an important issue and has caused a lot of discussion. Brown and Hagel provide a response.

Brown, J.S. and Hagel, J. (2003) Does IT Matter? *Harvard Business Review*, July 2003, Vol. 81 (7): 109–112.

Prahalad, C.K. and Krishnan, M.S. (2002) The Dynamic Synchronization of Strategy and Information Technology. *Sloan Management Review*, Summer, Vol. 43 (4): 24–33.

David, M. and Bradley R. (2008) Radically Simple IT. *Harvard Business Review*, March 2008, Vol. 86 (3): 118–124.

TALKING POINTS

Use these questions to help reflect on this chapter and explore the challenges of putting the ideas into practice:

1. What are the IT trends likely to have an impact on your industry?
2. What are the opportunities for disruptive innovation?
3. How might new developments create opportunities for:
   a. new products and services?
   b. new business models?
4. What are the outcomes from work on strategy?
5. How would you decide on the extent of work to develop or update the strategy and who to involve?
6. How (and when) can you judge the success of work on strategy?
7. Is work on strategy for a few people in the organization or for many?
8. What is your experience of strategy and business planning? What are the pitfalls? What contributes to success?
9. How does your experience relate to the work by Earl on what makes a successful approach to IT strategy?
10. How should we handle work on strategy when every business is a digital business?
11. How do you respond to the challenge that, given the pace of innovation and change, as well as the level of uncertainty, there is no point trying to take a long-term view?
12. What might be the contribution of suppliers and other external contacts to the strategy? What might be the value of consultants?
13. How would you balance effort and resources across the three approaches to strategy? (Consider: (i) exploiting the current business & IT infrastructure; (ii) responding to business priorities; (iii) exploring the opportunity for strategic change based on technology innovations.)
14. If strategy is a process, not a one-off activity, what are the implications?

Corporate strategy

An alternative perspective on strategy is to focus on corporate strategy, for example considering: what business and markets should we be in? What is the core business, and what do we outsource? How do we fund the business? How do we deliver value to shareholders and owners? What is the role of mergers, acquisitions and divestment?

How does this corporate strategy perspective fit with the approach taken in this chapter?

CASE STUDY 8.1

Sustainability is an important strategic driver with broad implications.

Journal of Information Technology Teaching Cases, Vol. 4 (2014): 41–48.

Implementing sustainable IT strategy: the case of Intel

Edward Curry and Brian Donnellan

Sustainable IT (Information Technology) involves the responsible management of resources (both IT and non-IT) encompassing environmental, economic and social dimensions. Sustainable IT has the potential to be a significant contributor to an organization's sustainability strategy. In this teaching case, we examine what Intel IT has done to transform its operations with Sustainable IT, resulting in the avoidance of significant CO_2 emissions and cost savings. This teaching case challenges the reader to analyse the Sustainable IT capability at Intel. The case includes insights into strategic and operational challenges of planning and managing Sustainable IT.

REFERENCES

Accenture (2014) Accenture Technology Vision 2014 – Every Business Is a Digital Business – From Digitally Disrupted to Digital Disrupter.

Ashurst, C., Doherty, N. and Peppard, J. (2008) Improving the Impact of IT Development Projects: The Benefits Realization Capability Model. *European Journal of Information Systems*, Vol. 17: 352–370.

Barney, J. (1995), Looking Inside for Competitive Advantage. *Academy of Management Executive*, Vol. 9 (4): 49–61.

Beinhocker, E. and Kaplan, S. (2002) Tired of Strategic Planning. *The McKinsey Quarterly*, Special Edition: Risk and Resilience.

Beinhocker, E. (1997) Strategy at the Edge of Chaos. *The McKinsey Quarterly*, 9 (1): 109–118.

Bryan, L. (2002) Just in Time Strategy. *The McKinsey Quarterly*, Special Edition: Risk and Resilience.

Collis, David J. and Montgomery, Cynthia A. (1995) Competing on Resources: Strategy in the 1990s. *Harvard Business Review*, July–August 1995, Vol. 73 (4): 118–128.

Doherty, N.F., Marples, C.G. and Suhaimi, A. (1999) The Relative Success of Alternative Approaches to Strategic Information Systems Planning: An Empirical Analysis. *Journal of Strategic Information Systems*, Vol. 8 (3): 263–283.

Earl, M. (1989) *Management Strategies for Information Technology*, Harlow: Prentice Hall.

Earl, M.J. (1993) Experiences in Strategic Information Systems Planning. *MIS Quarterly*, Vol. 17 (1): 1–24.

Herstatt, C. and Lettl, C. (2004) Management of 'Technology Push' Development Projects. *International Journal of Technology Management*, Vol. 27 (2–3): 155–175.

Johnson, G. and Scholes, K. (2002) *Exploring Corporate Strategy*, 6th edition, FT Prentice Hall.

Kim, W. and Mauborgne, R. (2005) *Blue Ocean Strategy*, Harvard Business School Press.

Melville, N., Kraemer, K. and Gurbaxani, V. (2004) Information Technology and Organizational Performance: An Integrative Model of IT Business Value. *MIS Quarterly*, Vol. 28 (2): 283–322.

Miles, R., Snow, C.C., Meyer, A. and Coleman, H. (1978) Organizational Strategy, Structure, and Process. *The Academy of Management Review*, Vol. 3 (3): 546–562.

Mintzberg, H. (1994) *The Rise and Fall of Strategic Planning*, New York: Free Press.

Murray, P. with Ward, J., Elvin, R. and Hemingway, C. (2001) Advanced Benefits Management, Cranfield School of Management, Information Systems Research Centre, Document Number – ISRC-200107.

Peppard, J. and Breu, K. (2003) Beyond Alignment – A Co-Evolutionary View of the IS Strategy Process, in *Proceedings of 24th International Conference on Information Systems (ICIS)*, Seattle, WA, pp. 743–750.

Peppard, J. and Ward, J. (2004) Beyond Strategic Information Systems: Towards an IS Capability. *Journal of Strategic Information Systems*, Vol. 13 (2): 167–194.

Rogers, E. (1995) *Diffusion of Innovations*, Free Press.

Ward, J. and Daniel, E. (2006) *Benefits Management*, John Wiley and Sons.

Ward, J. and Peppard, J. (2002) *Strategic Planning for Information Systems*, 3rd edition, John Wiley and Sons.

CHAPTER 9
MANAGING THE IT PORTFOLIO

IN THIS CHAPTER WE STUDY:

- portfolio management as a driver of benefits realization;
- practices for portfolio management related to competences for benefits realization;
- steps to develop the portfolio management capability.

PORTFOLIO MANAGEMENT AS A KEY DRIVER OF BENEFITS REALIZATION

For an organization seeking to improve benefits realization from IT action, at both project and portfolio levels, is almost certain to be required. This chapter tackles the portfolio perspective. It follows the discussion of strategy in Chapter 7, reflecting that portfolio management provides a bridge between strategy and implementation of change to enable *use* of IT to deliver business benefits.

SCOPE OF PORTFOLIO MANAGEMENT

It is important to note that in many organizations establishing a framework for portfolio management will be complex, partly due to the lack of a common language. In a recent workshop an IT director referred to a 'project' that had been running for six years. In this case, the 'project' included an operational (live/production) service and probably a 'programme' (i.e., a series of projects all contributing to strategic goal). In other situations, adoption of agile approaches involving rapid and incremental delivery of benefit from a series of releases, with planning taking place across multiple releases, blurs the boundary between a project and programme. We would take a pragmatic approach, starting with current usage in the organization, and aim to move to distinguish between project, programme and (operational) service. All of these are elements of the portfolio.

The scope of the 'portfolio' varies in other ways. For example, does it relate to all projects funded from the IT budget or owned by the IT department? Alternatively, perhaps it looks more broadly at all projects, which are affected by IT. There is also the time dimension: ideas for projects; live projects; completed projects; and operational systems or services. Again, we would take a pragmatic approach and make a start with the portfolio at a level that adds value in the short term. This might be a review of live projects or work on strategy that brings together ideas and priorities for future projects. A more comprehensive approach to managing the IT investment portfolio can then be developed over time.

A further important element to the scope of adoption of the portfolio is the organizational dimension. In virtually every medium or large organization the portfolio will be valuable at a number of organizational levels (team, department, business unit, etc.). The focus on benefits from IT-enabled change is the core aim. It does not matter whether the IT function (infrastructure and application development) is centralized or local; even with a highly centralized

IT infrastructure there is a need for a local business perspective on the portfolio. For example, the local portfolio needs to address the local implications of centrally driven projects, as there will be resource implications and presumably a need for local ownership of benefits realization. The local portfolio should also address local projects. There will usually be a range of important projects that can drive benefits realization that do not require central IT resource. For example, improved use of information or taking advantage of existing system features to improve efficiency or customer service (benefits exploitation). The portfolio has the nature of a 'fractal'; it can be usefully applied at any part of the organization.

This perspective also makes clear the organization-wide nature of the benefits realization capability reaching across central functions and local business units. There is value in adopting key practices very broadly.

PORTFOLIO MANAGEMENT AS A CRITICAL ELEMENT IN BENEFITS REALIZATION

Practices for the management of the IT investment portfolio emerged as a crucial theme at an early stage of my research in benefits realization from IT. Participants in the research projects provided many examples of how taking a portfolio perspective resulted in improved benefits realization.

The IT strategy director of a financial services company highlighted one of the major barriers to benefits realization: selecting the right projects. She and her business colleagues were unable to get approval for a number of projects that they agreed would enable business innovation and help the organization exploit new business opportunities. The rigid, cost-benefit approach to investment appraisal adopted by the organization meant that these projects could not be approved, as there could be no confirmation in advance of the potential benefits from innovation. We will never know what the benefits to the business might have been if they had been able to follow up these opportunities for innovation within the IT project portfolio.

The IT director at a public sector agency gave one example of saving £600,000 through the initiative of one of his project managers taking a cross-organization view of the project portfolio. The project manager was given the job of kicking off a new project – starting to establish requirements and build engagement with key business stakeholders. The budget for the project was £600,000. She had worked for the organization for some years and had good connections. As a result, she quickly discovered a second project, not connected with the IT function, that was tackling the same issues with a similar budget. Through the initiative of the project manager, and the influence of the IT director, the result was a single, combined project with a budget of £600,000 – hence the saving of £600,000.

A number of organizations highlighted a third opportunity for benefits realization: from better exploitation of existing systems and information. They had all made substantial investments in enterprise systems, yet there was no investment in continued exploitation of these assets other than reactive help desk and support services. The result, with changing business requirements and the impact of staff turnover, was frustration at the perceived lack of information and lack of flexibility of the systems.

Recent work has provided a definition of IT portfolio management:

> A continuous process to manage IT project, application, and infrastructure assets and their interdependencies, in order to maximize portfolio benefits, minimize risk and ensure alignment with organizational strategy, over the long run.
>
> (Kumar et al., 2008)

Our focus in this chapter is on the realization of benefits from the portfolio of investments in IT across an organization. The focus on the IT portfolio highlights crucial issues that are not visible when looking at individual projects or when looking at more general perspectives such as IT governance. To increase the benefits realized from IT, top management need to focus on practices for management of the IT portfolio. We have set out a number of management practices that contribute to improved benefits realization. We also identify a number of steps that can be taken to improve the IT portfolio management capability of the organization.

There are at least four compelling reasons why an explicit portfolio perspective will enhance the benefits realization capability of an organization:

1. Selecting which projects to invest in is crucial as 'the greatest gains come from doing the right things' (Earl and Feeny, 1994).

2. Benefits often stem from a number of related projects, rather than a single project.

3. Systems and projects have different characteristics – for example, in terms of benefits and risks – and they need to be managed in a way that reflects these differences.

4. Benefits realization practices need to be nurtured across an organization's complete IT portfolio.

A FRAMEWORK FOR MANAGING THE IT PORTFOLIO

An important starting-point for realizing value from investments in IT is the IT and Change Portfolio (Figure 9.1, based on Ward and Peppard (2002) and McFarlan (1981)). This describes the investments in IT-enabled business

Figure 9.1 IT and Change Portfolio (revised)
Source: Highlighting investments to develop the dynamic/transformational capability.

change, applications and services (those already in place, those planned and future possibilities), not in terms of technology but in terms of their role and contribution to business performance. The portfolio enables senior business and IT managers to work together to get a clearer focus on doing the right things: setting priorities and ensuring strategic alignment of investments in IT-enabled change.

The portfolio has been used to help plan a specific investment in benefits-driven change and also to plan the overall portfolio of investments as part of the work on strategy. In this chapter the emphasis is on managing the overall portfolio of investments in IT, building on earlier discussions.

Organizational maturity for portfolio management is low. In this chapter we present a number of practices, which contribute to improved portfolio management and provide a basis for improvisation and adaptation within organizations to contribute to benefits realization.

Figure 9.1 presents a revised version of the IT and Change Portfolio. The new category, 'Transformational', reflects investments that are designed to enhance the benefits realization/transformational capability of the organization. In Chapter 14 we link this capability with the focus on dynamic capabilities, which is a major strand of thinking related to strategic management.

PORTFOLIO PLANNING

One IT director highlighted how the gap between business and IT affected benefits planning:

> The project manager said to me: 'If I can get rid of all this complicated IT, I can make it deliver. The project initiation document wasn't originally shown to me. It said we will do this bit and IT will do the rest. Like we'll install the ATMs and IT will provide the rest of the bank. The way the project initiation document was written, it was a no-win for IT. I had to beg $20k to do some studies. To start off I had to use the stationery budget.

A key driver for work at a portfolio level is to bring together business and IT stakeholders, using the IT portfolio to help establish a common language focused on the contribution of investment to the organization and enable a 'joined-up' view of investments and investment priorities.

At the portfolio level the focus of benefits planning shifts to identifying which investments to make and getting an effective overall spread of investments. The emphasis is on strategy and also governance, in the sense of how decisions are taken across an organization by different individuals and business units.

Portfolio planning is particularly challenging. It requires good engagement across organizational units, professional disciplines and different levels of the hierarchy. There will be many challenges, including politics. There are also inherent uncertainties that must be taken into consideration in some way: how is the business context going to change during the lifetime of this investment? How will new technology innovations create opportunities, and when is the right time to make investments? These are not problems that have a 'solution', but a number of practices can help to tackle these complex, problematic situations.

One response is to adopt some of the project level practices at a portfolio level. For example, the tools of 'driver analysis' (Ward and Peppard, 2002) can be applied to the strategic question of 'Where should I invest in IT-enabled change?' as well as to the project level questions, which include 'How does this planned investment contribute to the strategic objectives of the organization?' Equally, the benefits dependency network (Ward and Daniel, 2006) can be applied at a strategy level, in which case the 'business changes' will represent programmes or strategic initiatives (covered in Chapter 8).

An architecture perspective is also valuable. This tackles the potentially adverse impact of a benefits-driven view of each project in isolation and looks across both the IT infrastructure and business organization (including business processes) to look at the big picture. Weill and Ross (2009) explore how to establish a 'digital platform' of coherent systems that allows accelerated innovation and benefits realization (see Chapter 10).

It is also important to adopt an agile perspective at a portfolio level to manage risk: speed of delivery and to maintain flexibility. A key agile principle is rapid, incremental delivery, which means that the portfolio will give priority to short projects delivering benefits over a series of 'releases' of an IT and business solution. For example, one organization works on the basis that the maximum duration on any project in the portfolio is 90 days.

A number of practices build on topics covered to date.

DEVELOPING WINNERS: SHARED MANAGEMENT OF A PIPELINE OF OPPORTUNITIES

A key concern of benefits planning is to focus on 'doing the right things'. In any organization there are many ideas for projects, and the ideas with the most vocal sponsors are not always the best. In many cases there are problems and opportunities that do not develop into specific ideas and proposals because of lack of knowledge of what is possible. There is far too little resource available to work up every idea into a full business case. Therefore the challenge is to find a way to identify and nurture these ideas and make informed decisions on priorities rather than simply select from the small sub-set that is pushed forward for consideration.

Organizations tackling these challenges take two complementary steps. Firstly, they establish an opportunity pipeline so that IT and business can work together and explore ideas prior to investment of resources in the development of a full business case. The pipeline needs decision-making gates at a number of stages to filter out less promising ideas. Some organizations are using limited seedcorn funds to enable the most promising ideas to be developed further. This idea of using gates is well known but is often only applied to projects in the IT portfolio once the business case is approved. The practice needs to be applied much earlier.

This practice is making effective use of Exploratory projects in a very targeted way to test out ideas and explore opportunities.

A second focus for 'doing the right things' is based on establishing good relationships so that IT have a 'seat at the table' and are present when business or business unit heads are discussing problems, opportunities or ideas. This is a crucial factor, as it enables IT to have an input in terms of what is possible and helps to avoid early rejection of options or early commitment to inappropriate approaches that would be hard to change at a later stage. Building relationships is an explicit strategy of senior IT management to get out into the business and explore possibilities, elicit good ideas and manage a pipeline of opportunities.

ADOPT PORTFOLIO-BASED CRITERIA FOR INVESTMENT APPRAISAL

Most organizations have traditional, financially based investment appraisal criteria, with some form of return on investment formula subject to varying levels of approval, based on the size of the project. This is a challenge, as increasingly projects are required where benefits are not directly financial. This is particularly the case in the public sector (consider: improved patient survival rates and patient experience; improved student experience, learning outcomes; increased research impact), but is not limited to the public sector. The IT strategy director at one financial services organization stressed the virtual impossibility of getting projects approved where the motivation is innovation. Consequently, business cases are being adapted to fit existing investment appraisal criteria; for example, estimates of the financial impact of non-financial benefits.

Criteria for deciding when to invest in a specific project, to compare projects and to explore the overall level and balance of investment are hard to determine. Specifically, we note that traditional, financially driven models (payback, net present value, etc.) are not a good fit for Competitive and Exploratory projects. This does not mean that rigorous assessment should be scrapped, but it would be helpful to have more appropriate criteria to help make these key decisions. Traditional methods favour projects with a direct and easy-to-measure financial return, rather than projects that provide value to customers and contribute to strategic objectives. As a result, there is over-investment in 'Support' projects at the expense of more strategic and innovative investments.

Organizations are now starting to explore a broader set of investment appraisal criteria and to relate these directly to the IT and Change Portfolio (see Box 9.1). For example, a traditional, financially based business case is entirely appropriate for a Support project. If the same approach is applied to Exploratory projects, none will ever be approved, as the purpose of the project is to explore potential benefits, and, by definition, it is not possible to put together a robust business case that is well supported with evidence.

Box 9.1　A broader view of investment appraisal

Organizations are starting to evolve an investment appraisal scorecard taking into account:

- **financial measures**: any appropriate measure can be used (net present value, etc.). The weighting would be much higher for Support projects.

- **strategic alignment**: the extent to which the project contributes to the strategic objectives of the organization. This could be given a high weight for a Competitive project.

- **organizational risk**: the business risk related to the business opportunity and the management of change.

- **future options**: an investment might create a range of opportunities that could be of value in the future – this puts a value on this flexibility.

- **contribution to architecture**: the contribution, in terms of services and/or functionality that the project might contribute that are of broader value to other projects.

- **technical risk**: an assessment of the technology risk.

The different factors are weighted according to the element of the portfolio. Financial measures are the key for Support projects. Strategic alignment is the primary focus for Competitive projects. For Exploratory projects, the key is spreading *limited* funds across a range of promising ideas and getting good learning. Who takes the decisions is also important – for Exploratory and Support projects, there are strong arguments that there should be some element of local autonomy and control, even in what is otherwise a centralized governance framework.

Figure 9.2 provides an example of a strategic alignment scorecard, which might form part of the appraisal process for Competitive and Qualifying projects. The matrix should be maintained for live programmes, to contribute to reassessment of priorities as part of regular reviews of the portfolio.

Criteria	Weight (e.g.)
Financial measures (say, NPV)	40%
Operational measures	
• Strategic alignment	30%
• Organization risk	(20)%
• Future options	10%
Technical measures	
• Contribution to IT architecture/infrastructure	20%
• Technical risk	(10)%

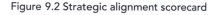
Weighting varies according to the portfolio category

Figure 9.2 Strategic alignment scorecard

A practice that can be combined with establishing portfolio-based evaluation criteria is to establish a 'benefits scorecard' linked to the strategy and portfolio. The scorecard defines key benefits metrics, and all investments are measured against their contribution to the scorecard.

The example in Figure 9.3 is from Intel and shows their IT 'value dials'; the example in Figure 9.4 is from an IT consultant and solutions provider and also provides a basis for assessing the benefits contribution of different projects. It is important to note that we will need to compare very different project proposals (like comparing apples and bananas), so we need some mechanism in addition to net present value to help make the right selections.

People take these decisions and the investment appraisal criteria are guidelines to help the people involved. It is important to have investment appraisal criteria that help people make good decisions. The portfolio-based approach helps establish a common language and approach, going some way to getting beyond depending on power and politics.

Value Dial	Definition/Valuation
Days of inventory	Reductions in days of inventory lead to value in finished goods, work in process or raw material inventories. (*value of 1 day*) x (*days of inventory removed*) x 15% (*weighted average cost of capital*)
Headcount reduction or avoidance	Solutions that reduce human resource requirements or absorb business growth without growing headcount. Employees can be moved to jobs with greater value. (*number of headcount reduced or avoided*) x (*average burden rate for location and job type*)
Employee productivity	Gains in headcount efficiencies or effectiveness. Headcount is expected to produce more through these gains due to the additional time efficiencies. (*number of employees affected*) x (*time*) x (*average burden rate*) x (*50%*)

Figure 9.3 Intel value dials – strategic scorecard

- Acquiring & retaining customers
- Raising quality, lowering costs
- Improving worker effectiveness, improving teamwork
- Providing accurate, timely management and control information
- Reducing business risk and protecting information and data

Figure 9.4 Example of criteria for a strategic scorecard – different projects in terms of how they contribute to improving the business
Source: www.waterstons.com.

One participant in a recent research project provided an excellent example of the importance of people in the decision-making process and specifically having the right knowledge involved from an early stage. The IT manager stressed the importance of procurement and vendor management and identified major savings that had been achieved:

They went out to tender. Z was one of two leading suppliers. They realized they had the whip hand. Z used high-pressure sales techniques – the sponsor and manager had no experience of resisting this. The vendor sent up a lot of high-profile people. I stepped in and stopped it. I had to convince the directors. Z threatened to sue. I'd been through it before – it didn't frighten me. I brought in a contract project manager who'd delivered eight of these.

We went out to tender again using his experience. They'd tried to oversell us on licences by £300k. We also saved £300k on services (from £500k to £200k) and we gained flexibility. It was a shame it wasn't sorted earlier.

Procurement and vendor management are revealed as important factors contributing to benefits realization, and must be managed at the portfolio level as part of the wider investment appraisal process to ensure that the best possible deals can be leveraged from suppliers.

ASSESSING COST IMPLICATIONS OVER THE LIFETIME OF THE INVESTMENT

The cost section of the business case is deceptively simple. Although Ward et al. (2007) identified this as the benefits-related practice organizations are most satisfied with (57%), in fact it is far from simple and is not effectively managed in many organizations. In particular, there are issues to consider in terms of IT vs. business costs, project vs. ongoing costs and direct vs. indirect costs.

A key challenge comes from having to compare opportunities for very different types of projects with very different cost profiles. Direct project and change costs (software and hardware purchase, consulting resources, etc.) are typically taken into account (71–85% of organizations), but other categories are less well accounted for, particularly indirect business change costs (see Box 9.2). The result is that, depending on the cost profile of the projects – for example, the balance between internal and external costs – the overall return will appear very different.

Box 9.2   Types of cost included in a business case

Project costs

Material purchase costs (85% always)
External human costs (75% always)
Internal human IS/IT costs (72% often–always)
Internal human business costs (51% often–always)

Change costs

Direct business change costs (71% often–always)
Indirect business change costs (63% never–rarely)
New operational costs (50% often–always)

Source: Ward et al. (2007)

There are also subtler factors to consider. For example, when rolling out a system in a branch or retail environment there will typically be local implementation and training. If this is budgeted for, it may turn into additional expenditure on hourly paid staff: a direct cost. If it is absorbed in existing local budgets, however, what might the impact be in terms of short cuts in training and potentially reduced benefits realization?

SETTING PRIORITIES: TAKING A LONG-TERM VIEW

A further significant challenge when considering strategic alignment and priority setting is that there is often no single, clearly defined set of priorities. Business unit priorities may differ from corporate priorities, for example. There is also a strong view from managers that the public sector faces particularly high levels of uncertainty, which makes the strategic alignment of the portfolio difficult. These organizations are always vulnerable to imposed changes of objectives and to these changes happening faster than they can deliver change programmes.

The time horizons of business and IT planning can be different, with IT often needing to consider three to five years or more, which goes well beyond typical business planning cycles. As a result, IT is potentially caught between different versions of business priorities and has to make a case for a longer-term perspective that is not directly aligned to short-term business priorities. Organizations with business control of IT priorities and budgets risk taking short-term decisions with adverse consequences in the long term. For example, a major enterprise system (ERP, CRM, supply chain) can easily have a life of 10–15 years, but there is a risk that replacement and major upgrade decisions are always put off for another day.

In this complex area, organizations are adopting a number of practices. In addition to building relationships and developing engagement with business strategy and planning processes at all levels of the organization, forward-looking IT organizations are developing an IT strategy including a three- to five-year architecture and technology roadmap so that they are gradually developing a strategic 'digital platform' (Weill and Ross, 2009). As a university IT director commented: 'We're working towards a long-term systems roadmap for each system with academic and non-academic colleague.'

RING-FENCE FUNDS FOR EXPLORATORY PROJECTS

Seedcorn funds and pilot projects are being used in a limited way by some organizations and represent first steps towards the explicit use of Exploratory projects to enable innovation and to reduce the risk of larger investments. There is a 'skunk works' element to these projects: one IT director admitted he had to use the stationery budget to fund some initial work on a potentially important project. There is also concern that any failures might be at the cost of the credibility of the IT function and of individual careers, so there is a need to establish a more entrepreneurial environment.

Organizations need to make use of the concept of Exploratory projects, and acknowledge that some will fail if they are indeed being used in exploratory, high-risk scenarios. Failure would be a good thing, as it provides an opportunity for learning and it avoids much greater losses on a Competitive or Qualifying project. A small element of budget (5% perhaps) is ring-fenced for Exploratory projects, and a simple selection process is established. Projects tackle interesting areas, with small teams and budgets adopting an agile approach (Highsmith, 2004). In many senses this venture capital approach provides funds in tranches and balances innovation and risk.

The governance framework for the portfolio needs to address the allocation of funds and resources for Exploratory projects. Is there a centralized decision-making process, or is there scope for local autonomy?

PLANNING FOR COMPETITIVE ADVANTAGE

Setting priorities at the portfolio level is a crucial enabler of benefits realization and competitive advantage. The portfolio encourages a holistic approach and consideration of the overall set of investments. Taking an agile approach using short projects as part of programmes of changes maintains flexibility.

PORTFOLIO DELIVERY AND REVIEW

Benefits delivery is about maintaining control of the overall portfolio to ensure benefits realization from the approved investments. At the portfolio level important issues will include: risk management, dependencies across projects, managing resource allocation across projects and exploring the business change impact of planned and current projects. Many issues become visible which will not be clear at an individual project level.

Issues of governance (i.e., which individuals and groups manage the portfolio) become important. Weill and Ross (2009) are helpful here, providing a framework for IT governance (Chapter 10). It is important to note that getting formal structures in place is only one factor. How people engage and behave is more important, as in the end effective governance will be determined by the individuals and their relationships.

At a portfolio level, many issues related to people become a priority. For example, what is the capacity for IT-enabled change, and how can the capacity be developed in the short, medium and longer term? Who are the best people for a specific project? How can the available resources and the demand for investment be matched up across the organization?

The portfolio perspective also relates to management of IT applications and infrastructure. The IT and Change Portfolio implies that different approaches can be adopted to technology and service management depending on where an application sits in the portfolio. For example, an 'Exploratory' development might depend on pre-release software to gain insights from new technology and working with a strategic supplier. It is unlikely that the same approach would be taken for Qualifying systems.

Important practices are as follows.

BUILDING MOMENTUM FOR BENEFITS REALIZATION

If you set out 'what does success look like' for benefits planning, hopefully you would go beyond having a business case documented and approved, to focus on having established a team of people who understand and are bought into the vision and are building momentum for the realization of benefits. There are many barriers, not least the fragmentation of project approval, which can mean there are delays between development of the business case, approval and mobilization of a project team.

An important practice for benefits delivery is project mobilization, building the core of the project team and gaining momentum for benefits realization. New people will come on board, and work is required, beyond giving them the business case to read, to get them effectively engaged. In addition, however well the planning has been done, there will be a need to get into greater detail as the project moves towards implementation, and there will inevitably be new insights, opportunities and problems to address.

The practice at a portfolio level reflects the importance of input to designing the project team and governance structures, with roles that fit with the individuals and context. There is also a need for advice to the project team to adapt the approach to the specific context and take on relevant lessons from other projects.

The approach taken will vary from project to project. One effective method is to use the workshop approach used in benefits planning. Over a period of several days a new team can work with input from key stakeholders to review and build on the benefits plan and develop project plan and designs in more detail, resulting most importantly in a shared understanding and establishing initial ways of working.

A critical influence of the portfolio at this stage is to help think through how to adapt the approach to each project to reflect the context.

Taking key aspects of project management – for example, leadership style, risk management, the extent to which agile practices are used and evolution is enabled through the project – the portfolio helps think through what is relevant.

Take leadership and, for example, the role of the project sponsor. A Qualifying project, for instance, will impact on many areas of operation of the current business. It might be sponsored by a chief operating officer or operations director and have senior operational managers engaged in governance, probably through an existing business governance mechanism. A senior, experienced operational manager with the ability to make things happen may well work on the project part- or full-time. Leadership will ensure project and development processes are carefully applied, with emphasis on testing, change management, risk management and contingency planning. The risk to the current business is significant, and risk management will ensure that resources are applied to minimizing risk and impact.

A Competitive project is critical to the future success of the organization. It might affect current business areas and will certainly involve significant change and innovation, potentially establishing new teams and ways of working. Senior business leadership is required, but now with a focus on the future of the organization. This might be a leader with credibility with the CEO and a stake in the success of the project. In terms of risk, the major issues are uncertainty about the business proposition: will this really work in the market, and will a good 'product' get to market at the right time? So the highly risk-averse approach of Qualifying projects might slow the project too much, and there will be a greater emphasis on speed and adaptability.

A Support project does not require the same level of senior leadership; in these situations it can even get in the way. A practical, pragmatic approach is required to make it happen without too much fuss, time or effort, so that costs and business impact are kept under control. Sound project practices are required as a way to make it happen effectively, and risk management will reflect the lower business risk and need for simplicity and low cost.

Exploratory projects can take many forms. They require entrepreneurial leadership and teams who have the expertise and determination to just get on and make it happen. A few rules might get broken, but there will be results. The leadership role might be very engaged or might be more hands-off, in which case a key role will be creating space for the team to work, free from bureaucracy and obstacles. An important leadership role reflects that not all Exploratory projects will succeed, so it is vital to create an environment when 'failure' is possible and learning is captured for the future. The key is to learn quickly and at low cost. Risk management is the driver for using an Exploratory project: limiting budgets and resources, and ensuring that the potential impact on the business is managed (e.g., that an output from an Exploratory project is not simply used organization-wide), and that additional funds and resources are not sucked in.

Practice	Outline description
Time-box	Time-boxing is a key practice – working to a deadline for the delivery of each phase and using this focus to enable innovation.
Incremental development/phased delivery	Totally linked with time-boxing is the focus on incremental or phased delivery. It results in smaller projects that are easier to manage, provides motivation for the team and is a quicker route to benefits and learning.
Manage trade-offs	The feature – time – resource trade-off is aligned with the time-boxed approach. The key driver is to deliver, shifting features to a later release if necessary.
Co-located team	The creation of a physical space for innovation can be vital. It allows sharing of tacit knowledge and effective ways of working with a minimum of paperwork and bureaucracy.
Phased funding	A venture capital model is adopted. Small tranches of funding until there is evidence of benefits and the team's ability to deliver.
Entrepreneurial team	The people are key. An entrepreneurial, multi-disciplinary team will make the project succeed. They might break a few rules along the way – just focus on creating the environment where they can innovate and make things happen.

Table 9.1 Key practices for Exploratory projects

Exploratory projects are ideal candidates for agile practices (Table 9.1). Many of the principles and practices also apply in other areas.

For many organizations explicitly introducing the concept of Exploratory projects is an important place to start adapting the approach.

In most organizations experienced project and programme managers will naturally be adapting the approach they take to individual projects. The portfolio provides a basis for a shared language and for enabling greater learning between projects and for designing the approach to a project as part of planning and mobilization.

MANAGING RISK: TAKE A PORTFOLIO PERSPECTIVE

We know a lot about managing risk on IT projects. Just look at any book on IT project management. Unfortunately, a focus on risks related to a specific project misses most of the big issues; for example, as the 'biggest gains come from doing the right things', risk management at a project level can be about trying to succeed with projects that should never have been started.

Once a portfolio view is established – that is, all projects are allocated to one of the quadrants and a core set of information is available on each project – it provides the basis for a much more strategic approach to risk management. For example: *Qualifying* projects are affecting critical business activities – this can be compared to changing the engine while the car is still moving. So there has to be a real focus on mitigating risks. *Exploratory* projects are very different. A risk-averse approach would mean that either these projects never take place or that they cost far too much. This is the place for innovation and taking risks – but limiting the potential damage by keeping the budgets and resources small. It also means recognizing that some of these projects will fail – and that is OK.

Taking a portfolio perspective is critical to effective IT risk management. The portfolio provides guidance on the attitude to risk on different projects. It also helps align the overall set of investments in IT with the business strategy – providing a real focus on business opportunities and risk. Risk management becomes a key element of the portfolio management and review process.

USE THE PORTFOLIO TO MANAGE APPLICATION LIFECYCLES

The portfolio helps to explore the management of software applications over time. Many organizations attempt to operate a centralized, monopolistic decision-making strategy related to IT application software. One micro-case study highlights some of the challenges (see Box 9.3).

The case illustrates the general practice that applications need to be periodically reassessed from a portfolio perspective. Applications will move around the portfolio as the positioning is related to strategy and competitive positioning. The key is to manage the movement so that the implications for management of the application are assessed and, for example, service levels adjusted accordingly.

Box 9.3   An example of issues in application lifecycle management

A university has a core e-Learning system used by 90% of its 20,000 students. It is reliable and effective. However, it looks dated and does not provide Web 2.0 features. A professor in Computer Science has developed a new e-Learning system, and usage is gradually growing in other departments. It looks up to date, and it has some clear functional advantages over the core university system. The system is hosted on a server under the professor's desk. It is becoming unreliable as usage grows, and no one other than the professor can provide support. The university structure is federal, with individual departments having a lot of autonomy; also individual, successful professors have considerable freedom of action.

*   *   *

Use the portfolio to examine the case. What actions are required?

*   *   *

The investment portfolio helps to identify a number of possible actions in response to the case study. For example: if the new e-Learning system is currently Exploratory, there might be an opportunity to move it to Qualifying or Competitive by IT taking on the management of the infrastructure professors system; and then investing in the core e-Learning system to add new functionality to replicate the system. Alternatively, IT could re-engineer the system to provide a sound basis for further development and production operation.

MANAGING THE PORTFOLIO

Portfolio management encompasses the entire lifecycle of an investment: from the pipeline of ideas and opportunities, through development of the benefits realization plan, to delivery of the project and then to ongoing benefits realization from use of the system and information and finally to retirement. The lifecycle becomes complex as a system is developed (versioned release) and upgraded through its life and as the business changes around it.

In terms of benefits delivery the focus is on control over the whole set of projects that are under way at any point in time. In many organizations this can easily be 100 or more. A first stumbling block to establishing portfolio management is often 'What do you mean by a project?' As a large percentage of IT budgets are spent on existing operations (>70%') and where organizations still have their own development teams, many projects can be carried out without external expenditure, so it is quite possible to hide projects as part of 'business as usual' activity. In addition, very significant 'IT projects' may be happening in other departments, funded from other budgets and with little or no input from the IT function.

The approach to projects set out in earlier chapters provides a basis for portfolio level control. Key milestones have been established and provide a basis for tracking progress. Business ownership and departments/processes affected should also be clear. So a portfolio-level view of all projects should provide a clear view of ownership and progress against key milestones, and provide a basis for communicating with process owners and business areas in a way that reflects the cumulative impact of the overall set of projects. At this level the overall interdependencies and business impacts become clear. As an IT function becomes effective at solution delivery, the bottleneck affecting the capacity for change often shifts quickly to front-line business areas where too much change undermines the ability to run the business and provide customer service in the short term.

CARRY OUT A PERIODIC REVIEW OF THE PORTFOLIO TO MAINTAIN ALIGNMENT AND CONTROL

The IT portfolio is a crucial link between the strategy of the organization and the implementation of change to deliver the strategic objectives. In the absence of a regular review of the portfolio, there is a risk of loss of control over significant investments of people and money, and the alignment with business strategy may drift as business priorities change.

A key element of control is provided by half-yearly reviews of the overall project portfolio, which are aligned with the business planning cycle. The reviews, varying between a day and half a day, provide an opportunity for an in-depth review of the portfolio. This provides an opportunity to reassess the strategic alignment of projects and to take a broader view of progress and lessons learned.

Initial sessions are likely to identify a range of issues and to help establish an effective governance framework. While there may be opportunities to consider the different constituents of the portfolio (current systems, current and future projects) in different sessions, it is normally helpful to maintain an overview of the entire portfolio. It is important to take a pragmatic approach to the portfolio and the review process. For example, in some cases it may be necessary to start with the IT function and IT projects. Clearly the goal is to move to consider all investments in IT-enabled change and preferably all investments in change.

Depending on the size and structure of the organization, the portfolio may exist at a number of different levels (e.g., each business unit and the organization as a whole), and reviews should take place at relevant levels. At all these levels it is important to ensure there is knowledge and expertise in portfolio management, as well as effective engagement from the individuals involved.

PORTFOLIO-LEVEL MONITORING OF BENEFITS REVIEWS AND FOLLOW-THROUGH OF LESSONS LEARNED

Benefits review highlights a crucial conundrum: everyone knows it is important to carry out post-implementation reviews of projects, yet they are only rarely carried out. This gap between what we know and what we do is a crucial barrier to the development of the IT portfolio management capability of an organization. Portfolio management needs to ensure that these project-level benefits reviews are carried out regularly and that action is taken as a result.

A key emphasis is on making sure that effective reviews take place and that lessons learned are shared between projects. The reviews need to take place for individual projects and then as a part of benefits exploitation, reviews should take place around live systems and business processes. There are significant challenges to enable both individuals and the organization as a whole to learn. It is important that the reviews do not become bureaucracy, but that they are used to enable learning and increasingly effective management of the portfolio.

DRIVING CONTINUOUS LEARNING AND IMPROVEMENT

Portfolio-level practices for benefits delivery and benefits review maintain visibility and control of the significant investments in IT and change and drive learning and improvement. A focus on people is vital: for example, to get strong leadership for projects and to build the capability and capacity of the organization for change.

CONTINUING TO REALIZE BENEFITS FROM THE PORTFOLIO

At the portfolio level benefits exploitation links strongly with service management. There is, however, an important change in perspective. The focus is on continuing to realize benefits rather than simply on managing an operational IT service.

Staff turnover with time, the changing business context and ongoing learning about the potential of the technology are just three reasons why a continued focus on benefits exploitation is required.

Usually, too much is left to chance. Organizations should focus more on benefits exploitation. The returns from management attention are likely to be good. In most cases incremental investment will be zero or small, and there will be valuable returns – for example, from better training and 'on-boarding' of new staff.

Existing systems are generally taken for granted. Often these are major enterprise systems, such as SAP, where post-implementation the emphasis has moved on, leaving a small support capability to resolve specific problems. There is a gradual loss of knowledge from the turnover of IT and business staff, resulting in less of the capabilities of these systems being used and an unnecessary inflexibility in the face of gradually changing business requirements. The loss of knowledge can easily be reinforced by bureaucracy, giving the impression of poor systems and a 'can't do' IT function.

Examples of practices for benefits exploitation are given in Box 9.4.

Box 9.4   Examples of practices for benefits exploitation

- Establish business owners for systems and services. There may need to be ownership at a local level as well as an overall 'owner'.

- Regular reviews of system usage, including an annual end-user survey, to understand satisfaction, identify problems, explore opportunities and provide input into future developments.

- An annual user conference is held to provide an opportunity for end-users to share how they are using the system and for good ideas to be communicated. The IT team provides additional input to the conference, based on their work with the solution provider and attendance at the user group meetings that include other organizations using the software.

- Regular updates are made to help guides and training courses that address how to get the most value from the system. Help information is provided in the form of a wiki, enabling broad participation in sharing ideas and advice.

- Consultancy services are provided to end-users and user departments by the IT function with the aim of tackling specific projects to help them realize additional value from using the system: 'We'll put in time to run a series of short seminars to provide updates on the new features and then we can work 1:1 with people who want specific advice.'

DEVELOPING THE PORTFOLIO MANAGEMENT CAPABILITY OF THE ORGANIZATION

Previous work on benefits realization from IT has largely focused at the project level. The main contribution of this chapter is to focus on the management of benefits at the portfolio level, and then identify a number of areas in which portfolio-level practices are emerging and can be adopted to improve benefits realization. Senior IT and business managers wanting to increase the benefits realized from IT in their organization should consider the actions they will take to improve IT portfolio management. Box 9.5 summarizes the practices discussed in this chapter.

ESTABLISH EFFECTIVE PORTFOLIO GOVERNANCE

Management of the portfolio becomes a key driver for benefits realization. It provides a link between strategy and implementation. Phased benefits delivery and an agile approach to projects will tend to mean more, shorter projects and a greater emphasis on learning and evolution of plans. The portfolio approach, and specifically the different types of investment, builds in an improved level of flexibility to enable the organization to respond to changing circumstances.

Effective governance structures for the IT portfolio are important. They need to bring together different stakeholders, specifically senior business leaders responsible for setting priorities and sponsoring change initiatives, with IT and other professionals involved in delivering the change programmes to realize the benefits. In some organizations this is a challenge because of the lack of status of the IT function and lack of involvement of the CIO with top management.

The governance framework is likely to evolve as the benefits realization capability develops. For example, a starting-point might be to establish effective portfolio-level control over all IT projects. A later stage might be to establish an organization-wide view of investments in change addressing setting priorities (strategy), delivery of benefits through change (implementation) and exploitation of existing systems, services and information. The governance framework must provide scope for flexibility, and the portfolio helps to manage this.

By itself, establishing a new, formal governance structure will not achieve the necessary improvements. Relationships are key, and it is vital to have the right people involved and committed to make it work. One approach is to embed management of the portfolio in existing structures, for a number of IT functions have representatives on business unit management teams and are tackling portfolio management in this forum.

TAKE A PORTFOLIO PERSPECTIVE ON PEOPLE AND SKILLS TO DRIVE BENEFITS REALIZATION

Benefits are achieved when a project specifically focuses on benefits realization from organizational change and not just technology implementation. We know that benefits-driven approaches have not been widely adopted and that most projects still have a technology focus. The interaction between the portfolio and the individual projects is a critical opportunity to influence the adoption of benefits-driven approaches and enable benefits realization.

At project initiation there is a portfolio-level role in finding the right people to be part of the project team, as well as helping to establish an approach to the project that is effective in the context of the investment portfolio.

There are a number of additional practices at a portfolio level, related to: developing people with relevant skills; getting people with the necessary skills allocated to projects and in appropriate roles; creating a career development framework that encourages the development of benefits-related skills in IT and business professionals; and also sharing practices for benefits realization.

THE CONTRIBUTION OF THE PROJECT OR VALUE MANAGEMENT OFFICE

The project management office (PMO) or more recently the value management office (VMO) can take many forms. The PMO can lapse into a bureaucratic role, policing adherence to the project method. Ideally the PMO/VMO will play a more strategic role, working with senior managers and project teams in a consulting role, demonstrating and sharing good practice.

Benefits planning

1. Developing winners: shared management of a pipeline of opportunities.

2. Adopting portfolio-based criteria for investment appraisal.

3. Setting priorities: taking a long-term view.

4. Ring-fencing funds for Exploratory projects.

Benefits delivery and review

5. Building momentum for benefits realization.

6. Adapting the approach to a project to reflect the portfolio.

7. Managing risk – taking a portfolio perspective.

8. Using the portfolio to manage application lifecycles.

9. Assessing cost implication over the lifetime of an investment.

10. Managing the portfolio: achieving effective control of the portfolio.

11. Carrying out a periodic review of the portfolio – maintaining alignment and control.

12. Portfolio-level monitoring of benefits reviews and follow-through.

13. Driving continuous learning and improvement.

Benefits exploitation: Continuing to realize benefits

14. Benefits review of operational services.

Note: Participants in a recent research project identified benefits exploitation as a priority – but we did not identify well-established practices in this area.

IN SUMMARY

Management of the portfolio of investments in IT is a key driver of benefits realization. Ideas and opportunities are explored and prioritized and become investment proposals. Further exploration results in the development of benefits realization plans. Project and programmes are managed with a focus on benefits realization. Focus remains on benefits realization through the working life of systems as they support business activities, and continuous improvement increases efficiency and reflects changing needs. At some point systems are retired and potentially replaced. Portfolio management is important at all these stages in the lifecycle of IT investments.

Portfolio management provides a vital linkage between strategy and individual projects. The portfolio provides an opportunity to address the overall balance of priorities and how best to use scarce resources. At a portfolio level there is a clear view of risk and the opportunities for innovation. The portfolio perspective also encourages a focus on sharing learning in terms of opportunities for benefits realization and practices that contribute to benefits realization.

The portfolio should be far more than a list of systems and projects. It provides an opportunity for active management of important resources for the organization. In the same way as most of the concepts and tools in this book, portfolio management can be applied at many levels of an organization as a way of increasing benefits from IT.

TAKING IT FURTHER

FURTHER READING AND RESOURCES

Jeffrey, M. and Leliveld, I. (2004) Best Practices in IT Portfolio Management. *MIT Sloan Management Review*, Spring: 41–49.

Meyer, A.D., Loch, C.H. and Pich, M.T. (2002) Managing Project Uncertainty: From Variation to Chaos. *MIT Sloan Management Review*, Winter: 60–67.

TALKING POINTS

Use these questions to help reflect on this chapter and explore the challenges of putting the ideas into practice:

1. How effective are portfolio management practices in your organization?
2. How can investment appraisal criteria be adapted to reflect the portfolio?
3. What issues would you face in trying to combine local and organization-wide use of the portfolio?
4. What guidelines, if any, could we agree for how to allocate resources across the portfolio?
5. How would you allocate resources to Exploratory projects?
6. How would you balance short- and long-term priorities in allocating resources?
7. What would be key questions/criteria to drive a review of the portfolio?
8. Who should be involved in portfolio governance?

9. How would you assess the effectiveness of portfolio management?

10. Where might you make a start introducing portfolio management into an organization?

11. What might be the next steps to improve portfolio management in your organization?

12. How could we increase the capacity of the organization for investments in change?

KEY DEBATES

Approaches to governance of the portfolio

In a large organization issues of governance and organizational design will interlink with portfolio management. Is there one IT function or several? Are systems organization-wide or local? A centralized, IT owned monopoly is common: is this effective and sustainable?

How would you approach governance of the portfolio in a large organization? What decisions have to be centralized? Which can be taken locally? What is the scope of the portfolio: all projects owned by the IT function? All projects involving IT? All investments in innovation and change?

CASE STUDY 9.1

Outsourcing is likely to play an important role in the IT portfolio. The case explores strategic issues.

Journal of Information Technology Teaching Cases, Vol. 3 (2013): 29–42.

Transforming a human resource function through shared services and joint-venture outsourcing: the BAE systems – Xchanging enterprise partnership 2001–2012

Leslie Willcocks, David Feeny and Mary Lacity

The call for new types of collaboration in outsourcing saw the development of the enterprise partnership model by Xchanging in 2001. The case looks at the history of one such partnership with BAE Systems. History shows why the model was attractive to BAE Systems against several other models. In Part 1 of the case we look at and ask students to assess the in-house, fee-for-service outsourcing and management consultancy options for transforming HR through shared services. In Part 2 the case details the distinctive features of a joint-venture model that was eventually adopted and of the supplier competencies needed. We follow the relationship through the phases of preparation, realignment, streamlining and continuous improvement, initially up to 2003. Students are asked to assess the model, progress and what the future holds. In the third part of the case we follow subsequent developments, including the change in the nature of outsourcing with BAE Systems from March 2007, the launch of Xchanging on the stock market in April 2007, its continued expansion, and its troubled history from 2010 to 2012. The case gives insight into the conduct of a distinctly different form of outsourcing, into how the client and the supplier deal with outsourcing over a number of years, and how a supplier navigates through a highly dynamic 21st-century global environment while trying to expand its market services and revenue growth.

REFERENCES

Earl, M. and Feeny, D. (1994) Is Your CIO Adding Value? *Sloan Management Review*, Spring, Vol. 35 (3): 11–20.

Highsmith, J. (2004) *Agile Project Management*, Boston: Addison-Wesley.

Kumar, R., Ajjan, H. and Niu, Y. (2008) Information Technology Portfolio Management: Literature Review, Framework & Research Issues. *Information Resources Management Journal*, Vol. 21 (3): 64–87.

McFarlan, F. (1981) Portfolio Approach to Information Systems. *Harvard Business Review*, Vol. 59 (5): 142–150.

Ward, J. and Daniel, E. (2006) *Benefits Management*, Weill Boston, MA: John Wiley & Sons Inc.

Ward, J., De Hertogh, S. and Viaene, S. (2007) Managing Benefits from IS/IT Investments: An Empirical Investigation into Current Practice 40th Annual Hawaii International Conference on System Sciences, Weill Boston: MA.

Ward, J. and Peppard, J. (2002) *Strategic Planning for Information Systems*, 3rd edition, Weill Boston, MA: John Wiley and Sons.

Weill, P. and Ross, J. (2009) *IT Savvy: What Top Executives Must Know to Go from Pain to Gain*, Weill Boston, MA: Harvard Business School Press.

CHAPTER 10
TAKING AN ARCHITECTURE PERSPECTIVE

IN THIS CHAPTER WE STUDY:

- governance for IT across the organization;
- the value of an architectural approach to benefits realization;
- service management as discipline to support benefits realization.

TAKING A BROADER PERSPECTIVE

It is vital to look beyond investments in IT considered as individual projects or as separate projects and programmes within a portfolio of investments. In this chapter we tackle three major topics that tackle important cross-organizational perspectives.

The issue of *governance* at the level of project and portfolio is tackled first. This important topic builds on earlier chapters to tackle issues of decision-making related to IT across the organization.

The overall business and IT '*architecture*' that underpins benefits realization is then explored. The architectural perspective helps achieve a coherent, cost-effective and agile IT infrastructure and is vital to benefits realization in the long term. Business and enterprise architecture perspectives and the role of the 'architect' have important implications for benefits realization.

The architecture perspective reflects different 'dimensions' of the organization: for example, strategy, organizational structures, locations, products, processes, systems and information. The different dimensions are interrelated: for instance, which organizational units and processes are in place at a particular location. The architectural perspective makes explicit the need to tackle the different dimensions when planning and delivering change, and helps keep in mind the importance of a bigger picture beyond an individual project. For example, there will often be benefits from taking a short cut at a project level, which will result in additional costs for the organization over the long term. The architect should understand the bigger picture.

The final topic addressed in the chapter is *service management*. This is a major topic and service management within IT and the business is an important discipline. This brief introduction builds on the coverage of Chapter 6 to address important management issues.

For each of these three topics the aim is to provide a brief introduction to major areas highlighting management issues related to benefits realization that cut across the organization as whole.

GOVERNING THE PORTFOLIO

PERSPECTIVES ON GOVERNANCE

IT governance is a broad and important topic. There are strong links with wider discussions of corporate governance. It also provides one of a number of starting-points for discussion of the IT capability of the organization. Most discussions of IT governance focus on the IT function, its relationship with the organization and how decisions related to the management of IT are taken.

What is governance? Definitions of governance include the following:

- Specifying the decision rights and accountability framework to encourage desirable behaviour in the use of IT (Weill and Woodham, 2002).

- The structure for making decisions regarding information, systems, technology and to encourage the behaviours that will lead to the achievement of business goals (Peppard, 2003).

- How authority for resources, risk, conflict resolution and responsibility for IT is shared (Luftman, quoted in Ward and Peppard, 2002, p. 46).

The IT-CMF (capability maturity framework) also provides a description as part of the IT leadership and governance capability (Box 10.1).

Box 10.1   IT leadership and governance

IT decision-making processes include:

- definition of responsibilities, and possible escalation of them;
- definition of the decision-making process and underlying decision criteria;
- establishment of a comprehensive system of reporting and oversight.

Governance addresses the establishment of appropriate decision rights and accountability mechanisms for IT throughout the organization.

Innovation Value Institute: IT Capability Maturity Framework (IT-CMF) (V 1.2.2)

(Note: various industry frameworks, such as CobiT and ITIL, also address governance.)

The definitions focus on authority, decision rights and, importantly, on behaviour. Peppard makes it clear that he is thinking broadly about information, systems and technology, and the aim is desirable behaviour that will lead to the achievement of business goals. It is clear that governance is *not* simply about structures and the formal organization. The focus on behaviour provides a good starting-point for linkage of the governance and capabilities perspectives.

GOVERNANCE AT A PROJECT LEVEL

We discussed governance at a project level in Chapter 4. It is helpful to have the right people involved and with clearly understood roles and responsibilities. The governance structure must be designed around benefits realization from business transformation and change, not IT solution delivery. This shift is significant and is likely to require much broader engagement in the project.

The governance framework should reflect engagement of all relevant stakeholders, not just management decision-making. Depending on the type of project – for example, Qualifying or Exploratory – there will be different governance issues to address and some flexibility of approach will be required. At the centre will be the project sponsor and a project board that brings together key stakeholders in a decision-making body with the sponsor and project manager.

De Meyer et al. (2002) set out different roles for the project manager and different approaches to managing tasks and relationships depending on the type/extent of uncertainty. In many cases there is an expectation of learning or unforeseen impacts, in which case agile and design approaches will be very important.

GOVERNANCE OF THE IT PORTFOLIO

Governance is an important aspect of the management of the overall IT portfolio. Cooper et al. (1999) identified three success factors in a study of product portfolio management:

- an explicit, consistently used approach, which is strongly supported by management and applied to all projects (the approach used is less important);
- multiple evaluation methods (e.g., financial, strategic);
- fit with the overall management style of the organization.

We envisage engagement of relevant stakeholders in decision-making on priorities and new investments, and monitoring progress across the portfolio of (IT-enabled) change initiatives. In many organizations structures will mean that there will be a need to establish portfolio governance at a number of levels: for example, at each business unit and organizational level.

GOVERNANCE FRAMEWORKS

Earl (1989) outlines the need for an information management strategy that, in the context of the increasing business dependence resulting from the pervasive use of IT, addresses governance. Objectives, policies and constraints, and plans and goals are required. Earl states that governance needs to:

- be written down;
- provide operational guidance;
- show management commitment;

- address strategy, style and commitment;
- include the capacity for change.

Ward and Peppard (2002) suggest that governance will need to vary based on the IT and Change Portfolio. For example, in a large organization there will be a strong argument for central control and provision of Qualifying systems. Integration is important, and these systems are expensive given the performance requirements, so it is important to avoid duplication of effort and to achieve economies of scale. In contrast, Support systems might be more locally controlled, justified from business unit budgets. Exploratory systems require entrepreneurial approaches, so freedom from the centralized planning, which might focus all resources on Qualifying, is required. Strategic investment decisions need senior business leadership and a focus on the future and competitive advantage rather than improving the current business, so again need to be considered as a group.

Weill (2004) sets out a framework that addresses decisions in relation to: (i) principles, including how IT will be used to create business value and the operating model; (ii) IT infrastructure, the set of shared services; (iii) enterprise architecture, the overall design of the organizations digital platform; (iv) business needs and project deliverables; and (v) investments and prioritization. In each of these five areas a number of overall management models are identified. See Figure 10.1 and Table 10.1.

Business monarchy	A group of business executives: for example, CxOs or/and individual. Includes committees of senior business executives, which may include the CIO.
IT monarchy	Individuals or groups of IT executives.
Feudal	Business unit leaders, key process owners of their delegates.
Federal	CxOs-level executives and at least one other group, such as business unit leaders. IT executives might participate.
IT duopoly	IT executives and one other group – CxO or business unit leader.
Anarchy	Individual users.

Table 10.1 Models for decision rights

In a large organization there will be a need for decision rights at various levels. For example, a business unit would expect to have, at the very least, a strong voice in terms of business needs and priorities (iv), but would probably have very little interest or influence in principles (i) and infrastructure (ii). Within the organization there will also be a need to look across different business units based on the operating model (iii) and to take decisions on overall investment priorities (v).

An Example…	IT Principles		Organizational needs		Infrastructure Strategy and architecture		Business applications		Investment and prioritization	
	Input	Decision	Input	Decision	Input	Decision	Input	Decision	Input	Decision
Management team		X		X		X		X		X
Manager information systems		X				X		X		
Head(s) of department	X		X		X		X		X	
IT governance team	X		X				X		X	

- IT principles – How will IT create business value?
- IT infrastructure strategies – How will we build shared services?
- IT architecture – What technical standards and guidelines will we use?
- Business applications – What applications do we need?
- IT investment and Prioritization – How much and where will we invest?

Figure 10.1 Organization-wide governance

The most appropriate model is said to depend on the goals of the organization and, for example, whether the objective is high growth or high profitability. Weill suggests that effective governance is the single most important factor contributing to getting value from IT.

Different models for decision rights are as follows:

ESTABLISHING EFFECTIVE GOVERNANCE

Peppard (2001) sets out a six-stage model for 'bridging the gap' between business and IT. There is a strong element of path dependence as the 'gap' is gradually closed. A key conclusion is that implementing better IT governance is not an end in itself. Building a better relationship between the business and IT function is vital, with the goal to realize the benefits that are the consequences of a strong relationship.

At a project and an enterprise level effective governance is a vital contributor to value from IT. We just need to keep in mind that by effective governance we mean the right people, working together effectively – it's about people and behaviour as much as structure. Building effective governance is a process and depends on relationships and trust. At different stages in the development of the organization as a whole and the IT function, different governance structures will be most appropriate. For example, if the IT function is struggling to keep services running, it can largely focus internally until it has got its own 'house in order' and built credibility with business users and management. Much further down the development path, an organization seeking competitive advantage from IT will need effective engagement from IT with senior business management in key business units.

In summary, key factors are as follows:

- Relationships and informal management processes/practices are key.
- Establishing effective governance is path-dependent: in other words, a gradual process.
- Bridging the IT–user gap is a key enabler for tackling business change and benefits realization issues.

ARCHITECTURE PERSPECTIVE – PROJECTS AND PROGRAMMES

INTRODUCTION

The architect, we know, is the designer of buildings. The architect has technical skills, knowledge of the properties of materials, fire regulations, building regulations and more, but their role goes beyond that to focus specifically on the design of the building and the experience of the people who live or work in it. The role of the IT architect is similar in many respects. They focus on the big picture, the overall solution, but also care and know about making it work because they understand the technology and its capabilities and limitations.

At a project or programme level the role of the architect can take several forms, and might be referred to as 'solution architect' or 'technical architect'. On a major project there might be an architecture team. In some cases the senior developer may also take on the role of architect, but on larger projects, where there will be various development teams working on different parts of an overall solution in different technologies, the role of the architect becomes extremely important.

The architect contributes from the very beginning of the project. Alongside others in a core team the architect can start exploring possible solutions in terms of business process, overall system design and technical issues and possibilities. They will also bring or develop an understanding of existing systems to help assess, for example, what information can be sourced from where, what services are available as part of the IT infrastructure, what policies and standards need to be adhered to.

The architect sees the project through from beginning to end, taking responsibility for the integrity of the overall IT solution, while others in the core team focus on benefits realization and project delivery.

OPPORTUNITY-BASED DESIGN

As work on benefits planning develops, you very quickly get to the point of wanting to consider what the available technology can do. At a certain level it will do what you need it to do, but of course some things are easier than others. In very many cases the project will draw on an existing software solution or service. This could be a package bought in for the project (perhaps a CRM system), existing software within the organization, an enterprise system such as SAP or software lower down the 'stack' such as Windows on the servers in the data centres, or perhaps a cloud-based service. In each of these cases the software comes with many capabilities that can be taken advantage of in the project, and some of these can be configured very easily, perhaps through options available to system administrators. Others would require development from scratch.

Opportunity-based design, as a practice, brings the perspective that at an early stage in the project it is vital to have within the team, or available to the team, the skills to explore what is possible. This will help in two major ways – as with early prototyping (see the discussion of design thinking in Chapter 7), it can help bring the scenario to life and help the team see new possibilities and also spot issues earlier. A very early demonstration based on the 'out of the box' capabilities of the system might be an important way to get a new perspective on potential benefits for stakeholders. A second important contribution is to get an early sense of the issues of delivery of the final system, which routes will be straightforward and cost-effective, where the major challenges and risks are.

FOCUS ON THE NON-FUNCTIONAL

The architect also provides an early focus on non-functional requirements. It is all too easy to forget about crucial factors that will have a major impact on the design and operation of the solution. These include: security, reliability, availability, response times and recoverability.

ARCHITECTURAL DESIGN

At a project or programme level it is good practice to have an architect in place from the beginning alongside others focusing on benefits and user experience, and also on project planning and management. At an early stage of the work on the benefits plan the architect will be sketching what the system might look like in broad terms. This will be at logical or functional level and probably also at a technical level.

As the work develops, they will consider whether key components already exist within the organization and can be used – for example, a service that allows user sign-on and access administration, perhaps a product database. It will also be important to consider whether to buy (a package or a service) or to build it. This, of course, raises questions of sourcing and procurement.

The architect will also help set priorities for features across different releases, ensuring core components are not neglected in favour of more visible elements. They might also lead work on technology validation, testing out critical decisions in advance of the main release schedule.

The role is challenging. It involves technical capability across a range of technologies, working closely with other team members and business stakeholders, and working on the big picture of the solution design.

ENTERPRISE ARCHITECTURE – A PORTFOLIO PERSPECTIVE

INTRODUCING ENTERPRISE ARCHITECTURE

Enterprise architecture involves a focus on the IT infrastructure and the organization as a whole and how individual systems and projects contribute. At its core, enterprise architecture is about looking at the many perspectives on the organization, networks, servers, desktops and other clients, information, systems and process, and locations, for example. Recognizing that IT is not about a set of discrete, unconnected systems but an integrated whole opens up many new issues and opportunities.

As an example, at a much earlier stage in my career I was working in retail. Two teams working on different aspects of ordering and distribution within the supply chain designed and implemented systems bringing into place different coding structures for products. Now the organization had the old coding structure and two new ones. So all three had to be maintained, and a complex look-up and translation process was required if the systems needed to talk to each other or when analytical and decision support systems were required to get an overview of the supply chain. An architectural approach would have been to ensure there was a single product coding system and that over time all systems migrated to using it, bringing in simplicity, enabling integration, reducing the risk of error and reducing the duplication of work.

Similar issues are common. A university recently did an audit and discovered it had 16 data centres scattered through different buildings; and in the business school we discover over 30 different sources of 'customer' information.

There are also important technology roadmap decisions to make: when do we move to Windows 8? Do we move to Google Docs? Do we virtualize the data centre? Which development environments do we use? Do we outsource? What can go in the cloud? When do we upgrade our integrated systems: for example, SAP? When do we bite the bullet and replace core systems that are still working but which we are struggling to maintain because they are 20 years old and all the staff expert in the relevant languages will have retired very soon?

The decisions are significant, and implementation is hard as there is a need to influence decision-making and solution delivery across the organization. A typical project manager and sponsor just want the project delivered quickly and cost-effectively. The architecture perspective is asking them to look at a bigger picture. There might be benefits, and certainly will be for the organization as a whole, but for the particular project there may be additional work. A second barrier to overcome is that some investments are required in the short term to build the agile, cost-effective infrastructure for the long term. But those are always competing with short-term business priorities. Why invest now in consolidating those 16 data centres into two; surely it's not a priority when we need a new student-friendly website?

In addition to the work to date on a business-oriented approach to IT strategy and to benefits-driven project planning and delivery, the architectural perspective is a crucial factor in benefits realization across the organization.

A valuable starting-point for consideration of the architecture within an organization is the business and IT operating model (Weill and Ross, 2009). As shown in Table 10.2, the model addresses the role of IT in integration and also standardization. What is the strategy and structure? Are activities centralized and tightly controlled, perhaps with centrally run shared services for HR, distribution and financial processing? Are sales and marketing activities localized based on geography or customer segment? To what extent is there synergy between different divisions?

The model (Figure 10.2) provides four operating model choices, which relate to business capabilities and then to the underlying systems and IT infrastructure (examples from Weill and Ross).

Diversification: low integration, low standardization. In this case the business units are independent, with different customers and expertise. They can be supported by shared services addressing some operational areas, but there will be much local autonomy and potential local systems in more customer related areas. For example: P&G.

Co-ordination: low standardization, high integration. In this case there is a need to share information, probably about the customer, but there is still considerable local autonomy and flexibility in processes and ways of working. For example: PepsiAmericas.

Replication: high standardization, low integration. A standardized platform of technologies is deployed in different locations supporting independent businesses, often consumer-oriented. For example: ING Direct, Tesco.

Unification: high standardization and high integration. In this case it is effectively a single business working with customers. A single set of systems and set of data underpin the global organization. For example: UPS, Swiss Re.

Challenges of scale and culture affect all these approaches in global organizations. For example, a US firm having made an acquisition in the UK might

		Low	High
Business process integration	**High**	Co-ordination Unique business units with a need to know each other's transactions	Unification Single business unit with global process standards and global data access
	Low	Diversification Independent business units with different customers and expertise	Replication Independent but similar business units sharing best practice
		Low	High
			Business process standardization

Figure 10.2 Architecture perspective – business operating model (Weill and Ross)

well be seeking to realize economies based on a unification or replication strategy. Yet in the US there may be thousands of staff and hundreds in the UK. There also tend to be very different styles of working. Even across academic schools in the university there might be ten Masters students in the Philosophy department and one programme secretary will know them all, and a few emails and a spreadsheet will be fine, and she will probably have a variety of other responsibilities as well, whereas in the Business School, with 800+ Masters students, the challenges will be different and there will be a dedicated postgraduate student support team. In principle the process are the same, but the challenges at these different scales are extremely different. The systems needs may in practice be different.

The operating model (Figure 10.2) provides a perspective on the organization as whole, but more importantly it provides a way to explore different capabilities or processes within an organization (Figure 10.3). At this level the model addresses the different competitive contributions of the different business activities and, for example, where scale and economy are vital or getting close to the customer and meeting their specific needs.

In a large organization, where there are multiple divisions, companies and business units, the operating model provides a portfolio perspective on the architecture that is an important element of defining strategy and investment priorities for the organization as a whole as the IT function or functions look across the organizational boundaries.

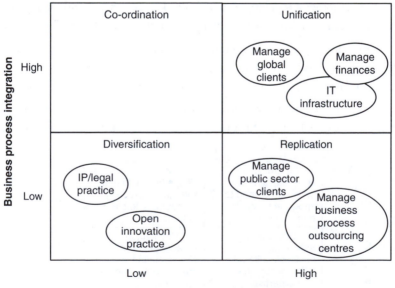

Figure 10.3 Using the operating model to consider specific business processes

START WITH THE END IN MIND: ESTABLISHING THE VISION

Establishing a single picture that provides an overview of the architecture is a very powerful practice. As shown in Figure 10.4, the aim is to capture multiple dimensions (information, process, etc.) and provide a visual representation of key aspects of the IT environment the organization is aiming to develop.

The pay-off as evidenced by the MIT research is greater value from IT based on flexibility and agility of the IT infrastructure and enabling more rapid and cost-effective delivery of new systems as they are able to draw on so much that is already in place. The one-page view then becomes a reference point for all technology investment decisions.

TAKING A LONG-TERM VIEW: ESTABLISHING A TECHNOLOGY ROADMAP

In a fast-moving world with continuing, rapid technology innovation it is possible and important to take a long-term view. For each main infrastructure component and system what is the target roadmap for change over the next three to five years? Consider the server operating system, desktop operating system, desktop software, enterprise systems and many others. Given that some larger organizations are still (at the time of writing in 2014) using Windows XP, which was launched in 2001 and sold until 2008, with support ending in April 2014, there is no excuse for not taking this long-term perspective. In longer time periods there is more guesswork, but planned product launch dates from key suppliers can be pencilled in and your organization can decide whether it is an early adopter or will wait and see how others get on.

Some changes may take place behind the scenes from a user perspective (for example, server virtualization). Others, such as moving to a Windows 8 desktop environment, will have a major impact on all users. Some benefits come directly from the switchover to a next generation, for example of smaller servers, which are much more powerful and cheaper to run in terms of electricity usage. Others come over time as a result of further projects that take advantage of the capabilities of the new technology: for example, using the Windows 8 'tiles' to provide personalized information for users.

An important benefit of the roadmap is that changes to the underlying systems and infrastructure can be linked to more customer-oriented development projects. For example, an Exploratory project might test out a potentially valuable new feature of the infrastructure, perhaps a simple way for web applications to share data and provide a more seamless customer experience (Figure 10.5). The learning from this could then feed into use of those same infrastructure capabilities in a system serving very different parts of the organization.

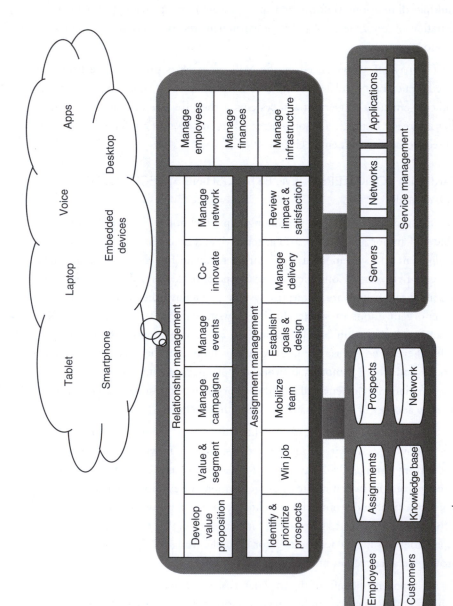

Figure 10.4 Architecture on a page – example

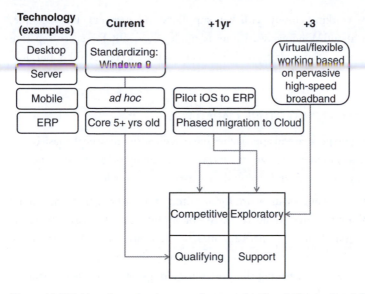

Figure 10.5 Linking the technology roadmap to the IT and Change Portfolio

ESTABLISHING A PIPELINE FOR INNOVATION

Around the technology roadmap there will be uncertainty at many levels. New technologies will be emerging rapidly. There will be competing suppliers and technical standards. Which choice is the right one? Which technologies are relevant for the organization, and when? When is it important to keep up with the latest versions and development? When is it OK just to take time, and perhaps not upgrade and miss a few new versions? When is it time to replace ageing infrastructure and systems – do the benefits outweigh the very considerable cost of change, often specifically the opportunity cost of doing something new and apparently more exciting? When is it right to trust a new supplier just entering the market and get the benefits of working very closely with them so you can later be a great case study for them as they seek to build their market? What are the benefits in terms of attracting and retaining excellent staff in terms of having an up-to-date infrastructure and investing in innovation?

The technology pipeline complements the technology roadmap and looks further ahead and further afield at emerging and new technologies. Research at conferences and with suppliers and small investments might then be used to test out views of potential benefits and to gain some early experience.

Key decisions in relation to the roadmap and pipeline relate to key aspects of the IT platform: for example, the .NET (Microsoft) vs. Java competition around software development environments. In virtually all organizations it will make sense to standardize, simplifying other decisions, making it possible to focus the expertise of people in specific areas and opening up the possibility of working closely with key suppliers and partners. For example, the decision about Windows vs. Linux is made once, not for every separate project. Even these major platform decisions then have to be revisited, but only periodically.

BUILDING AN ARCHITECTURE CAPABILITY

Architectural perspective and approaches have been adopted over the last 10–15 years and draw on older foundations. However, in many organizations there is still a long way to go and 'architectural maturity' is at a low level.

Ross (2003) sets out a framework for architectural maturity that needs to be built gradually over time (Table 10.2). As the architecture evolves, new capabilities are required, and the focus for management attention changes. A key message is that competing with IT requires an organization-wide architectural perspective as part of managing the portfolio, alongside the focus on benefits realization from projects and programmes.

There are important technical aspects to the architecture role, but it is far from a 'back room' role. To bring the architecture to life, it is vital to be engaged from the very early stage with new ideas, influencing project strategy and solution design and also contributing to consideration of what is and what will be possible.

A business architecture role is being established in some organizations. The role brings an organizational perspective to capabilities, processes, governance and other aspects of organizational design and change.

Stage	Outline
Application silo	Emphasis is on delivery and Return on Investment (ROI) of individual applications.
Standardized technology	Establishing standardized technology to control costs and improve IT service. Most firms in the research sample were at this stage. It requires senior management support of the CIO.
Rationalized data	Following standardization of technology, the focus becomes standardization of core data (product data, customer information, etc.) and processes. Benefits come from improved business process performance and integration.
Modular	The emphasis shifts to strategic agility from flexible and adaptable systems. Management practices and governance need to facilitate reusability.

Table 10.2 Stages of architecture maturity

SERVICE MANAGEMENT

Service management is another crucial perspective and discipline. Again we touch briefly on a major area. Detailed guidance can be found in ITIL and ISO 20000.

From a service management perspective the IT function can be considered as a set of services, perhaps represented as a service catalogue which defines the service, its customers, the service level etc. The definition is broad, so services are wide-ranging: the desktop service, the disaster recovery service, the help desk, capacity planning and management, as well as the activities covered directly in this book, including project management, portfolio management and strategy. These can all be considered as services.

Management of IT becomes the definition, provisioning and delivery of these services followed by ongoing continuous improvement. This perspective directly tackles the challenges of running IT day-to-day within the organization. As this requires (typically) 75% or more of the IT budget, it is important. Key areas of the management of IT relating to IT operations and infrastructure include the help desk and technical support, as well as ongoing maintenance of systems. The health of these services underpins day-to-day operations of the organization and supports what we have already discussed in terms of 'benefits harvesting'. From a more general perspective this approach is business process management and fits directly with conceptualizing the business as a bundle of services.

In terms of the coverage of this book, these areas are only given very brief coverage, as operations management addresses them within the overall management and MBA curriculum. Services marketing is also directly relevant. They are also specialist areas, in the sense that they are aspects of the management of the IT function and so less relevant to a general audience. The brief coverage here does not mean they are not important areas for benefits realization.

Given the broad definition of service, it is important to recognize that different services have very different characteristics and need to be managed in different ways. Peppard (2003) provides a further portfolio perspective, this time drawing on ideas from marketing, and specifically services marketing. He considers the activities of the IT department as a bundle of services (systems design, help desk, etc.) and then uses the service portfolio model as a way of exploring different approaches to managing and improving these different services (Figure 10.6). For example, management of the core server infrastructure (hardware, operating systems, etc.) requires much more rigid adherence to tried and tested processes. IT engagement with the business to develop IS strategy is

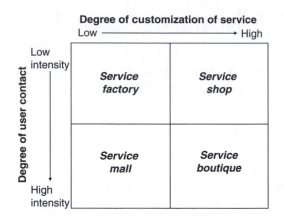

Figure 10.6 Managing the services portfolio

a much more fluid process, and it is not helpful to try and define or manage it in the same way.

A benefits perspective brings an important shift in mindset to the management of IT services, particularly the help desk and related education and support services. Traditionally the goal has been to teach people how to use new systems and then to deal with problems as and when they are reported. Success is having systems up and running and available to use, with no outstanding bugs. From a benefits perspective the goal goes much further: it is about enabling people to make the most of the information and systems to do their jobs effectively and to deliver benefits for stakeholders. This means, for example, promoting use of features over time, sharing good practices and helping users take advantage of the systems to work more effectively (see knowledge worker productivity in Chapter 6). This can never be the full responsibility of the IT function, but there is a opportunity for the IT function to take on a role as a catalyst and enabler of organizational learning to build digital literacy.

BRINGING IT ALL TOGETHER

This chapter has provided insights into architecture, governance and service management as major themes in the realization of business value from IT. It is important to understand the contribution of these areas and to be able to make use of key practices as well as to make connections with specialists working in these areas. Management of value from IT must look beyond individual projects.

All of us get involved in projects, and architecture, governance and service management are relevant at that level. Similarly, although only a few of us will get involved in enterprise architecture or designing governance at the enterprise level, they remain relevant if our authority and influence are more limited, perhaps within a business unit. The concepts help us understand the context we are working in, and the opportunities and constraints. Also we can make use of the ideas even where we have constraints on our ability to act.

The approach set out to all the topics in this chapter reflects a common philosophy with roots in agile and benefit-driven approaches and underpinned by academic perspectives on dynamic capabilities and the resource-based view of the firm. In particular, building capability takes time and is path-dependent: you need to start where you are, reflecting the specific context of your organization and develop gradually over time. You cannot leap from low to high maturity. Gradually adopting new practices as part of a wider change programme is an important contributor to maturity development. These practices themselves can contribute to broader changes in 'culture', and there is an opportunity for a 'flywheel' effect as more people get involved and change accelerates. The practices can be shared between organizations, but there is a need for some degree of unpacking and adaptation locally. These developments are about people, expertise, mindset and relationships and not (just) about structures and processes and policies.

TAKING IT FURTHER

FURTHER READING AND RESOURCES
Book
Ross, J., Weill, P. and Robertson, D. (2006) *Enterprise Architecture as Strategy*, Boston: Harvard Business School Press.

Articles
Ross, J. (2003) Creating a Strategic IT Architecture Competency: Learning in Stages. *MISQ Executive*, Vol. 2 (1): 31–43.

Kaplan, Robert S. and Norton, David, P. (2000) Having Trouble with Your Strategy? Then Map It, *Harvard Business Review*, Vol. 78 (5), Sep/Oct: 167–176.

Sauer, Chris and Willcocks, P. Leslie (2002) The Evolution of the Organizational Architect. *MIT Sloan Management Review*, Vol. 43 (3): 41–49.

TALKING POINTS
Use these questions to help reflect on this chapter and explore the challenges of putting the ideas into practice:

1. How could an architecture approach contribute to benefits realization?

2. What challenges would the architect face in making an impact?

3. How would the architecture perspective and role impact on a particular project?

4. How could the architecture perspective and role contribute to strategy development and implementation?

5. What architecture roles and practices are in place in your organization?

6. How effective is IT governance in your organization? Use the framework from Weill as a point of reference?

7. Why is IT governance so important? Do we focus on business governance in a similar way?

8. If governance is really about relationships, what are the implications?

9. How does the service management perspective contrast with business process management?

KEY DEBATES

IT value driven by IT governance

Weill sees IT governance as the key driver of business value from IT, establishing a clear and effective framework for who takes what decisions.

How does this perspective contrast with, and contribute to, the benefits-driven approach to change that is the focus of this book?

CASE STUDY 10.1

The case explores a journey of developing more effective governance of IT.

Journal of Information Technology Teaching Cases, Vol. 3 (2013): 60–69.

Improving enterprise governance of IT in a major airline: A teaching case

Steven De Haes and Wim Van Grembergen

A common and critical dilemma confronting enterprises today is how to ensure that they realize value from their large-scale investments in information technology (IT) and IT-enabled change. IT-enabled investments can bring huge rewards, but only with the right governance and management processes and full engagement from all management levels. This teaching case is about the tough but rewarding journey of the Dutch airline company KLM in improving the governance of IT, moving from managing the cost of IT towards managing the business value of IT. Although KLM still has challenges ahead, the changes in structures, processes and relational mechanisms have helped to restore trust between the business and the IT organization, and lowered business operating costs through a more rigorous selection and portfolio management process. The changes have also increased the resources allocated to IT innovation. Although KLM faced some unique challenges as it began the journey to transform its enterprise governance of IT, the realization of greater business value from today's significant and increasingly complex investments in IT is a concern for all businesses. We therefore believe that the practices and lessons learned at KLM can be applied by other organizations as they seek to engage their own business unit managers more fully in IT investment decision-making and in accountability for realizing business value.

REFERENCES

Cooper, R.G., Edgett, S.J. and Kleinschmidt, E.J. (1999) New Product Portfolio Management: Practices and Performance. *Journal of Product Innovation Management*, Vol. 16 (4): 333–350.

De Meyer, A.D., Loch, C.H. and Pich, M.T. (2002) Managing Project Uncertainty: From Variation to Chaos. *MIT Sloan Management Review*, Winter: 60–67.

Earl, M. (1989) *Management Strategies for Information Technology*, Harlow: Prentice Hall.

Peppard, J. (2001) Bridging the Gap between the IS Organization and the Rest of the Business: Plotting a Route. *Information Systems Journal*, Vol. 11 (3): 249–270.

Peppard, J. (2003) Managing IT as a Portfolio of Services. *European Management Journal*, Vol. 21 (4): 467–483.

Ross, J. (2003) Creating a Strategic IT Architecture Competency: Learning in Stages. *MISQ Executive*, Vol. 2 (1): 31–43.

Ward, J. and Peppard, J. (2002) *Strategic Planning for Information Systems*, 3rd edition, Chichester: John Wiley and Sons.

Weill, P. (2004) Don't Just Lead, Govern: How Top Performing Firms Govern IT. *MIS Quarterly Executive*, Vol. 3 (1): 1–17.

Weill, P. and Ross, J. (2009) *IT Savvy: What Top Executives Must Know to Go from Pain to Gain*, Boston: Harvard Business Press.

Weill, P. and Woodham, R. (2002) Don't Just Lead, Govern: Implementing Effective IT Governance, CISR Working Paper No. 326.

CHAPTER 11
EXPLORING THE DIGITAL BUSINESS

IN THIS CHAPTER WE STUDY:

- the growing role of IT, which means that every business is a digital business;
- important areas of digital business strategy and trends creating new business opportunities;
- the importance of social business and the power of collaboration and co-creation within and beyond the enterprise.

EVOLUTION OF THE DIGITAL BUSINESS

The history of information and information systems in organizations begins with people working together, not with the use of computers and data-processing, or information technology, as we refer to it now (Checkland and Holwell, 1999). Information has been stored and shared using clay tablets, paper and various other 'technologies'. It is a vital reminder to keep people and the use of information at the centre of our thinking, not the technology itself.

The use of IT in business gained momentum during the 1970s as most medium-size and large organizations used IT for some aspects of business processes. Typical starting-points were often financial processes, including purchasing, payroll and general ledger. Manufacturing became a second area of automation, often using very different technologies. Technology development continued with the introduction and adoption of the PC in the 1980s, followed later by the mouse and the graphical interface and then the Internet in the late 1990s. Over this period we have seen the coming together of a range of trends that have changed how we live and how we work.

In the 21st century it seems fairly safe to say that every business is a digital business. The impact of the PC, Internet and mobile technologies, to name just three of many innovations, has been radical. Among the many winners and losers, enormous value has been created. Critically, many organizations have a long way to go to make effective use of existing technologies. How are they going to cope in a world where technology innovation is accelerating, where there are more choices and options and where disruptive change is likely in many areas? We know there is still an 'IT attention deficit' and that key practices for successful management of benefits realization from IT-enabled change, transformation and innovation are far from universally and successfully adopted.

This book tackles management issues and practices that are applicable in a very wide range of situations and which have stood the test of time as technology has evolved and changed. In this chapter we take a slightly different focus and consider more directly the impact of technology on business. Firstly, we consider every business as a digital business and the need for a digital business strategy: what are the implications? Then we consider the specific impact of social technologies and the perspective of social business and the related thinking about socially responsible business. These are important scenarios for applying and testing out the principles and practices we have developed through the rest of the book.

For those who have been working with IT for 30 or more years, many of the current trends seem to have much in common with earlier waves of innovation. Are cloud-based enterprise applications really so different from time-sharing and then the idea of an 'application service provider'? Is the explosion of mobile devices connecting to enterprise systems all that different from the introduction of the PC and the development of end-user computing? Is this a radically new world, requiring new rules and new ways of thinking? To what extent is what we know, the expertise built up over many years, still valuable?

BUILDING A DIGITAL BUSINESS

THE DIGITAL VALUE CHAIN

Every business is a digital business – although the extent of digitization varies, with use of a laptop for email and basic record-keeping at the most basic small-business level. It is important not to see level of digitization as an issue of small vs. large business, as there are highly sophisticated, small digital businesses, and the availability of very sophisticated technologies to organizations of all sizes is one of the distinguishing features of the 'new world'.

The value chain (or network) remains a valuable model for understanding an organization. The focus on value creation fits directly with our focus on benefits, and the emphasis on information and flows of information provides a very natural fit with information systems and consideration of the digital business.

Figure 11.1 provides a value chain perspective on a single organization and indicates different technologies contributing to different aspects of the value chain along with the fit of terms such as business-to-consumer (B2C), business-to-business (B2B) and business-to-employee (B2E). It makes the point that IT can contribute to every aspect of the organization, although the effectiveness of how we make use of systems to create value will vary dramatically within and between organizations.

Using the value chain/network to understand value-creating activities, flows of information and the contribution of existing systems is a powerful way to gain an understanding of an organization. Essentially it provides a high-level process map, but one that looks beyond the boundaries of a specific organization.

A major limitation of Figure 11.1 is the focus on one organization. In reality it is in a complex network or organizations, and the systems (B2B and B2C) will reach out to other people and organizations.

The concept of social business looks within and beyond the walls of the organization and the formal business process views to people and communities (Mintzberg, 2009). Customer relationship management, even in a B2B context,

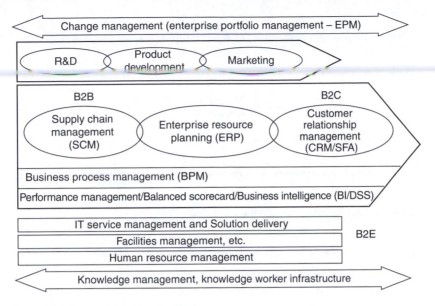

Figure 11.1 Systems and the value chain

recognizes the importance of relationships between people and not just orga-nizations. Social business represents a step-change in thinking and practice as new options for collaboration and value creation rapidly emerge. Wikipedia and Linux provided early examples of the way the Internet can enable collaboration with a purpose that happens regardless of formal organizational boundaries. Open innovation, crowd-sourcing, crowd-funding, co-creation of many forms are now evolving very rapidly as the Internet and mobile devices continue to reach out to more of the world.

USING INFORMATION TO MANAGE THE DIGITAL BUSINESS

Early uses of the value chain were in manufacturing, distribution and retail scenarios, often relating to physical products. This provides a starting-point for thinking about information and information flows at a transactional level: orders, stock replenishment, invoices and payments. Often a lack of informa-tion, or the difficulty of capturing information cost-effectively, was a challenge. Information is then used to manage and control these operational systems. Were orders complete and on time? Did the delivery match the order? Were customer queries responded to in line with planned service levels? This control information then feeds into key performance indicators, operational dashboards and management scorecards as key information is reported in summarized form in the context of targets and hopefully with the opportunity to 'drill down' and get insight into the reasons for any variances (Figure 11.2).

Establishing 'one version of the truth' remains a challenge as reporting draws on various sources of data and often there are still cottage industries of

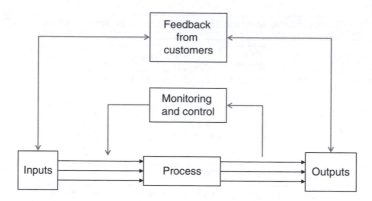

Figure 11.2 Information to manage the value chain

spreadsheets being created and used to deliver management reporting. Often this reflects the need for a variety of types of data to feed into key metrics and the difficulty of bringing the feeds from the different sources together.

An additional level, looking beyond control of the current system and business, is to consider the need for evolution and improvement. This might include looking beyond performance against current targets to changing targets in response to changing customer expectations, competitor action or new opportunities to improve performance and create value cost-effectively. There will also be drivers for more radical change, perhaps bringing in new product lines as others mature. At this level there will be more *ad hoc* analysis and exploration rather than routine reporting against specific targets; there will also be a need for qualitative and external data from many sources and of many different types. Examples of work include: benchmarking to gain insight into standards achieved by competitors; gaining an understanding of people or organizations who are not customers but who might be; understanding and sharing the reasons for good performance (or how to overcome problems).

In many organizations the levels blur as managers at different levels in different units have different needs. Consider a ward or a cancer team within a specific hospital. Control information is needed for the ward and the team, and is also required to provide relevant comparisons within and outside the hospital. Similarly wider management information is needed at all levels, as in the hospital and other knowledge work settings, responsibility for improvement is with the knowledge workers; they need the information to help them do this and part of this will be the external information, perhaps on other wards, cancer units in other hospitals or other countries.

One change that has happened and is happening is a breakdown of the assumptions of hierarchy and the link of different levels of information with different levels of management. If the front-line staff have responsibility for not just doing the job but also for improving the job, they need the information and the expertise to do that.

The challenges of explaining and using the information to understand what is possible, diagnose problems, plan and implement improvements require a very wide range of information (both structured – typically transactions and numbers in a database – and unstructured – all sorts of documents, videos and other media within and beyond an organization) and drive links between management information/decision support and the realms of knowledge management and organizational learning. To follow through the hospital example: is the example of the high-performing cancer team and another hospital relevant to us? What can we learn about the reasons for their improved performance, and are there any specific practices we can adopt that might work well in our context?

Although the broad challenges as described above could have been discussed in a similar way 10 or 20 years ago, what has changed dramatically is the availability of data and powerful analytical and visualization tools. From data often being too hard and expensive to capture we have had an explosion of data being captured easily and cost-effectively.

NEW PERSPECTIVES ON THE DIGITAL BUSINESS

Taking the view that technology is enabling a qualitatively different type of digital business – that is, not just doing what we did before faster and cheaper – it is worth considering what this does or might look like, how we get there and what the benefits could be.

Taking digital business strategy as 'organizational strategy formulated and executed by leveraging digital resources to create differential value', Bharadwaj et al. (2013) take a resource-based view and provide a helpful focus on differential business value, so going beyond consideration of efficiency and effectiveness to competing with IT. They go on to explore the scope of digital business strategy and the opportunities for value and identify the following broad areas.

Digitization of products and services

A major trend and source of value has been digitization of products and services. This is a rapid acceleration of a long-term trend as high-speed broadband connectivity becomes available to a majority of organizations and consumers in many markets. The roll-out of 4G mobile technologies is just another major step forward. Examples include Sony, where the TV becomes a smart TV providing Internet access and new features including films on demand. Amazon provides an example of moving rapidly from being an online retailer to a publisher and provider of digital content (MP3 music and e-books), to the provision of capability to read the content (Kindle software and device), to provision of a retail capabilities for other business and IT infrastructure services for other organizations (cloud storage, for example). Nike provides another consumer-oriented example where the sports products are being extended by information and services to help customers monitor health and performance. In a very different area, GE are bringing digital capabilities to aircraft engines and medical devices: for example, the engine effectively calling ahead to suggest priorities for preventive maintenance at the next scheduled stop.

Global processes: Extending to supply chains and flexible ecosystems

Links with suppliers – for example, through Electronic Data Interchange (EDI) – have been a focus of automation for decades and have provided considerable value. Walmart was a pioneer here and was able to share the transaction-level sales data from the tills in stores with suppliers to help them take on more responsibility for the supply chain and ensure their products were available on the shelves in each store.

More recently, with Internet technologies and standards, it has been possible to reduce costs and barriers to entry, enabling smaller firms to participate. New developments go beyond trading partner integration to the creation of new ecosystems based on digital resources (Apple: books and music; Amazon general retailing; Bharadwaj et al., 2013). As the Apple and Amazon examples illustrate, a major player often dominates these ecosystems and there are major network effects, as the scale of the networks becomes a major source of value. There seem to be increasing number of scenarios where network effects from digital connections are creating value.

Participation in these alliances, networks and ecosystems means an organization will have to adapt to reflect the standards set by others and adjust its systems to match. This goes beyond using the pervasive technical standards of the Internet to tackling some of the challenges familiar from EDI: for example, what fields of information you have on a purchase order or invoice.

Rapidly scalable infrastructure

Cloud-computing can provide virtualized IT resources that are available on demand on a self-service basis. It can provide a very flexible, rapidly scalable, pay-as-you-go capability, which could contribute to a strategic dynamic capability for an organization (Bharadwaj et al., 2013).

This provides a successful small organization with the ability to scale its service provision and cope with massive surges in demand that come with the Internet: for example, an online game or a successful e-commerce promotion. In the public sector the need for scalability is also critical, as potentially millions of people want access to a service: perhaps for last-minute filing of a tax return.

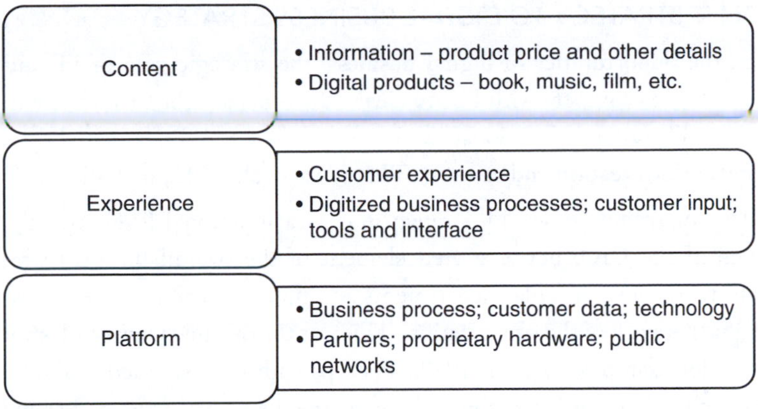

Content	• Information – product price and other details • Digital products – book, music, film, etc.
Experience	• Customer experience • Digitized business processes; customer input; tools and interface
Platform	• Business process; customer data; technology • Partners; proprietary hardware; public networks

Figure 11.3 Components of a digital business model

Information abundance

The rapid growth of the Internet with the explosion of mobile phones, tablets and other personal devices is being accelerated further by the 'Internet of Things' as machines and sensors in areas such as energy, environment, health and transportation are connected.

Changing business models

The components of a digital business model are explored by Weill and Woerner (2013) and include platform, experience and content (Figure 11.3).

LexisNexis has innovated in all three areas of its business model (Weill and Woerner, 2013). A major area of business has been information provision to the legal profession. With information being provided for free by Google and Bing – for example, the results of court cases – LexisNexis have invested in unique content (e.g., commentary from top lawyers). In terms of customer experience they have developed task-related mobile apps to enable customers to carry out time-sensitive tasks easily. They have also invested in a flexible global platform, which understands more about a user (cf. Amazon) and can target relevant information more effectively.

A second example is Apple, which has focused on an integrated platform (for example, iTunes, iPod, iPad) and the customer experience, and left content for others, as a result creating thriving ecosystems around music, video, books and apps.

Google provides a major example of a trend for 'multi-sided' business models. Something is provided for free (Android), but the revenue comes in other ways: in the case of Google, often through advertising. Many sectors have had to think differently about business models and sources of revenue, and power has shifted in the value chain as intermediaries have come and gone.

FROM IT STRATEGY TO DIGITAL BUSINESS STRATEGY

Given the opportunities of digital business, the strategic role of IT and the opportunity to compete with IT are clear: 'the time is right to shift our thinking about IT, not as a functional-level response, but as a fundamental driver of business value creation and capture' (Bharadwaj et al., 2013, p. 480).

It is important to see IT strategy not as a functional-level strategy, the domain of the CIO, but as a vital element of the overall business strategy, which transcends particular departments and functional silos and extends into the value network of the organization. This was the original view of IT strategy, set out, for example, by Earl (1989). Perhaps with the extended visibility and impact of IT, more organizations will overcome the IT attention deficit and the digital business strategy will provide a way to avoid islands of digitization across an organization and to enable competitive advantage.

DIGITAL OPTIONS FOR THE DIGITAL BUSINESS

Investments to build the digital business should generate value as a direct result of the investment. The investments also create value by creating *options* for the future: that is, the ability to respond more quickly or effectively to new events, threats or opportunities, drawing on the results of earlier investments.

Those options come from two broad sources. Firstly, the technology that has been put in place. This has always been the case, but as technologies become more flexible and adaptable, rapid evolution may be possible. For example, Amazon have leveraged their infrastructure of website and warehouse for selling books to extend rapidly the range of products sold. Secondly, previous investments will have contributed to the evolution of a broad set of business capabilities, including the people, practices and processes for running an agile digital business, which can quickly adapt and evolve. These capabilities also include the ability to innovate and change: the benefits realization capability. This change and benefits realization capability enables the organization to spot opportunities (entrepreneurial alertness) and to deliver improvements using an agile, benefits-driven approach, as well as manage a portfolio of investments across evolution of the existing business exploration to capture new sources of value.

To take advantage of these digital options, organizations need 'entrepreneurial alertness', or the ability to spot value-creating opportunities, and 'agility', the benefits realization capability, in the terms we have used (Sambamurthy and Bharadwaj, 2003). See Figure 11.4.

Business agility includes (Sambamurthy and Bharadwaj, 2003):

Operational agility: flexible processes offering speed, accuracy and cost-effectiveness. One example might be the ability to take on new customers and suppliers rapidly into integrated ordering, stock control and financial systems.

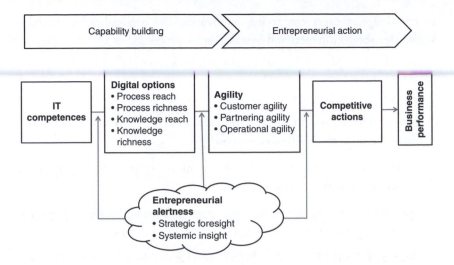

Figure 11.4 Creating value from digital options

Partnering agility: the ability to draw on the resources and capabilities of partners to create value, perhaps providing distribution, customer support and maintenance capabilities to an IT supplier.

Customer agility: providing flexibility for customers to adapt products and services and bringing them into the exploration and exploitation of opportunities as co-creators and testers.

Customer and partnering agility provide opportunities beyond traditional opportunities and are areas where open innovation and crowd-sourcing approaches are increasingly used.

One way to explore further the digital options available is to consider 'reach' and 'richness'. Reach is about the extent of connectivity – within and outside an organization. So at the extreme, anyone, anywhere can access the service. Richness is about depth of relationship and the way information is used to enhance it. Amazon knows about me, my reading and music interests, and much more besides, and uses that knowledge to offer me suggestions and promotions. Spotify does the same and provides me opportunities to connect with others and learn from their 'playlists' what music I might like. These services build 'stickiness' and create value for customers by bringing new opportunities – overcoming the barriers of 'you don't know what you don't know'.

Sambamurthy and Bharadwaj (2003) consider reach and richness in terms of process and knowledge. This fits well with the different perspectives on the organization we have developed in earlier chapters. How do these process and knowledge perspectives apply in different organizations? What digital options do they help uncover? For example, management consultancies and organizations such as BP and Shell have made major investments in various approaches to knowledge management, trying codification and personalization to share knowledge about customers and how to resolve problems.

Bharadwaj et al. (2013) use an alternative framework to explore digital business strategy:

Scope: What areas of the organization are priorities – products, services and participation in the business ecosystem?

Scale: How can the business and technical infrastructure scale up (and down) to take advantage of new opportunities?

Speed: How can the digital business speed up existing business operations and also the speed to market of new products and services?

Sources of value: In the digital business what are the new sources of value: from information; from new business models; from exploiting the digital architecture and capabilities?

These different frameworks for digital business provide new elements of our toolkit to help investigate the opportunities in a specific organization.

EXPLOITING THE CLOUD TO BUILD THE DIGITAL AND GLOBAL BUSINESS

'The cloud' is a general term for a very wide range of application and infrastructure services available via the Internet over mobile, wireless and broadband networks. It represents many strands of IT evolution coming together, not least virtualization, which means applications, run independently of specific physical servers and brings scalability and resilience. The cloud includes major enterprise applications such as customer relationship management, office applications such as Microsoft Office 365 and Google Docs, as well as a huge variety of 'apps' including such things as Dropbox (virtual storage for individuals and teams) and Evernote (one set of note books available across every device). We access cloud services from a variety of devices in a single day, perhaps a smartphone, a tablet, our own PC or laptop and a shared PC.

In a sense the cloud is very much here. Salesforce was founded 14 years ago and reached 1 million customers five years ago (Willcocks et al., 2014). At the same time we are in the early stages of the evolution and exploitation of the cloud.

Willcocks et al. (2014) set out a number of major challenges facing the industry and cloud adopters (Table 11.1).

There are significant opportunities for the digital business to exploit the cloud to enable innovation and transformational change. Growth and extension

1	Weighing up the security and legal risks	Concerns relate to availability of services and privacy of data. Legal issues include offshore data. There are many considerations. Providers will have extensive technical expertise, which would not be available to any but very large organizations. However, the reputational risks of failures are high.
2	Defining the relationship through contracting	Cloud contracts bring new issues. In particular, there is unlikely to be the service level agreement (SLA) associated with a more traditional outsourcing contract.
3	The lock-in dilemma	There is a risk of 'lock-in' to a cloud provider and potentially high switching costs. This is a major concern when core services and data are involved. However, it is just the next version of the existing issue of lock-in with enterprise application and other IT vendors.
4	Managing the cloud	Challenges include maintaining strategic control in a fast-changing environment and operational management of services.
5	Dealing with the integration challenge	The cloud brings a major risk of fragmentation of data and services. From an architectural perspective (Chapter 10) there is a risk that for the organization as a whole flexibility and agility will be undermined.

Table 11.1 Challenges of the cloud

of reach to become a global business can happen much more quickly than in earlier eras.

BUILDING MOMENTUM

Digital business opportunities and digital business strategy are topics that provide a good starting-point for getting senior management attention. There is an opportunity to use this approach to side-step the IT attention deficit and to build momentum for building the benefits realization capability of the organization.

We know that the future is already here – it's just unevenly distributed. This means that the opportunities are clear, even if we can't tell who the winners are going to be. We do know that capability comes from action and experience, so failing to take action to build the digital business is planning to fail.

Two case studies of the airline BA illustrate different aspects of digital business (Boxes 11.1 and 11.3).

Box 11.1 Bringing digital business to the core of the existing business

'A once-every-second-generation project'

BA operates with some of the most complex logistical parameters of any industry:

- a fleet of around 250 aircraft of various sizes, ages, makes and models;
- long-haul and short-haul cabin crew totalling 15,000 people;
- hundreds of routes serviced by scheduled passenger flights;
- 500 different rules and regulations to comply with Civil Aviation Authority (CAA) safety standards;
- Many long-standing employment terms and conditions agreements made with BA trade unions over time (for instance, over 20 different categories of cabin crew leave to adhere to!).
- It takes new users of the crew tracking system a year before they are fully trained in the use of the system.

Before any flight can take off, BA must ensure that the crew in charge of the aircraft are:

- qualified to fly;
- have had sufficient rest days prior to the flight;
- have the official capacity and designation to take on the duties required of them on the flight specified;
- are able to reach the designated point of departure in time and still be 'ready to fly'.

These are just some of the complex parameters and logic rules embedded in the legacy crew tracking system (referred to as TRACIE) that has been used by BA for around 35 years. TRACIE was bought by BA from KLM, and it has generally served the business well. TRACIE works well when there is no disruption to flight patterns and schedules. However, these parameters can often be suddenly and dramatically thrown into chaos by any number of external factors. Volcanic ash, severe snow, industrial action, terrorist activity and health epidemics have all shown their force in the last decade alone.

As soon as any one of these events occurs and disruption ensues, TRACIE becomes very tricky to use. Many pieces of exceptional data and amendments need to be inputted, often with very short turnaround. also connected to TRACIE are 108 downstream systems that must all be protected and maintained. Added to the fact that the technology platform is rapidly becoming obsolete, replacing TRACIE became imperative for BA.

John Hamilton is BA's Delivery Manager within the operations directorate. John describes this initiative as a 'once-every-second-generation project', that is expected to deliver business efficiency and benefits for 20 years. A first attempt at replacing TRACIE initially started 12 years ago. After two years this project was stopped because of software performance issues and the expense of the hardware at the time.

Maximizing engagement in a five-year programme – 'iFlightCrew'

In the five years since John Hamilton and his team started leading the TRACIE replacement, they have established it as a key strategic programme with 13 parallel work streams. The technology component has at its heart a third-party crew-tracking application.

The core objective of the programme is to enable each crew 'allocation', 'de-allocation' or 're-allocation' to be completed in a single transaction. With TRACIE, any of these activities requires dozens of paper-based and on-screen inputs. Operators are often dependent on faxed-in data sent by cabin crew personnel holed up in far-flung hotels.

The new system, iFlightCrew, replaces TRACIE with a best-of-breed new application. The management-of-change programme that has brought BA to this pre-implementation stage of readiness has been extensive and complex. John and his colleagues have undertaken a series of crucial activities to maximize engagement of all parties and increase the likelihood of successful adoption and implementation.

Acknowledgement: Thanks to Alison Freer for the work on this case study and to BA for allowing us to share it. It contributes to Ashurst et al. (2012).

TRENDS ENABLING THE DIGITAL BUSINESS

Many commentators are outlining trends that will have major impacts in the years ahead. Focusing specifically on IT rather than wider technology and geo-political developments (nano-technology, renewable energy, fracking, driverless cars...), Burgin et al. (2013) outline ten IT-enabled business trends for the decade ahead.

JOINING THE SOCIAL MATRIX

Organizations are reaching out to customers and engaging customers in marketing: for example, book reviews on Amazon, product reviews on many sites and 'likes' on Facebook. Organizations are also engaging customers and others in open innovation and co-creation. P&G and others have built broad engagement in technical problem-solving and research and development. Others have involved customers in deciding on colours for new clothing (Macy's) or toy promotions (Walmart).

The social matrix is also about connections between individuals within and across organizations. Knowledge workers are drowning in email: what if they could become 5 or 25% more productive by effective use of social technologies? Some organizations (such as Atos) are aiming to become zero-email organizations.

COMPETING WITH 'BIG DATA' AND ADVANCED ANALYTICS

'Big data' builds on the experience of retailers and others who have had access to vast quantities of customer data for many years. A retailer such as Tesco has built up huge experience of using transaction data and 'basket analysis' to target customer offers, for store layout improvements and to enable change in many areas of the value chain. Big data brings many new sources of data, from how people are using websites, to all the information available from social media, to the vast sources of information available from the 'Internet of Things' (see below). Burgin et al. (2013) provide the example of Acxiom, which provides big-data-related services handling 500 million customer profiles each with 1,500 data points drawn from 50 trillion transactions.

Value comes from using the data, and it's being used on the front line to provide an excellent customer experience: for examples as Amazon personalizes the results of a web search. There are also many opportunities for experimentation and gathering data to test out new options with samples of customers. This approach, known as A/B testing or 'champion' and 'challenger', allows rapid, cost-effective testing with low risk, as a website channels customers either to the existing page (etc.) or to the new alternative and tracks the relative outcomes.

As noted in Chapter 6, information capabilities are scarce and will be a key enabler of success with big data.

DEPLOYING THE INTERNET OF ALL THINGS

Falling costs mean that tiny sensors can be deployed *en masse* in a huge range of scenarios. This represents a step-change in capability beyond the passive, but still valuable, contribution of a Radio Frequency IDentification (RFID) tag to enabling tracking of items through a supply chain.

As an example, FedEx have a Sense Aware programme which involves a device the size of a mobile phone put into a package by a customer. It includes global positioning and temperature, light, humidity and pressure sensors. As a result, the customer has continuously updated information of the location and condition of the package.

There are fascinating opportunities for smart networks, smart cities and more, based on using these low-cost devices to gather information and bring intelligence to vast numbers of physical entities.

For individuals the 'quantified self' movement links these technologies – for example, in the form of wristbands – to apps and mobile devices and is enabling innovation in fitness, health and social care.

OFFERING ANYTHING AS A SERVICE

The trend of offering everything as a service is gathering speed. Buying a car reflects this: many schemes focus purely on the monthly cost, with the intention that a new contract will follow after two to three years, rather than on purchase of an asset. The video rental market, now based on access on demand over the Internet, has reflected this model for many years.

At a B2B level many organizations are looking to gain revenue from resources and capabilities. Amazon through its web services is leveraging digital capabilities. Others are using digital capabilities to increase revenue from physical assets by, for example, renting out idle trucks by the hour.

AUTOMATING KNOWLEDGE WORK

Use of IT to enhance knowledge work is a major opportunity (see Chapter 6), with an estimated 200 million knowledge workers. A developing trend is the automation of knowledge work. There is the potential for major change in many professional and knowledge work areas.

Beyond analytics and big data, machine learning is a major area. Bughin et al. (2013) provide two examples (Boxes 11.2 and 11.3).

Box 11.2   Machine learning: Examples

Clearwell Systems in Silicon Valley: scanned half a million documents as part of pre-trial discovery and pinpointed the 0.5% of them that were relevant to the upcoming trial. In three days they completed what would have taken a large team of lawyers weeks.

* * *

The IBM computer 'Watson' is tackling cancer research. It read 600,000 medical evidence reports, 1.5 million patient records and 2 million pages of clinical trial reports and medical journal articles. It is now providing decision support to specialist oncologists.

Source: Bughin et al. (2013).

Box 11.3   Using mobile technologies to enhance customer service

Exploration of new technologies and customer trends

Linda Dodsworth is BA's Delivery Manager within the flight operations directorate. Linda and her colleagues lead on delivery of a range of IT-enabled business improvement projects, most of which are dedicated to improving the airline's operational effectiveness. Among a challenging portfolio of projects, Linda and her team have made space to explore the opportunities to exploit the functionality provided by tablet computers and smartphones to deliver competitive advantages to BA's staff and customers.

A couple of years ago Linda anticipated that, with the dawn of the iPhone and the iPad, it would only be a matter of time before her team received requests to develop mobile apps. This was not an aspect of training covered by BA's technical training programmes. Linda identified a number of colleagues who had shown a personal interest in exploring the possibilities of this new enabling hardware, including Apple and Android products. In their early days of experimentation Linda's colleagues predominantly conducted their research in their own time, or made time alongside other project demands.

In parallel, BA's Director of Brand and Customer Experience, Frank van der Post, wanted to initiate a customer engagement project using iPads. Subsequently, Cabin Service Directors (CSDs) and senior members of cabin crew were given iPads for their personal use, with the investment funded by BA. Cabin service crews had noticed that more and more valued BA customers were bringing their iPads and smartphones onto flights and BA wanted to show that it too was embracing this rapidly expanding new technology.

Flight crew engagement

First steps for Linda and her colleagues were to engage their flight operations colleagues in discussions to identify the opportunities they could envisage for embracing the potential of mobile technology. At a workshop with these people a host of suggestions were generated which were then evaluated according to the relative ease of developing a solution and the potential impact each could have. From this exercise, six and then three ideas were selected and prioritized for further development.

Start simple

Linda and her colleagues decided to start with enabling an electronic form that flight crews could complete on an iPad. The aim was to bring the power of the BA employee self-service system to iPad users. This system had traditionally required PC-based log-in to the BA Intranet and was often unavailable to flight crews when working remotely. Now flight crew are able to complete these forms while they travel to their hotels on the crew bus, and they have a range of simple smart forms which can be completed and emailed in.

As a result, time-saving and empowerment were provided to the flight crew, and improved yet more timely data was provided to BA.

Future mobile app development

Air safety report forms are required to be completed by pilots at the end of their flight.

These paper-based forms have always been completed by hand. The purpose of the form is to record any in-flight safety issues, such as significant weather (e.g., turbulence encountered), route diversions and so on. Previously, pilots would hand it in for scanning and emailing to outsourcing data entry teams in India. Sometimes pilots have a very short turnaround between flights and may not have time to complete the form immediately, or to hand it in for processing. Consequently there has often been a time-lag in the required information being available.

The smart form designed by Linda's team cuts out at least two of these stages, and in the longer term there is plenty of opportunity to continue to increase the functionality available to eventually connect the data inputs directly to BA's safety management information system.

Having proved the concept of the potential benefits of relatively simple iPad app development, Linda envisages an internal 'App Store' for flight crews. This innovation has come about through a combination of technical experts and general users reaching mutual interest in and understanding of what's possible. This is a convergence of experimentation, collaboration and joint, agile development. What is also demonstrated here is that some business innovations can deliver benefits for relatively low investment in time and finance.

Acknowledgement: Thanks to Alison Freer for the work on this case study and to BA for allowing us to share it. It contributes to Ashurst et al. (2012).

ENGAGING THE NEXT 3 BILLION DIGITAL CITIZENS

Rapidly falling costs of smartphones will make Internet access available to billions more consumers. There will be many opportunities for new enterprises and opportunities to leapfrog established economies with industrial age legacy. For example, mobile payments have grown rapidly in emerging markets where consumers have no access to a traditional bank or bank account.

CHARTING EXPERIENCES WHERE DIGITAL MEETS PHYSICAL

The boundaries of the digital and physical worlds are becoming blurred and, as elsewhere, falling costs mean that technologies once costing millions of dollars for specialist research labs are now used in consumer applications.

The location sensor (GPS) in a smartphone is a starting-point for many of the opportunities, which include:

- augmented reality – for example, Google Glass projecting additional information based on our location;
- interaction with technology based on movement and gesture, as pioneered in the Microsoft Xbox;
- virtual changing rooms where customers can 'try on' new clothes;
- life-size virtual displays by retailers (such as Tesco) where shoppers can pick their groceries at the train station using a smartphone and have them delivered or waiting to pick up.

Within the organization there are many opportunities, and leading organizations are already realizing benefits: warehouse staff guided to the right aisle; maintenance engineers provided with relevant information based on their location; and the systems knowledge of the equipment in place and its status (Internet of Things).

There are threats to privacy, which will hold some organizations back. But others will focus on value for customers and other stakeholders, and experiment to create value.

FREEING YOUR BUSINESS MODEL THROUGH INTERNET-INSPIRED PERSONALIZATION AND SIMPLIFICATION

Customers increasingly expect service to be free, personalized and easy to use without instructions. Apple has become an industry leader based on user experience, and the initial success and momentum of Google were similarly based on user experience design and simplicity.

As a result, organizations need innovative models to find alternative sources of revenue.

BUYING AND SELLING AS DIGITAL COMMERCE LEAPS AHEAD

Mobile payment is a major development in digital commerce. New market-places and comparison services continue to spring up for hotels, travel and many more categories.

A major trend is the participation of the consumer and micro-business as seller and service provider. The barriers to entry are so low that there are new opportunities to reach a global market with both physical and digital products and services. Amazon and eBay may have started this development, but there are many new initiatives.

TRANSFORMING GOVERNMENT, HEALTH-CARE AND EDUCATION

The transformation in government, health-care and education is likely to exceed that in the private sector, if only because these massive sectors have been relatively late and risk-averse adopters.

There are huge opportunities in both the developed and the developing economies. In each case there may be disruptive change as the impact goes far beyond automation of current roles, structures and processes. Why do you need representative democracy when everyone can join in the voting? How can we change education not just by putting the lectures on the Internet, but by engaging people as a community of learners?

The case study in Box 11.4 illustrates opportunities in health-care.

Box 11.4 Innovation in health-care

Company overview

Founded in 2010 by Michael J Bell and Gavin Kipling, a core part of Digital Spark's vision is, 'to bring Apple-like user interface experiences to the clinical world'. Digital Spark develops data capture software that is easy to use by busy clinical staff in hospital settings. With a background in health-care strategy, user experience and web application development, Michael J. Bell and his colleagues set out to transform the way key clinical data is captured. In its first 18 months Digital Spark successfully developed and implemented CaptureStroke software for six hospitals in north-east England. Stroke patient data, from first arrival in Accident and Emergency, through to and beyond discharge from the hospital ward, is now fully captured. Now, crucial care performance information is already being gleaned from the system, and there is great potential for other clinical care pathways to benefit from this innovative data capture system.

Market context

For years doctors and nurses have complained of cumbersome and unreliable clinical data capture systems. Those that had been made available via the National Programme for IT (NPfIT) or via local trust procurement were often found to be under-utilized by staff. The extent and accuracy of clinical data capture have, until recently, been strongly dependent on users' diligence, IT competence and availability and access to static PCs. Not surprisingly, the potential benefits of such systems were never realized because staff simply didn't have time to input data. Any outputs from the systems were rendered inaccurate and often unreliable for clinical decision-making.

The UK National Health Service (NHS), like many large health service providers, is undergoing incredible structural change with two key goals being ever-present:

1. improving the quality of patient care;

2. reducing the cost of delivering health-care.

In the UK reducing deaths and severe disablement post-stroke remains a key health improvement target. Clinicians in north-east England have been eager to find new ways of understanding the condition, so that the treatment they give victims improves the health outcomes and also improves wider understanding of stroke prevention. Up until 2010 the stroke 'care pathway' involved collecting data from multiple sources, using a mix of manual and automated systems and duplicate data entry. The data that clinicians previously relied upon to affect service changes and track care delivery performance was generally not available in a timely manner, required extensive effort to uncover and was sometimes incomplete.

Responding to a call to action from the North of England Cardiovascular Network and the then Deputy Regional Director of Public Health at NHS North East, Digital Spark were presented with an opportunity to revolutionize the way stroke data is captured and used. CaptureStroke was developed to meet this need. Digital Spark also set out to prove the benefits of adopting innovations in touch-screen technology and intuitive user interface design, creating a system that could be used to collect data at the point of care to enhance data quality.

Digital Spark's data capture software delivers a number of key benefits:

1. Increased data accuracy and interoperability: CaptureStroke draws key patient data directly from the electronic patient record systems (Patient Administration System – PAS) already in place in

many hospitals. Coupled with mobile data capture capability, this means that data is both accurate and more highly available, and that duplication of effort is reduced.

2. Mobile data capture and real-time care statistics: CaptureStroke is an application clinicians can use on either fixed desktop PCs or on ward rounds, using the Panasonic Toughbook CF-H1. Toughbooks are iPad-like devices, specially designed for use in clinical settings, and can withstand dropping and spillages. The devices are also manufactured to meet the exacting hygiene management standards now in place in all NHS hospitals to support infection control. This enables data capture to happen at the point of care, thereby saving time, improving data accuracy and providing trusted, real-time information on patient care.

3. Ease of use: From the very start of development Digital Spark worked on the key user requirement, emphatically made by clinicians, that 'the system must be easy to use!' Gavin Kipling, Michael J. Bell's co-founder, fellow director and award-winning creative, ensures that all Digital Spark products are user-interface and design-led. CaptureStroke's screens are characterized by big, chunky user-interface components, surrounded with plenty of white space and red, amber and green colour schemes for ease of data input and visualization. All of CaptureStroke's user interfaces were designed with significant clinical input, and this proved invaluable in delivering a system that has seen mass adoption at current sites and delivery of key benefits ahead of time.

4. Clinical team organization and care delivery: CaptureStroke is used by a range of staff – both clinical and administrative – with ease and consistency. When shifts change, and when staff come and go, the dataset remains constant and can be interpreted easily by someone taking over the care of a patient, without having to spend time briefing and de-briefing on handovers. Crucially, the clinicians who are now using CaptureStroke to monitor and evaluate their patients' progress trust the system and the data they are working with. They have reduced their reliance on paper-based systems and have increased their time efficiency.

Innovation drivers

Digital Spark is growing at a time when a number of key factors are converging to make this health innovation possible:

- Mobile touchpad technology: the ubiquitous adoption of iPad-like devices in everyday life means that most users are already familiar with the touchpad user interface and can quickly understand and use Digital Spark applications.

- Preventative health-care: part of the transformation of health-care in the NHS is about finding new ways of preventing common conditions, including strokes.

- Clinician/user leadership: the drive for innovation in available technology has come from the key users themselves. There is a compelling desire to transform stroke care, and the very doctors and nurses involved in treating patients have demanded new software. In the new era of clinically led health-care commissioning, CaptureStroke is an early example of a successfully procured service.

- Cost and service delivery benefits: only two months after delivery, benefits are being realized by all key stakeholders, including clinicians, patients and the fund-holders concerned with cost vs. delivery. Under the current NHS financial model, another compelling driver is the ability confidently to demonstrate evidence of positive health outcomes following episodes of care for stroke patients. This is crucial in hospital trusts both to raise their profile and to receive necessary financial payments from central NHS funds.

All of these factors have combined to result in an idea successfully and widely applied, with clear evidence of benefits delivered.

Acknowledgement: Thanks to Alison Freer for the work on this case study and to Digital Spark for allowing us to share it. It contributes to Ashurst et al. (2012).

FROM SOCIAL TECHNOLOGIES TO SOCIAL BUSINESS

MAKING EFFECTIVE USE OF SOCIAL TECHNOLOGIES FOR BUSINESS VALUE

A wide range of technologies is resulting in rapid changes to how we communicate, collaborate and innovate. We are surrounded by different opportunities to communicate in our work and home lives. We still talk to people face to face, but there is also the mobile phone, instant messaging, Internet-based conferencing (Skype, Face Time, Lync, Adobe), social technologies such as Facebook, LinkedIn, Google+ and Twitter, and discussion forums both internally and in the public domain (Amazon, Trip Advisor, technical support for any product or

Search	Finding what you are looking for. A search facility or engine to efficiently discover relevant information based on an information input from one user.
Links	Using the links between pages, not just the content on pages, to influence search results.
Authorship	Making it easy for everyone to be an author via blogs, wikis and discussion.
Tags	Tags provide information about information, potentially user-generated 'likes' on Facebook.
Extensions	Extensions are the machine learning your interests and preferences: 'If you like that, you'll like this.'
Signals	Signals are the way in which users are notified about updates to the user-generated content that is relevant or importance to a particular user, user group or community. Signals are important, but can themselves become 'spam'.

Table 11.2 Technologies for enterprise 2.0 (based on McAfee, 2006)

technology). It is no wonder we struggle with passwords, how to use features, and how to make effective use of these tools to help us achieve our priorities.

These technologies are not just bringing new options for doing what we already do; they are also opening up major new opportunities for engagement within organizations, with customers and with individuals and organizations across the world. We are learning to think how and why people work in different ways. The technologies are resulting in radical changes to how we collaborate and innovate.

Management by carrot and stick around specific objectives set top-down by management seems strange in a world where unpaid collaboration has resulted in Linux, Wikipedia and many other developments. We are also seeing how much people have to offer in terms of innovation, assistance for others and problem-solving when given the chance.

This new collaborative enterprise has been called Enterprise 2.0 (McAfee, 2006) to reflect the extent of change. The SLATES framework (Table 11.2) outlines important technology capabilities that are enabling this development.

The strategic issue is social business rather than social technology. The definition 'a Social Business embraces networks of people to create business value' (IBM, 2011) provides a helpful emphasis on value creation.

Getting value from these technologies is a major challenge for management. They mean we need to rethink management (Birkinshaw, 2010) and specifically adopt styles that encourage the wisdom of crowds and support the intrinsic motivation of individuals to contribute.

In our recent research (Ashurst et al., 2012) we studied a number of cases of open innovation and found the approach being used by a range of large organizations to tackle a broad range of topics. It was clear that a pattern of good practice for applying open innovation is rapidly emerging as similar lessons are learned in different organizations.

From our sample key elements of good practice for open innovation are:

1. a launch date for a specific innovation challenge;

2. clear, focused questions;

3. evaluation criteria and process with well-informed participation in the review;

4. diverge to explore possibilities, then converge to focus on ideas for action;

5. rapid decision-making to turn ideas into action, encouraging contribution;

6. sponsorship and resource for the ideation project and to follow through good ideas.

The case study explores how social technologies are being used in one large organization (Box 11.5).

Box 11.5   Case study: Social business – Enabling innovation in a major organization

Company overview

Established in the 1950s and now employing over 90,000 people worldwide, CSC is one of the biggest and most pioneering IT services businesses (www.csc.com). Always at the vanguard of technology, CSC has most notably been the long-standing IT partner for NASA and was integral to the Shuttle programme, among other stellar projects. Today CSC's worldwide client portfolio is impressive and includes some of the leading global corporations, governments and institutions. An integral part of CSC's business strategy from the very start has been a clearly declared focus on innovation.

CSC is a global, multinational, multi-location business employing close to 100,000 professional knowledge workers. They work in matrix structures to deliver multiple projects, for multiple clients, across many professional disciplines and market sectors. CSC has the challenges of maximizing productivity on a massive scale amid considerable organizational complexity. For a business of this scale, face-to-face or in-person contact with tens of thousands of employees is almost impossible to achieve with any kind of authenticity. So CSC began to explore new ways of engaging its widely distributed workforce and, significantly, how best to tap into the combined knowledge and wisdom of this vast number of people.

Business context

CSC has consciously invested in exploring innovative enabling technologies, business models and services. This is a business for which 'innovation' is a central tenet, and Howard Smith is CSC's Global Lead for Collective Intelligence. Working together with colleagues in CSC's Office of Innovation and Leading Edge Forum, it is his remit to stimulate employees to respond to CSC business leader challenges and to innovate effectively across all its activities.

> CSC is here to do nothing but serve customers, so if they view something as innovative, that is the marker of the significance to them. We look at innovation all along the supply chain, from our suppliers through to customer delivery teams. Ultimately we aim to maximize the frequency of innovation.

Key innovation elements

Innovation for CSC is all about business growth. As a primarily service business, innovation is now a regular bid assessment criterion for the requests for proposals (RFPs) that CSC responds to. CSC has embedded a number of business innovation processes that provide employees and customers options for leveraging business benefits for all parties.

- **Customer Account Innovation Programmes**: Within the operationally driven environment of major outsourcing contracts it can be difficult for innovation to flourish. Therefore CSC teams are encouraged to plug into all the ways in which innovation can be provided for their customers. This includes drawing appropriately from a number of innovation resources and processes. Customer accounts use the innovation frameworks to understand what customers want from CSC within the scope of the contract.

- **Leading Edge Forum**: This best-practice network is available only to CSC customers on an elective, subscription basis. Members have access to thought leadership, study tours and bespoke research projects scoped by them.

- **Technical Excellence**: CSC constantly strives for excellence in different technical and business solutions for its clients. CSC customers value the thought leadership and intellectual property that are made available to them.

- **Innovation Frameworks**: All customer teams can draw on a rich vein of collateral, tools and thinking frameworks to give structure to innovation projects at all levels of a customer account. This can include service delivery innovation as well as business process innovation.

- **Ideation and Idea Management**: This is one of the tools available to account teams and can be used for specific customer projects as well as internal business innovation within CSC. It's a process based on the theory of the 'wisdom of crowds', as Howard Smith describes it; it's, 'a 21st-century employee suggestion box'. It is a rigorous 'end-to-end' process, which needs to be carefully facilitated, and CSC has been exploring the benefit of this approach for a number of years. The technique has been used by CSC on a number of occasions in the past five years, and ideation has since delivered considerable benefits for CSC and its customers.

- **Corporate Office of Innovation**: All of the elements are developed and promoted by Howard Smith and his colleagues in the Corporate Office of Innovation. This office was established to foster a greater focus on innovation across the CSC portfolio and organization. The team is often called on to facilitate innovation best practices across the business, in the form of ideation campaigns, client workshops and other engagement event forums. Team members are also responsible for accrediting 'Centers of Excellence' within divisions of CSC.

The 'wisdom of crowds' – ideation in action

Successful business innovation at CSC is achieved through leveraging the right combination of innovation best practices to suit the requirements of a team or client. Over the past few years CSC has been one of a few organizations at the forefront of applying newly realized social sciences understanding to wide staff engagement in idea and innovation management. The core concepts of ideation are based on embracing the so-called 'wisdom of crowds' to deliver business benefits from innovation.

During 2005 Howard began researching the principles and practices of ideation. He discovered that a number of companies were challenging their employees in more direct ways than had ever been possible using traditional suggestion schemes. During his investigations Howard discovered innovation process specialists Imaginatik (www.imaginatik.com). Imaginatik had produced a technology platform called Idea Central (now called Innovation Central), with which CSC decided to experiment.

Using features and functionality commonly found in social media channels and workflow systems, Idea Central meshed well with CSC's desire to engage employees more widely. Idea Central was piloted in 2006 at CSC, and immediately the potential was evident – so much so that a small group responsible for 'Collective Intelligence' was established. Howard Smith was appointed to his current role as Global Lead for Collective Intelligence, and he began working widely with business managers across CSC.

A number of pilot ideation campaigns ensued, using Idea Central as the platform. Idea Central can be specifically tailored to suit the different set of parameters required for each campaign, and the platform provides for 'one-to-many' and 'many-to-many' online collaboration. The following are some examples of how ideation has been used within CSC to solve key business questions.

1. **Maximizing the value of key customer accounts**

   One of the first ideation events was focused on customer account renewal. A newly appointed customer account director wanted staff to have their say and take the best of their thoughts and ideas about how to maximize opportunities within one of CSC's key customer accounts. Howard suggested that they experiment with Idea Central as a platform for ideation. Over a three-month period three separate ideation events were conducted using Idea Central as a focal point. This early campaign tested out the use of an interactive on-line forum to capture comments and ideas submitted to address the question 'How do we change and improve the relationship with this customer?'

   As in all ideation events, ideas 'flowed' through a build and evaluation process, leading to team recommendations and leadership decisions. This 'process' is what distinguishes idea management platforms from simpler collaboration technologies such as blogs, Wikis, intranets or social networking.

2. **Realizing R&D tax rebates**

   Another ideation campaign focused on realizing tax rebates for R&D investments made by CSC in different countries. For a business with wide global presence, this had proved a difficult area to get right, as each country has very different and specific laws on R&D tax rebates. Howard facilitated a unique event to flush out opportunities for relevant rebates. This ideation campaign took a week to design and ran for six weeks. The campaign uncovered the fact that R&D case studies were rarely compiled and therefore a lot of R&D work was unaccounted for. Implementing learning and ideas generated as a result of this ideation campaign then yielded £30 million in annual rebates in the UK alone. Following the success of this campaign, the rebate accounting process was adopted in other regions.

3. **Enabling conversations about 'elephants in the room'**

In 2008 CSC's then VP of Culture Change, Martha Johnson, recognized that ideation could be the perfect tool to enable employee engagement and consultation far beyond what was possible from gathering people in rooms for face-to-face workshops. Martha was looking at ways to enable culture change and first trialled ideation, using Idea Central as a mechanism, for a 'Women in Leadership' campaign. Having successfully galvanized the input of around 1,100 people, she became an advocate of the power of the ideation process, and of Idea Central as a suitable platform.

This experience paved the way for a bigger, more far-reaching, campaign with the title 'Elephants in the Room'. This campaign was co-designed with Howard's help and was, as the title implies, an opportunity for senior executives to table, in confidence, matters that they regarded to be holding the company back. This campaign was conducted with privacy and anonymity in mind, to promote maximum candour. The contributions aired during this campaign enabled senior leaders to engage in lots of well-informed thinking about CSC's future path, and demonstrated the power of ideation for generating honest dialogue. This campaign also succeeded in putting ideation firmly in CSC's innovation toolkit. However, there were still challenges to overcome.

Unlike 'bottom-up' technologies such as blogs and social networking which are 'always on', require no configuration and have no 'process' associated with them, ideation 'events' are business processes. Business processes, like any project designed to fulfil a clear objective, must be designed, launched and completed. All ideas must be seen to be considered, feedback given, conclusions drawn and actions assigned. Change in the organization must be delivered out of the back end of the process. In effect, all ideation events are 'business projects'. Since such ideation events involve far greater numbers of employees than a typical 'workgroup' project, they are a challenge to design and complete. They require careful design. Some CSC leaders found the up-front effort required onerous and did not take easily to the idea management approach. CSC, like other companies, is on a journey with respect to the embedded use of large-scale collaborative technologies epitomized by solutions such as Imaginatik. As the further examples below show, however, CSC has brought a level of maturity and best practice to the field.

4. **Engaging senior executives in redefining the corporate risk register**

CSC essentially takes on risks whenever it enters into a customer contract. The breadth and depth of the corporate risk register is highly complex, and it had always been very complicated for decision-makers to comprehend it fully. With the experience of other ideation campaigns to draw on, CSC's CEO decided to run a private/secure event across the global senior leader community to refresh the risk register.

The campaign was sponsored by CSC's Audit Office, and only very senior people within CSC – VP or Director level and above – were asked to participate. They posted their thoughts, experiences and ideas open to the Audit Office team. Options on the idea form allowed for anonymous posting, or posting in private to the Audit Office, or both. This highly sensitive campaign took months to plan and four weeks to run, to ensure that those invited to participate did so honestly and effectively. The campaign yielded fresher and more revealing insights into some of the previously unidentified or uncategorized business risks to create a far more accurate corporate risk register. This was reported in the CSC annual report in that year.

5. **Developing future business direction**

In 2009 CSC celebrated its 50th anniversary, and the CEO wanted to reach out to all staff in a 'two-way' communication process. (All previous mass communication campaigns from the CEO had been restricted by the sheer size of the company to one-way, top-down statements.) The CEO wanted to engage as many employees as possible in a discussion about 'What next for the company?' Howard and Martha Johnson worked with the CEO and Director of Strategy to plan the campaign, and when it was launched, all 90,000+ employees were invited. The campaign immediately yielded a good response rate and generated over 2,000 ideas. The review process evaluated some individual ideas and also led to the development of a range of business scenarios for the likely future direction of CSC.

The CEO challenge, as well as engaging the staff, was also designed to help other CSC leaders think more strategically about the company's future beyond the quarter-to-quarter management required of a publicly quoted company. The 'virtual' event for employees was therefore mirrored by a 'physical' event. At the annual sales conference senior attendees were asked to review a synthesis of the employee contributions by thinking through 200 different business scenarios crafted from various 'buckets' of ideas. Table groups of five to ten people evaluated the scenarios and fed their suggestions back at the conference. This thinking was incorporated into the corporate strategy for the future direction of the business.

Improving cash flow

IT contracting is a complex activity for CSC, given the scale, scope and duration of many of its key client accounts. There are many complicated variables involved in delivering on projects and programmes that are based on deploying people and contractors on a long-term basis. Cash flow was not always as CSC wanted it to be, particularly in the Federal side of the US business. Traditionally accountancy methods there meant that cash flow was measured as 'day sales outstanding': in other words, the number of person days CSC had paid for but which the client hadn't.

In a multi-billion dollar operation, cash-flow issues could have a significant impact on the profitability of some CSC programmes. The presidents of various business units had been trying to use business process re-engineering methods to help fix the issue, but with limited success and only small improvements achieved. The CFO decided to turn to ideation as the vehicle that could unlock some breakthroughs in a persistent problem.

At the outset, Howard spent around six weeks interviewing a wide range of people in the cash operations business. He used a problem definition questionnaire as the basis for these structured interviews. He then meshed the feedback together to enable the identification of the key questions that needed to be asked and how ideas generated by an ideation campaign could be subsequently evaluated. Finally the event could be planned to include:

- a launch date;
- the key 'challenge' questions;
- evaluation criteria in the form of a financial scorecard;
- 20 named review team members from the business unit's CFO office;
- a clearly understood review process.

The subsequent six-week event was launched, and around 3,000 people participated from across the multi-disciplinary business community.

Careful evaluation and speed were of the essence in the review process. Idea Central was structured so all ideas were reviewed by every review team member. A time horizon was established for all the ideas, some of which could be implemented straight away, while others would be deferred to a later date. Recommended ideas were pitched to the CFO, who selected those he considered to be most significant in making a difference to the cash-flow issue. The subsequent programme of ideas for implementation yielded a very significant $64 to $128 million of additional free cash flow, per year, on a continuous basis. While some of the ideas were, in actual fact, quite obvious, the ideation process galvanized consensus about specific ideas and consensus to act. A community of people most involved with programme delivery informed decisions, so there was momentum and ownership. This campaign was further evidence from CSC of the power of using ideation for addressing internal business issues.

*   *   *

Since the effort to organize such events is large, it should, in CSC's opinion, only be attempted for the most serious issues facing the company. A good test of whether ideation is appropriate is to ask whether the topic is clearly focused on one of the top five agenda items of the sponsoring business leader. Does this mean idea management is a niche business discipline? Howard Smith claims not. His view is that different organizations will adopt different styles of collaboration. There are no hard and fast rules as to how idea management solutions are deployed. A lot depends on what other technologies are deployed. If blogs, wikis and social networking are allowed to dominate, it may be hard to find a role for idea management in anything other than the larger 'one-off' efforts. By contrast, another corporate client of Imaginatik, operating in the life sciences sector, uses Idea Central at all times and instead of *ad hoc* collaboration, even for short-term projects involving just 20 to 50 participants. Smith also claims that using idea management has benefits when a company wishes to implement 'open innovation' with partners or clients. His view is that, without a 'process', open collaboration is very hard to manage, and that it can be dangerous without the controls that a clear workflow and role-based interface can provide.

Acknowledgement: Thanks to Alison Freer for the work on this case study and to CSC for allowing us to share it. It contributes to Ashurst et al. (2012).

SOCIAL(LY RESPONSIBLE) BUSINESS

A second perspective on social business is the socially responsible business. Major organizations are looking beyond existing customers and markets either with philanthropic goals or with the aim of creating different products, services and business models directly around a new value proposition. See the examples in Table 11.3.

Organizations are increasingly recognizing the value of social responsibility in terms of customer and employee engagement.

In our experience, the benefits-driven framework for projects and strategy set out in this book provides a clear focus on value for stakeholders and fits directly with the challenges of social business and social responsibility.

Organization	Initiative
Intel	Trained more than 10 million teachers in the use of technology to improve educational outcomes, turning education into a profitable business for the company.
Mars	Catalysed a cross-sector coalition to transform farms and surrounding communities in Ivory Coast with the aim of avoiding looming cocoa shortages.
Novartis	Provided essential medicines and health services to 42 million people in 33,000 rural villages in India through a social business model that became profitable after 31 months.

Table 11.3 Socially responsible business in action
Source: Pfitzer et al. (2013).

DEVELOPING DIGITAL BUSINESS STRATEGY

Business leaders must engage in the development of a digital business strategy. It is too important to ignore, and it is clearly not a technology issue. The tools and principles in this book apply directly to the digital organization.

We will increasingly see islands of systems as different areas of the organization go to different suppliers and partners, taking advantage of the pay-as-you-go business models to make progress rapidly without the need for major investments. We need to retain an architectural perspective to avoid costs escalating and organizational agility being undermined by the fragmentation.

To gain competitive advantage in the digital business we need to encourage experimentation, avoid chaos and establish an overall digital business strategy. In our approaches to strategy we need to take time to explore possibilities and take creative approaches to allow us to envisage the future. Scenario planning may become important as we try and cope with uncertainty. We must not fall into the trap of focusing on the technology and not on the people; the falling costs of technology deployment will only encourage us to make that mistake.

TAKING IT FURTHER

FURTHER READING AND RESOURCES

This area is very fast-moving. Look at *McKinsey Quarterly*, *Harvard Business Review* and *MIT Sloan Management Review* for new developments.

TALKING POINTS

Use these questions to help reflect on this chapter and explore the challenges of putting the ideas into practice:

1. How 'digital' is your organization?
2. To what extent does work on strategy engage senior management in exploring digital options?
3. How effectively are social technologies being used?
4. What are the opportunities for open innovation?
5. How should our approach to strategy development and execution change to reflect the digital world?
6. How does our social use of technology (smartphones, tablets, apps, etc.) relate to and contribute to our use of IT in organizations?
7. What are the key features of the approaches to projects and strategy covered in this book that help build readiness for the digital world?

KEY DEBATES

A new normal?

One perspective is that 'everything has changed'. The extent and pace of innovation mean that the digital business is radically different from the past.

An alternative perspective is that we have seen much of this before in the various phases of IT evolution (time-sharing, the information centre, application service providers, etc.). While there has been a breakthrough in terms of reach, range and cost-effectiveness of the technology, many of the management issues are familiar.

Is one of these perspectives correct? What are the implications for benefits realization?

CASE STUDY 11.1

Digital businesses of any size can be global businesses. The case illustrates a range of strategic issues.

Journal of Information Technology Teaching Cases, Vol. 2 (2012): 107–109.

Healthware S.p.A. – from an underdeveloped region of Italy – can it be a global firm?

Erran Carmel and Giovanni Vaia

Healthware, a digital communication agency specializing in health-care, is based in Salerno, Italy. The firm has 72 employees in two countries as well as clients in 14 countries. The case illustrates the location trade-offs of operating – and growing – a global digital company far from the epicentre of Italian business. The theme is universal. Once the firm is far from a nation's epicentre, a dynamism may be absent, but the advantages are quite tangible: lower costs and employee stability. This teaching case is based on actual companies, people and events, although some details have been dramatized or disguised.

REFERENCES

Ashurst, C., Freer, A., Ekdahl, J. and Gibbons, C. (2012) Exploring IT-Enabled Innovation: A New Paradigm? *International Journal of Information Management*, Vol. 32 (4): 326–336.

Bharadwaj, A., El Sawy, O., Pavlou, P. and Venkatraman, N. (2013) Digital Business Strategy: Towards a Next Generation of Insights. *MIS Quarterly*, Vol. 37 (2): 471–482.

Birkinshaw, J. (2010) *Reinventing Management*, Chichester: John Wiley and Sons.

Bughin, J., Chui, M. and Manyika, J. (2013) Ten IT-Enabled Business Trends for the Decade Ahead. *McKinsey Quarterly*. May.

Burgin, J., Chui, M. and Manyika, J. (2013) Ten IT-Enabled Business Trends for the Decade Ahead. *McKinsey Quarterly*, May.

Checkland, P. and Holwell, S. (1999) *Information, Systems, and Information Systems: Making Sense of the Field*, John Wiley and Sons.

Earl, M. (1989) *Management Strategies for Information Technology*, Prentice Hall.

IBM (2011) *The Social Business: Advent of a New Age*.

McAfee, A. (2006) Enterprise 2.0: The Dawn of Emergent Collaboration. *MIT Sloan Management Review*, Vol. 47 (3): 21–28.

Mintzberg, H. (2009) *Rebuilding Companies as Communities*, Harvard Business Review, Vol. 87 (7/8): 140–143.

Pfitzer, M. Bocksette, V. and Stamp, M. (2013) Innovating for Shared Value. *Harvard Business Review*, September, Vol. 91 (9): 100–107.

Sambamurthy, V. and Bharadwaj, A. (2003) Shaping Agility through Digital Options: Reconceptualizing the Role of Information Technology in Contemporary Firms. *MIS Quarterly*, Vol. 27 (2): 237–263.

Weill, P. and Woerner, S.L. (2013) The Future of the CIO in a Digital Economy. *MIS Quarterly Executive*, Vol. 12 (2): 65–75.

Willcocks, L., Venters, W. and Whitley, A. (2014) *Moving to the Cloud Corporation*, Basingstoke: Palgrave Macmillan.

CHAPTER 12
IMPLICATIONS FOR THE CIO AND IT FUNCTION

IN THIS CHAPTER WE STUDY:

- the role of the chief information officer (CIO) and IT function;
- managing IT across the organization;
- funding IT;
- managing talent for IT;
- the business leader's role in making the most of IT.

CHALLENGING TIMES FOR IT LEADERS

The role of IT has evolved rapidly over the last 30 years. Even in the last five years the impact of the Internet and mobile devices has been huge. The implications for the IT Manager, IT Director or CIO or whatever the role is called have been significant.

In some organizations an IT Manager still reports to the finance director, as was common in the past, and plays a broadly technical and operational role. In other organizations, still surprisingly few, a CIO is a full member of the top management team.

In some organizations, after a period of relative stability and centralization of the management of IT, new roles and initiatives are springing up outside the IT function, perhaps a Director of Innovation, or a Director of Digital Business.

While our primary focus is on the organization-wide impact of IT, we can't neglect the IT function and roles/structures for the management of IT within an organization.

WHAT IS THE ROLE OF THE IT FUNCTION?

The challenge of benefits realization from IT is a 'value trap' that sucks in top management in many organizations to respond to the perceived problems with changes to the IT function – only. Change the CIO, cut the IT budget, outsource. It is almost certain that these are only tackling a part of the problem.

This chapter focuses specifically on the management of the IT function, but it is vital to retain awareness of the much bigger picture.

What is the role of the IT function? The answer will vary between organizations and over time. There is a clear maturity or development model as organizations develop and as the role of IT evolves. In essence, the evolution goes from a focus on delivering a secure, reliable, cost-effective IT service, to a focus on realizing benefits from investments in IT (typically these made by the IT function), then to a focus on working with the management and wider organization to realize the strategic potential of IT and compete with IT. Substantial mindset shifts are required in moving from stage to stage, and as a result it is not a smooth or easy progression.

It is important to judge the current situation and respond accordingly. There is little point trying to engage senior colleagues in discussions of competitive advantage if their perception is of poor value for money and unreliable systems.

In the 'new world' environment of pervasive IT, with powerful mobile devices and enterprise services available from cloud platforms over the Internet, there are particular challenges for the IT function. In many respects it is similar to the early years of the PC era, when PCs and new PC-based applications sprang up outside the IT function, and the use of IT expanded rapidly beyond existing mainframe and mini-computer applications. Now the opportunities are even greater, and they affect staff, customers and partners in the value chain. The opportunities for new IT-based services and solutions are huge, and in many cases this is happening outside the IT function (Ashurst et al., 2012).

Our focus is on competitive advantage from IT, and this is a challenge for the organization as a whole. What role do the IT function and the CIO have?

WHAT IS THE ROLE OF THE CIO?

The role of the CIO varies from organization to organization. Weill and Woerner (2013) identified four different aspects of the role (Box 12.1).

Box 12.1   The role of the CIO

IT services activities: managing the IT organization and its people and external partners to ensure delivery of IT infrastructure, applications, projects and related services across the enterprise.

Embedded activities: working with non-IT colleagues, both enterprise-wide and within business units, addressing issues such as business strategy, business process optimization, new product or service development, regulatory compliance and risk, and IT investment prioritization.

External customer activities: meeting with the company's external customers, partners and colleagues as part of the sales or service delivery process, including electronic linkages with customers.

Enterprise process activities: managing enterprise processes and the associated digital platform, including shared services, product development, operations, corporate responsibility, green issues and a range of special projects.

One starting-point is to distinguish the CIO, who should be part of the overall business leadership team and play a strategic role in enabling competitive advantage from IT, from the IT Director, where the focus is much more about 'keeping the lights on'.

Peppard (2010) suggests there has been too much emphasis on the CIO as an individual, when value realization and competitive advantage depend on a broad range of factors. These include: the capability of the IT leadership team and the IT-savviness of the CEO and CxOs, and the IT value realization process.

The CIO has a wide range of responsibilities. From a benefits perspective it is vital to be closely involved in strategic thinking across an organization. Often IT is brought into discussions far too late, and solutions and plans are already well defined. At this stage input from IT will tend to be perceived as obstructive and to reinforce a perception of IT being a barrier. The CIO needs to lead the engagement of the IT function from the beginning of work on a major challenge or opportunity to help explore the issues and provide insights into what's possible. Alongside this contribution to strategic thinking, the CIO has to work with colleagues to lead transformational change and the management of the wider IT investment portfolio. The third broad area of responsibility is the management of the IT infrastructure and day-to-day operation and continuous improvement of IT systems and services.

It is asking a lot of one individual to span these three areas and the different competences and management styles involved. The team around the CIO is clearly vital.

Weill and Woerner (2013) suggest that successful CIOs free up their time by establishing effective governance mechanisms and mentoring colleagues in order to allow others to manage IT services so they can spend time with business colleagues and/or customers to create business value.

As noted above, there is a natural evolution of the role of IT relating to the maturity of the organization and also to changes in technology. Alongside this there is an evolution in the role of the CIO and IT function. Key considerations include:

The extent of outsourcing. Traditionally this has included formal contracts with major service providers to run all or parts of the IT infrastructure and application services. More recently, with business process outsourcing, this has been extended to taking on responsibility for running business services as well as the underlying IT solutions.

Less often called outsourcing, the decisions on whether to buy or build applications are important in defining the role of the IT function. In the early days of corporate IT firms might build their own PCs and develop their own word processors. As the market has evolved, ERP and wider categories of enterprise systems also became systems to buy (or rent) rather than build. The trend continues. Key decisions are how to work with suppliers, and what is the role of in-house development and system integration skills.

With cloud-based services outsourcing can happen more easily technically, and also take place 'under the radar', with much less central visibility and control. What are the governance arrangements required to achieve security, privacy, data and systems integration, value for money and to enable flexibility?

Transformation and change. As benefits come from business change, effective leadership of broad change programmes will be key to success, rather than the implementation of IT solutions. What is the role of the IT function? Does it provide project, programme and change management capabilities? Or do these sit within a separate central function or in business units? Do the IT function and CIO act as champion and centre of expertise for the development of these capabilities? If not, who does? Is there a distinction between major, transformational change programmes and the ongoing change at a local level in response to legislation, cost pressures and the drive to improve services? What investment is there in the capabilities for building these capabilities for local change and for effective participation in centrally owned and transformational programmes?

Use of information. How is the organization handling the provision of information and the tools to access, explore, analyse and present it? The expertise required can be significant.

Does the role of the IT function go beyond providing some form of data warehouse along with Excel and other analysis and visualization tools? Where is the expertise to provide reports and analysis, to make use of powerful 'end-user' tools and also to share learning and resources across the organization, avoiding armies of people reinventing the wheel and perhaps providing inaccurate information very inefficiently?

Building organization-wide capability. In many areas, specifically related to the use of information and benefits-driven change, there is a need for broad competences across the organization. Development of these competences might involve provision of formal education/training, but goes far beyond that. What role does IT have, working with others (e.g., a strategically oriented HR and organizational development function or corporate university) to build these capabilities? Does the role of 'experts' include helping others develop in their area of expertise as part of a learning community? Are specialists recruited and developed to have these abilities?

There may be a mismatch between the needs of the organization and the ability of the IT function to take on the required roles: for example, the credibility of the IT function because of past poor performance may mean that getting into a position where the focus can be on benefits driven change can be hard. There can be a perception that 'the CIO is telling me how to run my business (unit) when he should be focused on sorting out the mess in IT'. This, of course, requires very effective communication and relationship-building. The benefits approach set out earlier provides principle and practices, forming a shared language that can help as part of relationship, credibility and capability-building efforts. The need for strategic leadership from the CIO is arguably greater than ever before, given the opportunities for exploiting the cloud to become a digital business (see Willcocks et al., 2014).

MANAGING IT ACROSS THE ORGANIZATION

Given that the goal is to realize benefits from IT across the organization, and not simply manage the IT function, it is important to consider broader issues than the role of the CIO and IT function.

TOP MANAGEMENT ENGAGEMENT

The 'IT attention deficit' is one manifestation of the issues (see Box 12.2). Often the CIO is not fully engaged as part of the top management team, and IT issues are not considered at the right time. As a result, decisions are made and presented to the CIO as requests to implement an agreed solution, when earlier involvement would have allowed different and better approaches. The CIO of an organization commented, having received a business case from the operations department of a transport organization seeking to implement new ticketing systems: 'they were effectively saying we'll implement the ATMs, you provide the rest of the bank. There was no consultation and it was signed off.'

Box 12.2 Information technology and the board of directors: Is there an IT attention deficit?

IT attention deficit

Given the ever-increasing importance of information technology (IT) to corporate success, board scrutiny of IT activities is a critical issue. This study conducted interviews with board chairs and board members of 17 medium to large corporations, most with global operations. Our question to them: 'How much attention does your board give to a range of IT-related issues, specifically, the CIO's IT vision for the company, the IT strategic plan, major IT application decisions, IT leadership, IT functional structure, IT function effectiveness, IT risk and exposure, and whether or not IT applications provide competitive advantage?' We also interviewed the CIOs at these 17 firms about their view of what their boards ought to be considering.

We found an **'IT attention deficit'** in these boards. The CIOs were nearly unanimous that boards should pay attention to: the IT vision, the IT strategic plan, IT competitive advantage, IT effectiveness, IT risk, and very large application development decisions and projects. All 17 boards were unanimous only on paying attention to IT risk. Only one-half the boards of the financial services firms had discussed the other topics. But none of the boards of the primary resource firms (energy, mining, forestry, agricultural products, and oil exploration and extraction) had discussed the other topics.

After recounting the specifics of this research, we suggest six ways boards can reduce their IT attention deficit: (1) include IT on the board agenda, (2) invite the CIO to board meetings, (3) elicit brief CIO presentations, (4) recruit IT experience onto the board, (5) get the board talking about IT, and (6) realize that boards now operate in an IT era.

Sid Huff and Michael Maher, *MIS Quarterly Executive*, Vol. 5. No. 2, June 2006.

A clear sign of a good relationship between the CIO and the rest of the senior management team is being involved from the very beginning in discussions of possibilities and initiatives. This is 'having a seat at the table', overcoming the 'IT attention deficit' (Huff et al., 2006), and is a vital enabler of a co-evolutionary approach to strategy moving from separate IS and business strategies to a digital business strategy.

BUILDING RELATIONSHIPS BETWEEN IT AND OTHER BUSINESS UNITS

The factors involved in building relationships between IT and other business units are complex. Issues of language, management style and trust are particularly important. The CIO/IT management can be perceived as being from a different world because of differences in language from their colleagues. Every discipline has its own jargon and abbreviations; it is helpful if business-facing IT managers can become bilingual, dropping much of the IT-speak and blending in with their business colleagues. The IT language can then be used when talking with IT colleagues. Benefits and agile approaches can be used very successfully to enable engagement at the right level and in business language. It is just important to avoid turning them into another formal method driven by IT and building a new barrier.

In terms of management style, there is a considerable risk that adherence to policy and process – for example, for project management and software delivery – will make the IT function seem slow and bureaucratic in relation to more commercially oriented business areas, who from an IT perspective may not have significant expertise in leading major programmes and change initiatives. Ideally, there is an opportunity to meet in the middle, with IT adopting a commercial approach and business areas building expertise and engaging in effective project and service management.

Trust is almost certainly the most important factor. Does the relationship between business and IT colleagues, and also within and across other groups of stakeholders involved in projects, programmes and the management of IT, allow effective working? Trust in this context will draw on many things, including inter-personal relationships, but it is also about providing an effective service and delivering results. This goes beyond individual relationships to the ability of the department as a whole to deliver against service promises.

BUILDING BENEFITS REALIZATION CAPABILITIES ACROSS THE ORGANIZATION

Value from IT depends on a complex mix of competences: information management, transformational change and business process management are just examples. The existence or otherwise of these competences within an organization will be major enablers or blockers of value realization.

Very often this will be an issue, and at best these competences will exist in pockets across an organization. Similarly in many organizations programme and project management competence is scarce, or at least not available to contribute to investments in IT. As a result, building the ability of the organization to realize value from IT is underpinned by the ability to build this complex of management competences across the organization (see the discussion in Chapter 6). The growth of competences can happen at different speeds in different places, just as ice crystals might form at different speeds as frost takes hold on a window.

The different benefits tools can be used locally by very small teams and departments (for example, the portfolio, stakeholder mapping or the benefits realization plan), or they can be used for major organization-wide projects and the overall portfolio of investments in IT and change. The organization-wide capability comes to life through these pockets of expertise, which grow and join up so they are embedded through the organization.

MANAGING IT RELATIONSHIPS ACROSS THE VALUE CHAIN

No organization is an island. Competing with IT is enabled by effective management of IT across the value chain. There are a number of perspectives to consider.

WORKING WITH SUPPLIERS AND PARTNERS

IT integration with suppliers has been a focus of activity over many years, with retail and automotive industries being major examples. Beyond links with existing suppliers, IT has reshaped organizations and supply chains. IT and business process outsourcing provide a basic example where one organization draws on core competences to operate processes on behalf of another.

Though not typically called outsourcing, the preference to buy rather than build many aspects of IT capabilities brings interdependencies with many organizations. They are not suppliers in a traditional sense, as in many cases they have deep expertise in how their products can be used (think about SAP, for example, or other enterprise software suppliers). There is an opportunity to work with at least some of these organizations as partners and to work with their other customers to influence future product developments and to share how to make the most of product capabilities.

In some cases developments happen on an even larger scale. Apple (and others) have created new industries, around iTunes and the App Store. Essentially a new ecosystem evolves, in this case with a major player at the centre as standard-setter and gatekeeper. In other cases there may be a looser grouping around common, open standards. This is more like the way Google has used Android.

FOCUSING ON VALUE FOR THE CUSTOMER'S CUSTOMER

For many organizations it is valuable to go beyond a focus on the customer to thinking about innovation and value creation for the customer's customer. This can open up new insights into the real drivers for products and services and new opportunities for working with the initial customer in different ways to create value. For example, Microsoft might work with Barclays to create a new banking 'app'.

SOURCING

I remember visiting one large organization as a very junior member of the audit team and learning that they made their own PCs. Apparently they thought they had very specific requirements. It was over 30 years ago. I'd be quite surprised to find that today. Why not produce your own electricity as well, if you want to control all aspects of production?

Clearly, at some level, all organizations outsource aspects of their IT. You would not write your own versions of Word, PowerPoint, etc., or your own web browser, and most organizations do not develop their own enterprise systems (Salesforce, Sage, Dynamix, SAP).

Where do you draw the line? What are the factors that contribute to the decision?

There have been many examples of major outsourcing deals that have failed dramatically. Some have related to virtually the whole IT function and others to major development projects. Often a major driver of these deals is a perspective of IT as a problem by top business management and a total lack of recognition that the real issue is business value from IT, which is an organizational issue not an IT function issue. They didn't understand the problem and applied an inappropriate solution. A classic case of the IT attention deficit. Much has been learned about outsourcing, and it can make a very valuable contribution to the IT capability of an organization (see Willcocks et al., 2006).

Accepting (a) that outsourcing of the realization of business value from IT is completely impossible, (b) that outsourcing the total IT function is also likely to be a major mistake, and at the very least you must retain strategy, architecture, and supplier management expertise, and (c) that some level of 'outsourcing' is inevitable in terms of relying on software and hardware suppliers as well as making buy vs. build decisions for new systems, what are the issues for your organization? Where can outsourcing add value? Have you got the internal capabilities you need to manage the outsourcing successfully (Cullen et al., 2014)?

Ross and Beath (2006) identify three broad models for outsourcing and link them to different stages of architecture maturity:

Transaction exchange: targets quality and cost per transaction, providing access to world-class processes and economies of scale.

Co-sourcing alliance: targets project success and provides access to project management and specialist expertise on demand.

Strategic partnership: targets bottom-line impact and provides broad management and specialized service capabilities.

Supply chain is just one area where the focus is business capabilities, not IT system outsourcing. Lacity and Willcocks (2013) indicate that, while the driver is often saving money, success is more likely if the focus is on innovation. Cullen et al. (2014) suggest that outsourcing is a strategic decision for the business and should be on the CEO agenda.

Two matrices can be used to help take outsourcing decisions (Figures 12.1 and 12.2). The first stage, as in Figure 12.1, is to assess the business activity being considered for outsourcing. Does the activity contribute to competitive positioning, and how critical is it to current business operations?

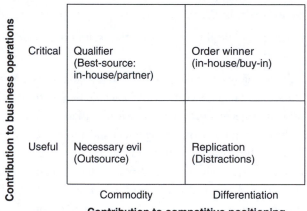

Figure 12.1 Sourcing decisions by business contribution
Source: Cullen et al., 2014.

The second stage, using Figure 12.2, is to consider the cost and capability of in-house and market options. This provides a sound decision-making framework, but these are not easy decisions to make, with competitive positioning changing over time and the in-house vs. market comparison complex.

Expertise is required in many areas to succeed with outsourcing. Procurement and supplier management is a key area. Given that major suppliers

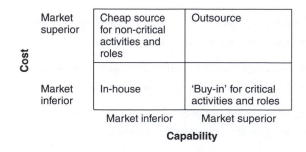

Figure 12.2 Sourcing decision matrix – by market comparison
Source: Cullen et al., 2014.

have extensive and specialist expertise – for example, in writing legal contracts – how are you going to ensure your contract is at a fair price and on reasonable terms? Pricing is not transparent, and major suppliers are liable to charge very different prices to different customers for hardware, software and services.

Legal and regulatory expertise is also vital. What are the privacy issues related to using a cloud provider? How does the Data Protection Act really apply? When are the directors personally liable? What about the business process outsource provider having access to all your customer information?

Perhaps even more important is the ability to build and manage strategic relationships and partnerships. This can be hard in the public sector, where procurement rules seem to drive open tendering for everything, or risky, long-term outsourcing deals. Savvy IT managers will work closely with a number of strategic partners, taking advantage of their deep expertise.

Cullen et al. (2014) build on earlier work by Feeny and Willcocks (1998a, 1998b) to establish a framework of the IT competences required by an organization. There is a strong emphasis on working with suppliers/vendors and the capability for outsourcing with capabilities for informed buying, contract facilitation, vendor development and contract monitoring (Figure 12.3). These capabilities relate to the original decision-making, the contract negotiation and managing the contract/relationship over its lifetime.

The explosion of cloud capabilities and services brings new opportunities and challenges (Willcocks et al., 2014). From a sourcing perspective, the

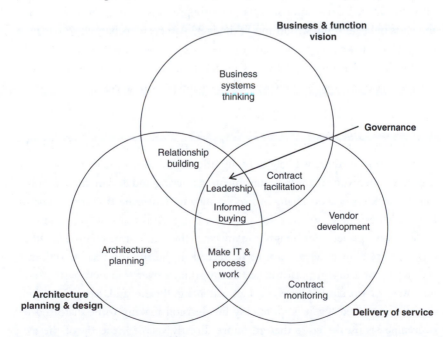

Figure 12.3 IT capabilities framework

pay-as-you-go business models and ease of set-up provides exciting opportunities for speed and experimentation, but it also means that strategic decision-making and IT infrastructure can become fragmented. There will be challenges for the CEO and CIO in terms of the management model they want to apply (Birkinshaw, 2010). The shift in the role of the CIO and IT function is potentially significant.

FUNDING IT

The funding of IT is another area where there are many different approaches. In earlier discussions of investment appraisal and governance we have explored the criteria and responsibilities for decision-making, particularly in relation to approval and funding of specific investments. There are wider questions on where the money comes from. Does the IT function own the budget, and is there effective business input into decision-making on major expenditure? Are budgets allocated to business units for expenditure on IT projects? Are business units free to use external suppliers and bypass the IT function? If so, what are the implications for the coherence of the IT architecture and IT operational costs?

OPERATIONAL COSTS

How to handle IT operational costs similarly presents a range of options. Are the costs held centrally within the IT budget? Are costs recharged to business units? If so, on what basis (as many of the costs will be shared and not directly attributable)? Whatever approach is taken, what are the incentives to reduce costs and also to invest to improve resilience and performance?

END-USER COSTS

End-user costs are a major element of both project and operational costs. In terms of projects, there is likely to be significant end-user time throughout the lifecycle from involvement in requirements-gathering and design, through testing, to work on process change to receiving and delivering training. Some of these costs can be captured – for example, the payroll costs of someone seconded onto a project – although it many cases this will not be recorded. Other elements are almost certain not to be recorded: the time to receive training, the impact of a dip in performance during the cutover to a new system and new ways of working. These costs are often significant, and, as they are not directly accounted for, it is quite easy for decision-making to be distorted by overemphasis on the costs that are more directly visible – the tip of the iceberg. For example, savings made on the project budget reducing the effort to ensure the user interface is intuitive and that there are very effective online help and training resources could result in significantly increased training costs and slower ramp-up to full effectiveness on the system. The total impact would be very negative, but the project budget would not reflect this.

IMPACT ON BENEFITS REALIZATION

From the perspective of a specific business unit it is simply important to be aware of the funding arrangements in place and their implications for accountability and decision-making. At more senior levels in the organization there may be more degrees of freedom to influence these funding arrangements.

In terms of value from IT, a key issue is to build the perception and understanding of value for money. A key starting-point is to establish a set of metrics, a scorecard to help understand the performance of the IT function and drive improvement in key areas. Inevitably the scorecard will evolve as the IT capability develops, moving from an initial focus on cost to a greater emphasis on value realization (Figure 10.2). There is a clear risk that the emphasis gets stuck on cost control and reduction, reducing opportunities for longer-term value creation and competitive advantage (Table 12.1).

The understanding that value realization from IT is an issue for the organization as a whole means that metrics and scorecards at a business unit level

Category	Example metrics
Cost controls	IT cost performance – hardware, software, outsourcing, networks
Operational excellence	Critical outages Average resolution for service request
Financial controls	IT spend in relation to business metrics (turnover, people)
Human capital	Staff turnover Time to fill open positions
Customer satisfaction	User ratings of support experience and comments
Business impact and alignment	Percentage of staff working on new developments Percentage of staff by line of business
Application development	Progress vs. schedule and costs Benefits vs. top-level scorecard (growing revenue, cost reduction, etc.)
Capacity planning	Percentage utilization at peak load (web servers, network, storage)

Table 12.1 Example of metrics benefits scorecard (based on Hunter and Westerman, 2009)

should also reflect priorities for value realization. At least in part this should be reflected in wider targets for process and performance improvement where IT is making a contribution to wider change programmes.

A perennial question is 'how much should we invest in IT?', often thinking in terms of percentage of sales. It's an important question, given the significant sums spent on IT and one that is very difficult to answer.

Research by Weill and Brynjolfsson shows that there is no simple correlation between expenditure and value, and that really the key question is how effectively any funding is used. This is the primary focus of this book. It is possible to get some sense of performance by benchmarking, but this is most helpful in relation to costs, so, although useful, it has its dangers.

A management focus on IT costs and benchmarking can be a signal that there are wider issues: does expenditure on marketing, finance and other functions receive similar scrutiny?

MANAGING TALENT

Underpinning our efforts to realize value from IT is the recruitment and development of talent both within the IT function and across the wider organization.

Within any IT organization there are many disciplines, often with very different skills and working practices and with different qualifications and allegiance to different professions. A few examples include: IT network and infrastructure, software development, IT operations, help desk, usability and user experience, testing, project management, architecture. A key challenge for the CIO is creating an environment where the different disciplines can work together and with colleagues from across the organization, so that the 'whole is greater than the sum of the parts'.

This section provides a brief introduction to a major topic.

BALANCING AGILITY AND DISCIPLINE

A key assumption underpinning this book is that in many organizations a priority is to encourage and enable employees, and the role of managers as leaders is primarily to create an environment for individuals and teams to succeed. Goals should still be challenging, and there should be a strong determination to succeed and (self-)disciplined working. This is very different from the carrot and stick view and from the idea that you need top-down management control to get anything done.

Various writers have made the analogy of management with the improvisation of jazz. Skilled musicians are able to play together and to improvise around shared knowledge of chord sequences. The toolkit of practices shared across a multi-disciplinary team plays the role of the chord sequences, and context is provided by the shared mindset of the benefits-driven approach, of an agile, multi-disciplinary team.

In a sense the shared practices provide 'boundary objects' (Carlile, 2002) between the different disciplines, allowing them to work together effectively but allowing them space for their own specialist practices within their individual domains.

The use of practices (tools) provides a basis for continuous improvement as the use of practices evolves and new practices are introduced. It also enables new members of the team to get engaged quickly: for example, by focusing their learning on an initial set of practices, and then by contributing practices from their own experience.

CREATING FLEXIBLE CAREER PATHS FOR IT PROFESSIONALS

The early stages of an IT career are often in a specific technical discipline, such as infrastructure, software development or project management. At more senior levels there is often a need for a broader role and a shift from a technical focus to managing people and relationships. The transition can be difficult to make. Differences in management culture between IT can business areas can also be a source of problems.

A specific challenge for many IT functions is to provide a technical career path to retain senior technicians in technical roles rather than limiting progression to those who move into more general management roles.

DEVELOPING LEADERS OF BENEFITS REALIZATION ACROSS THE ORGANIZATION

A direct implication of the perspective that value from IT is delivered through competences across the organization is that leaders across an organization need a range of skills related to leading benefit-led change. These need to be developed through education and experience as part of overall initiatives for talent management and leadership development.

Similarly, as noted in Chapter 6, there should be a broad emphasis on digital literacy and enabling staff to develop their ability continually to take advantage of a broad range of IT systems and services to work effectively and improve efficiency and effectiveness.

THE CHANGING ROLE OF THE IT FUNCTION

DRIVERS FOR CHANGE

Rapid innovation in technology has had a dramatic impact on our customers and other stakeholders and on the society in which they live. Our employees, as part of society and as customers of many organizations, have also been affected by these changes. The organization itself is also seeing major changes in the sourcing and operation of IT systems. All these factors have major implications for the CIO and the IT function.

Rapid innovation has enabled a large percentage of the population in many parts of the world to have access to the Internet from phones, tablets, laptops and PCs. Staff and customers are increasingly 'digital natives' who have grown up using PC and mobile technologies. They have high expectations of ease of use, availability and connectivity, with new 'apps' available within a few seconds and often for free.

There are also new expectations of participation, from the self-service provided by Amazon and others to the ability to contribute – for example, through Twitter, Facebook or blogs or YouTube – and to self-published books, again perhaps through Amazon.

There may be a major disconnect between their use of technology in their day-to-day lives and the use of IT in the workplace. Many systems remain complex and hard to use, with interfaces that don't adapt well to different devices.

There are tensions between the expectation of 'bringing your own device' to access work systems and the challenge of maintaining a work–life balance and finding space to switch off from email and the (perceived?) expectation to be available 24 hours a day and seven days a week.

Within the organization, 'enterprise' applications and services are now available over the Internet. Services in the cloud have rapidly come of age. There is a huge range, from an application like Dropbox allowing files to be shared across devices, through a virtual drive, to sophisticated customer relationship management and other enterprise systems such as Salesforce.com. Some can be accessed by individuals at zero cost, and others can simply be adopted on a pay-per-user per-month basis. The ease of adoption, apparent low cost and flexibility make these options very attractive; new systems could be operational while a slot is being put in the diary for a meeting to discuss changes to internal systems with the IT function.

These trends of ease of use, rapid innovation and broad availability at any time and from any device are well established. As a result, there are many implications for the IT function.

IMPLICATIONS FOR THE CIO AND IT FUNCTION

The implications for the CIO and IT function are significant. At one extreme the outlook in the short to medium term is for Internet-based developments related to social media, 'apps' and cloud-based systems happening outside the IT function, either in a new innovation group or just within a range of organizational units. In this case the IT function will be left maintaining a set of 'legacy systems' and potentially carrying the can for anything that goes wrong, but not being seen as a player in the new, exciting and strategic developments.

In a slightly less extreme version of the future there are still major implications. In an extension of a long-established trend the IT function becomes a broker – providing insight into new possibilities and building relationships with suppliers and partners. There is a major shift away from actually developing software and delivering services.

The changes in IT can be compared to the evolution of the library – where the librarian is no longer just providing access to books but also offering the skills to help people search for and access information. Similarly the IT function is no longer providing all the systems; they are offering their skills, including vendor management and systems integration, to help users find, and deploy cost-effectively, systems that will add value.

Many practical steps are possible: for example, in a large organization IT could work with vendors and internal early adopters to run a 'showcase' of new opportunities and work hard to communicate innovations by end-users widely across the organization.

A major discussion relates to the need for structural change. It is possible that we now need two IT functions – essentially the existing function with the focus on exploiting existing systems and technology, and a new function where the aim is to explore and bring innovation to the organization and to be part of innovative new projects and ventures seeking to develop the organization for the future (Cash et al., 2008). The split into two functions allows very different cultures and processes to be established and for staff to be recruited with relevant skills and attitudes, rather than expecting one department to meet two very different needs, each requiring different skills and management styles.

The changes in technology and the wider environment require a new mix of skills and a different relationship between IT and the wider organization. Some individuals and teams will struggle to adapt.

We think it will be desirable for the CIO and IT function to retain a strategic role as champions of benefits realization from IT and to provide leadership for development of competences across the organization. Recent experience, however, suggests that in many organizations the CIO is playing only a marginal role in a range of developments.

IMPLICATIONS FOR THE ORGANIZATION

For the organization, the pace and scale of change bring both risks and opportunities. Many CIOs and IT functions will be hoping that, when end-user groups find out the hard way that running IT systems isn't as easy as they think, it doesn't bring the entire organization crashing down. There are certainly security and privacy issues to be addressed. There is also a major risk of fragmentation of systems and information. As when the PC came in and key information was often processed and stored on individual PCs (with limited security or back-up), now crucial information and processes are supported by external systems, and, even if they are reliable and secure, there is certainly a risk and cost of fragmentation.

It will be important to revisit governance arrangements to reflect the new opportunities available to end-user groups and the ability to bring in new systems on a pay-per-user per-month basis outside existing capital expenditure and project controls.

There are also important implications for skills within end-user areas. Are there skills for system selection, design, implementation, vendor management, training, process design and change: in other words, all the practices that contribute to an agile, benefits-driven approach to change?

From the perspective of the IT function there may be an opportunity for a shift from 'doing' to supporting and enabling others to do: for example, to work within an end-user team or to advise an end-user project manager. This will be challenging.

From the perspective of the organization, structures and roles are secondary: benefits realization is the key driver. New technologies are increasingly enabling rapid and low-cost delivery of new solutions, and the organization needs to build its capability for innovation to explore and realize value from the many possibilities.

IMPLICATIONS FOR THE COMPETENCES REQUIRED

New skills are required within the IT function and across the organization. These include the practices of agile, benefits-driven projects.

In Chapter 14 we explore further how to develop the IT/benefits realization capability of the organization.

MAKING THE MOST OF YOUR IT AND IT FUNCTION

Gaining competitive advantage from IT is very clearly the responsibility of the CEO and the management team as a whole, not just the IT function. The focus should be on action taken across the organization to realize value from IT and not just on better management of the IT function. For non-IT managers the question should be: how can I provide leadership in realizing value for IT and make the most of the information, systems and services provided by the IT function?

Becoming 'IT Savvy' is a good starting-point (Weill and Ross, 2009). The aim is to understand the issues of managing IT for business value rather than developing expertise in the technology itself. One element of this would be ensuring that business leaders have knowledge and expertise in benefits-driven change. This can only come from a mixture of relevant education and, more importantly, from experience.

In addition, it is vital to develop digital literacy across all employees. This needs to go beyond the social and personal use of smartphones of the digital natives to skilled use of information and systems to work effectively and to innovate in how work gets done at a local level. Within each department and team there are opportunities to develop expert or power users across a range of systems who can become local experts and advisers in how to make the most of key systems that are critical to getting the job done.

For leaders in the modern, digital business there is no escaping responsibility for exploiting IT to run and develop the business and to work effectively with the IT function to make it possible.

TAKING IT FURTHER

FURTHER READING AND RESOURCES

Austin, Robert D., Nolan, Richard and O'Donnell, Shannon (2009) *The Adventures of an IT Leader*, Boston: Harvard Business Press.

TALKING POINTS

Use these questions to help reflect on this chapter and explore the challenges of putting the ideas into practice:

1. Is a senior manager brought in from outside the IT function likely to succeed? What would be the challenges and opportunities?

2. Is it time to accept that IT is a commodity and that cost and efficiency should be the key drivers for management? If so, who provides leadership for innovation and benefits realization?

3. Does your organization have or need a CIO with a strategic leadership role?

4. How do you balance specialist and generalist career paths (development opportunities, reward, performance criteria)?

5. How do you make your organization attractive to technical and specialist employees?

6. What management competences do you need to make the most of IT in your business unit?

7. What steps could you take to work more effectively with your IT function?

8. How are the new technology developments (cloud, mobile, etc.) affecting the role of IT?

KEY DEBATE

Is there a strategic role for the CIO and IT function?

There are multiple perspectives on the strategic role of the CIO and IT function. Consider just a few options:

- IT is a commodity. The role is not strategic.

- IT is strategic, but the role of the IT function is operational – developing and running systems. Business leaders are taking on the strategic leadership of IT.

- IT is strategic, but strategic leadership will not come from the IT function. A new innovation or digital business director and team will lead on the strategic direction and opportunities.

Is there a right answer? What is the way forward for your organization? What are the risks and opportunities? How do you balance the theory with what works in practice?

CASE STUDY 12.1

The exploration of the evolution of IT governance provides an opportunity to reflect on the role of the CIO and IT function.

Journal of Information Technology Teaching Cases, Vol. 3 (2013): 88–95.

Reshaping the IT governance in Octo Telematics to gain IT–business alignment

Giovanni Vaia and Erran Carmel

The case shows how a technology services company shaped and reshaped – and reshaped again – its IT governance structure to integrate the IT function better with business clients. The company is a large Italian telematics provider – Octo Telematics – which is specialized in the provision of telematic services and systems for the insurance and automotive markets. During the period described in this case, the company was growing and globalizing rapidly. The desired alignment between IT and the business units is needed to promote behaviours consistent with the organization's mission and strategy. As Octo experimented with new processes, committees and reorganizations, the company 'travelled' through several governance archetypes.

REFERENCES

Ashurst, C., Freer, A., Ekdahl, J. and Gibbons, C. (2012) Exploring IT-Enabled Innovation: A New Paradigm? *International Journal of Information Management*, Vol. 32 (4): 326–336.

Birkinshaw, J. (2010) *Reinventing Management*, San Francisco, CA: Jossey-Bass.

Carlile, P. (2002) A Pragmatic View of Knowledge and Boundaries: Boundary Objects in New Product Development. *Organization Science*, Vol. 13 (4) July: 442–455.

Cash Jr., J.I., Earl, M.J. and Morison, R. (2008) Teaming Up to Crack Innovation and Enterprise Integration. *Harvard Business Review*, Vol. 86 (11): 90–100.

Cullen, S., Lacity, M. and Willcocks, L. (2014) *Outsourcing: All You Need to Know*, Marston Gate: White Plume Publishing.

Feeny, D. and Willcocks, L. (1998a) Re-Designing the IS Function around Core Capabilities. *Long Range Planning*, Vol. 31 (3): 354–367.

Feeny, D. and Willcocks, L. (1998b) Core Capabilities for Exploiting Information Technology. *Sloan Management Review*, Spring, Vol. 39 (3): 9–21.

Huff, S., Maher, M. and Munro, M. (2006) Information Technology and the Board of Directors: Is There an IT Attention Deficit? *MIS Quarterly Executive*, Vol. 5 (1): 55–68.

Hunter, R. and Westerman, G. (2009) *The Real Business of IT*, Boston MA: Harvard Business Press.

Lacity, M. and Willcocks, L. (2013) Outsourcing Business Processes for Innovation. *MIT Sloan Management Review*, Spring, Vol. 54 (3): 63–69.

Peppard, J. (2010) Unlocking the Performance of the Chief Information Officer (CIO). *California Management Review*, Vol. 52 (4): 73–99.

Ross, J. and Beath, C. (2006) Sustainable IT Outsourcing: Let Enterprise Architecture Be Your Guide. *MIS Quarterly Executive*, Vol. 5 (4): 181–192.

Weill, P. and Ross, J. (2009) *IT Savvy*, Boston MA: Harvard Business Press.

Weill, P. and Woerner, S.L. (2013) The Future of the CIO in a Digital Economy. *MIS Quarterly Executive*, Vol. 12 (2): 65–75.

Willcocks, L., Feeny, D. and Olson, N. (2006) IT Outsourcing and Retained IS Capabilities: Challenges and Lessons. *European Management Journal*, February, Vol. 19 (6): 568–590.

Willcocks, L., Venters, W. and Whitley, A. (2014) *Moving to the Cloud Corporation*, Basingstoke: Palgrave Macmillan.

CHAPTER 13
ENABLING BUSINESS INNOVATION

PERSPECTIVES ON INNOVATION

SHIFTING THE FOCUS TO INNOVATION

As organizations build their capability to realize benefits from IT, it is natural to focus more on business innovation enabled by IT to contribute to strategic objectives and competitive advantage for the organization.

DRIVERS FOR INNOVATION

In 1986 Tushman and Nadler stressed that 'organizations can gain competitive advantage only by managing effectively for today while simultaneously creating innovation for tomorrow' and suggested that 'there is perhaps no more pressing managerial problem than the sustained management of innovation' (p. 74). Being more innovative is a key goal of many organizations. We feel it is right to make innovation a high priority, given the business environment and the ongoing rapid innovation in IT.

Brynjolfsson (2010) suggests that doubts about the value of IT and the contribution to business performance have been replaced with emerging evidence that leaders in the exploitation of IT are pulling ahead of their competitors:

> I really think that the way companies implement business processes, organizational change, and IT-driven innovation is what differentiates the leaders from the lagers. Rather than leveling the playing field, IT is actually leading to greater discrepancies. In most industries the top companies are pulling further away from the companies in the middle and the bottom of the competitive spectrum. (p. 55)

From this perspective IT-driven innovation is an element in a complex mix of capabilities contributing to competitive advantage.

There are many perspectives on innovation and many factors that contribute to it. Tushman and Nadler (1986) identify visionary leadership and also people, structures and values as important factors that affect whether an organization realizes benefits from innovation. Baldwin and von Hippel (2011) explore different approaches, from individual innovators to open collaborative innovation, and have identified the role of the customer as innovator (Thomke and von Hippel, 2002). Cash, Earl and Morison (2008) considered the implications of the need simultaneously to explore and exploit for the organization and management of IT.

It is useful to note that innovation does not necessarily require new technology: 'If all technological progress in the economy stopped today, would productivity growth grind to a halt? We don't think so. On the contrary, we believe that there are decades worth of potential innovations to be made in creatively combining (and making use of) inventions that we already have' (Brynjolfsson and Saunders, 2009, p. 95).

Our key assumptions are that the continuing innovation in IT is an important enabler of business innovation and transformation, and also that this IT innovation is not going to stop in the foreseeable future. Knowledgeable commentators, including Bill Gates, suggest that 'we ain't seen nothing yet' and the pace of innovation is likely to accelerate.

The challenge is to enable innovation to happen: to give it every possible encouragement, without creating unnecessary risks. Having established the foundations of a benefits-driven approach, a next step is to focus on projects and programmes of IT-enabled change to succeed with business innovation.

A key question is: what business opportunities do new and emerging technologies create? These might be new products and services, or significantly different ways of approaching existing activities. The focus remains on the business and benefits for stakeholders: this is not about technology for its own sake or technology research and development.

A key challenge for many CIOs and IT functions is how to become more effective at enabling business innovation and transformation. There is a risk that innovation happens outside the IT function, with a new Director of Innovation, and that IT are left with management of existing systems. For the organization as a whole this may be the right solution.

MANY DIMENSIONS OF INNOVATION

'Innovation is the specific tool of entrepreneurs, the means by which they exploit change as an opportunity for a different business or service' (Peter Drucker, 1985). This does not limit entrepreneurs to the small business: innovation comes from entrepreneurial behaviour in even the largest firms. Innovation does not require new technology, although it is often a factor.

Innovation strategies can be classified into the 'four Ps': product innovation, process innovation (changing the way products and services are created or delivered), position innovation (changing the context – for example, the market – in which products and services are introduced) and paradigm innovation (changing the underlying mental and business models which frame what an organization does) (Tidd et al., 2005 – see Figure 11.1). A second dimension is the degree of novelty involved. Is the innovation incremental, a change at the component level, doing something better? Or, on the other hand, is it a radical innovation, a change at the system level, doing something new (Box 13.1)?

LEADING INNOVATION

Innovation has a different role to play in each organization, depending on the strategic context and objectives. Birkinshaw and Goddard (2009) provide a way of putting innovation in context as part of the overall management framework of the organization.

Tushman and Nadler (1986) indicate the importance of a range of factors, including people, structures and values, in the management of innovation. The research considered how activities are organized and decisions taken as a way to explore aspects of the management framework. Birkinshaw (2010, p. 38) develops a management model, firstly exploring four dimensions of management (Figure 13.1) and then bringing this into an overall model which consider *ends* (objectives) and *means* (how the objectives are set and achieved) (Figure 13.2; see p. 174). A key message is that managers need to be thinking about and designing their management model, including enabling innovation. From

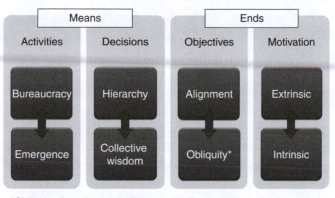

*Obliquity: focusing on indirect goals. For example, value to society rather than direct financial results.

Figure 13.1 Dimensions of management

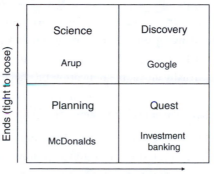

Figure 13.2 Four models of management

this perspective, management and the management model are themselves a potential source of competitive advantages (or disadvantage).

INTELLECTUAL TECHNOLOGIES: IMPLICATIONS FOR INNOVATION

A major factor to consider is that many IT innovations are not straightforward cases of 'adoption' of new technology. The new technology can be put to a very wide variety of uses within an organization, and benefits realization depends not just on the technology but also on complementary organizational resources and competences (Melville, et al., 2004). Lee (1999, p. 7) makes a similar point and suggests that 'Management Information Systems – MIS involves not just information technology but also its instantiation': 'There are rich organizational and political processes whereby a set of information technology is instantiated and there are also rich organizational and political processes pertaining to the continual managing, maintaining and changing of the information technology instantiation' (Lee, 1999, p. 7).

Lee (1999) also suggests 'MIS involves information technology as a form of intellectual technology'. Information technology is an intellectual technology rather than an industrial technology in that it has properties that are not fixed on implementation but which can be 'innovated endlessly, depending on its interaction with the intellect of the human beings who implement and use it' (Lee, 1999, p. 8). This can lead to an ongoing cycle of innovation and change as the technology extends the intellects of its users, leading to further innovation. This suggests a much more complex process than 'adoption' or diffusion of an innovation. Thomke and von Hippel (2002) make a related point in their proposal for the provision of 'toolkits' to enable customers to be a key part of innovation activity.

Taking the perspective of the knowledge worker is one example. In some sense Microsoft Word can be seen as a toolkit. It provides a set of functionality that users can adopt and adapt. If the user chooses to, they will be able to continue to discover features that help them work more effectively as their competence and confidence grows. There are group and social dimensions as well, as knowledge is shared around different parts of an organization. A similar process occurs with virtually any app, application or system; in some scenarios innovation is restricted to using the features of the software (however versatile it is), and in others there is feedback into new versions and releases.

Previous work on innovation provides important foundations for this research. The ideas of adoption or diffusion of innovations (Rogers, 2003), disruptive innovation (Christensen, 1997) and open vs. closed innovation (Chesbrough, 2003) are relevant.

TECHNOLOGY ADOPTION LIFECYCLE

A widely used framework when exploring innovation is the technology or product adoption lifecycle (Figure 13.3). The model helps us think about the gradual adoption of a technology (or product or idea) into a market-place (also referred to as diffusion of innovation (Rogers, 2003)).

In *Crossing the Chasm*, Geoffrey Moore (1998) explores the characteristics of the different sections of the market and how to accelerate adoption. It is interesting to reflect the comparatively long adoption cycles associated with many 'new' technologies. I first came across radio frequency ID tags (RFID) over 20 years ago, and they are still 'new' in many areas. Microsoft introduced tablet PCs in 2001, but mass-market appeal only came with Apple's iPad in 2010.

In many cases, innovators have opportunities to use exploratory projects to learn and build capabilities. A key decision is when to adopt early, taking into account that later adopters will still have to face some degree of learning curve to be able to exploit the opportunities.

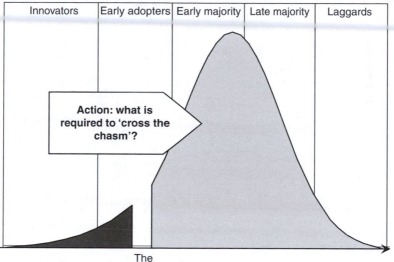

The challenge is to develop innovative uses of technology and to create the customer demand to cross the chasm

| Innovators | Early adopters | Early majority | Late majority | Laggards |

Action: what is required to 'cross the chasm'?

The chasm

Figure 13.3 The technology adoption lifecycle

DISRUPTIVE INNOVATION

A second perspective is 'disruptive innovation', where Clayton Christensen (www.claytonchristensen.com) is the primary author. Disruptive technologies change the basis of competition: the memory stick has made the diskette obsolete, for example. My current 16Gb memory stick is the equivalent of 16,000 diskettes, which, interestingly, are still available from our stationery cupboard. This disruption is also affecting whole industries, with the demise of Blockbuster video rentals and of the Kodak dominance of colour photography as two classic examples.

As Figure 13.4 indicates, in an established market the incumbent usually has the economies of scale to improve price performance more quickly than new entrants. The opportunity for new entrants is to disrupt the market by introducing a new technology or tackling the problem in a new way. Incumbents often react much more slowly and are left behind as the new technology improves and gains broad adoption. The challenge, of course, is to have the vision to see the threat or opportunity and then to react quickly enough and with enough resources to do something about it.

OPEN INNOVATION

Recent work on social media (e.g., Hagel et al., 2010) suggests that new services enabled by IT are changing the way organizations innovate. The ability to

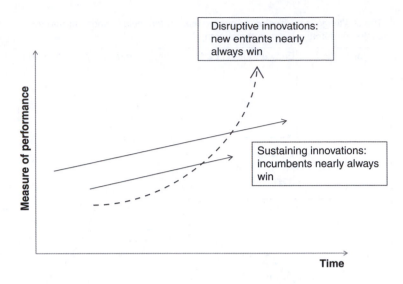

Figure 13.4 Disruptive innovation

connect with people at a distance is creating opportunities for new forms of sharing problems, ideas and solutions within and across organizations (McAfee, 2006). Shirky also suggests (2010) that the adoption of social media is creating opportunities for new forms of collaboration, as individuals devote time and expertise to tackling a wide variety of issues in ways that are made possible by the new technologies.

Organizations are adopting 'crowd-sourcing' as part of open-innovation initiatives. This reflects the 'collective wisdom' approach to management (Birkinshaw, 2010, p. 38). These activities are underpinned by social technologies and are gaining widespread engagement from inside and outside the organizations (professional connections of individuals, value chains of organizations, including customers).

In our recent research (Ashurst et al., 2012) we found clear leadership for innovation activities in a number of case study organizations, but there was also good evidence of the intrinsic motivation for individuals to contribute (a fourth dimension of the management framework put forward by Birkinshaw, 2010, p. 38). Organizations seem to be rapidly evolving clear practices for how they make use of the technologies involved to get value from open innovation in relation to organizational priorities.

VALUE INNOVATION

A further angle is presented by Kim and Mauborgne in their book *Blue Ocean Strategy* (2005). They suggest that success and profitability come from 'value innovation'. Rather than fierce competition on price and performance in existing markets (red oceans), innovators see the world from a different perspective and create new market spaces (blue oceans), with a different basis of competition. They give many examples, including a very simple mobile phone, avoiding the race to add more features and functions and concentrating instead on ease of use for the section of the market that still just want to make voice calls.

Blue Ocean Strategy also suggests that, if the proposition is right, it is possible to bypass the technology adoption cycle and go straight for the mass market.

INNOVATION FOR ALL

There are so many perspectives on innovation (Figure 13.5). This section has provided a brief introduction to a few of the major ones. All are important and relevant; the context is the key in terms of determining relevance in a specific situation.

As an over-riding perspective on innovation we focus on 'innovation for all'. Innovation is certainly not the domain of a few specialists. In the sense of *ideas successfully applied* and making a difference in terms of creating additional value, or finding new and better ways to get the job done, anyone and everyone can and should play a part. That doesn't exclude the need for some to have a much greater focus on innovation and to be seeking radical change to develop the organization for the future.

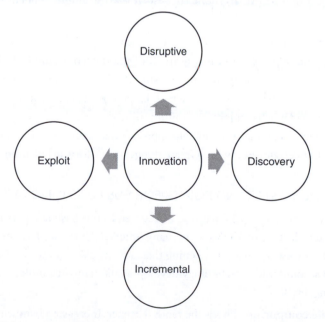

Figure 13.5 Dimensions of innovation

FOUNDATIONS FOR BUSINESS INNOVATION: RAPID TECHNOLOGY DEVELOPMENT

FROM AUTOMATION AND INTEGRATION TO INNOVATION

Early uses of IT focused on automating and integrating existing processes, often replacing people with technology to enable great speed, scale and cost-effectiveness. This is still a major driver for IT investments. Over the last decade IT has increasingly become a driver and enabler of innovation in products, services and ways of working.

In his book *The World Is Flat* Thomas Friedman (2007) discusses '10 Flatteners' that together have resulted in transformational change over the last five to ten years. The only flattener that is not directly based on IT is the fall of the Berlin Wall. The outline in Wikipedia provides a good summary of the core argument: http://en.wikipedia.org/wiki/The_World_Is_Flat.

The world is clearly not (yet) flat, with billions still excluded by poverty. However, the core argument that the convergence of broadband, the PC, open standards and powerful software has created huge challenges and opportunities is convincing. Friedman potentially underestimates the importance of social relationships and the power of inertia, but it would be a risk to rely on these factors as insulation from the forces of change. A recent news article discussing the prospect of a $25 smartphone suggests the world might suddenly get even flatter.

Friedman argues that the flat world crept up on us while we were asleep, distracted and depressed in the aftermath of the dot-com bubble and bust. In our exploration of benefits from innovation, it is important to consider our response to these flatteners and other IT-based business and social trends. We can also consider what might be coming next, so we are not caught sleeping again. Scenario planning is a valuable approach that provides a way to view the significant uncertainties involved in any longer-term forward planning.

KEY TRENDS – STARTING POINTS FOR BUSINESS INNOVATION

This section provides a personal view of key trends. It is based on personal experience and reflecting on the views of many others. Clearly, we have no claim to have a better view of what is happening than anyone else, and these ideas do not take into account wider technology developments (nano-technology, quantum computing, etc.).

Mobile computing. This is the tenth flattener. Increasing bandwidth, more reliable connectivity and the power of new devices mean that new opportunities are emerging rapidly. We are moving to a situation where we have constant access to a full range of IT services and our own data across a wide range of devices. This is 'Martini' computing; any time, any place.

There are many challenges – security, work–home boundaries and the digital divide – but there are also huge opportunities. In hindsight, we will probably see today as an experimental period where we were just starting to explore the potential of the tools available to us, and learning how to exploit them.

Enabling knowledge work. There is a lot of terminology to consider, as different commentators talk about the knowledge economy and knowledge-intensive businesses. In essence, there is a switch in focus from using IT to *automate* transactions to using it to *informate* and contribute to the creativity and productivity of people. Many aspects of technology are relevant to the effectiveness of individuals, teams and organizations as they compete on adding value. Some of these technologies – for example, related to collaboration and supporting virtual teams – have very broad application. Others are much more specialized. Friedman gives an example of how freely available software is changing the basis of competition in creative industries (artwork for advertising).

Again, many technologies are available, but we have hardly begun to learn to exploit their potential.

Information management. New technology is providing organizations with vast stores of data: for example, the 'click stream' data of website usage or 'basket data' from retailer loyalty systems. The challenge is making use of this data to gain insight into how to create value for customers and to improve decision-making. Many tools, for example for data visualization, are becoming more widely available to help analysis and decision-making. At a more basic level, in many organizations there are many opportunities to get more out of widely available tools such as Excel.

Cloud computing. We are using this as a broad term encompassing web services, software as a service and utility computing. These developments are making powerful, enterprise-level software and scalable IT infrastructures available on a pay-as-you-go basis. The open, Internet standards also mean that there are many opportunities for integration between systems and organizations. As a result, small organizations are much better placed to compete with large organizations, and large organizations have a range of new options to consider when planning how to supply their IT needs.

CHALLENGES OF INNOVATION

There are a number of major challenges for organizations trying to make sense of these new developments and to identify where to make investments.

Pace of change. The pace of change is certainly high, but paradoxically many new developments have a long lead-time, as they take years or even decades to go from a technical proof of concept to mainstream, cost-effective, robust deployments. RFID is one example which enthusiasts were experimenting with in the mid-1990s but was only having an impact a decade later. Similarly we were working on projects to replace invoices with EDI 20 years ago, but organizations are still making major investments to scan invoices and introduce workflow software, so the invoice is nowhere near being eliminated.

Variety/uncertainty. Closely related are the issues of variety and uncertainty. In many areas (consider Web 2.0 technologies) there are very many competing products and services, and it is far from clear which, if any, has a future and might emerge as a reliable, long-term choice. IT departments have always faced this issue; perhaps today the extent of variety and the pace of change are greater.

Ultimately competitive advantage will come not from specific technologies or innovations but from the ability to explore, experiment and act to realize value across a whole portfolio of opportunities. A common factor is the increasing ease and opportunity for low-cost experimentation if organizations have the structures and processes to allow it to happen.

BUILDING ON EXISTING FOUNDATIONS TO ENABLE INNOVATION

INNOVATION AT ALL LEVELS

There are a number of areas where we can build on the benefits-led approach to enable successful business innovation. In the following sections we highlight how practices related to the management of the IT and Change Portfolio and agile, benefits-driven projects make an important contribution to innovation. In addition to practices at the project and portfolio levels there are important factors at the organizational level to consider.

THE PORTFOLIO: PROVIDING A FOCUS

A traditional view of IS strategy has been that it is a response to 'demand-pull' from the business strategy (Earl, 1993). A 'technology-push' perspective is also well established (Herstatt and Lettl, 2004). In this case a technology opportunity drives business change – the major wave of outsourcing is an example. These perspectives reflect the (planned) alignment of business and

IS/IT strategies. The concept of co-evolution reflects a third perspective, often reflecting the messy reality of interaction of business, IS and IT (Peppard and Breu, 2003). In this case there is a strong emphasis on learning by doing as business and IT groups work together.

The IT and Change Portfolio provides a key framework that accommodates business demand-pull, technology-push and co-evolution as drivers for investment. The portfolio includes Exploratory investments, which are an important enabler of innovation.

Investments which *may* be important in achieving future success are exploratory. Often neglected, this is business R&D, not technology experimentation. Exploratory projects can be about new products and services or new ways of working. They might involve adopting and adapting ideas from elsewhere. They are often about building new business capabilities through people, process and technology. Many knowledge management, customer relationship management and e-Learning initiatives would have been good opportunities for Exploratory projects. There is clearly a business opportunity – but the detail of how to realize it is not clear.

The starting-point for innovation is to set aside a percentage of the budget and IT resources for investments in Exploratory projects. Small, high-calibre teams need to be given small budgets and tight timescales to have a go and see what's possible. They won't all work – but some of them will provide valuable innovations that will lead to Competitive projects later on. Exploratory projects will also reduce the risks of much bigger failures – from launching into Competitive projects without really understanding what is possible or what customers and other stakeholders really want.

Exploratory projects require close engagement between senior business and IT managers. It is through this close relationship that the ideas emerge and opportunities are identified. They also require trust, a willingness to have a go and the leadership to ensure that red tape does not stifle the innovation and learning at birth.

In essence, this is taking a venture capital or incubator approach. Small initial funding is topped up based on early success.

PROJECTS: ADAPTING THE APPROACH

Having spotted an opportunity and decided *where* to invest, the next challenge is to consider *how* to approach the project. Most approaches to IT projects are risk-averse and designed for an age when IT was mainly about automating well-defined and well-understood business processes. This is almost certainly not the case in an Exploratory project: by definition, you are doing something new. How effective will you be at defining the requirements in detail before going into a design stage? How effectively can you specify the requirements for something new and innovative before you go into design and development? Ideas of design thinking and prototyping to explore possibilities are critical (see Chapter 7).

Peppard et al. (2007) describe how a benefits dependency network (BDN) can be used for business-objective-driven investments in IT focused on specific benefits (benefits-led). This is similar to the concept of alignment when considering strategy. The BDN can also be used for IT innovation-based investments (Peppard et al., 2007). This second situation, of opportunity- or discovery-driven investments, is similar to the strategic perspective of co-evolution.

Exploratory projects are the ideal opportunity for following an agile approach and adopting relevant agile practices. An initial high-level vision and a small, multi-disciplinary team exploring what is possible replace upfront definitions of requirements. Key practices include:

Prototyping: human-centred design, getting a deep understanding of the user and using rapid prototyping as part of a design-thinking approach.

Co-location: bringing the team members together so they can work together face to face with the minimum of paperwork. Their interaction will be the source of innovation.

Multi-disciplinary team: ensuring that key skills are in the team from day one, representing the organization, the customer and the technology possibilities.

Milestone-based control: based on the idea of a 'time-box': tight timescales contribute to innovation. The team needs to work to clearly defined timescales and stick to them, to ensure that the exploration and innovation do not drift. On exploratory projects there should be a major milestone every two to three weeks. The focus on milestones keeps up momentum and motivation while avoiding too much micro-management. The key is to get a solution to the 'customer' and start learning.

Daily meetings: a 30-minute daily meeting might become the primary means of controlling the project and responding to problems and opportunities.

Agile approaches are not new. The 'Agile Manifesto' was written in 2001 (www.agilemanifesto.org), and many of the principles and practices have been around for much longer. Why aren't more organizations adopting agile approaches, particularly for exploratory projects?

Unfortunately, blame cultures and fear of failure get in the way of approaches that are more effective. It is safer to go by the book, even if it's unlikely to result in real innovation.

For the entrepreneurial CIO, who is working closely with senior business colleagues, there is a real opportunity. Adopt the IT and Change Portfolio,

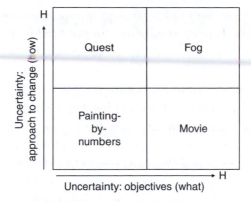

Figure 13.6 Adapting the approach to projects

ring-fence a small percentage of the IT budget for some exploratory projects, build some small, high-calibre teams and let them have a go. Be ready to take responsibility if things go wrong on one or two of them, and recognize the efforts of the teams that succeed.

Competitive projects are critical to achieving strategic objectives. The goal is competitive advantage, a major shift in products and services or ways of working to create value for customers. They involve doing something new, often with the added pressure of the need for rapid results. They are central to business innovation.

These major investments must be managed in a way that allows learning and innovation. Phased, incremental delivery is vital so that the learning is managed at both programme and portfolio levels. At a project level it is also important to allow for exploration and learning. The agile, benefits-led approach set out in Chapters 2–4, combined with design-led practices (Chapter 7), provides a strong foundation for innovation at a project level.

Obeng (2003) provides a framework to help explore relevant approaches to projects (Figure 13.6). He makes the point that most approaches to projects are fit for purpose only if the scenario is 'painting by numbers', with both goals and approach clear (Ends and Means cf. Figure 13.3). Unfortunately, many projects are not in this category.

INNOVATION – THROUGH BENEFITS EXPLOITATION

If all technological progress in the economy stopped today, would productivity growth grind to a halt? We don't think so. On the contrary, we believe that there are decades worth of potential innovations to be made in creatively combining and making use of inventions that we already have.

Brynjolfsson and Saunders, 2009, p. 95

Innovation is not just about new technology and spending more money. What about all the technology we already have in place and have barely begun to exploit? Why not start with Word, the rest of Microsoft Office, SharePoint or even your ERP system? Without a doubt, you can quickly find some innovations that make a real difference to individuals, teams or your wider organization. Perhaps you can start a bigger process of building a climate where innovation happens. You might start by helping people discover some functionality that will make a real difference: surprisingly Styles, Table of Contents, Document Map in Word, Smart Art in PowerPoint and using Outlook to set up meetings are still good starting-points. You might go on and look at the potential of a range of 'apps' for tablets and how they can contribute to improved productivity.

For most organizations, these opportunities just fall through the gaps between the help desk, which fixes problems, and the investment of technical skills in major projects. It is important to free up some resources to enable innovation when realizing benefits from existing IT investments. The cumulative impact can be significant.

PEOPLE: REMOVING THE BARRIERS

At the organizational level there will be many factors that enable or inhibit innovation. Management at every level can do a lot to provide leadership to establish 'how we do things around here' and enable people across the organization to be innovators.

In some organizations there is a very strong focus on hierarchy and managing to tightly defined targets. This can be accompanied by fear and intimidation. Bonuses and rewards may be used, but based on very specific results related to the current business. They might not provide any scope for initiative and innovation. As part of this there may be a 'not invented here' attitude, where managers know best and ideas are not encouraged. There may be a very narrow focus on specific performance measures related to the team or individuals and a disregard for the wider organization and the needs of the customer. Managers will need to work hard to overturn these features of the culture if innovation is to flourish. In some organizations change would have to come from the very top, and that might only happen if there are significant changes in the top management team.

A lack of strategic focus can inhibit innovation; there can be too much being busy due to initiative overload without the chance really to see things through to results. The lack of focus also makes it very difficult to judge where innovation will add value.

Managers and management teams should reflect on their own behaviour and consider whether they are creating a climate that encourages innovation and how they can remove any barriers they identify. They should also consider specific mechanisms, such as individual and team performance targets and staff performance reviews, to consider how they can encourage innovation relevant to the local context.

In many cases small steps can start to change the climate and build momentum for innovation. Following through ideas and suggestion from the team, and encouraging people to act on their own initiative, will soon start to make a difference.

CREATING THE ENVIRONMENT FOR INNOVATION

Beyond project and portfolio management there are many broader factors that contribute to an environment that enables innovation.

Learning by doing – building capability. In traditional IT projects the starting-point is to prepare a detailed set of requirements and a business case, typically to automate an existing process, reducing costs and increasing speed. If the opportunity is for innovation, these approaches are a bad fit. From both business and IT perspectives it is important to learn by doing – to explore how to add value and how to use the technology. The exploration is also building capability (knowledge and skills), so that if opportunities become competitive, the risks of major investment are much reduced.

Architectural approach. Paradoxically, an architectural approach to IT – establishing a coherent technical and application infrastructure – may be an important enabler of innovation. It can ensure that the core infrastructure is robust and reliable and that there is good information integrity and depth of skills in key areas, which provides a platform for innovation around this foundation.

Shift the focus from governance to relationships. IT people like to talk about governance; we put a lot of effort into setting up structures and processes. It is important to remember that outside the IT bunker this is not how real organizations work, at least not at the top level. Too much focus on formal structures indicates the CIO is not part of the top team.

Governance structures are simply *a means to an end*: that is, getting the right people together to take decisions. It is far better to take a different approach and focus on building relationships – person to person. It is out of these relationships, not the IT governance committee, that innovation will grow.

From the wisdom of the leader to the wisdom of crowds. Is the CIO (or the CEO or any other leader) going to be one who has all the good ideas? No. We need to get much broader involvement in innovation. Our staff, customers, suppliers, competitors, perhaps even the local business school and university, should all be contributing.

The CIO needs to: go out and find the innovators and learn from their ideas; provide opportunities for sharing ideas; and provide some (limited) resources to support people to put their ideas into practice. Specific events and activities can be used to encourage innovation (Box 13.2).

Box 13.2   Events and activities to facilitate innovation

Innovation lab: people and a workspace to use design-thinking practices to tackle specific projects in intensive burst of activity.

Showcase: a market-place of ideas and innovations, a 'show-and-tell' on a grand scale, bringing people together from across one or more organizations.

Conference: a more formal version of the Showcase, with presentations and demonstrations from recognized thought leaders.

Jams: the IBM term for open innovation.

Prizes: to recognize good ideas and the delivery of innovations.

Funding: to invest in a range of innovation proposals.

BUILDING THE TOOLKIT FOR INNOVATION

The toolkit approach proposed through this book is intended as an enabler of innovation. The tools are simple, and the barriers to entry are low. They are intended to help multi-disciplinary teams draw on tried and tested good practice and rapidly establish a common language and shared, effective way of working. They are flexible and provide scope for improvisation as a team develops and in response to different challenges.

Core aspects of the toolkit have been introduced in earlier chapters. Innovation is about how these tools are used, and particularly the overall mindset or paradigm of the user. The emphasis of virtually all the tools is on enabling people to work together constructively, energetically and creatively.

SOCIAL TECHNOLOGIES ENABLING INNOVATION

Social technologies have become critical enablers of innovation, connecting people and ideas across the boundaries of time and place and organizational structure. We have explored their contribution in Chapter 11.

INNOVATION: MAKING A START

AVOIDING THE DARK SIDE

There are places where too much innovation is a bad thing. Qualifying systems, for example, must not be put at risk. This means that the CIO and IT department, as a whole, need to be able to adopt different approaches in different situations. This is certainly a challenge.

OPPORTUNITIES FOR NEXT STEPS

There are many opportunities for action to enable innovation. Box 13.3 summarizes potential starting-points. A series of small steps can rapidly start to demonstrate a very different approach.

Box 13.3   Innovation: Options for action

- Adoption of more agile approaches to projects.
- Adoption of the idea of Exploratory projects.
- Making small, staged investments in a range of opportunities. Investing further, as and when there is a clearer understanding of the potential.
- Emphasis on learning by doing – so that prototypes and pilots can provide feedback and learning.
- Allocation of key technical people to Exploratory projects and Exploitation activities.
- Emphasis on phased benefits delivery through a series of short projects.
- Building skills in collaborative, multi-disciplinary teamwork and effective stakeholder engagement.
- Exploring and taking advantage of the practices of 'design thinking'.
- Ensuring that, as part of strategy and architecture activities, there is a technology roadmap. This could, for example, look one year and three-to-five years ahead at known and potential developments and provide a basis for planning exploratory investments and developing skills. The roadmap could be linked to the idea of the product adoption lifecycle.
- Taking proactive steps to facilitate the sharing of learning and opportunities across the organization and with key suppliers/partners.

Effective relationships between business and IT staff at all levels are critical if IT is to play its part as an enabler of business innovation. These relationships will depend on many factors, including hiring and staff development practices. They are also underpinned by getting the basics right – in other words: do current systems work reliably?

A NEW PARADIGM

Many of the practices contributing to innovation are familiar from previous work, for example on agile and benefits-led approaches. On the other hand, something is very different. I have made a similar point (Ashurst, 2007, 2012) in relation to the difference between benefits-led and technology-focused approaches to IT investments, suggesting that the issue is not different methods but different 'paradigms'. Steel (2000) says 'a paradigm is a self-consistent set of ideas and beliefs which acts as a filter, influencing how we perceive and how we make sense'. My conclusion is that an innovation approach to IT represents a 'third paradigm', which is significantly different from previous paradigms (technology implementation and benefits-led). The difference is the attitude or mindset, more than the specific practices, and the challenge of making a paradigm shift will be the major barrier to developing the capability for IT-enabled business innovation in many organizations and IT functions.

Five questions for further consideration:

1. How can/will the role of the CIO and IT function evolve to encompass IT-enabled business innovation? Will IT be marginalized as other areas of the organization take the lead? If IT is not taking the lead, who will?

2. Would it be helpful to reinterpret work on benefits practices to provide a clear focus on innovation? Would this be helpful in communicating the creative collaboration/design paradigm that contributes to innovation?

3. How can practices of innovation (and the role of the IT function) evolve to address IT as intellectual technology more directly? Agile and design approaches do this to an extent, but they do not seem to be the final answer and in any case are not (yet) widely adopted.

4. What guidance can be provided for applying innovation principles and practices in a very wide range of scenarios, and how can this be developed as a core element of establishing on organization-wide innovation capability?

5. How can the learning from these early adopters of innovation practices be shared more widely in these large organizations and among other organizations? How can the significant barriers to the adoption of agile approaches and design thinking be overcome?

TAKING IT FURTHER

FURTHER READING AND RESOURCES

Any of these books provides practical insight into design thinking and innovation:

Brown, Tim (2009) *Change by Design: How Design Thinking Creates New Alternatives for Business and Society: How Design Thinking Can Transform Organizations and Inspire*, Collins Business.

Kelley, D. and Kelley, T. (2013) *Creative Confidence*, London: William Collins.

Kelley, Tom (2001) *The Art of Innovation: Lessons in Creativity from IDEO, America's Leading Design Firm*, London: Harper Collins Business.

Kelley, Tom (2008) *The Ten Faces of Innovation: Strategies for Heightening Creativity*, Profile Business

TALKING POINTS

Use these questions to help reflect on this chapter and explore the challenges of putting the ideas into practice:

1. What are the barriers to taking a more innovative approach to projects?

2. How might you make a start in building innovation at a project level?

3. How do you establish a business case of an innovation project?

4. How can the IT & Change Portfolio enable innovation?

5. Is innovation part of everyone's job?

6. Who provides leadership for innovation?

7. How can a large organization balance allowing opportunities for innovation and maintaining a focus on the vision and mission?

8. How can you handle the inevitable failure of some innovation initiatives?

9. Does your industry face threats of disruptive innovation?

10. What else should be in the innovator's toolkit?

KEY DEBATES

Innovation: For a few or for all?

As an organization explores becoming more innovative, a key debate is whether innovation is for a few specialists or for all. Is there a need for a Director of Innovation and an innovation team? Should innovation be pervasive – part of everyone's job? Does the answer depend on the organization/market? Can the two approaches be usefully combined?

As you consider this issue, remember that not all innovation is radical, disruptive or organization-wide, depends on new technology or is easily replicated and adopted across an organization. Innovation in the sense of 'ideas successfully applied' may be valuable but incremental, local and simple.

CASE STUDY 13.1

IT has been a driver of business model innovation across a range of industries. It is likely to keep happening.

Journal of Information Technology Teaching Cases, Vol. 3 (2013): 78–87.

How IT enables business model innovation at the VDAB

Stijn Viaene and Saskia Broeckx

This case study invites students to discuss strategic value creation through the use of IT. It raises issues of business model innovation, IT strategy, digital platforms, ecosystems, business–IT alignment and leadership. The key character in the case is the Chief Information Officer, Paul Danneels, who is ready to drive the strategic transformation of the VDAB, the Flemish Employment Agency, from a service provider to a labour market conductor. Starting from a firm understanding of the VDAB's strategic choices, students should be able to discuss the positioning and role of the IT department as well as its views on value delivery.

REFERENCES

Ashurst, C. (2007) Realizing Benefits from IS/IT: Exploring the Practices and Competences Required to Succeed, PhD thesis, Loughborough University, UK.

Ashurst, C. (2012) *Benefits Realization from Information Technology*, Basingstoke: Palgrave Macmillan.

Ashurst, C., Freer, A., Ekdahl, J. and Gibbons, C. (2012) Exploring IT-Enabled Innovation: A New Paradigm? *International Journal of Information Management*, Vol. 32 (4): 326–336.

Baldwin, C. and von Hippel, E. (2011) Modeling a Paradigm Shift: From Producer Innovation to User and Open Collaborative Innovation. *Organization Science*, Vol. 22 (6): 1399–1417.

Birkinshaw, J. (2010) *Reinventing Management*, San Francisco, CA: Jossey-Bass.

Birkinshaw, J. and Goddard, J. (2009) What Is Your Management Model? *Sloan Management Review*, Winter, Vol. 50 (2): 81–90.

Brynjolfsson, E. (2010) The Four Ways IT Is Revolutionizing Innovation: An Interview with Erik Brynjolfsson by M.S. Hopkins. *MIT Sloan Management Review*, Vol. 51 (3): 51–56.

Brynjolfsson, E. and Saunders, A. (2009) *Wired for Innovation: How Information-Technology Is Reshaping the Economy*, MIT Press.

Cash, J.I., Earl, M.J. and Morison, R. (2008) Teaming Up to Crack Innovation & Enterprise Integration. *Harvard Business Review*, Vol. 86 (11): 90–100.

Chesbrough, H.W. (2003) The Era of Open Innovation. *MIT Sloan Management Review*, Vol. 44 (3): 35–41.

Christensen, C.M. (1997) *The Innovator's Dilemma: When New Technologies Cause Great Firms to Fail*, Boston, MA: Harvard Business School Press.

Drucker, P. (1985) *Innovation and Entrepreneurship*, Harper & Row.

Earl, M.J. (1993) Experiences in Strategic Information Systems Planning. *MIS Quarterly*, Vol. 17 (1): 1–24.

Friedman, T.L. (2007) *The World Is Flat: The Globalized World in the Twenty-First Century*, Penguin.

Hagel, J., Seely Brown, J. and Davison, L. (2010) *The Power of Pull*, New York: Basic Books.

Herstatt, C. and Lettl, C. (2004) Management of 'Technology Push' Development Projects. *International Journal of Technology Management*, Vol. 27 (2–3): 155–175.

Kim, W. Chan and Mauborgne, R. (2005) *Blue Ocean Strategy*, Harvard Business School Press.

Lee, A.S. (1999) Researching MIS, in Currie, W. and Galliers, B. (eds.) *Rethinking Management Information Systems*, Oxford: Oxford University Press, pp. 7–27.

McAfee, A. (2006) Enterprise 2.0: The Dawn of Emergent Collaboration. *MIT Sloan Management Review*, Vol. 47 (3): 21–28.

Melville, N., Kraemer, K. and Gurbaxani, V. (2004) Information Technology and Organizational Performance: An Integrative Model of IT Business Value. *MIS Quarterly*, Vol. 28 (2): 283–322.

Moore, G. (1998) *Crossing the Chasm*, Capstone.

Obeng, E. (2003) *Perfect Projects*, Pentacle Works the Virtual Media Company.

Peppard, J. (2007) The Conundrum of IT Management. *European Journal of Information Systems*, Vol. 16: 336–345.

Peppard, J. and Breu, K. (2003) Beyond Alignment – A Co-Evolutionary View of the IS Strategy Process, in Proceedings of 24th International Conference on Information Systems, (ICIS) Seattle, WA, pp. 743–750.

Peppard, J., Ward, J. and Daniel, E. (2007) Managing the Realization of Business Benefits from IT Investments. *MIS Quarterly Executive*, Vol. 6 (1): 1–11.

Rogers, E.M. (2003) *Diffusion of Innovations*, 5th edition, New York: Free Press.

Shirky, C. (2010) *Cognitive Surplus*, London: Penguin Group.

Steel, R. (2000) New Insights on Organizational Change. *Organisations & People*, Vol. 7 (2): 2–9.

Thomke, S. and von Hippel, E. (2002) Customers as Innovators: A New Way to Create Value. *Harvard Business Review*, Vol. 80 (4): 74–81.

Tidd J., Bessant, J. and Pavitt, K. (2005) *Managing Innovation: Integrating Technological, Market and Organizational Change*, 3rd edition, Chichester, West Sussex: John Wiley and Sons.

Tushman, M. and Nadler, D. (1986) Organizing for Innovation. *California Management Review*, Vol. 28 (3): 74–92.

CHAPTER 14
BUILDING THE IT CAPABILITY OF THE ORGANIZATION

IN THIS CHAPTER WE STUDY:

- a project perspective on competences for benefits realization;
- a portfolio perspective on competences for benefits realization;
- wider organizational issues affecting competences for benefits realization;
- the implications of a dynamic capability perspective;
- steps to build a capability for benefits realization.

COMPETITIVE ADVANTAGE FROM IT

Benefits realization and competitive advantage from IT are an issue for the organization as a whole. They depend on a complex set of organizational competences embedded in the IT function, and particularly in management teams and business units across the organization (Figure 12.1). Advantage comes from investments in change that deliver a stream of benefits, from improving the current business and from new products, services and ways of working.

The perspective of organizational competences is powerful because it provides an insight into the complexity of organizations and does not prescribe specific processes or structures. This is also its weakness. It can be hard to use it to develop practical guidance for individuals and teams in organizations who are working to make improvements.

In this chapter the focus is on the model of competences for benefits realization. Firstly, we consider the model in relation to specific investments in IT-enabled change. Then we consider the implications for managing the overall portfolio of investments. As a third stage, the relationship with the wider organizational context is also explored. These sections provide a brief recap on the book, related directly to the competences model. The final part of the chapter focuses on the crucial issue of how to approach *developing* these

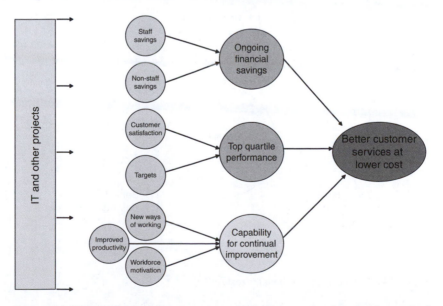

Figure 14.1 High-level transformation programme roadmap showing development of capability for continual improvement

competences in order to develop the overall capability of the organization to achieve competitive advantage from IT.

Leading a digital business is about developing these competences through efforts to realize value from current information and systems as well as incremental and transformational change. The simplified benefits roadmap from a case study reported in Ashurst (2012) shows how development of the capability for continual improvement (i.e., transformation or benefits realization capability) is one of the goals of a major organizational transformation programme (Figure 14.1).

ORGANIZATIONAL COMPETENCES FOR BENEFITS REALIZATION: PROJECT PERSPECTIVE

The project perspective was a key starting-point for the design of the model of competences for benefits realization (Figure 14.2). The practices identified in Ashurst et al. (2008) demonstrate this as they are largely at the project level. The project perspective remains a valuable use of the model.

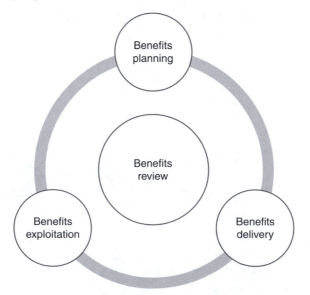

Figure 14.2 Competences for benefits realization

There is a broad similarity between the competences model and a project or investment lifecycle, which is useful. It is important to remember that these competences ('the ability of the organization to ...') are not just stages in a lifecycle. Activities related to the different competences are likely to be taking place in parallel through much of the life of a project and investment. For example, benefits planning should continue through the life of a project to maintain a focus on benefits as new information becomes available and new opportunities are identified. Benefits exploitation is important from the beginning of a project, as planning for sustaining and developing benefits after 'going live' and completion of the original project is likely to be an important factor in successful benefits realization.

BENEFITS PLANNING

Benefits planning takes an idea for a project and develops a clear understanding of the potential benefits for relevant stakeholders and the organization. It also involves exploring how the benefits can be realized. The benefits realization plan is one way to bring together the understanding of *what* the benefits are and the plan for *how* they will be achieved.

Benefits planning goes beyond the delivery of a business case, which all too often addresses the *what* and not the *how*. Business cases are often of limited value for benefits realization because they are written to gain approval of funding for the project, not to contribute to the actual realization of benefits. The gap can be surprisingly large: for example, a business case might put a financial value on time saved across a large number of people from introducing a new e-procurement system. This says nothing about whether the benefits can actually be realized by reducing headcount or in other ways.

Benefits planning is, or should be, an ongoing activity through the project. In a fairly straightforward situation, reviews at key milestones will help ensure that a project remains on track to deliver the intended benefits. In many other situations, where there is a greater element of innovation, there will be a need to revisit benefits planning at each stage. The understanding of the problem and/or opportunity will have evolved, and there will be fresh insights into the potential benefits and how to realize them.

Benefits planning is also the best place to stop bad projects if the benefits aren't clear, the costs of realizing them are too high or the sponsorship for the required business changes is not in evidence. There is a clear link to the portfolio perspective. If bad ideas don't get translated into failing projects, resources can be focused on projects with the potential for adding greater value.

A number of well-established practices underpin the competence for benefits planning. It is vital to use relevant practices to bring together the high-level vision and the detailed planning for benefits realization, as well as linking to the design for the IT solution and the organizational changes.

BENEFITS DELIVERY

Benefits delivery takes the benefits realization plan and addresses the delivery of the IT solution and organizational changes required to achieve the potential benefits. It includes virtually all aspects of the 'IT project' that delivers the technology solution, related training, support materials and the support infrastructure. The IT project is now only one strand of a wider change project.

The toolkit for benefits delivery is also well established and draws on much of what we know about project management. Two of the most challenging areas are adapting the approach to a specific scenario and achieving the desired outcomes from the business changes.

Individuals involved in a project will adapt the approach they take, based on the context and their experience. This is often fairly informal, and there are opportunities for many organizations to evolve this adaptation so that it is less *ad hoc* and dependent on the individuals who happen to be involved. The IT and Change Portfolio can be used to help think through how to adapt the approach to a specific project and can be one source of guidance for the senior management team responsible for the 'IT portfolio'.

IT has evolved from automating transaction processing (payroll, financial transaction and accounting) to a much wider range of scenarios, which involve communication and collaboration between individuals and where the technology is used to informate, rather than automate. In these cases, often involving professional or knowledge workers, the end-user often has a lot of discretion about how (or whether) they use the technology and the information provided. This brings a number of challenges: not least, that designing and managing change become extremely hard. It is important to look beyond changes to business processes, particularly where these are taken as about transactions, to a wider view of what is being changed: working practices, performance measures, skills, behaviours, etc. Models such as the 'cultural web' and '7-S' are relevant. The link between cause and effect also becomes less certain.

BENEFITS REVIEW

Benefits review includes a number of different activities. One starting-point is to reinvent the traditional post-implementation review to address benefits realization and lessons learned. The review explores the benefits realized (planned and unplanned), the reasons for changes from the plan and also opportunities for further benefits. The 'lessons learned' element considers what worked well and what didn't in terms of the practices that contributed to benefits realization. The review effectively reflects on the *what* and the *how* of the benefits realization plan. Lessons learned need to be addressed in later stages of the current project (programme) and other projects in the organization as relevant.

Note: there is real risk of confusion here as the competence and the practice are both referred to as 'benefits review'. For the moment, we do not see a way out of this conundrum and hope that it is clear from the context which is intended.

Benefits review can be considered as an ongoing activity during a project and the lifetime of an investment. There is certainly a need for focus at key project milestones:

- Is the project still on track to deliver the intended benefits?

- Have new opportunities for benefits been identified?

- Does the latest information on costs and the feasibility of the changes required to realize the benefits affect the project?

- Is the project still a priority for use of resources, given the *current* level of knowledge and latest strategic context?

Benefits review is a great example of the 'knowing–doing gap'. I suspect virtually every project method has some form of a post-implementation or benefits review and every project manager knows its importance. Yet reviews are only carried out in around 25% of cases. The goal is not to reinvent a post-implementation review as a benefits review. What is important is to get benefits reviews to happen consistently and to get benefits from carrying them out.

BENEFITS EXPLOITATION

Benefits exploitation goes beyond the end-point of a project into service management (where ITIL is the dominant framework). IT investments often have long lifetimes, even in these days of rapid change and innovation. Core business systems can easily be 10–20 years old, and even relatively fast-moving technologies such as word processors and intranet software can often be five years old. Benefits exploitation includes sustaining business changes and ensuring continued benefits realization over the lifetime of these investments. This can include provision of training to help maintain knowledge as staff leave the organization, new staff join and others change roles. It also includes adapting to changes in customer needs and business priorities over these long periods of time. Crucially, benefits exploitation also reflects that these are often 'intellectual technologies' that have properties that are not fixed on implementation but can be innovated endlessly, depending on the interaction with the intellect of the human beings who implement and use them. As we learn more, we start to see new possibilities and become equipped for a further cycle of learning.

In most organizations benefits exploitation is neglected. IT effort goes into maintenance and keeping the systems running smoothly, but between the business areas and IT there is not enough focus on continued benefits realization.

Practices in the area of benefits realization are not well established. Our toolkit of practices for benefits realization has some initial ideas. Exploratory work on knowledge worker productivity has highlighted the importance of this area and indicated opportunities for organizations to take action.

BUILDING BENEFITS COMPETENCES AT A PROJECT LEVEL

There are a number of possible starting-points for developing competences for benefits realization (Box 14.1 provides some examples).

It is often valuable to start with benefits review. There will always be projects that have just completed or are in progress that would benefit from input in this area. An initial review can often be based around a two- to three-hour workshop, so the effort required is small. Reviews of a number of projects should add value to the projects themselves and enable realization of further benefits if the project itself is complete. The reviews will also provide insights in common issues and opportunities, and provide a starting-point for planning wider action.

Box 14.1   Project-level starting-points for developing benefits realization competences

Benefits review

Carry out a benefits review of a small number of recently completed projects.

Benefits review

Carry out a benefits review of a small number of ongoing projects.

Benefits planning

Pilot a benefits planning process on two or three projects.

PORTFOLIO PERSPECTIVE

The portfolio perspective is an important part of the model of benefits realization competences For an organization seeking to improve benefits realization from IT, action at both project and portfolio levels is almost certain to be required. Recent work (Chapter 9) has started to extend the toolkit of practices for benefits realization to the portfolio level.

It is important to note that in many organizations the situation will be complex, partly due to the lack of a common language. As noted in Chapter 9, what is classed as a project may be far from clear.

The scope of the 'portfolio' varies in other ways. For example, does it relate to all projects funded from the IT budget or owned by the IT department? Alternatively, perhaps it looks more broadly at all projects that are affected by IT. There is also the time dimension: ideas for projects, live projects, completed projects and operational systems or services. Again, we would take a pragmatic approach and make a start with the portfolio at a level that adds value in the short term. This might be a review of live projects or work on strategy that brings together ideas and priorities for future projects. A more comprehensive approach to managing the IT investment portfolio can then be developed over time.

A further important element to the scope of adoption of the portfolio is the organizational dimension. In virtually every medium or large organization the portfolio will be valuable at a number of organizational levels (team, department, business unit, etc.). The focus on benefits from IT-enabled change is the key. It does not matter if the IT function (along with the infrastructure and application development) is centralized or local; even with a highly centralized IT infrastructure there is a need for a local business perspective on the portfolio. For example, the local portfolio needs to address the local implications of centrally driven projects, as there will be resource implications and presumably a need for local ownership of benefits realization. The local portfolio should also address local projects. There will usually be a range of important projects that can drive benefits realization that do not require central IT resource. For example, improved use of information or taking advantage of existing system features to improve efficiency or customer service (benefits exploitation). The portfolio has the nature of a 'fractal'; it can be usefully applied at any part of the organization.

This perspective also makes clear the organization-wide nature of the benefits realization capability. There is value in adopting key practices very broadly.

BENEFITS PLANNING

At the portfolio level the focus of benefits planning shifts to identifying which investments to make and to getting an effective overall spread of investments. The emphasis is on strategy and also governance, in the sense of how decisions are taken across an organization by different individuals and business units.

The competence is particularly challenging. It requires good engagement across organizational units, professional disciplines and different levels of the hierarchy. There will be many challenges, including politics. There are also inherent uncertainties that must be taken into consideration in some way: how is the business context going to change during the lifetime of this investment?

How will new technology innovations create opportunities, and when is the right time to make investments? These are not problems that have a 'solution', but a number of practices can help to tackle these complex, problematic situations.

One response is to adopt some of the project-level practices at a portfolio level. For example, the tools of 'driver analysis' (Ward and Peppard, 2002) can be applied to the strategic question of 'Where should I invest in IT-enabled change?' as well as to the project level questions, which include 'How does this planned investment contribute to the strategic objectives of the organization?' Equally, the 'benefits dependency network' (Ward and Daniel, 2006) can be applied at a strategy level, in which case the 'business changes' will represent programmes or strategic initiatives.

An architecture perspective is also valuable. This tackles the potentially adverse impact of a benefits-driven view of each project in isolation and looks across both the IT infrastructure and business organization (including business processes) to look at the big picture. Weill and Ross (2009) explore how to establish a 'digital platform' of coherent systems that allows accelerated innovation and benefits realization.

It is also important to adopt an agile perspective at a portfolio level to manage risk and speed of delivery and to maintain flexibility. A key agile principle is rapid, incremental delivery, which means that the portfolio will give priority to short projects delivering benefits over a series of 'releases' of an IT and business solution. From a portfolio perspective it is important to ensure that the approach to projects is adapted to reflect their specific context, using the portfolio as a guide. It will be important to introduce Exploratory projects if an equivalent concept is not already in use.

BENEFITS DELIVERY

Benefits delivery is about maintaining control of the overall portfolio to ensure benefits realization. At the portfolio level important issues will include risk management, dependencies across projects, managing resource allocation across projects and exploring the business change impact of planned and current projects. Many issues become visible that will not be clear at an individual project level.

Issues of governance become important: that is, which individuals and groups manage the portfolio. Weill and Ross (2009) are helpful here as well, providing a framework for IT governance. It is important to note that getting formal structures in place is only one factor. How people engage and behave is more important, as in the end effective governance will be determined by the individuals and their relationships.

At a portfolio level, many issues related to people become a priority. For example, what is the capacity for IT-enabled change, and how can the capacity be developed in the short, medium and longer term? Who are the best people for a specific project? How can the available resources and the demand for investment be matched up across the organization?

The portfolio perspective also relates to management of IT applications and infrastructure. The IT and Change Portfolio implies that different approaches can be adopted to technology and service management, depending on where an application sits in the portfolio. For example, an 'Exploratory' development might depend on pre-release software to gain insights from new technology and working with a strategic supplier. It is unlikely that the same approach will be taken for Qualifying systems.

BENEFITS EXPLOITATION

At the portfolio level benefits exploitation links strongly with service management. There is, however, an important change in perspective. The focus is continuing to realize benefits rather than simply to manage an operational IT service.

Staff turnover with time, the changing business context and ongoing learning about the potential of the technology are just three reasons why a continued focus on benefits exploitation is required.

Usually, too much is left to chance. Organizations should focus more on benefits exploitation. The returns from management attention are likely to be good. In most cases incremental investment will be zero or small, and there will be valuable returns.

BENEFITS REVIEW

Benefits review is as critical at the portfolio level as at the project level. Investment appraisal is one area to focus on. Criteria for deciding when to invest in a specific project, to compare projects and to explore the overall level and balance of investment are hard to determine. Specifically, we note that traditional, financially driven models (payback, net present value, etc.) are not a good fit for Strategic and Exploratory projects. This does not mean that rigorous assessment should be scrapped, but it would be helpful to have more appropriate criteria to help make these key decisions. Traditional methods favour projects with a direct and easy-to-measure financial return, rather than projects that provide value to customers and contribute to strategic objectives. As a result, there is over-investment in 'Support' projects.

The benefits review concept is also critical at the portfolio level. Here a key emphasis is on making sure that effective project reviews take place and that lessons learned are shared between projects. The reviews need to take place for individual projects and then as a part of benefits exploitation reviews should take place around live systems and business processes. There are significant challenges to enable both individuals and the organization as a whole to learn. It is important that the reviews do not become bureaucracy, but that they are used to drive learning and increasingly effective management of the portfolio.

It is usually helpful to extend benefits reviews to a periodic review of the portfolio itself and related portfolio management practices. Review at this level can help reassess priorities and realign resources and will typically take place every three or at most six months.

BUILDING BENEFITS COMPETENCES AT A PORTFOLIO LEVEL

It is inherent in the thinking behind the benefits competence model that developing the required competences is a complex and often challenging process of organizational change. The steps that are feasible and that will provide benefits will vary from organization to organization, depending on a range of factors.

At a portfolio level a number of initial or next steps are usually fairly straightforward. Box 14.2 provides suggestions.

Box 14.2   Practical steps to build benefits competences at a portfolio level

Benefits planning

Introduce the IT and Change Portfolio as a way of categorizing projects and use as part of planning and approval.

Benefits delivery

Carry out interim benefits reviews of 'important' projects to ensure that the current portfolio is in good shape.

Provide advice/coaching as new projects are established to ensure strong teams and governance, use of benefits practices, adaptation to reflect the portfolio.

Benefits exploitation

Review a sample of projects completed 6–18 months ago and explore opportunities for benefits realization.

Review a sample of major business systems/services and explore opportunities for benefits realization.

> **Benefits review**
>
> Review investment appraisal criteria in the context of the IT and Change Portfolio.
>
> Monitor benefits reviews taking place at a project level. Ensure there is clear ownership for sharing lessons learned.
>
> Carry out an initial review of the project portfolio using benefits criteria.
>
> Introduce regular reviews of the portfolio with a suitable management group(s).

Making use of IT solutions to contribute to effective portfolio management

It is vital to keep the focus on organizational change, not IT implementation. But here, as in other areas, IT can be an important enabler of change. Combinations of portfolio management software and Web 2.0 approaches enabling collaboration and knowledge-sharing can help develop competences for benefits realization at a number of levels. They can provide a clear framework for project and portfolio management, improving efficiency and effectiveness. For example, a clear project lifecycle can be established and used consistently, with agreed templates for key deliverables. It can enable collaborative working at a project level and can facilitate effective management of the portfolio by providing increased visibility of key project information: for example, 'traffic light' reporting of project status and progress against key milestones. Key benefits tools can be supported: for example, by consistent ways of capturing key information, for instance from a stakeholder analysis. Approached in the right way, the technology can enable creative and flexible working by saving time on areas that don't add much value, by enabling collaborative working and improving communication. The Web 2.0 emphasis can also be valuable in enabling organizational learning and knowledge-sharing. For example, collaboration around specific tools can be valuable and can help individuals and teams apply those tools effectively.

The ideal situation is to embed adoption of IT support into a wider programme of change to develop the enhanced competences for benefits realization.

ORGANIZATIONAL PERSPECTIVE

The organizational context is an important influence on benefits realization. Recent work by Brynjolfsson and Saunders (2009), drawing on a whole series of earlier studies, provides strong evidence of a number of organizational-level factors that contribute to benefits realization. This perspective is a valuable addition to our findings at project and portfolio levels.

In the right context there can be broader benefits from individual investments in IT. For example, Microsoft made a major push to get rid of paper forms and succeeded something like 15 years ago. At one level this would be a series of support investments with relatively limited payback. Over all, however it provided a strategic initiative to push the boundaries of what was possible and to find out how to resolve problems such as meeting legislative requirements and handling the need for signatures. The learning could be shared with customers, and there were wider benefits in terms of the agile, low-bureaucracy work environment that made a contribution to priorities such as attracting and keeping talent and being a great place to work.

From our earliest work on benefits realization we have identified a range of factors at an organizational level. These include (but are not limited to):

- The role of the CIO, including his/her relationship with other senior leaders and the leadership they provide for developing a benefits focus.

- The general organizational culture and climate and the extent to which learning is possible. For example, one case study provided an example of an organization where it was very difficult to say that something had gone wrong or that improvements were needed, so that it was very difficult to learn and improve.

- The impact of HR policies and practices: for example, the role of project managers and how performance is defined. Does the focus remains on delivery to time and budget rather than consideration of benefits? Is there a development path that encourages business 'high flyers' to get involved in leading change projects? Is there openness to cross-organizational working?

OTHER PERSPECTIVES

Previous work has considered the skills and competences of individuals including the CEO (Earl and Feeny, 2000), the CIO (Earl and Feeny, 1994) and organizational competences such as competences for information management (Marchand et al., 2000). In the context of the IT function, Feeny and Willcocks (1998a, 1998b) have explored the concept of IT capabilities, and have proposed a framework of nine distinct capabilities necessary for its effective management. That the necessary capabilities can be developed within the scope of the IT function is at odds with the research that highlights the need for enterprise-wide co-operation and involvement to realize the benefits from IT investments. Peppard and Ward (2004) have addressed this and proposed a model of IS competences across the organization.

The framework put forward in this chapter draws on these foundations and, in particular, the perspective that competing with IT is an organization-wide capability.

DYNAMIC CAPABILITY

WHAT ARE DYNAMIC CAPABILITIES?

Many practices that contribute to successful realization of benefits from IT have been identified. The primary problem is that they are not widely, consistently and effectively adopted (B.C.S., 2004). In an initial report (Ashurst et al., 2008) we explored the challenges of realizing benefits from investments in IT from a resource-based perspective, and developed a model of an organizational benefits realization capability and a framework of practices for benefits realization. In this section we explore the implications of previous work on *dynamic capabilities* for our understanding of benefits realization, and the development and effectiveness of a benefits realization capability.

The resource-based view of the firm has become a major strand of strategic management research and as a result provides an important starting-point when considering the realization of value from IT: 'the theoretical and practical importance of developing and applying dynamic capabilities to sustain a firm's competitive advantage in complex, and volatile external environments has catapulted this issue to the research agenda of many scholars' (Zahra et al., 2006). An increasing number of authors have considered the concept of the 'dynamic capabilities' of an organization (Ambrosini and Bowman, 2009).

The idea of a 'dynamic capability' can be traced back to early work by Teece and then to Penrose and Schumpeter: 'the mechanisms by which firms learn and accumulate new skills and capabilities and the forces that limit the rate and direction of this process'. Dynamic capabilities can also be defined as:

> The firm's processes that use resources – specifically the processes to integrate, reconfigure, gain and release resources – to match and even create market change. Dynamic capabilities thus are the organizational and strategic routines by which firms achieve new resource configurations as markets emerge, collide, split, evolve, and die.
>
> (Eisenhardt and Martin, 2000)

Zahra et al. (2006) refer to a dynamic capability as the 'dynamic capability to change or reconfigure existing substantive capabilities'. This requires a definition of *substantive* capabilities, which they give as 'the ability to solve a problem' (p. 921). A dynamic capability is the ability to change the way a 'firm solves its problems'. If an organization does not have or use dynamic capabilities, any advantage from substantive capabilities may be short-lived due to changes in the environment or competitor action.

Bowman and Ambrosini (2003) explain that dynamic capabilities comprise four main processes:

- 'Reconfiguration: transformation and recombination of assets and resources
- Leveraging: replicating a process or system that is operating in one business unit into another, or extending a resource by deploying it into a new domain
- Learning: to perform tasks more effectively and efficiently as an outcome of experimentation, reflecting on failure and success
- Creative integration: ability to integrate assets and resources resulting in a new resource configuration'

Two further elements of dynamic capabilities are (Augier and Teece, 2008; Teece 2007):

- 'Search identifying opportunities & threats
- Sensing – changing customer requirements'.

Also dynamic capabilities are not synonymous with strategic change. For example, changes may occur through *ad hoc* interventions, through emergent processes that have not been deployed by managers or by luck (Ambrosini and Bowman, 2009). There is also room for some exploration of what represents a dynamic capability in a particular organization: differing from Eisenhardt and Martin (2000), Zahra et al. (2006) see new product development as a substantive capability, and the ability to change how the firm develops new products as a dynamic capability (p. 921).

VALUE FROM DYNAMIC CAPABILITIES

Organizations realize value from their dynamic capabilities in the choices they make in how they are applied to develop new or improved 'substantive capabilities' (Zahra et al., 2006). Value is then realized through the resulting substantive capabilities. This parallels the way value is realized from IT, with the direct impact being on business process performance, which in turn contributes to improved organizational performance (Melville et al., 2004). As a result, a key contributor to realizing value from dynamic capabilities is the 'entrepreneurial alertness' (Sambamurthy and Bharadwaj, 2003) that helps an organization recognize the opportunities and take action. Lockett (2005) builds on work by Penrose and emphasizes the need for entrepreneurial skills, including imagination, to contribute to change and gaining competitive advantage and not just managerial competence in running the current business.

In order to make good decisions about how to apply dynamic capabilities, management need to be able to consider a range of possible futures and assess the value that can be realized (Amit and Schoemaker, 1993; Srivastava et al., 2001). Zahra et al. (2006) relate this ability to the level of knowledge of the organization. There is also a risk that options are ignored because of a lack of knowledge or overlooked because of an inability to see beyond the current frame or paradigm (Eisenhardt and Martin, 2000). In addition, as Sambamurthy and Bharadwaj (2003) note, value is provided by the 'digital options' represented by investments in business and IT substantive capabilities that open up new possibilities not planned at the time of the original investment. These options contribute to agility, which is extremely important in a changing and unpredictable business environment. Teece et al. (1997) also note that there are situations where local autonomy to allow a decentralized approach to change may be important.

DEVELOPING DYNAMIC CAPABILITIES

Organizational capabilities, both dynamic and substantive capabilities, are developed through learning and application (Prahalad and Hamel, 1990; Grant, 1996b; Powell and Dent Micallef, 1997). Zollo and Winter (2002, p. 344) suggest, 'dynamic capabilities emerge from the co-evolution of tacit experience accumulation processes with explicit knowledge articulation and codification activities.' A dynamic capability has some patterned element; it is repeatable (Zollo and Winter, 2002).

Ambrosini and Bowman (2009) refer to the importance of social capital, particularly individuals' internal and external social ties, to enable information-sharing and to contribute to innovation.

There is also a risk of decay or loss of capabilities through lack of use, and substantive capabilities may become difficult to change if they are left unchanged for a period of time (Eisenhardt and Martin, 2000). Dynamic capabilities are built rather than bought in the market. The development of dynamic capabilities is path-dependent, and it is likely that there is a natural sequence of development (Eisenhardt and Martin, 2000). They also suggest that they are 'equifinal'. As a specific example, Ross (2003) notes that the development of IT architecture capabilities must be in stages, and it is very unlikely that an organization will be successful if it tries to miss out a stage of development. The ability to learn, and to develop, dynamic capabilities is in itself a higher-order dynamic capability (Ambrosini and Bowman, 2009). Developing and maintaining dynamic capabilities is expensive (Zollo and Winter, 2002; Ambrosini and Bowman, 2009).

The dynamic capability requires a range of individuals with different knowledge and skills working together in multi-disciplinary, cross-functional teams. To be effective there is a need for a common language and some level of common experience and common process (sequencing, rules and directives) (Grant,

1996a; Eisenhardt and Martin, 2000). In addition, as Grant notes (1996a), 'rules and directives', and group problem-solving are important in the effectiveness of this knowledge-intensive work. The degree of codification of the routines that is helpful will vary according to the velocity of markets (Eisenhardt and Martin, 2000). Similarly, Bohn (1994) explores the appropriate degree of proceduralization, depending on the level of knowledge of a business process.

As we have noted (Ashurst et al., 2008), these routines are practices, representing the work people do. They can be the basis for establishing a common approach, or a specific way of working as part of a substantive or dynamic organizational capability. These practices, which contribute to a capability, can be shared within an organization and also between organizations. As Teece et al. (1997) indicate, there is value in inter-organizational learning.

THE CONTRIBUTION OF PRACTICES

Practices open up the 'black box' of productive performance and provide a specific mechanism to translate resource inputs into productive activity. They also provide a potential way to connect an investment in skills to a contribution to improved productivity by helping shape what people do in the workplace. Research has suggested that the adoption of practices needs to be approached as a strategic change programme, and in many cases this does not happen (Leseure et al., 2004). One of the barriers to adoption of practices for business transformation is lack of awareness of a need and as a result a lack of demand for adoption. This is an example of a more general issue affecting the sharing of knowledge (Bessant et al., 2005). In the terms used by Siebers et al. (2008) there is often a lack of 'needs pull'. This is the problem of 'we don't know what we don't know' and the difficulty of acquiring professional knowledge (Schon, 1983) in another guise. This could be related to the point made by Eisenhardt and Martin (2000), using the example of acquisitions, that there is a need for some level of initial knowledge, so that more advanced knowledge can be developed through a variety of experiences.

Our initial research has made a number of contributions in relation to the adoption and effective application of practices to contribute to the successful realization of benefits from IT in organizations. It established a framework of practices for benefits realization, which can be further developed and refined. It also supported the value of the practice 'lens' from research and practitioner perspectives. Practices appear to be a good fit with how people work and provide a good basis for sharing knowledge. This alignment with how people actually work suggests that the practices perspective has the potential to make an impact on what actually happens in organizations. Recent research by Ward et al. (2007) provides evidence of the importance of practices and their link with

IS project success. In addition, our research provided insights into the factors inhibiting the adoption of benefits-driven approaches.

IMPLICATIONS OF WORK ON DYNAMIC CAPABILITY FOR THE BENEFITS REALIZATION CAPABILITY

The benefits realization capability is the means by which an organization realizes value from IT. The capability is organization-wide, not just embedded in the IT function (Bharadwaj, 2000; Peppard and Ward, 2004; Peppard, 2007). The capability has transformational (dynamic) and operational elements (Ravichandran and Lertwongsatien, 2005). Value realization depends on fusing IT with complementary, firm-specific, human and business resources (Powell and Dent-Micallef, 1997).

The 'greatest gains come from doing the right things' (Earl and Feeny, 1994): the strategic choices that are the result of entrepreneurial alertness and activities lead to value being realized when dynamic capabilities are deployed within the business to establish new or improved substantive capabilities (Sambamurthy and Bharadwaj, 2003). The operational (substantive) element of the benefits realization capability includes the exploitation of IT to contribute to value creation as part of wider, substantive business capabilities.

The benefits practices relate to both dynamic and substantive elements of the benefits realization capability, and provide a response to the need to match the degree of codification to the velocity of markets and other factors (Eisenhardt and Martin, 2000).

In summary, key propositions from the large body of work on dynamic capabilities that relate to our work on developing the benefits realization capability of an organization include:

1. There are substantive and dynamic elements to the benefits realization capability.

2. It is organization-wide.

3. Value from the dynamic aspects of the capability depends on the choices made as to how it is applied. Making the right decisions depends on insight into possible futures and on being able to see beyond the frame of the current situation.

4. Value from IT is realized in conjunction with complementary business and human resources as part of both substantive and dynamic capabilities.

5. Practices (routines) are an important contributor to organizational capabilities. The practices that contribute to dynamic capabilities have much in common across organizations.

6. Practices can be codified to an extent, and the level of codification, which is valuable, will differ depending on the velocity of the market.

7. There are times when completely new capabilities are needed – organizations must watch out for this, as they could get stuck by their expertise in old, irrelevant ways of doing things.

8. Routines (practices) are part of a wider approach to effective working in a knowledge intensive environment. Wider factors include establishing a common language, a framework provided by rules, directives and sequencing (i.e., the formal organization of policy, structure and process) and effective teamwork, including group decision-making and problem-solving.

9. Capabilities are developed through intra- and inter-organizational learning and from learning by doing.

10. There is at least some element of a natural sequence of adoption of practices. The path of development of a benefits realization capability will have some similarities across organizations.

11. Adoption of new practices and competence development is a process of strategic change.

12. Dynamic capabilities and the changes they result in are costly, and the level of change/capability required will vary. It is not cost-effective for every part of every organization to have a high level of dynamic capability. The cost of change will, to some extent, decrease with experience.

13. Different substantive capabilities *may* need different dynamic capabilities to succeed with change (Zahra et al., p. 947).

14. As Prahalad and Hamel (1990) note, there should be more management focus on planning for the development of core competences rather than just on financial budgeting. The lack of focus on building dynamic capabilities (specifically, the benefits realization capability) is an example of organizations/management being stuck in an outdated frame/paradigm and therefore being unable to see the need for a new way of doing things.

These propositions provide a good starting-point for planning to build the benefits realization capability of an organization.

BUILDING THE CAPABILITY TO COMPETE WITH IT: LEADING THE DIGITAL BUSINESS

The project, portfolio and organizational perspectives on the competences for benefits realization outlined in this chapter provide further insight into the capability to compete with IT. Leaders in the digital business need to be able to put in place many of the practices outlined in this book to establish these competences.

Gradual adoption of practices for benefits realization with an emphasis on building skills and effective enactment of the practices is an important element of the change programme to develop the organizational capability for competing with IT. A common language (provided by clear principles for benefits realization) and a common project framework are also important. The perspective of organizational learning provides useful insights into the change programme to develop competences.

The change programme to build benefits realization competences is not following the classic 'unfreeze – change – freeze' model. The organization is moving to state of continuous change. Effectively a key goal is to build the dynamic capability of the organization. Value is realized from both the dynamic and substantive elements of the benefits realization capability (see Figure 14.3).

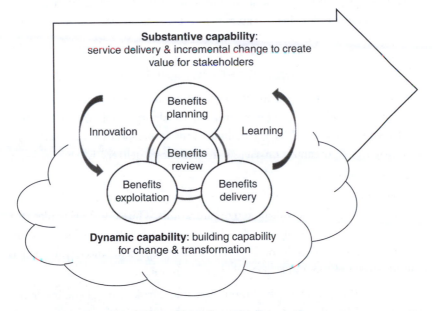

Figure 14.3 Dynamic capability and benefits realization

PRACTICES FOR BENEFITS REALIZATION

The first element of the change programme is the phased adoption of improved *practices* for benefits realization. Often the gradual introduction of new 'tools' is linked to a programme of education and the provision of guidance and coaching for those learning how to apply them.

An important finding that emerged from the research is that a range of practices, for example risk management or phased delivery, can be applied to IT solution delivery or to a benefits realization project. The shift from solution delivery to benefits realization is subtle, for example affecting who is involved and the emphasis taken. For many practices, the shift from solution delivery to benefits realization is more about the new paradigm, or mindset, than a substantial change in the actual practice. There is a potential bonus that, once the shift in perspective is made, a lot of what is already known is very valuable in the new paradigm.

PROCESS – COMMON FRAMEWORK FOR BENEFITS REALIZATION ON PROJECTS

An overall framework or process for a benefits-driven approach is also required. From our research, a simple overall framework provides a structure for projects and the basis for a shared understanding and common approach. This is important, as project teams are formed from across an organization and often across multiple organizations. Our e^{4+1} framework is a response to this need. The principles and process provide a starting-point for a common language and effective teamwork. An effective approach to the management of the portfolio of projects is also required.

PRINCIPLES – A PARADIGM SHIFT

The fundamental success factor is to recognize the real problem: that there is a need to develop a benefits realization capability. Adoption of benefits-focused approaches to IT is a 'paradigm shift' in perspective (mindset). The large majority of organizations act as if technology delivery is what makes a project successful.

Making the shift to a real focus on benefits realization is potentially a significant challenge for individuals and organizations. The explicit principles that articulate the foundation of a benefits-driven approach help to enable this shift. The principles, for example, of 'IT as an enabler' represent 'know-why', which is an important element in a major change programme.

Without this paradigm shift there is a major risk that a benefits-driven approach will be adopted as yet another 'methodology', with no real change to attitudes and without the development of a new understanding. We saw this in another organization, where the result was just painful compliance with yet another set of rules.

Gradual adoption of key practices for benefits realization, as part of a new way of working, can help contribute to this paradigm shift in perspective. Getting broad engagement in a core set of creative, collaborative practices, perhaps – stakeholder mapping, benefits mapping, and using the IT and Change Portfolio – allows people to *experience* a new approach. This experience is a valuable step towards a new perspective and a change in mindset.

Benefits realization requires high levels of skills from the people involved. As individuals and multi-disciplinary teams, they have to work effectively with each other and a very wide range of stakeholders.

Craftsmen are passionate about the job. They are also expert in using their tools to get the job done. Their expertise takes time to develop. The expert's tools are often the same as those used by the novice, but they can achieve much more.

The principles, process and practices are designed to enable effective teamwork and engagement with stakeholders as project teams build a shared language and way of working. The tools are simple and common sense, but they make a vital contribution to benefits realization. The tools embrace key aspects of leadership and teamwork, which are often discounted as 'soft skills' in approaches to projects.

Relationships are also a vital element of the competences for benefits realization (Ashurst and Hodges, 2010). The practices help to build a common language, mindset and way of working, but the importance of relationships goes much further. Leaders use their relationships and networks to get fresh insights and to get things done. Leaders build relationships to gain commitment, and energetic and enthusiastic support for change (Box 14.3).

Box 14.3   Adopting a benefits-led approach

Principles

The principles of a benefits-driven approach establish a new paradigm ('mindset').

Adherence to the new principles will require consistent and sustained communication from the leadership team.

An education programme may be a very effective way to introduce key practices and establish the principles and process. In our experience the education can provide hands-on experience to develop expertise in using specific practices and can exemplify the creative and collaborative way of working that contributes to benefits realization.

Process

An overall process or framework for a project establishes a common language and facilitates different groups working together.

In many cases it will be possible to evolve a framework for a benefits-driven approach from existing approaches in use within an organization.

Practices

Many existing organizational practices will be valuable in the new 'benefits-driven' paradigm, and other practices can be adopted from elsewhere (for example, our evolving toolkit).

Phased development of a benefits focus for existing practices and adoption of a 'toolkit' of new practices for benefits realization contribute to the development of individual skills and organizational competences.

People

Underpinning everything are the skills of individuals and multi-disciplinary teams. The toolkit supports sharing of working practices and the building of 'craft' skills.

MAKING A START

The goal is clear. The scope can be a specific project or projects within a team or across an organization. The starting-point depends on you. It usually makes sense to start small, take a phased approach and learn by doing.

First steps might be to:

- adopt a benefits-driven approach on one or two pilot projects; and/or
- carry out benefits reviews of a small number of recently completed projects.

One approach we have found valuable is to work with representatives from a number of project teams and a number of other stakeholders as a pilot group. At one organization we worked with the IT Director, his management team and representatives from five projects and other influential individuals from within and outside IT, on a programme of five one-day workshops spread over eight months. In the workshops we introduced elements of the benefits-driven toolkit, applying them there and then to the five projects. We also worked on skills for more effective stakeholder engagement and a more innovative, collaborative way of working.

It is important to see this as more than a quick win. The principles for benefits realization encapsulate a benefits 'mindset' which provides a crucial foundation for a benefits-driven approach to be successfully adopted. Developing this mindset will need sustained leadership.

Steps after the initial pilot(s) might include a benefits review of the overall project portfolio, wider education and adoption on a second group of projects. Box 14.4 gives an outline of a benefits realization plan for developing the benefits realization capability.

Box 14.4 Outline of a benefits plan for adopting a benefits-driven approach

Drivers

In an increasingly competitive business environment, product and service innovation, as well as cost reduction, depend on IT.

Currently the IT function is successful in delivering technology, but less so engaging with the business areas to focus on benefits realization.

Objectives

Establish a benefits-driven approach as 'business as usual'.

Establish a culture of continuous improvement to develop the overall benefits realization capability.

Benefits

Better selection of investment opportunities.

Faster return on investment.

Increased return on investment.

Increased ability to innovate and create value in addition to cutting costs through IT.

Increased staff energy and motivation.

Changes

Follow a consistent project framework and use a common set of tools.

Close business and IT working through multi-disciplinary teams.

Enablers

Education for project sponsors and teams.

Support for pilot adopters of benefits-driven approaches.

Clear business ownership for adoption of benefits-driven approaches.

Regular review sessions to reflect on progress and drive learning and improvement.

Broad changes at the organizational level are typically important at some point in the change programme: for example, changes to management education and progression criteria. Also the learning organization (Chapter 5) provides a framework for building momentum following initial changes.

DEVELOPING THE MATURITY OF THE BENEFITS REALIZATION CAPABILITY

Capability frameworks, such as IT-CMF, typically have a number of levels of maturity. An organization carries out an assessment to determine its current level of maturity (often on a 1–5 scale), considers the maturity levels required for different capabilities and then plans a change programme to deliver the improvement. For a large organization moving up a maturity level, say from 2 to 3, is often a significant effort over 18–24 months. A key step at each stage is adoption of relevant practices.

An important goal of current research is to establish 'playbooks' to help guide organizations at different maturity levels to move forward.

BREAKING OUT OF 'CATCH-22'

In our research we identified many organizations struggling and failing to improve their capability for benefits realization. We needed to get a better understanding of the underlying issues.

The fact that many organizations have a limited benefits realization capability (i.e., a low maturity in terms of their ability to realize benefits from investments in organizational change), means that they will struggle to improve, at least at the early stages. This is because developing the benefits realization capability is itself an organizational change, and that is what they are not good at. Essentially that's what having a limited benefits realization capability means. Organizations are stuck in a classic 'Catch-22' situation.

> **Catch-22 of benefits realization**. The organization is not good at benefits realization. Benefits realization is essentially about leading organizational change. Developing the benefits realization capability is itself a complex organizational change. You need to change to get better at change!

> **Catch-22 – another example** from the UK: to work as a professional actor you need a union membership card from the actors' trade union. To become a member of the union you need to be working as a professional actor. As a newcomer, how do you break into this world?

Breaking out of Catch-22 needs vision and determination, and a willingness to take small steps. As benefits approaches are adopted on specific projects, a pool of people with new knowledge and expertise develops, and this can provide the catalyst for wider development of the benefits realization capability (see the case study reported in Ashurst, 2012); in effect, there is an opportunity for a 'flywheel' effect (Collins, 2001).

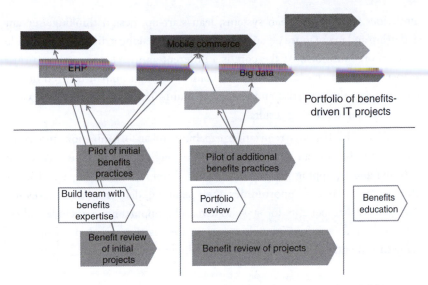

Capability development programme: interlinked with core project portfolio

Figure 14.4 Breaking out of Catch-22

Figure 14.4 illustrates how to break out of Catch-22. It is how the change programme illustrated in Figure 14.1 was brought to life. Essentially the individual change projects and programmes have embedded within them objectives to develop the overall benefits realization capability. This includes broadening and deepening the capability of leaders of change, as well as gradually testing out and embedding practices for benefits realization. The focus remains on delivery of benefits for the customer and organization, but all the time the underlying dynamic and benefits realization capability evolves.

FINAL COMMENTS

It's a digital world, and to succeed we need digital literacy and digital leaders of digital business. We've gone beyond business and IT strategies to digital business strategy. Has anything really changed, or is it all another wave of hype?

My view is that there is a major opportunity for very many organizations. The speed of change has certainly increased, and the barriers to test out new ideas and technologies are much lower than they were, bringing the opportunity for speed, experimentation and learning. There is also a groundswell of new approaches to managing which tackle some of the same core issues. We see similarities across agile, lean systems, lean start-up, design thinking, servant leadership and many more perspectives, which are making a difference in a wide range of organizations. At the core is a different approach to people – a shift to focusing on the customer and stakeholders through human-centred design and engaging the expertise and energy of multi-disciplinary teams and wider stakeholders in delivering results.

Building the benefits realization capability of an organization and competing with IT are an important thread through this cauldron. It's about inspiring and equipping people all across an organization to be part of identifying and developing opportunities, then planning, delivering and harvesting change to realize benefits for stakeholders. The opportunities include radical innovation and transformational change as well as the cumulative impact of many incremental changes. It is about developing agents of change across the organization.

I think that Brynjolfsson and Saunders (2009) are right and that the leaders, the more effective organizations, are pulling further away from the rest. There is clearly a learning curve, and there is a risk that others will find it hard to close the gap. What works is fairly clear: the challenge is to close the 'knowing–doing gap' in your organization (team, department, business unit).

What are the next steps you will take to make a difference?

TAKING IT FURTHER

FURTHER READING AND RESOURCES

Austin, Robert D., Nolan, Richard and O'Donnell, Shannon (2009) *The Adventures of an IT Leader*, Boston: Harvard Business Press.

Told as a story, this book provides an excellent insight into issues of IT leadership and competing with IT.

Ashurst, C. and Hodges, J. (2010) Exploring Business Transformation: The Challenges of Developing a Benefits Realization Capability. *Journal of Change Management*, Vol. 10 (2): 217–237.

TALKING POINTS

Use these questions to help reflect on this chapter and explore the challenges of putting the ideas into practice:

1. Are the principles and practices discussed in the book really about benefits from IT, or is this really a more general approach to change?

2. What can you learn from experience – yours or your organization's – about the challenges of developing the benefits realization capability of an organization? Try and focus on specific experience and evidence.

3. How is the dynamic capability represented in your organizational strategy? Is capability development a priority?

4. Who provides leadership for the development of the benefits realization or dynamic capability?

5. What are the implications for the competences required from managers across the organization?

6. Contrast different types of change: from local and incremental to radical, innovative and organization-wide. How do the practices and capabilities required differ?

7. Why is capability development 'path-dependent'?

8. How can you facilitate/encourage a mindset shift (for example, from technology delivery to benefits realization) as part of capability development?

9. What are the opportunities and next steps to develop the benefits realization capability in your organization at a project level?

10. How can you ensure projects deliver the intended benefits and also make a contribution to the development of the overall benefits realization capability? What would be the implications for how you approach a project?

11. What are the opportunities and next steps to develop the benefits realization capability in your organization at the portfolio level?

12. What are the opportunities and next steps to develop the benefits realization capability in your organization at an organizational level?

13. How would you make a start in developing the benefits realization capability? What can you do?

14. What is the role of business leaders in benefits realization and capability development?

KEY DEBATES

Taking a longer view

Given the short-term nature of performance targets and the rapid movement of successful and senior managers from job to job within and between organizations, a focus on the longer-term issues of capability development is never going to be a priority. It's fine in theory, but in practice it is just not going to happen.

What do you think? What is your experience?

How can we respond to the pressures for short-termism?

CASE STUDY 14.1

The case illustrates a journey of business transformation. Also consider the development of the benefits realization (transformation/dynamic) capability.

Journal of Information Technology Teaching Cases, Vol. 4 (2014): 20–26.

From products to product-service systems: IT-driven transformation of a medical equipment manufacturer

Jens Fähling, Felix Köbler, Jan Marco Leimeister and Helmut Krcmar

Meditec is a German manufacturer of instruments for surgeries. The company is quality leader in this sector and supplies many German and international hospitals. However, the opportunities for differentiation against competitors decrease continuously. New competitors from emerging markets are challenging the market position of established companies in this industry. Meditec is therefore forced to change its strategy and business model in order to survive in this novel competitive environment. The management of Meditec has decided to shift from being a pure product manufacturer to being a customer-centric solution provider. This transformation requires the development of new processes, competencies and capabilities – especially with respect to IT and IT services. This teaching case helps in understanding the role of IT in product-service systems (PSS) and PSS-based business models. Therefore the case illustrates why IT is necessary to establish a PSS-based business model and why a customer-centric view is important for this kind of business model.

REFERENCES

Ambrosini, V. and Bowman, C. (2009) What Are Dynamic Capabilities and Are They a Useful Construct in Strategic Management? *International Journal of Management Reviews*, Vol. 11 (1): 29–50.

Amit, R. and Schoemaker, P.J.H. (1993) Strategic Assets and Organizational Rent. *Strategic Management Journal*, Vol. 14: 33–46.

Ashurst, C. (2012) *Benefits Realization from Information Technology*, Basingstoke: Palgrave Macmillan.

Ashurst, C. and Hodges, J. (2010) Exploring Business Transformation: The Challenges of Developing a Benefits Realization Capability. *Journal of Change Management*, Vol.10 (2): 217–237.

Ashurst, C., Doherty, N. and Peppard, J. (2008) Improving the Impact of IT Development Projects: The Benefits Realization Capability Model. *European Journal of Information Systems*, Vol. 17: 352–370.

Augier, M. and Teece, D. (2008) Strategy as Evolution with Design: Dynamic Capabilities and the Design and Evolution of the Business Enterprise. *Organization Studies*, Vol. 29: 1187–1208.

B.C.S. (2004) *The Challenges of Complex IT Projects*, British Computer Society

Bessant, J., Phelps, B. and Adams, R. (2005) External Knowledge: A Review of the Literature Addressing the Role of External Knowledge and Expertise at Key Stages of Business Growth and Development: Final Report, *Advanced Institute of Management*.

Bharadwaj, A. (2000) A Resource-Based Perspective on Information Technology Capability and Firm Performance: An Empirical Investigation. *MIS Quarterly*, Vol. 21 (1): 169–196.

Bohn, R.E. (1994) Measuring and Managing Technological Knowledge. *MIT Sloan Management Review*, Fall: 61–73.

Bowman, C. and Ambrosini, V. (2003) How the Resource-Based and the Dynamic Capability Views of the Firm Inform Competitive and Corporate Level Strategy. *British Journal of Management*, Vol. 14: 289–303.

Brynjolfsson, E. and Saunders, A. (2009) *Wired for Innovation: How Information-Technology Is Reshaping the Economy*, MIT Press, Boston.

Collins, J. (2001) *Good to Great*, Random House Business, London.

Earl, M. and Feeny, D. (1994) Is Your CIO Adding Value? *Sloan Management Review*, Spring 1994, Vol. 35 (3): 11–20.

Earl, M. and Feeny, D. (2000) How to Be a CEO for the Information Age. *Sloan Management Review*, Winter 2000, Vol. 41 (2): 11–23.

Eisenhardt, K. and Martin J. (2000) Dynamic Capabilities: What Are They? *Strategic Management Journal*, Vol. 21: 1105–1121.

Feeny, D. and Willcocks, L. (1998a) Re-Designing the IS Function around Core Capabilities. *Long Range Planning*, Vol. 31 (3): 354–367.

Feeny, D. and Willcocks, L. (1998b) Core Capabilities for Exploiting Information Technology. *Sloan Management Review*, Spring 1998, Vol. 39 (3): 9–21.

Grant, R. (1996a) Toward a Knowledge-Based Theory of the Firm. *Strategic Management Journal*, Vol. 17: 109–122.

Grant, R. (1996b) Prospering in Dynamically Competitive Environments: Organizational Capability as Knowledge Integration. *Organization Science*, Vol. 7: 375–387.

Leseure, M., Birdi, K., Bauer, J., Denyer, D. and Neely, A. (2004) Adoption of Promising Practice: A Systematic Review of the Literature. *Advanced Institute of Management*.

Lockett, A. (2005) Edith Penrose's Legacy to the Resource-Based View. *Managerial and Decision Economics*, Vol. 26: 83–98.

Marchand, D.A., Kettinger, W.J. and Rollins, J.D. (2000) Information Orientation: People Technology and the Bottom Line. *MIT Sloan Management Review*, Summer 2000, Vol. 41 (4): 69–80.

Melville, N., Kraemer, K. and Gurbaxani, V. (2004) Information Technology and Organizational Performance: An Integrative Model of IT Business Value. *MIS Quarterly*, Vol. 28 (2): 283–332.

Peppard, J. (2007) The Conundrum of IT Management. *European Journal of Information Systems*, Vol. 16: 336–345.

Peppard, J. and Ward, J. (2004) Beyond Strategic Information Systems: Towards an IS Capability. *Journal of Strategic Information Systems*, Vol. 13: 167–194.

Powell, M. and Dent-Micallef, A. (1997) Information Technology as Competitive Advantage: The Role of Human, Business, and Technology Resources. *Strategic Management Journal*, Vol. 18 (5): 375–405.

Prahalad, C.K. and Hamel, G. (1990) The Core Competencies of the Corporation. *Harvard Business Review*, Vol. 68 (3): 79–91.

Ravichandran, T. and Lertwongsatien, C. (2005) Effect of Information Systems Resources and Capabilities on Firm Performance: A Resource-Based Perspective. *Journal of Management Information Systems*, Vol. 21 (4): 237–327.

Ross, J. (2003) Creating a Strategic IT Architecture Competency: Learning in Stages. *MISQ Executive*, Vol. 2 (1): 31–43.

Sambamurthy, V. and Bharadwaj, A. (2003) Shaping Agility through Digital Options: Reconceptualizing the Role of Information Technology in Contemporary Firms. *MIS Quarterly*, Vol. 27 (2): 237–263.

Schon, D (1983) *The Reflective Practitioner: How Professionals Think in Action*, New York: Basic Books.

Siebers, P., Battisiti, G., Celia, H., Clegg, C.W., Fu, X., De Hoyos, R., Iona, A., Petrescu, A. and Peixoto, A. (2008) Enhancing Productivity: The Role of Management Practices, *AIM Research Working Paper Series*.

Srivastava, R., Fahey, L. and Christensen, H. (2001) The Resource-Based View and Marketing: The Role of Market-Based Assets in Gaining Competitive Advantage. *Journal of Management*, Vol. 27 (6): 777–802.

Teece, D. (2007) Explicating Dynamic Capabilities: The Nature and Microfoundations of (Sustainable) Enterprise Performance. *Strategic Management Journal*, Vol. 28 (13): 1319–1350.

Teece, D., Pisano, G. and Shuen, A. (1997) Dynamic Capabilities and Strategic Management. *Strategic Management Journal*, Vol. 18 (7): 509–533.

Ward, J. and Daniel, E. (2006) *Benefits Management*, Chichester: John Wiley and Sons.

Ward, J. and Peppard, J. (2002) *Strategic Planning for Information Systems*, 3rd edition, Chichester: John Wiley and Sons.

Ward, J., De Hertogh, S. and Viaene, S. (2007) Managing Benefits from IS/IT Investments: An Empirical Investigation into Current Practice. 40th Annual Hawaii International Conference on System Sciences.

Weill, P. and Ross, J. (2009) *IT Savvy: What Top Executives Must Know to Go from Pain to Gain*, Boston: Harvard Business School Press.

Zahra, S., Sapienza, J. and Davidsson, P. (2006) Entrepreneurship and Dynamic Capabilities: A Review, Model and Research Agenda. *Journal of Management Studies*, Vol. 42 (4): 917–955.

Zollo, M. and Winter, S. (2002) Deliberate Learning and the Evolution of Dynamic Capabilities. *Organization Science*, Vol. 13 (3): 339–351.

INDEX

CONTENTS

PREFACE

This approach to understanding and reducing emotional distress in family caregivers of older relatives with dementia was developed over the past 9 years at the Tingstad Older Adult Counseling Center and the Alzheimer's Disease Research Center (a National Institute on Aging [NIA] funded research center, Caleb Finch, principal investigator [PI]) at the University of Southern California (USC) Andrus Gerontology Center. As is the case in any long-term research and development program, a large number of people have contributed to the work that is reported in this volume.

In 1989, I received a grant from the Robert Ellis Simon Foundation which funded the first version of caregiving interventions that eventually developed into the stress reduction training program. In that first year, we worked with caregivers in groups and used an approach that focused on education about dementing illnesses (Alzheimer's disease, vascular dementias, and so forth) and discussed problem-solving strategies as well as use of relaxation training and other stress reduction strategies.

At around the same time, Hortense Tingstad (whose endowment has supported the continued operation of the Tingstad Older Adult Counseling Center) was lending enthusiastic support to the development of stress reduction strategies over lunch in the tearoom at the old Bullock's Wilshire in Los Angeles and during early morning phone calls. Ms. Tingstad had benefitted from a short stress reduction treatment from a psychologist at her health maintenance organization (HMO) during an early phase of caring for her husband.

Also about the same time, stress and coping models began to emerge as the dominant conceptual paradigm for thinking about outcomes of caregiving, including caregivers' emotional distress. Our current thinking about stress and coping models for caregiver distress is outlined in chapter 1. This thinking is influenced largely by Folkman and Lazarus's theoretical models of stress and coping as well as by the work of Leonard Pearlin and of Peter Vitaliano.

In 1989–1990, we received a budget augmentation from the NIA to USC's Alzheimer's Disease Research Center, which was used to fund additional psychoeducational groups for caregivers and to develop manuals and videotapes for problem-solving training and stress reduction training. Both approaches included education about dementia, education about community resources, and sections on using social support wisely. The problem-solving approach follows the strategies outlined in Zarit, Orr, and Zarit's *The Hidden Victims of Alzheimer's Disease: Families Under Stress* (1985). It focuses primarily on teaching caregivers problem-solving skills and behavioral techniques to reduce problems with the care recipient which, in turn, should reduce caregivers' distress. The stress reduction manual contained the elements of the approach described here: relaxation training, scheduling of relaxing events, and cognitive restructuring. As described in chapters 4 and 6, relaxation training and cognitive restructuring are common elements of cognitive behavioral therapy and have been used widely for stress reduction in other populations by, among others, Donald Meichenbaum and Albert Ellis. The relaxing events notion was directly adapted from the pleasant events component of Peter Lewinsohn's behavioral therapy for depression (see chapter 5). These techniques are designed to directly reduce the caregiver's emotional distress. Anne Katz headed up the development of these manuals, with substantial assistance from Jacque Lehn, Marie Liston, Jodi Olshevski, Susan Thurgood, Richard Wurster, Mark Beers, Richard A. Lehn, Richard M. Lehn, and Brad Williams.

From late 1989 through 1992, we were funded by the Alzheimer's Disease Research Program of the California Department of Health Services (the "tax checkoff" monies) to do research on the stress and coping model of caregiving and to compare the problem-solving therapy and stress reduction training approaches. Jodi Olshevski, then a student in the master's degree program in gerontology at USC and Steven Lutzky, then a doctoral student in gerontology at USC, were the key research assistants in that project. At this point, we switched to individual stress reduction training, with most of the training being in the caregivers' homes. The group training sessions in 1989 had not proven to be cost-effective for us because groups were hard to arrange and tended to disband quickly if one or two members became ill, placed their relatives, or took a vacation. We also came to realize that recruiting caregivers who could leave the relative with dementia at home and come to a group every week tended to screen out caregivers of relatives with more severe impairments and caregivers who were more seriously distressed—the very people that we wanted to interview and to help.

At the end of this project, we evaluated the outcomes of the two approaches and also reflected on our experiences with the two types of training. The quantitative evaluation results are summarized in chapter 7. Although this clearly was a small, pilot study, we felt that the results favored stress reduction training. Our trainers unanimously reported that caregivers preferred the stress reduction approach and seemed to find it more helpful. There were aspects of this version of the training that we felt needed revision and improvement. A key issue was the feeling that we were trying to cover too much material in too short a time and that there was only limited time to follow up with the caregivers to see if they were regularly using the interventions and to identify problems that came up in using these strategies so that they could be individualized for each caregiver's unique situation and personal needs.

We then decided to delete education about dementing illnesses in order to leave more time to focus on the stress reduction interventions. In our evaluations of this pilot project, knowledge about dementia was uncorrelated with distress and did not change much during the training. Our observation was that most caregivers already knew a lot about dementing illnesses. When they did not, it was easy to give them information to read or to refer them to educational events in the community. We also found that, after a certain basic orientation to the illness, more information about dementia is not necessarily helpful in terms of reducing distress.

We also put the information about community resources "outside of" the stress reduction training sessions. The issue here is that this background information is needed by stress reduction trainers so that they can make accurate referrals as needed for caregivers' specific problems. However, it is unnecessary to educate each individual caregiver about the full range of community resources, many of which will not be relevant. Chapter 8 provides an overview of typical community resources for caregiving families. We have tried to make it as general as possible, but services, resources, and laws vary from state to state and often from community to community. As I have argued elsewhere about psychotherapy with older adults (Knight, 1996), it is necessary to understand the context of community services for frail older people, and especially for adults with dementia and their families, in order to perform effective psychological interventions.

These changes produced a version of stress reduction training which essentially is focused entirely on the three change techniques, beginning with teaching caregivers to monitor their stress levels (as described in chapter 3). Monitoring stress is key to understanding the sources of stress and of relaxation and to help the caregiver notice the small, gradual changes that are typical during the training. As described in chapter 3, stress monitoring itself sometimes can reduce perceived stress, especially by disproving the perception that one is stressed to the same extent all of the time.

By focusing on fewer techniques, more time is available to work with the caregivers to be sure that they use the techniques at home and to analyze and solve problems that arise in using the techniques in the individual situation of the specific caregiver. This approach has been used in our project under the direction of Donna Benton at the Alzheimer's Disease Research Center since 1994. As this volume goes to press, we are preparing to analyze the data from this second pilot study.

Since 1994, we also have become increasingly interested in the influence of ethnicity and of cultural values on caregivers' stress and coping strategies. Chapter 2, written by T. J. McCallum who presently is a doctoral candidate in clinical psychology and aging at USC, summarizes our thinking about ethnic issues, especially with regard to African American caregivers. While still in very early stages of development, we expect that theories of caregiving and interventions to help caregivers (including this one) will need to be adapted to work with different ethnic groups and in other nations.

There are many other people who deserve recognition for contributing to this project. Dozens of graduate and undergraduate students in gerontology, clinical psychology, and social work have worked on the stress reduction project at one time or another since 1989. They drove all over Los Angeles County and sometimes into Orange and Ventura Counties to interview or to teach stress reduction training. And, of course, the caregivers themselves deserve credit for sharing their lives, caregiving experiences, and perceptions of their own stress and coping.

The stress reduction training program for caregivers is still a work in progress. The experience of doing the revised version (the model presented in this volume) generally has seemed positive to us. We have had fewer dropouts and fewer times when we have thought the caregivers have not been applying the techniques in their daily lives, and both trainers and caregivers have seemed more satisfied. Of course, analyzing the data from this second pilot study may lead to more revisions. Before we truly can be confident in recommending the use of this approach, larger scale intervention research is needed.

In the meantime, we offer stress reduction training for caregivers as a developing approach that is strongly grounded in research and theory on caregiving within the stress and coping model and which uses cognitive behavioral techniques that are strongly grounded in research on stress reduction in other populations.

Bob G. Knight

Stress and Coping Models of Caregiving Distress

Demographic trends in the United States, as in other industrialized countries, show an increase in the relative percentage and absolute numbers of the older population (65+ years old). In 1900, 4% of the population was age 65 or older, whereas by 1990, the percentage had grown to 12.5% (U.S. Bureau of the Census, 1995). In addition, the oldest old segment of the population (85+ years old) will increase dramatically before the year 2000 (National Institute on Aging, 1987). This projection will have several consequences on society, not only in economic terms, but also in the composition of society and in the roles expectation related to the care of older people.

According to Melcher (1988), the increase in life expectancy, the aging of the population, and the advances in medical technology and medicine will lead to an increase in the number of frail older people who will require care from their family or from society. Does the increase in life expectancy imply a higher percentage of disease among the oldest segment of the population? According to Peterson (1994), as a person ages, his or her biological and physiological systems deteriorate. Peterson postulated possible interactions between the aging process and disease; disease is more likely to occur with

This chapter, and especially the introduction to it, was written with the assistance of Elena Fernandez. It draws upon the introduction to her master's thesis in gerontology at USC's Leonard Davis School of Gerontology. Ms. Fernandez is currently a doctoral student in clinical psychology at the Universidad de Barcelona (Catalonia, Spain).

1

older age. On the other hand, he also supported the premise that aging is not equivalent to disease. Crimmins, Saito, and Ingegneri (1989) has argued that the average period of frailty has remained constant, at about 3 years before death, as life expectancy has increased. Taking as an example the probability of dementia, George, Blazer, Winfield-Laird, Leaf, and Fischbach (1988) estimated the prevalence of mild cognitive impairment at 13% for persons age 65 to 74, increasing to 24% for those age 85 or older.

As the percentage of frail and dependent older people increases, the number of families involved in the care of this segment of the population also increases. Research has found that almost half of older people live with their spouse, while about 15% live with a nonspousal relative (Chappel, 1991). Most help is thought to be provided by unpaid caregivers who are family members and friends. Twenty-nine percent are adult daughters, 23% wives, 12.5% husbands, 8.5% sons, and 27% other relatives (such as siblings or grandchildren) and nonrelatives including sons-in-law or daughters-in-law (Finucane & Burton, 1994).

Family caregivers perform the first line of care for frail older people by providing needed services at home, usually for several years before seeking institutional care (Horowitz, 1985). In the United States, a large number of families take on the responsibility of a family member with a chronic or deteriorating disability or disease. But, what is a family caregiver? Family caregivers can be defined in several ways. Based on the American Association of Retired Persons (AARP) and the Travelers Companies Foundations survey (1988), *caregivers* are defined as individuals who provide unpaid assistance, for at least two instrumental activities of daily living or one activity of daily living within 12 months to a person age 50 or older. This definition is somewhat restrictive, however. Caring for someone includes all types of care—from giving companionship to the patient to providing 24 hours of nursing care. A person may be considered the primary family caregiver because he or she has the *responsibility* to provide or obtain proper care or services for the patient. Such objective definitions do not capture the process by which individuals come to think of themselves as caregivers. We have found that some family members provide a lot of care without having identified themselves as caregivers, whereas others have come to see themselves as highly burdened caregivers while doing little besides worrying about a parent. The system of professional services, self-help groups, and advocacy groups for caregivers undoubtedly plays a role in this labeling process.

In most of the families studied, a primary caregiver has been identified (Lebowitz & Light, 1993). In the White U.S. caregivers who have been the primary focus of research so far, the primary caregiver has been selected according to a hierarchy. If available, the first line of defense is a spouse, then a daughter, and then a daughter-in-law (Gatz, Bengtson, & Blum, 1990; Horowitz, 1985). This selection hierarchy clearly is culturally determined.

In Japan and Korea, the oldest son is responsible for his parents, with the personal care being performed by his wife (Choi, 1993; Sung, 1992). In African American families, spousal caregivers are less common, with care more frequently being provided by children and by extended family or fictive kin (see chapter 2 for more on this point). Aranda and Knight (1997) speculated that, in some other cultures (e.g., U.S. Latinos), it may be more appropriate to think of the family system as the caregiving unit. In other words, the whole notion of primary caregiver rather than shared caregiving responsibility may be culture dependent.

☐ Stress and Coping Models

The simplest model of caregiving distress is to think that caregiving always is stressful, that it is stressful because caregiving is hard work, and that caregiving distress follows a "wear and tear" model. That is, the longer caregiving goes on, the more stressful it becomes. Research has suggested that none of these statements are true. These discoveries have then led to thinking of caregiving in a more complex and more accurate way.

Emotional Distress

In this section, we examine emotional distress outcomes for caregivers and then discuss the less frequently studied links of caregiving stress to perceived physical health and to more objective health measures.

There are estimates that symptoms of emotional distress appear in 85% of caregivers (Rabins, Mace, & Lucas, 1982) and that depressive symptoms appear in over 40% (Cohen et al., 1990; Haley, Levine, Brown, Berry, & Hughes, 1987). Gallagher, Rose, Rivera, and Lovett (1989) used the Schedule for Affective Disorders and Schizophrenia (SADS) interview schedule to diagnose affective disorders in caregivers. Dura, Stukenberg, and Kiecolt-Glaser (1991) used the Diagnostic Interview Schedule (DIS) to diagnose affective and anxiety disorders in caregivers. Caregivers reported higher levels of depression and anxiety than noncaregiver comparison samples. The evidence for higher than normal levels of emotional distress outcomes, including syndromal depression and anxiety seems quite clear, at least for White U.S. caregivers.

However, it is important to note that not all caregivers become emotionally distressed. Most research has been done on caregivers who have been seeking help. Even among help seekers, most caregivers have not reported feeling severely emotionally distressed. When non–help-seeking caregivers have been interviewed, they have shown considerably lower rates of depression and other types of distress. For example, Gallagher et al. (1989) found that about half of help seekers, but only about one in five non–help seekers, were depressed. This selection bias is a common problem in clinical research of all kinds (medical and psychosocial) and simply reflects the reality that people seek help when they are feeling bad. The studies of help-seeking caregivers are valuable in understanding other help-seeking caregivers, but they are not representative of all caregivers, many of whom seem to be doing reasonably well.

Researchers also have found evidence that caregiving can lead to higher levels of life satisfaction (Motenko, 1989). From national estimates in 1987, almost three fourths of all caregivers interviewed reported that the caregiving role made them feel useful, and that it contributed to their self-worth (Schulz, Visintainer, & Williamson, 1990; U.S. House of Representatives, Select Committee on Aging, 1987). To complicate the matter further, some researchers, such as Lawton and his colleagues (Lawton, Moss, Kleban, Glicksman, & Rovine, 1991) reported that caregiving satisfaction and caregiving burden sometimes go hand in hand. That is, caregiving can be both positive and negative at the same time.

Summary

Caregiving appears to operate as a form of chronic stress that makes caregivers more susceptible to emotional distress and to clinical disorders such as depression and anxiety. Caregiving also has a positive dimension, which sometimes is mixed with the emotional distress. One issue, as yet not resolved by research, is whether caregivers develop specific emotional reactions (depression, anxiety, anger) or whether all of these emotions are a part of a more general emotional distress response as occurs with other life stress reactions (Stephens & Hobfoll, 1990). Hooker and her colleagues (Hooker, Monahan, Bowman, Frazier, & Shifren, 1998; Hooker, Monahan, Shifren, & Hutchinson, 1992) have modeled the emotional outcomes of caregiving as a single factor, a result which favors the general distress model and which we have replicated in our research (Fox, Knight, & Chou, 1997). This result would provide theoretical support for psychological interventions that are aimed at stress reactions in general over those aimed at specific emotions.

In our psychoeducational intervention strategies, we attempt to directly reduce the emotional distress reaction by the use of progressive relaxation training (also a key element in Meichenbaum's *Stress Inoculation Training*, 1985) and by increasing relaxing events in the caregiver's life, a strategy adapted from the use of pleasant events in Lewinsohn, Munoz, Youngren, and Zeiss's (1986) intervention for depression. Both of these interventions help to increase positive affect and to decrease negative affect.

Perceived Physical Health

Although less clearly established than emotional distress outcomes, caregivers generally have reported that their perception of their own health is lower than that reported by appropriate matched controls or by population norms for age- and gender-matched groups. Stone, Cafferata, and Sangl (1987) found that caregivers in the Informal Caregivers Survey perceived their health as being worse than did age peers in the U.S. population. Lower perceived health ratings also have been reported by other researchers, including Baumgarten, Battista, Infante-Rivard, Hanley, Becker, and Gauthier (Canada; 1992) and Grafstrom, Fratiglioni, Sandman, and Winblad (Sweden; 1992). Snyder and Keefe (1985) reported that 70% of caregivers in their sample attributed declines in physical health to caregiving. Chenoweth and Spencer (1986) found that 21% of caregivers in their sample reported ill health as a primary reason for institutionalizing a relative with dementia. As discussed by Schulz, O'Brien, Bookwala, and Fleissner (1995), perceived physical health in caregivers seems to be determined by risk factors that are similar to those of the larger population (e.g., lower income, high psychological distress, low social support). The factors specific to caregiving seem to be different than those for emotional distress: cognitive impairment in the recipient rather than behavior problems and a much less clear role for the appraisal of caregiving as burdensome (Schulz et al., 1995).

The connection between perceived physical health and objective health outcomes (such as diseases) is not entirely clear. On the one hand, perceived physical health is clearly related to health status, functional ability, and mortality in longitudinal studies (George, 1996). On the other hand, perceived physical health also is related to depression, the personality factor neuroticism, and to other psychological variables (e.g., Hooker et al., 1992, 1998). The perception of physical health is almost certainly influenced both by actual physical health and by psychological distress.

Objective Health Measures

As noted in two extensive reviews by Schulz and his colleagues (Schulz et al., 1990, 1995), objective reports of caregiver health have been far less clear in showing a health difference. Symptom checklists for physical health, number of diseases, medication use, and medical utilization all have shown tremendous variability across samples, with at least as many nonsignificant differences reported as significant ones. Schulz et al. (1990) noted that the extensive use of convenience samples and the likelihood of selection pressures favoring inclusion of healthy caregivers (both because many caregivers are married and married persons are healthier and because health is a factor in becoming and remaining a caregiver as well as in willingness to participate in research) make the interpretation of this null result inconclusive. At present, the clearest result with regard to objective physical health effects is that aspects of immunological functioning are impaired in caregivers and that this leads to higher levels of respiratory infections (Kiecolt-Glaser, Dura, Speicher, & Trask, 1991; Kiecolt-Glaser et al., 1987).

Summary

In short, caregivers are at higher risk of emotional distress, perceive their health as being impaired, and experience changes in immune functioning and a higher prevalence of infectious diseases. As noted above, not all caregivers experience these problems and some people seem to find caregiving a positive experience. If not all caregivers become distressed, and if some feel good about caregiving, then the obvious question for researchers, professionals, and caregivers is, What makes the difference? In what follows, we explore common ideas about why caregiving would be stressful for at least some caregivers, including that caregiving is hard work and therefore stressful and that certain phases of the course of caregiving are stressful, and return to the stress and coping model with its focus on how caregivers' appraise the experience of caregiving.

☐ Is Caregiving Stressful Because It Is Hard Work?

The simplest way of thinking about the connection between stressors and distress reactions is to expect that distress is worse when the stressors are worse. This does not seem to be the case for caregiving. Total caregiving workload, the care receiver's level of illness or disability, and other objective measures of caregiving stressors are not clearly or strongly related to the caregiver's perception of caregiving as burdensome or to health and mental health outcomes. There are a few exceptions. For White U.S. caregivers, the number of behavior problems in the care receiver usually is related to mental health outcomes, and the level of memory impairment often is related to perceived physical health outcomes (see Schulz et al., 1995). Functional disability, number of hours spent caregiving, duration of illness, number of tasks performed for the care recipient, and other objective measures generally are independent of how the caregiver feels. While there is limited cross-cultural evidence, it appears that these findings may be different for other ethnic groups (see chapter 2).

As will be seen in the more detailed discussion of stress and coping models below, this finding is not uncommon in psychological research on stress and its outcomes. It is not so much the objective stressors which we face, but our interpretation of them and the resources which we have for dealing with stressors that determine our health and mental health reactions.

☐ The Course of Caregiving Distress

As we suggested above, the most common view is that caregiving should get worse as time goes on. This view is especially compelling when the disease process is chronic and progressive (like most dementing illnesses). However, it is far from clear that this is the case. Haley and Pardo (1989) suggested that caregiving may be most stressful in the middle period of a dementing illness, which is the time with the highest frequency of behavior problems (wandering, suspiciousness, anger, and so forth). Gatz, Bengtson, and Blum (1990) discussed the different potential paths of caregiving distress over time and added another: Caregiving could be like grieving, in which the highest level of distress is at the beginning when the caregiver recognizes the problem and begins to make changes in life to allow for caregiving. Once this adjustment occurs, caregiving could get better over time, because caregivers get better at the job of caregiving. These observations of time courses for caregiving distress, which depart from the wear and tear model, call attention to differing aspects of the caregiving experience that could be experienced as stressful: specific types of problems in caring or adjusting to the diagnosis of the care recipient and to the tasks of caregiving. The focus on what is experienced as stressful about caregiving takes us to the stress and coping model, with its emphasis on the appraisal of experiences as stressful.

☐ Stress and Coping Models and the Intervention Presented in This Volume

The understanding of caregiver distress is based on the stress and coping theory developed by Lazarus and Folkman and their colleagues (Folkman, Lazarus, Pimley, & Novacek, 1987; Lazarus & Folkman, 1984). In general, stress and coping models include the following categories of variables: (a) context variables such as gender, age, socioeconomic status, caregiving history, and relationship of the caregiver to the patient; (b) demands on the caregiver: objective stressors or objective burden; (c) the caregiver's appraisal of demands as stressful or satisfying: subjective caregiver burden; (d) the potential mediators between appraisal and outcomes: coping styles and social support; and (e) the consequences of caregiving demands: emotional distress and health outcomes. (See Figure 1-1.)

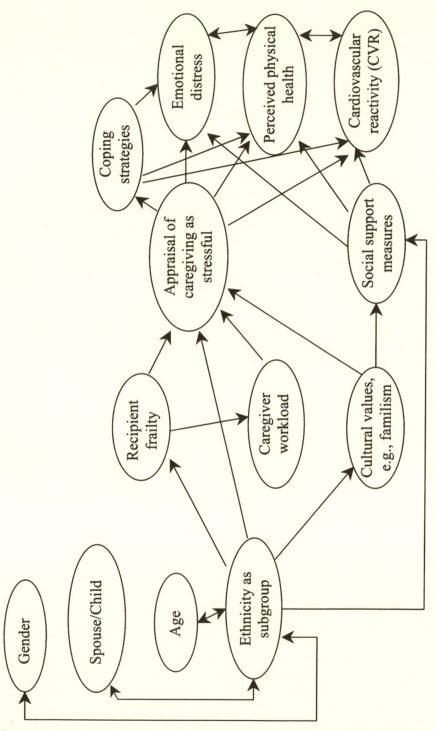

FIGURE 1-1. Sociocultural stress and coping model.

Appraisal of Stressors

A key step in the stress and coping model is appraisal of the situation as stressful or not stressful. Some caregivers obviously appraise (or perceive) caregiving to be highly stressful, whereas others, as discussed above, find it a challenge in a positive sense or even find it enjoyable. Why this is so for different individuals may not always be clear. Cultural values and beliefs likely play a role. Aranda and Knight (1997) argued that the finding that African American caregivers often report lower levels of burden may be due to cultural differences, such as a greater emphasis on family rather than on individuality. In research by Hooker et al. (1998) and in our research, the personality factor neuroticism has been shown to play a role in influencing the appraisal of caregiving as stressful. Individuals high in neuroticism tend to experience negative emotions in response to life stresses, to focus more on their internal reactions, and to often use ineffective coping strategies like avoidance coping (see section below on coping).

Regardless of the reason, this aspect may be changeable, within realistic limits. Ellis (1962; specifically applied to stress reduction in Ellis, Gordon, Neenan, & Palmer, 1997), the originator of a type of cognitive therapy called rational emotive therapy, argued that much emotional distress comes from unrealistically negative appraisals of stressful situations. That is, a person looks at a bad situation and perceives it as a hopeless catastrophe. This also is likely to be true for some caregivers. Many caregiving stressors are undeniably bad (including the fact of a relative with dementia), but caregivers may be able to reduce distress by changing the thoughts that are repeated to themselves about the caregiving and about the illness (see chapter 6).

The relationship of self-talk to stress is also a key component of Stress Inoculation Training as developed by Meichenbaum (1985). Modifying what people say to themselves about objective stressors changes their response to the stress situation. Meichenbaum's approach to cognitive restructuring was more general than that of Ellis, who specifically emphasized the irrationality of thought styles like catastrophizing. In our view, both ways of approaching cognitive restructuring are potential strategies for changing appraisals of caregiving as highly stressful to more neutral.

Coping Styles

Coping styles have long been recognized as an important influence on mental health outcomes among caregivers. Within the stress and coping model, coping styles are mobilized by the appraisal of an objective event as being stressful. Styles of cognitive coping in stressful situations often are more important in determining the emotional response to stress than the objective stressor itself (Folkman et al., 1987; Folkman & Lazarus, 1984; Haley, Levine, Brown, & Bartolucci, 1987). Within the Folkman and Lazarus model, coping styles are generally characterized as active coping (changing or solving the problem situation) or as emotion regulation (changing the emotional reaction to the stressor). Cognitive coping strategies have been strongly related to emotional distress in caregivers of persons with dementia (Haley et al., 1996; Pruchno & Resch, 1989; Stephens, Norris, Kinney, Ritchie, & Grotz, 1988).

While in theory, emotion regulation coping can have positive outcomes, the particular styles studied in caregivers have tended to have negative outcomes, making the emotional distress reaction worse rather than better. Emotion-focused coping styles such as escape-avoidance coping and self-blame have been linked to high levels of emotional distress in caregivers (Fox et al., 1997; Pruchno & Resch, 1989; Stephens et al., 1988). Haley et al. (1996) reported a structural equation model of stress and coping processes in caregivers that showed a significant relationship between avoidance coping and depression. In general, the strategies that are ineffective (e.g., escape-avoidance coping, self-blame) are more clear than the strategies that work, especially for chronic stressors without action-oriented solutions, like caregiving for a family member with dementia.

Very few problems can be solved by avoiding them or wishing they would go away. Accepting responsibility (or, more negatively, self-blame) also is sometimes found to be associated with higher levels of emotional distress in caregivers (Knight, 1992). It seems likely that this coping style may be helpful in some situations (perhaps in working out problems with a cognitively intact spouse or family member), but is not helpful when it amounts to blaming oneself for the problems caused by the dementing illness.

Since avoidance coping does not work, it would be tempting to assume that directly confronting and solving the problems of caregiving would be a good way to avoid emotional distress. However, this coping style often is found to be unrelated to distress outcomes among caregivers. Many of the problems associated with dementia are not really solvable. Vitaliano, De-Wolfe, Maiuro, Russo, and Katon (1990) found that, unlike persons dealing with work problems or physical health problems, dementia caregivers who appraised their stress as changeable reported higher levels of stress. Williamson and Schulz (1993) examined coping among dementia caregivers in a more problem-specific way and reported that some issues respond to problem-solving coping (e.g., seeking social support for coping with the recipient's decline) and others do not (e.g., direct action for problems due to the memory impairment).

We think that the better overall strategy for dementia caregivers is acceptance coping, and some recent data from our research provides preliminary support for this idea. Acceptance coping means accepting a problem rather than avoiding it and then realizing that the situation must be adjusted to rather than actively changed. For the dementia caregiver, this means that the dementia and the changes in the family member will not change. The caregiver can then focus attention on changing his or her reaction to the caregiving stressors rather than trying to solve unsolvable problems. In general, this has been operationalized in our intervention as a guideline for changing self-talk. That is, when altering what caregivers say to themselves about stress events using cognitive restructuring strategies (Ellis et al., 1997; Meichenbaum, 1985), we try to encourage the use of self-statements that reflect acceptance of the reality of the dementia and an acceptance of the behaviors of the person with dementia, as appropriate. Of course, it still is important to solve the specific problems that can be solved.

Social Support

The effects of quantitative social support on caregiver distress are unclear at this time. Caregivers with high levels of support have been found both to be less burdened (Zarit, Reever, & Bach-Peterson, 1980) and more burdened (Knight, 1991; Scott, Roberto, & Hutton, 1986) than other caregivers. Recently, there has been more attention to the costs of social support for caregivers (Schulz, Tompkins, Wood, & Decker, 1987) and to the quality of social support. Conflict with persons in the support system often is linked with high levels of depression (Pagel, Erdly, & Becker, 1987; Rook, 1984).

Many people who should be sources of support are, or are perceived to be, unhelpful and critical of the caregiver. Sometimes there are disagreements about what type of care is needed, how problems should be handled, or even whether the relative has dementia or not. Sometimes advice that is intended to be helpful is taken as criticism because the caregiver already has tried what is being suggested and has found that it does not work.

The relationship between the size of the support network and burden often is positive or zero. It may be that the most important thing is having at least one person who is supportive, and that more is not necessarily better. It may be that quality is more important than quantity. It may be that the relationship works in the opposite direction so that, as caregiving is appraised as being more stressful, the caregiver recruits more helpers into the support network. Highly stressed dementia caregivers may experience stress while maintaining the support system, because persons in the support network expect to receive help and emotional support as well as to provide it, and because support networks also expose members to other people's stress. In any case, it can be useful to keep in mind that not all support is good support, and to maximize the positive and minimize the negative. We only indirectly address changing the social support system, through the focus on monitoring stress and discovering causes of stress (some of which may turn out to be conflicts with presumed social support network members) and increasing the number of relaxing events (which, at least for extroverted caregivers, will involve contact with other people).

☐ Summary

Our intended focus is emotional distress outcomes. As we have discussed earlier in this chapter, it is clear that caregivers have higher levels of emotional distress and higher levels of clinical disorders (like depression and anxiety) than do noncaregivers of similar age and sex. In research from our project (Fox et al., 1997) and in research by Hooker et al. (1992, 1998) emotional distress outcomes for dementia caregivers have been found to be best modeled by a single latent factor of emotional distress. We interpret this as being in support of the view that caregivers, like others responding to severe stressors, experience a wide range of emotional and other responses to that stress. That is, we think it is appropriate to anticipate a variety of emotional distress responses, including depression, anxiety, and hostility, rather than to focus on single emotional responses to caregiving (e.g., on depression only). Thus, in our attempts to help caregivers, we ask them to rate their daily stress level rather than any one emotion, and our targets focus on alleviating stress in general rather than on targeting a specific emotion.

We also mean this to be a specific goal of treatment. That is, our aim is to change emotional outcomes and alleviate the caregiver's felt distress. We do not know if this will affect other outcomes such as health. We believe that interventions specifically aimed at health outcomes will be needed to improve caregiver health, but the research does not support any position on this issue at present.

We also are not convinced that improving the mental health of caregivers necessarily will keep the relative with dementia out of institutional care. A colleague's dissertation research (Lutzky, 1995) found no correlations between stress and coping model variables and decisions to place relatives in institutional care. Clinical experience suggests that sometimes the decision to place the patient is the appropriate decision for all involved. We also have found that reducing emotional distress makes it easier for some caregivers to continue providing care and for others to make the decision that it is time to seek 24-hour care.

In our view, these decisions are highly individual, and most likely are affected by factors other than caregiver emotional distress and the stress and coping model. These observations may explain in part why both psychosocial interventions and respite care seem to help caregivers feel better, but have little or no impact on prolonging family caregiving at home (see Knight, Lutzky & Macofsky-Urban, 1993; Weissert, Cready, & Pawelak, 1988). In any case, our aim is to help caregivers reduce emotional distress, as it is broadly defined. We are not claiming to also do other things.

With these limitations noted, we do feel that the approach described in this volume is helpful in reducing emotional distress when working with caregivers of older adults with dementia. This approach is based on current research knowledge with regard to stress and coping among dementia caregivers. It also draws on long-established psychological intervention techniques from behavioral and cognitive-behavioral approaches to stress reduction. In the chapters that follow, we describe the techniques, the caregivers' individual responses to them, and suggestions for responding to common problems that arise when using these strategies with caregivers.

☐ References

American Association of Retired Persons and Travelers Companies Foundation. (1988). *A national survey of caregivers. Final report. Health advocacy section*. Washington, DC: Opinion Research Corporation.

Aranda, M. P., & Knight, B. G. (1997). The influence of ethnicity and culture on the caregiver stress and coping process: A sociocultural review and analysis. *Gerontologist, 37,* 342–354.

Baumgarten, M., Battista, R. N., Infante-Rivard, C., Hanley, J. A., Becker, R., & Gauthier, S. (1992). The psychological and physical health of family members caring for an elderly person with dementia. *Journal of Clinical Epidemiology, 45,* 61–70.

Chappel, N. (1991). Living arrangements and sources of caregiving. *Journal of Gerontology. Social Sciences, 46,* S1–8.

Chenowith, B., & Spencer, B. (1986). Dementia: The experience of family caregivers. *The Gerontologist, 26,* 267–272.

Choi, H. (1993). Cultural and noncultural factors as determinants of caregiver burden for the impaired elderly in South Korea. *The Gerontologist, 33,* 8–15.

Cohen, D., Luchins, D., Eisdorfer, C., Paveza, G. J., Ashford, J. W., Gorelick, P., Hirschman, R., Freels, S., Levy, P., Semla, T., & Shaw, H. (1990). Caregivng for relatives with Alzheimer's disease: The mental health risks to spouses, adult children and other family members. *Behavior, Health, and Aging, 1,* 171–182.

Crimmins, E., Saito, Y., & Ingegneri, D. (1989). Changes in life expectancy and disability-free life expectancy in the United States. *Population and Development Review, 15,* 235–267.

Dura, J. R., Stukenberg, K. W., & Kiecolt-Glaser, J. (1991). Anxiety and depressive disorders in adult children caring for demented parents. *Psychology and Aging, 6,* 467–473.

Ellis, A. (1962). *Reason and emotion in psychotherapy*. New York: Lyle Stuart.

Ellis, A., Gordon, J., Neenan, M., & Palmer, S. (1997). *Stress counseling: A rational emotive behaviour approach*. London: Cassell.

Finucane, T., & Burton, J. (1994). Community-based long-term care. In W. Hazzard, E. Bierman, J. P. Blass, W. H. Ettinger, Jr., & J. B. Halter (Eds.), *Principles of geriatric medicine and gerontology* (3rd ed.). New Baskerville, USA: McGraw-Hill, Inc.

Folkman, S., Lazarus, R. S., Pimley, S., & Novacek, J. (1987). Age differences in stress and coping processes. *Psychology and Aging, 2,* 171–184.

Fox, L. S., Knight, B. G., & Chou, C. (1997, November). Caregiver burden: Stress appraisal or outcome measure? Presented at the Annual Meeting of the Gerontological Society of America, Cincinnati, OH.

Gallagher, D., Rose, J., Rivera, P., Lovett, S. (1989). Prevalence of depression in family caregivers. *Gerontologist, 29,* 449–456

Gatz, M., Bengston, V. L., & Blum, M. J. (1990). Caregiving families. In J. E. Birren & K. W. Schaie (Eds.), *Handbook of the psychology of aging* (3rd ed.), (pp. 405–426). San Diego, CA: Academic Press.

George, L. (1996). Social factors and illness. In R. Binstock & L. George (Eds.), *Handbook of aging and the social sciences* (4th ed., pp. 229–252). San Diego, CA: Academic Press.

George, L., Blazer, D., Winfield-Laird, I., Leaf, P., & Fischbach, R. (1988). Psychiatric disorders and mental health service use in later life: Evidence from the epidemiological catchment area programs. In J. Brody & G. Maddox (Eds.), *Epidemiology and aging: An international perspective* (pp. 189–219). New York: Springer.

Grafstrom, M., Fratiglioni, L., Sandman. P. O., & Winblad, B. (1992). Health and social consequences for relatives of demented and nondemented elderly: A population-based study. *Journal of Clinical Epidemiology, 45,* 861–870.

Haley, W., Bartolucci, A., Brown, S. L., & Bartolucci, A. A. (1987). Stress, appraisal, coping and social support as predictors of adaptational outcome among dementia caregivers. *Psychology and Aging, 2,* 323–330.

Haley, W. E., Levine, E. G., Brown, S. L., Berry, J. W., & Hughes, G. H. (1987). Psychological, social, and health consequences of caring for a relative with senile dementia. *Journal of the American Geriatrics Society, 35,* 405–411.

Haley, W. E., & Pardo, K. M. (1989). Relationship of severity of dementia to caregiving stressors. *Psychology and Aging, 4,* 389–392.

Haley, W. E., Roth, D. L., Coleton, M. I., Ford, G. R., West, C. A. C., Collins, R. P., & Isobe, T. L. (1996). Appraisal, coping, and social support as mediators of well-being in Black and White family caregivers of patients with Alzheimer's disease. *Journal of Consulting and Clinical Psychology, 64,* 121–129.

Hooker, K., Monahan, D. J., Bowman, S. R., Frazier, L. D., & Shifren, K. (1998). Personality counts for a lot: Predictors of mental and physical health of spouse caregivers in two disease groups. *Journal of Gerontology: Psychological Sciences, 53B,* 75–85.

Hooker, K., Monahan, D., Shifren, K., & Hutchinson, C. (1992). Mental and physical health of caregivers: The role of personality. *Psychology and Aging, 7,* 386–392.

Horowitz, A. (1985). Family caregiving to the frail elderly. *Annual Review of Gerontology and Geriatrics, 5,* 194–246.

Kiecolt-Glaser, J., Dura, J. R., Speicher, C. E., & Trask, O. (1991). Spousal caregivers of dementia victims: Longitudinal changes in immunity and health. *Psychosomatic Medicine, 54,* 345–362.

Kiecolt-Glaser, J., Glaser, R., Shuttleworth, E., Dyer, C., Ogrocki, P., & Speicher, C. (1987). Chronic stress and immunity in family caregivers of Alzheimer's disease victims. *Psychosomatic Medicine, 49,* 523–535.

Knight, B. (1991). Predicting life satisfaction and distress of in-home spouse dementia caregivers. *American Journal of Alzheimer's Care and Research and Related Disorders, 6,* 40–45.

Knight, B. (1992). Emotional distress and diagnosis among helpseekers: A comparison of dementia caregivers and depressed older adults. *Journal of Applied Gerontology, 11*, 361–372.

Knight, B. G., Lutzky, S. M., & Macofsky-Urban, F. (1993). A meta-analytic review of interventions for caregiver distress: Recommendations for future research. *The Gerontologist, 33*, 240–249.

Lawton, M. P., Moss, M., Kleban, M. H., Glicksman, A., & Rovine, M. (1991). A two-factor model of caregiving appraisal and psychological well-being. *Journal of Gerontology, 46*, 181–189.

Lazarus, R. S., & Folkman, S. (1984). *Stress, appraisal, and coping*. New York: Springer.

Lebowitz, B., & Light, E. (1993). Caregiver stress. In T. Yoshikawa, E. L. Cobbs, & K. Brummel-Smith (Eds.), *Ambulatory geriatric care* (pp. 47–54). St. Louis, Mo: Mosby-Year Book, Inc.

Lewinsohn, P., Munoz, R., Youngren, M., & Zeiss, A. (1986). *Control your depression*. Englewood Cliffs, NJ: Prentice Hall.

Lutzky, S. M. (1995). *Understanding of caregiver distress and the decision to place: Applying a stress and coping model*. Unpublished doctoral dissertation, School of Gerontology, University of Southern California, Los Angeles.

Meichenbaum, D. (1985). *Stress inoculation training*. New York: Pergamon Press.

Melcher, J. (1988). Keeping our elderly out of institutions by putting them back in their homes. *American Psychologist, 43*, 643–647.

Motenko, A. (1989). The frustrations, gratifications, and well-being of dementia caregivers. *Gerontologist, 29*, 166–172.

National Institute on Aging (1987). *Personnel for health needs of the elderly through the year 2020*. Bethesda, Maryland: Public Health Services; Department of Health and Human Services.

Pagel, M., Erdly, W., & Becker, J. (1987). Social networks: We get by with (and in spite of) a little help from our friends. *Journal of Personality and Social Psychology, 53*, 793–804.

Peterson, M. (1994). Physical aspects of aging: Is there such a thing as 'normal'?. *Geriatrics, 49*, 45–49.

Pruchno, R. A., & Resch, N. L. (1989). Mental health of caregiving spouses: Coping as mediator, moderator, or main effect? *Psychology and Aging, 4*, 454–463.

Rabins, P., Mace, N. L., & Lucas, M. J. (1982). Impact of dementia on the family. *Journal of the American Medical Association, 248*, 333–335.

Rook, K. S. (1984). The negative side of social interaction: Impact on psychological well-being. *Journal of Personality and Social Psychology, 46*, 1097–1108.

Scott, J. P., Roberto, K. A., & Hutton, T. (1986). Families of Alzheimer's victims: Family support to the caregivers. *Journal of the American Geriatrics Society, 34*, 348–354.

Schulz, R., O'Brien, A. T., Bookwala, J., & Fleissner, K. (1995). Psychiatric and physical morbidity effects of dementia caregiving: Prevalence, correlates, and causes. *Gerontologist, 35*, 771–791.

Schulz, R., Tompkins, C. A., Wood, D., & Decker, S. (1987). The social psychology of caregiving: Physical and psychological costs of providing support to the disabled. *Journal of Applied Social Psychology, 17*, 401–428.

Schulz, R., Visintainer, P., & Williamson, G. M. (1990). Psychiatric and physical morbidity effects of caregiving. *Journal of Gerontology, 45*, 181–191.

Snyder, B., & Keefe, K. (1985). The unmet needs of family caregivers for frail and disabled adults. *Social Work in Health Care, 19*, 1–13.

Stephens, M. A. P., & Hobfoll, S. E. (1990). Ecological perspectives on stress and coping in later-life families. In M. A. P. Stephens, J. H. Crowther, S. E. Hobfoll, & D. L. Tennenbaum (Eds.), *Stress and coping in later-life families* (pp. 287–304). New York: Hemisphere.

Stephens, M. A. P., Norris, V. K., Kinney, J. M., Ritchie, S. W., & Grotz, R. C. (1988). Stressful situations in caregiving: Relations between caregiver coping and well-being. *Psychology and Aging, 3,* 208–209.

Stone, R., Cafferata, G. L., & Sangl, J. (1987). Caregivers of the frail elderly: A national profile. *The Gerontologist, 27,* 616–626.

Sung, K. (1992). Motivations for parent care: The case of filial children in Korea. *International Journal of Aging and Human Development, 34,* 109–124.

U.S. Bureau of the Census. (1995). *Sixty-five plus in the United States.* Washington, DC: U.S. Government Printing Office.

Vitaliano, P. P., DeWolfe, D. J., Maiuro, R. D., Russo, J., & Katon, W. (1990). Appraised changeability of a stressor as a modifier of the relationship between coping and depression: A test of the hypothesis of fit. *Journal of Personality and Social Psychology, 59,* 582–592.

Weissert, W. G., Cready, C. M., & Pawelak, J. (1988). The past and future of home and community based long term care. *The Milbank Quarterly, 66,* 309–388.

Williamson, G. M., & Schulz, R. (1993). Coping with specific stressors in Alzheimer's disease caregiving. *Gerontologist, 6,* 747–755.

Zarit, S. H., Reever, K., & Bach-Peterson, J. (1980). Relatives of the impaired elderly: Correlates of feelings of burden. *Gerontologist, 20,* 373–377.

CHAPTER 2

T. J. McCallum

Dementia Caregiver Burden and Ethnicity

While the literature on caregiving in general continues to expand, research on caregiving among ethnic minorities remains notably limited. When differentiated by specific ethnicity, this lack becomes even more apparent. Within the past several years, only a handful of studies investigating Latino and Asian caregivers in the United States have been published. Studies on African American caregivers, still few and far between, total more than that of any other ethnic group. It is due to this dearth of research on varied minorities that this chapter is limited to a discussion of African American caregivers. Accordingly, although the chapter admittedly is incomplete, it represents an analysis of the most comprehensive body of existing literature on minority caregivers.

For nearly 20 years, caring for an older relative with dementia has been recognized as a source of burden for the caregiver (Zarit, Reever, & Bach-Peterson, 1980). In addition, as the caregiving career can span decades, the process has become a prime exemplar of the effects of chronic stress on physical health and mental health outcomes. The literature documenting the effects of caregiving on self-report emotional distress largely has been a literature of White caregivers in the United States (Schulz, O'Brien, Bookwalla, & Fleissner, 1995). Results from a number of research studies, on the other hand, strongly suggest that African American caregivers appraise caregiving as less burdensome than do White caregivers (Fredman, Daly, & Lazur, 1995; Lawton, Rajagopal, Brody, & Kleban, 1992; Morycz, Malloy,

17

Bozich, & Martz 1987). At present, few researchers have investigated the so-cial, psychological, and physiological aspects associated with dementia care-giving in general, and particularly in the African American community. Accompanying this research void is a lack of theoretical models to account for these differences (Dilworth-Anderson & Anderson, 1994), with the exception of recent studies by Haley et al. (1995, 1996) and Knight and McCallum (1998).

According to Dilworth-Anderson and Anderson (1994), any model attempting to investigate caregiver stress in the African American population should examine sociocultural factors such as social supports and strains, psychological factors such as coping resources, and physiological change factors such as cardiovascular reactivity (CVR). This chapter is an attempt to bring together the present research connecting these factors in relation to the African American caregiver and stress.

☐ Sociocultural Factors and Social Support

There are a wide variety of sociocultural factors that differentiate African Americans and Whites in this country, such as years of education, employ-ment, and geographical distribution. In the realm of caregiving, however, several similarities among ethnicities should be noted. Most caregivers are women, many are not married and are of low income, and many report being in fair to poor health (Fredman et al., 1995; Haley, Levine, Brown, & Bartolucci, 1987; Knight & McCallum, 1998).

Some have argued that social support is a conceptual offshoot of extended families and is fundamental to well-being in the African American commu-nity (Neighbors, 1997). *Social support*, defined here as those interpersonal transactions involving aid, affect, or affirmation (Kahn & Antonucci, 1980), has been extensively examined in the context of caregiving over the past two decades. Within this context, a number of studies investigating the social support networks of African American caregivers, as well as a few on network comparisons between African American and White caregivers have been conducted. Despite evidence of more variation within social sup-port networks (Burton et al., 1995; Gibson, 1982), African American care-giver networks have not been shown to be significantly larger than those of White caregivers (Burton et al., 1995; Haley et al., 1995). This chapter examines the factors most relevant to caregiving according to Dilworth-Anderson and Anderson (1994): the cultural characteristics (cultural tradi-tion, family dynamics, the role of the church) and coping style of African Americans.

☐ **Cultural Tradition**

Many cultural characteristics of African Americans can be traced to African culture and traditions (Nobles, 1980). One such African tradition present in African American culture is the importance of the extended family, which often includes both blood relatives and non–blood-related individuals who may be given similar status to blood relatives (Nobles, 1974). This is in sharp contrast to the concept of the nuclear family prevalent in White American culture, a concept which may create clear and distinct roles for relatives and lesser or nonexistent roles for those outside of the immediate family. These group differences in familial organization may begin to explain differences in caregiving.

Lawton et al. (1992) examined "traditional caregiving ideology," and found that African Americans scored higher than Whites in this category (although it should be noted that traditional caregiving ideology did not correlate with burden). Traditional caregiving ideology is based on the Barresi and Menon (1990) notion that African Americans are socialized or inculcated with attitudes that encourage providing respect and assistance to older family members. Lawton et al. (1992) described the ideology as continuing a family tradition of mutual concern.

This suggestion of a stronger mutual concern within the African American community has been described by Johnson and Barer (1990). In their study of older inner-city African Americans and Whites selected from medical clinics, they found that the former group had a more active social support network. The authors employed focused interview techniques involving open-ended questions which, due to questionable validity, are more common to theoretical rather than empirical research, and did not report validity coefficients. Their measures regarding support networks lacked necessary detail, particularly in the area of emotional support. Information about overall mood also was extracted from life review techniques. This information suggested that mechanisms within African American families which serve to expand network membership in two distinct ways. Networks expand through the mobilization of relatives on the periphery of the kinship network (cousins, nieces, and nephews), and through the extension of the kinship network through the creation of *fictive kin*, or individuals given the status and responsibilities of relatives who are not blood relations. A 1995 study found that older disabled African Americans had a greater likelihood of having at least one caregiver who was not part of the immediate family, controlling for variables such as network size (Burton et al., 1995). While Burton et al. found no differences in the total size of social support network, there were significant differences between the two populations that call into question their comparability and thus the generalizability of these results.

African Americans in this study were younger, had significantly less education, and over half lived under the poverty line. Also, reported cognitive status differences were vast, with 46% of the African Americans scoring in the impaired range of the brief screening instrument versus only 25% of the Whites. Though the authors noted the potential confound with level of education on their cognitive function measure, the Short Portable Mental Status Questionnaire, a more comprehensive measure of cognitive function should have been employed. Despite these differences and limitations, this study does support the idea of a more varied network of support among older African Americans based on the aforementioned methods of expansion. For example, grandparents may raise the offspring of distant relatives or friends who, in later life, may come to serve as caregivers even though they do not possess biological ties. Such fictive kin may serve important emotional and instrumental needs for older African Americans that biological relations may not. While fictive kin may have its roots in African tradition, its present day use also can be connected to the relationship dynamics in African American families.

☐ Family Dynamics

Over the past few decades, major trends affecting African American family structure, such as increases in cohabitation and nonmarital births, delays in marriage formation, marriage dissolution, and remarriage and an increase in the number of blended families in this country have impacted and altered family dynamics in African American families. Longitudinal studies examining the African American family have found that Blacks are more likely than Whites to live in extended family households. Furthermore, there is some evidence that one of the benefits of the extended family is the ability to care for impaired family members (Taylor, Tucker, Chatters, & Jayakody, 1997). Factors such as the increase in the number of births to unmarried women, the subsequent rise in the number of female-headed families, the increase in coresident living arrangements in female-headed families, and the rise in never-married African Americans. Other factors include increased cohabitation and the increase in multigenerational households not directly defined by blood linkages. Generally, cohabiting unions are less stable and of shorter duration than legal marriages (Bumpass, Sweet, & Cherlin, 1991), furthermore, African American cohabitating couples are a great deal more likely than White cohabitating couples to have children (McLanahan & Casper, 1995). According to Johnson and Barer (1990), the results of their study of families and networks among older, inner-city African Americans reflect the lack of stable, long-term marriages in the inner-city African American community, with only 14% of their sample reporting currently being married or cohabiting. Over half of their sample reported being divorced, and many within that group reported multiple marriages. High divorce rates and multiple marriages create a network of relatives that may become quite flexible and able to adapt to the needs of those within the system. In the context of caregiving, this results in fewer spouse and blood-related caregivers than in the White caregiving population. The 1992 Lawton et al. study reported that far fewer African American caregivers (27.3%) were spouses, as compared with the White sample (51.2%), and that many more African American caregivers either were other relatives (not children-in-law or siblings) or friends (17.6% vs. 4.2%). Haley et al. (1995) found similar distributions of spouses and adult children in the caregiving role, and also reported that the percentage of divorced caregivers in their study was eight times higher for African American caregivers (25%) than for White caregivers (3%). For older African Americans, this extended family network system provides a greater number of relatives from which to choose when assistance is needed, and this may partially explain the large number of nonspousal, nonchild caregivers within the African American community. The following case example outlines the life of one such African American nonspousal, grandchild caregiver.

☐ Case Example

Ms. Carson

Ms. Carson is a single African American woman in her late thirties who serves as a caregiver for her 76-year-old grandmother. Ms. Carson's caregiving role began 3 years ago, after her aunt suffered a fatal stroke. Her aunt had lived with her grandmother for 20 years, the past 4 as a caregiver. Ms. Carson's grandmother was diagnosed with probable Alzheimer's disease 7 years ago.

Ms. Carson previously had been a secondary caregiver, assisting her aunt in the care of her grandmother on weekends and after work. Though she lived about 40 miles from her older relatives, Ms. Carson considered it to be her familial duty to help out as much as possible. She decided to move in with her grandmother after her aunt's death, despite the fact that the once nice neighborhood had deteriorated badly. Her grandmother's large old house also was in need of many repairs.

Ms. Carson had worked full time for a large metropolitan newspaper for 15 years, and finally had to take an unpaid leave of absence to stay with her grandmother. Over the past 3 years, she had used up all of her vacation and sick leave to assist her grandmother with various appointments and to repair parts of the house.

As the only grandchild in contact with her deceased mother's side of the family, Ms. Carson believes it is her duty to care for her grandmother. She feels strongly about caring for her grandmother herself, despite suggestions from several of her friends that she place her grandmother in a nursing home.

The behavior of her grandmother is erratic, but Ms. Carson handles it quite well. The pair maintain a very regimented schedule, which seems to help reduce the grandmother's general confusion. The biggest problems faced by Ms. Carson include her grandmother's unpredictable angry and violent tirades, her grandmother's attempt to cook despite having started two fires by leaving food on the stove and forgetting about it, and her grandmother's sleeplessness. Ms. Carson has the most difficulty in encouraging her grandmother to sleep through the night, and reports that her own sleeplessness is beginning to wear her down physically.

Ms. Carson's social life has suffered somewhat over the past 3 years, but she did not engage in a large number of social events before her life as a primary caregiver. Her long-time boyfriend understands and has accepted the change. Although the couple's dates are less frequent now, they speak on the phone every day, which is more often than they had done previously.

The church has become central in the lives of both Ms. Carson and her grandmother. Not only do they attend church together on Sundays, but many members of the church assist Ms. Carson in various ways. Members visit several times a week to allow Ms. Carson time for grocery shopping and an occasional movie, and other caregivers from the church have created a phone network to check up on each other a few times a week.

Ms. Carson's grandmother remains in excellent physical health, and may live for another 20 years. Through her religious faith, Ms. Carson accepts her role and the difficulties inherent in it. She does not intend to place her grandmother in a nursing home, unless her grandmother requires medical assistance that she cannot provide. Though small, her social support system, fulfills her needs at the present time.

☐ The Role of the Church

An additional source of assistance for older African Americans is the church, the importance of which reflects another cultural remnant from Africa that has ramifications for caregiving. The church, along with support from family and friends, composes a mutual aid system for many older African Americans. Within the mutual aid system, older African Americans and their adult children provide care and support to each other, at higher rates than do older Whites and their offspring (Mutran, 1985). Walls and Zarit (1991) also concluded that African American churches serve as a strong support network for older African Americans. Although they found that the family was the strongest source of support, the informal networks derived through the church tended to complement that support, with both networks predicting well-being. The church, therefore, may add both qualitative and quantitative social support to older African Americans. Last, there is evidence that the church also facilitates the utilization of specific coping styles in the African American community.

□ Caregiver Ethnicity and Coping Style

Just as social support is hypothesized to differentiate African American and White caregivers, there is some evidence that coping style also may differentiate the groups. Past research in the field has demonstrated that a caregiver's negative appraisal of the situation, more than specific situational characteristics, leads to distress and depression (Picot, Debanne, Namazi, & Wykle, 1997). It follows that the style or method by which caregivers cope may be linked to their appraisal of the situation and, in the case of caregiving, perhaps to their view of illness.

According to Landrine and Klonoff (1992), important cultural differences in health-related beliefs and schemas exist between African Americans and Whites, in that many Whites tend to view illness as a person-centered, temporally bounded, and discontinuous event, whereas many ethnic and cultural minority groups in the United States view illness as a long-term, fluid, and continuous manifestation of changing relationships and dysfunctions in the family, the community, or nature. Landrine and Klonoff further suggested that many minority groups view treatment as a long-term, informal, highly personal, and cooperative process in which the healer, victim, and family atone for the wrongdoing and improve the habits and relationships that are construed to be the cause of illness. This view may begin to explain differences between African American and White caregivers in the perception and appraisal of stress in the caregiving role. In other words, if African Americans view dementing illness as fluid and long term, and Whites view the illness as discrete, then African American caregivers may adjust better psychologically to the role strains inherent in long-term caregiving.

A number of caregiving researchers have found several differences between African American and White caregivers which support the idea that African American caregivers do in fact appraise the caregiving role differently than do White caregivers. Morycz, Malloy, Bozich, and Martz (1987) found that African American caregivers experienced less strain, were less likely to institutionalize, and differed from White caregivers in the factors that predicted burden. Fredman et al. (1995) reported similar findings in relation to burden, despite the fact that the African American caregivers in their study reported caring for people with greater functional and cognitive impairment. In their 1992 study, Lawton et al. found that African American caregivers scored higher than White caregivers on scales of mastery and satisfaction, and scored lower on scales designed to test subjective burden, sense of intrusion, and depression. Most recently, Haley and his colleagues (1995) found a higher incidence of depression and decreased life satisfaction in White caregivers when compared with African American caregivers. Knight and McCallum (1998) also found similar evidence of differences in the appraisal of caregiving between ethnicities.

However, according to Lazarus and Folkman (1984), appraisal of a situation is only part of the equation when facing a stressor. Individuals also actively choose how to cope when placed in a potentially stressful situation. The coping style literature contains precious little research on older African Americans, and even less on ethnic caregiving. Nevertheless, work which has been done suggests that older African Americans employ coping styles quite different from older Whites. Picot et al. (1997) found significant differences in the relationship between caregiver ethnicity and the perceived rewards and comfort attained from prayer. This is not surprising in light of earlier findings from religiosity studies indicating higher levels of religiosity among African Americans, females, and older adults (Chatters, Levin, & Taylor, 1992). Specifically, the group found that African American caregivers scored higher on prayer and comfort from religion scales. This result lead Picot et al. (1997) to suggest that religiosity serves as a coping resource variable, which in turn operates as a stress deterrent, as opposed to a stress buffer (Wheaton, 1985). As a resource variable, the function of religious coping may be to raise the African American caregiver's threshold for stress. African American caregivers in this study prayed more frequently, a behavior which may have preceded their caregiving career, and therefore they may have perceived less stress than White caregivers when confronted by the same caregiving situation. Similarly, Krause and Van Tran (1992) found that older African Americans use religious involvement as a counterbalance to offset deleterious effects of stressful circumstances. Though their research indicated that life stresses tended to erode feelings of mastery and self-worth, the negative effects were offset when religious involvement was high. In a study of older African Americans, Neighbors and his colleagues found prayer to be the most frequently mentioned coping resource utilized among this group when faced with a serious personal problem. They also found that the tendency to report prayer as most helpful was highest among those with the most severe personal problems and that, after physicians, ministers were ranked highest among professionals from whom to seek help. Although the aforementioned study did not examine it directly, one need not jump far to make the connection to coping with caregiving as a serious personal problem.

Religious coping also has been considered a path through which African American caregivers cognitively redefine a stressful situation (Skaff, 1995). *Cognitive redefinition*, also known as positive reappraisal, is the act of reframing a potentially stressful event into a more positive light. Though theorized to be utilized more frequently by African Americans, little empirical work has been done on the subject. In perhaps the only study to examine this type of coping with African American caregivers, Knight and McCallum (1998), found significant differences between African American and White caregivers. African American caregivers were found to use positive reappraisal more often than their White counterparts. Furthermore, they found evidence that this coping style may not be useful for Whites. In the study, caregivers of both ethnicities that showed significant CVR levels during two stressful tasks were compared. As expected, positive reappraisal and depression were inversely related for African Americans when the subject shared a stressful story about caregiving. Surprisingly, White caregivers showed a positive relationship between positive reappraisal and depression in both stress conditions. In other words, positive reappraisal appeared to be an effective coping style for African American caregivers, but positively correlated with depression for White caregivers.

The evidence that African American caregivers appraise and cope with the stress inherent in the caregiving role differently than White caregivers is mounting. Positive reappraisal and religious coping are two related styles of coping with the stresses of caregiving that may be used more often and with greater success by African American caregivers than by their White counterparts. Furthermore, the connection between positive reappraisal, CVR, and caregiver ethnicity is important for two reasons. First, it connects physiological measures with psychological ones, adding information not obtainable through paper-and-pencil measures, which in turn adds incremental validity to caregiving research as a whole. Second, the finding that African American caregivers show an inverse relationship to CVR when using positive reappraisal, while White caregivers show a positive relationship between the two, indicates that this particular style of coping may be more useful to reduce stress in one group than the other. In other words, White caregivers may not be able to successfully apply the techniques that seem to aid African American caregivers in reducing caregiving stress. It follows that researchers now entertain the possibility that efficacious stress reduction techniques may differ between these two groups.

☐ Theoretical Explanations

There have been a number of theoretical explanations put forth to explain the paradox of lower reported burden in African American caregivers.

Dilworth-Anderson and Anderson (1994) suggested that caregiving may not be the most salient stressor for many low-income African Americans. Financial stress, child rearing, or job stress may be more important than caregiving in some instances. In attempting to explore these issues, Haley et al. (1996) recently examined stress appraisal, coping, and social support as mediators of well-being in African American and White caregivers. They concluded that the stress process was similar in African American and White caregivers, but suggested that "cultural mechanisms" may explain why the former group appraised and coped with stress more effectively than the latter group. Thus, some aspect of African American culture may facilitate the more effective use of social support or the development of a coping style that differs from White caregivers allowing for more effective coping and, consequently, less burden. Dilworth-Anderson and Anderson (1994) suggested that aspects of caregiving also may increase a personal sense of mastery or increase family cohesiveness in light of a lifetime of other stressors, thus shedding more light on cultural mechanisms at work. The Haley et al. (1996) study found no significant differences in social support, however. Without an empirical link to social support in ethnic caregiving research, the literature simply is unable to explain these consistent ethnic differences in caregiver burden.

Knight and McCallum (1998) hypothesized that reporting bias may explain the ethnic differences in caregiver burden. These authors sought to examine physiological measures of stress in order to compare the two ethnicities and determine if comparable physiological stress measures would indicate that African Americans actually were experiencing similar stress from a physiological vantage point, but were reporting lower levels of stress on psychological inventories. The results of this study did not support such a conclusion. However, more studies attempting to connect physiological stress with psychological stress may uncover some, thus far, elusive answers.

☐ Stress Buffering

Stress researchers have long noted that some individuals are more psychologically vulnerable or responsive to stress than others, even if exposed to similar types or levels of stressors. Further research has suggested that people connected with strong family and friendship networks are less susceptible to the effects of stress and, therefore, are more likely to enjoy higher levels of mental health (Cohen & Willis, 1985). Networks of friends and families are hypothesized to protect members by providing them with emotional or tangible resources that are used to cope with problems or difficulties. While research in the African American community has shown the existence of and importance of elaborate social networks, including extended family, friends, and church members (Chatters, Taylor, & Jackson, 1986), only scant evidence exists in support of a buffering effect against stress.

☐ Physiological Research

As mentioned above, researchers have been examining the effects of caregiving for the past 20 years. When compared to age-matched peers, predominantly White samples of caregivers consistently have been shown to exhibit more depressive symptoms, higher rates of burden, and more perceived hassles (Haley et al., 1987). Lacking in the literature, thus far, have been objective examinations of the physical toll exacted by caregiving as measured by specific physiological markers. Recent studies of immune response and metabolic changes are two avenues by which the physiological effects of caregiving are just beginning to be investigated. This underdeveloped area of research is important not only in that it adds to the cannon of general caregiving literature, but also because it may help shed further light on the consistent and inadequately explained finding of ethnic differences in caregiver burden.

☐ Caregiving and Physiological Stress: A Review of the Literature

Studies of caregiving historically have focused on a variety of concepts of stress. Dozens of models and measures which were designed to explain the impact of stress on the caregiver presently are in use. Researchers, while citing the importance of both mental and physical aspects of stress, often employ measures insufficient to the task of investigating the physiological components of stress, particularly when comparing health outcomes. This is a criticism relevant to the majority of caregiving studies cited in the earlier sections of this chapter. The following is a review of several recent studies that attempt to connect caregiver stress with immunity and metabolic function.

Kiecolt-Glaser, Esterling, and their colleagues have been at the forefront of examining specific health outcomes of caregiving. In a 1987 study, Kiecolt-Glaser et al. conducted one of the first experiments linking caregivers and chronic physiological stress. Theorizing that the long-term stressor of caregiving may have an adverse impact on the immune system, Kiecolt-Glaser et al. compared a predominantly White sample of Alzheimer's caregivers with matched controls employing immunological analyses. They found that caregivers had significantly lower percentages of T lymphocytes and helper T lymphocytes, as well as significantly lower helper suppressor cell ratios. The results suggest that caregivers or, more specifically, White caregivers, possess poorer immunologic adaptation than noncaregivers. Of course, only studies including African American caregivers would validate this finding for that group.

In 1991, Kiecolt-Glaser, Dura, Speicher, Trask, and Glaser launched a longitudinal study in order to examine caregiver immunity and health over time. Again, it is assumed that this study included a predominantly White sample as most of the literature in this realm does not note ethnicity. Between the initial intake and the approximate 13 months later, caregivers showed decrements in immunity and more infectious illness, particularly upper respiratory infection. The study also found that caregivers who reported lower levels of social support at intake and who were most distressed by dementia-related behaviors showed significantly negative changes in immune function at follow up. The connection of social support indicators with aspects of immune function is noteworthy, as this is the first example of an essentially psychosocial indicator having been shown to correspond with a purely physiological measure.

Three years later (Esterling, Kiecolt-Glaser, Bodnar, & Glaser, 1994), the group expanded their scope to examine former and present caregivers, as well as controls along the dimensions of stress and social support. Here they sought to determine whether or not problems such as anxiety, depression, and slowed-down immune system regulation would subside for caregivers with the death of the patient. They found that former caregivers were immunologically indistinguishable from present caregivers. Both groups were significantly more depressed and displayed a poorer immune system response than the controls.

The findings of the previous study were replicated a year later. Castle, Wilkins, Heck, Tanzy, and Fahey (1995) also examined caregivers and immunity. They likewise concluded that a link exists between chronic stress and a lowered immune response which, when adding the variable of age, may combine to increase the risk of disease for caregivers. However, similar to their psychologically and sociologically oriented brethren, these researchers failed to include strong measures from the other realms, rendering their results difficult to generally apply.

Similarly, Mills et al. (1997) matched caregivers and controls while looking at plasma catecholine levels and lymphocyte receptor alterations. They found the chronic stress of caregiving to relate to changes in receptor physiology, and suggested that such stress may alter cellular immunity.

Using all White samples, other researchers also have reported immunological differences between caregivers and noncaregivers. Recently, Vitaliano, Russo, Young, Teri, and Maiuro (1996) investigated the links between metabolic variables, stress, and caregiving. Employing a longitudinal design and a chronic stress perspective, these researchers measured insulin and glucose in caregivers and noncaregiving controls twice over a 15- to 18-month period. They found that caregivers had significantly higher insulin levels than controls at intake and time 2, even when variables of obesity, gender, exercise, age, alcoholic drinks, hormone replacement therapy, lipids, and hypertension were considered in the analysis. They also found psychological distress to be positively associated with glucose at time 2. While Vitaliano et al. did include controls and incorporated strong psychological measures, they did not include any African American caregivers in their study.

In contrast, Knight and McCallum (1998), recently conducted a study investigating ethnic differences in burden, which incorporated commonly used measures from sociological, psychological, and physiological realms. The main findings, mentioned above, suggested that positive reappraisal may be an effective coping style for African American caregivers, but not for Whites. The relationship to positive reappraisal was unexpectedly positive for Whites, with higher reported use of positive reappraisal leading to higher levels of CVR and corresponding with high levels of depression, rather than providing the protective effect as in African Americans. For African American caregivers, the inverse relationship was found.

☐   Caregiving and Poor Health Outcomes

Evidence for the negative impact of physiological caregiving stress on health outcomes is mounting, though it is based on predominantly White caregiving samples. While some may argue that the process of aging alone leads to some of the immunity and metabolic changes suggested by the aforementioned studies, it cannot explain significant differences found between the age-matched controls and the caregivers. In other words, these studies strongly suggested that, due to the stress of caregiving, caregivers may enter higher health risk categories than those dictated by age alone. Specifically, this cross section of studies suggests that caregivers possess poorer immunologic adaptation than noncaregivers, that caregivers show more infectious illness than noncaregivers, and that former caregivers are immunologically indistinguishable from present caregivers.

At present, the physiological caregiving research remains in its infancy as it just begins to empirically examine physiological forms of stress related to caregiving. In some sense, this is where the field of research began 20 years ago. There are, however, some important differences. The caregiving research incorporating physiological information today can benefit from and add to the existing sociological and psychological findings of the past 20 years. In doing so, physiological research holds the key to many advancements in the study of caregiver burden and can elucidate information that exists on ethnic differences.

☐ Summary

Historically, little research has been conducted investigating African American caregivers and stress. The research which has been done can be divided into three distinct areas: sociological research, psychological research, and, more recently, physiological research. In the sociological realm, the social support research conducted has underlined the importance of cultural traditions of an expanded kinship network, the complex family dynamics marked by divorce and multigenerational households, and the role of the church in facilitating and supplementing this family system in relation to caregiving. Researchers in psychology have explored differences in the view of illness and in coping style between African American caregivers and their White counterparts, concluding that both factors impact the stress appraisal process in a manner that may begin to explain why African American caregivers report lower burden in the caregiving role. The physiological research has included few African American participants, but suggests that caregivers are at greater health risks due to poorer immune function. Perhaps the most consequential work that has been done thus far, however, combines aspects of these three areas. Kiecolt-Glaser et al.'s (1991) work connecting poor immune function to low social support and the Knight and McCallum (1998) study linking coping style to CVR serve as examplars of the next step in this line of research.

The ultimate benefit of this line of research would be seen in the creation of models of caregiver stress that would isolate the points of impact wherein stress reduction techniques can be employed. Simultaneously, researchers can work to determine if physiological system function parallels that of the complex emotional system that leads to caregiver burden. In other words, they can explore the possibility that social support and coping style directly impact immune function. As consistent reporters of low levels of burden, continued integrated research on African American caregivers and stress is paramount if these goals are to be realized.

☐ References

Barresi, C., & Menon, G. (1990). Diversity in Black family caregiving. In Z. Harel, E. Mc Kinney, & M. Williams (Eds.), Black Aged (pp. 221–235). Newbury Park, CA: Sage.

Bumpass, L., Sweet, J., & Cherlin, A. (1991). The role of cohabitation in declining rates of marriage. *Journal of Marriage and the Family, 53*, 913–927.

Burton, L., Kasper, J., Shore, A., Cagney, K., La Veist, T., Cubbin, C., & German, P. (1995). The structure of informal care: Are there differences by race? *The Gerontologist, 35*, 744–752.

Castle, S., Wilkins, S., Heck, E., Tanzy, K., & Fahey, J. (1995). Depression in caregivers of demented patients is associated with altered immunity: Impaired proliferative capacity, increased CD8, and a decline in lymphocytes with surface signal transduction molecules and a cytotoxicity marker. *Clinical Experimental Immunology, 101*, 487–493.

Chatters, L., Taylor, R, & Jayakody, R. (1994). Fictive kin relationships in Black extended families. *Journal of Comparative Family Studies, 25*, 297–312.

Chatters, L., Levin, J., & Taylor, R. (1992). Antecedents and dimensions of religious involvement among older Black adults. *Journal of Gerontology: Social Sciences, 47*, S269–S278.

Chatters, L., Taylor, R., & Jackson, R. (1986). Aged black's choice for an informal helper network. *Journal of Gerontology, 41*, 94–100.

Cohen, S., & Wills, T. (1985). Stress, social support, and the buffering process. *Psychological Bulletin, 98*, 310–357.

Dilworth-Anderson, P., & Anderson, N. B. (1994). Dementia caregiving in Blacks: A contextual approach to research. In B. Lebowitz, E. Light, & G. Niederehe (Eds.), Stress effects on family caregivers of Alzheimer's patients (pp. 385–409). New York: Springer.

Esterling, B., Kiecolt-Glaser, J., Bodnar, J., & Glaser, R. (1994). Chronic stress, social support persistent alterations in the natural killer cells response to cytokines in older adults. *Health Psychology, 13 (4)*, 291–298.

Fredman, L., Daly, M., & Lazur, A. (1995). Burden among White and Black caregivers to elderly adults. *Journals of Gerontology: Social Sciences, 50*, 110–118.

Gibson, R. (1982). Blacks at middle and late life: Resources and coping. *Annals of the American Academy of Political and Social Science, 464*, 79–90.

Haley, W., Levine, E., Brown, S., & Bartolucci, A. (1987). Stress, appraisal, coping, and social support as predictors of adaptational outcome among dementia caregivers. *Psychology and Aging, 2*, 323–330.

Haley, W., Roth, D., Coleton, M., Ford, G., West, C., Collins, R., & Isobe, T. (1996). Appraisal, coping, and social support as mediators of well being in Black and White family caregivers of patients with Alzheimer's disease. *Journal of Consulting and Clinical Psychology, 64*, 121–129.

Haley, W., West, C., Wadley, V., Ford, G., White, Barrett, J., Harrell, L., & Roth, D. (1995). Psychological, social, and health impact of caregiving: A comparison of Black and White dementia family caregivers and noncaregivers. *Psychology and Aging, 10*, 540–552.

Jackson, J., Jayakody, R., & Antonucci, T. (1996). Exchanges within Black American three generation families: The family environment context model. *Journal of Marriage and the Family, 55*, 261–276.

Johnson, C., & Barer, B. (1990). Families and networks among older inner-city Blacks. *The Gerontologist, 30*, 726–733.

Kahn, R., & Antonucci, T. (1980). Convoys over the life course: Attachment, roles, and social support. In P. Baltes and O. Brim (Eds.), Life-span development and behavior (Vol. 3, pp. 253–286). Lexington, MA: Lexington Books.

Kiecolt-Glaser, J., Dura, J., Speicher, C., Trask, O., & Glaser, R. (1991). Spousal caregivers of dementia victims: Longitudinal changes in immunity and health. *Psychosomatic Medicine, 53*, 345–362.

Kiecolt-Glaser, J., Glaser, R., Shuttleworth, E., Dyer, C., Ogrocki, P., & Speicher, C. (1987). Chronic stress and immunity in family caregivers of Alzheimer's disease patients. *Psychosomatic Medicine, 49*, 523–535.

Knight, B., & McCallum, T. (1998). Heart rate reactivity and depression in African-American and White dementia caregivers: Reporting bias or positive coping? *Aging and Mental Health, 2*, 212–221.

Krause, N. (1992). Stress, religiosity, and psychological well-being among older Blacks. *Journal of Aging and Health, 4*, 412–439.

Landrine, H., & Klonoff, E. (1992). Culture and health-related schema's: A review and proposal for interdisciplinary integration. *Health Psychology, 11*, 267–276.

Lawton, M., Rajagopal, D., Brody, E., & Kleban, M. (1992). The dynamics of caregiving for a demented elder among Black and White families. *Journal of Gerontology: Social Sciences, 47*, 156–164.

Lazarus, R., & Folkman, S. (1984). Stress, appraisal, and coping. New York: Springer.

McLanahan, S., & Casper, L. (1995). Growing diversity and inequality in the American family. In R. Farley (Ed.), State of the union: America in the 1990s. Vol. 2: Social trends (pp. 1–45). New York: Sage.

Miller, B., Campbell, R., Farran, C., Kaufman, J., & Davis (1995). Race, control, mastery, and caregiver distress. *Journal of Gerontology: Social Sciences, 50*, 374–382.

Mills, P., Ziegler, M., Patterson, T., Dimsdale, J., Hauger, R., Irwin, M., & Grant, I. (1997). Plasma catecholine and lymphocyte beta-2 adrenergic receptor alterations in elderly Alzheimer's caregivers under stress. *Psychosomatic Medicine, 59*, 251–256.

Morycz, R., Malloy, J., Bozich, M., & Martz, P. (1987). Racial differences in family burden: Clinical implications for social work. In R. Dubroff (Ed.), Gerontological social work with families (pp. 133–154). New York: Haworth Press.

Mutran, E. (1985). Intergenerational family support among Blacks and Whites: Response to culture and socioeconomic differences. *Journal of Gerontology, 34*, 48–54.

Neighbors, H. (1997). Husbands, wives, familiy and friends: Sources of stress, sources of support. In R. Taylor, J. Jackson, & L. Chatters (Eds.), Family life in Black America (pp. 279–294). Thousand Oaks: Sage.

Nobles, W. (1980). African philosophy: Foundations for black psychology. In R. L. Jones (Ed.), *Black psychology* 2nd Edition. New York: Harper & Row.

Nobles, W. (1974). Africanity: It's role in Black families. *The Black Scholar*, 10–16.

Picot, S., Debanne, B., Namazi, K., & Wykle, M. (1997). Perceived rewards and religiosity among Black and White caregivers. *The Gerontologist, 37*, 612–619.

Schulz, R., O'Brien, D., Bookwalla, F., & Fleissner, J. (1995). Examining caregiver burden. *The Gerontologist, 35*, 181–191.

Skaff, M. (1995). Religion in the stress process: Coping with caregiving. Paper presented at the Annual Scientific Meeting of the Gerontological Society of America, Los Angeles, CA.

Taylor, R., Chatters, L., & Jackson, J. (Eds.). (1997). Family life in Black America. Thousand Oaks: Sage.

Taylor, R., Tucker, B., Chatters, L., & Jayakody. (1997). Recent demographic trends in African American family structure. In R. Taylor, J. Jackson, & L. Chatters (Eds.), Family life in Black America (pp. 14–62). Thousand Oaks: Sage.

U.S. Bureau of the Census. (1990). The need for personal assistance with everyday activities: Recipients and caregivers. Washington, DC: U.S. Government Office.

Vitaliano, P., Russo, J., Young, H., Teri, L., & Maiuro, R. (1991). Predictors of burden in spouse caregivers of individuals with Alzheimer's disease. *Psychology and Aging, 6*, 392–402.

Walls, C., & Zarit, S. (1991). Informal support from Black churches and the well-being of elderly Blacks. *The Gerontologist, 31,* 490–495.

Wheaton, R. (1985). Models of stress-buffering functions of coping resources. *Journal of Health and Social Behavior, 26,* 352–364.

Zarit, S., Reever, K., & Bach-Peterson, J. (1980). Relatives of impaired elderly: Correlates of feelings of burden. *The Gerontologist, 20,* 373–377.

3

CHAPTER

Stress Level Monitoring

In this chapter, the foremost strategy of the Stress Reduction Technique—Stress Level Monitoring—is laid out. A description of stress and the cycle of distress is first provided, and following is the introduction of stress monitoring which includes the Daily Stress Rating (DSR) Form. There is a discussion of how to chart one's stress level, and the chapter closes with several case examples that demonstrate the use of this technique.

☐ Understanding Stress

The first step in introducing the strategies of the Stress Reduction Technique to caregivers is to provide an overview and basic definition of stress. It is important that this groundwork be laid for several reasons. First, the term *stress* is used differently by most people and it is a good starting place to make sure that there is general agreement about what, in fact, is being discussed and targeted. Second, caregivers will benefit from having a reference point throughout the learning process. Often, caregivers will have difficulty understanding how a particular strategy relates to the original problem of stress, and it is through this professional reminder of the basic description of stress that caregivers will be able to grasp the connection.

Different definitions of stress abound in the literature. Selye began writing about stress in the 1930s and has done extensive work on the stress process. Selye defined stress as "the nonspecific response of the body to any demand" (1980, p. 127) and his work has focused primarily on the body's physiological response to these demands. In the 1960s, Lazarus expanded the meaning of stress to include the environment and introduced the concepts of appraisal and coping. Lazarus and his colleague, Folkman defined psychological stress as "a relationship between the person and the environment that is appraised by the person as taxing or exceeding his or her resources and endangering his or her well-being" (1984, p. 19). This definition moved beyond Selye's tradition that stress is a singular response (Hobfoll, 1988). Within the Lazarus model, *appraisal* is the process by which a person assesses the stressfulness of a situation or circumstance (Holroyd & Lazarus, 1982; Lazarus, 1966). And *coping* is a person's efforts to manage both environmental and internal demands as well as conflicts between demands (Holroyd & Lazarus, 1982; Lazarus, 1966).

A definition of stress that has been widely used by stress researchers is that of McGrath (Hobfoll, 1988). He defined stress as a "substantial imbalance between environmental demand and the response capability of the focal organism" (McGrath, 1970, p. 17). McGrath proposed that *imbalance* is based on subjective perceptions, and *demand* involves quantitative and qualitative properties. An additional definition of stress was offered by Kaplan who stated that psychological stress "reflects the subject's inability to forestall or diminish perception, recall, anticipation, or imagination of disvalued circumstances, those that in reality or fantasy signify great and/or increased distance from desirable (valued) experiential states, and consequently, evoke a need to approximate the valued states" (Kaplan, 1983, p. 196). Hobfoll combined Kaplan's and McGrath's definitions to suggest that "stress is the state in which individuals judge their response capabilities as unable to meet the threat to the loss of desirable experiential states— states that are dictated by their values and expectations" (Hobfoll, 1988, p. 19).

This is a small sampling of some of the definitions of stress that exist and, clearly, there are countless others. Although there are many ways to view the term *stress*, it generally is acknowledged that stress involves not only a stressor, but also an individual's appraisal of the stressor. In working with caregivers, a very basic definition of stress serves useful: Stress is a response to change. This simple and concise statement is effective because it allows caregivers to understand that stress can be either positive or negative, and it also suggests that, although caregivers may not be able to control the caregiving situation, they can control their reaction to change. It is caregivers' awareness both of this reaction and of their ability to impact the appraisal process that is critical in order for them to believe they can affect their stress level.

Stress can be positive, on one hand, because it can be a motivating factor that stimulates better performance and accomplishments. For example, the change in an older relative's ambulation abilities may motivate the caregiver to take the relative to a physician, resulting in physical therapy to help the relative walk better. This result allows the caregiver to feel successful in this role, satisfied that he or she is helping to keep the relative's quality of life as high as possible, and also reduces the amount of physical care that the caregiver has to provide.

On the other hand, negative stress is a response to a change that yields no constructive outcome. For example, the day-to-day stressors of caregiving, such as when the relative continually is obstinate about personal care tasks, can add up and become overwhelming for the caregiver. A negative response would occur if the caregiver does nothing to try to counterbalance the stress and merely becomes more and more frustrated. This emotional reaction to negative stress can be described as distress. *Distress* implies mental strain imposed by emotional pain, worry, or constant demands. Often, distress is manifested as fear, anger, frustration, and anxiety. If the demands or stressors are continual, distress often can evolve into depression or anxiety disorders such as phobias. Physical responses can include increased blood pressure and heart rate, muscle tension, dizziness due to an increase in rate of breathing, and an increase in perspiration.

Prolonged stress can affect both physical and emotional health. Negative stress that is extended or frequent can wear on the entire body and eventually can cause permanent damage and disease. For example, increased blood pressure, when perpetuated, can cause cardiovascular disorders such as heart attack or stroke. Ongoing stomach tension as a result of stress is related to gastrointestinal problems, and constant muscle tension can lead to chronic fatigue, headaches, backaches, and muscle pain. Research indicates that stress is related to many different illnesses including gastrointestinal disorders, cardiovascular disease, atherosclerosis, hypertension, cancer, endocrine disease, hyperthyroidism, pulmonary disease, bronchial asthma, chronic obstructive pulmonary disease, and hematological disease (Bunney et al., 1982). Furthermore, stress is believed to impact the entire body's immune system, making a person more vulnerable to illness (Minter & Kimball, 1980). According to Zegans, "There appears to be anatomical, physiological, and neurochemical evidence that cognitive-affective responses to stress can alter the functioning of those vital hypothalamic-pituitary pathways that modulate endocrine, autonomic, and immune processes. Alteration of these systems and of the brain sets the stage for the onset of disease" (1982, p. 150).

Ongoing stress also can have an impact on emotional health. Unrelenting distress can lead to a variety of emotional reactions, including depression, anxiety, and frustration. Mrs. Strickland is an 80-year-old African American woman who has been caring for her husband for the past 8 years. He recently became incontinent. When asked to describe some emotional reactions she had to this added stressor, she broke down in tears and replied,

"I guess I don't have to tell you what my emotional reaction is." Further discussion with Mrs. Strickland resulted in her sharing that she cries every day, but has gotten used to it; it has become a normal way of living. With long-term stress, these emotional reactions may last a long time. Caregivers may become used to these distressing emotions and come to consider them as normal and usual feelings, whereas these emotions would have been recognized as problems in less stressful times.

Given the potential impact of ongoing distress on the caregiver's health, it is important to begin to explore various means of helping the caregiver reduce this stress once a general understanding of stress is established. The first strategy of Stress Level Monitoring takes caregivers' understanding of stress to another level, allowing them to personalize the stress that they are experiencing. It is the first step in the Stress Reduction Technique and it will help caregivers determine when stress reduction strategies are needed.

☐ The Cycle of Distress

For caregivers, there will be moments when they feel relaxed for one reason or another, and times when they will feel distressed. If they do not deal with the stress when they first experience it, it likely will become a vicious cycle and develop into a pattern that maintains or heightens their stress level. For example, caregivers may feel distress over lack of family support. This distress may be manifested as anger or lashing out at a family member. Caregivers may then develop feelings of guilt over their behavior, thereby compounding their feelings of distress. In the case of Ms. Strickland, although she considered daily crying as normal, she complained about her daughter and son who rarely came to visit. When they did come, the visit inevitably would end up in an argument after which they would leave. Afterward she would feel guilty for starting the argument, and would feel even more distressed about her caregiving situation. When caregivers experience distress on a continual basis without any relief, they place themselves at increased risk of emotional health problems, as with Ms. Strickland, and also physical health problems. Therefore, it is important that caregivers have a daily awareness of where they are in the cycle.

Every person experiences stress differently; hence, it is important for caregivers to have a baseline of what is stressful for them while trying to determine where they are in the cycle of distress. For example, one caregiver may find a day full of doctors' appointments very distressing, while another caregiver may not. Furthermore, it is not merely the events that may cause stress for caregivers, but also what else is going on in their life on a particular day.

☐ The Use of Monitoring

An important way for caregivers to understand their baseline or average level of stress and also assess where they are in the cycle of distress is to begin monitoring their stress level on a daily basis. This concept has been used by Lewinsohn, Munoz, Youngren, and Zeiss (1992, p. 38) in treating depression. Lewinsohn's approach is that, by tracking one's level of mood, one is able to evaluate how successful one is at improving it. It is used as a tool in helping a person "look carefully at her activities and interactions to determine which activities lead to positive outcomes and which activities are associated with negative outcomes." Also, it allows people to increase awareness of the impact of events on their mood. Likewise, this same approach can be applied to managing stress. All caregivers have stress, and it is important to first have caregivers describe some of the stress they are experiencing. The professional can write down the stress as the caregivers describe it and keep it for reviewing in later discussions. This will help to individualize the program and serve as a reference later when introducing the DSR (discussed below).

In order to help caregivers grasp the role of monitoring their stress level, the following three points should be kept in mind. First, it is critical that they learn to recognize exactly when they feel distressed. What situations are occurring when they have these negative feelings? They should be reminded that both positive and negative situations can cause them to feel distressed. For example, they may feel distressed at a family gathering (a positive situation) because of fear of how other relatives may react to the behavior of the person with dementia. Or, they may feel distressed when their relative begins to wander from home (a negative situation).

Second, caregivers should learn to identify what specifically about a situation makes them feel calm and what makes them feel distressed. Often there are good and bad components to an event, so caregivers need to determine what about a situation helps them feel calm and minimizes distress, and then focus on maximizing these positive aspects. For example, when caregivers are taking their spouse to the doctor, they may find that if they allow plenty of time and first stop to eat at a restaurant, their spouse is better adjusted by the time they reach the doctor's office. On the other hand, if caregivers do not allow enough time and have to rush to make the appointment, their spouse may become more irritable and therefore cause the caregivers to feel distressed. Realizing this, caregivers can allow for extra time on their next visit to the doctor, which will help them to feel less stressed.

Third, in addition to recognizing when caregivers feel distressed and what causes the distress, caregivers should learn to ascertain where they are in the distress cycle. It is important for caregivers to not generalize their position. Few people are highly stressed all of the time. Most people have "good" and "bad" days. It may be useful to have caregivers compare their present position in the cycle to those times when they have felt more or less distress, in order to accurately perceive where they now are in the cycle. Once caregivers recognize these three basic ideas—the when, the what, and the where of the distress cycle—they are ready to be introduced to the DSR form.

☐ The Daily Stress Rating Form

Although few people are highly stressed all the time, most people fail to recognize this and feel that they are constantly under stress. The DSR form provides a method of tracking the caregiver's stress level in order to demonstrate that there truly are "good" days and "bad" days. It also provides the first step toward changing the caregiver's stress level: identifying when the stress happens.

The DSR is fairly easy to understand. It includes a scale that is meant to be a numeric representation of the overall stress level for each day, ranging from "very calm" (9) to "very distressed" (1). The idea is for caregivers to take 2 to 3 minutes at the end of the day to reflect on the events that took place, compare and contrast their images of calm events and distressing ones in a nondetailed manner, and then record an overall impression of the day on the DSR sheet. Figure 3-1 gives a sample of the DSR form.

The caregiver should be aware that few people have a day that is a 9, which might be compared to feeling as if one is basking in the sun on a deserted island. Likewise, few people are on the other end of the scale with a 1, feeling as if everything that could go wrong did, and are completely overwhelmed. The purpose of this form is that, by having caregivers look at their daily stress level, they will avoid generalizing and saying that they have nothing but stressful days. Instead, caregivers will recognize that days, like feelings, are different. It also is hoped that caregivers will realize that they have some days that actually are good.

By allowing caregivers to look back on the events and feelings of the day, the DSR can show caregivers that their feelings affect their stress level. It highlights the connection between the events of the day, the caregivers' behavior or reactions to those events, and their overall distress level. The key to understanding this connection is knowing what is happening at the time caregivers are having these distressing feelings.

After explaining the process to the caregivers, it is useful for the professional to go through an example. The professional should give the caregivers a copy of the DSR and have them rate the day's distress feelings. Then the

Please rate your level of stress for this day, i.e. how calm or distressed you feel, using the nine-point scale shown below. Enter the date in column 2 and your stress score in column 3. If you felt really calm (the best you have ever felt or can imagine yourself feeling), mark 9. If you felt really distressed (the worst you have ever felt or can imagine yourself feeling), mark 1. If it was a "so-so" (or mixed) day, mark 5. If you felt worse than "so-so," mark a number between 2 and 4. If you felt better than "so-so," mark a number between 6 and 8. **Remember, a low number signifies that you felt distressed, and a high number means that you felt calm today.**

Very Distressed 1   2   3   4   5   6   7   8   9   Very Calm

Monitoring Day	Date	Stress Score	Monitoring Day	Date	Stress Score	Monitoring Day	Date	Stress Score
1			16			31		
2			17			32		
3			18			33		
4			19			34		
5			20			35		
6			21			36		
7			22			37		
8			23			38		
9			24			39		
10			25			40		
11			26			41		
12			27			42		
13			28			43		
14			29			44		
15			30			45		

FIGURE 3-1. Daily Stress Rating (DSR) form.

professional should help the caregivers fill out the form, and offer feedback to the caregivers on how they have used the form. The caregivers should be given the form to use for several days, and may need help from the professional to work toward using it independently.

The Use of Charting

Once the caregivers have become familiar and comfortable with using the DSR form, helping them chart their stress level for a week at a time will enhance their ability to monitor their stress level. They should be able

The scale provided is meant to be a numeric representation of the day overall, ranging from "very calm" (9) to "very distressed" (1). The idea is for you to take two to three minutes at the end of the day to reflect on the events that took place. Compare and contrast your images of calm events and distressing ones in a non-detailed manner, then record an overall impression of the day and the date on the sheet.

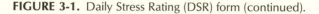

Very Distressed __ __ __ __ __ __ __ __ __ Very Calm
1 2 3 4 5 6 7 8 9

DAY	DATE	STRESS SCORE
1		

- Take 2 to 3 minutes to reflect on the day.
- Compare and contrast events of the day.
- Record the number that correlates with your overall impression.

FIGURE 3-1. Daily Stress Rating (DSR) form (continued).

to determine what their personal average distress level is by averaging their previous stress scores on the DSR; this can be used as a baseline for measuring where their stress level is in any given week. A caregiver's chart may look like Figure 3-2 for one week.

Note that the level of distress fluctuates from day to day; some days are less stressful than others, which is to be expected. It may be helpful for

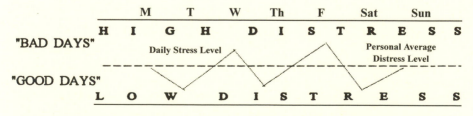

FIGURE 3-2. Example of a caregiver's charted stress level for one week.

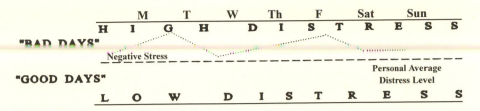

FIGURE 3-3. Example of a caregiver's charted stress that may indicate a negative stress level.

caregivers to think of the ups and downs in terms of "good" days and "bad" days. Another chart for the same caregiver in a different week may look like Figure 3-3.

Note that, during this second week, the caregiver continually stays above his or her personal average distress level (Figure 3-3). This often is an indication that the caregiver's stress level has become negative and potentially can be harmful if the caregiver does not seek ways to intervene in the cycle. Appropriate use of interventions at this point can change the direction of the spiral of increasing stress. Hence, charting can allow caregivers to visualize both their average daily stress level and if they are deviating from that average.

☐ Case Examples

Generally speaking, this first strategy is readily embraced by caregivers. It is easy for most caregivers to grasp, and most important, it takes very little time and thought. The challenge, however, is to help caregivers maintain continual use of this strategy and utilize it as a tool to indicate the need for further interventions. The following cases demonstrate this more fully.

Mr. Ramos

Mr. Ramos is a single man in his early forties. He has been caring for his mother, who has dementia, since the death of his father in 1985. A man who considers himself a natural to the role of caregiving, Mr. Ramos has accepted caregiving as his familial obligation, despite the stress that comes from providing care and the loss of personal freedom.

Mr. Ramos's caregiving role actually began before the death of his father, who soon after retirement began displaying symptoms of Parkinson's disease. Then, his father suffered a stroke and became even more functionally impaired. Mr. Ramos's mother became the primary caregiver for her long-time spouse, and Mr. Ramos became his mother's support. As he observed the amount of stress his mother was under, he shifted more and more into supporting and caring for her. Before his father's death, as Mr. Ramos gradually became more involved, his mother began demonstrating symptoms of dementia. She began to require assistance, and her son was "the obvious" caregiver.

There was a strong sense of reciprocity between Mr. Ramos and his parents, and this was especially true with his mother, to whom he was always close. When he was growing up, his mother seemed depressed, particularly in the 1960s when she was a "stereotypical housewife." Whereas his brother seemed to "block everything out," as a child Mr. Ramos felt his mother's depression and did his best to help her feel better. He also tried to make up for the fact that his father worked long hours while his mother was alone at home.

In spite of the fact that Mr. Ramos felt that being a caregiver was the right thing to do, he inevitably experienced a lot of stress from the role. First, his work was a source of distress. Mr. Ramos had a high-pressure job during the first few years of his mother's illness, and it increasingly became impossible for him to perform well in addition to giving her adequate care. His mother constantly would call him while he was at work, and he had difficulty concentrating. When it reached a point of culmination, he made the difficult decision to leave his job and move in with his mother to become her full-time caregiver. Although Mr. Ramos feels good about this decision, it is a constant source of worry because he wonders about the future of his career, and when and if he should reenter the workforce.

Second, Mr. Ramos finds that trying to access resources for his mother is a constant source of stress. He will not consider placing his mother in a nursing home, as he promised long ago never to do this. He has found adult day care centers unfriendly to him as a caregiver due to their limited hours and inability to handle his mother's behavioral problems like resistance and agitation. Cost also is an issue for Mr. Ramos, and he feels strongly that professionals do not recognize the reality of this factor when recommending respite.

Third, Mr. Ramos has had great difficulty maintaining personal relationships while being a caregiver. His friends do not seem willing to understand his position, and he looks to them mainly for occasional social interaction. Also, while being a caregiver, he started a relationship with a woman, but became unable to continue it because she wanted to talk about their future and Mr. Ramos could not consider giving up his role as caregiver.

When Mr. Ramos began to learn the Stress Reduction Technique, he was under a great deal of stress which was manifesting itself in both physical and emotional symptoms. He had great difficulty distinguishing between what aspects of his role were stressful and what aspects were not; to him, it was entirely stressful all of the time. When the concept of Stress Level Monitoring was introduced to Mr. Ramos, he thought it would be easy to do, and was convinced that he would be rating every day a 1. Due to his busy daily schedule and the fact that he rarely had a minute to himself, it was necessary to strategize with him as to when he would use the DSR form in order to ensure that it would be used every day. After going through in detail how Mr. Ramos spent his days, he agreed that the best time to try to use the form was after dinner, when his mother usually was content to watch television for 30 minutes.

After trying the DSR form for 1 week, Mr. Ramos reported that it was not what he had expected. While he agreed that it was very easy to use, he was having difficulty remembering to use it daily, and finding time for it at the end of the day. On this particular week, his mother had been increasingly agitated after dinner and Mr. Ramos found that he could not leave her unattended. By the time he got his mother to bed, he had forgotten about the form and was so exhausted he collapsed into bed. Also, Mr. Ramos indicated that he had a hard time determining where he fell on the scale. He did indeed feel that every day had been a 1.

Further discussion and problem solving resulted in a different plan for Mr. Ramos on week 2. Mr. Ramos agreed that he would leave the form on his bedside stand under his alarm clock, and try to use it every morning when he awoke to record a score for the previous day. He was able to recognize that mornings were generally calmer regardless of his mother's agitation level, as she usually needed to be awakened by Mr. Ramos and he typically had some time to himself before doing this. Trying to help him comprehend the DSR scale was a little more challenging. Considerable time was spent going over examples and then asking Mr. Ramos to recall a day where he felt less stressed than he had during the past week. It was necessary for Mr. Ramos to recall a day several months previous, but eventually he was able to agree that on that day he felt less stressed than he had been during the previous week. Using this as a reference, Mr. Ramos was then able to utilize the DSR scale and reflect on the prior week, resulting in a different score for each day. As a result of helping Mr. Ramos identify a better time to try to record his daily stress level, and assisting him in understanding how to apply the scale, Mr. Ramos was willing to continue using the DSR for a second week.

Following the second week, Mr. Ramos reported that he was successful in utilizing the form, and that it made more sense to him. Since he had 1 full week of scores, the next step was to chart his week in order to help him visualize his stress level. This proved to be very useful for Mr. Ramos, as he was able to identify that the middle of the week was most stressful for him. He recalled the events of the middle of the week and was able to ascertain what about the situation was distressing. From this, he was able to consider ways to help alleviate his stress should the situation occur.

Mr. Ramos continued to utilize the DSR form and charting to learn more about his stress. It became a very simple and quick way for him to be in touch with how he was managing, and it slowly diminished his tendency to catastrophize how stressful his role was. It also allowed him to move on and learn the other strategies in the Stress Reduction Technique.

Ms. Duncan

Ms. Duncan is a middle-aged woman who has been caring for her mother for many years. It all started when her father was diagnosed with cancer and had surgery. Ms. Duncan's parents were living in Texas and, following her father's surgery, she temporarily moved to Texas to help out. During this time, she noticed that her mother also was declining. After an evaluation, her mother was diagnosed with Alzheimer's disease. Ms. Duncan moved to southern California and decided to bring both parents along to live with her. Her father recovered from the surgery, but her mother continued to deteriorate cognitively.

Ms. Duncan reflects that she always has been a loving person and, as a child, she cared for her grandmother. She sees herself as a "people pleaser," which explains why she decided to care for her parents when her older sister claimed she was too busy and her brother asserted that he could not impose on his wife. Ms. Duncan reports that she saw a need and stepped in; there was no other way to handle the situation. It was clear that her mother could not help care for father during his recovery, and neither could her father help her mother. So, Ms. Duncan moved her parents into the small mobile home where she and her husband resided.

What developed in the following years was not easy. Ms. Duncan's husband was not supportive of her decision to move both parents into their small home, and this became a great source of contention in their marriage. Ms. Duncan often felt angry not only because she lacked her husband's support, but also because it was a constant source of conflict between them. After several years of their being unable to resolve this conflict, Ms. Duncan's husband left her and moved to Washington.

Ms. Duncan recognized that her home was a difficult environment to live in. Her mother constantly was wandering around the small space, seemingly in circles and agitated, and her father could not accept that it was a disease and that her mother could not control her behavior. In addition, although Ms. Duncan had lived apart from her parents for many years, her father seemed to slip back into his previous role of father once they moved in together. He expected Ms. Duncan to wait on him constantly, and he frequently voiced his opinion and disapproval of her daily activities. Once her husband left, her father seemed to constantly vacillate on how terrible that was. Ms. Duncan increasingly felt frustrated at the fact that her home was no longer hers, but continued to feel the need to provide the care she was giving.

Ms. Duncan worked at a private religious school nearby, and frequently had to leave during the workday to help with a crisis such as her mother leaving the home and her father being unable to manage the situation. There also were constant phone calls and she often found it hard to concentrate. However, in spite of the stressors that seemed to impede her work life, Ms. Duncan also reported that it has been her coworkers and friends at her church who provided the greatest support to her during the most trying days.

As her mother's condition progressively worsened, Ms. Duncan came to the difficult realization that she could no longer keep her at home. Along with the increased agitation, memory loss, and confusion, her mother was starting to fall frequently. Her father had hernia surgery and was unable to provide the hands-on care that Ms. Duncan's mother was beginning to require. Ms. Duncan could not quit her job as this was her only source of income. So, with the encouragement of her friends, she made the decision to place her mother in a nursing home. This was one of the most difficult and painful parts of being a caregiver, according to Ms. Duncan. Once she went through this troublesome process and got to the place where she was able to limit her visits to the nursing home, she began to rebuild her life. However, her father still continued to live with her and she resented how this was holding her back from moving on.

It was during the demanding stage of her mother's worsening health that Ms. Duncan was introduced to the Stress Reduction Technique. She was enthusiastic about trying the strategies because she felt she would collapse unless she got some help in dealing with the situation. When the DSR form was introduced to Ms. Duncan, she was anxious to begin to understand more about her stress level. She decided that she would try to fill out the form at the end of the day after dinner, as she usually had some time to sit down and relax once the dishes were done.

After the first week, Ms. Duncan was surprised that, although it seemed easy to sit down and rate her day, she had difficulty doing it consistently every day. She had failed to realize that 2 days a week she had to rush to activities at her church following dinner. And, on the nights that she was at home, her mother's increasing agitation in the evening made it difficult for her to find time after the dishes were done. Also, her stress level often went up after she had rated her day, because getting her mother to follow through with personal hygiene tasks before bedtime was becoming more challenging. Following some discussion, Ms. Duncan decided that a better approach would be to fill out the form as part of her own bedtime routine. Ms. Duncan seemed to understand how to rate her stress level, but she just had not been able to do it for more than 3 days that week. Ms. Duncan was determined to complete all 7 days for the second week.

After the second week, Ms. Duncan did indeed find that the later time worked better for her in recording her stress level. She had managed to rate her stress level for 7 days, and the next step was to help her chart the week. Once this was done and she could look at a visual representation of the week, Ms. Duncan was very surprised that she rated her stress level as high for only 3 out of the 7 days. When asked how her week went, she had responded that it was very stressful. On further discussion, however, Ms. Duncan was able to realize that it was not that every day was stressful, but it was that the amount of stress she experienced on 3 of the days was so high. She recalled the events of those 3 days and was able to identify particular situations that were very distressing. For example, when her mother refused to eat at the dinner table, it not only was the frustration of trying to coerce her into eating that was disturbing, but also her father's yelling at her mother was particularly upsetting. Ms. Duncan was able to gain a new perspective on specifically what caused her to feel distressed, and to use this information when she learned the additional strategies of the technique. For example, she was able to recognize that, when dinner was particularly disturbing, she needed to utilize a strategy to help bring her stress level down before trying to go to sleep. Once Ms. Duncan was able to make the connection between rating, charting, and taking steps to reduce her stress, she was convinced that this was the only way to manage on a daily basis and continued to use the DSR throughout her entire caregiving career.

☐ Summary

Helping caregivers understand stress and begin to utilize Stress Level Monitoring is the first step in introducing the Stress Reduction Technique. It is critical that enough time be spent at this early stage to help caregivers grasp the reason for and use of this basic tool in order for the remaining strategies to be effective. Unless caregivers can be empowered to recognize when they feel distressed, what specifically about the situation makes them feel calm and what makes them feel distressed, and where they are in the distress cycle, they will have great difficulty taking the next step to reduce their stress. However, if caregivers can master these steps with the use of the DSR form and weekly charting, they will be able to learn the additional strategies central to the technique and move forward in alleviating their distress.

☐ **References**

Hobfoll, S. E. (1988). *The ecology of stress*. New York: Hemisphere.

Holroyd, K. A., & Lazarus, R. S. (1982). Stress, coping, and somatic adaptation. In L. Goldberger & S. Brezniz (Eds.), *Handbook of stress: Theoretical and clinical aspects* (pp. 21–35). New York: The Free Press.

Kaplan, H. B. (1983). Psychological distress in sociological context: Toward a general theory of psychosocial stress. In H. B. Kaplan (Ed.), *Psychosocial stress: Trends in theory and research* (pp. 195–264). New York: Academic Press.

Lazarus, R. S. (1966). *Psychological stress and the coping process*. New York: McGraw-Hill.

Lazarus, R. S., & Folkman, S. (1984). *Stress, appraisal, and coping*. New York: Springer.

Lewinsohn, P. M., Munoz, R. F., Youngren, M., & Zeiss, A. M. (1992). *Control your depression*. New York: Fireside, Simon & Shuster.

McGrath, J. E. (1970). A conceptual formulation for research on stress. In J. E. McGrath (Ed.), *Social and psychological factors in stress* (pp. 10–21). New York: Holt, Rinehart & Winston.

Minter, R. E., & Kimball, C. P. (1980). Life events, personality traits, and illness. In I. L. Kutash, L. B. Schlesinger & Associates (Eds.), *Handbook on stress and anxiety: Contemporary knowledge, theory, and treatment* (pp. 189–206). San Francisco: Jossey-Bass.

Selye, H. (1980). The stress concept today. In I. L. Kutash, L. B. Schlesinger & Associates (Eds.), *Handbook on stress and anxiety: Contemporary knowledge, theory, and treatment* (pp. 127–143). San Francisco: Jossey-Bass.

Zegans, L. S. (1982). Stress and the development of somatic disorders. In L. Goldberger & S. Brezniz (Eds.), *Handbook of stress: Theoretical and clinical aspects* (pp. 134–152). New York: The Free Press.

Progressive Relaxation and Visualization

An important aspect of assisting caregivers in managing their stress is helping them recognize the usefulness of strategies that can reduce the symptoms of stress. In this chapter, two tools that are useful for caregivers to learn will be presented: progressive relaxation and visualization. A short review and history of progressive relaxation will be presented, and then each strategy will be described. Also included are instructions for progressive relaxation and visualization which can be used with caregivers. As with chapter 3, this chapter will conclude with three case studies.

☐ Progressive Relaxation

Progressive relaxation is unique to the many other existing forms of relaxation in that it requires muscle tension release cycles. The actual term *progressive relaxation* was coined in 1929 by Jacobson, and was used to describe a method that "could quiet the nerve-muscle system, including what is commonly called the 'mind'" (Jacobson, 1929; 1957, p. 87). Jacobson proposed that, even when one lies on a couch and tries to relax, there still remains "residual tension" that can dissipate only through concentrated relaxation of each part of the body. In effect, he suggested that, if one could relax the muscles, inevitably one could then relax mentally; the more relaxed the muscles, the more relaxed one would feel inside (Woolfolk &

Richardson, 1979). In its original form as developed by Jacobson, progressive relaxation could involve as much as 40 individual sessions, covering nearly 30 to 39 muscle groups (Carlson & Hoyle, 1993; Jacobson, 1929; Woolfolk & Richardson, 1979). In 1973, Bernstein and Borkovec produced a more abbreviated form of the technique in a manual which involves 8 to 12 sessions, covering 16 muscle groups. This streamlined version of the technique has allowed it to be greatly utilized by clinicians.

Many studies have been performed to evaluate the effectiveness of progressive relaxation in treating various physiological and psychological disorders. A quantitative review of research studies between 1981 and 1992 that used Bernstein and Borkovec's abbreviated progressive relaxation training (ABRT) was undertaken by Carlson and Hoyle (1993). They concluded that, on the whole, ABRT has been found to be an effective treatment for a range of disorders, including tension headaches, hypertension, cancer, and psychophysiological disorders, often involving pain management. Several studies also have been done on the effects of progressive relaxation in reducing insomnia in older adults (Engle-Friedman, Hazlewood, Bootzin, & Tsao, 1992; Gustafson, 1992; Piercy & Lohr, 1989), demonstrating that it is a useful form of treatment. However, it also has been noted that, for some older adults, progressive relaxation can be ineffective because of physical limitations that contraindicate muscle tension release procedures (Scogin, Rickard, Keith, Wilson, & McElreath, 1992). Scogin et al. (1992) suggested that imaginal relaxation, which requires passive focusing on physiological sensations, is a beneficial alternate option for those older adults unable to engage in progressive relaxation—in particular, older adults experiencing anxiety-related symptoms. Progressive relaxation, then, appears to be an effective tool for treating various stress-related symptoms, with the exception of older adults who may have chronic conditions which preclude them from using the technique. For these older adults, a similar exercise can be used, but they should be instructed to imagine these operations as opposed to actually tensing the muscles.

For caregivers, progressive relaxation can help them become aware of and control various muscles that may become tense and contribute to stress. Also, when caregivers are relaxed, they are less likely to become anxious and depressed. Learning to relax is similar to learning a skill and, with regular practice, caregivers can control their bodily tension and experience a greater degree of relaxation more of the time. It is recommended that caregivers practice progressive relaxation from 10 to 20 minutes, at least once a day. They should not worry if their progress seems slow. As long as caregivers work at the procedure and practice conscientiously, they will gradually experience an enjoyable state of relaxation. The key is to not try too hard and to not rush through the relaxation exercises.

Some common problems that caregivers may experience when doing relaxation therapy include external distractions, distracting thoughts, and physical reactions. First, external distractions can be avoided by encouraging caregivers to carefully select a time and place where they will not be disturbed. This may be very difficult given the constant attention that care recipients may require. It should be suggested that caregivers come up with creative times and places to perform the exercise. Some examples that caregivers may try include waking up 30 minutes before the care recipient wakes, performing the technique after the care recipient is asleep, trying to occupy the care recipient with an independent task (i.e., folding clothes), or suggesting that the care recipient take a short nap. After a while, caregivers will be less and less disturbed by minor distractions, such as worrying about the care recipient or hearing the care recipient in the other room. Second, caregivers' minds may wander during practice sessions and they may be plagued by distracting thoughts. This is common for people under a great deal of stress, so they should not become discouraged. Instead, caregivers should try to redirect their attention to their breathing or to relaxing their muscles. Third, at times, caregivers may experience small muscle spasms, jerks, or tingling sensations while they relax. These physical reactions actually are signs that they are relaxing and, with further practice, these reactions will decrease or become so familiar that they no longer will be distracting. These three common difficulties should be addressed and explained to caregivers before starting the technique, to ensure that, if they occur, caregivers will not automatically abandon the method.

Progressive relaxation consists of tensing and relaxing various muscles, and slow deep breathing. The muscle tensing and relaxing occurs in five steps. First, caregivers turn their attention to the muscles to be relaxed. Second, they tense the muscles, not so that it hurts, but enough so that they can feel the tension. If caregivers happen to have chronic pain in any part of their body, they should not tense these parts. As suggested by Scogin et al. (1992), caregivers should be instructed to use imaginal relaxation if chronic pain is experienced during the tensing of muscles, whether this be for particular muscles or for the entire exercise. For example, if caregivers have arthritis in their wrists, they may wish to utilize progressive relaxation techniques in other muscle groups of their bodies but, when they relax their arms and hands, they should use imaginal relaxation and simply imagine the relaxing of these muscles. Third, caregivers gradually let the tension go and feel the muscles unwind. Fourth, they tense the muscles again, but not as much as before. Last, caregivers gradually let the tension go and feel the muscles unwind completely. Slow deep breathing, which occurs in conjunction with the muscle relaxation, involves inhaling, holding the breath briefly, and then slowly letting out one's breath between slightly parted lips. As one breathes out, it is important to also let the tension go. These two techniques are essential for caregivers to learn, in order for progressive relaxation to be effective.

It is important for caregivers to realize that relaxation is a skill and, therefore, it may not work for them the first time they try it. But, with practice, caregivers can learn how to gain control over their muscle tension and begin to enjoy the feelings of relaxation. After caregivers have learned the technique, they can experience it on their own whenever they feel distressed.

Instructions

The following is a script that the professional can use with caregivers for progressive relaxation. The professional should take care to move very slowly and methodically through the exercise, making sure to pause after each step. The exercise should take at least 20 minutes, and every effort should be made to make sure caregivers are in a quiet place, free from distractions. It may be helpful to play soft music if noise distractions cannot be minimized.

Caregivers should be encouraged to follow each instruction carefully, even though it may seem uncomfortable at first. The purpose of going through the exercise with caregivers is to allow them to experience it and therefore increase the possibility that they will continue to use the technique regularly. If possible, the professional should go through the relaxation exercise with caregivers on a weekly basis for several weeks. The exercise goes as follows:

> Settle back as comfortably as you can. Let yourself relax to the best of your ability. Now, close your eyes. Take a few deep breaths. Inhale. Exhale. Inhale. Feel the tension building as you inhale. Exhale. Feel the tension leaving your body as you exhale; all the tensions of the day are going out of your body. Inhale once again. Hold your breath. Exhale.
>
> I'm going to ask you to tense each muscle two times. The first time, tense quite hard; the second time, only half as much. Now, let us begin.
>
> Tighten your feet muscles. Hold it, relax. Experience the sensation of relaxation when you relax your feet. As you feel the tension leaving your feet, allow this soothing feeling to move upward to your ankles. Repeat.
>
> To relax your calf muscles, press your feet and toes downward, away from your face, so your calf muscles become tense. Hold for a few seconds, then relax. Repeat once again. This time, bend your feet toward your face so that you feel tension along your shins. Bring your toes right up. Relax again. The second time, tense half as much.
>
> Tighten the muscles in your thighs by pushing them against the chair. Hold. Relax. Once again.

Tighten your buttocks muscles. Hold. Release. Again. Hold. Relax.

Pull the muscles of your stomach inward. Try to visualize your navel pressing against your spine and organs inside. I seem to hold a lot of tension in my stomach; maybe you do, too. I like to think of all my organs as rubber bands. Hold. Relax. The second time only half as hard. Tense. Release.

Next, you are going to relax your shoulders and upper back. You have two choices: Pull your shoulders back as though you were trying to touch your shoulder blades together, or you may want to try an alternate movement by raising your shoulders as though you were trying to touch your ears with the tops of your shoulders. Hold. Release. Repeat once again.

Hold your arms out and make a fist. Hold. Release. Repeat, the second time half as hard. Relax.

For the neck, there are two techniques to choose from. Pull your chin toward your chest using the muscles in the front of your neck, or you may wish to pull your head back with the muscles pushing back toward the wall. Begin tensing your muscles. Hold. Relax. Experience the relaxation for a brief period of time, then repeat.

Clench your teeth and pull back the corners of your mouth. At the same time, press your tongue firmly against the roof of your mouth. Hold. Release. Repeat once again.

Make a face. Raise your eyebrows as high as they will go. Wrinkle your brows and nose. Shut your eyelids tightly together. Hold for several seconds. Relax. Repeat again.

Now as you sit in your chair, with eyes closed, explore each of the regions you have relaxed. Think about your feet, calves and shins, thighs, buttocks, stomach, upper back, shoulders, arms, neck, mouth, and face. Try to be aware of any tension left in these muscles. If you are now free from tension, just quietly savor the feelings of calmness and relaxation. (Adapted from Woolfolk & Richardson, 1979, pp. 152–155).

☐ Visualization

Visualization is a technique that should follow the progressive relaxation exercise, but it also can be done on its own. It involves creating an image in one's mind that is tranquil and restful, and allowing oneself to be in that place for a period. Visualization allows one to imagine relaxation spreading through one's body. It enables one to escape a stressful environment for a brief duration, visit a very serene place, and then return to the stressful environment refreshed and with more energy. There is little empirical research available to demonstrate the effectiveness of visualization, but it is a technique that seems to be part of most current popular stress reduction material and it often is practiced in cancer and pain centers. Visualization is a particularly useful tool to use with caregivers because often caregivers are surrounded by stressors.

Instructions

The following is a script the professional can use with caregivers as a visualization exercise. It should follow the progressive relaxation technique for optimum effectiveness. As is true with progressive relaxation, the professional should take care to move very slowly and methodically through the exercise, making sure to pause after each statement. Caregivers should be encouraged to form mental sense impressions and involve all of their senses. This exercise should take an additional 10 to 15 minutes.

> Now, I want you to picture a blank screen in your mind. It may look like a TV or movie screen. Now, that you have the screen in mind, I want you to start with a dot of color in the middle of it. Choose a color that you find relaxing. For some people, that color may be yellow, blue, or orange. Choose any color that you find soothing. Now, let that color fill your screen. Once you have the color filling the screen, we will paint a picture on the screen. Now that you are relaxed, imagine yourself in a calm and peaceful place. Continue to take deep breaths. As your breathing gets deeper and slower, take yourself to a favorite spot. You may picture yourself in the mountains, at the beach, or in any tranquil environment that you like. This is a place just for you. It is warm, timeless, and tranquil. Your breathing is long and slow. There is no tension in your body and your mind is calm and relaxed. You feel at peace with yourself and fully relaxed. Your breathing is slow, deep, and steady, and you are enjoying your state of being. This is a time just for you. You are safe, calm, and warm. Time has disappeared and you may find yourself drifting. You continue to breathe slowly and enjoy your state of deep relaxation.
>
> When you are ready, slowly begin to ease back into the present. Your breathing is still relaxed and slow. You are still feeling relaxed, refreshed, and peaceful. When you wish to end this relaxation exercise, tell yourself that you can reach this gentle state of relaxation anytime you wish. When you open your eyes, you should feel refreshed, wide awake, and calm. Slowly open your eyes when you are ready. Remember, it is important to practice 20 to 35 minutes daily, in order to gradually experience a enjoyable state of relaxation.

☐ Case Examples

Both the progressive relaxation technique and visualization can be very useful for caregivers, regardless of the particulars of their situation. The following case examples describe the complex situations of three caregivers, and demonstrate how these techniques can be useful.

Ms. Brown

Ms. Brown is a middle-aged African American woman who has cared for her aunt who is in her eighties and has dementia. Ms. Brown's aunt moved into her home around the time of her eightieth birthday. It seemed silly for both of them to be living alone and, since they both enjoyed each other's company so much, it seemed like a natural step. At this point, Ms. Brown's aunt seemed very active and able bodied, but Ms. Brown had begun to notice that her aunt would not eat unless she was accompanied, her checkbook was unbalanced, and she constantly phoned Ms. Brown. Ms. Brown thought these problems would be taken care of once her aunt moved in with her.

And, it seemed easy for Ms. Brown to become the caregiver. She felt indebted to her aunt for the care she had given her as a child. Ms. Brown used to spend much time at her aunt's house when she was a child. Her aunt had no children of her own, so Ms. Brown was her aunt's "little girl." They had a warm, close relationship and Ms. Brown had many fond memories of all that her aunt had done for her. For Ms. Brown, becoming her aunt's caregiver was "just her": Her aunt required help and she merely was responding to a need.

However, the longer her aunt was with her, the more Ms. Brown realized how much assistance her aunt really required. Their relationship changed, and Ms. Brown started providing more and more care for her aunt. Providing assistance with personal care was especially difficult for Ms. Brown, as her aunt always had been so independent. The physical strain of changing dirtied undergarments, bathing her aunt, and helping her dress became overwhelming. Also, they seemed to have frequent conflicts, and they often would argue over how to do tasks and about how much supervision her aunt really needed. Between all of these strains, Ms. Brown found herself feeling more and more drained.

In addition to being her aunt's caregiver, Ms. Brown also worked full time as a director of a non-profit organization. She had a demanding job with long hours, many meetings, and regular out-of-town trips. It took all of her energy just to complete the tasks at work for which she was responsible. Between working and caregiving, Ms. Brown often was busy from first thing in the morning to late in the evening.

For Ms. Brown, progressive relaxation became an effective way to reduce her stress symptoms. Because she was going almost all hours of the day, she often found it difficult to relax. At first, Ms. Brown found it challenging to take the time to sit quietly and move slowly through the exercise; it was difficult for her to take her mind off of the many tasks she worried about daily. As soon as she sat down and was still, her thoughts turned to such worries as how she was going to rush home from work later to pick up her aunt from the local adult day care center, how she would manage to get her aunt to consent to a bath, and how she should use her aunt's money to ensure that she would get the best care possible. Also, Ms. Brown initially thought that she really was wasting too much time if she took 20 to 30 minutes for herself; she could accomplish many tasks in that time.

Gradually, Ms. Brown recognized that, in order for her to move through the progressive relaxation exercise, she would have to clear her mind and focus on relaxing each muscle. She started small by telling herself, when she had a distracting thought, that she could think about that concern later and should turn her attention to relaxing her body. And, once Ms. Brown began to feel the positive effects of being relaxed, she learned that the amount of time was worth it; she actually felt more energized to complete the tasks required of her. So, after trying out the technique several times and making an effort to take the time and concentration necessary, it seemed to work well.

Once Ms. Brown was able to recognize the usefulness of the technique, the next step was to determine when to use it and how often. Ms. Brown soon realized that doing relaxation techniques every morning before she started her busy day would help to reduce the amount of tension and stress she experienced throughout the day. By relaxing her mind and body at the start of every day, Ms. Brown found it easier to move through the day slowly, without trying to accomplish everything at once. Along with the relaxation techniques, Ms. Brown used visualization exercises to help her reach a place of quiet and serenity. In fact, she even tried out visualization at her church's prayer group that she attended two mornings a week and found it to work well. Ms. Brown liked to envision herself walking in the mountains around a cool, calm lake, with nothing to worry about. This served to be a point of focus for her while she was at work, trying to get everything completed before picking up her aunt. Because she took the time in the morning to visualize this peaceful place, she was able to reflect on it when feeling distressed and it helped her to relax during the busyness of the day.

Ms. Brown continued using the progressive relaxation techniques and visualization throughout her caregiving role. This was especially true during the period when Ms. Brown started facing the reality that she may have to place her aunt in a skilled nursing facility (SNF). She would pick up her aunt from the adult day care center after work, and then would spend the evening trying to bathe her aunt. Ms. Brown had to deal with her aunt's uncooperativeness and the physical demands of assisting with her personal care. Ms. Brown often felt exhausted after helping her aunt get into bed, but found it difficult to relax enough to sleep. She decided to try using the technique to sleep, and was successful. The same technique that helped her start her day and maintain a sense of control during the day also helped her go to sleep and get the rest that she needed. She experimented with different ways of using the exercise at night and found that listening to soothing music while lying in bed and moving through the technique was the most useful.

Once Ms. Brown placed her aunt in a nearby SNF, she found it particularly stressful to visit her aunt because she begged to go home. Even though

Ms. Brown felt she had the strong support of her church community, she found herself feeling exhausted and guilty when returning home after a visit. So, she tried using the technique to clear her mind immediately following a visit, and this also was useful. Although using progressive relaxation and visualization could not prevent Ms. Brown from being affected by the many stressors of caregiving, it helped her manage her symptoms of stress, and often helped her to better manage the challenges and tasks of the role.

Ms. Gomez

Ms. Gomez is a middle-aged woman who has been caregiving for her mother for several years. Ms. Gomez's mother lives with her in Ms. Gomez's apartment, along with Ms. Gomez's son who is in his mid-twenties. Her mother has dementia, and requires constant care and supervision.

Ms. Gomez has lived with her mother most of her life, from the time she was a child through her early adult years when she had a son as a single parent. In fact, Ms. Gomez's mother always has provided support for her: She helped out financially and with child care as Ms. Gomez struggled to rear her son in earlier years. Because of this, Ms. Gomez always has felt indebted to her mother. Several years before Ms. Gomez assumed the role of caregiver, her mother had moved to Florida to live with Ms. Gomez's sister and to be near to Ms. Gomez's son who was in Florida for a while and with whom her mother was very close. During this time, her mother began exhibiting symptoms of dementia and, because Ms. Gomez was concerned about the quality of care that her sister was providing to her mother, she made plans to move her mother back in with her when her son returned home.

The following years became much more than Ms. Gomez had anticipated. As her mother deteriorated and, due to the dementia, became more dependent, Ms. Gomez became increasingly frustrated with the constraints imposed on her because of caregiving. Her mother was very demanding and expected her to do everything. Almost suddenly, their once-close relationship seemed to disappear. Also, her mother increasingly favored her son, and demanded that Ms. Gomez do more and more for him. Ms. Gomez felt the need to be constantly available for her mother, and experienced unending pressure from her mother to also "wait on" her son.

In addition to feeling pulled at home, Ms. Gomez worked full time and had a lengthy commute to her workplace. Her caregiver role greatly affected her work performance, and she often found it difficult to concentrate and keep up with her workload. She was unable to be flexible at work, because unless she left the office promptly at the end of each day, she would not make it home in time to relieve the in-home worker who demanded to leave at a certain time. So, Ms. Gomez felt pressures both at work and at home and, as a result, easily became irritated and upset.

For Ms. Gomez, muscle tension was a part of daily life, and progressive relaxation seemed to help her deal with this symptom of stress. When Ms. Gomez first started using the technique, she was so relaxed by the end of the exercise that she began to fall asleep. It seemed as if she was so exhausted by the end of the day that, when she actually gave herself permission to stop and was quiet, she relaxed rather quickly. However, without the technique, it was difficult to set aside time for herself and her tension seemed to run from one day into the next.

In addition to using the exercise at the end of her day when Ms. Gomez felt fatigued, she also learned to use it to reduce specific tensions. Ms. Gomez found that, as she became accustomed to feeling relaxed, she also became cognizant of when she was experiencing tension and in what part of her body. She quickly realized that, when she had a conflict with her mother (particularly when it was related to Ms. Gomez's son), she would hold tension in her shoulders. Once aware, Ms. Gomez applied the progressive relaxation technique and was able to release the tension in this part of her body. Visualization added an extra measure and allowed Ms. Gomez to escape the stressors that surrounded her and to imagine a place that was calming. Again, she found this helpful following a stressful interaction with her mother, which seemed to occur daily. From this she gained a new energy. Ms. Gomez found the techniques quite helpful and reported that she continued to utilize them throughout her many years as a caregiver.

Ms. Schmidt

Ms. Schmidt is a woman in her forties who has been caring for her mother for several years. She had been living in St. Thomas and working at an art gallery, but returned to the United States after noticing her parents' need for care on one of her visits home. Her parents had immigrated from Germany when Ms. Schmidt was a young girl and, being an only child, she felt indebted to them for all that they had provided for her. After her father died, Ms. Schmidt moved in with her mother, and became her only and constant support.

Ms. Schmidt openly admits that she spent most of her adult life trying to "free herself" from her parents, and then ended up becoming dependent on them again. She worked hard to develop a healthy relationship with them while living away from them but, when she returned, all of her hard work seemed to dissipate. In order to care for them, she felt it necessary to give up all possibilities of working and to devote her entire energies to their needs. Their care needs were constant, and Ms. Schmidt thought it unacceptable to have anyone but herself fulfill these needs. After all, her parents expected this of her. Therefore, she no longer received her own paycheck, paid her own bills, lived in her own home, spent time alone, or nurtured her own friendships—all aspects of independence she had worked hard to develop. This, she says, was the most stressful part of being her mother's caregiver. Ms. Schmidt felt like she was socially, intellectually, emotionally, and economically putting her life on hold. She felt very isolated most of the time, and also felt hostile toward her mother because of all that she was sacrificing.

Ms. Schmidt was with her mother constantly, with little relief. Her routine began in the morning with waking her mother, dressing her, and transferring her to the couch in the living room. Then she prepared breakfast and tried to get her mother to eat. This was a challenge, as her mother frequently was agitated and uncooperative. After this was completed, Ms. Schmidt would try to get herself bathed and dressed, and then went about keeping her mother stimulated while at the same time managing the household tasks. She did not have a social life as her mother required constant supervision, and Ms. Schmidt found it challenging just to run out to get groceries and run errands. This day in and day out caregiving caused Ms. Schmidt to often battle feelings of anxiety and depression.

This was particularly true toward the end of her mother's life, when her physical care became increasingly taxing. Her mother was incontinent and pulled off her undergarments, often after Ms. Schmidt had bathed her. Also, her mother became "dead weight" and it was awkward to try to lift her out of bed, dress her, and sit her in the living room on the couch for the day. Her mother seemed to have more frequent mood swings and constantly was angry at Ms. Schmidt, making it difficult for her to have patience with her.

Ms. Schmidt often found herself tense and unable to relax; she constantly felt the need to think about what her mother needed and to be one step ahead of her. She agreed to try progressive relaxation training to attempt to mitigate this tension and stress, but initially was doubtful that it would work. First, her mother expected her to be at her beck and call, and Ms. Schmidt was unsure when she could set aside a time where she would not be distracted. Second, she did not think she actually could relax.

To begin, Ms. Schmidt tried setting aside time when her mother was napping in the afternoon, but she immediately found that she was easily distracted by the need to complete the tasks she usually was able to do during this time. So, Ms. Schmidt attempted to try the exercise once her mother was in bed. Although this allowed her to have time to herself, she found that it was not very beneficial because she never had trouble relaxing before bed, but did find herself feeling tense in the middle of the day. After some thought, Ms. Schmidt decided to complete the tasks that she usually did during her mother's afternoon nap in the evening after her mother was asleep, and to utilize progressive relaxation during the afternoon nap. This allowed Ms. Schmidt to experience the technique during the time of the day that she most needed it, and prevented her from being plagued with thoughts of tasks that needed to be done.

Once she had identified the optimum time, she then had to take the time to move through the exercise. It took several weeks before she was able to complete the entire exercise and feel the effects of it. In spite of her doubts about her ability to relax, she was determined to try to alleviate her tension. She started small and, at first, spent only 10 minutes moving through the relaxation technique. As she began to feel the positive effects of the exercise, she gradually increased her time to 30 minutes. Ms. Schmidt found visualization to be easier, as she immediately was taken back to the picturesque beaches of St. Thomas, which she had left several years before. This allowed her to return to a place that she had loved and to a time in her life that was more enjoyable.

After Ms. Schmidt realized that these techniques could have some positive effects, the challenge was to be consistent with the exercises and to continually make time for them. This was particularly true when she had a difficult day with her mother, although she quickly recognized that, on these difficult days, she benefited most from the techniques. With constant repetition and regular exploration of reasons why she was not using the exercises at particular times, she was able to integrate them into her daily life.

Over time, she found progressive relaxation and visualization to be effective tools in reducing her stress level. By using them in the middle of the day, she was able to go through the rest of the day without increasing her tension level. The methods became useful in reducing the sense of anxiousness that previously had plagued her, and they allowed her to continue caregiving until her mother's death.

☐ Summary

Progressive relaxation and visualization are interrelated, and they encompass a perspective on dealing with stress that caregivers may not have thought about much. They are methods that should be discussed with caregivers in-depth, to allow caregivers to fully understand them, experiment with them, and then use them on a daily basis. At first, caregivers may be reluctant to consider these ways of addressing stress, and the professional may be required to spend a good amount of time going over the concepts and practicing various techniques with them until they are able to realize their effectiveness. The end result, however, should be that caregivers have learned additional ways to deal with the stressors of caregiving. These ways may seem alternative to caregivers at first glance, but eventually may offer an innovative manner by which caregivers can approach coping with the daily effects of caregiving.

 # References

Bernstein, D. A., & Borkovec, T. D. (1973). *Progressive relaxation training*. Champaign, IL: Research Press.

Carlson, C., & Hoyle R. (1993). Efficacy of abbreviated progressive muscle relaxation training: A quantitative review of behavioral medicine research. *Journal of Consulting and Clinical Psychology, 61*, 1059–1067.

Engle-Friedman, M., Hazlewood, L., Bootzin, R., & Tsao, C. (1992). An evaluation of behavioral treatments for insomnia in the older adult. *Journal of Clinical Psychology, 48*, 77–90.

Gustafson, R. (1992). Treating insomnia with a self-administered muscle relaxation training program: A follow-up. *Psychological Reports, 70*, 124–126.

Jacobson, E. (1929). *Progressive relaxation*. Chicago: University of Chicago Press.

Jacobson, E. (1957). *You must relax*. New York: McGraw-Hill.

Piercy, J., & Lohr, J. (1989). Progressive relaxation in the treatment of an elderly patient with insomnia. *Clinical Gerontologist, 8*, 3–11.

Scogin, F., Rickard, H., Keith, S., Wilson, J., & McElreath, L. (1992). Progressive and imaginal relaxation training for elderly persons with subjective anxiety. *Psychology and Aging, 3*, 219–424.

Woolfolk, R., & Richardson, F. (1979). *Stress, sanity and survival*. New York: Signet.

The Relaxing Events Schedule

The Relaxing Events Schedule is a method that can help caregivers gain control over their time; at the same time, it can allow them to experience a sense of enjoyment and gratification in the midst of the stress of everyday caregiving. The schedule can provide caregivers permission to engage in activities that are relaxing. This chapter will start by highlighting the issue of caregivers caring for themselves, and then it will describe the Pleasant Events Theory on which this strategy is based. The role of relaxing events in managing and relieving caregiver stress will be discussed, followed by an in-depth description of this strategy. To demonstrate how the Relaxing Events Schedule can be utilized with caregivers, the chapter will end with a case example.

☐ Caring for Self

Given the high level of burden and distress that caregivers may experience (Schulz, O'Brien, Bookwala, & Fleissner, 1995), one of the most elementary aspects of trying to help caregivers manage their stress involves caring for themselves. Caregivers usually will acknowledge that they must take better care of themselves, but rarely will do so. Most of the time, caregivers will take better care of their family members than themselves. They may routinely report stress-related symptoms, such as anxiety, depression, and fatigue. Also, caregivers often may experience feelings of anger, resentment, and guilt over not doing enough, even though they may spend 24 hours a day with the person being cared for (Zarit, Orr, & Zarit, 1985).

The burden of caring for a person who has dementia can be emotional as well as physical, and may lead caregivers to feel sad, discouraged, frustrated, or trapped; they also may feel tired and overwhelmed. Many times, caregivers put aside their own needs for rest, friends, and time alone in order to care for the person with dementia. It is not unusual for caregivers to feel alone as friends disappear, and they may not know any other people who are involved in caregiving. It also may become impossible for caregivers to get out of the house and they may become socially isolated.

Because of these typical factors, it is critical that caregivers schedule time into their routines to spend on themselves (Mace & Rabins, 1981). When caregivers no longer participate in activities that they enjoy, the greater is their feeling of distress and burden. It can become a vicious circle—the less caregivers do for themselves, the more stressed and burdened they feel; the more burdened they feel, the less they feel like caring for themselves. Caregivers can begin to feel trapped in a downward spiral. It is this very process that the Relaxing Events Schedule serves to address both by preventing and intervening in the spiral.

☐ Pleasant Events Theory

Lewinsohn, Munoz, Youngren, and Zeiss's social learning model of depression (1986) introduced the idea that pleasant events are linked to depression. Although people do not experience depression in the same way, depression typically is accompanied by feelings of hopelessness and helplessness. These feelings contribute to the attitude that there is very little control over life and the future. The approach of Lewinsohn et al. suggests that people can get help in controlling their own depression by working with a counselor who can offer encouragement and support while monitoring their progress.

In their concept of pleasant activities, Lewinsohn et al. asserted that, if one feels depressed, it is likely that he or she is not involved in many pleasant activities, or perhaps is involved in activities that do not produce much pleasure. When one experiences few activities that are considered to be pleasant, one feels depressed; when one feels depressed, one does not feel like doing the kinds of activities that are likely to be pleasurable or satisfying. It is similar to the chicken or the egg phenomenon: Does a low number of pleasant activities cause one to feel depressed, or does feeling depressed cause one to be inactive? Lewinsohn et al. proposed that it works both ways: Being involved in only a few pleasant activities causes one to feel depressed, and being depressed causes one to be inactive. This approach considers there to be a relationship between the number of pleasant activities and mood, and provides a potential handle on managing depression. By increasing pleasant activities, one can help oneself feel better. This model of depression, created in 1978, was used primarily with depressed younger individuals.

Although Lewinsohn et al.'s model was used primarily with depressed younger adults, a study performed by Gallagher and Thompson in 1982 examined Lewinsohn's earlier behavioral model as a way to treat depressed older adults. In their study, they evaluated three distinct forms of treatment: Lewinsohn et al.'s behavioral model, Beck's cognitive model (1967, 1974), and a more traditional brief relational and insight treatment approach. Participants in the cognitive and the behavioral treatment groups appeared to maintain gains longer than those in the relational and insight therapy condition. Those in the cognitive and the behavioral groups appeared to have acquired skills that they used on a regular basis over time. Skills taught in the behavioral model included overt and covert relaxation techniques, management of time, social skills, and problem solving. In addition, participants were taught to monitor their moods and track pleasant and unpleasant activities on a daily basis. Clearly then, this study raised the possibility that Lewinsohn et al.'s model could be applied to older adults experiencing depression.

Taking the application of the model one step further, a study performed in 1988 by Gallagher and Lovett demonstrated its use among the caregiver population. Given the reality that caregivers often find that time available for their own pleasant activities is minimized because of the constant, and often unpleasant, demands of the caregiver role, this study considered the link between caregivers' level of emotional distress and the number of pleasant and unpleasant events experienced. More specifically, they looked at caregivers' *self-efficacy* (individuals' perception of their ability to perform specific behaviors) for problem solving, using the model of D'Zurila (1986), and self-efficacy for maintaining pleasant events, using the model of Lewinsohn et al. They predicted that self-efficacy levels would be inversely related to emotional distress.

Results indicated several notable findings. First, in agreement with other similar studies, the caregivers in their study showed higher rates of depression than the general older adult population. Second, efficacy for maintaining pleasant activities and problem solving was positively related to caregivers' level of morale and negatively related to level of depression. Third, Lewinsohn et al.'s social learning model of depression, along with the social problem-solving model of D'Zurilla and the notion of self-efficacy, appeared to be useful in approaching caregiver stress and the development of interventions. Last, the study suggested that psychoeducational classes are not always feasible interventions for depressed caregivers because they often are unable to leave their caregiving duties; more specialized interventions were recommended to treat this population.

It is interesting to note that the Pleasant Events Theory also has been applied with successful results to the care recipient population. Teri and Uomoto (1991) performed a study that assessed whether there was a significant relationship between depressed mood and pleasant activities among individuals with Alzheimer's disease, and also looked at the feasibility of training caregivers to be successful at increasing the level of pleasant events experienced by the care recipients and thereby improving their depressed mood. Caregivers were taught behavioral management skills to alleviate depression in the person receiving care. Although the sample was quite small, the results indicated that depressed mood was related to the frequency and duration of pleasant activities, with more frequent and longer duration of pleasant events significantly related to less depressed mood. Worth noting was the suggestion from the results of the study that caregivers who may be depressed prior to treatment also may benefit from the intervention.

☐ Caregiver Stress and Relaxing Events

Given the apparent relationship between pleasant events and mood among caregivers, there is reason to consider the application of this approach to caregivers experiencing distress. The fact that relaxation techniques can be used to relieve distress suggests that relaxing events is a more appropriate way to apply the Pleasant Events Theory to distressed caregivers. Similar to the Pleasant Events Theory, the Relaxing Events Theory holds that stress is a result of too few relaxing events and too many stressful events. The basis of the theory rests on the idea that the combination of the two produces and maintains the distress cycle and, in order to reduce feelings of distress and increase feelings of relaxation, caregivers have to schedule more relaxing events into their lives.

As a result of all the duties and responsibilities that caregivers must perform for their relatives with dementia (e.g., the seemingly endless demands on time, energy, money), it is likely that there are too few activities caregivers engage in that are strictly for their own relaxation. What is necessary to manage the stress is a balance between the nonrelaxing, but necessary, tasks of caregiving and the activities that caregivers find relaxing. By increasing relaxing events, caregivers can lessen their stress and gain some control over their distress cycle.

☐ The Relaxing Events Schedule

The Relaxing Events Schedule is a method to help caregivers take time for themselves. The technique requires that caregivers take time to identify events in their lives that they find relaxing and write them down in a calendar or a daily planner. The goal is to accomplish a modest increase in relaxing events. This may involve an increase in activities that caregivers have done and found relaxing in the past, or it may involve engaging in activities that they never have done before, but which they think may be relaxing.

The first step in helping caregivers develop a Relaxing Events Schedule is to have caregivers set aside a specific time to develop the plan in writing. According to Lewinsohn et al. (1986), this step is critical for five reasons. First, it allows caregivers to commit to the plan. The process of writing down specific events for each day of the forthcoming week formalizes an agreement and helps caregivers prioritize the relaxing activities. Second, planning helps caregivers find balance between the activities that must be accomplished and the activities that they really want to do. Third, having a clear plan permits caregivers to look ahead and examine if there will be any difficulties that may interfere with the plan. For example, if caregivers want to go to the movies on Friday afternoon, they may have to arrange for someone to come and stay with the care recipient. It is critical for caregivers to think ahead so that they can make necessary arrangements for care in order to follow through with the planned relaxing activity. Fourth, putting the plan in writing will contribute to caregivers' abilities to resist the countless demands that might otherwise conflict with the plan. Fifth, the process of planning will give caregivers a sense of control. Given the fact that caregivers may feel out of control on many levels, this is an important element that will add to caregivers' abilities to feel control over their time and, consequently, over their lives.

The process of setting aside time to plan the Relaxing Events Schedule often can seem overwhelming and almost an impossible task to caregivers. However, if the professional can keep these five aspects of planning in mind when discussing the schedule, caregivers will have a better chance of being successful. By making a commitment to write down relaxing events with activities caregivers really want to do, by looking ahead to make sure there are no conflicts, by following through on what is on the written page, and by resisting demands on this set aside time, caregivers will feel more in control and thus more likely to continue with the Relaxing Events Schedule as a tool to decrease their feelings of distress.

Once caregivers understand the importance of setting aside time to write down and schedule relaxing events, they are ready to start. The Relaxing

Events Schedule involves three steps. First, caregivers must identify relaxing events in their lives. Second, they must decide when to schedule events and write them in the appropriate space for the designated time. Third, caregivers have to follow the schedule.

Identifying Relaxing Events

In this first step, the professional should keep in mind that a relaxing event is a subjective one, since what may be relaxing to one caregiver may be stressful to another. For example, one caregiver may find going to a restaurant very stressful, while another caregiver may find this relaxing. It is important to allow caregivers to identify what they find relaxing, regardless of how it may seem to others. Caregivers may have difficulty identifying a relaxing event and it may take some coaching from the professional. Caregivers may have to think about years past in order to identify a relaxing event. It may be helpful for the professional to assist caregivers in identifying events by exploring how their lives were prior to being caregivers, what things they enjoyed doing then. It also may help to have them discuss activities that other people enjoy doing which they may wish to try; for example, they may be aware that a friend enjoys reading poetry and, although they never have done this, they may want to consider it. It is important to discuss specific examples of relaxing events; for example, talking with a friend, reading the newspaper, taking a bath, stretching and exercising, taking a walk, reading, watching a movie, or working on a hobby. Figure 5-1 can be used as a handout if caregivers are having a hard time thinking of a relaxing event. However, the examples should not be a substitute for caregivers' own lists, but should be used as a starting place to prompt caregivers to think of what they find relaxing.

The following case examples demonstrate the subjective nature of relaxing events and the fact that they should be simple activities. Ms. Rubinov, a 52-year-old woman originally from Russia, was caring for her mother who was incontinent and dirtied her clothes and bedding multiple times a day. This problem created an abundance of laundry that had to be done. When asked to identify a relaxing event, Ms. Rubinov explained that folding the sheets and clothes was very relaxing to her; she found the warmth and softness of the clothes a comfort. However, Mr. Morrison, a 62-year-old White caregiver, complained that, after working all day, coming home, preparing dinner, and helping his wife who was in the early stages of dementia get ready for bed, the last task he wanted to do was laundry. Just the thought of having to do it caused him a great deal of stress. Clearly then, it is important for caregivers to identify for themselves what they find relaxing.

Sitting in the sun.
Doing a project your own way.
Listening to music.
Going to a restaurant.
Exercising.
Watching a movie.
Talking about philosophy or religion.
Helping someone.
Doing a crossword puzzle.
Observing nature.
Planning trips or vacations.
Playing with a pet.
Reading a newspaper, magazine, or novel.
Learning something new.
Working on a hobby.
Laughing.
Taking time to relax.
Watching television.
Being with friends.
Breathing fresh air.
Eating a good meal or snack.
Showering or bathing.
Wearing informal clothes.
Having coffee, tea, and so forth with friends.
Thinking about your problems.
Singing.
Solving a problem.
Getting or giving a massage.
Having your hair or nails done.
Sleeping or napping.
Looking at the stars or moon.
Going to a support group.
Taking relaxation training.
Having peace and quiet.

FIGURE 5-1. Examples of relaxing events. Adapted from Lewinsohn's Pleasant Events Schedule, first published in MacPhillamy, D. J., and Lewinsohn, P. M. (1982). The pleasant events schedule: Reliability, validity, and scale intercorrelation. *Journal of Consulting and Clinical Psychology, 50*, 363–380. Used with permission.

TABLE 5-1. Daily planner

	Sunday	Monday	Tuesday	Wednesday	Thursday	Friday	Saturday
7:00							
8:00							
9:00							
10:00							
11:00							
12:00							
1:00							
2:00							
3:00							
4:00							
5:00							
6:00							
7:00							
8:00							
9:00							
10:00							

Often, caregivers may be hesitant to say that they have anything relaxing associated with their situation, and this usually is because they do not realize how simple a relaxing event can be. In fact, this was the case with Mr. Morrison. When he started exploring relaxing events, he identified many events that sounded very complicated to accomplish. For example, he thought of golfing, which involved arranging care for his wife, arranging for someone to play with, and setting up a tee time. He never considered the fact that sometimes just sitting and doing nothing was relaxing for him. It is important for caregivers to realize that relaxing events can be simple and they also should be realistic and easy to accomplish, so that the events themselves do not create additional stress.

Deciding When to Schedule

After helping caregivers identify relaxing events, the next step is to assist caregivers in taking the events that they have identified as relaxing and write them in on the Relaxing Events Schedule. Caregivers should be encouraged to write down at least one relaxing event each day for an entire week. Table 5-1 is a sample of a daily planner that can be used to schedule relaxing events.

It may be necessary to take a significant amount of time to help caregivers go through this process because it is likely at this stage that caregivers will indicate resistance to this scheduling notion. This resistance commonly takes two forms. First, although it is common for caregivers to acknowledge that they do not have many relaxing activities in their lives, they may be gripped by the picture that it is too overwhelming for them to think of *what* they can fit into their schedules. It is helpful to present the activity of scheduling as a chance for caregivers to begin changing this picture, and then suggest that the hour per week spent with the professional to go over the stress reduction program be the first item on the planner. For example, Mr. Morrison felt that he had no relaxing time anymore, much less time to himself. His first reaction to scheduling in relaxing events was that he could not schedule anything further into his week. It was suggested that the hour he spent with the professional going over Stress Reduction Techniques be the first scheduled relaxing event. Mr. Morrison agreed. Since he already was meeting with the professional once a week, this suggestion seemed like a good plan. Likewise, if caregivers already are engaging in some relaxing activities, these activities should be included in the planner so they are able to recognize what they already are doing.

In helping caregivers decide what events should be scheduled in, it is essential to reinforce that a relaxing event does not need to take a great deal of time and that it can be very simple in nature. For example, another caregiver, Ms. Hayworth, had listed reading the newspaper as a relaxing event but, when it came time to fill out the Relaxing Events Schedule, she questioned whether this in fact was a relaxing event since it usually took only 10 minutes. Once she was able to recognize that indeed this activity was a relaxing way for her to start the day and that, since becoming a caregiver, she never made time for it and instead found herself stacking the delivered newspaper day after day with regret that she had not had time to read it, she realized that it was a worthwhile event to schedule in. So, caregivers may require some reinforcement to help them appreciate the significance of scheduling in simple and time-limited activities.

Second, another common form of resistance is that caregivers may have difficulty recognizing *how* they can fit these events into their schedules; they may think that they do not have 1 minute to spare in the week to schedule in anything else. When under distress, it is typical for caregivers to generalize about their time. They may feel as if they always have to attend to their relative. For example, for Ms. Rolm, the most stressful aspect about caregiving was the fact that her life was controlled by the need for her mother to be supervised 24 hours a day, 7 days a week. She did not feel she had a moment to herself, let alone 15 minutes. For most caregivers, this is a common complaint. Often, caregivers will describe their situation as one in which they feel imprisoned. Ms. Rolm did not even think she could go to the bathroom without her mother calling her name or needing something. It is important for the professional to validate caregivers' feelings, but then gently challenge what may be a cognitive distortion, by helping caregivers break down how they spend their time. In the process of talking out her daily routine, Ms. Rolm indicated that her mother slept in until 8 a.m., and went to sleep consistently at 10 p.m. When the professional pointed out that this allowed some time in the morning and some before she went to bed, Ms. Rolm replied that it often was difficult for her to relax during this time for fear that her mother would awaken and need her assistance. After some discussion, however, Ms. Rolm was able to see that, by scheduling in several relaxing activities during this time, it would allow her to maximize time to herself and help her to relax. And, Ms. Rolm was able to recognize that her mother had never awakened during this time and that, although this was a very real fear, it was unlikely that it would happen. Even though Ms. Rolm was able to see her own cognitive distortion and, in doing so, felt less fearful of using this time for herself, she decided a further way to allay her fear would be to try out activities that would allow for interruptions by her mother. This example demonstrates the critical nature of the discussion between the professional and caregivers to help identify how to fit in relaxing events.

These two forms of resistance—the what and the how of scheduling relaxing events—are the most common, but certainly many more may emerge. During this step, caregivers should be encouraged to voice any resistance they may have about the Relaxing Events Schedule so that the professional can help provide validation, help them understand the resistance, and then move beyond it.

Following the Schedule

Once caregivers have identified relaxing events and decided when to schedule them in, caregivers should be encouraged to follow the schedule for 1 week. After this week, it is important for the professional to follow up and find out if the caregivers were able to complete the relaxing event as scheduled. If the caregivers were able to complete the schedule, a discussion should occur as to whether caregivers found the schedule helpful in terms of their stress levels. Reference to the Daily Stress Rating (DSR) Form will be useful at this stage to see if the relaxing events impacted caregivers' daily stress ratings. Typically, it takes more than 1 week for caregivers to see an impact on their distress levels but, at this early stage, it is helpful to allow caregivers to recognize the connection between the Relaxing Events Schedule and their stress levels. Once the association is clear, caregivers will be more likely to continue utilizing the schedule, with the understanding that it should eventually impact their stress levels.

If caregivers were unable to follow the schedule, the professional should investigate the reasons why, and help caregivers problem solve so that the following week will be successful. Some of the common reasons caregivers will give as to why they were unable to follow through with the schedule include busyness, an unexpected problem with the care recipient (i.e., medical difficulty, falling, not sleeping), tiredness, and thoughts such as "I'm not worth it" and "It won't help." Each of these reasons are worth exploring further, as they are often reality based. First, if caregivers found they were too busy to fit in the scheduled relaxing events, perhaps it is necessary to take a second look as to whether the events identified were simple enough and whether they were scheduled in at the best times. Second, if there was an unexpected problem with the care recipient, the professional should inquire if this consumed the caregivers' entire week or if it made it difficult for the caregivers to follow through. Often it is helpful for caregivers to realize that, if it did not take up the whole week, it could have been advantageous for them to go back to the schedule after the incidents in order to relieve the additional stress that was created. Third, if tiredness is given as a reason for not following the schedule, perhaps caregivers should try to complete the activities only 3 days out of the week. Assisting caregivers in taking small steps can help them take care of themselves; eventually they will be able to recognize that, even when they feel tired, the relaxing activities can be beneficial. Fourth, an in-depth conversation about the underlying feelings behind the thoughts caregivers may be having will help to get them to the next step of trying the technique. For example, after 1 week, Ms. Rolm admitted that she had thoughts such as "I'm not worth it." In discussion with the professional, it became apparent that, since caring for her mother, she had quit her job which was a strong source of self-esteem. Also, since childhood, her relationship with her mother had not been good, and she always had felt her mother was judgmental. Ms. Rolm believed that, since her mother had developed Alzheimer's disease, she seemed to be more critical and more demanding of her. Once she was able to talk about her thoughts of not being worthwhile and to gain awareness of the emotional source of these thoughts, she was able tell herself that indeed she had an identity beyond being her mother's daughter and caregiver, and that she was worth spending time on. Each reason given for lack of follow through on the schedule usually is reflective of the challenges of the particular caregiving situation and there is value in discussing each further.

Also, it is important to remember that setting a specific goal that is reasonable is a critical part of the plan. Caregivers should be reminded that it is more important to be successful than to try for a large increase in relaxing events, but fail to accomplish them. One way to help caregivers follow through with the schedule is to include in the plan a contract for rewarding themselves. Caregivers should include only those rewards which they can give themselves and that are not dependent on someone else's behavior. For example, caregivers may choose a reward of buying themselves flowers. This will help to reinforce how difficult the task is, but how important it is to their well-being.

☐ Case Example

The following case example demonstrates the role that the Relaxing Events Schedule can play in helping caregivers reduce their stress.

Ms. Sheffield

Ms. Sheffield, in her early fifties, has been caring for her husband who is in his sixties and has had Alzheimer's disease for several years. Currently, her husband is receiving care in an Alzheimer's care unit, but the years preceding his placement were very challenging for her. When Mr. Sheffield first began exhibiting symptoms of memory loss, Ms. Sheffield found it extremely stressful because it seemed that he purposely was being difficult. She often would get into arguments and tried intently to tell him what to do so that he would not keep making the same mistakes. This was one of the most frustrating periods for Ms. Sheffield.

Another troublesome aspect of dealing with her husband in the early stages of the disease was the fact that Ms. Sheffield was working full time. She had a good job in the defense industry, and had worked hard to get there. However, it increasingly became hard for her to juggle work and caregiving. Not only was it was difficult for Ms. Sheffield to leave her husband alone at home but, once she was at work, he called her constantly and it was almost impossible for her to concentrate on her job. And, when she was able to focus, she had a constant underlying sense of worry about what could go wrong at home. Likewise, once she got home, she felt tired from working and had little energy or patience to deal with the taxing aspects of the disease.

Once Mr. Sheffield was diagnosed, Ms. Sheffield was given educational materials on the disease which helped her to realize that the disease was causing her husband's behaviors and that he was not intentionally trying to antagonize her. Along with this understanding came the realization that he would continue to need more and more care. Mr. Sheffield was diagnosed in March and, in July, Ms. Sheffield made the painful decision to leave her job. Part of what made it so difficult was the fact that she knew she could never go back to the same industry because, during this time period, the defense industry was being downsized. So, Ms. Sheffield chose to give up her career because she knew her husband desperately needed her to provide him with 100% of her attention.

It was quite a change for Ms. Sheffield to be at home every day and to be solely focused on the care of her husband. Gradually, her role began to shift and she took on more of what he used to do. This shift was quite a stark one, since Mr. Sheffield previously had made all of the decisions in the household. At first, Ms. Sheffield talked to her husband about decisions but, eventually, she became the sole decision maker. Ms. Sheffield thought that she would never be able to keep up all that she was doing, as it seemed so painful.

An additional stressor in the situation was the reality that Mr. Sheffield had little patience, had a quick temper, and was easily agitated. Ms. Sheffield struggled to figure out how best to handle him. This was a complete change from how she had related to her husband prior to the onset of the disease, and it was a constant source of strife. She would argue with him constantly, which only seemed to upset him more. Slowly, she learned that arguing did not accomplish much, but it was a arduous process to learn a new way of relating to him that did not involve engaging his behaviors.

Although Ms. Sheffield had a lot of emotional support from her children, her son was a student at Stanford Law School and her daughter was a freshman at the University of California, Los Angeles, so their availability was limited. Ms. Sheffield was determined to care for her husband at home for as long as possible but she was afraid that, without much direct support, this would not be possible unless she learned how to manage the stress involved. It was in this context that Ms. Sheffield began learning the Stress Reduction Technique and, in particular, the Relaxing Events Schedule.

When the schedule was first described to Ms. Sheffield, she thought the concept was good and made sense, but she voiced great doubt that it would work for her. It was clear that she did not need to be sold on the idea itself, but that she would need a lot of assistance in applying it to her situation. Because she was able to recognize that since she started caring for her husband, she had stopped doing anything relaxing or enjoyable, she was willing to try the Relaxing Events Schedule and easily agreed to set aside time to write out the plan.

In approaching the first step of identifying relaxing events, Ms. Sheffield had difficulty thinking of what she found relaxing. It was clear that it had been a while since she had had time to herself for enjoyment, so it was necessary to have her reflect on years past to discover what she found relaxing. At first, everything she identified and described involved events that she had shared with her husband, and it was important for her to talk about her sadness of losing his companionship. It became evident that

Ms. Sheffield had done very little by herself and, therefore, it was necessary to reconstruct those events she previously had enjoyed with her husband into activities that she could visualize enjoying on her own. Also, most of the activities were complicated and would have involved a lot of coordination, such as going out to breakfast, going to a movie, or going to the beach for a weekend. While these activities were important ones for Ms. Sheffield to think about doing on an occasional basis, she was encouraged to think about activities that did not take a lot of time and could be done on a daily basis with little effort. After a lot of discussion, she identified several simple activities that she thought she would find relaxing: taking a hot bath, reading the newspaper, reading a novel, riding her exercise bike, and going for a walk.

The next step of scheduling these activities was an involved process. Ms. Sheffield was able to identify when she had time to herself, such as when her husband took a nap or when he was content to watch television. But, she was quick to add that these times were unpredictable and, when they did occur, she completed household tasks which were impossible to do when her husband was following her around. She was encouraged to think about whether there were any predictable times when she knew she had time to herself. This entailed a process of reviewing her typical week. After retracing the events of each day, she was able to see that her husband usually would fall asleep before she did, and she often would have around 15 minutes before she would feel ready to go to sleep herself. Ms. Sheffield decided that she would schedule in certain activities, such as taking a hot bath and reading the newspaper, at this time and that she would have a second level of activities she would keep in mind for those occasions when Mr. Sheffield took a nap or watched television. During those times, she thought she would try to go for a walk in the yard and ride her exercise bike.

After the first week of trying to follow the schedule, Ms. Sheffield reported that it was very challenging. She often found that, once her husband was asleep, she was so exhausted from the day, and so worried about the next day, that she could not follow through with taking a hot bath or reading the newspaper. It then was suggested that she try relaxation exercises during this time for the next week, with the hope that this would get her used to relaxing at the end of the day so she could integrate in these enjoyable activities. Also, Ms. Sheffield found that, as she had thought, when her husband had taken a nap 1 day out of the week, she immediately began completing household tasks she had found difficult to finish earlier in the day. Again, Ms. Sheffield was encouraged to try to change this pattern, and she agreed to make another attempt. A discussion followed that helped Ms. Sheffield consider getting a housekeeper to help with household chores so that she would be able to spend time with enjoyable activities.

After the second and third weeks, Ms. Sheffield had made some progress and seemed convinced that it actually was possible for her to follow through with relaxing activities, provided she took little steps each week. She found that, after trying relaxation exercises a few nights, she was able to clear her mind and get into a pattern of using the last part of the day to enjoy herself, instead of worrying about the situation. The third week, she managed to take a hot bath 2 nights out of the week and found that, on those days, her stress level was reduced. Also, on one occasion when her husband had taken a nap, she spent time walking in her garden and found that this gave her time to think about the importance of her role.

Although it took Ms. Sheffield several months to integrate relaxing events into her daily routine, it was a useful strategy for her. It not only allowed her to reduce her stress and feel that she was spending time on herself, but it also assisted her in the process of adjusting to her new position in life as a spousal caregiver without the companionship of her husband. In effect, it helped her to create an ability to experience pleasure alone, in a way that she had not done before.

☐ Summary

The Relaxing Events Schedule is a strategy that can seem very basic at first glance but, nonetheless, it is a key aspect of helping caregivers reduce their stress levels. Once caregivers are able to identify relaxing events and give themselves permission to engage in the activities, this tool can be a great source of tension release. It also fits in well with the other strategies that caregivers learn as part of the Stress Reduction Technique because, once caregivers are comfortable with scheduling in relaxing activities, they can apply this same principle to scheduling in the various strategies.

☐ References

Beck, A. (1967). *Depression: Clinical, experimental, and theoretical aspects*. New York: Harper & Row.

Beck, A. (1974). The development of depression: A cognitive model. In R. Friedman & M. Katz (Eds.), *The psychology of depression* (pp. 3–24). Washington, DC: Winston.

D'Zurilla, T. (1986). *Problem-solving therapy*. New York: Springer.

Gallagher, D., & Lovett, S. (1988). Psychoeducational interventions for family caregivers: Preliminary efficacy data. *Behavior Therapy, 19*, 321–330.

Gallagher, D., & Thompson, L. (1982). Treatment of major depressive disorder in older adult outpatients with brief psychotherapies. *Psychotherapy: Theory, Research and Practice, 19*, 482–489.

Lewinsohn, P. (1974a). A behavioral approach to depression. In R. Friedman & M. Katz (Eds.), *The psychology of depression* (pp. 157–178). Washington, DC: Winston.

Lewinsohn, P. (1974b). Clinical and theoretical aspects of depression. In K. Calhoun, H. Adams, & K. Michell (Eds.), *Innovative Treatment Methods of Psychopathology* (pp. 63–120). New York: Wiley.

Lewinsohn, P., Munoz, R., Youngren, M., & Zeiss, A. (1986). *Control your depression* (Rev. ed.). New York: Fireside, Simon & Schuster.

Mace, N., & Rabins, P. (1981). *The 36-hour day*. Baltimore: Johns Hopkins Press.

Schulz, R., O'Brien, A., Bookwala, J., & Fleissner, K. (1995). Psychiatric and physical morbidity effects of dementia caregiving: Prevalence, correlates, and causes. *The Gerontologist, 35*, 771–791.

Teri, L., & Uomoto, J. (1991). Reducing excess disability in dementia patients: Training caregivers to manage patient depression. *Clinical Gerontologist, 10*, 49–63.

Zarit, S., Orr, N., & Zarit, J. (1985). *The hidden victims of Alzheimer's disease: Families under stress*. New York: New York University Press.

6
CHAPTER

Stress-Neutral Thoughts

This chapter describes the last strategy of the Stress Reduction Technique: Stress-Neutral Thoughts. This strategy is based on the method of cognitive restructuring which is a basic component utilized in the cognitive-behavioral approach to therapy. A brief history of cognitive restructuring will be provided to set the context, followed by a description of the role of worried thoughts in the stress process experienced by caregivers. Next, the Thought Tracking Record (TTR) will be introduced. The course of reducing worried thoughts and increasing Stress-Neutral Thoughts will be discussed, and the chapter will end with several case examples.

☐ Cognitive Restructuring

Cognitive restructuring is a key method utilized in many therapies that fall broadly into the category of cognitive-behavioral approaches (Mahoney & Arnkoff, 1978). Simply put, cognitive restructuring rests on the premise that thoughts (or internal dialogue) impact emotion, and that negative or worried thoughts generally are related to emotional distress; therefore, the most effective way to relieve emotional distress is to "restructure" one's thoughts, or replace negative thoughts with positive thoughts. Typically, when cognitive restructuring is utilized, some form of self-monitoring of thoughts is practiced.

There have been many influences on the development of cognitive restructuring but, given the purpose of this chapter, only three will be highlighted: Beck, Ellis, and Meichenbaum. Beck began his work in the 1950s and, by the early 1960s, he outlined the fundamental principles of his approach, which he called "cognitive therapy," in a series of papers (Burns, 1980; Wright, Thase, Beck, & Ludgate, 1993). Beck's model continued to develop and was published in 1976 in the book, *Cognitive Therapy and the Emotional Disorders*. Beck's "cognitive therapy" asserted that individuals' internal thoughts are directly related to the emotions that they feel. Specifically, Beck believed that an individual may have "faulty" or self-defeating thoughts, and these types of thoughts are directly related to emotional distress. He asserted that, by changing these "erroneous beliefs, we can dampen down or alter excessive, inappropriate emotional reactions" (Beck, 1976, p. 214). The goal of Beck's cognitive therapy was to help relieve this emotional distress. The means of achieving this involved helping individuals to identify, observe, and monitor their own thoughts (Beck, Rush, Shaw, & Emery, 1979). By helping one to understand the relationship between affect and cognition, an individual is able to alter distorted thoughts and, thereby, impact psychological distress (Corey, 1986).

Around the same time that Beck developed his approach to cognitive restructuring, Ellis constructed what he called rational-emotive therapy (RET). Ellis claimed that emotional disturbances "are the result of 'attitudes' and 'sentiments'" (p. 46) which are related to irrational thoughts. To Ellis, maximizing rational thoughts and minimizing irrational thoughts was the key to overcoming emotional disturbance (Ellis, 1963). Three steps are essential to Ellis's approach. First, external events that precipitated the distressing emotion must be identified. Second, the specific thoughts and underlying beliefs that make up the internal response causing the negative emotion must be determined. And, third, these thoughts and beliefs must be replaced with rational ones (Meichenbaum, 1977; Rimm & Masters, 1974). Assumed in RET is that, once people recognize their irrational beliefs, they will then wish to change these beliefs to be rational (Corey, 1986). Both Beck and Ellis applied their respective versions of cognitive restructuring to successful treatment of many disorders, including depression and anxiety.

In the 1970s, Meichenbaum (1977) articulated a notion of cognitive restructuring as an element of what both he and Mahoney (1974) called cognitive-behavioral modification. Cognitive-behavioral modification, according to Meichenbaum and Mahoney, viewed cognitions as critical determinants of behavior; therefore, cognitive factors can enhance the effectiveness of behavior modification (Schwartz, 1982). Within this context, Meichenbaum viewed self-instructional training as key to cognitive restructuring (Mahoney & Arnkoff, 1978). Self-instructional training made "subjects aware of negative self-statements" (p. 61) and Meichenbaum put the focus on the learning of problem-solving and coping skills (1977). He proposed that distressed people are different from nondistressed people in their learned means of coping (Mahoney & Arnkoff, 1978).

Beck, Ellis, and Meichenbaum made use of slightly different means, but all pointed to the central goal of cognitive restructuring: bringing about more adaptive thought patterns (Mahoney & Arnkoff, 1978). Beck's techniques were meant to allow clients to discover for themselves that their thoughts were self-defeating, while Ellis's approach was more straightforward and confrontational in that he focused on the destruction of irrational beliefs. Meichenbaum's self-instructional method, on the other hand, emphasized the development of a constructive set of skills (Mahoney & Arnkoff, 1978).

In addition to Beck, Ellis, and Meichenbaum, a more recent promoter of cognitive restructuring is Burns, who popularized this approach in 1980 in his best-selling book, *Feeling Good: The New Mood Therapy*. In this book, Burns (a student of Beck) presented, in simple language, effective methods for identifying "cognitive distortions" (p. 180) and replacing them with "rational responses" (p. 218). Burns presented the basic premises of cognitive restructuring in a clear and easy-to-read manner and, as a result, many people have embraced this viewpoint on treating depression and general emotional distress.

While the concept of cognitive restructuring within its many forms has been widely recognized and utilized since its inception, this is not to say that it has been accepted without critique. Many have pointed to the fact that worried or negative thoughts are not as maladaptive as the approach suggests. Coyne and Gotlib (1983) asserted that Beck's model is incomplete in explaining depression. Their research reported that depressed persons do present themselves negatively, but less consistently than the literature suggests. They proposed that equal consideration should be given to a depressed person's relationship to the environment, when trying to understand verbalized negative thoughts. Mahoney (1974) critiqued Ellis's approach on two fronts. First, he questioned Ellis's assertion that the discovery of irrationality in self-statements automatically motivates adjustment. And, second, Mahoney challenged the thought that "all forms of subjective distress are unreasonable" (p. 184). He suggested that, while it is obviously irrational to be extremely upset, it is not necessarily logical to be entirely without distress. In other words, the goal of eliminating all distress or negative thoughts may be the wrong goal.

Beyond questioning the role of negative thoughts, others have proposed that the relationship between negative and positive thoughts and emotional distress is more complex than that put forth by cognitive restructuring. Schwartz has written extensively on the connection between the two types of thoughts. He questioned the simplistic view that negative thoughts should be eliminated and positive thoughts should be increased, and has instead suggested that "negative thoughts interfere with coping more than positive thoughts facilitate it" (Schwartz, 1986, p. 599). Schwartz and Garonomi (1989) developed the States of Mind (SOM) model which proposes an optimal balance between positive and negative cognition's. This model suggests that it is the balance between the two that influences dysfunction, not merely the presence of negative thoughts. Kendall and colleagues also have contributed to the notion that the balance between positive and negative thoughts is critical. Hollon and Kendall created an inventory to assess internal dialogue (1980), and Kendall and others consequently put forth the idea that it is important to reduce negative thinking rather than just increase positive thinking (Kendall, 1983; Kendall, Howard, & Hays,1989; Kendall & Korgeski,1979). This pattern was dubbed the "power of non-negative thinking" (Kendall, 1984, p. 69; Kendall & Hollon, 1981, p. 110).

In summary then, cognitive restructuring can take many forms, but it primarily is geared toward changing maladaptive thoughts in order to reduce distress. Given this, however, one should not assume that maladaptive thoughts are the only element that may influence distress. And, one also should keep in mind that this process of restructuring thoughts is a complex one—it actually is the balance between negative and positive thoughts that is important, and relieving negative thoughts is more critical than just increasing positive thoughts.

☐ Cognitive Restructuring: Caregivers and Older Adults

Several recent studies have evaluated the benefits of utilizing some form of cognitive restructuring, within the context of cognitive-behavioral strategies, to reduce symptoms of distress among caregivers of older relatives. DeVries and Gallagher-Thompson (1993) demonstrated that, among caregivers experiencing anger and frustration around caring for an older relative, cognitive and behavioral treatments can effectively help caregivers manage these feelings by producing positive mood and decreasing anger and tension. Likewise in 1994, Gallagher-Thompson and Steffen demonstrated the usefulness of cognitive-behavioral therapy (as well as brief psychodynamic therapy) in treating clinically depressed family caregivers. In particular, the cognitive-behavioral approach seemed to be the more beneficial treatment among long-term caregivers of 44 months or longer. This suggests that, as caregivers experience stressors over time, there are clear benefits from structured, skill-oriented interventions rather than forms of therapy that focus on the sense of loss that is being experienced.

Gendron, Poitras, Dastoor, and Perodeau (1996) found that an 8-week group intervention program with spousal caregivers demonstrated the "potential benefit of cognitive-behavioral interventions with caregivers and in particular to the usefulness of assertion training and cognitive-restructuring" (p. 13). Several additional studies (Gallagher-Thompson, 1994; Gallagher-Thompson & Thompson, 1995; Kaplan & Gallagher-Thompson, 1995) have demonstrated the use of this approach with family caregivers.

Cognitive restructuring, as one of several cognitive-behavioral strategies, also has been effective as a means of treating various disorders among the general older adult population, to which older caregivers also are susceptible. Morin, Kowatch, Barry, and Walton (1993) used this approach to treat late-life insomnia, and it was found to be a successful means of treatment. In fact, among the participants in the study, sleep improvements appeared to be maintained well at follow up, indicating that the cognitive-behavioral treatment produced durable changes in the sleep patterns of these older individuals. Stanley, Beck, and Glassco (1996) found that cognitive-behavioral therapy (and supportive psychotherapy) was effective in treating older adults suffering from generalized anxiety disorder; the treatment was administered through a small group format. Several studies performed with older adults who were experiencing an episode of major depressive disorder indicated the efficacy of cognitive or behavioral therapies with this population (Gallagher & Thompson, 1982, 1983; Gallagher-Thompson, Hanley-Peterson, & Thompson, 1990; Thompson & Gallagher, 1984; Thompson, Gallagher, & Brekenridge, 1987). Teri, Curtis, Gallagher-Thompson, and Thompson (1994) summarized 20 outcome studies and concluded that cognitive-behavioral therapies are useful in treating late-life depression.

The various studies mentioned, as well as the history of the effectiveness of the cognitive approach, make evident the benefits that caregivers stand to gain from learning these techniques. Given that caregivers deal with an immense amount of distress, ranging from anxiety to anger and sleep disturbances to depression, cognitive restructuring can be an effective tool in helping them cope better with the daily challenges of the role.

In applying cognitive restructuring among other cognitive-behavioral strategies with the older adult population, certain modifications may be useful. Gallagher-Thompson and Thompson (1995) suggested three factors to keep in mind. First, the professional should be active during sessions and keep the older person focused on pertinent topics. Second, these strategies may progress at a slower pace if the older person has reduced visual or auditory acuity. And, third, if compensation for cognitive slowing or sensory deficits is required, it may be useful to present important information in several different sensory modalities. These recommendations should help to ensure the success of utilizing these techniques with the older population.

The aim of the Stress-Neutral Thoughts strategy is to draw from the most effectual element of cognitive restructuring—namely, that negative thoughts impact emotion—and apply it to the distress of caregivers. The way that cognitive restructuring is used in our strategy is by assisting care-givers to identify worried thoughts related to giving care, and then help-ing caregivers to replace these negative thoughts with what we call Stress-Neutral Thoughts. This process takes into account the findings cited earlier in the chapter on the relationship of negative to positive thoughts; it focuses on neutralizing the worried thoughts, as opposed to just identifying them, and then increasing positive thoughts. It considers what Kendall called "the power of non-negative thinking" (Kendall, 1984, p. 69; Kendall & Hollon, 1981, p. 110).

☐ Worried Thoughts

It is not uncommon for caregivers who are under constant distress to have worried thoughts that often make it difficult to envision anything construc-tive in a situation. Often, caregivers' reactions to a stressful event can be determined by the strength of these worried thoughts. Worried thoughts of-ten become so automatic that caregivers may be unaware that they even are thinking them. These thoughts typically are extremely negative and detri-mental to caregivers' feelings of self-worth, and thus can promote the cycle of distress. For example, when encountered with a troublesome situation, caregivers may reinforce their distress by thinking such thoughts as: "I am not doing enough," "I can't handle this," "I should have done it this way," "If I knew what I was doing, Mom wouldn't be getting worse." Although these types of thoughts may seem very natural and understandable given the caregiving situation, they actually can induce increased feelings of dis-tress. Worrying is simply a process of repeating these types of stress-inducing thoughts. Eventually, caregivers think the worried thought automatically, and they begin to feel as if they cannot stop the thought from occurring. At this point, worrying can become a habit—a learned behavior that repeats itself at different times in different situations. If worrying is viewed as a habit, it is reasonable to expect that it can be replaced with a new learned behavior that is productive.

Replacing these worried thoughts with Stress-Neutral Thoughts can help to lessen the perpetuation of the distress, and may even serve to relieve feel-ings of distress. Stress-Neutral Thoughts are realistic thoughts that reduce the threat of a particular situation and, at the same time, increase caregivers' self-confidence in handling situations. Examples of Stress-Neutral Thoughts include: "I did everything I could," "Worrying won't help the situation," "I've handled this before," "I did what I felt was best at the time." These thoughts all are realistic, but optimistic thoughts, and therefore can elevate caregivers' levels of self-esteem. They are the type of thoughts that can re-verse the cycle of distress at any point. The key is simply in recognizing the worried thoughts when they happen, and then replacing them with Stress-Neutral Thoughts.

☐ The Thought Tracking Record

The first step for caregivers in replacing worried thoughts with Stress-Neutral Thoughts, is recognizing worried thoughts when they occur. The thought tracking record (TTR) is a tool that can help caregivers identify specifically what thoughts they are having, when they are having them, and how they are being affected by them. Table 6-1 is a sample of the TTR form.

The first column is for writing down the event that precipitated the worried thought. In the second column, caregivers should write down specifically what the thought expresses. They should be encouraged to stop for a minute and examine what occurred as a result of their thought. Finally, in the third column, caregivers should write down a thought that is more realistic and stress neutral to use in the future. Table 6-2 is an example of how the TTR works.

Caregivers often are hesitant to substitute Stress-Neutral Thoughts for worried thoughts because they do not really believe them. Although caregivers may not believe them from the start—and this is acceptable—it is important to go through the process anyway. As the new thoughts are substituted on an ongoing basis, caregivers will be able to accept them and they will become a habit, replacing the worried thoughts.

The goal is that, as caregivers continue this process, they will notice some changes in the way that they deal with stressful situations. However, changing habits takes practice and work, so they should expect that there will be times when they may not see all the differences that they may like. It is important for caregivers to keep in mind that, as they continue to replace their worried thoughts with Stress-Neutral Thoughts, the worried thoughts will soon dissipate and confidence-building thoughts will replace

TABLE 6-1. Thought Tracking Record

Day _____	Date:	
Situation	Worried Thought	Stress-Reducing Thought
Actual event leading to unpleasant emotion	Write thought that preceded emotion	Write realistic response

TABLE 6-2. Thought Tracking Record (TTR)

Date: 12/5/97		
Situation	Worried Thought	Stress-Neutral Thought
The adult day care center calls; they are unable to provide transportation for your relative today.	"People are always doing this to me." Leads to: Feelings of frustration and self pity, problem-solving ability impaired, stress level increases.	"They have been good to us in the past." Leads to: Clearer thinking, ability to problem solve, less stress.

them. Changing caregivers' thought processes often is the start of reversing or avoiding the cycle of distress.

Once the TTR has been explained to caregivers and an example similar to Table 6-2 has been presented, the professional should work with caregivers to identify a situation that has occurred for them during the previous week, and proceed to fill in the chart. If it seems arduous for caregivers to think of a stressful situation and identify a worried thought associated with the event, the professional may want to identify a commonplace scenario that many caregivers are faced with in order to help facilitate the discussion. One such example is a situation where a friend or relative urges a caregiver to place their relative in a nursing home. Faced with this circumstance, the caregiver may have the following thought, "No one loves my relative and they don't care about how I'll feel if I place my relative there." In response to this worried thought, a Stress-Neutral Thought would be, "I know they mean well and, by suggesting that I put my relative in a home, my stress would be reduced." This example may prompt caregivers to think of a real situation and identify a worried thought, and the discussion can then proceed.

Caregivers should be encouraged to use the TTR at least once a day, provided an event occurs that causes distress. It should be suggested that caregivers fill out the chart as soon as they can following an event that leads to a distressing emotion. If they do not have the chart when the event occurs, caregivers should be instructed to simply jot down the event and emotion on any available piece of paper, and fill in the chart later. If caregivers have difficulty thinking of Stress-Neutral Thoughts on their own, they should leave this column blank and it can be worked on when they meet with the professional. Also, the professional should inquire whether caregivers anticipate any problems keeping the chart, and if they do, the professional should work with caregivers to find a comfortable way for them to do so.

☐ Reducing Worried Thoughts and Increasing Stress-Neutral Thoughts

Once caregivers are using the TTR and recognize the importance of identifying worried thoughts and replacing these thoughts, the next step is to help caregivers realize that working on thoughts is a good avenue for change. First, caregivers' thoughts are always with them; therefore, they can work on them anytime and anywhere. Second, caregivers' thoughts are under their control alone and, hence, so is the ability to change them. These two points identify the fact that thoughts are within caregivers' control, and actually are something caregivers can work on within themselves, even if the situations cannot be changed.

Several techniques may help caregivers learn how to better manage and decrease worried thoughts. First, caregivers can use self-talk. They can learn to recognize that they are having a worried thought by using the TTR and, once the thought has been identified, caregivers can learn to interrupt the worried thought. For example, as soon as caregivers have a worried thought, they can tell themselves either aloud or internally, "I am going to stop thinking about this now," and then think about something that is stress neutral. This is one of the simplest methods of managing worried thoughts. A second technique involves having caregivers yell the word, "Stop," as loudly as they can as soon as they have a worried thought. The automatic thought will be pushed aside for a few seconds and they can then substitute it with a Stress-Neutral Thought. After some practice aloud, caregivers should be able to do this mentally and get the same result. Third, caregivers can utilize a mild punishment for a worried thought. Although this approach may seem ridiculous to some caregivers, it actually may work for others. Each time caregivers notice themselves thinking a worried thought, they can snap a rubber band worn on their wrists. Then, they can think a Stress-Neutral Thought instead. If this is done consistently, they will begin to catch their worried thoughts as soon as they occur, and the frequency will begin to decrease.

Becoming familiar and comfortable with Stress-Neutral Thoughts also may be a learning process for caregivers. Several techniques are available to help caregivers identify Stress-Neutral Thoughts with which they can replace the worried thoughts. One technique designed to increase caregivers' use of more realistic thoughts is to put together a list of stress-reducing thoughts. They should be put on 3 × 5 index cards, one thought per card. It may be helpful for caregivers to use the TTR to write some realistic responses to the thoughts caregivers already have had. The next time caregivers find themselves having a worried thought, they either should have a card available, or they can imagine themselves turning over one of the cards, and then they should use this realistic response to replace the worried thought. A variation of using 3 × 5 cards, or in addition to using them, is the use of cues. Caregivers can use frequent behaviors as reminders that they should have a Stress-Neutral Thought. For example, caregivers can remind themselves to think a realistic thought each time they eat, brush their teeth, talk on the phone, read something, get in the car, and so forth.

By using one or two of these techniques, caregivers are stopping themselves when they are having a worried thought and, at the same time, are increasing the frequency of their realistic thoughts. Therefore, they also are augmenting the likelihood that these realistic thoughts will become a habit. Again, caregivers should understand that it is most important to concentrate on breaking the cycle of worried thoughts, and it is not necessary for them to believe the stress-reducing thoughts initially. As these realistic thoughts become a habit, they will begin to accept them more and more.

☐ Elements of Self-Change

It is critical for caregivers to be aware that self-change often is difficult, and the process of changing one's thought patterns can be a challenging process. Four elements of self-change identified by Lewinsohn, Munoz, Youngren, and Zeiss (1992) can provide caregivers with a framework for approaching self-change. The first element is self-reward. Caregivers should be encouraged to make a specific agreement to reward themselves for sticking to their stress reducing techniques, such as changing their thoughts. The rewards or reinforcers can range from self-praise to having a special treat, like a walk in the evening or taking a weekend trip. These rewards should be realistic, obtainable, and under the caregivers' control. The second element is step-by-step change. It is important that caregivers be instructed to notice small changes in their thinking. For example, if they replace one worried thought with a Stress-Neutral Thought per week, they are being successful at their self-change plans. They should not expect to change all stress-inducing thoughts at once, because this is not a realistic goal. The third element of self-change suggested by Lewinsohn is modeling. Caregivers should imagine how some nondistressed person they like might think and act. They should ask themselves what their model would do to reduce their worried thoughts, and how they would feel about increasing Stress-Neutral Thoughts. The last element of self-change is self-observation. Keeping records makes it easier for caregivers to pay attention to their self-change process. It also helps with self-reinforcement, as it gives caregivers a clear picture of how much they are changing and how much they should or should not reward themselves. These four aspects of self-change are important elements to be remembered as caregivers are attempting to integrate the changes required in the Stress-Neutral Thoughts strategy.

☐ Case Examples

The technique of Stress-Neutral Thoughts can be an effective tool for caregivers to learn and apply. Although it may take some time, along with assistance from the professional, for caregivers to begin to see the usefulness of the technique, it can provide caregivers with many benefits in reducing their stress levels. The following two case examples demonstrate how cognitive restructuring can be used in helping caregivers reduce their stress levels.

Ms. White

Ms. White is a middle-aged, married woman who is one of four children and has been the designated caregiver for her mother for the past 12 years. Ms. White's mother always had been a very dependent woman, even prior to her diagnosis of dementia. When her mother moved to Los Angeles after being widowed, Ms. White began helping her with locating a new home, transportation, and daily tasks. Ms. White always was the strong, take-charge member of the family, and she had difficulty tolerating her mother's dependent nature even at this stage.

Then, Ms. White's mother moved to northern California to be closer to Ms. White's brother and to give Ms. White a break from caregiving. Shortly after the move, Ms. White's mother began showing signs of forgetfulness and seemed to require increased care. Not only did she have memory problems, but she also developed allergies, bronchitis, and emphysema; she was hospitalized often, and Ms. White made frequent visits as she doubted her brother's ability to manage her mother's situation. Over time, it became clear to Ms. White that her mother was deteriorating rapidly and was needing more and more help.

Finally, following one of her mother's numerous hospitalizations, Ms. White moved her mother back to Los Angeles to the home that she shared with her husband. Before long this was the source of a bitter conflict between Ms. White and her husband. He refused to help in any way, and provided no support on any level. He constantly pressured Ms. White to discontinue the care that she was providing for her mother, and eventually demanded that she place her mother in a facility outside of the home. Once

Ms. White went through the painful process of placing her mother, she soon learned that this did not necessarily lighten her load. She found herself making daily telephone calls to her mother as well as frequent trips back and forth to the facility to provide reassurance. Ms. White found it taxing to juggle the constant demands of her mother with her marriage, her job, and her own health problems. She also found it very stressful to maintain her relationship with her brother in northern California, whom she blamed for not providing adequate care and causing her to assume full responsibility of her mother. In addition, she found the physical hands-on care of others arduous; the stress of caregiving was physically hard on Ms. White's rheumatoid arthritis.

Ms. White frequently found herself overwhelmed with the responsibilities involved in caregiving. When the concept of Stress-Neutral Thoughts was introduced to her, she initially was doubtful it could help her. Although it appeared in conversation that she had many thoughts of a worried nature, she had great difficulty when it came time for her to identify those thoughts. It was suggested that Ms. White start using the TTR and begin with a situation that seemed to be a daily source of distress for her: leaving the care facility after visiting her mother. As this situation was discussed, Ms. White revealed that, when she left, she often had the thought that she was abandoning her mother. This was identified as a worried thought that led to feelings of guilt and frustration. Once this step occurred, Ms. White was asked to identify a Stress-Neutral Thought that could replace this thought. Again, Ms. White had great trouble coming up with this sort of a thought. The suggestion was made that perhaps a Stress-Neutral Thought would be one such as, "It is difficult to leave my mother, but I know that the staff at the facility will take care of her needs." Once this suggestion was made, Ms. White was able to distinguish between a worried thought and a Stress-Neutral Thought, and she indicated that she was willing to try to use the technique.

The next step was for Ms. White to practice replacing this particular thought as suggested. Ms. White was encouraged to focus on this thought alone and that, as she was able to realize how this could be helpful, she could then work to identify and replace additional thoughts. Ms. White made a commitment to try to use the method of replacing her thought every time she had the worried thought about abandoning her mother. After a week, Ms. White reported that, although she was able to recognize when she was having the worried thought, she was unable to take it to the next step; she actually found it troublesome to get her mind off of the thought. For the next week, Ms. White was instructed to practice interrupting the thought by telling herself she would stop thinking the thought. Then, Ms. White decided to try the technique of writing the Stress-Neutral Thought on an index card, and have it available to her in the car as she drove home from her mother's care facility. After the second week, Ms. White reported that interrupting her worried thought, and using the index card to remind her to replace this thought with a Stress-Neutral Thought, was working.

However, although at this stage Ms. White was able to utilize the technique, she again doubted the fact that this process actually would help her because she did not really believe the stress-reducing thought. She constantly was unsure that the staff at the care facility could help her mother as much as she could. Ms. White was encouraged to proceed with identifying and replacing her worried thought, even though she felt she did not really believe the Stress-Neutral Thought. It was suggested that the more the Stress-Neutral Thought became a habit, she would begin to accept it. So, Ms. White agreed to proceed with the technique, even though she was unsure it would impact her stress level.

After several weeks of continued working on this one particular thought, Ms. White finally reported that she noticed a difference in the way she was feeling, and that it was easier for her to leave her mother's facility. One positive outgrowth was that Ms. White found it easier to concentrate on her own work and household tasks on returning home, and therefore felt she was thinking clearer and was less distressed.

Once Ms. White reached the point where she was able to recognize the benefits of the technique, she was ready to go back to the TTR and identify additional worried thoughts she was having. Again, she started by recalling situations that she found stressful, and then used that as a springboard to identify the worried thought that was associated with each situation. It was hard work for Ms. White to get to the stage where she was able to accept the Stress-Neutral Thought for each worried thought she had but, after several months, she became convinced that this was a useful way to reduce her stress. Ms. White remarked that, while she could not control her mother's dementia, the fact that her husband was not supportive, or her own declining health, she could control her own thoughts, her reactions to stressful situations, and her own stress level. She also was able to see how her natural tendency to problem solve fit in well with the structured steps involved in replacing her stressful thoughts. Although using the Stress-Neutral Thoughts strategy was not a "quick fix" approach to her stress, Ms. White found that, with some work, it became a tool that greatly helped the way she handled the stress associated with the care of her mother.

Ms. Martinez

Ms. Martinez, a woman in her sixties, has been caregiving for her husband for the past 4 years, during which time he was diagnosed with dementia. Ms. Martinez had imagined her early retirement years would be quite different from the way they turned out to be. Although she had prepared to spend these years in close relation with her husband, she had thought they would be traveling together—both active and healthy. She was raised with the strong value that her role as a wife meant that she should care for her husband, regardless of how great his needs became. Her parents were from Mexico and, at an early age, she realized that caregiving was an expected part of being a woman and a wife. This value is a big reason why Ms. Martinez moved into the role of caregiver during the time she and her husband had planned on retiring, without ever questioning what it involved.

The role, however, was not one that Ms. Martinez easily embraced. The stress created by all of the changes seemed to be more than she could handle. Initially, she thought her husband was malcontent on purpose and felt he was aware of the arguments he seemed to be starting. It was painful to think that he was intentionally fighting with her and causing unnecessary problems. She asked herself, What is happening to our marriage? She also found it stressful to be forced into taking over many tasks her spouse always had done. Ms. Martinez was used to her husband being "in charge." Suddenly, she was in charge of finances, household matters, and decisions, in addition to caring for him. She felt angry about this shift and hated taking over his role in their marriage. How could he do this to her? Often, guilt would inevitably set in from her feelings of anger. She loved him, and wondered why she felt so much anger toward him. The interplay of various emotions and the shift in roles made the seemingly simple task of caregiving so overwhelming that she often was immobilized.

Mr. Martinez's condition made it almost impossible for the couple to attend social events. It seemed too burdensome to try to juggle light conversation with friends, while constantly ensuring that Mr. Martinez's behaviors were not causing problems for others. It became tiresome to explain his condition to others. Her other choice was to leave him at home, but she was uncomfortable socializing alone. After all, she had shared life with him for many years. She felt more at ease taking her husband to family events, but this was not easy either. She essentially was dependent on her family to take over when she arrived, so that she could enjoy the event. Getting out of the house for enjoyment took more and more energy and, consequently, Ms. Martinez went out less and less.

Once Ms. Martinez understood more about dementia and why her husband was behaving the way he was, it became easier for her to adjust to the changes. However, over time, he began to require more than only supervision as he also declined physically. She increasingly found it toilsome to care for Mr. Martinez, day after day. She did hire in-home workers to relieve her for periods of time, but this was a financial strain and she could not afford a 24-hour worker, which is what her husband came to require. Also, due to Mr. Martinez's reluctance to relinquish control over his personal care needs, the in-home workers were not always able to be very helpful. Ms. Martinez often found herself having great difficulty handling her husband physically during bathing and, on occasion, he fell in the process. The progression of the dementia and the demands of constant caregiving seemed to drain Ms. Martinez to the point that she often wondered how long she could continue to cope with providing his care in their home.

It was during this difficult stage that the Stress-Neutral Thoughts strategy was introduced to Ms. Martinez. Ms. Martinez was eager to try anything, as she felt she was experiencing more and more distress on a daily basis. It was easy for her to think of a situation and a related thought that was full of worry. For Ms. Martinez, the situation involved the daily task of providing personal care to her husband. As it became increasingly difficult to provide this heavy hands-on care, she often found herself thinking that she may need to consider placing her husband in a skilled nursing facility (SNF); she then had the counteracting thought that she should be able to handle the situation and do more to care for him and keep him at home. This inevitably led her down the spiral of distress, as she then thought she had no choice but to continue trying harder even though she was getting to the point of exhaustion in the process. Ms. Martinez was aware that this was a worried and unrealistic thought, but was not sure how to deal with it.

Although Ms. Martinez was enthusiastic about getting started in learning to use the Stress-Neutral Thoughts strategy, once she took the initial step of identifying the first worried thought to focus on, she was unable to move to the next step of thinking of a Stress-Neutral Thought. After much discussion Ms. Martinez was able to formulate a more realistic thought; namely, that she was doing everything she could to keep her husband at home. Once she was able to verbalize this Stress-Neutral Thought, she was able to say what before may have been impossible for her to say: that it may be best for both herself and her husband if she considered placement at some point. So, Ms. Martinez was determined, at this point, to begin the process of actually trying to utilize the technique by working on this one thought.

In spite of Ms. Martinez's determination, however, she reluctantly admitted at the end of the first week that she was unable to actually utilize the technique. She had been so busy with trying to cope with the daily challenges of caring for her husband that she had little energy to even think about focusing on her thoughts. Ms. Martinez realized that she needed something to remind her on a daily basis to identify when she was having this particular worried thought. She decided to utilize the technique of wearing a rubber band and write on it a phrase that would serve as a reminder. The following week, this method proved to be effective, and Ms. Martinez was able to identify the many times per day she had the worried thought that she should be able to handle the situation better than she was.

Once this identification was made, Ms. Martinez knew she had to move forward and actually try to stop the thought, and then replace it with the more realistic thought she had previously identified. She utilized the process of saying "Stop" out loud to herself when she recognized the worried thought, and this proved to be effective. Replacing the thought was a little more challenging because Ms. Martinez found it problematic to think a thought that she really did not believe. The values of her childhood seeped into her thought process and this new thought seemed counterintuitive. It took Ms. Martinez several weeks to determine that this was a worthwhile task, and she did decide to at least try to replace her thought. It did not come easily but, after 3 to 4 weeks, she found herself replacing the worried thought with ease and actually began to believe it.

This process was timely for Ms. Martinez as, during the same time, she was dealing with the painful decision of whether to place her husband in a SNF or to continue trying to care for him at home. Through this technique of replacing her unrealistic thought with a stress-neutral one, she was able to reach the conclusion that the best decision was to move forward in placing Mr. Martinez in a facility down the street from her home. The decision still was very agonizing, but she was able to recognize that it was okay for her to reach a point where she was unable to continue providing care for her husband at home.

Once Ms. Martinez placed her husband, she proceeded to use the technique in dealing with the many worried thoughts that resulted from the transition. Over time, the process became easier to use and she was able to replace her worried thoughts with less effort. For Ms. Martinez, utilizing Stress-Neutral Thoughts became a beneficial method of managing her distress level. It was effective throughout the entire course of caring for her husband at home, placing him in a facility, and learning to move on with her life.

☐ Summary

The Stress-Neutral Thoughts strategy can be a remarkable tool for caregivers to learn to utilize in managing distress. It is not necessarily an easy technique for caregivers to learn, and it may necessitate persistent instruction from the professional involved. Creativity in adapting the basic method to a particular situation is essential in helping caregivers embrace the concept. Caregivers may be tempted at various stages to give up the technique, and the role of the professional is to continuously reinforce the benefits of pushing through this stage to realize the full potential of the approach. After some time, and with ongoing support, caregivers should realize the usefulness of the technique and be able to adapt it to many different situations.

☐ References

Beck, A. (1976). *Cognitive therapy and the emotional disorders.* New York: International Universities Press.

Beck, A., Rush, A., Shaw, B., & Emery, G. (1979). *Cognitive therapy of depression.* New York: The Guildford Press.

Burns, D. (1980). *Feeling good: The new mood therapy.* New York: Signet Books.

Corey, G. (1986). *Theory and practice of counseling and psychotherapy.* Pacific Grove, CA: Brooks/Cole.

Coyne, J., & Gotlib, I. (1983). The role of cognition in depression: A critical appraisal. *Psychological Bulletin, 94,* 473–505.

DeVries, H., & Gallagher-Thompson, D. (1993). Cognitive/behavioral therapy and the angry caregiver. *Clinical Gerontologist, 13,* 53–56.

Ellis, A. (1963). *Reason and emotion in psychotherapy.* New York: Lyle Stuart.

Gallagher, D., & Thompson, L. (1982). Treatment of major depressive disorder in older adult outpatients with brief psychotherapies. *Psychotherapy: Therapy, Research, and Practice, 19,* 482–490.

Gallagher, D., & Thompson, L. (1983). Effectiveness of psychotherapy for both endogenous and nonendogenous depression in older adult outpatients. *Journal of Gerontology, 38,* 707–712.

Gallagher-Thompson, D. (1994). Clinical intervention strategies for distressed family caregivers: Rationale and development of psychoeducational approaches. In E. Light, G. Niederehe, & B. Lebowitz (Eds.), *Stress effects on family caregivers of Alzheimer's patients* (pp. 260–277). New York: Springer.

Gallagher-Thompson, D., Hanley-Peterson, P., & Thompson, L. (1990). Maintenance of gains versus relapse following brief psychotherapy for depression. *Journal of Consulting and Clinical Psychology, 58,* 371–374.

Gallagher-Thompson, D., & Steffen, A. (1993). Comparative effects of cognitive-behavioral and brief psychodynamic psychotherapies for depressed family caregivers. *Journal of Consulting and Clinical Psychology, 62,* 543–549.

Gallagher-Thompson, D., & Thompson, L. (1995). Psychotherapy with older adults in theory and practice. In B. Bonger & L. Beutler (Eds.), *Comprehensive textbook of psychotherapy* (pp. 357–359). New York: Oxford University Press.

Gendron, C., Poitras, L., Dastoor, D., & Perodeau, G. (1996). Cognitive-behavioral group intervention for spousal caregivers: Findings and clinical considerations. *Clinical Gerontologist, 17,* 3–19.

Hollon, S., & Kendall, P. (1980). Cognitive self-statements in depression: Development of an automatic thoughts questionnaire. *Cognitive Therapy and Research, 4,* 383–395.

Kaplan, C., & Gallagher-Thompson, D. (1995). The treatment of clinical depression in caregivers of spouses with dementia. *Journal of Cognitive Psychotherapy: An International Quarterly, 9,* 35–44.

Kendall, P. (1983). Methodology and cognitive-behavioral assessment. *Behavioural Psychotherapy, 11,* 285–301.

Kendall, P. (1984). Behavior assessment and methodology. *Annual Review of Behavior Therapy: Theory & Practice, 10,* 47–86.

Kendall, P., & Hollon, S. (1981). Assessing self-referent speech: Methods in the measurement of self-statements. In P. Kendall & S. Hollon (Eds.), *Assessment strategies for cognitive-behavioral interventions* (pp. 85–118). New York: Academic Press.

Kendall, P., Howard, B., & Hays, R. (1989). Self referent speech and psychopathology: The balance of positive and negative thinking. *Cognitive Therapy and Research, 13,* 583–598.

Kendall, P., & Korgeski, G. (1979). Assessment and cognitive-behavioral interventions. *Cognitive Therapy and Research, 3,* 1–21.

Lewinsohn, P., Munoz, R., Youngren, M., & Zeiss, A. (1992). *Control Your Depression.* New York: Fireside Simon & Schuster.

Mahoney, M. (1974). *Cognition and behavior modification.* Cambridge, MA: Ballinger.

Mahoney, M., & Arnkoff, D. (1978). Cognitive and self-control therapies. In S. L. Garfield & A. Bergin (Eds.), *Handbook of psychotherapy and behavior change: An empirical analysis* (2nd ed.), (pp. 689–722). New York: Wiley and Sons.

Meichenbaum, D. (1977). *Cognitive-behavior modification: An integrative approach.* New York: Plenum Press.

Morin, C., Kowatch, R., Barry, T., & Walton, E. (1993). Cognitive-behavior therapy for late-life insomnia. *Journal of Consulting and Clinical Psychology, 61,* 137–146.

Rimm, D., & Masters, J. (1974). *Behavior therapy: Techniques and empirical findings.* New York: Academic Press.

Schwartz, R. (1982). Cognitive-behavior modification: A conceptual review. *Clinical Psychology Review, 2,* 267–293.

Schwartz, R. (1986). The internal dialogue: On the asymmetry between positive and negative coping thoughts. *Cognitive Therapy and Research, 10,* 591–605.

Schwartz, R., & Garamoni, G. (1989). Cognitive balance and psychopathology: Evaluation or an information processing model of positive and negative states of mind. *Clinical Psychology Review, 9,* 271–294.

Stanley, M., Beck, G., & Glassco, J. (1996). Treatment of generalized anxiety in older adults: A preliminary comparison of cognitive-behavioral and supportive approaches. *Behavior Therapy, 27,* 565–581.

Teri, L., Curtis, J., Gallagher-Thompson, D., & Thompson, L. (1994). Cognitive-behavioral therapy with depressed older adults. In L. Schneider, C. Reynolds, B. Lebowitz, & A. Friedhoff (Eds.), *Diagnosis and treatment of depression in late life: Results of the NIH consensus development conference* (pp. 279–291). Washington, DC: American Psychiatric Press.

Thompson, L., & Gallagher, D. (1984). Efficacy of psychotherapy in the treatment of late-life depression. *Advances in Behavior Research and Therapy, 6,* 127–139.

Thompson, L., Gallagher, D., & Breckenridge, J. (1987). Comparative effectiveness of psychotherapies for depressed elders. *Journal of Consulting and Clinical Psychology, 55,* 385–390.

Wright, J., Thase, M., Beck, A., & Ludgate, J. (1993). *Cognitive therapy with inpatients: Developing a cognitive milieu.* New York: The Guilford Press.

The Effectiveness of the Stress Reduction Technique

When learning and preparing to implement the Stress Reduction Technique, an important question to consider is, What is its effectiveness? This chapter will address the question by first providing a brief review of the literature on interventions aimed at alleviating caregiver distress. While this review is by no means a comprehensive analysis, it will lay the groundwork for understanding how the technique fits into the larger context of interventions. Second, an examination of preliminary outcomes from a study performed by Bob Knight, Steven Lutzky, and Jodi Olshevski will provide a framework for understanding the effectiveness of the Stress Reduction Technique in reducing anxiety and distress, and how the technique compares to another method, the Problem-Solving Technique. Critical in trying to ascertain the usefulness of the Stress Reduction Technique are the qualitative experiences that caregivers have in learning and using the technique; these will be highlighted in the form of case studies.

☐ A Brief Review of the Interventions

From the emergence of studies on caregiver burden in the early 1980s to present-day literature, the interventions developed and tried in alleviating caregiver distress have been many, and they have differed in approach and method. Typically, interventions for caregivers have been psychoeducational

99

in nature, teaching caregivers about the disease(s) affecting the care recipient and about common caregiving problems. Most have emphasized a mix of group support and problem solving. See Tables 7-1 and 7-2 for a summary of the studies that follow below.

Early reviews of evaluations of interventions with caregivers were not encouraging. A review compiled by Gallagher (1985) looked at programs that utilized education and support, behavioral and psychotherapeutic techniques, self-help groups, and respite care to alleviate caregiver distress. She concluded that more controlled evaluations of the interventions were needed in order to more accurately evaluate the impact of the intervention. Toseland and Rossiter (1989) performed a study that systematically reviewed 29 studies on psychosocial group interventions which included both education and support. Most of the groups were based on information about the care receiver's situation, the group as a mutual support system, the emotional impact of caregiving, self-care, problematic interpersonal relationships, the development and use of support systems outside the group, and home care skills. It was concluded that impressionistic reports by caregivers and group leaders almost always were positive but, when structured measures of emotional distress were used and when comparison group designs were employed, there was little evidence of change.

Several studies have tested different intervention approaches using improved methodological designs. Lovett and Gallagher (1988) tested the efficacy of a 10-week psychoeducational program designed to teach specific skills for coping more effectively with caregiving. There were two approaches: The first focused on increasing the level of caregivers' pleasant events and the second provided training in social problem-solving skills. Both interventions decreased self-reported depression and increased self-reported morale among the caregivers who participated. Greene and Monahan (1989) evaluated the effects of an 8-week group intervention with caregivers that included group support, education about caregiving, and relaxation training. Results indicated statistically significant reductions in anxiety and depression among those caregivers screened for relatively high prior stress levels. Toseland and Smith (1990) utilized an individual intervention of 8 weekly sessions that included problem identification, problem solving, stress reduction, time management, and behavioral and cognitive coping strategies. Those caregivers who received the treatment demonstrated significant change on self-reported psychological symptoms and emotional well-being, as compared with participants in a no-treatment control condition.

While these three studies demonstrated improvement in design and results that are encouraging, they all either mixed dementia caregivers with caregivers of physically frail older adults or used only caregivers of physically frail older adults. Therefore, it is unclear whether the positive out-

TABLE 7-1. Caregiver intervention studies

Author	Year	Intervention	Population	Type	Length	Measures	Outcome
Lovett & Gallagher	1988	Psychoeducational interventions	107 caregivers of frail older patients	Psychoeducational groups: life satisfaction skills, problem-solving skills.	10 weekly 2-hr sessions	Perceived Stress Scale, Philadelphia Geriatric Center Morale Scale, Beck Depression Inventory, Schedule for Affective Disorders and Schizophrenia (SADS), Index of Unpleasant Events, Reduction of Pleasant Events, Social Support Scale, Self-Efficacy Scale.	Both groups reported decreased depression and increased morale.
Greene & Monahan	1989	Support and education program	289 primary caregivers	3-component intervention: discussion, education, relaxation training.	8 weekly 2-hr sessions	SCL-90 Modified Burden Scale, Activities of Daily Living (ADL)/Instrumental Activities of Daily Living (IADL), cognitive dysfunction, psychological and psychobehavioral problems.	Significant reductions in anxiety and depression, little effect for burden and hostility.
Toseland & Smith	1990	Individual counseling	87 primary caregivers of frail older parents (daughters and daughters-in-law)	Professional counseling vs. peer counseling, problem identification, problem solving, stress reduction, time management, behavioral and cognitive coping strategies.	8 weekly 1-hr sessions	Bradburn Affect Balance Scale, Zarit Burden Interview, Brief Symptom Inventory, informal social support, Community Resources Scale, self-appraisal of change.	Participants receiving professional counseling demonstrated better outcomes on subjective well-being, psychiatric symptomatology, and perceived change in relationship.

TABLE 7-2. Caregiver intervention reviews

Author	Year	No. of studies reviewed	Types of studies reviewed	Categories of interventions	Results
Gallagher	1985	Not applicable	Not applicable	Education and support programs, behavioral and psychotherapeutic techniques, self-help groups, respite care.	Controlled experiments are needed to study the impact of various kinds of interventions.
Toseland & Rossiter	1989	29	Group interventions.	Support groups.	No clear link between participants' satisfaction and measurable outcomes. Studies with truly randomized designs have had mixed results.
Zarit	1990	4	Support groups and psychoeducational interventions.	Problem solving, respite care, support/stress management, individual and family counselors, support groups.	
Knight, Lutzky, & Macofsky-Urban	1993	20	Controlled studies (1980–1990) that attempted to change caregiver emotional distress.	Individual psychosocial, group psychosocial, respite care.	Individual psychosocial interventions and respite care show moderately strong effects. Group psychosocial interventions demonstrate small, but positive, effects.
Bourgeois, Schulz, & Burgio	1996	69	Exhaustive (15 yr)	Support groups, individual and family counseling, respite care, skills training, comprehensive, multicomponent interventions.	Support groups show evidence of improved knowledge, psychological gains, and development of informal networks, but only suggest quantitative treatment effects. Counseling provided for narrowly defined problems to individual caregivers is effective. Respite care appears to have only modest benefits. Skills training successfully changes caregiver behavior and, sometimes, patient behavior. Multicomponent interventions appear to contribute to positive outcomes.

comes would generalize to dementia caregivers. Also, two of the studies used quasi-experimental designs with nonrandom assignment to the no-treatment comparison group. In a more recent survey of the same types of interventions, Zarit (1991) noted that the few studies with truly randomized designs have had mixed results.

As is apparent, a difficulty in assessing effectiveness of interventions, by looking at both individual studies and reviews, is that the methodologies used in the studies surveyed often are inconsistent. In attempt to correct this, Knight, Lutzky, and Macofsky-Urban (1993) reviewed articles from 1980 to 1990 on psychosocial interventions and respite care for caregivers. The review was limited to controlled studies that attempted to change emotional distress in caregivers. Two criteria were used in selecting studies to be reviewed. First, the studies measured caregiver distress, which was defined broadly to include subjective burden, depression, anxiety, hostility, and other measures of negative affect. Second, the studies included a comparison group that did not receive the intervention. Meta-analytic techniques were applied to these studies. A total of 18 studies were examined, and no restriction was placed on the type of intervention used. Interventions included psychosocial approaches, respite care, and case planning.

This meta-analytic review concluded that individual psychosocial interventions and respite care programs have had a moderately strong effect on caregiver distress. Group psychosocial interventions appear to have had a small, but positive, effect on caregiver distress. And, although studies on social and health care services other than respite care seem frequently to report important effects for caregivers, these effects do not consistently seem to include lowering caregiver dysphoria. A clear message sent by the authors is that interventions are most effective when they are targeted to caregivers with specific needs, and this targeting should be based on assessment of need and not self-selection by the caregivers.

In a shift away from examining outcomes and methodologies used, Bourgeois, Shulz, and Burgio (1996) reviewed 69 published manuscripts with a focus on the content and process of the actual interventions. They provided a broad examination of both descriptive and quantitative studies, and grouped the studies into the following categories: support groups; individual and family counseling; respite care; skills training; and comprehensive, multi-component interventions. Consistent with previous reviews, Bourgeois et al. found that studies on support groups demonstrated increased knowledge and psychological gains for participants, while quantitative treatment effects (i.e., perceived burden) were only suggestive. In terms of individual and family counseling interventions, they reported that the literature provides several studies that demonstrated effective treatment when counseling was delivered to individual caregivers. On the other hand, respite care intervention studies were reported to demonstrate only moderate benefits. The skills training intervention literature, which includes those interventions that change caregiver behavior and sometimes patient behavior, appear to provide the "most robust and rigorously evaluated treatments," according to Bourgeois et al. (p. 77). And, last, what the authors called multicomponent interventions (comprehensive service delivery programs) appeared to add to positive outcomes for caregivers who were interested in the program offerings.

Bourgeois et al. concluded that measurement validity is important, but should not disguise the importance of clinical impact. They suggested that it is not just statistical significance and consistent methodology that is important in looking at interventions, but whether caregivers actually feel that their involvement in the intervention helped to significantly alter their own or their families' lives. They proposed that the critical factors to ensure an intervention is effective are determination of caregivers' needs, expectations of the intervention, and realistic treatment goals.

The literature on caregiver interventions, then, offers several insights to evaluating the effectiveness of the Stress Reduction Technique. First, the success of the technique is dependent not just on the strategies themselves, but also on how the intervention is targeted, described, and applied to caregivers' situations. Second, in the context of the various interventions reviewed, the Stress Reduction Technique can be viewed in a number of ways, given the inconsistent terminology used in categorizing treatment studies. In terms of the meta-analytic study by Knight et al. (1993), the Stress Reduction Technique could be considered an "individual psychosocial intervention" (p. 246); while according to the review by Bourgeois et al. (1996), the Stress Reduction Technique could be considered either an "individual and family counseling" (pp. 72–73) intervention or a "skills training" (pp. 75–77) intervention. In either case, it is apparent that the type of intervention provided by the Stress Reduction Technique fits into categories that have shown fairly effective treatment results.

In order to gain a more precise picture of how the Stress Reduction Technique impacts caregiver distress, an examination will now be made of the preliminary outcomes from a study performed by Knight, Lutzky, and Olshevski.

☐ The Effects of Psychoeducational Intervention on Self-Reported Distress in Caregivers

The study involved an 8-week psychoeducational program of individual tutoring in stress reduction training as well as problem-solving training. Participants were randomly assigned either to the stress reduction training, the problem-solving training, or a wait list. All participants were primary caregivers of older adults with dementia and were prescreened for high levels of burden. Prescreening for high levels of perceived stress assured that caregivers needed the intervention and minimized the possibility of floor effects for change in outcome variables.

Stress reduction training emphasized the caregiver's own emotional state. Caregivers were taught to monitor distress levels on a daily basis, to use progressive relaxation, to plan relaxing activities on a weekly basis, and to change stress enhancing thoughts to stress reducing or Stress-Neutral Thoughts. The problem-solving training focused more on improving the caregiver's problem-solving ability and ability to manage the care recipient. This model followed the Zarit, Orr, and Zarit (1985) approach and focused on monitoring the care recipient's behavior, devising behavioral management strategies to solve the older adult's care problems, and evaluating and refining these interventions.

Method

Subjects

The participants were selected from a larger investigation of caregiver distress on the basis of high scores on the Zarit Burden Interview (ZBI; Zarit, Reever, & Bach-Peterson, 1980). The larger sample was recruited from caregivers of older adults with dementia who contacted the telephone information lines of the Alzheimer's Association of Los Angeles County or the Los Angeles Caregiver Resource Center (a social service program for caregivers of adults with brain impairments). All were caregivers of persons with a dementing illness, and either lived with the recipient or provided more than 8 hours per week of care. All caregivers in the larger sample who scored 40 or more on the ZBI were asked to participate in the intervention study. Seventy-four of 121 caregivers met this requirement. High burden caregivers were randomly assigned to stress reduction training, problem-solving training, or to the wait list. Persons assigned to the wait list were reinterviewed 8 weeks later, and then randomly assigned to one of the two intervention conditions. All subjects were interviewed within 2 weeks after the end of the intervention, and then again for a follow-up assessment approximately 2 months after the intervention ended. Fifty of the 74 caregivers completed the 8-week intervention or wait list period and the posttest assessment.

Measures

The screening variable used, as previously mentioned, was the ZBI. Several scales were used to measure caregivers' self-reported distress: the Brief

Symptom Inventory, the Spielberger State-Trait Anxiety Inventory, and the Center for Epidemiological Studies Depression Scale. Systolic blood pressure-reactivity (SBP-R) also was measured by an Orion biofeedback monitor with a SC 700A automatic blood pressure cuff. Systolic blood pressure was sampled once per 3-minute interval during each of three 12-minute periods with the mean of the four 3-minute samples used as the measure for each task (a rest period and two task periods). One stress task was a mental effort task (counting backward by 7s from 500). The other task was to discuss the most stressful caregiving problem that occurred in the preceding month. Cardiovascular reactivity (CVR) was calculated as the difference between mean systolic blood pressure for each task period minus the mean for the rest period. And, last, cognitive coping styles of caregivers were measured by the Folkman and Lazarus scale (1988).

Procedure

The initial interview consisted of demographic questions, questions about the circumstances of the caregiving situation, the paper-and-pencil self-report questionnaires, the CVR procedure, and the coping questionnaire. Interviews were conducted in the caregiver's home or on campus at the caregiver's convenience. Initial interviews averaged about 3 hours in length. The intervention sessions lasted about 1 hour each and were scheduled weekly for 8 weeks. After material was introduced, there was considerable emphasis on practicing techniques. Caregivers were encouraged to provide feedback on results and the trainers provided troubleshooting advice on how to use the techniques to optimum effect.

Design

The paper-and-pencil measures and the CVR procedure were given at the initial interview and were repeated within 2 weeks of the final treatment session (posttest). The test of initial outcomes compares the three groups at posttest using a doubly multivariate repeated measures ANOVA. With the crossover design, wait list subjects went into treatment after 8 weeks on the wait list and posttest, and then were retested after treatment (treatment posttest) and for the 2-month follow up. The test of maintenance of gain at follow up includes wait list subjects in the two treatment groups and compares stress reduction training to problem-solving training using a doubly multivariate repeated measures ANOVA of scores at pretest, treatment posttest, and follow up. In addition, correlational analyses were conducted to explore whether changes in process variables would predict changes in outcome measures.

Results

Outcome Measures

The three-group comparison of stress reduction training, problem-solving training, and wait list was analyzed with a doubly multivariate repeated measures MANOVA. Since the sample size for this analysis is small, the averaged univariate F test was used because it has greater power with small samples. The Maunchly sphericity test rejected the assumptions of equal variances and zero covariances in the covariance matrix (chi-square = 218.8, $p < .001$). The degrees of freedom for the repeated measures test were adjusted using the Huynh-Feldt epsilon correction. The treatment $\times$ time interaction effect was significant (F (7, 40) = 2.61, $p < .01$). Neither the main effect for treatment nor the main effect for time were significant. The associated univariate tests show that this effect is due to change in systolic reactivity during caregiving story, to change in Global Symptom Index (GSI), and to change in state anxiety. Tukey's post hoc comparisons of group means with alpha set at .05 reveal that these differences are due to stress reduction training being superior to wait list in reduction of state anxiety and in reduction of GSI. Stress reduction training was more effective than problem-solving training in reducing state anxiety. SBP-R *increased* significantly more in the problem-solving training as compared to stress reduction training. No comparisons of the problem-solving group and the wait list reached significance. However, the standard deviation of SBP-R was considerably higher in the wait list group than in the interventions; if the standard error was based on the pooled variance of the other groups, the SBP-R change in the problem-solving group would be significantly higher than the wait list group.

In assessing the follow-up effects, the Maunchly sphericity test again was significant (chi-square = 329.0, $p < .001$) and so the Huynh-Feldt epsilon was used to adjust degrees of freedom for the averaged F test. The main effect for time was significant (F (6,54) = 2.33, $p < .05$). The associated univariate tests suggest that this effect was due to change in GSI and in state anxiety. Planned post hoc paired t tests were performed using a Bonferroni correction. GSI and state anxiety showed significant change from baseline to immediate posttest (t (37) = 3.63 and 2.75 respectively, $p < .009$). Neither GSI nor state anxiety showed a significant difference between immediate posttest and 2-month follow up. The direct comparison of baseline to follow up shows that GSI is significantly different (t (30) = 3.30, $p < .002$); however, state anxiety is not different from baseline at follow up, suggesting a tendency to rebound once treatment is terminated. Neither main effect for group nor the group by time interaction effects were significant. The group by time interaction approached significance; given the low power of this test, the failure to reach significance must be considered inconclusive.

Process Measures

Correlational analyses were used to see if changes in process variables predicted changes in outcome variables. In stress reduction training, declines in the use of escape avoidance strategies and in the use of distancing predicted lowered CVR ($r = .40$ and $.52$) respectively, ($p < .05$). Lower use of self-blame led to declines in GSI and state anxiety ($r = .45$ and $.52$) respectively, ($p < .05$). In the problem-solving training group, increased use of self-control strategies was associated with higher CVR ($r = .56$).

Discussion

Although the results of this randomized evaluation of psychoeducational interventions for dementia caregivers should be viewed as preliminary, they provide support for the effectiveness of using Stress Reduction Techniques with this population. Stress reduction training appears to have an effect on psychological symptoms and state anxiety at posttest and this effect does not change significantly over a 2-month follow up. In contrast, caregivers showed increased cardiovascular reactivity in the problem-solving condition. While further study with larger samples clearly is needed, the Stress Reduction Technique appears to be more effective than the problem-solving training in lowering anxiety.

The experimental outcome data and the correlational data on processes tend to confirm the premise of stress and coping models for understanding the distress of this population and for designing interventions to assist them. These findings strengthen the evidence for the effectiveness of psychological approaches to helping dementia caregivers by adding experimental evidence to the quasi-experimental designs of Greene and Monahan (1989) and Toseland and Smith (1990). Along with these earlier studies, this investigation supports the importance of prescreening caregivers for interventions, a step which arguably equates caregiver intervention studies with other intervention studies which use subjects that have a clinical diagnosis or who are actively seeking clinical treatment.

The correlations between changes in cognitive coping styles during psychoeducational interventions and change in SBP-R can begin to extend our understanding of the role of coping responses in changing psychophysiological stress responses. The study showed that decreased use of escapist coping is correlated with lower levels of CVR. The finding that less use of distancing was correlated with lower CVR in stress reduction training and that higher CVR levels in the problem-solving technique were correlated with increased use of self-control strategies, support the argument that suppression of emotions leads to increased psychophysiological distress (see Rodin & Salovey, 1989). These tentative findings on coping styles suggest that interventions should work on decreasing avoidant coping and self-blame and on increasing emotional expression. A lower frequency of self-blame (accepting responsibility) also led to less anxiety in the stress reduction training condition. The effects on CVR and the correlation of CVR to coping styles provides empirical support for the use of psychophysiological outcome measures and for links between coping styles and CVR.

There clearly are limitations in this investigation that need to be considered in generalizing the findings. The small size of the sample limits the power of the statistical tests and clearly calls for replication. The small sample also precludes testing for specific treatment effects by subgroups (gender, relationship to recipient, ethnicity). Also, the attrition over repeated times of testing affects the generalizability of the results in unknown ways.

☐ Case Examples

The preceding study points toward the effectiveness of the Stress Reduction Technique as evaluated by quantitative methods. Also important in assessing the effectiveness of the technique is looking at how an individual caregiver has experienced the technique and whether, on an individual level, a caregiver finds it helpful in reducing the level of distress. The following two cases demonstrate this point.

Ms. Groth

Ms. Groth has been a caregiver for her husband for over 3 years. She is a woman in her late fifties and her husband is many years older. Her husband not only has dementia but also is bedbound and requires almost total care, needing attention around the clock. According to Ms. Groth, her husband's care is somewhat easier now, compared to the time during which he was ambulatory and she felt as if she had to follow him around all the time to make sure he did not place himself in danger. However, although he no longer requires the vigilance of Ms. Groth in following him around, he cannot be left alone due to his extensive care needs. And, he requires heavy hands-on care, such as lifting, turning, changing incontinence undergarments, and bathing, all of which Ms. Groth finds physically exhausting.

Ms. Groth has been the primary caregiver for her husband. Although her daughter lives in a small house behind Ms. Groth's home, she has a husband and a young daughter and has not been available on a regular basis to relieve Ms. Groth of the tasks of helping her husband with personal care. Ms. Groth also has a son, but he does not live nearby and has been unable to assist much with the hands-on care.

Ms. Groth has found the role of caregiving to be very distressing. In fact, she has reported frequently feeling depressed. She has felt trapped by having to remain in her home almost constantly to ensure care for her husband's needs. She has hated the routine and the confinement. And, since her husband is so much older than herself, she has felt this role was placed on her prematurely. She is at the age where she wants to enjoy having her children grown and out of the house, and she has plenty of things that she had intended to do during this time in her life. She also has felt that she has been unable to enjoy her granddaughter as much as she wished. It has seemed as if the only time she has been able to spend with her has been when her granddaughter has come over to the house, and then Ms. Groth has been unable to enjoy her entirely because she always has been distracted by her husband's needs. Also, Ms. Groth has felt that her granddaughter has not been able to truly enjoy her as a grandmother; she speculates that her granddaughter has been resentful that her grandmother has had to tend to her sick grandfather instead of playing with her for hours.

Ms. Groth has had some formal support as a visiting nurse has stopped by on a weekly basis to check her husband's vitals, but this never has been long enough to relieve her of her responsibilities. It has only given her 15 minutes to run to the store and get groceries. Ms. Groth also has seemed reluctant to accept additional formal help. She has felt that she has the best sense of how to care for her husband since he often has been resistant to receiving care and she has had to coerce him into turning or getting bathed.

It was in this context that Ms. Groth started to learn the Stress Reduction Technique. Clearly, she had a high level of distress, both in terms of self-report and also as indicated by the screening tool. As the various methods were taught to Ms. Groth, she seemed very eager to learn them. When she talked about her caregiving situation and what was most difficult, she often was tearful and angry. Although she was ready for any and all help available, the most challenging aspect of utilizing the technique was trying to find the time required, and trying to do this on a consistent basis.

Often this would be so frustrating to her that, during weekly sessions, it seemed necessary to let her talk about her frustrations first, and then gently try to help her identify ways that she could try using the methods. For example, she found it impossible to find 20 minutes a day when she could be alone and not interrupted by her husband's cries for help. She wanted to try using relaxation techniques, but just could not seem to do it. Discussion about her time revealed that her husband did seem to sleep for 6 hours at night, and this often was the time when she tried to get household tasks done before sleeping herself for around 5 hours per night. After some ideas were brought up about how she could take care of the household tasks in other ways, it was suggested that she try utilizing the relaxation technique once her husband was asleep and she was ready to go to sleep. After a week of trying this, Ms. Groth reported that she was able to use relaxation two times during the week, and that it helped her to feel rested, relaxed, and ready to face the next day. It was this type of problem solving that was necessary to help Ms. Groth actually use the various Stress Reduction Techniques. At the end of the sessions, she seemed to have identified ways to make the time necessary for her to use the methods she had been taught. Ms. Groth also reported that she felt better about her ability to manage her feelings of stress but, clearly, her caregiver role would continue to cause distress and only time would reveal how effective the technique would be for her.

A follow-up interview was arranged with Ms. Groth approximately 2 years after she had received the training sessions on the Stress Reduction Technique. Her husband had continued to deteriorate, had become nonverbal, and required a feeding tube. Although she reported that his worsening condition was difficult, she also had the sense that he was at the latter stages of his life and this gave her hope that the end was imminent. At the same time, she reported feeling afraid of the end of her role, since she had grown accustomed to it. She indicated that she had a sense of satisfaction about caregiving in that she was doing something good. Ms. Groth also voiced a strong sense that she was better off as a person as a result of caregiving, and that she had moved beyond her anger into understanding and acceptance of the situation. She felt as if she had become a stronger person, both mentally and physically.

The formal supports Ms. Groth utilized had increased. She had a visiting nurse two times per week; a home health aide for bathing three times per week; and an aide 4 hours per day, 4 days per week for a period of time. Also, her son had moved in with her, and he helped with care at night and with lifting. Ms. Groth also had accessed her neighbors and friends for emotional support.

In reflecting on the Stress Reduction Technique and whether it was helpful, Ms. Groth reported that she clearly had benefited from it and that it had helped her immensely. She had found it useful to think about replacing her worried thoughts and had written out Stress-Neutral Thoughts on cards which she used frequently. She continued to use relaxation and visualization at night, and found this very beneficial. Ms. Groth also was now in the habit of spending an hour per day on herself, which had grown out of the technique of identifying and scheduling relaxing events. She said this was especially helpful to her.

So, Ms. Groth is an example of a caregiver who seemed to benefit greatly from the Stress Reduction Technique and, for her, it was an effective means of managing her distress. Clearly, many other changes had occurred in the 2 years between the introduction of the technique and the follow-up interview but, as reported by Ms. Groth, the technique was a central part of learning to manage her distress.

Ms. Duncan

Ms. Duncan is an older woman who provided care to her husband for around 10 years. In a sense, she always had been a caregiver to her husband because he was a long-standing alcoholic and, prior to his acquiring Korsakoff's syndrome, she had been a helper to him. Once he began to experience small strokes and exhibit signs of dementia, however, her helper role was heightened. She then found it imperative to keep him away from alcohol and also to provide the constant supervision he required.

Mr. Duncan was not an easy person for whom to provide care. He frequently became agitated and often refused to cooperate with Ms. Duncan when she was trying to help him with his personal care tasks. She found herself adapting her life on a daily basis so that her husband would not become agitated. For example, he would hover over her and become very nervous when she was talking to someone on the telephone. Therefore, Ms. Duncan tried to make her telephone conversations as short as possible.

Adapting to her husband's condition was very difficult, especially since Ms. Duncan had a daughter and several grandchildren who lived out of the area. The only way she could keep in touch with them was over the telephone. When her daughter had a new baby, Ms. Duncan had to plan months in advance in order to arrange a visit and make sure that her husband could tolerate the road trip. This became increasingly difficult as he deteriorated further and, eventually, she had to ask her son who lived nearby to stay with him. She was never without worry, however, and always was fearful of him wandering away from the house, which he did on several occasions. Her distress seemed to be constant and seemed to increase as her husband's dementia symptoms worsened.

Ms. Duncan tried several different types of formal supports. The most effective seemed to be a local adult day care center where he went for a few days per week. She found in-home care to be ineffective. Her husband was resistant to care and having someone with whom he was not familiar trying to help him was intolerable; he seemed to become that much more agitated and difficult to deal with. Ms. Duncan tried out several different providers and, during one period a male home health aide seemed to be a good match; however, when he had to discontinue his help, Mr. Duncan was unable to adjust to any of the other providers.

Ms. Duncan found support for herself in many ways, but primarily through the use of support groups. She had attended Al-Anon for many years, and thus was very comfortable with this format. She became part of several ongoing caregiver support groups and collected a group of friends through the groups with whom she stayed in regular contact.

Ms. Duncan was interested in learning about the Stress Reduction Technique and was curious about anything that could help her manage her distress level. She met the criteria when she was screened and also reported feeling distressed. As she was taught the various methods, she exhibited enthusiasm about trying them out. She also had a lot to talk about during the sessions, however, and it often was difficult to get her to focus on the actual technique. This was complicated by the fact that the sessions were held in her home where her husband also was present, and often he would wander into the room and she would have to attend to him.

She found most of the techniques helpful; especially, the relaxation techniques during which she inevitably fell asleep while practicing with the instructor. The thought restructuring seemed a little more difficult for her to grasp, and she frequently reported that she was too busy to try out various methods for changing her negative thoughts to positive ones. But, she repeatedly voiced how helpful it was for her to meet with the instructor on a weekly basis and to hear about ways to reduce her distress.

A follow-up interview was conducted approximately 2 years following the sessions. Ms. Duncan reported that her husband recently had been placed in a locked Alzheimer's unit, and that there were repeated problems with his compliance. She said that she had found it increasingly difficult to manage him at home and, since in-home care was not an option, she was left with no choice other than to place him. She said that she was not as tearful as she had been while caring for him at home, but that she had been very frustrated with the details of the placement and consumed with trying to make it work. Ms. Duncan indicated that she felt she was better off because of caregiving, although she was unable to recognize this when she was in the thick of caring for her husband at home, and could only see this now that she could look back over it all.

In looking back over the effectiveness of the Stress Reduction Technique, she responded that it gave her good food for thought, but that she was unable to remember the details. When reminded of the various techniques, she reported that the relaxation technique was helpful and she had continued to utilize this every once in a while. She reported that, although she had been unable to maintain the scheduling of relaxing events, she recently had been able to do this since her husband had been placed. Overall,

Ms. Duncan seemed to indicate that just having someone she could talk to one-on-one on a weekly basis was helpful to her.

Ms. Duncan is an example of a caregiver who felt the process was helpful, but had difficulty identifying how the techniques helped; she could not recall all of the details associated with the methods. It seemed to play some part in her ability to manage the distress related to her caregiving, but it was not clear exactly what part it played.

☐ Summary

As has been demonstrated by the brief review of the caregiver intervention literature, the outcomes from the study performed by Knight, Lutzky, and Olshevski, and the two case examples, the Stress Reduction Technique can be an effective means of helping caregivers cope with their distress. Several factors are important to consider in ensuring that this technique is effective, however. First, it is clear that caregivers should first be assessed to make sure they are experiencing distress and are good candidates for the method. This technique should be targeted to caregivers who demonstrate a need for reducing their distress. Second, caregivers most likely will need assistance from the professional in making sure the techniques are understood, utilized, and helpful. Third, caregivers should be assessed at periodic times following the conclusion of the sessions to evaluate if the techniques have been helpful and to provide any needed follow up.

☐ References

Bourgeois, M., Shulz, R., & Burgio, L. (1996). Interventions for caregivers of patients with Alzheimer's disease: A review and analysis of content, process, and outcomes. *International Journal of Aging and Human Development, 43*, 35–92.

Folkman, S., & Lazarus, R. S. (1988). *Manual for the Ways of Coping Questionnaire*. Palo Alto, CA: Consulting Psychologists Press.

Gallagher, D. E. (1985). Intervention strategies to assist caregivers of frail elders: Current research status and future research directions. *Annual Review of Gerontology and Geriatrics, 5*, 249–282.

Greene, V. L., & Monahan, D. J. (1989). The effect of a support and education program on stress and burden among family caregivers to frail elderly persons. *The Gerontologist, 29*, 472–477.

Knight, B. G., Lutzky, S. M., & Macofsky-Urban, F. (1993). A meta-analytic review of interventions for caregiver distress: Recommendations for future research. *The Gerontologist, 33*, 240–248.

Lovett, S., & Gallagher, D. (1988). Psychoeducational interventions for family caregivers: Preliminary efficacy data. *Behavior Therapy, 19*, 321–330.

Rodin, J., & Salovey, P. (1989). Health psychology. *Annual Review of Psychology, 40*, 533–579.

Toseland, R. W., & Rossiter, C. M. (1989). Group interventions to support family caregivers: A review and analysis. *The Gerontologist, 29,* 438–448.

Toseland, R. W., & Smith, G. C. (1990). Effectiveness of individual counseling by professional and peer helpers for family caregivers of the elderly. *Psychology and Aging, 5,* 256–263.

Zarit, S. H. (1991). Interventions with frail elders and their families: Are they effective and why? In M. A. P. Stephens, J. H. Crowther, S. E. Hobfoll, & D. L. Tennenbaum (Eds.), *Stress and coping in later-life families.* New York: Hemisphere.

Zarit, S. H., Orr, N., & Zarit, J. (1985). *Hidden victims: Caregivers under stress.* New York: New York University Press.

Zarit, S. H., Reever, K. E., & Bach-Peterson, J. (1980). Relatives of the impaired elderly: Correlates of feelings of burden. *The Gerontologist, 20,* 649–655.

The Context of Stress Reduction: Community Services and Resources for Caregivers

This chapter is an overview of information that caregivers and their helpers should be aware of in order to effectively carry out stress reduction. It is important to understand the social context of older adults and something about case management in order to work with this population. Finding and receiving respite care—regular time off from giving care—will be discussed. In addition, a brief definition of the different types of respite services and community-based care will be covered. The California Statewide System of Caregiver Resource Centers model, which is recognized as a model program, will be used so that the context of this method can be understood and utilized. Next, the importance of planning ahead by engaging in legal and financial planning will be discussed. Last, additional counseling referrals for people who still need help at the end of the stress reduction program will be included.

☐ Respite Services and Community-Based Services

Respite care emphasizes meeting the mental and physical health care needs of the caregiver and care recipient. Respite care comes in many forms, settings and duration. In 1984, California enacted landmark legislation to replicate the model caregiver support program developed by the San Francisco-based Family Caregiver Alliance. The program addresses the emotional, financial, and care providing concerns of the caregiver.

California's Department of Mental Health was required to establish a statewide system of Caregiver Resource Centers (CRCs), modeled after the Family Caregiver Alliance. The CRCs provide a multitude of services to help caregivers, from early intervention to assistance through the various stages of care. The hallmarks of the CRC respite program are flexibility, choice, and consumer control. CRC respite services are provided through the flexible and creative use of local resources, including (but not limited to) in-home care, adult day care services, group care, temporary placement in a facility, and transportation.

Respite care as defined in the CRC's enabling legislation is "Substitute care or supervision in support of the caregiver for the purposes of providing relief from the stresses of constant care provision and so as to enable the caregiver to pursue a normal routine and responsibilities" (Friss-Feinberg, & Kelly, 1995, p. 701). Respite programs such as adult day care, in-home care, and short-term residential placements have the potential to relieve some of the stress on caregivers. Some studies (Gallagher-Thompson, 1994, Knight, Lutzky, & Macofsky-Urban, 1993) have shown that caregivers who have formal help and respite care are better adjusted than those who do not have outside help. It often is difficult to assess the definite impact of community-based services on stress levels of caregivers, because caregivers typically do not access this type of help until late in the course of caregiving when they may be exhausted.

Assistance from social service agencies, when informal support systems are not available from family and friends, can make a caregiver's task a lot easier. Many people have mixed feelings about seeking and receiving outside help. Even though caregivers know they must have help, they may feel that outsiders will not do the job as well as themselves, or that the person they are caring for may be upset by the change. The cost of outside help also is a concern to most people.

> Ms. K, a 65-year-old White woman, was caring for her husband of 44 years and was very distressed. She felt like she did not have any time for herself and did not want to ask her friends or family for assistance in caregiving. She did not want to hire outside help because no one could care for her husband like she did and she did not feel as though she could afford the luxury.

By far, the services most often requested by caregivers are for someone to come into the home and relieve them or to provide housekeeping services. Caregivers can hire their own help or there are a variety of home health agencies in almost every community that can provide a wide range of services, including physical, speech and occupational therapy, nursing care, home health aides, homemakers, and respite care. These agencies vary in the cost per hour of service the minimum number of hours required, and the particular services provided. It would be beneficial for caregivers to contact a few and compare each to their specific needs.

> It was suggested to Ms. K that there were many services she could try. She had mentioned that there was a local high school down the street, where they had a friendly visitor program. She thought she might call and request a male high school student to come over while she remained at home. By starting slowly, she could see what her own comfort level was with the student as well as her husband's comfort level.

When contacting an agency, it is important for caregivers to have the following information available:

1. The type of service you are seeking. Be as specific as possible.
2. Information about the special needs or problems of the care recipient.
3. Your method of payment.

In order to get the services they need, caregivers may have to make quite a few phone calls and speak with several different people. Here are some tips for caregivers that can help make the process a little easier:

- Write down the name of the person you speak to, in case you need to reach them again.
- Be persistent; polite, but firm.
- You may need to explain your problem more than once; try not to lose your temper and hang up.
- If you are not sure where to start, call your Area Agency on Aging, or 24-hour information and referral service in your area for guidance.

> Ms. K did call the friendly visitor program, but felt like she was getting the runaround. They told her they did not have any male visitors at the present time and were not sure when they might have one available. Ms. K was encouraged to call other programs, and someone she talked to at a local senior center happened to know of a young man who was looking for an after-school job. Ms. K and her husband agreed to meet Sam and see if he would be compatible. After a few visits, Ms. K went for a walk around the block. When she returned, her husband and Sam were engaged in a checker game and appeared to be doing fine together. Ms. K reported that she may try to go for a longer period of time, next week.

Various respite options that offer a range of services are available in most communities. These include in-home respite, homemaker and home health aide services, home-delivered meals, transportation and escort services, chore workers, friendly visitor programs, adult day care programs, overnight out-of-home respite programs, and short-term and overnight respite in a facility.

In-Home Respite

Generally, in-home respite is available 7 days a week, 24 hours a day, and may be scheduled in any way desired by the caregiver. The cost per hour of service varies, depending on whether caregivers find their own helper or whether they hire someone through an agency.

Visiting Nurse Associations and Home Health Agencies

Visiting nurse associations and home health agencies send professional nurses and therapists into the home to provide specific care, including skilled nursing care, physical therapy, occupational therapy, speech therapy, and medical social services. The service must be ordered by a physician in order to qualify for Medicare reimbursement.

Homemaker Services

Homemakers primarily assist with day-to-day household chores. The services provided may include changing beds, doing shopping, and doing light housework. It is important that caregivers interview and select their aide carefully. They should find out about the homemaker's experience and ask for references. They also should inform the homemaker about the physical and mental condition of the care recipient and the services that will be needed. It is important that the homemaker and the care recipient are comfortable with each other. Homemakers sometimes are available to low-income families on a limited basis.

Friendly Visitor Program

Friendly visitors often are students or retirees who come to visit on a regular basis to talk and spend time with homebound older people.

Home-Delivered Meals

Home-delivered meals programs, such as Meals-on-Wheels, deliver a hot, well-balanced lunch and, sometimes, a cold evening meal directly to the home, usually at a reduced cost.

Home Modification

This approach assesses the home setting and develops specific recommendations for environmental modifications. Although little empirical research has been reported on this type of assistance which documents the success of these modifications on reducing troublesome patient behaviors, it seems evident that this type of basic intervention cannot help but improve daily living for caregivers (Pynoos, 1995).

Adult Day Care Respite

Adult day care centers offer part-time respite care. Most offer services on a daily basis, but not overnight or weekend care. There are four types of adult day care centers:

1. Social adult day care. These centers offer social activities and recreational programs. They provide a supervised environment with opportunities to meet new friends and participate in group activities. While most adult day care centers will accept people with Alzheimer's disease, they usually will not accept individuals who are incontinent, wander, or behave in aggressive ways. Staffing will vary according to the needs of each program. Fees will vary but Medicare, Medicaid (Medi-Cal in California), and private insurance typically are not accepted.
2. Alzheimer's day care centers. These centers are special social day care centers that serve people in the moderate to severe stages of Alzheimer's disease or other related dementias. These centers are able to manage participants who are incontinent or who exhibit other problem behaviors.
3. Adult day health care. These centers specialize in providing medical, rehabilitative, and social services for adults over age 18 who have physical or mental impairments. Staff will include nurses and a variety of professional therapists and medical consultants. Fees vary, but Medicare, Medicaid or Medi-Cal, and private insurance typically are accepted.
4. Adult day treatment. These centers specialize in psychological treatment as well as social and recreational activities. Staff will include nurses, social workers, and mental health professionals. Fees vary, but Medicare, Medicaid or Medi-Cal, and private insurance usually are accepted.

It is important to shop around when looking for an adult day care center. Some centers will not accept people with Alzheimer's disease. It is important to question the staff about stipulations concerning wandering, incontinence, and memory impairment. Selecting the best place means asking many questions and visiting the various centers. Most centers encourage caregivers to bring the participant for a visit. Before setting up a visit, caregivers may want to ask the following questions:

• What are the days and hours?
• What is the cost? Is there a sliding scale fee? Are there scholarships available?

- Is transportation available?
- Are there meals or snacks?
- How many participants attend?
- What languages are spoken?
- Does the center serve people with Alzheimer's or other related dementias?
- Is the staff experienced in working with people like my relative?
- Does the staff have any specialized training?
- Can people who wander be safely supervised?

During the visit, caregivers may want to see how the staff members interact with the participants. Ask for, and review, any written material about the center and its policies, activities, menus, and other schedules. Most day care staff will want involvement of caregivers and will answer all their questions and concerns.

Attending an adult day care center can be frightening to the person with dementia as well as to the caregiver. Oftentimes, people do not know what to expect from an adult day care, or they have preconceived notions of what it will be like. It is important for the care recipient to attend regularly and for the caregiver to offer reassurance to the care recipient to make the transition easier. Often, participation in adult day care may become the high point of the week for both the caregiver and the care recipient.

Overnight Out-of-Home Respite Programs

Overnight respite services for caregivers can occur in a variety of settings. Most overnight respite programs provide care to the care recipient for a night, a weekend, or longer. Some of the facilities are traditional care settings, such as a residential care facility or a skilled nursing home, while other programs for care recipients are offered in a "camp" facility. Some programs focus on taking the caregiver, rather than the care recipient, out of the home temporarily for a rest while 24-hour care is provided in the home.

Short-Term, Overnight Respite in a Facility

This option is for caregivers who want relief from the day in and day out duties of caregiving. Relief is available from as little as 24 hours to several weeks. "Reasons expressed by caregivers for this service include need for rest (sleep), or relief, attending family events away from the area, or recuperating from surgery or illness" (Friss-Feinberg, & Kelly, 1995, p. 704). In order to qualify, care recipients must be ambulatory and without severe behavioral problems.

Community-based care is very useful when a caregiver is trying to keep the care recipient in their own home. There may come a time when this will not be possible and 24-hour care in a facility will be necessary.

Senior Centers

Senior centers offer a wide range of activities, social interactions, physical activities, therapy, crafts, congregate meals, legal services, preventive health care, and transportation services. They also may be a valuable source of information for available resources needed to provide respite care.

Case Management Services

Case management is a widely used service that involves assessment, information, and referral data and coordination of services. It serves to cut down the fragmentation of community-based services. Case management is especially useful when a caregiver lives a far distance from the care recipient. Research data appears to be mixed with regard to the efficacy of case management for prevention of long-term institutionalization, but there are results of controlled studies which are positive in that caregivers have used this service heavily when it has been available and have strongly endorsed this model (Gallagher-Thompson, 1994).

☐ Placement in 24-Hour Care

"Although families often go to great lengths to keep aged loved ones at home, they may not be able to provide the best physical and emotional care without experiencing undue stress. When home care and community services are no longer adequate, a person must decide on the best alternative arrangement for meeting personal and health care needs" (*NIA Age Page*, 1996). Placement in a facility depends on the level of care necessary, the functional capacity of the older person, and the amount of behavioral disturbance exhibited. The four types of facilities listed below are in order of the amount of nursing supervision provided, functional capacity of the residents, and cost per month.

Residential Care Facility

Residential care facilities (RCFs) are for individuals who are unable to live alone but do not warrant skilled nursing services. RCFs provide room and board, including special diets of a nontechnical nature, housekeeping, assistance with personal hygiene and grooming, and bedside care during periods of minor or temporary illness. The resident, in general, must be fairly independent. RCFs also provide some recreational and social activities. Some RCFs specialize in care of older people, people with mental disabilities, or people with developmental disabilities. It is suggested that caregivers check out each facility and talk with the owners. RCFs usually are the lowest in cost per month.

Assisted Living

Assisted living facilities accept individuals who are relatively independent but who need assistance with bathing, dressing, getting out of bed, and so forth. These facilities provide some nursing care but do not offer continual nursing services or supervision. Because they provide lower amounts of skilled nursing services, assisted living facilities usually are lower in cost than skilled nursing facilities (SNFs).

Skilled Nursing Facility

SNFs provide continuous nursing services under a registered nurse or licensed vocational nurse. Assistance with activities of daily living (walking, bathing, getting dressed, eating) also are provided. SNFs are required by law to provide recreational activities for the residents. Some SNFs have different levels of care within their facility. Many of these facilities have dementia care units with specially trained staff and accomodations for a person with dementia. Placing a family member in a nursing home can be a difficult decision to make and it often takes time. Many times, families have tried everything else first. Caregivers frequently meet with family resistance and guilt. However, a time may come in the process of caring for a person with dementia when nursing home placement becomes the most responsible decision that a family can make. Going to live in a nursing home is a major change for the frail older person. Their ability to respond to this change will be influenced by how ill they are. Caregivers will want to help them participate in this move and adjust to this change as much as they are able.

When caregivers meet with nursing home administrators, they should discuss financial arrangements in detail and not take anything for granted. If there are things they do not understand, they should not hesitate to ask. All financial agreements should be in writing and caregivers should have a copy of the final arrangements.

It is important to note that the caregiving experience does not stop here. In fact, burden may not decrease . Studies have shown that after placement caregivers often feel even more burdened (Zarit, 1996; Zarit & Whitlatch, 1992; Aneshensel, Pearlin, Mullan, Zarit, & Whitlatch, 1995). Caregivers may feel like they have to be at the facility every day or, if they are not at the facility, they feel guilty or are concerned that their loved one is not being cared for properly.

Psychiatric Locked Facilities

These facilities provide 24-hour nursing services for people with problems such as wandering or violent, disruptive behavior. Unlike SNFs, locked facilities have doors that lock from the inside and walking areas that are secured.

Using respite services and community-based care or placement in a 24-hour care facility may help to reduce some of the distress a caregiver may be feeling, but it is not guaranteed to reduce stress if it is the only strategy used. It is important to combine as many strategies as possible.

Again, it is very helpful if a caregiver can visit several facilities and, if possible, involve the care recipient in selecting one that is the most acceptable. What should caregivers look for and ask when visiting a long-term care facility? Here are some of the things they will want to know:

- Do most of the residents seem reasonably happy and clean?
- Can specific needs, such as diet or physical therapy, be provided?
- What activities and services are available for the residents? Are they encouraged to participate?
- What are the qualifications of the staff?
- How long has the administrator or director of nursing been at the facility?
- What part of the stay will be paid for by Medicare, Medicaid, or private insurance? How much will the resident pay directly?
- You have the right to ask about past or present health department violations. . . . Ask!

Often, finding the right facility may be difficult. Frequently, the best facilities have long waiting lists or have no vacancies when a caregiver needs it. It would be advantageous for caregivers to begin looking for a suitable facility in advance of when they think they might need it. Names of facilities can be obtained from doctors, clergy, local hospital discharge planners, friends, support group members, local senior centers, or other information and referral services. As mentioned above, it is important to plan ahead. Another area where it is important to plan is the legal and financial aspect of caregiving. The following section will provide more specifics about the legal and financial planning aspect of taking care of a person with dementia.

☐ Legal Alternatives

Managing finances, paying bills, signing contracts, and even the ability to properly understand what ownership means become progressively more difficult for a person with dementia. Often, people simply will give away savings or other assets. In addition, there may be less and less ability to make proper health care decisions.

Depending on the particular situation, there are certain steps or legal alternatives that can be taken to prevent problems in the future. Of course, while some of these steps can be taken without the aid of a lawyer, it may be beneficial in some situations to seek legal advice. The information given here is not to be considered as legal advice.

Generally, there are two categories of systems for legal alternatives. First, for those who plan ahead there are: (a) power of attorney, (b) durable power of attorney, (c) durable power of attorney for health care, and the (d) living trust. Second, for those who do not plan ahead there is conservatorship.

Power of Attorney

The power of attorney gives the caregiver, or whomever is so designated by the individual, the authority to act legally on his or her behalf concerning financial matters. This person is named the attorney-in-fact. The individual may specify either broad areas or very limited areas in which the attorney-in-fact may act on his or her behalf. The power of attorney may be revoked at any time.

The power of attorney is really only valid in the early stages of Alzheimer's disease while the individual is still competent.

Durable Power of Attorney

The durable power of attorney (DPA) is very similar to the power of attorney. It does, however, remain in effect even after the individual is no longer considered competent. In fact, the DPA may contain instructions on when a person is considered incompetent and, therefore, when the DPA will go into effect. This document, often called a springing DPA, may go into effect, for example, only if the individual becomes incapacitated. This may be determined, for instance, when two or more people, such as family members or a physician, state in writing that the person has lost mental capacity. This allows the DPA to go into effect without the oftentimes humiliating court process of determining incompetence. The DPA must be signed while the individual is still competent.

The document itself is fairly simple and is inexpensive to create, but careful thought is necessary when choosing the appointed holder of the DPA. The DPA allows the holder to sign checks, to pay bills or buy necessities, or to sign a contract, for instance, for nursing home care if needed. Gifts can be made by the holder. Often, this may be done to protect the individual's family in an emergency. If the individual develops a tendency to give property away to strangers, the holder can take the property out of the person's hands by putting it into a living trust (discussed below).

Coholders may be appointed. This means that two or more people will act together to manage the individual's assets. This may be used as a safeguard against misconduct by the appointed holders. In contrast to a conservatorship, the holder of the DPA is not under strict court supervision to account for all transactions and, therefore, is subject to mismanagement.

The DPA has been criticized because its acceptance is not mandatory. Some institutions may be unfamiliar with the DPA or suspicious of it and, therefore, may choose not to accept it. This decision would be within their legal rights.

Another potential drawback of the DPA is that, if it becomes necessary to place the individual in an SNF, the holder is not authorized to do so without voluntary consent of the individual. This may be a problem if the individual has become unmanageable at home.

Durable Power of Attorney for Health Care

The DPA for health care authorizes an individual or individuals to make medical decisions for a person if the person is incapacitated and cannot make these decisions. The holder can make the decisions to stop the use of life support machines, to consent to surgical or other medical interventions, or to refuse or terminate treatment. The holder also can decide on donation of the brain after death. He or she is allowed access to medical records and may make them available to others.

The DPA for health care is effective for 7 years from the date signed, unless the document specifies a shorter time period or the person remains unable to make decisions for himself or herself. The DPA for health care remains in effect until the person is able to make his or her own decisions.

The document must be witnessed either by a notary or by two persons, one of whom is not related to the person who has an impairment and is not an heir to that person. The document may not be witnessed by the person granted power of attorney, any health care provider or employee, or any community facility director or employee. The DPA for health care may not be held by the treating health care provider or community care facility or their employees, unless they are related to the patient.

In addition, the holder may not consent to sterilization, psychosurgery, shock treatment, or mental health treatment including outpatient care or commitment to a mental health facility.

The same individual may act as holder of both the DPA for property and the DPA for health care. Both of these powers of attorney may be included in a single document.

The Living Will

The living will is related to the DPA for health care. It is a directive to a person's physician indicating that he or she does not want to be kept alive by artificial means. The living will also allows individuals to appoint someone they trust to make medical decisions for them by including a DPA for health care.

The Living Trust

The living trust appoints a trustee to hold the title to an individual's assets. He or she is obligated to manage these assets according to the terms of the trust. The trust is revocable while the individual is alive, so changes can be easily enforced. At death, the living trust becomes irrevocable and will govern how the trust property is dealt with. Married couples often make a single revocable trust designating themselves as cotrustees. Then, if a patient is deemed incompetent, the healthy spouse acts as sole trustee.

There are many laws governing trusts and the duties of the trustees. There also are wide-ranging legal, financial, and tax implications that may be very complicated. Therefore, good legal advice should be sought when setting up a living trust.

Similar to the DPA, the living trust is less expensive than a conservatorship. For one thing, the trustee does not have to make annual accountings to the court and thus does not need to annually spend money on attorney's fees. Also, if appropriately composed, the living trust for a husband and wife can save a large proportion of the costs of probate. It also can be an excellent tax planning tool.

Conversely, because legal assistance is needed, the living trust itself may be expensive to establish—costing between $750 and $1,000. Also, when the trust becomes irrevocable, there generally will be an immediate tax cost to the estate.

While the living trust probably would deter misuse of the person's assets more efficiently than the DPA, its tighter limitations may make some situations more difficult. The trustee may use assets only for what is stipulated in the trust document. With the DPA, the assets may be used for whatever purpose seems best under the circumstances.

Finally, like the DPA, the living trust does not allow for involuntary placement in an institution.

☐ Options after Incapacity

Guardianship or Conservatorship

A conservatorship may be created through a petition requesting a hearing from the court at which time the conservator of the patient will be appointed. At the hearing, the judge will give the petitioner an opportunity to explain the situation and to discuss requests. Close family members will be notified of the hearing so that they may attend to support or oppose the petition. More than one person may be appointed as coconservators.

There are two types of conservatorships in many states. A person's legal needs will determine which one is appropriate. The first type of conservatorship falls under probate law. Within this category, there are two varieties. First, there is conservatorship of the person. This type of conservatorship is used when a person is no longer able to satisfactorily take care of his or her personal needs, such as health needs, food, clothing, or shelter. Conservatorship of the person also is an option if a person becomes unmanageable and must be placed in a nursing home. Thereafter, should the person demand to be released, the nursing home can legally keep him or her in that protective setting. If this type of conservatorship has not been assigned prior to a placement, a nursing home cannot legally detain a person if he or she wishes to leave.

The second form of probate conservatorship is a conservatorship of the estate. If a person is shown to be unable to manage his or her own finances or to resist fraud or undue influence, this type of conservatorship may be appropriate.

With the conservatorship of the estate, it is possible to divide the community property of a person and his or her healthy spouse into equal shares. This can protect one half of the community property from the financial drain that many husbands and wives experience when they have to place their spouse in a nursing home. Conservatorship also can be used to make a gift of the home to the person's spouse. In this instance, the person no longer has the legal capacity to make gifts to anyone, or to enter into legal contracts.

The same person may be appointed as conservator of the estate and conservator of the person. The central duties of the conservator are to preserve the person's assets. The conservator is responsible for making an accounting of how he or she has managed the person's finances after the first year, and every 2 years following. A conservator must ask the court to approve all expenditures made. The conservator also may ask to be paid for his or her services and be reimbursed for any money advanced for the patient. An attorney is needed to carry out the accounting as well as to implement the conservatorship. As a result, this legal alternative may be expensive. The proper price range for a simple, uncontested conservatorship is between $1,000 and $5,000.

The second type of conservatorship is called the psychiatric conservatorship. This is a more specialized and more limited form of conservatorship than the probate conservatorship. The psychiatric conservatorship permits involuntary commitment to a psychiatric institution for treatment if the individual is harmful to himself or herself or to others or unable to take care of the basic needs of food, shelter, and clothing by reason of a mental disorder.

Involuntary commitment can be ordered by a court only after a full hearing that contains several procedural safeguards. A separate portion of the psychiatric laws provides for involuntary commitment without judicial safeguards for short periods for purposes of emergency treatment and psychiatric evaluation. However, in most states, this temporary commitment must be followed by proper and thorough judicial procedures before long-term involuntary commitment can be ordered.

The question of how to pay for long-term care is a concern for many people. Unfortunately, there are few options. A person can use personal savings, buy long-term care insurance, or, if eligible, apply for Medicaid or Medi-Cal.

☐ Medicaid and Medi-Cal

Medicaid (Medi-Cal in California) is a joint federal and state program that covers the costs of long-term nursing home care for older adults and adults with disabilities, and, in some cases, in-home care (long-term care Medicaid). Coverage varies from state to state. It may cover care in a nursing home, provided the nursing home accepts Medicaid reimbursment. It also can help pay for many of the medical services not covered by Medicare. In some states, it provides medical care for impoverished people (community-based Medicaid). Its purpose is to provide medical care to persons who are in need and do not have sufficient insurance or funds to pay for such care or to provide for those whose medical expenses exceed their income.

Every state establishes its own eligibility standards and administers its own program. Eligibility is based on income and assets. Since every state has different eligiblity requirements, we cannot offer exact figures but can provide an overview; caregivers can refer to state offices for details. A lawyer who is familiar with Medicaid law should be consulted if a person has specific questions about the estate and so forth.

Long-Term Medicaid

Applicants must meet both income asset requirements. There are income limits, and two basic models are used by states. In 20 states, the income eligiblity cutoff is set as a multiple of the state's poverty standard; in 1997, the limit was $1,452 in most of these states. In 30 states, applicants also are eligible if monthly income is less than the monthly cost of nursing home care. When a person qualifies, monthly income must be used to pay for nursing home care; Medicaid pays the balance. The resident is allowed to keep a small amount for a personal needs allowance. A majority of states set a limit at $2,000 for an individual, but this can range from $1,000 to $4,000. The following are examples of what is not included: a home (if a spouse or child with a disability resides there), an automobile, and life insurance (if below an amount specified by the state). Long-term care must be "medically necessary," and each state has a system for making this determination. The criteria vary, and most states use a combination of medical and functional criteria.

In order to prevent the "healthy" spouse from impoverishment, states provide certain protections for income and assets. The rules vary from state to state so it is useful to consult with an attorney. In general, the spouse at home is entitled to keep a monthly maintenance needs allowance (the 1997 federal guidelines were $1,295.00 to $1,975.50). The community spouse also is entitled to keep a portion of the liquid assets. The spousal resource allowance in the 1997 federal guidelines was $15,804 to $79,020. The amount allocated to the spouse in the nursing home must be spent down to the asset level set by the state. The states may deny Medicaid to people who have transferred any asset, including a home, for less than fair market value within 36 months before applying for assistance (look-back period). Anyone needing nursing home care should consult with an attorney before considering asset transfers.

Under certain circumstances, the federal government requires states to try to collect money from the recipient's estate as a way to recoup costs. This is done after determination, through a fair hearing process, that the individual cannot return home and that no one protected under recovery law (spouse, a child who is disabled or a dependent child, certain siblings) is living in the house. The state can seek recovery after a person's death from property other than a house. Estate recovery laws are complex and, again, it is important to consult with an attorney.

Many states have home- and community-based waivers to avoid institutionalizing people in nursing homes when home-based care is a reasonable alternative. Services can include case management; homemaker services; home health aides; personal care services; and adult day health, rehabilitation, and respite care. Not every state offers this, and programs differ from state to state. Programs often have wait lists and are limited in scope.

For more information on legal and financial alternatives, see:

> *Family Survival Handbook: A Guide to the Financial, Legal and Social Problems of Brain-Damaged Adults* by J. Bosshardt, D. Gibson, and M. Snyder. Available through the Family Caregiver Alliance for Brain-Damaged Adults, Inc., 425 Bush Street, Suite 500, San Francisco, CA 94108. Telephone (800) 445-8106.

Many times, finding and utilizing community resources, attempting to get financial and legal affairs in order, and understanding all of the programs available can be stressful. If a caregiver is feeling the need for emotional support, psychosocial interventions also are available .

☐ Psychosocial Interventions

What can caregivers do if they have tried all of the techniques in the book and everything they know to reduce their level of stress, and still feel emotionally and physically exhausted and depleted, or if reducing their level of stress has made them feel better but they still feel like they need help? It then is helpful to explain that sometimes even the most resourceful person needs to seek outside professional help. Some people say they are afraid to ask for professional help because others will think they are "crazy" or "mentally ill." A person does not have to be "crazy" or "mentally ill" to benefit from help. People have many reasons for seeking professional help. Seeking professional help can be a useful and positive way to learn how to reduce one's level of stress. It may mean that:

1. People care enough about themselves to take active steps to reduce their levels of stress.
2. They have developed an awareness of themselves and want to learn how to strengthen their coping skills.
3. They have learned that it is okay to ask for support from others.
4. They care about their family, loved ones, and relationships. They want to be less stressed so that they can be there for their relationships.

Where Can a Person Go For Help?

There are a number of places that a person can go to seek professional help. Some of the possibilities are:

1. Churches or synagogues often have counselors on staff. If they cannot help caregivers, they should be able to refer them to someone who can.
2. Community mental health clinics offer a variety of services. These clinics usually offer various kinds of counseling (individual counseling, family counseling, group counseling, support groups, crisis counseling). Community-based clinics often will see clients for a minimal fee, and many clinics operate with a sliding scale fee schedule where fees are based on income.
3. Universities, colleges, or professional schools often can recommend an appropriate counselor who is in private practice for particular problems. Counselors or therapists in private practice can have varied educations and experiences. They can be social workers, psychologists, marriage and family therapists, or medical doctors. To find a therapist that is appropriate, caregivers can get referrals from professional organizations, health professionals, universities, family members, or friends.

Regardless of where a referral is received, it always is a good idea for caregivers to "interview" the potential counselor, because only caregivers can decide if they will be able to work together with the counselor to gain new skills and a new understanding about their problems.

Questions like, How do I find someone to talk to? What do I look for? Should I go to a group or to individual counseling? and How do I choose someone? often are asked. The most important thing is that the caregiver likes and feels comfortable with the counselor. The caregiver will want to make sure that the professional has experience with dementia and caregiving. Find out where counselors were educated, if they have a degree or specialization in gerontology or aging, what type of approach they use, and the costs of their services. Does insurance cover their services or do they have a payment plan?

Individual Counseling

Individual counseling can help ease the burden and identify positive steps to take, and may assist caregivers in deriving meaning and growth from stressful encounters. Individual psychotherapy has been shown to be effective in helping to manage stress, and is especially important if caregivers are clinically depressed.

Family Meetings

A family meeting can help a family solve a situational problem and provide information to members in order to increase their control over the situation. "Often family meetings are arranged to coordinate and facilitate cooperation among all family members to meet the common goal of caring for the patient" (Bourgeois, Schulz, & Burgio, 1996). In the CRC model, the family meeting usually takes place in one session, but more sessions are available if needed. The meeting should focus on responding to changes occurring in the care recipient or related issues involved in providing care, and should not concentrate on long-standing family conflicts or pathologies. Family meetings can address the tensions and imbalances in the family system created by the care recipient's disabilities (Zarit, Orr, & Zarit, 1985), and also can address the issue of providing more support to the primary caregiver.

Support Groups

A support group may be invaluable to caregivers of people who have memory impairments. Sharing experiences with others who also are trying to cope with a caregiving situation can be both an educational and an encouraging experience.

Caregivers are most likely to receive assistance from a support group than any other type of intervention. Support groups can offer information, emotional support, and the exchange of ideas about managing difficulties. They may assist caregivers in changing their perception of the stressfulness of demands, and help to produce a change in the appraisal of the problem. Membership in a support group may vary. Groups may be specialized for adult children or spouses, or they may be mixed. The group may be led by a professional, or by peers. Some studies (Fitting, Rabins, Lucas, & Eastham, 1986) have demonstrated that male caregivers may have different needs in a support group than female caregivers, and have suggested that perhaps males should be given the opportunity to form their own groups with cofacilitation by a male professional. Studies (Fitting et al., 1986) have shown that male caregivers tend to be more isolated than female caregivers, may be unfamiliar with nontraditional sex role behaviors, and may be uncomfortable with expressing negative feelings.

☐ Summary

The importance of understanding the network of community resources and the options for legal and financial planning cannot be emphasized enough.

Also, in order to avoid the stress related to having to make decisions at times of crisis, it is critical that caregivers plan ahead. This awareness will be useful to caregivers and their helpers in increasing their abilities to carry out stress reduction effectively.

 # References

Aneshensel, C., Pearlin, L., Mullan, J., Zarit, S., & Whitlatch, C. (1995). *Profiles of Caregiving: The Unexpected Career*. San Diego, CA: Academic Press.

Burgeois, M., Schulz, R., & Burgio, L. (1996). Interventions for caregivers of patients with Alzheimer's disease: A review and analysis of content, process, and outcomes. *International Journal of Aging and Human Development, 43*, 35–92.

Friss-Feinberg, L., & Kelly, K. (1995). A well-deserved break: Respite programs offered by California's Statewide System of Caregiver Resources Centers. *The Gerontologist, 35*, 701–705.

Fitting, M., Rabins, P., Lucas, M., & Eastham, J. (1986). Caregivers for dementia patients: A comparison of husbands and wives. *The Gerontologist, 26*, 248–251.

Gallagher-Thompson, D. (1994). Direct services and interventions for caregivers: A review of extant programs and a look to the future. In M. Cantor (Ed.), *Family caregiving: Agenda for the future* (pp. 102–122). San Francisco: American Society on Aging.

Gonyea, J. (1989). Alzheimer's disease support groups: An analysis of their structure, format and perceived benefits. *Social Work in Health Care, 14*, 61–72.

Kahan, J., Kemp, B., Staples, F., & Brummel-Smith, K. (1985). Decreasing burden in families caring for a relative with a dementing illness: A controlled study. *Journal of the American Geriatric Society, 33*, 664–670.

Knight, B., Lutzky, S., & Macofsky-Urban, F. (1993). A meta-analytic review of interventions for caregiver distress: Recommendations for the future research. *The Gerontologist, 33*, 240–249.

Pynoos, J. (1995). Supportive Services? Fine. But how about supportive surrounding? *Perspective on Aging, 24, no. 4*, 20–23.

Quayhagen, M. P., & Quayhagen, M. (1988). Alzheimer's stress: Coping with the caregiving role. *The Gerontologist, 28*, 391–396.

Zarit, S. (1996). Interventions with family caregivers. In S. Zarite and B. Knight (Eds.), *A Guide to Psychotherapy and Aging* (pp. 139–159). Washington, DC: American Psychological Association.

Zarit, S., Orr, N., & Zarit, J., (1985). *The Hidden Victims of Alzheimer's Disease: Families Under Stress*. New York: New York University Press.

Zarit, S., & Whitlatch, C. (1992). Institutional placement: Phases of the transition. *The Gerontologist, 32*, 665–672.

INDEX
(f, figure; t, table)

137